D1451838

CRIMINAL LAW AND PROCEDURE

JOHN L. WORRALL

University of Texas at Dallas

JENNIFER L. MOORE

DeSales University

PEARSON

Boston   Columbus   Indianapolis   New York   San Francisco   Upper Saddle River
Amsterdam   Cape Town   Dubai   London   Madrid   Milan   Munich   Paris   Montreal   Toronto
Delhi   Mexico City   São Paulo   Sydney   Hong Kong   Seoul   Singapore   Taipei   Tokyo

Editorial Director: Vernon R. Anthony
Editor, Digital Projects: Nichole Caldwell
Acquisitions Editor: Gary Bauer
Associate Editor: Megan Moffo
Editorial Assistant: Tanika Henderson
Director of Marketing: David Gesell
Senior Marketing Manager: Mary Salzman
Senior Marketing Coordinator: Alicia Wozniak
Marketing Assistant: Les Roberts
Production Manager: Fran Russello
Creative Director: Jayne Conte
Cover Designer: Bruce Kenselaar
Full Service Project Management/Composition: Niraj Bhatt/Aptara®, Inc.
Printer/Binder: Edwards Brothers
Cover Printer: Lehigh Phoenix
Text Font: Sabon LT Std

DEDICATION

For my wife, Sabrina, and my kids, Dylan and Jordyn.
J. W.

For my husband, Brian; my family; and the students
who served as my inspiration.
J.M.

Credits and acknowledgments borrowed from other sources and reproduced, with permission, in this textbook appear on the appropriate page within the text.

Cover Image Credits (clockwise from top left): © Aleksey Dmetsov/Fotolia, © James Steidl/Fotolia, © Junial Enterprises/Fotolia, © Marina Krasnovid/Fotolia, © Stephen Coburn/Fotolia.

Many of the designations by manufacturers and sellers to distinguish their products are claimed as trademarks. Where those designations appear in this book, and the publisher was aware of a trademark claim, the designations have been printed in initial caps or all caps.

Library of Congress Cataloging-in-Publication Data
Worrall, John L.
    Criminal law and procedure/John L. Worrall, University of Texas at Dallas, Jennifer L. Moore,
        DeSales University.
    pages cm
    ISBN-13: 978-0-13-237577-1
    ISBN-10: 0-13-237577-X
    1. Criminal law—United States. 2. Criminal procedure—United States.
        I. Moore, Jennifer L. (Esquire) II. Title.
    KF9219.W675 2014
    345.73—dc23

                                                      2012043919

ISBN 10:   0-13-237577-X
ISBN 13: 978-0-13-237577-1

PREFACE

Welcome to the first edition of *Criminal Law and Procedure*. Each of us has taught these subjects for several years and have become quite familiar with other texts in the area. As we grew familiar with them, we saw an increasing need to write our own book, one that adopts a fresh and contemporary take on criminal law and procedure. Due to the large volume of information a combined course in criminal law and procedure needs to cover, we also determined that there is a need for a new format for the book. The format we have adopted is modular in nature.

Our book's modular format sets it apart from others in the market. Like chapters in a traditional text, modular chapters begin with a set of chapter objectives. Learning objectives, however, are then broken up and organized into modules. Each module is a stand-alone section. There are two to five modules per chapter in our book. Each module follows a consistent organization and contains the following elements:

1. Standard criminal law or criminal procedure content, covering all the major topics. This material is found under the "Core Concepts" headings throughout the book.
2. "Court Decisions," featuring excerpts from real cases. These explore in detail the logic behind important court decisions governing different aspects of criminal law and procedure.
3. Exercises affording the reader an opportunity to decide a particular case. We call these "Your Decision."
4. Concise bulleted summary.

Each chapter concludes with a list of learning objectives, review questions, and key terms, organized by module. This summary format gives readers the ability to quickly link specific terms, questions, and objectives to the modules associated with them.

Presenting material in a modular format gives instructors the flexibility of assigning the modules they feel are most pertinent. It also ensures that each main topic in the text is supported by an application ("Your Decision") and a case example ("Court Decision").

DISTINGUISHING FEATURES

Interesting and Controversial Cases

We make liberal use of interesting, fresh, and controversial cases. A large number of our cases were decided in the last few years, making the material as current as possible. We also present classic cases (e.g., *Miranda* v. *Arizona*) where warranted. All in all, the cases are specifically targeted to engage young students with unique and relatable factual scenarios and encourage lively class discussions.

Exercises

Each module contains scenarios that emulate the approach taken in Singer and LaFond's *Criminal Law: Examples and Explanations* (Wolters Kluwer) and Worrall's *Criminal Procedure: From First Contact to Appeal* (Pearson). Students are presented with a hypothetical scenario that puts them in the position of judge or jury. We call this feature "Your Decision." Two such exercises appear at the end of each module. *Answers are available to instructors in the instructor's resource materials.* This promotes classroom discussion.

Equal Balance of Course Material

Other texts covering both criminal law and procedure fail to give equal coverage to both aspects of the course. Our text achieves a better balance of the two subjects, allocating sufficient attention to all key legal issues. Throughout the text, "connections" between the two subjects are frequently noted and the students are directed to other relevant portions of the text when necessary.

Instructor Resources

The following supplementary materials are available to support instructors' use of the main text:

- *eBooks. Criminal Law and Procedure* is available in two eBook formats, *CourseSmart* and Adobe Reader. *CourseSmart* is an exciting new choice for students looking to save money. As an alternative to purchasing the printed textbook, students can purchase an electronic version of the same content. With a *CourseSmart* eTextbook, students can search the text, make notes online, print out reading assignments that incorporate lecture notes, and bookmark important passages for later review. For more information, or to purchase access to the *CourseSmart* eTextbook, visit **www.coursesmart.com**.

- *TestBank* and *MyTest*. These supplements represent a new standard in testing material. Whether you use the basic *TestBank* or generate

questions electronically through *MyTest*, every question is linked to the text's learning objective, page number, and level of difficulty. This allows for quick reference in the text and an easy way to check the difficulty level and variety of your questions. *MyTest* can be accessed at **www.PearsonMyTest.com**.

- *Interactive Lecture PowerPoint Presentation* This supplement will enhance lectures like never before. Award-winning presentation designers worked with our authors to develop *Power-Points* that truly engage the student. Much like the text, the *PowerPoints* are full of instructionally sound graphics, tables, charts, and photos that do what presentation software was meant to do: support and enhance your lecture. Data and difficult concepts are presented in a truly interactive way, helping students connect the dots and stay focused on the lecture. The *Interactive Lecture PowerPoints* also include in-depth

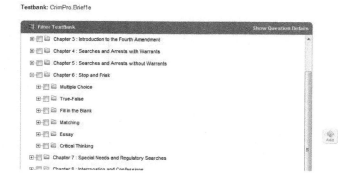

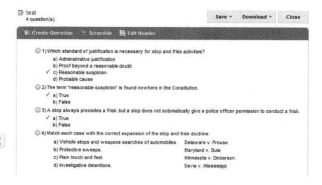

lecture notes and teaching tips so that you have all your lecture material in one place.

- *The Pearson Criminal Justice Online Community* Available at **www.mycriminaljusticecommunity.com**, this site is a place for educators to connect, and to exchange ideas and advice on courses, content, *CJ Interactive*, and so much more.

- *Instructor's Manual with Case Briefs and Test Bank* This instructor's manual contains case briefs, proposed responses to the Your Decision questions in the text, and a test bank with answer key. The authors have prepared a pack of case briefs that correspond to the excerpted cases that appear in each chapter. These case briefs essentially serve as a one-page summary of the key elements of the various cases, similar

to the approach used by students during law school. We feel this is an important addition because it aids the instructor in preparing for class. One difficulty often encountered by instructors in courses that use the "text-case" approach is remembering all of the details of each case for class. These briefs provide summaries of the key material and greatly decrease the preparation time needed. In addition, they make switching to the new text an easier transition.

To access these supplementary materials online, instructors need to request an instructor access code at **www.pearsonhighered.com/irc**. Within 48 hours after registering, you will receive a confirmation e-mail that includes an instructor access code. When you receive your code, go to the site and log on for full instructions on downloading materials you wish to use.

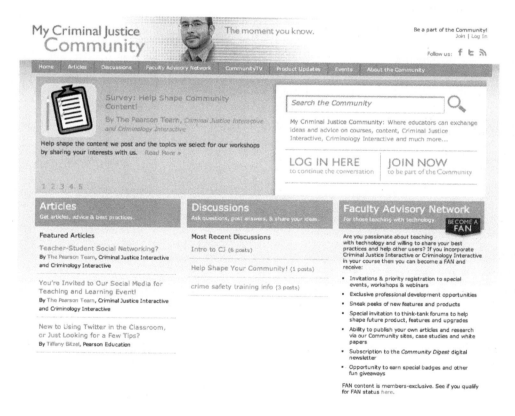

ABOUT THE AUTHORS

John L. Worrall is Professor of Criminology and Department Head at the University of Texas at Dallas. A Seattle native, he received both his M.A. (criminal justice) and Ph.D. (political science) from Washington State University, where he graduated in 1999. From 1999 to 2006, he was a member of the criminal justice faculty at California State University, San Bernardino. He joined the University of Texas at Dallas in the fall of 2006. Dr. Worrall has published articles and book chapters on a variety of topics, ranging from legal issues in policing to crime measurement. He is also the author or coauthor of numerous textbooks, including *Introduction to Criminal Justice* (with Larry J. Siegel, 14th ed., Cengage, 2014) and *Criminal Procedure: From First Contact to Appeal* (4th ed., Prentice Hall, 2013); coeditor of *The Changing Role of the American Prosecutor* (SUNY, 2009); and editor of the journal *Police Quarterly*.

Jennifer L. Moore is Associate Professor of Criminal Justice at DeSales University in Center Valley, Pennsylvania. She obtained her B.A. in government from Dartmouth College in Hanover, New Hampshire, and her J.D. with honors from Emory University School of Law in Atlanta, Georgia. Prior to entering academics, Professor Moore practiced at a large law firm in Atlanta, Georgia. Her legal practice included corporate litigation, antitrust litigation, and white-collar criminal defense. Professor Moore has also published articles on a wide range of legal topics, with a specific focus on criminal-law issues. She also coauthored the first edition of *Criminal Law and Procedure* (Prentice Hall, 2013) with John L. Worrall.

ACKNOWLEDGMENTS

Many people contributed to this project. We would like to thank everyone at Pearson, including Gary Bauer, Megan Moffo, and Tanika Henderson. We also thank our copy editor Khumanthem Seilesh and project manager Niraj Bhatt for improving the overall quality of this textbook.

We would also like to thank the reviewers. They were Dorinda Davis, Columbus State University; Cari Keller, Northeastern State University; Shana Maier, Widener University; Nicholas Meier, Kalamazoo Valley Community College; Terry Miller, Valencia College; Cheryn Rowell, Stanly Community College; Cortney Waid-Lindberg, North Dakota State University; and Alfonzo Williams, Augusta Technical College.

Finally, we would like to thank our families for their continued love and support.

BRIEF CONTENTS

CONTENTS

1

LEGAL FOUNDATIONS

MODULE 1.1 **PRELIMINARY INFORMATION**
Learning Objectives
- Explain the difference between substantive criminal law and criminal procedure.
- Describe the various classifications of crime.
- Identify the sources of law.

MODULE 1.2 **REACHING A VERDICT**
Learning Objectives
- Describe the adversarial system.
- Identify courtroom participants.

MODULE 1.3 **COURT ORGANIZATION**
Learning Objectives
- Describe the structure of the U.S. legal system, including jurisdiction.
- Understand the parts of a court case.
- Explain the practical meaning of a verdict.

MODULE 1.1

PRELIMINARY INFORMATION

Learning Objectives

- **Explain the difference between substantive criminal law and criminal procedure.**
- **Describe the various classifications of crime.**
- **Identify the sources of law.**

CORE CONCEPTS

criminal law Specifies what kinds of behavior are illegal, what punishments are available for dealing with offenders, and what defenses can be invoked by individuals who break it.

criminal procedure A vast set of rules and guidelines that describe how suspected and accused criminals are to be handled and processed by the justice system.

defendant The individual charged with committing a crime.

Criminal law is the bedrock of the American criminal justice system. It specifies what kinds of behavior are illegal, what punishments are available for dealing with offenders, and what defenses can be invoked by individuals who find themselves on the wrong side of the law. Without the criminal law, there would be no crimes, no criminals, and perhaps no means of controlling undesirable behavior. Certainly violence would still exist, property would be stolen, and order would be threatened, but these activities, harmful as they are, would not be considered illegal. Our system of criminal laws ensures that something can be done in response to behaviors that are widely deemed unacceptable.

Criminal procedure consists of a vast set of rules and guidelines that describe how suspected and accused criminals are to be handled and processed by the justice system. Of great significance is the relationship between the police and the people suspected of criminal activity. Criminal procedure arms the police with the knowledge necessary to preserve the rights of individuals who are seized, searched, arrested, and otherwise inconvenienced by law enforcement officials. It also arms other actors—such as judges, prosecutors, and defense attorneys—with the necessary information to preserve the rights of individuals accused of criminal activity. In short, criminal procedure begins when the police first contact a person and ends well after his or her conviction.

Comparing Criminal Law to Criminal Procedure

The substantive criminal law is separate and distinct from the law of criminal procedure. Criminal procedure emphasizes *procedure* over substance. Constitutional guidelines pertaining to search and seizure, confessions and interrogations, due process, and the like are all-important in criminal procedure. A grasp of criminal procedure arms one with an understanding of how criminal justice officials are supposed to process criminal suspects, criminal defendants (the individual charged with a crime is called the **defendant**), and even the convicted.

In contrast, criminal law is about the *substance* of the law, what it prohibits and what types of individuals can be punished for violating it. It focuses on a number of critical topics, including the basic elements of crime, the defenses available to criminal conduct, the rules governing criminal activity that stops short of completion, and liability for people who conspire together in furtherance of their illegal actions. Criminal law is also concerned with the differences between the many types of illegal activity named in criminal statutes at the federal, state, and local level. For example, what is the difference between robbery and burglary? When is a person guilty of first-degree murder instead of second-degree murder? What sets terrorism apart from homicide?

More simply, criminal law is the "what" and criminal procedure is the "how." That is, criminal law defines what is treated as criminal. Criminal procedure is about *how* people charged with crime should be treated and processed by the criminal justice system. This book looks in depth at both issues by combining criminal law and criminal procedure. After we lay a foundation in this introductory chapter, we turn attention to criminal law. The last part of the book is devoted to criminal procedure.

The Classification of Crimes

Criminal statutes tend to classify crimes in terms of felonies and misdemeanors, the former being more serious than the latter. This classification scheme, though, is somewhat arbitrary and may not reflect the true harms that one crime causes compared to another. For that reason, it is helpful to think of the "evil" that underlies a certain type of activity. Some behaviors are simply more evil than others.

Felonies and Misdemeanors

felony A crime punishable by death or confinement in prison for more than 12 months.

misdemeanor A crime punishable by a fine or a period of incarceration *less than* 12 months.

The classification of crimes into felonies and misdemeanors is age-old, popular, and found in nearly every penal code. In general, a **felony** is a crime punishable by death or confinement in prison for more than 12 months. Obviously death is reserved for the most serious felonies, such as first-degree murder. Lesser felonies, such as theft of goods valued at a certain amount, result in imprisonment rather than capital punishment. A **misdemeanor**, by contrast, is a crime punishable by a fine or a period of incarceration *less than* 12 months.

Importantly, a crime is defined as a felony or a misdemeanor based on possible, not actual punishment. For example, in one case, a woman was sentenced to one year in prison for driving under the influence, but the judge "probated" her sentence, meaning he suspended it, and instead required her to serve 120 days in home confinement. She later argued she was a misdemeanant, not a felon, but an appeals court said that "a person whose . . . felony sentence is reduced . . . does not become a misdemeanant by virtue of the reduction but remains a felon."[1]

Why should we care about the distinction between felonies and misdemeanors, other than by the punishments that can be imposed? A key reason is that trial procedures differ for felonies and misdemeanors. For example, jury trials are not

---

[1]*Commonwealth* v. *Rhodes*, 920 S.W. 2d 531 (1996), p. 533.

required in misdemeanor cases where the punishment does not exceed six months' confinement.[2] Also, felony trials tend to be more drawn-out and elaborate due to the stakes involved, which could include capital punishment for the offender in serious cases. Another reason it is important to classify crimes in this way is because certain offenses require it. For example, some statutes define burglary in terms of unlawful entry with intent to commit a felony inside. If a misdemeanor is committed inside, then the crime is not burglary. We look at burglary in more detail in Chapter 7.

It is also useful to distinguish between felonies and misdemeanors in terms of the consequences associated with each. A felony conviction bars a person from employment in certain fields, may deny that individual the right to vote, usually prohibits the individual from legally owning a firearm, and can carry with it a number of other harsh consequences. State laws usually dictate the consequences. In contrast, a misdemeanor conviction is usually not as damaging, but this is not to say there are no undesirable consequences. Depending on the state, a misdemeanor conviction could lead to eviction, suspension of a driver's license, limited employment opportunities, and a host of other outcomes.

Malum in Se versus Malum Prohibitum

malum in se An act that is wrong or evil in itself.

malum prohibitum An act that is wrong or evil because it is defined as such.

Malum in se (or the plural form, *mala in se*) is a Latin phrase meaning wrong or evil in itself. In contrast, *malum prohibitum* (or *mala prohibita*) means wrong or evil because it is defined as such. Certain crimes are simply wrong in themselves. For example, it is all but impossible to convince someone that an unjustified and inexcusable murder is acceptable. Other examples of *mala in se* offenses include robbery, larceny (theft), and rape, among others. Crimes like prostitution or drug possession, some would argue, are not as serious as violent crime and, so, should not be criminalized.

The line between what is wrong in itself and what is wrong because legislators defined it that way is difficult to draw. Is drug possession wrong in itself? What about speeding? Speeding arguably poses risks to other drivers, so is it inherently wrong? If not, could it be once a driver exceeds a certain speed, say 100 miles per hour? There are no easy answers. The distinction between *malum in se* and *malum prohibitum* is largely academic these days because for the majority of offenses, it is difficult to objectively place them in one category over another.

Sources of Law

We have already offered definitions of "criminal law" and "criminal procedure," but we have *not* just yet discussed where the law of both comes from. What are the origins of the law? There are many of them, some ancient, others more modern. Here we look at five sources of the law: early legal codes, the common law, modern statutes, the Model Penal Code, and constitutional sources. Each is best viewed as a piece of a broader puzzle (see Figure 1.1).

---

[2]*Baldwin v. New York*, 399 U.S. 66 (1970).

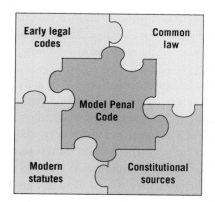

Figure 1.1
Sources of Law

Code of Hammurabi The earliest known example of a formal written legal code. It expressed a strong "eye for an eye" philosophy on punishment.

Twelve Tables The first secular written legal code.

common law Also known as case law or judge-made law, the law developed in early England by judges who wrote down their decisions and circulated them to other judges. The law "in common."

special law In contrast to common law, the laws of specific villages and localities that were in effect in medieval England and that were often enforced by canonical (i.e., religious) courts.

Early Legal Codes

Perhaps the earliest known example of a formal written legal code was the **Code of Hammurabi**. Also known as Hammurabi's Code and assembled by the sixth Babylonian king, Hammurabi, in 1760 B.C., the code expressed a strong "eye for an eye" philosophy. To illustrate, here is the seventh of the code's "code of laws":

> If anyone buy from the son or the slave of another man, without witnesses or a contract, silver or gold, a male or female slave, an ox or a sheep, an ass or anything, or if he take it in charge, he is considered a thief and shall be put to death.[3]

Roman law provides another example of formally codified legal principles. The so-called **Twelve Tables** (450 B.C.) was the first secular (i.e., not regarded as religious) written legal code.[4] The code was named as such because the laws were literally written onto 12 ivory tablets. The tablets were then posted so that all Romans could read them. The Twelve Tables, like Hammurabi's Code, contained a strong element of retributive justice. One of the laws "*Si membrum rupsit, ni cum eo pacit, talio esto*" translates as follows: "If one has maimed another and does not buy his peace, let there be retaliation in kind."[5]

Despite their shortcomings and harsh character, these early legal codes are important because they signaled the emergence of formalized "law." And while it is difficult to define the term with precision, **law** generally refers to formal rules, principles, and guidelines enforced by **political authority**. This political authority is what began to take dispute resolution out of the hands of citizens and put it under control of governments. Legal codes have changed and evolved considerably over the years, but the use of political or governmental authority to enforce such codes has remained pretty constant.

Common Law

After the Norman conquest of England (A.D. 1066), King William and his Norman dukes and barons moved quickly to consolidate their hold over newly won territories. One method was to take control of the preexisting legal/court system. Once they did this, the judges in their courts not only issued decisions but also wrote them down. These decisions were subsequently circulated to other judges. The result was a measure of uniformity from one court to the next. This was literally the law "in common" throughout England, and it came to be known as the **common law**.

The common law can be better understood when it is contrasted with **special law**, which refers to the laws of specific villages and localities that were in effect in medieval England and that were often enforced by canonical (i.e., religious) courts. Under the reign of Henry II (1154–1189), national law was introduced, but not through legislative authority as is customary today. Rather, Henry II implemented a

[3]Ancient History Sourcebook, *Code of Hammurabi*, c. 1780 B.C., from http://www.fordham.edu/halsall/ancient/hamcode.html (accessed January 1, 2010).
[4]O.J. Thatcher (ed.), *The Library of Original Sources* (Milwaukee, WI: University Research Extension Co., 1901), Vol. III: *The Roman World*, pp. 9–11.
[5]Ibid.

system whereby judges from his own central court went out into the countryside to preside over disputes. They resolved these disputes based on what they perceived as custom. The judges effectively created law, as there was no democratic law-forming process in place at the time.

As more and more judges began to record their decisions, the principles of *stare decisis* and precedent were developed. **Precedent** refers, generally, to some prior action that guides current action. In the common law context, this meant that judges' decisions were guided by earlier decisions. Precedent thus ensured continuity and predictability. If decisions changed radically from one judge to the next or from place to place, or both, the "common" law would be anything but common. It was also easier for judges to fall back on earlier decisions, otherwise they would have to continually reinvent the wheel. **Stare decisis**, which is Latin for "to stand by things decided," is thus the formal practice of adhering to precedent.

While the common law is usually viewed as a legal concept, it also had social implications: The medieval judge was entrusted with the collective wisdom, values, and morals established by the community and was trusted to apply them to solve disputes between citizens. Even when appointed by the king, the medieval judge represented the community and applied the community's (not the king's) law, thereby maintaining its age-old customs and values.

precedent In general, some prior action that guides current action. In the context of courts, letting judges' decisions be guided by earlier decisions.

stare decisis A Latin term meaning "to stand by things decided," or to adhere to precedent.

Modern Statutes

Modern statutes differ from early legal codes because they exist at different levels of government and come in many different forms. The United States Code, which is passed by the United States Congress, contains federal laws, and violations of its provisions can lead to federal prosecution. States have their own respective criminal codes passed by their state legislature. Other units of government, such as counties and cities, often have their own ordinances. These legal codes exist in several varieties. States such as California list criminal offenses in more than one code. There, most crimes are spelled out in the Penal Code, but the Health and Safety Code criminalizes drug-law violations. The state has 29 separate legal codes![6]

Having multiple legal codes at various levels of government makes it nearly impossible to develop a full understanding of criminal law and criminal procedure. This book cannot thoroughly cover the legal code of each state, as it would be excessively lengthy. Of course, an attorney who wishes to practice criminal law in a particular state will need to become well-versed in the laws of his or her state, but for a general introduction to criminal law and criminal procedure, we cannot afford to delve too deeply into the laws of any given state. Fortunately, there is considerable overlap in the criminal laws of various jurisdictions.

The Model Penal Code

In our federal system of government, each state is free—within certain constitutional limitations—to develop its own common and statutory law. This led to considerable

---

[6]See, e.g., http://www.leginfo.ca.gov/calaw.html (accessed January 1, 2010).

American Law Institute A private organization of lawyers, judges, and legal scholars that wrote and adopted the Model Penal Code.

Model Penal Code A model set of criminal laws adopted by the American Law Institute for states to emulate as they see fit.

variation from state to state. In 1962, however, the **American Law Institute**, a private organization of lawyers, judges, and legal scholars, adopted a **Model Penal Code**. The Code was intended to serve as just that, a "model" for states to follow. Since 1962, several states have adopted the Model Penal Code, either in whole or in part. This is beneficial in at least two respects. First, it promotes consistency across the states. Second, it makes the study of the criminal law more manageable. As such, we will, throughout this book, introduce criminal law concepts through the lens of the Model Penal Code. But bear in mind that the federal system has not adopted it, nor has California, the nation's most populous state.

The Model Penal Code is more concerned with criminal law than criminal procedure. We will refer to it rather extensively in Part 2 of this book, but it will not receive much attention in the criminal procedure section. Part 3 of this book will examine the next source of law—constitutions, particularly the U.S. Constitution—in depth.

Constitutional Sources

Constitutions are perhaps the most significant source of law. Unlike penal codes, constitutions generally do not prohibit actions on the part of private citizens. Rather, constitutions generally place limits on government authority. They define, in broad terms, government structure and organization; they also spell out various rights that people enjoy, how government officials will be selected, and what roles various government branches will take on.

The U.S. Constitution is so important to criminal law and criminal procedure that we come back to it on multiple occasions throughout this book. From a criminal law standpoint, we will look at the Constitution's prohibition against so-called *ex post facto* laws. We will look in detail at the concept of equal protection and consider issues of vagueness and overbreadth in the criminal law. From a criminal procedure standpoint, we will look at how the U.S. Constitution constrains the actions of criminal justice professionals as they come into contact with suspects, make arrests, conduct searches, and charge and try offenders.

Bill of Rights The first ten amendments to the U.S. Constitution.

The **Bill of Rights** (see Figure 1.2), consisting of the first ten amendments, also announces important limitations on government authority with respect to the investigation and prosecution of crime. The Fourth Amendment, for example, spells out warrant requirements, and the Fifth Amendment protects people, in part, from being forced to incriminate themselves. The Eighth Amendment prohibits cruel and unusual punishment.

While the federal Constitution receives the most attention due to its status as the supreme law of the United States, it is important to note that each state has its own constitution. These often mirror the federal Constitution, but they often go into much more detail. Some states use an initiative process, where every November voters can decide the fate of proposed constitutional amendments. Other states have used their constitutions to more clearly spell out what they consider prohibited actions, whereas a close read of the federal Constitution suggests the founding fathers intended something different. In any case, constitutions work together with legal codes, administrative regulations, and the common law to provide an interesting basis for criminal justice as we know it.

Amendment I

Congress shall make no law respecting an establishment of religion, or prohibiting the free exercise thereof; or abridging the freedom of speech, or of the press; or the right of the people peaceably to assemble, and to petition the government for a redress of grievances.

Amendment II

A well regulated militia, being necessary to the security of a free state, the right of the people to keep and bear arms, shall not be infringed.

Amendment III

No soldier shall, in time of peace be quartered in any house, without the consent of the owner, nor in time of war, but in a manner to be prescribed by law.

Amendment IV

The right of the people to be secure in their persons, houses, papers, and effects, against unreasonable searches and seizures, shall not be violated, and no warrants shall issue, but upon probable cause, supported by oath or affi rmation, and particularly describing the place to be searched, and the persons or things to be seized.

Amendment V

No person shall be held to answer for a capital, or otherwise infamous crime, unless on a presentment or indictment of a grand jury, except in cases arising in the land or naval forces, or in the militia, when in actual service in time of war or public danger; nor shall any person be subject for the same offense to be twice put in jeopardy of life or limb; nor shall be compelled in any criminal case to be a witness against himself, nor be deprived of life, liberty, or property, without due process of law; nor shall private property be taken for public use, without just compensation.

Amendment VI

In all criminal prosecutions, the accused shall enjoy the right to a speedy and public trial, by an impartial jury of the state and district wherein the crime shall have been committed, which district shall have been previously ascertained by law, and to be informed of the nature and cause of the accusation; to be confronted with the witnesses against him; to have compulsory process for obtaining witnesses in his favor, and to have the assistance of counsel for his defense.

Amendment VII

In suits at common law, where the value in controversy shall exceed twenty dollars, the right of trial by jury shall be preserved, and no fact tried by a jury, shall be otherwise reexamined in any court of the United States, than according to the rules of the common law.

Amendment VIII

Excessive bail shall not be required, nor excessive fi nes imposed, nor cruel and unusual punishments infl icted.

Amendment IX

The enumeration in the Constitution, of certain rights, shall not be construed to deny or disparage others retained by the people.

Amendment X

The powers not delegated to the United States by the Constitution, nor prohibited by it to the states, are reserved to the states respectively, or to the people.

Figure 1.2
Bill of Rights

State constitutions can be more restrictive than the U.S. Constitution, but no state can relax protections spelled out in the U.S. Constitution. For example, the U.S. Constitution's Fourth Amendment spells out search warrant requirements, but the Fourth Amendment is vague in terms of whether a warrant is required in all circumstances. In theory, a state could require warrants for *all* searches, but as a practical matter, most states have followed the U.S. Constitution's lead—and the Supreme Court's interpretation of it.

YOUR DECISION

1. Armed with a Swiss Army knife, Jeffrey Biggins robbed the local convenience store and made off with $700 in cash. The police were able to apprehend Biggins and charged him with the crime of armed robbery, which has a potential prison sentence of up to five years. Biggins pleaded guilty to the crime. Since this was Biggins' first criminal offense, the judge sentenced him to 6 months in jail and 100 hours of community service. Is the crime of armed robbery a felony or a misdemeanor? Why?

2. Martin Drake is being charged with first-degree murder in Florida and wants to raise the defense of insanity. Drake and his lawyer believe that he has the best chance of winning under the Model Penal Code's "substantial capacity" test for insanity. Drake's lawyer asks the Florida court to apply the Model Penal Code's test. Does the trial court in Florida need to use the Model Penal Code test? Why or why not?

Summary

- Criminal law specifies what kinds of behavior are illegal, what punishments are available for dealing with offenders, and what defenses can be invoked by individuals who find themselves on the wrong side of the law.

- Criminal procedure is a vast system of laws and guidelines that details how suspected and accused criminals are to be processed and handled by the criminal justice system.

- A felony is a crime punishable by death or confinement in prison for more than 12 months. A misdemeanor, by contrast, is a crime punishable by a fine or a period of incarceration *less than* 12 months.

- *Malum in se* (or the plural form, *mala in se*) is a Latin phrase meaning wrong or evil in itself. In contrast, *malum prohibitum* (or *mala prohibita*) means wrong or evil because it is defined as such.

- Five sources of law are early legal codes, the common law, modern statutes, the Model Penal Code, and constitutional sources. One of the earliest known examples of a formal written legal code was the Code of Hammurabi. The so-called "Twelve Tables" was the first secular written legal code.

- Common law is "the law in common," meaning that as one judge wrote down a decision and circulated it to other judges, consistency developed as they began to apply the same principles. The common law was not unique to any particular place; it was the law "in common" throughout England. Special law refers to the laws of specific villages and localities.

- The United States Code contains federal laws, and violations of its provisions can lead to federal prosecution. States have their own legal codes that define what is and is not criminal. Other units of government, such as counties and cities, often have their own ordinances that define legal and illegal behaviors.

- The Model Penal Code, developed by the American Law Institute, is a *sample* legal code that many states have adopted.

- Constitutions are perhaps the most significant source of law. Unlike penal codes, constitutions generally do not prohibit actions on the part of private citizens. Rather, constitutions generally place limits on government authority. The U.S. Constitution, including the Bill of Rights, is very influential in American criminal law and criminal procedure.

MODULE

1.2   REACHING A VERDICT

Learning Objectives

- **Describe the adversarial system.**
- **Identify courtroom participants.**

CORE CONCEPTS

This book makes extensive use of cases involving actual people charged with and convicted of crimes. The problem is that most published court decisions hail from the appellate courts—after someone has been convicted. This is a critically important point to keep in mind. Nearly every published case involves some person who was already convicted of a crime and who decided to appeal that conviction for one reason or another.

The appellate stage of the criminal process comes *after* adjudication, that is, after the defendant has been tried, convicted, and sentenced in court. It is thus easy to lose sight of some of the important procedures and considerations that lead up to the publishing of a court case. In this section, we look at several of them: the adversary system, the burden of proof in criminal trials, presumptions, the roles of the prosecutor and the defense attorney, and the roles of the judge and jury.

Adversarial System

adversarial justice system A system of justice that pits two parties against each other in the pursuit of the truth.

Ours is an adversarial justice system. It is adversarial because it pits two parties against each other in the pursuit of the truth. Our adversarial system is not what it is, though, because attorneys love to hate each other. Rather, adversarialism is based on the many protections our Constitution and laws afford people.

When criminal defendants assert their rights, this sometimes amounts to one side saying the other is wrong, which ultimately leads to an impasse that must be resolved by a judge. If the defendant's attorney seeks suppression of the key evidence that may have been obtained improperly, the prosecutor will probably disagree; after all, such evidence could form the basis of his or her case. The judge must rule to settle the matter. This is the essence of adversarialism—two competing sets of interests (the defendant's and the government's) working against each other.

Why else is ours an adversarial system? Another more fundamental explanation lies in the founding fathers' concerns with oppressive governments. Adversarialism promotes argument, debate, and openness. With no defense attorneys and only prosecutors having any say in a defendant's case, there would be untold numbers of rights violations, rushes to judgment, and so on.

Hollywood loves to make it look like prosecutors and defense attorneys cannot stand each other, and they are constantly springing surprise witnesses on one another, arguing with each other to the point of fighting, and so on. While it is true that some prosecutors and defense attorneys are not the best of friends, most know each other and work together on a routine basis. Some prosecutors were once defense attorneys and vice versa. These days, collaboration is popular, too, as prosecutors and defense attorneys are coming to realize that the traditional hard-line adversarial approach to meting out justice is not always helpful for the accused.

Inquisitorial Justice

inquisitorial system The opposite of an adversarial system. The accused does not enjoy the same protections, and decision-making authority is placed in the hands of one or very few individuals.

Adversarial justice can be better understood when compared to its opposite, namely inquisitorial justice, which is characteristic of an **inquisitorial system**. There are several features of inquisitorial systems that differ from adversarial systems. First, inquisitorial systems do not provide the same protections to the accused (e.g., right to counsel); second, inquisitorial systems place decision making in the hands of one or a very few individuals. Third, juries are often the exception in inquisitorial systems. Finally, the attorneys in inquisitorial systems are much more passive than in adversarial systems, and judges take on a more prominent role in the pursuit of the truth.

Inquisitorial justice is often likened to justice from the past, such as in medieval England, and particularly at the hands of the early Christian church. For the most part, this perception is accurate, but some borderline inquisitorial systems are very much alive and well in this day and age, even in modern industrialized nations. For example, in France, the "juge d'instruction" (i.e., investigating magistrate) engages in fact-finding and performs investigations in cases of serious and complex crimes. American judges, in contrast, focus on legal matters, and in trials by jury, they never engage in fact-finding.

Until as recently as 1996, China had a full-blown inquisitorial system. Since the Chinese adopted significant reforms to their legal system, that has changed. As one researcher observed,

> [U]nder China's inquisitorial system, judges were required to engage in evidence-gathering and criminal investigations. Judges in the post-reform period, however, should be more likely to serve as impartial adjudicators who hear evidence and arguments from both sides and render a decision based solely on this information.[7]

---

[7]H. Lu, "Confessions and Criminal Case Disposition in China," *Law and Society Review,* Vol. 37(2003), pp. 549–578, 555.

burden of proof The requirement that a particular party convince the jury with regard to a particular issue. In the criminal law context, the burden of proof falls on the prosecutor to establish the defendant's guilt.

proof beyond a reasonable doubt The standard of proof necessary in a criminal case, roughly akin to 95% certainty.

preponderance of evidence The standard of proof in a civil case, equivalent to "more certain than not."

burden of persuasion In a criminal case, the requirement that the prosecution persuade the jury that the defendant committed the crime.

burden of production One party's (the prosecutor's in a criminal case) obligation to present sufficient evidence to have the issue decided by a fact-finder. The burden of production is a question of law.

directed verdict A judge's order that one side or the other wins without the need to move on to fact-finding (in which the defense would introduce evidence, call witnesses, etc.).

presumption A fact assumed to be true under the law.

Burden of Proof

The **burden of proof** in a criminal prosecution first falls on the government. This means that it is the government's responsibility to prove that a person committed a crime. In a criminal case, the prosecutor must present **proof beyond a reasonable doubt** that the defendant committed the crime, which is roughly the same as 95% certainty. In contrast, the burden of proof in a civil case falls on the plaintiff, the party bringing suit. Also, the standard of proof in a civil trial is lower. It is generally the **preponderance of evidence**, roughly akin to "more certain than not."

The prosecution must *persuade* the jury that the defendant should be held accountable. This is known as the **burden of persuasion**. Related to the burden of proof is the **burden of production**. The burden of production is one party's (the state's or the government's, argued by the prosecutor) obligation to present sufficient evidence to have the issue decided by a fact-finder. If the prosecutor does not meet the burden of production, the case may result in a **directed verdict**, which is a judge's order that one side or the other wins without the need to move on to fact-finding (in which the defense would introduce evidence, call witnesses, etc.).

If proof beyond a reasonable doubt amounts to 95% certainty, then reasonable doubt is that other 5%. It is in the defense's interest to exploit that 5%, to get members of the jury thinking that there is a *chance* the defendant did not commit the crime.

If the defendant chooses to assert an affirmative defense, then he or she must meet the burden of production and the burden of persuasion as far as that defense goes. For example, if the defendant in a murder trial claims he was insane at the time of the crime, then it will be his burden to prove as much. States vary in their burden of proof requirements for affirmative defenses, and the level of proof necessary is usually less than proof beyond a reasonable doubt.[8]

Presumptions

A **presumption** is a fact assumed to be true under the law. In the world of criminal law, there are many types of presumptions. Conclusive presumptions require that all parties agree with something assumed to be true. An example of this would be that a child born to a married couple that lives together is the couple's child. It is likely that both parties to a case would agree to this presumption. In contrast to this kind of a conclusive presumption, a *rebuttable* presumption is one that could reasonably be disagreed with. Here is an example of a rebuttable presumption: "Because a letter was mailed, it was received by its intended recipient." This is rebuttable because the letter could actually be lost due to a mistake made by the post office.

Every person charged with a crime is assumed, in advance, to be innocent, which is known as the **presumption of innocence**. The presumption of innocence is both a presumption of law (because it is required from the outset) and a rebuttable presumption (because the prosecutor will present evidence to show the defendant, or

---

[8]See J. Dressler, *Understanding Criminal Law*, 5th ed. (Danvers, MA: Lexis-Nexis, 2009), Chapter 7.

- *Presumption of sanity.* All defendants are presumed sane; the burden falls on the defense to prove otherwise.
- *Presumption of death.* It is presumed that a person who has disappeared and is continually absent from his or her customary location (usually after seven years) is dead.
- *Presumption against suicide.* It is assumed that when a person dies, the cause is not suicide.
- *Presumption of a guilty mind following possession of the fruits of crime.* The jury can usually infer guilt if a person is caught "red-handed" with the fruits of crime.
- *Presumption of knowledge of the law.* Ignorance is not a defense to criminal liability.
- *Presumption of the regularity of official acts.* It is assumed, for example, that a proper chain of custody exists, unless the defense can show otherwise.
- *Presumption that young children cannot commit crimes.* Some states presume that children under a certain threshold age (e.g., age seven) cannot form criminal intent and thus cannot commit crime.
- *Presumption that people intend the results of their voluntary actions.* If a person voluntarily shoots another, the jury can presume the shooter intended to do so.

Figure 1.3
Common Presumptions

presumption of innocence A bedrock presumption in the American criminal justice system, the notion that the accused is not guilty until proven as such in a criminal trial.

the person charged with the crime, is not guilty). The presumption of innocence is a bedrock legal principle. One classic court decision put it this way:

> The presumption of innocence is not a mere belief at the beginning of the trial that the accused is probably innocent. It is not a will-o'-the-wisp, which appears and disappears as the trial progresses. It is a legal presumption which the jurors must consider along with the evidence and the inferences arising from the evidence, when they come finally to pass upon the case. In this sense, the presumption of innocence does accompany the accused through every stage of the trial.[9]

Presumptions are essential to the smooth operation of criminal justice. They serve, basically, as substitutes for evidence. Without them, every minute issue that could possibly be disputed would come up during trials. Without presumptions such as these, the process would be slowed down considerably because every minor event, no matter how likely, would have to be proven in court. (Figure 1.3 shows popular presumptions that arise in criminal justice.)

The Prosecutor and the Defense Attorney

opening statements The statements made by both the prosecutor and defense attorney at the outset of a criminal trial wherein each side lays out for the jury, in overview form, what they will prove throughout the trial.

Trials begin with **opening statements**. In their opening statements, both the prosecutor and the defense attorney lay out for the jury, in overview form, what they will prove throughout the trial. Opening statements are a crucial part of the trial. They give the attorneys a chance to bond with the jury. Studies reveal, indeed, that jurors frequently decide in favor of the party they are most impressed with during the opening statements phase of the trial[10]; they also give attorneys an early shot at summarizing the whole argument that lies ahead. This may resonate better with the jury

---

[9]*Dodson v. United States*, 23 F.2d 401 (1928).
[10]J.J. Eannace, "Art—Not a Science: A Prosecutor's Perspective on Opening Statements," *The Prosecutor*, Vol. 31(1997), pp. 32–37.

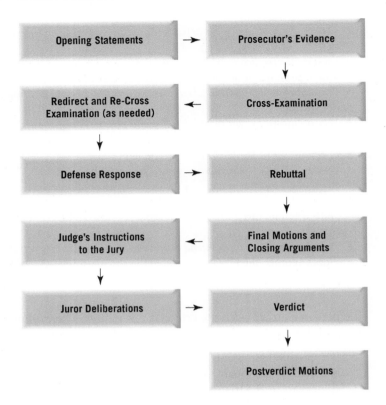

Figure 1.4
Summary of Steps in a
Criminal Trial

than a long, arduous process of rolling out exhibit after exhibit and witness after witness. See Figure 1.4 for a summary of the full trial process.

The Prosecutor

Once opening statements have concluded, the government (via the prosecutor) has the opportunity to present its case. As prosecutors make their case, they present evidence. Evidence can be thought of in many different ways. **Direct evidence** is "evidence that proves a fact without the need for the juror to infer anything from it,"[11] an example of direct evidence being testimony by a witness that the accused committed the crime. By contrast, **circumstantial evidence** is "evidence that *indirectly* proves a fact."[12] Circumstantial evidence needs to be combined with other evidence to allow a fact-finder to infer a conclusion. An example of circumstantial evidence is evidence of the defendant's ability to commit the crime or his or her possible motives; for instance, the prospect of receiving a life insurance settlement could serve as someone's motive to kill. Fingerprints are also circumstantial. They could prove that the defendant was at the crime scene, but not necessarily that he or she committed the crime.

It is also useful to think in terms of real, testimonial, and demonstrative evidence. **Real evidence** refers to "any tangible item that can be perceived with the

direct evidence Evidence that proves a fact without the need for the juror to infer anything from it.

circumstantial evidence Evidence that indirectly proves a fact.

real evidence Any tangible item that can be perceived with the five senses.

---

[11]J.L. Worrall and C. Hemmens, *Criminal Evidence: An Introduction* (Los Angeles: Roxbury, 2005), p. 71.
[12]Ibid.

Defense attorneys perform a valuable function, providing legal representation for those accused of crime.

testimonial evidence
Most often, testimonial evidence consists of verbal statements given by someone who is under oath.

demonstrative evidence
Evidence that seeks to demonstrate a certain point (e.g., drawings and illustrations).

material evidence
Evidence that is relevant and goes to substantial matters in dispute, or has legitimate influence or bearing on the decision of the case.

five senses."[13] Real evidence can consist of everything from clothing and footprints to weapons and drugs, as well as documents, contracts, letters, and the like, and it can include scientific evidence, such as blood samples, fingerprints, and lab test results. **Testimonial evidence** refers to what someone says, usually someone who is under oath and giving testimony in a trial. Finally, **demonstrative evidence** is evidence that seeks to demonstrate a certain point, such as drawings, diagrams, illustrations, and computer simulations that are used to help jurors understand how a crime was likely committed.

Not just any of these forms of evidence will do. In the case of real evidence, what is introduced must be relevant, and evidence is relevant when it sheds light on a matter that is in dispute. Real evidence also has to be competent, meaning it was not secured illegally or in violation of the Constitution. Finally, real evidence must be material. **Material evidence** is "that which is relevant and goes to substantial matters in dispute, or has legitimate influence or bearing on the decision of the case."[14] Distinguish between relevant and material evidence in this way: The former relates to the issue in question; the latter is concerned with how significant the evidence is.

The Defense Attorney

Once the prosecution rests its case, the defense gets its turn. The main concern is with establishing reasonable doubt to ensure the prosecution fails to meet its burden. One strategy the defense may resort to is challenging the prosecution's scientific evidence, and another may be to present on one of many affirmative defenses. **Affirmative defenses** are those that go beyond simply denying that a crime took place or that the defendant committed it; examples include everything from alibi defenses and self-defense to duress and entrapment. We look at these defenses in some depth later on (Chapter 9).

Interestingly, a defendant in a criminal trial cannot be compelled to testify under *any* circumstances because defendants enjoy absolute Fifth Amendment protection from self-incrimination during criminal proceedings. However, once a defendant takes the stand, he or she can be compelled to answer questions related to the facts of the case at hand.[15] Otherwise the defense attorney, not the defendant, is the one who challenges the prosecution's case in an effort to create reasonable doubt.

[13]Ibid.
[14]Ibid., p. 407.
[15]See, e.g., *Brown* v. *United States*, 356 U.S. 148 (1958); *Rogers* v. *United States*, 340 U.S. 367 (1951).

© Junial Enterprises/Shutterstock

The Judge and the Jury

affirmative defense A
criminal law defense that
goes beyond simply
denying that a crime took
place or that the
defendant committed it.

The judge presides over the proceedings, from before trial all the way through to the reading of the verdict. Judges are required to remain neutral and detached throughout the proceedings. Prior to reading the verdict, the judge will give instructions to the jury (in a jury trial). This section thus looks at the role of judges and juries in the criminal process.

The Role of the Judge

trier of law One who is
tasked with resolving any
legal matter that comes
before a court, most often
a judge. Opposite of a
trier of fact.

Judges are often described as **triers of law** (or finders of law), meaning that they are generally tasked with resolving any *legal* matter that comes before the court. For example, if one of the attorneys in a case goes too far in questioning a particular witness, such as by leading the person in a particular direction, the judge will make a ruling on the propriety of such action if the opposing party objects; in other words, the judge will determine whether the questioning can proceed. In a criminal case, the defendant's attorney may seek exclusion of evidence that was allegedly obtained improperly, and the judge, being familiar with the Fourth Amendment and relevant state and local rules governing the admissibility of evidence, will decide on the matter. His or her decision will amount to applying the law, either as spelled out in statutes or as interpreted by other courts' decisions.

trier of fact Someone
who listens to the
evidence and renders a
decision, a judge in a
bench trial or a jury
member in a jury trial.
Opposite of trier of law.

The opposite of a trier of law is a **trier of fact** (or finder of fact), someone who listens to the evidence and renders a decision. Assuming there is a jury trial, jurors are the triers of fact; in a criminal case, they listen to the facts presented by the prosecution and the defense and then render a decision based on which side made the more convincing case. (Remember that the "facts" presented by the prosecution and the "facts" presented by the defense can differ because what happened before the trial is often disputed). Since jurors were not present for the crime, they are forced to interpret the facts as presented to them by the prosecution and defense. Jurors' decisions ultimately affect whether the defendant will be held accountable for the crime. At no point does a jury decide on what the law says or how it is to be interpreted. At the most, members of a jury may be presented with different options for verdicts, but these options are presented to them by a judge.

bench trial A trial in
which the judge, rather
than a jury, decides the
proper verdict.

In some cases, judges serve as triers of law *and* fact. This occurs in a **bench trial**, a trial in which the judge basically replaces the jury. Sometimes defendants waive their constitutional right to a jury trial. In other situations, especially those involving low-level offenses like misdemeanors, jury trials are rare, if not barred altogether, which requires that the judges do more than just decide on the legal minutia in the cases. Judges even act as triers of fact to some extent in jury trials, especially in the sentencing phase. They weigh aggravating and mitigating factors and settle on a sanction that is fair relative to the crime in question, something that requires at least some degree of attention to what happened during the case or at least to what the defendant's background was leading up to the case.

The Judge's Instructions to the Jury.
Once final motions and closing arguments have been made, the judge will give his or her instructions to the jurors before they head off to deliberate. First, the judge gives the jurors something of a crash

course in basic legal principles, discussing burdens and standards of proof. Second, the judge discusses the specific offenses in question, and the particular elements of each. Third, if an affirmative defense was raised, the judge will advise the jury of the standards or tests that need to be used to determine whether such a defense is meritorious. Finally, the judge will inform jurors of the verdicts that can be selected and may also discuss the prospect of a guilty verdict for a lesser included offense. In the homicide context, for example, jurors may find the defendant guilty of second- instead of first-degree murder. Second-degree murder is less serious than first-degree murder, but its elements are the same as first-degree murder (deliberate killing); first-degree murder just adds premeditation.

All of this is usually preceded by a charging conference. In a criminal case, this is where the prosecutor, defense attorney, and judge meet out of earshot of the jury to decide on what the instructions to the jurors will be. Jury instructions are important insofar as they can serve as the basis for an appeal; that is, if what the judge tells the jury is wrong, then the defendant may have a basis for challenging a conviction. Unfortunately, even if the judge's instructions to jurors are flawless, getting jurors to understand them is a different matter entirely—researchers have found that many jurors, even well-educated ones, have difficulty comprehending the instructions they are given.

The Jury

The Sixth Amendment states, in part, that the "accused shall enjoy the right to a speedy and public trial, by an impartial jury of the state." While this seems straightforward on its face, it is a qualified right. In *Duncan* v. *Louisiana,* the Supreme Court prohibited jury trials for petty offenses, and in *Baldwin* v. *New York,* the Court announced its reason for this: The "disadvantages, onerous though they may be," of denying a jury trial for petty crimes are "outweighed by the benefits that result from speedy and inexpensive nonjury adjudication."[16]

The right to a jury trial can also be waived. If the case is particularly inflammatory or is one with which the community is intimately familiar, then obtaining a fair jury may be difficult, so in such a situation, the defendant may opt for a bench trial. Interestingly, the waiver of the right to a jury trial can be vetoed by the trial judge; that is, the judge can require a jury trial even if the defendant desires otherwise; often, such a veto comes at the request of the prosecutor. Indeed, the Supreme Court has upheld at least one federal statute permitting vetoes of this nature.[17]

Assuming the right to a jury trial applies and that the right is not waived, jury selection takes place. The process behind selecting an impartial jury is rather complicated. Before *voir dire* (the process of examining potential jurors for bias) commences, a list of potential or prospective jurors must be compiled, and the creation of this list is critical; without an impartial list, the final jury will not reflect a fair cross-section of the community. Once a list is put together, then a panel of jurors is selected. This is where individuals are selected, usually randomly, for jury duty. Think

---

[16]*Baldwin* v. *New York,* 399 U.S. 66 (1970), p. 73.
[17]*Singer* v. *United States,* 380 U.S. 24 (1965).

of jury selection, then, as a three-stage process: A list of potential jurors must be compiled, potential jurors are selected from that list, and only then is the jury itself is chosen from the potential jurors who are selected.

There are three main steps in the *voir dire* process. *Voir dire* usually begins with the judge asking questions concerning potential jurors' familiarity with the case, attitudes toward one or other party to the case, demographic information, and so on. This is often done to guide the attorneys in their *voir dire* questioning. Next, during *voir dire,* both the defense and the prosecution have an unlimited number of so-called **challenges for cause**, which are used to exclude potential jurors from service on the jury because of bias or a similar reason. For example, if a member of the jury panel is related to the defendant, a challenge for cause will almost certainly succeed, or if the potential juror served on a past jury in a case dealing with a similar crime, a challenge for cause could probably succeed. Next, each attorney is afforded a certain number of **peremptory challenges**. These call for the removal of potential jurors without any type of argument. Think of the peremptory challenge as a fall-back measure. If, say, the defense fails with a challenge for cause to exclude a potential juror whom it believes will be biased against the defendant, a peremptory challenge can be used.

Jury Decision Making. Once the jury leaves the courtroom to deliberate, this becomes the "black box" phase of the criminal process. Jury deliberations, as we mentioned earlier, are secretive. If jurors need anything (such as to view an exhibit a second time), they will ask the bailiff, otherwise jurors are more or less shut off from the rest of the courtroom actors. The reason for this should be obvious: Preserving the jury's neutrality and objectivity is of paramount concern. As we saw earlier, though, it is somewhat naive to think of jurors as entirely objective and concerned solely with the facts as presented.

If the jury cannot reach a verdict and becomes hopelessly deadlocked, this is known as a **hung jury**. If this occurs, the result is generally a **mistrial**, and a new trial will then be held. Mistrials can occur for various reasons, not just deadlocked juries, as this explanation illustrates: "[A mistrial is] a trial which has been terminated and declared invalid by the court because of some circumstance which creates a substantial and uncorrectable prejudice to the conduct of a fair trial, or which makes it impossible to continue the trial in accordance with prescribed procedures."[18]

Juries rarely become deadlocked in their deliberations, meaning that rates of hung juries are exceptionally low.[19] Even so, in the event that a jury cannot reach an agreement, one result may be an **Allen charge** (named after the Supreme Court's decision in *Allen v. United States*[20]), which is a set of instructions given to jurors after they become deadlocked that instructs them to reexamine their opinions in an effort to reach a verdict.

challenge for cause The opportunity for a prosecutor or defense attorney to excuse a prospective juror for cause (e.g., racial prejudice). Challenges for cause or unlimited.

peremptory challenge The opportunity for a prosecutor or defense attorney to excuse a prospective juror for any reason. Peremptory challenges are limited, and race cannot be used as a basis for exercising peremptory challenges.

hung jury A deadlocked jury, one that cannot reach a verdict.

mistrial An end to the trial, such as a when the jury becomes hopelessly deadlocked. A new trial is usually held.

Allen charge Instructions given to jurors after they become deadlocked that instructs them to reexamine their opinions in an effort to reach a verdict.

---

[18]U.S. Department of Justice, *Dictionary of Criminal Justice Data Terminology,* p. 132.
[19]P.L. Hannaford, V.P. Hans, and G.T. Munsterman, "How Much Justice Hangs in the Balance? A New Look at Hung Jury Rates," *Judicature,* Vol. 83(1999), pp. 59–67.
[20]*Allen v. United States,* 164 U.S. 492 (1896).

Jury Nullification. Sometimes juries act strangely and run amok, returning decisions that are altogether opposite of what would be expected by tradition, process, or law. They sometimes return a guilty verdict in cases where the defendant is clearly not guilty and/or return a not-guilty verdict in cases where the defendant is guilty. This practice of either ignoring or misapplying the law in a certain situation is known as **jury nullification**. Jury nullification sounds counter to the way the jury system should operate, but there can be an upside to it. Back in 1997, an Aurora (Illinois) bar owner, Jessie Ingram, booby-trapped his bar after it was burglarized three times. He put warning signs outside the windows that had been broken during previous burglaries, announcing that anyone entering the premises without permission would be subject to electric shock. One burglar ignored the signs and broke a window; on climbing through it, he was shocked to death by a piece of electrified steel that Ingram had adhered to the windowsill. The grand jury refused to indict Ingram on homicide charges (interestingly, though, he was later held civilly liable for the burglar's death). This was a grand jury case, not a trial jury case, but the same logic applies—sometimes justice can be served (or so the grand jurors felt) by going somewhat counter to what the law requires.

There is precedent for jurors ignoring the law and deciding what they feel is best. During Prohibition, for example, jurors routinely refused to convict people charged with liquor-law violations.[21] But jury nullification can also live up to its negative connotations. Historically, southern juries often refused to convict white defendants who were charged with offenses against black victims despite the presence of evidence that would warrant conviction.[22] Some have argued that jury nullification can also be used for political purposes and has little to do with the facts of the case at hand or even with juror characteristics. For example, the acquittal of O.J. Simpson may have been little more than an effort on jurors' part to show that the Los Angeles Police Department (LAPD) was racist.[23]

Is jury nullification really a problem? One study showed, for example, that as penalties become more severe, jurors become less likely to convict, possibly suggesting nullification.[24] In another study, researchers used mock jurors to decide the fate of a hypothetical physician who was accused of knowingly transfusing a patient with blood he knew hadn't been screened for HIV; the researchers found that the jurors were less likely to convict if the penalty was severe (e.g., prison instead of a fine).[25] These studies do not provide clear evidence of jury nullification, but they at least illustrate there can be apprehension on jurors' part to apply the law to the letter, meaning jurors sometimes do what *they* think will best serve the ends of justice.

jury nullification Jurors' practice of either ignoring or misapplying the law in a certain situation.

---

[21]A. Scheflin and J. Van Dyke, "Jury Nullification: The Contours of Controversy," *Law and Contemporary Problems,* Vol. 43(1980), pp. 51–115.

[22]See, e.g., W.W. Hodes, "Lord Brougham, the Dream Team, and Jury Nullification of the Third Kind," *University of Colorado Law Review,* Vol. 67(1996), pp.1075–1108.

[23]J. Rosen, "The Bloods and the Crits: O.J. Simpson, Critical Race Theory, and the Law and the Triumph of Color in America," *New Republic* (December 9, 1996), pp. 27–42.

[24]N.L. Kerr, "Severity of Penalty and Mock Jurors' Verdicts," *Journal of Personality and Social Psychology,* Vol. 36(1978), pp. 1431–1442.

[25]K.E. Niedermeier, I.A. Horowitz, and N.L. Kerr, "Informing Jurors of Their Nullification Power: A Route to a Just Verdict or Judicial Chaos," *Law and Human Behavior,* Vol. 23(1999), pp. 331–351.

jury vilification The opposite of jury nullification.

The flipside of jury nullification has been called **jury vilification**[26]: "Juries may return verdicts that reflect prejudiced or bigoted community standards and convict when the evidence does not warrant a conviction."[27] Jury vilification is exceptionally rare; more often, if a person is unjustifiably convicted, the decision is more likely due to jurors' failure to understand important dimensions of the case.

YOUR DECISION

1. Jodie Matthews is the lead prosecutor on a murder trial that is currently in the process of jury selection. Juror #2, Lane Smith, claims that he was a college roommate of the defense attorney. Juror #6, Jack Sproule, is wearing a T-shirt that reads "Down with the Police." And Juror #12, Mary Murphy, is falling asleep during the questioning process. Jodie is trying to decide which of these jurors, if any, to eliminate. What types of challenges, if any, could Jodie use to eliminate these potential jurors?

2. Amy Jones was physically and mentally abused by her husband, Mark, for the last ten years of their marriage. Amy routinely ended up in the hospital as a result of Mark's terrible beatings. One evening while Mark slept, Amy finally decided she'd had enough. She shot Mark in the chest, killing him instantly. At her murder trial, Amy presented gruesome evidence regarding the abuse she suffered during her marriage. She failed, however, to prove that she was in any danger at the moment she killed Mark. You are on the jury and feel that Mark "got what he deserved" and would like to find Amy not guilty. If you find Amy not guilty, are you engaging in jury nullification? Why or why not?

Summary

- An adversarial system pits two parties (prosecution and defense) against one another in the pursuit of the truth. The American system of justice is adversarial. An inquisitorial system is the opposite of an adversarial system.

- The burden of proof in a criminal trial is proof beyond a reasonable doubt.

- A presumption is a fact assumed to be true under the law. The most widely known presumption in American criminal law is the presumption of innocence.

- The prosecutor presents the government's case. The defense attorney represents the defendant and seeks to establish reasonable doubt in the minds of the jurors (or judge in a bench trial).

- Judges (called triers of law) are tasked with resolving *legal* matters that come before the court and making sure that the law is followed.

- The practice of either ignoring or misapplying the law in a certain situation is known as jury nullification. Jury vilification occurs when jurors convict if the evidence does not warrant a conviction.

---

[26]I.A. Horowitz, N.L. Kerr, and K.E. Niedermeier, "Jury Nullification: Legal and Psychological Perspectives," *Brooklyn Law Review*, Vol. 66(2001), pp. 1207–1249.
[27]Ibid., p. 1210.

COURT ORGANIZATION

Learning Objectives

- **Describe the structure of the U.S. legal system, including jurisdiction.**
- **Understand the parts of a court case.**
- **Explain the practical meaning of a verdict**

CORE CONCEPTS

The law lies more or less dormant until someone is charged with a crime. Once someone is charged with violating the law, as we have seen, a trial takes place. Trials take place at different levels, however. Federal criminal trials involve suspected violations of federal law. State criminal trials apply to violations of state laws. To further gain a grasp of this arrangement, it is important to consider both the structure and hierarchy of the court system in the United States.

Dual Court System

dual federalism A system in which the only powers of the federal government are those explicitly listed, with the rest being left to the states.

dual court system The American court system, one that separates federal and state courts.

cooperative federalism A system of federalism in which the lines between federal and state power are blurred.

Ours is a **dual court system** that separates federal and state courts. The dual court system is advantageous and desirable because it parallels federalism, a system of government where power is constitutionally divided between a central governing body (i.e., the federal government) and various constituent units (i.e., the states). Federalism requires that laws are made by the central governing authority and by the constituent units. In the United States, the federal government makes law, but federalism also gives the states power to make their own laws.

A quick glance at the U.S. Constitution reveals a system of **dual federalism**, where the only powers of the federal government are those explicitly listed, with the rest being left to the states. In reality, though, ours is more of a system of **cooperative federalism**, meaning some of the lines between federal and state power are blurred. Article I, Section 8, of the U.S. Constitution gives the federal government the power to regulate interstate commerce, but this authority has been interpreted broadly such that the federal government can control much of what happens at the state level.

While a dual court system is desirable from a federalism standpoint, it also promotes complication and confusion. It would be neat and tidy if the federal criminal law was separate and distinct from state criminal law, but in reality both overlap. For example, certain criminal acts, such as those involving firearms, are violations of *both* federal and state criminal law. This leads to confusion over where it would be best to try offenders or whether they should be tried twice in the two different systems.

courts of limited jurisdiction Courts that have jurisdiction over relatively minor offenses and infractions. A traffic court fits in this category.

courts of general jurisdiction Courts that try several types of cases, so-called "trial courts."

superior courts The name commonly used for courts of general jurisdiction. Often found at the county level.

intermediate appellate courts Courts to which verdicts from courts of general jurisdiction can be appealed.

state supreme court The highest court in a state.

district court Federal trial court. There are 94 in the United States, the District of Columbia, and the U.S. territories.

Court Levels

The dual court system is only part of the story. At each level, there is a distinct court hierarchy. States often have limited jurisdiction courts (such as traffic courts), trial courts, appellate courts, and supreme courts. At the federal level, there are trial courts, appellate courts, and the U.S. Supreme Court. Each trial court adjudicates different offenses. Appellate courts consider different matters depending on where they lie in the court hierarchy. Appeals from state courts can sometimes be heard in the federal courts. Higher-level courts can control the actions and decisions of lower courts, but not the other way around. Despite the apparent complexity, each court has its place.

There is no way to succinctly describe all the variations in state court structures, but, generally, they resemble one another. Typically, the lowest-level courts in a given state are **courts of limited jurisdiction**, which have jurisdiction over relatively minor offenses and infractions. A traffic court fits in this category. Next are the trial courts, also called **courts of general jurisdiction**, which try several types of cases. Courts of general jurisdiction are often county-level courts and are frequently called **superior courts**. At the next highest level are the **intermediate appellate courts**; verdicts from courts of general jurisdiction are appealed to these courts. Finally, each state has its own **state supreme court**, the highest court in the state. Figure 1.5 shows California's relatively simple court structure. Importantly, state courts try cases involving state laws (and, depending on the level of the court, some county, city, and other local ordinances).

Federal courts try cases involving federal law. The *federal* court structure can be described succinctly because, for our purposes, it consists of three specific types of courts (we do not discuss federal magistrate courts, as their role is primarily one of assisting federal trial courts[28]). The federal trial courts are called **district courts**.

U.S. Supreme Court building.

---

[28]For more on the role of federal magistrate judges, see http://www.fedjudge.org/ (accessed April 10, 2012).

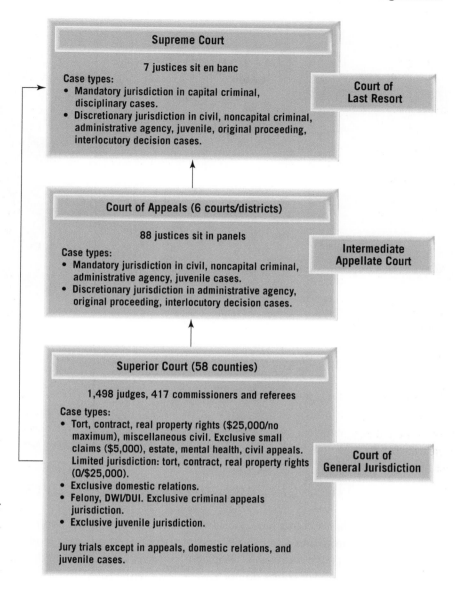

Figure 1.5

California Court System
Source: D.B. Rottman and S.M. Strickland, State Court Organizations, 2004 (Arlington, VA: National Center for State Courts, 2006). Available at: http://www.ojp.usdoj.gov/bjs/pub/pdf/sco8704.pdf

U.S. Court of Appeals
The federal appellate court. There are 13 in the United States: 12 regional courts and 1 federal circuit.

U.S. Supreme Court The highest court in the federal system.

There are 94 federal district courts in the United States (as of this writing), including 89 district courts in the 50 states and 1 each in Puerto Rico, the Virgin Islands, the District of Columbia, Guam, and the Northern Mariana Islands. At the next level are the **U.S. Court of Appeals**. There are 13 of these so-called circuit courts of appeals: 12 regional courts and 1 for the federal circuit. Each is charged with hearing appeals from several of the district courts that fall within its circuit. Figure 1.6 illustrates how the U.S. Courts of Appeal are divided geographically in the United States. Finally, the **U.S. Supreme Court** is the highest court in the federal system.

Most of the cases we will look at in this book hail from either the appellate courts or the Supreme Court. Again, this is because trial courts rarely publish their decisions. This point cannot be overemphasized because there are untold numbers of cases that never make their way into criminal law texts or classrooms simply because they are not published. See Figure 1.7 for an overview of how cases arrive at the U.S. Supreme Court.

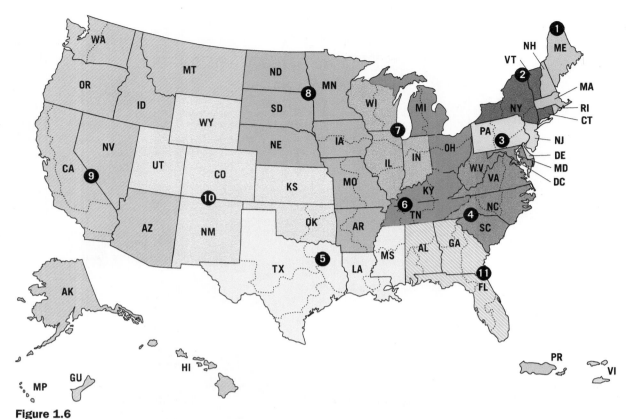

Figure 1.6
Geographic Boundaries of the U.S. Courts of Appeal
Source: Administrative Office of the U.S. Courts. http://www.uscourts.gov/Court_Locator.aspx (accessed April 25, 2011)

The Relationships between Courts

Higher courts have considerable influence over lower courts due to the hierarchical structure pointed out in the previous section. At the state level, for example, appellate and supreme courts issue decisions that lower courts are—on their face—required to abide by. Yet lower courts do not always "follow the rules" to the letter. Also, many of them have developed various means to cope with influential decisions from the higher courts.

Nearly all high-court decisions are subject to interpretation simply by the way they are written. For example, in the famous school desegregation case of *Brown* v. *Board of Education,*[29] Chief Justice Warren's implementation order (also called an implementation decree, issued following the Court's opinion in the case, spelling out details on how the decision was to be implemented by the lower courts) said the following:

> [T]he cases are remanded to the District Courts to take such proceedings and enter such orders and decrees consistent with this opinion as are necessary and proper to admit the parties to these cases to public schools on a racially nondiscriminatory basis with all deliberate speed.[30]

---

[29]*Brown* v. *Board of Education*, 347 U.S. 483 (1954).
[30]*Brown* v. *Board of Education*, 349 U.S. 294 (1955), p. 301.

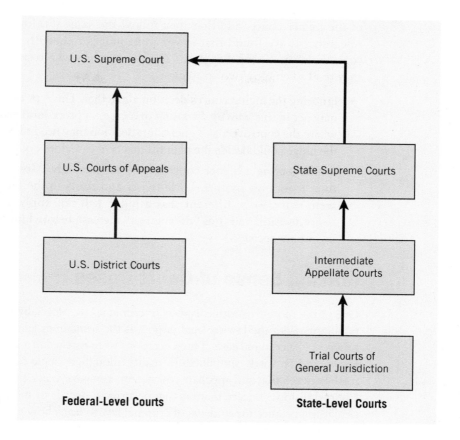

Figure 1.7

How Cases Arrive at the U.S. Supreme Court

What is meant by "all deliberate speed"? There was no easy answer to this question, which meant the lower courts had considerable license to interpret it. The implementation order also referenced a "prompt and reasonable start toward full compliance with the ruling."[31] What did Chief Justice Warren mean by this? Again, there was no easy answer, and the result was room for interpretation by the lower courts.

Consider a criminal justice example. In the landmark *Katz* v. *United States*[32] decision, the Supreme Court defined a search as consisting of government action that infringes on a "reasonable expectation of privacy." What is a reasonable expectation of privacy? Yet again, there is no easy answer.

Lower courts employ a range of methods for dealing with higher-court decisions simply because of how many of the former there are. Researchers are mixed on the issue of how compliant lower-court judges are with higher-court decisions.[33] A number of studies have found that lower-court judges' decisions closely mirror those

---

[31]Ibid., p. 300.
[32]*Katz* v. *United States*, 389 U.S. 347 (1967).
[33]D.R. Songer, J.A. Segal, and C.M. Cameron, "The Hierarchy of Justice: Testing a Principal-Agent Model of Supreme Court-Circuit Court Interactions," *American Journal of Political Science*, Vol. 38(1994), pp. 673–696.

of the higher courts and that they follow the same ideological trends.[34] But other researchers have found that lower-court judges frequently resist higher-court decisions with which they disagree.[35] For those judges who resist higher-court decisions, they tend to employ two strategies:

- **Ignoring the higher court's decision altogether.** This type of defiance is rare. A judge may act in this way by disposing of a case on procedural grounds before the point where the controversial higher-court decision may need to be applied. For example, the judge could decide the plaintiff in a civil case does not have standing to sue.

- **Implementing a higher court's decision sparingly.** Most cases are factually distinct from one another. Little twists and turns in the facts can make one case seem sufficiently different that a judge will not apply a controversial higher-court decision and thus "distinguish" the case before him or her, effectively issuing a new decision.

Making Sense of Court Cases

One of the more frustrating aspects of criminal law, especially for those who have little familiarity with the law or legal jargon, is the sometimes laborious task of tracing the progress of a criminal case. If final decisions were reached in a single court, then criminal law would be vastly simplified. In reality, though, a single case can bounce back and forth between trial and appellate courts, sometimes for years. Indeed, many U.S. Supreme Court decisions concern matters that occurred a decade or more ago. Thus, it is of particular importance for students of criminal law to learn how to trace a criminal case.

There are several essential steps to tracing the progress of a criminal case. First, it is necessary to have a basic understanding of the nation's court structure. This requires knowing where the criminal trial in question took place. If it took place in a federal circuit court, then tracing the progress of the case will be fairly easy. As you read earlier, there are only three possible courts—district court, circuit appellate court, and the Supreme Court—that may have handed down decisions on the matter. If the case originated in state court, however, it can be decidedly more difficult to trace the case over time. Familiarity with the state court structure is needed, as well as an understanding of how cases can jump back and forth between the state and federal courts, which will be discussed later in this section.

Second, to adequately follow the progress of a criminal case, it is also necessary to understand the legal jargon, beginning with the parties to the case. The *parties* to the case are the people involved. At the trial level, the parties of interest are the defendant

---

[34]For just a few examples, see L. Baum, "Response of Federal District Judges to Court of Appeals Policies: An Exploration," *Western Political Quarterly,* Vol. 3(1980), pp. 217–224; S.C. Benesh, *The U.S. Court of Appeals and the Law of Confessions: Perspectives on the Hierarchy of Justice* (New York: LFB Scholarly, 2002); J. Gruhl, "The Supreme Court's Impact on the Law of Libel: Compliance by Lower Federal Courts," *Western Political Quarterly,* Vol. 33(1980), pp. 502–519; D. Songer and R.S. Sheehan, "Supreme Court Impact on Compliance and Outcomes: *Miranda* and *New York Times* in the United States Courts of Appeals," *Western Political Quarterly,* Vol. 43(1990), pp. 297–319.

[35]See, e.g., J.W. Peltason, *Fifty-Eight Lonely Men: Southern Federal Judges and School Desegregation* (New York: Harcourt Brace, 1961); N.T. Romans, "The Role of State Supreme Courts in Judicial Policy Making," *Western Political Quarterly,* Vol. 27(1974), pp. 38–59.

prosecutor The official who charges the defendant and is tasked with representing the government in court.

appellant The party of appeals.

appellee The party appealed against.

reverse In the appeals context, what happens when an appellate court nullifies or sets aside a lower court's verdict.

vacate In the appeals context, basically the same as a reversal.

remand In the appeals context, what happens when an appellate court sends a case back to the lower court for further action consistent with its decision.

affirm In the appeals context, the act of an appellate court agreeing with a lower court's decision.

(as defined above, the person charged with the crime in question), and the government, represented by the **prosecutor**. At the appellate level, these parties are no longer called *defendant* and *prosecutor* but rather **appellant** and **appellee**. The *appellant* is the party that appeals; both the prosecutor and defendant can appeal, but the defendant appeals more often than the prosecutor. The *appellee* (sometimes called the *respondent*) is the party appealed against. Most cases favor the defense on appeal, as the prosecution is permitted to appeal only in very limited circumstances due to certain constitutional constraints, such as double jeopardy (discussed in the next chapter).

Next, to follow a criminal case, it is essential to have an understanding of how cases are decided and what possible decisions can be reached. At the trial level, two decisions can result: guilty and not guilty. At the appellate level, however, the picture becomes more complex. Assume, for example, that a defendant is found guilty in a federal district court and appeals to one of the circuit courts of appeals. Assuming that the court agrees to hear the case, it can hand down one of several decisions. It could **reverse** the lower court's decision, which is akin to nullifying or setting it aside. Sometimes the appellate court **vacates** the lower court's decision, which is basically the same as reversing it. A reversal does *not* always have the effect of setting the defendant free, however. The appellate court could also **remand** the case back to the lower court. When a case is remanded, it is sent back to the lower court for further action consistent with the appellate court's decision. Cases can also be reversed and remanded together. The appellate court can also **affirm** the lower court's decision, in which case it agrees with the lower court.

If there was only one appellate court, tracing the progress of a case would be fairly simple. Unfortunately, multiple appellate courts exist, which means the decisions from court to court can change. This is a very important point. Assume, for example, that a defendant is found guilty in a state trial court. He or she could appeal to the state's intermediate appellate court, which could reverse the defendant's conviction. The case could then go to the state's supreme court, which could reverse the appellate court's decision and basically uphold the defendant's conviction. Finally, the case could go to the U.S. Supreme Court, which could again reverse the defendant's conviction. Believe it or not, this is a fairly simple progression. Nothing prevents a single case from going from the trial court to the appellate court, back to the trial court, up to the appellate court again, then up to the state supreme court, back to the intermediate appellate court, and so on.

It is essential to understand what has happened with a criminal case before making any claims as to its importance or influence. In other words, doing incomplete legal research can be a recipe for disaster. If, for instance, a researcher finds a state supreme court decision that supports a point he or she wants to make but that decision was later reversed, say, by the U.S. Supreme Court, whatever argument he or she makes in reliance on that state supreme court case will be inaccurate. Thus, in tracing the progress of a criminal case, it is necessary to understand whether the issue in question has been resolved or may currently be on the docket of an appellate court, which could render an altogether different decision.

Understanding the Parts of a Court Decision

In tracing a criminal case, especially when interpreting one decided at the appellate level, it is important to understand the components of a published decision. An

opinion The rationale for an appellate court's decision subscribed to by the majority of judges or justices, usually authored by one judge or justice.

concurring opinion An opinion that agrees with the majority decision but for different reasons.

dissent A minority opinion that is at odds with the majority opinion.

appellate court often consists of a panel of judges who may not always agree with one another, even though the court reaches a single decision. For example, a 5–4 decision by the U.S. Supreme Court is one in which the Court reached a single decision because of a majority, but four of the justices disagreed. The **opinion** is the voice of the five justices (or the voice of the majority of the judges in a lower appellate court decision), although one or more of the five may opt to write a **concurring opinion**, which supports the majority's decision but with different legal logic. The four remaining justices will probably write a **dissent**, in which they argue why they disagree with the majority's decision. If they wanted to, each of the four minority justices could write his or her own individual dissent. Either way, it is important to distinguish between a given court's opinion and possible concurring and dissenting opinions. Finally, there is the potential for a plurality opinion, which occurs when no single opinion received the support of the majority of the court's members.

In addition to the opinion and dissent (if there is a dissent), cases also include a prior history, the disposition, the judges who decided the case, the facts of the case, the decision, and the procedural history. Sometimes these elements are clearly spelled out. Other times some of them are "buried" within the case. For example, the facts of the case, the recounting of what happened, are often included near the beginning of the opinion. Likewise, decisions do not always stand out in their own section. They are often included in the language near the end of the opinion. And unfortunately, no case as the same is the next, and multiple formats are followed. Thus, it takes a certain amount of practice to read cases.

We invite the reader to examine Appendix B, as it provides a brief tutorial on briefing cases. This is another exercise that can help students make sense out of complicated (and lengthy) court cases and distill them down to their most basic elements in summary form.

The Practical Meaning of Verdicts

There are some important points that need to be borne in mind with respect to verdicts. First, the two main verdicts that can be reached in a trial—guilty and not guilty—do not speak to *factual* guilt or innocence. Just because a defendant is found not guilty does not mean he or she is innocent. It just means that the prosecution could not meet its burden of proving beyond a reasonable doubt that the defendant committed the crime. Likewise, a verdict of guilty means, simply, that the government met its burden. It does not mean the defendant is factually guilty (i.e., committed the crime), but this may certainly be the case.

Second, the "verdicts" reached at the appellate stage have equally unusual meanings. If an appellate court sides with an appellant, it is not stating the individual is innocent. Indeed, appellate courts do not focus on the "facts" of the case and decide whether a defendant is guilty or not guilty. Instead, they focus on legal issues and whether proper procedures were followed at the trial level. It is not uncommon for an appellate court to side with the appellant who then spends the rest of his or her sentence in prison. Other times, the appellant court may require a new trial, which could result in a guilty verdict just as easily as it could result in a not guilty verdict.

YOUR DECISION

1. James Garfalo was arrested for selling 10 grams of cocaine to an undercover police officer. At his jury trial in the state trial court, James was convicted and sentenced to two years in prison. James believes his constitutional rights were violated during the trial and wishes to appeal. What court will hear James's appeal? Assume instead that James's trial happened in a federal district court. What federal court would hear his appeal?

2. Assume that the U.S. Supreme Court issues an opinion declaring that the Sixth Amendment to the U.S. Constitution requires all criminal defendants to have a trial with 24 jurors instead of the traditional 12. The lower courts are not happy with this decision because their jury boxes only accommodate 12 people comfortably, not 24. Do the lower courts have to follow the U.S. Supreme Court's decision? Why or why not?

Summary

- America's is a dual court system that separates federal and state courts. The dual court system, while ideal from a federalism standpoint, promotes complication and confusion (e.g., in the precise relationship between the courts).

- There is a distinct court hierarchy at both the state and federal levels. States often have limited jurisdiction courts (such as traffic courts), trial courts, appellate courts, and supreme courts. At the federal level, there are trial courts, appellate courts, and the U.S. Supreme Court.

- Higher courts have considerable influence over lower courts due to the hierarchical structure of court systems. Lower courts do not always "follow the rules" to the letter; many have developed creative means to cope with influential decisions from the higher courts.

- At the trial level, the parties of interest are the defendant (the person charged with the crime in question) and the prosecutor (the official representing the government). At the appellate level, these parties are no longer called *defendant* and *prosecutor* but rather appellant and appellee.

- Appellate courts can issue several decisions. They *reverse* the lower court's decision, which is akin to nullifying or setting it aside. Sometimes appellate courts vacate the lower court's decision, which is basically the same as reversing it. They can also *remand* the case back to the lower court. Finally, appellate courts can *affirm* the lower court's decision, in which case they agree with the lower court.

- The opinion is the voice of the majority. A concurring opinion supports the majority's decision, but with different logic. A dissent (not written in a unanimous decision) is an argument that disagrees with the majority's decision.

- In addition to the opinion and dissent (if there is a dissent), court cases also often include a prior history, the disposition, the judges who decided the case, the attorneys who represented the government and the defendant, the facts of the case, the decision, and the procedural history.

- If an appellate court sides with an appellant, it is not stating the individual is innocent. It is not uncommon for an appellate court to side with the appellant who then spends the rest of his or her sentence in prison.

Chapter Review

PRELIMINARY INFORMATION

Learning Objectives

- Explain the difference between substantive criminal law and criminal procedure.
- Describe the various classifications of crime.
- Identify the sources of law.

Review Questions

1. In what ways is the criminal law different from the law of criminal procedure?
2. How are crimes classified?
3. What effect did early legal codes have on the modern criminal law?
4. What is the common law and why is it important?
5. At what levels of government are modern statutes found?
6. What are the constitutional sources of the criminal law?

Key Terms

criminal law

criminal procedure

defendant

felony

misdemeanor

malum in se

malum prohibitum

Code of Hammurabi

Twelve Tables

common law

special law

precedent

stare decisis

American Law Institute

Model Penal Code

Bill of Rights

REACHING A VERDICT

Learning Objectives

- Describe the adversarial system.
- Identify courtroom participants.

Review Questions

1. Distinguish between adversarial and inquisitorial justice.
2. What is the burden of proof in a criminal trial? How does it compare to the burden of proof in a civil trial?
3. What are presumptions and why are they important?
4. Distinguish between the roles of the prosecutor and defense attorney.
5. What is the role of the judge?
6. How does jury selection play out?
7. What is the difference between jury nullification and vilification?

Key Terms

adversarial justice system

inquisitorial system

burden of proof

burden of persuasion

burden of production

directed verdict

proof beyond a reasonable doubt

preponderance of evidence

presumption

presumption of innocence

opening statements

direct evidence

circumstantial evidence

real evidence

testimonial evidence

demonstrative evidence

material evidence

affirmative defense

trier of law

trier of fact

bench trial

challenge for cause

peremptory challenge

hung jury

mistrial

Allen charge

jury nullification

jury vilification

MODULE **1.3**   COURT ORGANIZATION

Learning Objectives

- Describe the structure of the U.S. legal system, including jurisdiction.
- Outline the stages of a criminal case.
- Explain the practical meaning of a verdict

Review Questions

1. What does it mean to say America's is a dual court system?
2. Distinguish between dual and cooperative federalism.
3. Explain the concept of court hierarchy.
4. Summarize the typical state court structure (i.e., what are the courts at each level and what do they do?). Do the same for the courts at the federal level.
5. Explain the relationship (real and ideal) between higher and lower courts.
6. Identify the parties to a case at both the trial and federal level.
7. Explain the various decisions that can be reached at the appellate level.

Key Terms

dual court system

dual federalism

cooperative federalism

courts of limited jurisdiction

courts of general jurisdiction

superior courts

intermediate appellate courts

state supreme court

district court

U.S. Court of Appeals

U.S. Supreme Court

prosecutor

appellant

appellee

reverse

vacate

remand

affirm

opinion

concurring opinion

dissent

Chapter Synthesis Questions

1. Is it possible to define as criminal all potential harms? Why or why not?

2. The American system of law is built upon several sources. What, in your opinion, are the advantages and disadvantages of this?

3. Is the adversarial system a help or a hindrance? Why do you feel this way?

4. There is a formal relationship between the courts, but reality deviates from this relationship. Should it? Why or why not?

2

LIMITATIONS ON THE CRIMINAL LAW

MODULE 2.1 GOVERNMENT'S LAW-MAKING AUTHORITY AND GENERAL LIMITATIONS ON THE CRIMINAL LAW

Learning Objectives

- Explain how the separation of powers and federalism limit the government's law-making authority.
- Describe the principle of legality.
- Describe the principle of lenity.

MODULE 2.2 CONSTITUTIONAL LIMITATIONS ON THE CRIMINAL LAW, PART 1

Learning Objectives

- Describe the Fourteenth Amendment's equal protection clause.
- Summarize the prohibition of *ex post facto* laws and bills of attainder.
- Summarize the void for vagueness principle.
- Explain the void for overbreadth doctrine.

MODULE 2.3 CONSTITUTIONAL LIMITATIONS ON THE CRIMINAL LAW, PART 2

Learning Objectives

- Describe the protections against cruel and unusual punishment.
- Explain the guarantee against double jeopardy.

MODULE

2.1

GOVERNMENT'S LAW-MAKING AUTHORITY AND GENERAL LIMITATIONS ON THE CRIMINAL LAW

Learning Objectives

- **Explain how the separation of powers and federalism limit the government's law-making authority.**
- **Describe the principle of legality.**
- **Describe the principle of lenity.**

CORE CONCEPTS

While the criminal law is designed primarily to protect individuals and society from harm, it also safeguards the person accused of a crime. All defendants are innocent until proven guilty and maintain numerous rights throughout the criminal justice process. Offender protection occurs through the state's involvement in prosecuting offenders, proportionate punishment schemes, and procedural rules. Certain procedural protections, such as the right to counsel and the right to an impartial jury trial, hail from the U.S. Constitution and will be discussed in detail in the criminal procedure section of the text. They are *direct* protections, as they lay out the procedures by which an individual who is arrested and prosecuted will (or at least should) be treated by the criminal justice system. There are also *indirect* means of protecting offenders. For example, the U.S. Constitution prohibits laws that are vague and overreaching. This promotes offender protection indirectly because the focus becomes a specific law rather than the treatment of one individual. Certain common law principles, namely legality and lenity, also place limits on the criminal law. These indirect methods are the focus of the present chapter. They are *indirect* protections in the sense that they are more concerned with the criminal law itself than they are with the treatment of individuals. We begin by examining general limitations on the criminal law, then we conclude with a look at various constitutional limitations. First, however, we offer a brief refresher on government's law-making authority.

Government's Law-Making Authority

How far can the government go in terms of criminalizing behavior? For example, can a state legalize medical marijuana while the federal government makes it illegal? Alternatively, at what point should the courts get involved in deciding on whether certain criminal statutes go "too far?" To answer these questions, we need, first, to be mindful of the separation of powers and of federalism, two key elements of the American system of government.

Separation of Powers

The U.S. Constitution divides governmental authority into three branches: executive, legislative, and judicial. In general, the legislative branch makes the laws, the executive branch enforces the laws, and the judicial branch interprets the laws. Members of the executive branch include high-level officials like the president and his cabinet all the way down to municipal police officers and local prosecutors. The legislative branch consists mainly of Congress (the House of Representatives and the Senate) and has law-making authority. The judiciary is the court system. Some of the judiciary's key functions, especially relevant in this book, are deciding on the meaning of laws, how these laws are applied, and when and whether they become unconstitutional. In an ideal world, these three powers are separate and distinct. In reality, however, the lines between each are blurry.

There is a natural hesitancy on the judiciary's part to intrude on the legislative branch's law-making authority. This is so for at least two reasons. First, the people elect legislators, so presumably the laws reflect the interests of all people. It would run counter to this core feature of democracy for the courts to constantly meddle in legislative affairs. Second, if the courts routinely decided on matters of legislation, the result would be arbitrariness and confusion. Court A's decision could be at odds with Court B's. The courts thus *presume* that all laws are constitutional. If someone wishes to challenge the constitutionality of a statute, the burden falls on that party to bring the issue to the courts. Consequently, courts only get involved in matters of legislation when someone challenges the constitutionality of a statute.

Federalism

federalism A system of government where power is constitutionally divided between a central governing body and various constituent units.

Federalism is a system of government where power is constitutionally divided between a central governing body (the federal government, for example) and various constituent units (the states). In a federalist system, laws are made by the central governing authority and by the constituent units. This is obviously the case in the United States. The federal government makes law, but federalism also gives the states power to make their own laws. For example, both the federal government and each state have their own legal codes regulating the conduct of citizens. This is in contrast to a unified system of government, where all power is vested in a central authority. It is also distinct from a **confederation**, where there is no strong central government.

confederation A system of government that lacks a strong central authority.

dual federalism An interpretation of the U.S. Constitution that suggests a system in which the only powers vested in the federal government are those explicitly listed in the document, with the remaining powers being left to the states.

Ours is a system of **dual federalism**, where the only powers vested with the federal government are those explicitly named in the Constitution—the rest is left to the states. This is what we might call the "textbook" definition of federalism. In reality, however, ours is more of a system of cooperative federalism, meaning some of the lines between federal and state power are blurred, or at least that they have fluctuated over time. For example, Article I, Section 8, of the U.S. Constitution gives the federal government the power to regulate interstate commerce, but this authority has been interpreted broadly such that the federal government can control much of what happens at the state level. To this day, we see plenty of federal influence over even local criminal justice activities.

Regarding what activities the federal government can criminalize compared to the state, one must become familiar with Article I, Section 8, of the U.S. Constitution (see Figure 2.1). It specifies the law-making authority of the federal government. And a quick read of Section 8 makes it clear that the federal government's law-making authority is limited. This is why criminal codes vary so much from state to state. With few exceptions, the federal government is not in the business of criminalizing

The Congress shall have power to lay and collect taxes, duties, imposts and excises, to pay the debts and provide for the common defense and general welfare of the United States; but all duties, imposts and excises shall be uniform throughout the United States;

To borrow money on the credit of the United States;

To regulate commerce with foreign nations, and among the several states, and with the Indian tribes;

To establish a uniform rule of naturalization, and uniform laws on the subject of bankruptcies throughout the United States;

To coin money, regulate the value thereof, and of foreign coin, and fix the standard of weights and measures;

To provide for the punishment of counterfeiting the securities and current coin of the United States;

To establish post offices and post roads;

To promote the progress of science and useful arts, by securing for limited times to authors and inventors the exclusive right to their respective writings and discoveries;

To constitute tribunals inferior to the Supreme Court;

To define and punish piracies and felonies committed on the high seas, and offenses against the law of nations;

To declare war, grant letters of marque and reprisal, and make rules concerning captures on land and water;

To raise and support armies, but no appropriation of money to that use shall be for a longer term than two years;

To provide and maintain a navy;

To make rules for the government and regulation of the land and naval forces;

To provide for calling forth the militia to execute the laws of the union, suppress insurrections and repel invasions;

To provide for organizing, arming, and disciplining, the militia, and for governing such part of them as may be employed in the service of the United States, reserving to the states respectively, the appointment of the officers, and the authority of training the militia according to the discipline prescribed by Congress;

To exercise exclusive legislation in all cases whatsoever, over such District (not exceeding ten miles square) as may, by cession of particular states, and the acceptance of Congress, become the seat of the government of the United States, and to exercise like authority over all places purchased by the consent of the legislature of the state in which the same shall be, for the erection of forts, magazines, arsenals, dockyards, and other needful buildings;—And

To make all laws which shall be necessary and proper for carrying into execution the foregoing powers, and all other powers vested by this Constitution in the government of the United States, or in any department or officer thereof.

Figure 2.1

U.S. Constitution, Article I, Section 8

the types of behaviors most state criminal codes consider illegal. Instead, its focus is more on matters of interstate commerce, relationships with other countries, taxes, currency, and the nation's defense.

There are times, however, when a federal law criminalizes behavior while a state legalizes the same behavior. Whenever federal and states laws are at odds like this, the federal law supersedes. Returning to the subject of medical marijuana, this is why federal agents sometimes raid medical marijuana establishments in states like California and Colorado; such businesses are sanctioned under state law, but violate federal law.

General Limitations on the Criminal Law

Governmental authority to criminalize behavior is not absolute. In order to prevent abuse and provide guidance to citizens, state and the federal criminal statutes must be specifically crafted according to legal guidelines. Two distinct principles form the foundation of these criminal codes: legality and lenity.

Legality

principle of legality A legal principle stating that a defendant cannot be convicted of a crime unless there is specific legislation making it illegal and defining the potential punishment.

The **principle of legality** is often expressed through the Latin maxim, "*Nullemcrimen, nullapoena, sinelege.*" This translates into, "There is no crime without law, no punishment without law." It means that a defendant cannot be convicted of a crime unless there is specific legislation making it illegal and defining the potential punishment.

The advantage of the legality principle is that a criminal code provides prior notice to the people of what behavior is illegal. Even though in reality the vast majority of citizens do not read the criminal code from start to finish, the principle of legality prevents governmental abuse. Yet its downside is a lack of flexibility. The criminal law has a hard time keeping pace with new actions that, although harmful, are not yet considered criminal. People are continually inventing new ways to inflict harm on others (either physically or monetarily), while legislators struggle to stay one step ahead.

Consider terrorism. With all the public pressure on the government to do something about it, prosecutors often find themselves in an awkward predicament because they are the ones who must ultimately file charges against known and suspect terrorists. The problem is that most of the available laws they would use to prosecute require completion of a criminal act. So, what is a prosecutor to do in the case of terrorism? Wait around until a serious attack occurs? Certainly not. Prosecutors have two options. One is to wait until lawmakers criminalize actions that are committed in furtherance of a criminal attack. This has happened, and continues to happen, but it certainly wasn't a major priority before the September 11, 2001, terrorist attacks. Another is for prosecutors to get creative in their efforts to prosecute would-be terrorists, such as by using statutes that haven't traditionally been used to target would-be terrorists.[1]

---

[1] R. Chesney, "Anticipatory Prosecution in the War on Terror," in John L. Worrall and M. Elaine Nugent-Borakove, eds., *The Changing Role of the American Prosecutor* (Albany: SUNY Press, 2008).

Lenity

principle of lenity A legal principle requiring that any ambiguity in a statute should benefit the defendant, not the government.

Related to legality is the **principle of lenity**. Lenity requires that the courts construe a statute as favorably as possible to the defendant. If there is any ambiguity in a statute, that ambiguity should benefit the defendant, not the government. In the next section, we consider several means by which lenity is applied. When statutes are overly vague, for example, that vagueness should be resolved in favor of the defendant.

It bears mentioning that there is a downside to the rule of lenity. Many statutes are not completely clear in their wording, meaning there is plenty of room for interpretation in the language of the criminal law. As such, taken to the extreme, the rule of lenity can be used to interpret a statute in a manner that is at odds with legislative intent. For this reason, many states have abolished the rule of lenity.[2] Indeed, the Model Penal Code does not even recognize lenity, opting instead that any ambiguity in the criminal law be resolved in favor of furthering the legislative priorities behind the law, not the defendant.[3]

YOUR DECISION

1. Dr. Feelgood, a self-proclaimed new age doctor in San Francisco, convinced his female patients that he could cure their illnesses if they had sexual intercourse with him. Unaware that he was a fraud, the women willingly complied. The rape statute in California at the time of the incidents required that the defendant act "with force or threat of force" against the victims. Can Dr. Feelgood be charged with the rape of his patients?

2. The drug trade from Central and South America is causing a dramatic increase in criminal activity in New Mexico. The New Mexico legislature wants to take action. They pass a statute with this language: "Any person found transporting illegal substances, including but not limited to, heroin, cocaine and marijuana, into New Mexico will be punished to the full extent of the law." Is this criminal statute enforceable? Why or why not?

Summary

- Legislatures enact the law.
- Courts are naturally hesitant to intrude on the legislature's law-making authority.
- Federalism is a system of government where power is constitutionally divided between a central governing body (the federal government, for example) and various constituent units (the states).
- Ours is a system of dual federalism, where the only powers vested with the federal government are those explicitly named in the Constitution—the rest being left to the states.
- With few exceptions, the federal government is not in the business of criminalizing the types of behaviors most state criminal codes consider illegal. Instead,

[2]J. C. Jeffries, Jr., "Legality, Vagueness, and the Construction of Penal Statutes," *Virginia Law Review*, Vol. 71 (1985), p. 189.
[3]Model Penal Code Section 1.02(3).

its focus is more on matters of interstate commerce, relationships with other countries, taxes, currency, and the nation's defense.

- The legality principle holds that there is no crime without a law prohibiting it and specifying the potential punishment.

- The problem with legality is that the criminal law struggles to keep pace with new and emerging types of harmful behavior.

- Lenity requires that the courts construe a statute as favorably as possible to the defendant.

- Taken to the extreme, the rule of lenity can be used to interpret a statute in a manner that is at odds with legislative intent. For this reason, many states have abolished the rule of lenity.

MODULE 2.2

CONSTITUTIONAL LIMITATIONS ON THE CRIMINAL LAW, PART 1

Learning Objectives

- **Describe the Fourteenth Amendment's equal protection clause.**
- **Summarize the prohibition of *ex post facto* laws and bills of attainder.**
- **Summarize the void for vagueness principle.**
- **Explain the void for overbreadth doctrine.**

CORE CONCEPTS

To reiterate an earlier point, the courts only get involved in reviewing statutes when there is a clear possibility that a statute violates some specific constitutional provision. There are also fairly clear dividing lines, because of federalism, between the law-making authority of the federal government and the law-making authority of the states. With this backdrop in place, we can now delve into the constitutional limitations on the criminal law. There are six of them that we will take up in this chapter: equal protection of the laws, the *ex post facto* law prohibition, the void for vagueness doctrine, the void for overbreadth doctrine, the cruel and unusual punishment provision of the Eighth Amendment, and the double jeopardy clause of the Fifth Amendment. Each places a specific limit on the criminal law. We consider the first four in this module and the last two in the next module.

Equal Protection

equal protection clause
A clause in the Fourteenth Amendment of the U.S. Constitution requiring that the government justify any differential treatment on the basis of race, gender, age, sexual orientation, or other characteristic with a state interest.

The U.S. Constitution's Fourteenth Amendment requires that "no state shall deny to any person within its jurisdiction the equal protection of the laws." This is known as the **equal protection clause** and affects various aspects of criminal justice and criminal procedure, not just the criminal law. For example, convicted criminals have used

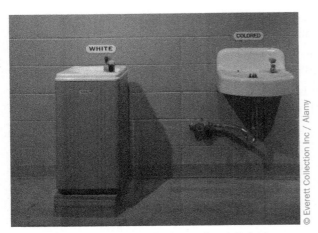

Even after the Civil War and prior to the civil rights era, some states retained separate facilities for whites and blacks. This picture depicts separate drinking fountains in North Carolina, circa 1950.

© Everett Collection Inc / Alamy

the equal protection clause to challenge jury composition. In *Strauder* v. *Virginia*,[4] the Supreme Court declared unconstitutional a statute that explicitly barred African-Americans from jury service. In the criminal-law context, however, equal protection challenges relate mainly to who is targeted by the statute. Essentially, a criminal statute cannot "discriminate" or treat a person differently based on a specific characteristic without a legitimate reason.

Before the end of the Civil War, many southern states retained separate systems of laws for whites and blacks. During the colonial period, black slaves who killed whites in Georgia, for whatever reason, were automatically executed.[5] At about the same time, Georgia's penal code provided that rape of a white woman by a black man was punishable by death, yet the rape of blacks was punishable "by fine and imprisonment, at the discretion of the court."[6] Likewise, a black person who assaulted a white person could be put to death, but it was considered a "minor" offense for a white person to commit the same offense against a black person. These forms of unequal treatment are absent from contemporary penal codes. Today, race-based classifications in the criminal law are not allowed.

While states no longer maintain separate penal codes for blacks and whites, there are other areas where equal protection challenges continue to creep up. For example, in *Michael M.* v. *Superior Court*,[7] the Supreme Court was tasked with deciding whether California's statutory rape law, which defined unlawful sexual intercourse as "an act of sexual intercourse accomplished with a female not the wife of the perpetrator, where the female is under the age of 18 years," discriminated against males. In other words, the petitioner, Michael M., claimed that the statute unfairly discriminated against men because only men were criminally liable under the statute. On its face, this argument seems to have some merit, but the Supreme Court concluded that a more inclusive statute would complicate enforcement. It said this:

> There is no merit in petitioner's contention that the statute is impermissibly underinclusive, and must, in order to pass judicial scrutiny, be broadened so as to hold the female as criminally liable as the male. . . . [A] gender-neutral statute would frustrate the State's interest in effective enforcement, since a female would be less likely to report violations of the statute if she herself would be subject to prosecution. The Equal Protection Clause does not require a legislature to enact a statute so broad that it may well be incapable of enforcement.[8]

The Court went on to note that gender-based classifications are not "inherently suspect." It further noted that so long as they bear a "fair and substantial relationship"

---

[4]100 U.S. 303 (1879).
[5]*McCleskey* v. *Kemp*, 481 U.S. 279 (1987) (Brennan, J., dissenting).
[6]Ibid.
[7]450 U.S. 464 (1981).
[8]Ibid., p. 465.

to legitimate state goals, such classification schemes do not violate the Fourteenth Amendment's equal protection clause. The legitimate state interest in this case was a desire to prevent illegitimate teenage pregnancies.

The *Michael M.* case raises an important point concerning equal protection, namely that the government is not required to treat *everyone* exactly the same. Although we have yet to discuss them in more detail, consider the differences between various levels of homicide. State homicide statutes treat first-degree murderers differently from those who commit negligent homicide, yet the end result of each offense is the same (i.e., the death of another). Why? One is fundamentally more serious than the next. First-degree murder requires planning and intent, while negligent homicide occurs only when a person acts negligently. It would not be fair to treat each offender as exactly the same.

Another example of a modern equal protection challenge is found in *Vacco* v. *Quill*.[9] In that case, three New York physicians challenged two seemingly contradictory sets of state statutes. One expressly prohibited physician-assisted suicide, meaning a doctor was not permitted to assist a patient in ending his or her life. The other statutes permitted a competent person to refuse lifesaving medical treatment. The distinction between the two is subtle but important. On the one hand, physicians were prohibited from actively *helping* patients end their lives. On the other hand, they were permitted to sit idly by and let the patients refuse treatment, which often resulted in death. The physicians argued that a patient's refusal to accept lifesaving treatment is basically the same as physician-assisted suicide, meaning that New York's assisted-suicide ban violated equal protection. The Supreme Court disagreed, noting a distinction between both actions:

> [W]hen a patient refuses life-sustaining medical treatment, he dies from an underlying fatal disease or pathology; but if a patient ingests lethal medication prescribed by a physician, he is killed by that medication. . . . Furthermore, a physician who withdraws, or honors a patient's refusal to begin, life-sustaining medical treatment purposefully intends, or may so intend, only to respect his patient's wishes. . . . The same is true when a doctor provides aggressive palliative care; in some cases, painkilling drugs may hasten a patient's death, but the physician's purpose and intent is, or may be, only to ease his patient's pain. A doctor who assists a suicide, however, "must, necessarily and indubitably, intend primarily that the patient be made dead." Similarly, a patient who commits suicide with a doctor's aid necessarily has the specific intent to end his or her own life, while a patient who refuses or discontinues treatment might not.[10]

The Supreme Court basically said that New York had a rational basis for treating both actions differently. Thus, there was no equal protection violation.

Standards of Scrutiny in Equal Protection Cases

To decide whether a statute violates equal protection, the courts now apply one of three tests depending on the classification in question. If a law classifies people based on race or national origin, it is unconstitutional unless the law is "narrowly tailored" to serve a "compelling" government interest. What's more, there must be no "less restrictive" alternative available. This is known as **strict scrutiny**.[11] If a law categorizes based on

strict scrutiny A test used under the Equal Protection Clause of the Fourteenth Amendment for classifications based on race. The law must be "narrowly tailored" to serve a "compelling" government interest. What's more, there must be no "less restrictive" alternative available.

---

[9]521 U.S. 793 (1997).
[10]Ibid., pp. 801–802.
[11]*Loving* v. *Virginia*, 388 U.S. 1 (1967), p. 11.

gender, it is unconstitutional unless it is "substantially related" to an "important" government interest. This is known as **intermediate scrutiny.**[12] Finally, a law that classifies people on any other basis is subjected to a **rational basis** test.[13] This means that law is constitutional so long as it is "reasonably related" to a "legitimate" government interest. See the accompanying Court Decision for more on equal protection. In it, we take a look at the 1996 Virginia Military Institute case, *United States* v. *Virginia*.

COURT DECISION

The Logic Behind the Equal Protection Clause and Gender

United States v. *Virginia*
518 U.S. 515 (1996)

Decision: The exclusion of women from the Virginia Military Institute violates the Equal Protection Clause of the United States Constitution.

Reason: Virginia's public institutions of higher learning include an incomparable military college, Virginia Military Institute (VMI). The United States maintains that the Constitution's equal protection guarantee precludes Virginia from reserving exclusively to men the unique educational opportunities VMI affords. We agree.

. . . In 1971, for the first time in our Nation's history, this Court ruled in favor of a woman who complained that her State had denied her the equal protection of its laws. Since *Reed*, the Court has repeatedly recognized that neither federal nor state government acts compatibly with the equal protection principle when a law or official policy denies to women, simply because they are women, full citizenship stature—equal opportunity to aspire, achieve, participate in and contribute to society based on their individual talents and capacities.

. . . To summarize the Court's current directions for cases of official classification based on gender: Focusing on the differential treatment or denial of opportunity for which relief is sought, the reviewing court must determine whether the proffered justification is "exceedingly persuasive." The burden of justification is demanding and it rests entirely on the State. The State must show "at least that the [challenged] classification serves 'important governmental objectives and that the discriminatory means employed' are 'substantially related to the achievement of those objectives.'". The justification must be genuine, not hypothesized or invented post hoc in response to litigation. And it must not rely on overbroad generalizations about the different talents, capacities, or preferences of males and females.

. . . "Inherent differences" between men and women, we have come to appreciate, remain cause for celebration, but not for denigration of the members of either sex or for artificial constraints on an individual's opportunity. Sex classifications may be used to compensate women "for particular economic disabilities [they have] suffered," to "promot[e] equal employment opportunity," to advance full development of the talent and capacities of our Nation's people. But such classifications may not be used, as they once were, to create or perpetuate the legal, social, and economic inferiority of women.

---

[12]*Craig* v. *Boren*, 429 U.S. 190 (1976), p. 197.
[13]*Turner* v. *Safley*, 482 U.S. 78 (1987).

Intermediate scrutiny A test used under the Equal Protection Clause of the Fourteenth Amendment for classifications based on gender. The law must be "substantially related" to an "important" government interest.

rational basis A test used under the Equal Protection Clause of the Fourteenth Amendment for classifications. The law must be "reasonably related" to a "legitimate" government interest.

ex post facto laws A law enacted in order to retroactively punish behavior. *Ex post facto is* Latin for "after the fact."

The *Ex Post Facto* Law Prohibition

Just as the Fourteenth Amendment requires equal protection, the Constitution bans so-called **ex post facto** laws in Article I, Section 9. *Ex post facto* is Latin for "after the fact," or "from after the action." Basically, an *ex post facto* law is one enacted in order to retroactively punish behavior. The ban on *ex post facto* laws makes perfect sense, as it would be unfair to punish someone for an action that wasn't illegal when it was committed. So important is the ban on *ex post facto* laws that it is found not only in the U.S. Constitution (Article I, Section 9), but also in the language of most state constitutions.

While the main type of *ex post facto* law is one that retroactively criminalizes behavior, there are three means by which a law can run afoul of the Constitution:

1. The law criminalizes an act that was legal when it was committed.
2. The law increases the punishment for an act after it was committed.
3. It takes away a defense that was available when the crime was committed.[14]

It is relatively uncommon for statutes to retroactively criminalize behavior. Legislatures carefully guard against this problem, which means that most *ex post facto* cases deal with different, sometimes more tedious issues. For example, if a new statute changes the element of a crime after it is committed, does the new statute violate Article I, Section 9? Assume a state decides to define a juvenile as someone under the age of 16, not the usual 18. Assume further that a 17-year-old committed robbery before the change. To suddenly try him or her as an adult could constitute an *ex post facto* violation.

Consider the 1970 California case, *Keeler v. Superior Court*.[15] In that case, Robert Keeler learned that his ex-wife was pregnant with another man's child, became very angry, and said, "I'm going to stomp it out of you." He pushed her up against a car, kneed her in the abdomen, and struck her in the face. She fainted, but by the time she regained consciousness, Keeler had departed. She managed to drive herself to a nearby hospital where a Caesarian section was performed. Doctors determined that the fetus's head was severely fractured and it was delivered stillborn. Keeler was charged with murder in violation of a California Penal Code provision that defined the offense as "the unlawful killing of a human being, with malice aforethought." The question taken up by the court was whether the fetus could be considered a human being. Keeler claimed that if a fetus is not a human being, it would be akin to an *ex post facto* violation to convict him after the fact of an act that was not considered murder when he committed it. At worst, in his view, he committed assault (or possibly an abortion), but not murder.

What did the court decide? Interestingly, it sided with Mr. Keeler. The court began with a lengthy examination of the legislative history behind the statute. It found that the law's authors felt a child in its mother's womb was not a human being. The court also noted that the state is supposed to construe statutes as favorably as possible to the defendant (recall the principle of lenity). The defendant, the court said, "is entitled to the benefit of every reasonable doubt as to the true interpretation of words or the construction of language used in a statute."[16] Against this

---

[14]*Beazell* v. *Ohio*, 269 U.S. 167 (1925).
[15]2 Cal. 3d 619 (1970).
[16]Ibid., p. 631.

backdrop, the court declined to interpret the statute to mean Keeler committed murder. In other words, Keeler had no "fair warning" that what he did was murder. Certainly he knew it was wrong, but the court felt he could not have known it was murder. The court said,

> This requirement of fair warning is reflected in the constitutional prohibition against the enactment of ex post facto laws. . . . When a new penal statute is applied retrospectively to make punishable an act which was not criminal at the time it was performed, the defendant has been given no advance notice consistent with due process. And precisely the same effect occurs when such an act is made punishable under a preexisting statute but by means of an unforeseeable judicial enlargement thereof.[17]

Lynce v. *Mathis*[18] raises the issue of whether an *ex post facto* violation occurs when the punishment scheme for an offense is altered after its commission. In 1986, Kenneth Lynce received a 22-year prison sentence following a conviction for attempted murder. He was released in 1992, however, because he accumulated early release credits totaling 5,668 days, including 1,860 "provisional credits" that were awarded because of the state's prison overcrowding problem. Shortly after his release, he was rearrested pursuant to an opinion issued by the attorney general that interpreted a 1992 statute as cancelling provisional credits for people convicted of murder and attempted murder. In effect, he was required to spend more time in prison making up the 1,860 provisional credit days. Lynce challenged this, arguing that it violated the Constitution's *ex post facto* law provision. In a unanimous decision, U.S. Supreme Court sided with Lynce, holding that the 1992 statute in question violated the Constitution's *ex post facto* clause. The logic was straightforward; the new law retroactively increased Lynce's punishment by an additional 1,860 days.

A related issue arose in the case of *Garner* v. *Jones*.[19] In that case, Robert Jones, who was serving a life sentence in prison for murder, escaped and committed another murder. He was convicted and sentenced to another life term. At the time Jones committed the second murder, the state's board of pardons and parole permitted parole reviews every three years following an initial consideration after seven years. After Jones started serving his second term, the board amended its rules, which it was authorized to do by law, such that a parole review would take place every eight years for inmates serving life sentences and who were denied parole in the past. Jones was affected by this policy change and claimed that it constituted an *ex post facto* violation. The Court of Appeals for the Eleventh Circuit agreed with him, but the Supreme Court did not, holding that the increased interval for parole review "created only the most speculative . . . possibility of . . . increasing the measure of punishment."[20] In his concurring opinion, Justice Scalia made this argument:

> Just as the Ex Post Facto Clause gives respondent [Jones] no cause to complain that the Board in place at the time of his offense has been replaced by a new, tough-on-crime Board that is much more parsimonious with parole, it gives him no cause to complain that it has been replaced by a new, big-on-efficiency Board that cuts back on reconsiderations without cause. And the change in policy is irrelevant, in my view,

---

[17]Ibid., p. 634.
[18]519 U.S. 433 (1997).
[19]529 U.S. 244 (2000).
[20]Ibid., p. 251.

whether or not the pre-existing policy happens to have been embodied in a policy statement or regulation. To make the constitutional prohibition turn upon that feature would be to ignore reality and to discourage measures that promote fairness and consistency. Such a policy statement or regulation, in the context of a system conferring complete discretion as to substance and as to the timing of hearings, upon the Parole Board, simply creates no reasonable expectation of entitlement, except perhaps among prisoners whose parole hearings are held (or are scheduled to be held) while the regulation is in effect. This is not an expectation of the sort that can give rise to ex post facto concerns.[21]

We wrap up our examination of the *ex post facto* prohibition with a look at *Smith* v. *Doe*, a 2003 Supreme Court case.[22] It involved a challenge to an Alaska law that required sex offenders to register with law enforcement authorities, share certain personal information with them, and inform them as to any changes as they come up. Two convicted sex offenders challenged the statute, claiming it retroactively punished them for actions committed before the registration requirement was put in place. The Court held that Alaska's sex offender registration statute was regulatory and nonpunitive. It stated, in part, that "the Act does not subject respondents to an affirmative disability or restraint. It imposes no physical restraint, and so does not resemble imprisonment."[23]

Article I, Section 9, of the Constitution also bans bills of attainder. A **bill of attainder** is a law that criminalizes conduct without the benefit of a trial. In other words, it is unconstitutional to for Congress to perform the judicial function, to hold "trial by legislature."

bill of attainder A law that criminalizes conduct without the benefit of a trial.

Void for Vagueness

If a criminal statute stated only that "it is a crime to be bad," citizens would be left to wonder exactly what conduct was prohibited. The U.S. Supreme Court has repeatedly struck down laws that are so vague that a normal person could not reasonably understand them or determine when they can be applied.[24] The Court has also struck down laws that give excessive discretion to law enforcement officials to decide who is arrested or prosecuted—and to judges to decide what conduct is prohibited. In contrast to the *ex post facto* prohibition, there is no specific constitutional provision that bans overly vague laws. Instead, the **void for vagueness** doctrine is based on the Fifth and Fourteenth Amendments due process clauses. Void for vagueness cases have historically fallen into two categories—those dealing with obscenity laws and those dealing with loitering and vagrancy statutes.

void for vagueness A constitutional doctrine based on the Fifth and Fourteenth Amendments to the U.S. Constitution requiring that laws be written with sufficient clarity and specificity.

Obscenity Cases

In an early case, *Winters* v. *New York*,[25] the Supreme Court was confronted with the question of whether a New York statute relating to the print and distribution of

---

[21]Ibid., p. 259.
[22]538 U.S. 84 (2003).
[23]Ibid., p. 84.
[24] *Connally v. General Construction Company*, 269 U.S. 385 (1926).
[25]333 U.S. 507 (1948).

obscene articles was overly vague. A person was guilty of a misdemeanor if that person printed, published, or sold "printed paper devoted to the publication, and principally made up of criminal news, police reports, or accounts of criminal deeds, or pictures, or stories of deeds of bloodshed, lust or crime" in "such a way as to incite crime." A book dealer who was convicted under the statute claimed it was overly vague and succeeded. In its decision, the Court focused heavily on the "incite crime" clause. It said, in part:

> The clause proposes to punish the printing and circulation of publications that courts or juries may think influence generally persons to commit crimes of violence against the person. No conspiracy to commit a crime is required. . . . It is not an effective notice of new crime. The clause has no technical or common law meaning. Nor can light as to the meaning be gained from the section as a whole or the Article of the Penal Law under which it appears.[26]

State v. *Metzger*[27] is another interesting case. In it, the Nebraska Supreme Court was tasked with deciding whether a Lincoln city ordinance was void for vagueness. The law in question provided that "[i]t shall be unlawful for any person within the City of Lincoln…to commit any indecent, immodest or filthy act in the presence of any person, or in such a situation that persons passing might ordinarily see the same."[28] Metzger was observed standing near his apartment window naked and was convicted. He argued that nudity is not necessarily obscene and is a form of free expression guaranteed by the First Amendment. He also argued that the ordinance was overly vague. The court, focusing on the vagueness issue, noted that there is little agreement as to what constitutes an "indecent, immodest, or filthy act":

> There may be those few who believe persons of opposite sex holding hands in public are immodest, and certainly more who might believe that kissing in public is immodest. Such acts cannot constitute a crime. Certainly one could find many who would conclude that today's swimming attire found on many beaches or beside many pools is immodest. Yet, the fact that it is immodest does not thereby make it illegal, absent some requirement related to the health, safety, or welfare of the community. The dividing line between what is lawful and what is unlawful in terms of "indecent," "immodest," or "filthy" is simply too broad to satisfy the constitutional requirements of due process. Both lawful and unlawful acts can be embraced within such broad definitions. That cannot be permitted.[29]

The Nebraska Supreme Court thus invalidated the statute, declaring that it was too vague.

Loitering and Vagrancy

Several cases have also dealt with the meaning of loitering and vagrancy statutes. For example, in *Kolender* v. *Lawson*,[30] the law at issue said that a any person who "loiters or wanders upon the streets or from place to place without apparent reason

---

[26]Ibid., p. 519.
[27]319 N.W. 2d 459 (Neb. 1982).
[28]Ibid., p. 595.
[29]Ibid., pp. 598–599.
[30]461 U.S. 352 (1983).

or business and who refuses to identify himself and to account for his presence when requested by any peace officer so to do" is guilty of a misdemeanor. Edward Lawson was detained and arrested on approximately 15 separate occasions. He was prosecuted only twice, however, and convicted just once. After his one conviction, he challenged the constitutionality of the statute, arguing that it was unconstitutionally vague. The Supreme Court agreed, holding that:

> As presently drafted and as construed by the state courts, [the statute] contains no standard for determining what a suspect has to do in order to satisfy the requirement to provide a "credible and reliable" identification. As such, the statute vests virtually complete discretion in the hands of the police to determine whether the suspect has satisfied the statute and must be permitted to go on his way in the absence of probable cause to arrest. An individual, whom police may think is suspicious but do not have probable cause to believe has committed a crime, is entitled to continue to walk the public streets "only at the whim of any police officer" who happens to stop that individual under [the statute]."[31]

Papachristou v. *City of Jacksonville*[32] dealt with a similar statute, this time in Florida. The law in question, a Jacksonville ordinance, defined vagrants as any of the following:

> Rogues and vagabonds, or dissolute persons who go about begging, common gamblers, persons who use juggling or unlawful games or plays, common drunkards, common night walkers, thieves, pilferers or pickpockets, traders in stolen property, lewd, wanton and lascivious persons, keepers of gambling places, common railers and brawlers, persons wandering or strolling around from place to place without any lawful purpose or object, habitual loafers, disorderly persons, persons neglecting all lawful business and habitually spending their time by frequenting houses of ill fame, gaming houses, or places where alcoholic beverages are sold or served, persons able to work but habitually living upon the earnings of their wives or minor children.[33]

Eight defendants were convicted in Florida municipal court pursuant to the statute. Their convictions were affirmed by the Florida Circuit Court, but their appeal to the Florida appellate court was denied. They petitioned the U.S. Supreme Court for *certiorari*. The Supreme Court agreed to hear their consolidated case and reversed their convictions, holding in part that the statute "fails to give a person of ordinary intelligence fair notice that his contemplated conduct is forbidden by the statute... and because it encourages arbitrary and erratic arrests and convictions."[34]

The cases we just reviewed may give the impression that it is easy for defendants to challenge statutes on vagueness grounds. Nothing could be further from the truth. Courts presume that laws are constitutional. The burden of proving otherwise thus falls on the defendant. And meeting that burden is not easy, as the Ohio Supreme Court remarked:

> [The defendant]. . . must show that upon examining the statute, an individual of ordinary intelligence would not understand what he is required to do under the law.

---

[31]Ibid., p. 358.
[32]405 U.S. 156 (1983).
[33]Ibid., p. 158.
[34]Ibid., p. 162.

Thus, to escape responsibility . . . [the defendant] must prove that he could not reasonably understand that…[the law in question] prohibited the acts in which he engaged. . . . The party alleging that a statute is unconstitutional must prove this assertion beyond a reasonable doubt.[35]

The Void for Overbreadth Doctrine

The equal protection requirement, the ban on *ex post facto* laws, and the ban on overly vague statutes apply to all criminal laws at all times. There is another more specific limitation on the criminal law—namely, the **void for overbreadth** doctrine. In general, a law will be void for overbreadth if it prohibits action that is protected by the Constitution. For example, a law that criminalized "starting a riot and saying anything bad about the president of the United States" would be overly broad and unconstitutional. While it is permissible to outlaw starting a riot, the ability to peacefully criticize our politicians is protected under the First Amendment and cannot be criminalized.

Overbreadth cases frequently involve the First Amendment, which protects the freedom of religion, assembly, and speech. It is the latter that is of interest to us here. The free speech clause says, "Congress shall make no law . . . abridging the freedom of speech, or of the press. . . ." Over the years, the Supreme Court has interpreted this language rather loosely to include not just things people say, but also the written word[36] and actions that communicate words and ideas. The First Amendment's free speech clause has also been made binding on the states, underscoring its importance.[37]

In general, Congress cannot ban free speech, but the Supreme Court has sanctioned such bans in a few important areas. These include certain forms of obscenity, profanity, libelous speech, and so-called fighting words.[38] These forms of free speech and expression are not sanctioned because they are not, according to the Supreme Court, an "essential element of any exposition of ideas, and are of such slight value as a step to truth that any benefit that may be derived from them is clearly outweighed by the social interest in order and morality."[39]

The Court has been confronted with a number of free speech cases over the years, mostly in the areas of seditious speech and libel, fighting words and threats to the peace, and so-called group libel, or hate speech. Before continuing, let us define some of these terms. **Libel** is defamation by the written or printed word. **Defamation**, simply, is an attack on the good reputation of another. **Seditious speech** is that which advocates rebellion against the government. (See Figure 2.2 for a list of speech that is not protected by the First Amendment.)

void for overbreadth A constitutional principle requiring that laws do not infringe on constitutionally protected behavior.

libel Defamation by the written or printed word.

defamation Written or spoken words that damage the reputation of the object of the speech.

seditious speech Speech that advocates rebellion against the government.

Speech that is NOT protected under the First Amendment:

- Obscenity
- Defamation
  - ○ Libel: Written word
  - ○ Slander: Spoken word
- Fighting words
- Child pornography
- Solicitations to commit crimes
- True threats
- Blackmail
- Perjury
- Incitement to lawless action

Figure 2.2

Speech That is NOT Protected Under the First Amendment

---

[35] *State* v. *Anderson*, 566 N.E. 2d 1224 (Ohio 1991).

[36] *Texas* v. *Johnson*, 491 U.S. 397 (1989).

[37] *Gitlow* v. *New York*, 268 U.S. 652 (1925).

[38] *Chaplinsky* v. *New Hampshire*, 315 U.S. 568 (1942), p. 573.

[39] *Gitlow* v. *New York*, p. 572.

Seditious Speech and Libel

Our system of government welcomes citizen protests, but seditious utterances are basically prohibited. For example, the Sedition Act of 1798 made criminal any writings that defamed, brought into disrepute, or bolstered the hatred of the people toward the government.

This is a delicate area, one in which a number of cases have been decided over the years. In one interesting case, *Brandenburg* v. *Ohio*,[40] the Court decided on the constitutionality of Ohio's Criminal Syndicalism statute. A Ku Klux Klan leader was convicted under the statute for "advocate[ing] . . . the duty, necessity, or propriety of crime, sabotage, violence, or unlawful methods of terrorism as a means of accomplishing industrial or political reform" and for "voluntarily assembl[ing] with any society, group or assemblage of persons formed to teach or advocate the doctrines of criminal syndicalism." The statute was declared unconstitutional for these reasons:

> Since the statute, by its words and as applied, purports to punish mere advocacy and to forbid, on pain of criminal punishment, assembly with others merely to advocate the described type of action, it falls within the condemnation of the First [Amendment].... Freedoms of speech and press do not permit a State to forbid advocacy of the use of force or of law violation except where such advocacy is directed to inciting or producing imminent lawless action and is likely to incite or produce such action.[41]

The Court felt that because the statute did not distinguish between (1) teaching the need for violence and (2) actually calling for it, the statute infringed on the First Amendment's free speech clause.

Fighting Words and Threats to the Peace

In *Chaplinksy* v. *New Hampshire*, the Supreme Court sanctioned a conviction under a statute that prohibited "any offense, derisive, or annoying word" addressed to anyone in a public place. The Court felt that statute was "narrowly drawn and limited to define and punish specific conduct lying within the domain of state power, the use in a public place of words likely to cause a breach of the peace."[42] The case is most famous for Justice Murphy's observation:

> [I]t is well understood that the right of free speech is not absolute at all times and under all circumstances. There are certain well-defined and narrowly limited classes of speech, the prevention and punishment of which have never been thought to raise any Constitutional problem. These include the lewd and obscene, the profane, the libelous, and the insulting or "fighting" words—those which by their very utterance inflict injury or tend to incite an immediate breach of the peace. It has been well observed that such utterances are no essential part of any exposition of ideas, and are of such slight social value as a step to truth that any benefit that may be derived from them is clearly outweighed by the social interest in order and morality.

---

[40]395 U.S. 444 (1969).
[41]Ibid., p. 444.
[42]Ibid., p. 573.

Importantly, the government cannot prohibit fighting words simply because they are offensive. Rather, they must have a tendency to cause acts of violence by the people against whom they are directed. Consider the case of *Gooding* v. *Wilson*,[43] a case involving a Georgia statute providing that "any person who shall, without provocation, use to or of another, and in his presence . . . opprobrious words or abusive language, tending to cause a breach of the peace . . . shall be guilty of a misdemeanor." The Court invalidated the statute, claiming that it was overly broad. It said, in part, that "the term 'breach of peace' is generic, and includes all violations of the public peace or order, or decorum; in other words, it signifies the offense of disturbing the public peace or tranquility enjoyed by the citizens of a community. . . . This definition makes it a 'breach of peace' merely to speak words offensive to some who hear them, and so sweeps too broadly."[44] In essence, the Court held that the statute was void for overbreadth. This is now the standard that the courts use to decide whether a statute seeking to restrict free speech runs afoul of the First Amendment.[45]

See the accompanying Court Decision for more on the role of the First Amendment in criminal law. It features the case of *Texas* v. *Johnson*, in which the Supreme Court addressed the constitutionality of a Texas criminal statute that outlawed burning the American flag.

Flag burning is considered expressive conduct and is protected under the First Amendment.

© Richard Levine/Alamy

---

[43]405 U.S. 518 (1972).

[44]Ibid., p. 527.

[45]For other cases dealing with supposed fighting words, see *Hess* v. *Indiana*, 414 U.S. 105 (1973); *Lewis* v. *City of New Orleans*, 415 U.S. 130 (1974); *Lucas* v. *Arkansas*, 416 U.S. 919 (1974); *Kelly* v. *Ohio*, 416 U.S. 923 (1974); *Karlan* v. *City of Cincinnati*, 416 U.S. 924 (1974); *Rosen* v. *California*, 416 U.S. 924 (1974); and *Eaton* v. *City of Tulsa*, 416 U.S. 697 (1974).

| **COURT DECISION** | **The Logic behind Flag Burning as a Form of Expression** |

Texas v. Johnson
491 U.S. 397 (1989)

Decision: Burning an American flag is expressive conduct protected under the First Amendment to the United States Constitution.

Reason: After publicly burning an American flag as a means of political protest, Gregory Lee Johnson was convicted of desecrating a flag in violation of Texas law. This case presents the question whether his conviction is consistent with the First Amendment. We hold that it is not.

. . . The First Amendment literally forbids the abridgment only of "speech," but we have long recognized that its protection does not end at the spoken or written word. While we have rejected "the view that an apparently limitless variety of conduct can be labeled 'speech' whenever the person engaging in the conduct intends thereby to express an idea," *United States* v. *O'Brien, 391 U.S.* at 376, we have acknowledged that conduct may be "sufficiently imbued with elements of communication to fall within the scope of the First and Fourteenth Amendments."

. . . Johnson burned an American flag as part—indeed, as the culmination—of a political demonstration that coincided with the convening of the Republican Party and its renomination of Ronald Reagan for President. The expressive, overtly political nature of this conduct was both intentional and overwhelmingly apparent. At his trial, Johnson explained his reasons for burning the flag as follows: "The American Flag was burned as Ronald Reagan was being renominated as President. And a more powerful statement of symbolic speech, whether you agree with it or not, couldn't have been made at that time. It's quite a just position [juxtaposition]. We had new patriotism and no patriotism." In these circumstances, Johnson's burning of the flag was conduct "sufficiently imbued with elements of communication," *Spence,* 418 U.S., at 409, to implicate the First Amendment.

. . . If there is a bedrock principle underlying the First Amendment, it is that the government may not prohibit the expression of an idea simply because society finds the idea itself offensive or disagreeable.

. . . Johnson was convicted for engaging in expressive conduct. The State's interest in preventing breaches of the peace does not support his conviction because Johnson's conduct did not threaten to disturb the peace. Nor does the State's interest in preserving the flag as a symbol of nationhood and national unity justify his criminal conviction for engaging in political expression. The judgment of the Texas Court of Criminal Appeals is therefore *Affirmed.*

Group Libel

The courts have also sanctioned laws that ban speech that defames a certain group or class of people—or is "libelous" toward a specific group. In *Beauharnais* v. *Illinois,*[46]

---

[46]343 U.S. 250 (1952).

a man was convicted under a libel law for distributing a leaflet that called for keeping African-Americans out of white neighborhoods. The Supreme Court held that the law complied with the First Amendment.

Subsequent decisions, however, have complicated matters. For example, in *R.A.V. v. City of St. Paul*,[47] a juvenile was alleged to have burned a cross on a black family's front lawn. He was charged with violating the city's Bias-Motivated Crime Ordinance, which made it a misdemeanor for anyone to place "on public or private property a symbol, object, appellation, characterization or graffiti, including, but not limited to, a burning cross or Nazi swastika, which one knows or has reasonable grounds to know arouses anger, alarm or resentment in others on the basis of race, color, creed, religion or gender...."[48] The Court ruled that the statute was unconstitutional and decided it was overly broad because "the First Amendment does not permit [the city] to impose special prohibitions on those speakers who express views on disfavored subjects."[49]

The Court's logic in *R.A.V.* is tedious, but a few points bear mention. First, the law was limited only to race, color, creed, religion, and gender. If someone wanted to use fighting words in connection with some other ideas not covered by the law (e.g., homosexuality or political beliefs), that person would be allowed to. This, the Court said, is content discrimination and is prohibited. Second, the Court felt that law imposed viewpoint discrimination. Justice Scalia, author of the Court's opinion, said on this point that fighting words that "do not themselves invoke race, color, creed, religion, or gender—aspersions upon a person's mother, for example—would seemingly be usable *ad libitum* in the placards of those arguing *in favor* of racial, color, etc., tolerance and equality, but could not be used by those speakers' opponents." Finally, the Court implied that the ordinance could have been written differently and satisfied the First Amendment: "An ordinance not limited to the favored topics, for example, would have..."[50] helped protect the rights of groups that have, throughout history, been discriminated against.

YOUR DECISION

1. Concerned with its growing gang problem, the city of New York passes a law making it a crime to be a member of "a criminal street gang." Jose Perez is a 19-year-old citizen of Mexican descent. He is seen in a high-crime area wearing the color yellow, which is typically the color worn by members of the Latin Kings gang. He is arrested and charged with violating the new statute. Perez argues that the statute fails to adequately define what "a criminal street gang" is and leads to discriminatory enforcement by police. Is the New York City statute constitutional?

2. As the Olympic torch passed through Juneau, Alaska, Joseph Frederick and a number of his classmates held up a sign that read "BONG HiTS 4 JESUS." On a break from school, the high school principal confiscated the sign and suspended

---

[47]505 U.S. 377 (1992).
[48]Ibid., p. 380.
[49]Ibid., p. 391.
[50]Ibid., p. 395.

Frederick from school. Frederick claimed that he had the constitutional right to display the banner. Does the First Amendment protect Frederick and his classmates?

Summary

- Constitutional limitations on the criminal law include equal protection of the laws, the *ex post facto* law prohibition, the void for vagueness doctrine, the void for overbreadth doctrine, the cruel and unusual punishment provision of the Eighth Amendment, and the double jeopardy clause of the Fifth Amendment.
- The Fourteenth Amendment states, in part, that "no state shall deny to any person within its jurisdiction the equal protection of the laws."
- The equal protection clause has been interpreted to ban separate criminal codes for separate classes of people.
- Three separate standards are used in equal protection clause analysis: strict scrutiny for classifications based on race, intermediate scrutiny for gender, and rational basis for all other classifications.
- An *ex post facto* law is one enacted in order to retroactively punish behavior.
- *Ex post facto* laws are banned by the U.S. Constitution, Article I, Section 9.
- An *ex post facto* violation occurs when (1) the law criminalizes an act that was legal when it was committed, (2) the law increases the punishment for an act after it was committed, or (3) it takes away a defense that was available when the crime was committed.
- The U.S. Supreme Court has repeatedly struck down laws that are so vague that a normal person could not reasonably understand them or determine when they can be applied.
- The void for vagueness doctrine is based on the Fifth and Fourteenth Amendments due process clauses.
- Obscenity, loitering, and vagrancy statutes have been challenged on multiple occasions as overly vague.
- Statutes that are overly broad in their language and that infringe on free speech and expression violate the First Amendment.
- In general, seditious speech, certain fighting words, and "group libel," or hate speech, can be criminalized without running counter to the First Amendment.

MODULE

2.3

CONSTITUTIONAL LIMITATIONS ON THE CRIMINAL LAW, PART 2

Learning Objectives
- **Describe the protections against cruel and unusual punishment.**
- **Explain the guarantee against double jeopardy.**

CORE CONCEPTS

Cruel and Unusual Punishment

The Eighth Amendment to the U.S. Constitution prohibits "cruel and unusual punishment." Both the federal government *and* the states are bound by this constitutional limitation.[51] In general, the Eighth Amendment prohibits barbaric punishments and disproportionate sentencing (i.e., getting sentenced for an inordinately long time for a minor offense).

In 1910, the Supreme Court expressed a preference that "punishment for crime. . . be graduated and proportioned to [the] offense."[52] This means, basically, that a punishment that seems excessive in light of the underlying offense could be deemed unconstitutional. We say *could* because many a punishment has been sanctioned that would seem to the untrained observer a gross violation of the Eighth Amendment.

Two broad classes of Eighth Amendment cruel and unusual punishments have come before the Supreme Court over the years: death penalty cases and cases challenging the length of a sentence.

The electric chair is used to carry out executions in nine states (as of this writing).

Death Penalty Cases

When someone is convicted of intentional murder, the death penalty (aka *capital punishment*) is a legally authorized punishment in the states that continue the practice. A common argument raised by death row inmate and opponents to capital punishment is that putting someone to death violates the cruel and unusual punishment provision of the Eighth Amendment. While the Supreme Court has never held that the death penalty itself constitutes cruel and unusual punishment, in a 1972 case, *Furman* v. *Georgia,*[53] the Court decided that the death penalty, *as it was being carried out at the time*, was unconstitutional. Each of the Court's nine justices authored separate opinions in this 5–4 decision. Three of them raised discrimination concerns: Justice Douglas argued that death penalty procedures were "pregnant with discrimination"[54]; Justice Stewart pointed out that the death penalty was "so wantonly and so freakishly imposed"[55]; and Justice White found "no meaningful basis for distinguishing the few cases in which [the death penalty] is imposed from the many cases in which it is not."[56]

---

[51]*Robinson* v. *California*, 370 U.S. 660 (1962).
[52]*Weems* v. *United States*, 217 U.S. 349 (1910), p. 367.
[53] *Furman* v. *Georgia*, 408 U.S. 238 (1972).
[54]Ibid., p. 257.
[55]Ibid., p. 310.
[56]Ibid., p. 313.

The *Furman* decision was far-reaching. It brought executions to a halt and "emptied death rows across the country."[57] It also invalidated death penalty statutes in 39 states. Most of the states responded by enacting new laws aimed at curbing the discretion of judges and jurors in death penalty cases to ensure fairness and even-handedness in the process.[58] The new laws were of two varieties—some provided for the death penalty in cases of first-degree murder and others provided for the death penalty in several offenses based on the presence of aggravating or mitigating circumstances,[59] which are now called **guided-discretion laws**.

guided-discretion laws
Laws that provide for the death penalty based on weighing aggravating and mitigating circumstances.

In the wake of *Furman*, the Court decided additional death penalty cases to clarify the law. In *Woodson* v. *North Carolina*[60] and *Roberts* v. *Louisiana*,[61] the Court held that North Carolina's and Louisiana's mandatory death penalty statutes were unconstitutional—both states' laws gave jurors no opportunity to consider aggravating and mitigating circumstances. In contrast, the Court looked favorably on the guided-discretion laws in the states of Florida, Georgia, and Texas.[62] For example, in *Gregg* v. *Georgia,* the Court held that Georgia's statute limited the jury's discretion and thus minimized the chances that the death penalty would be arbitrarily imposed[63]:

> No longer can a jury wantonly and freakishly impose the death sentence; it is always circumscribed by the legislative guidelines. In addition, the review function of the Supreme Court of Georgia affords additional assurance that the concerns that prompted our decision in *Furman* are not present to any significant degree in the Georgia procedure applied here.[64]

The practical result of the *Gregg* decision was that the death penalty was reinstated as long as the state statutes complied with the new constitutional guidelines. (See Figure 2.3 for a map of the United States showing the use of the death penalty by state).

Other cases have dealt with the question of whether death is an appropriate sanction for offenses other than murder. *Coker* v. *Georgia,*[65] for example, involved a man who committed two rapes, was convicted and imprisoned, escaped, and raped again. He was sentenced to death for his post-escape rape. The Supreme Court held that the sentence was grossly disproportional. Rape, the Court opined, "does not compare with murder, which...involve[s] the unjustified taking of human life. . . . The murderer kills; the rapist, if no more than that, does not."[66]

The *Coker* decision was limited to cases involving the rape of adult women. After the decision was handed down, several states enacted laws sanctioning the death penalty for child rapists, those convicted of raping children under the age of 12. Were

---

[57]S. R. Gross and R. Mauro, *Death and Discrimination: Racial Disparities in Capital Sentencing* (Boston: Northeastern University Press, 1989), p. 215.
[58]Walker, Spohn, and DeLone, *The Color of Justice,* p. 293.
[59]Ibid.
[60]*Woodson* v. *North Carolina,* 428 U.S. 280 (1976).
[61]*Roberts* v. *Louisiana,* 428 U.S. 280 (1976).
[62]*Proffitt* v. *Florida,* 428 U.S. 242 (1976); *Gregg* v. *Georgia,* 428 U.S. 153 (1976); *Jurek* v. *Texas,* 428 U.S. 262 (1976).
[63]*Gregg* v. *Georgia,* 428 U.S. 153 (1976).
[64]Ibid., pp. 206–207.
[65]433 U.S. 584 (1977).
[66]Ibid., p. 598.

Figure 2.3
Death Penalty Use in the United States
Source: Death Penalty Information Center, http://www.deathpenaltyinfo.org/states-and-without-death-penalty (accessed July 10, 2012).

such laws constitutional? The answer came only recently in the 2008 case of *Kennedy* v. *Louisiana*.[67] The Court held that even the rape of a child, where the rape does not result in death, is also unconstitutional. This despite the fact that the case involved a stepfather's rape of his eight-year-old stepdaughter. The Court noted the heinous nature of the crime:

> Here the victim's fright, the sense of betrayal, and the nature of her injuries caused more prolonged physical and mental suffering than, say, a sudden killing by an unseen assassin. The attack was not just on her but on her childhood. . . . Rape has a permanent psychological, emotional, and sometimes physical impact on the child. . . . We cannot dismiss the years of long anguish that must be endured by the victim of child rape.[68]

Even so, the Court said that "[i]t does not follow . . . that capital punishment is a proportionate penalty for the crime." Why? Here is the Court's logic:

> [W]e conclude that, in determining whether the death penalty is excessive, there is a distinction between intentional . . . murder on the one hand and nonhomicide crimes

---

[67]128 S.Ct. 2641 (2008).
[68]Ibid., p. 2660.

against individual persons, including child rape, on the other. The latter crimes may be devastating in their harm, as here, but . . . "in terms of moral depravity and of the injury to the person and to the public," they cannot be compared to murder in their . . ."severity and irrevocability."[69]

In summary, the death penalty is a permissible punishment for intentional murder. Recently, however, the Supreme Court ruled that it is only constitutional in cases involving offenders who were 18 years old or older at the time of their capital offenses.[70] Also, it is unconstitutional to execute a mentally retarded murderer.[71] Capital punishment is *not* allowed in rape cases, no matter the circumstances.

The method of execution, such as electric chair, firing squad or lethal injection, has also been challenged under the cruel and unusual punishment provision. See the accompanying Court Decision for more on the role of the Eight Amendment in death penalty cases. It features the case of *Baze* v. *Rees*, a recent case in which the Supreme Court reviewed the constitutionality of lethal injection as a form of execution.

COURT DECISION

The Logic behind Lethal Injection and the Eighth Amendment

Baze v. *Rees*
553 U.S. 35 (2008)

Decision: The three-drug method of execution by lethal injection does not violate the Eighth Amendment's cruel and unusual punishment provision.

Reason . . . Petitioners in this case—each convicted of double homicide—acknowledge that the lethal injection procedure, if applied as intended, will result in a humane death. They nevertheless contend that the lethal injection protocol is unconstitutional under the Eighth Amendment's ban on "cruel and unusual punishments," because of the risk that the protocol's terms might not be properly followed, resulting in significant pain.

. . . This Court has never invalidated a State's chosen procedure for carrying out a sentence of death as the infliction of cruel and unusual punishment. In *Wilkerson* v. *Utah*, we upheld a sentence to death by firing squad imposed by a territorial court, rejecting the argument that such a sentence constituted cruel and unusual punishment. We noted there the difficulty of "defin[ing] with exactness the extent of the constitutional provision which provides that cruel and unusual punishments shall not be inflicted." Rather than undertake such an effort, the *Wilkerson* Court simply noted that "it is safe to affirm that punishments of torture,. . . and all others in the same line of unnecessary cruelty, are forbidden" by the Eighth Amendment. By way of example, the Court cited cases from England in which "terror, pain, or disgrace were sometimes superadded" to the sentence, such as where the condemned was "embowelled alive, beheaded, and quartered," or instances of "public dissection in murder, and burning alive." In contrast, we observed that the firing squad was routinely

(continued)

---

[69] Ibid., p. 2660.
[70] *Roper* v. *Simmons*, 543 U.S. 551 (2005).
[71] *Atkins* v. *Virginia*, 122 S.Ct. 2242 (2002).

used as a method of execution for military officers. What each of the forbidden punishments had in common was the deliberate infliction of pain for the sake of pain—"superadd[ing]" pain to the death sentence through torture and the like.

Petitioners do not claim that lethal injection or the proper administration of the particular protocol adopted by Kentucky by themselves constitute the cruel or wanton infliction of pain . . . Instead, petitioners claim that there is a significant risk that the procedures will *not* be properly followed—in particular, that the sodium thiopental will not be properly administered to achieve its intended effect—resulting in severe pain when the other chemicals are administered. Our cases recognize that subjecting individuals to a risk of future harm—not simply actually inflicting pain—can qualify as cruel and unusual punishment. To establish that such exposure violates the Eighth Amendment, however, the conditions presenting the risk must be "*sure or very likely* to cause serious illness and needless suffering," and give rise to "sufficiently *imminent* dangers." *Helling* v. *McKinney,* 509 U.S. 25, 33, 34-35 (1993). We have explained that to prevail on such a claim there must be a "substantial risk of serious harm," an "objectively intolerable risk of harm" that prevents prison officials from pleading that they were "subjectively blameless for purposes of the Eighth Amendment." *Farmer* v. *Brennan,* 511 U.S. 825, 842, 846, and n. 9 (1994).

Simply because an execution method may result in pain, either by accident or as an inescapable consequence of death, does not establish the sort of "objectively intolerable risk of harm" that qualifies as cruel and unusual. In *Louisiana ex rel. Francis* v. *Resweber*, a plurality of the Court upheld a second attempt at executing a prisoner by electrocution after a mechanical malfunction had interfered with the first attempt. The principal opinion noted that "[a]ccidents happen for which no man is to blame," and concluded that such "an accident, with no suggestion of malevolence," did not give rise to an Eighth Amendment violation . . . The judgment below concluding that Kentucky's procedure is consistent with the Eighth Amendment is, accordingly, affirmed.

Sentence Length and the Eighth Amendment

While there is a bright line distinction between what types of offenses can result in death and what types cannot, it is substantially less clear when a prison sentence is disproportionate to a crime in violation of the Eighth Amendment. In *Rummel* v. *Estelle,*[72] a man was sentenced to life in prison under Texas's habitual offender law. He was convicted of obtaining a check for $120.75 by false pretenses, then cashing it, but he had previously been convicted of theft on two occasions. The Supreme Court sanctioned his life sentence, stating that "[T]he interest of the State of Texas here is not simply that of making criminal the unlawful acquisition of another person's property; it is in addition the interest...in dealing in a harsher manner with those who by repeated criminal acts have shown that they are simply incapable of conforming to the norms of society established by its criminal law."[73]

---

[72]445 U.S. 263 (1980).
[73]Ibid., p. 276.

Contrast *Rummel* with *Solem* v. *Helm*,[74] a case involving the life sentence (without parole) of a man who was convicted of passing a "no account" check for $100.00. It was his seventh conviction. Even so, the Supreme Court decided that the sentence was cruel and unusual. It also noted that the "without parole" part of the sentence was determinative. The Court noted that Texas had a more liberal parole policy, which is why the *Rummel* sentence was deemed constitutional (he could have been paroled).

But further contrast *Solem* with the Supreme Court's 1991 decision in *Harmelin* v. *Michigan*.[75] That case involved a first-time offender who was convicted of possessing 672 grams of cocaine and sentenced to life in prison without the possibility of parole. The Supreme Court held that the sentence was constitutional. In essence, the Court felt the underlying offense was more serious than that in the *Solem* case. A similar decision was reached in *Ewing* v. *California*,[76] a case involving an application of California's punitive three-strikes laws. Ewing, a twice previously convicted felon, was sentence to 25 years to life in prison for stealing three golf clubs, each worth $399, which made his offense "grand theft," a felony under California law. The Court found no Eighth Amendment violation:

> Throughout the States, legislatures enacting three-strikes laws [have] made a deliberate policy choice that individuals who have repeatedly engaged in serious or violent criminal behavior, and whose conduct has not been deterred by more conventional approaches to punishment, must be isolated from society in order to protect the public safety. Though three-strikes laws may be relatively new, our tradition of deferring to state legislatures in making and implementing such important policy decisions is longstanding.[77]

These decisions make it more than a little difficult to determine when a long prison term violates the Eighth Amendment. In deciding what length of term is appropriate, courts must consider various factors, including (1) the gravity of the offense compared to the sentence, (2) the penalties imposed on other offenders in the same state for the same offense, (3) the penalties imposed in other states for the same offense, and (4) the defendant's recidivism. Courts are not required to consider all these criteria, however. To this day, there is some uncertainty as to which (if any) combination is important.

Double Jeopardy

double jeopardy A principle found in the Fifth Amendment to the U.S. Constitution that prevents an individual from being tried twice for the same crime.

The Fifth Amendment protection against **double jeopardy** is designed to ensure that a person who has been convicted or acquitted of a crime is not tried or punished for the same offense twice. Double jeopardy occurs when, for the same offense, a person is (1) reprosecuted after acquittal, (2) reprosecuted after conviction, or (3) subjected to separate punishments for the same offense. Double jeopardy does not apply, however, to prosecutions brought by separate sovereigns. The federal government, each state government, and each Native American tribe is considered a separate sovereign.

---

[74]463 U.S. 277 (1983).
[75]501 U.S. 957 (1991).
[76]538 U.S. 11 (2003).
[77]Ibid., p. 24.

Early English common law contains the foundations of the modern-day protection against double jeopardy. The rule of *autrefois acquit* prohibited the retrial of a defendant who was found not guilty. The rule of *autrefois convict*, on the other hand, prohibited the retrial of a defendant who *was* found guilty. These rules were adopted by the American colonies.

Today, every state provides double jeopardy protection because of the Supreme Court's decision in *Benton* v. *Maryland*,[78] in which the Court declared that the Fifth Amendment's protection against double jeopardy is a fundamental right:

> The fundamental nature of the guarantee against double jeopardy can hardly be doubted. Its origins can be traced to Greek and Roman times, and it became established in the common law of England long before this Nation's independence. . . . As with many other elements of the common law, it was carried into the jurisprudence of this Country through the medium of Blackstone, who codified the doctrine in his Commentaries. "The plea of *autrefoits acquit*, or a former acquittal," he wrote, "is grounded on this universal maxim of the common law of England, that no man is to be brought into jeopardy of his life more than once for the same offence." . . . Today, every State incorporates some form of the prohibition in its constitution or common law.[79]

When Double Jeopardy Protection Applies

The Fifth Amendment suggests that double jeopardy occurs when a person's "life or limb" is threatened. This language has been taken to mean that double jeopardy applies in all criminal proceedings. Determining whether a proceeding is criminal, however, is not always easy. Courts will often look to the legislature's intent in writing the statute that is the basis for prosecution. For example, in *Kansas* v. *Hendricks*,[80] the Supreme Court found that a statute providing for a "sexual predator" proceeding, in addition to a criminal proceeding, did not place the defendant in double jeopardy because it provided for *civil* confinement. The Court stated:

> Because we have determined that the Kansas Act is civil in nature, initiation of its commitment proceedings does not constitute a second prosecution. . . . Moreover, as commitment under the Act is not tantamount to "punishment," Hendricks' involuntary detention does not violate the Double Jeopardy Clause, even though that confinement may follow a prison term.[81]

The courts will also examine the punitiveness of the sanctions involved in determining whether a proceeding is criminal. In *Helvering* v. *Mitchell*,[82] the Supreme Court upheld the constitutionality of a tax proceeding that was used to recover back taxes from a person *after* the person was acquitted on criminal charges. The Court declared that the proceeding was designed as a remedial sanction to reimburse the government. Because it was not considered punitive, double jeopardy did not apply.

---

[78]395 U.S. 784 (1969).
[79]Ibid., pp. 795–796.
[80]521 U.S. 346 (1997).
[81]Ibid., pp. 369–370.
[82]303 U.S. 391 (1938).

The *Blockburger* Rule

Double jeopardy prevents a second prosecution for the *same offense*. A rather complicated issue in double jeopardy jurisprudence concerns the definition of what constitutes the same offense. In *Blockburger* v. *United States*,[83] the Supreme Court developed a test that states that "[w]here the same act or transaction constitutes a violation of two distinct statutory provisions, the test to be applied to determine whether there are two offenses or only one, is whether each requires proof of an additional fact which the other does not."[84] This test came to be known as the *Blockburger* Rule.

> *Blockburger* Rule An offense is considered the "same offense" for purposes of double jeopardy if two separate statutes that define the offense both contain the same elements.

According to the *Blockburger* Rule, an offense is considered the same offense if two separate statutes that define the offense both contain elements A, B, and C. Moreover, if one crime contains elements A, B, and C, and the other has elements A and B, both are considered the same offense because neither statute requires proof of a fact that the other does not. For example, assume that the offense of first-degree murder contains elements A (premeditated), B (deliberate), and C (killing), and that the offense of second-degree murder contains elements B (deliberate) and C (killing). Both offenses are considered the same for double jeopardy purposes because second-degree murder does not require proof of another element that first-degree murder does not. If a person is convicted of first-degree murder, then, according to this example, that person cannot be charged with second-degree murder.

Separate offenses can be identified when, for example, one crime contains elements A, B, and C, and the other contains elements A, B, and D. Both crimes require proof of an additional element that the other does not. For example, assume the offense of joyriding contains elements A (unlawful taking), B (of an automobile), and C (the intent to *temporarily* deprive the owner of possession). Assume also that the offense of car theft contains elements A (unlawful taking), B (of an automobile), and D (the intent to *permanently* deprive the owner of possession). These are considered separate offenses because each offense requires proof of an element that the other does not. Thus, a person who is found guilty of joyriding can also be charged with the crime of car theft.[85]

When Double Jeopardy Protection Does Not Apply

There are four main exceptions to the *Blockburger* Rule, which means that there are four situations in which double jeopardy protection does *not* apply.

Conduct Committed after the First Prosecution. Double jeopardy does not apply if the second prosecution is based on conduct committed after the first prosecution. This was the decision reached in *Diaz* v. *United States*.[86] There, the defendant was convicted of assault and battery. When the victim later died, the defendant was charged with homicide. The Court stated, "The death of the injured person was the principal element of the homicide, but was no part of the assault and battery. At the time of the trial for the latter the death had not ensued, and not until

---

[83]284 U.S. 299 (1932).
[84]Ibid., p. 304.
[85]See, e.g., *Brown* v. *Ohio*, 432 U.S. 161 (1977).
[86]223 U.S. 442 (1912).

it did ensue was the homicide committed. Then, and not before, was it possible to put the accused in jeopardy for that offense."[87]

Defendant Responsible for the Second Prosecution.

If the defendant is responsible for the second prosecution, double jeopardy does not apply. In *Jeffers* v. *United States*,[88] the defendant was convicted in two separate trials for essentially the same offense. In the first, he was convicted of conspiring with others to distribute cocaine. In the second, he was convicted of violating drug laws. The state sought joinder on the charges (i.e., sought to combine them together such that the defendant was tried for both in the same trial), but the defendant successfully moved to have the charges tried separately. The Supreme Court sanctioned this approach because the defendant was opposed to trying both offenses in the same trial.

Court Hearing the First Offense Lacks Jurisdiction.

Double jeopardy does not apply when the court hearing the first offense lacks jurisdiction to try the second offense. This exception came from the Supreme Court's decision in *Fugate* v. *New Mexico*.[89] There, the Court held that a defendant's conviction on drunk-driving charges in municipal court did not bar prosecution in a higher court for vehicular homicide tied to the same incident. The Court noted that the municipal court did not have jurisdiction to try a homicide case, so double jeopardy protections did not apply.

Defense Plea Bargains over the Prosecution's Objection.

If the defense plea bargains over the prosecution's objection, double jeopardy protections do not apply. In *Ohio* v. *Johnson*,[90] the defendant succeeded in convincing the judge to dismiss certain charges against him, over the prosecution's objection. The defendant was later tried on the dismissed charges, and the Court held that double jeopardy protections did not apply. Had the prosecution acquiesced to the dismissal, the result would have been different. Indeed, it is unlikely the defendant would have been prosecuted on the dismissed charges if the prosecution had agreed with the judge's decision.

There are still other exceptions in which reprosecution for the same offense is permissible. First, if a defendant successfully appeals a criminal conviction or otherwise succeeds in overturning a conviction, he or she may be reprosecuted. In *United States* v. *Tateo*,[91] the Court held:

> It would be a high price indeed for society to pay were every accused granted immunity from punishment because of any defect sufficient to constitute reversible error in the proceedings leading to conviction. From the standpoint of a defendant, it is at least doubtful that appellate courts would be as zealous as they now are in protecting against the effects of improprieties at the trial or pretrial stage if they knew that reversal of a conviction would put the accused irrevocably beyond the reach of further prosecution. In reality, therefore, the practice of retrial serves defendants' rights as well as society's interest. The underlying purpose of permitting retrial is as much furthered by application of the rule to this case as it has been in cases previously decided.[92]

---

[87]Ibid., p. 449.
[88]432 U.S. 137 (1977).
[89]471 U.S. 1112 (1985).
[90]467 U.S. 493 (1984).
[91]377 U.S. 463 (1964).
[92]Ibid., p. 466.

Second, if a case is dismissed by the judge but the defendant is not acquitted, he or she may be reprosecuted. In *United States* v. *Scott*,[93] the Court held, in part, that "where a *defendant* successfully seeks to avoid his trial prior to its conclusion by a motion for a [dismissal], the Double Jeopardy Clause is not offended by a second prosecution. Such a motion by the defendant is deemed to be a deliberate election on his part to forgo his valued right to have his guilt or innocence determined by the first trier of fact."[94]

Finally, reprosecution is permissible if a *mistrial* occurs over the defendant's objections and is a "manifest necessity." That is, reprosecution is permissible following a mistrial "when the defendant's interest in proceeding to verdict is outweighed by the competing and equally legitimate demand for public justice."[95] Also, the defendant may be reprosecuted if the judge declares a mistrial with the defendant's consent or by the defendant's motion, provided that the prosecution does not agree to the defendant's consent or motion in bad faith (e.g., by intending to pursue a subsequent retrial for the purpose of subjecting the defendant to the harassment of multiple trials).[96]

Double Jeopardy and Sentencing

Double jeopardy protection also extends to sentencing increases. First, the Supreme Court has considered whether double jeopardy is violated with the use of *consecutive punishments* (i.e., back-to-back punishments)—say, when the defendant is sentenced to a total of 10 years for convictions on two counts that each carries a 5-year sentence. The Court has held that this determination depends on legislative intent.[97] That is, if the criminal law permits such punishment, double jeopardy does not occur.

Questions about double jeopardy have also been raised when a defendant is resentenced following some important development in the case. Increasing the sentence for the same charge (i.e., as opposed to increasing the sentence for separate charges, as in the case of cumulative punishments) after it has been imposed is permissible (1) when a conviction is reversed by an appeal[98]; (2) after the prosecution has appealed a sentence, provided there is legal authorization to do so (a rare occurrence)[99]; and (3) after the discovery of a legal defect in the first sentence.[100]

In a recent—and controversial—case, *Sattazahn* v. *Pennsylvania*,[101] an individual was charged with capital murder, but the jury could not unanimously conclude that the death penalty was warranted. As required by a Pennsylvania statute, the judge then sentenced the offender to life in prison. The defendant was then retried and sentenced to death. He argued that the Fifth Amendment's double jeopardy clause was violated, but the Supreme Court disagreed. The Court argued that the deadlocked jury did not amount to a "death penalty acquittal," so it saw no constitutional problems with retrying the offender.

---

[93] 437 U.S. 82 (1978).
[94] Ibid., p. 92.
[95] *Illinois* v. *Somerville*, 410 U.S. 458 (1973).
[96] See, e.g., *Lee* v. *United States*, 432 U.S. 23 (1977); *Oregon* v. *Kennedy*, 456 U.S. 667 (1982).
[97] See, e.g., *Albernaz* v. *United States*, 450 U.S. 333 (1981).
[98] *North Carolina* v. *Pierce*, 395 U.S. 711 (1969).
[99] *United States* v. *DiFrancesco*, 449 U.S. 117 (1980).
[100] See, e.g., *In re Bradley*, 318 U.S. 50 (1943).
[101] 537 U.S. 101 (2003).

**YOUR
DECISION**

1. Assume that a state law gives the trial judge authority to sentence to death a defendant convicted of a capital crime but also requires the judge to consider the jury's recommendation as to whether the death penalty should be imposed. Assume further that a man has been sentenced to death by the judge in his trial, even though the jury that convicted him recommended life in prison. The man appeals, claiming that the statute is unconstitutional because it does not specify the weight the judge must give to the jury's sentencing recommendation and thus permits the arbitrary imposition of the death penalty. He further claims that the judge should be forced to give "great weight" to the jury's recommendation. How should the appellate court rule?

2. The police found marijuana and growing equipment when they searched a man's house. He was prosecuted criminally, but the federal government also sought civil forfeiture of his house, pursuant to a federal law. The man challenged this action, claiming that the proposed forfeiture of his house would amount to double jeopardy, a violation of the Fifth Amendment. Does civil asset forfeiture in addition to criminal prosecution place a person in double jeopardy?

Summary

- The Eighth Amendment prohibits cruel and unusual punishment.

- The death penalty is permissible for intentional murder, but not for murderers who were 18 years old or younger at the time of their crimes, and not for the mentally retarded. Likewise, the death penalty is not allowed in rape cases.

- In deciding whether a term of imprisonment violates the Eighth Amendment, courts must consider various factors, including (1) the gravity of the offense compared to the sentence, (2) the penalties imposed on other offenders in the same state for the same offense, (3) the penalties imposed in other states for the same offense, and (4) the defendant's recidivism.

- Double jeopardy occurs when, for the same offense, a person is (1) reprosecuted after acquittal, (2) reprosecuted after conviction, or (3) subjected to separate punishments for the same offense.

- Double jeopardy protection applies in all criminal proceedings.

- In *Blockburger* v. *United States*, the Supreme Court developed a test that states that "[w]here the same act or transaction constitutes a violation of two distinct statutory provisions, the test to be applied to determine whether there are two offenses or only one, is whether each requires proof of an additional fact which the other does not."

- Double jeopardy does not apply when (1) the second prosecution is based on conduct committed after the first prosecution, (2) if the defendant is responsible for the second prosecution, (3) when the court hearing the first offense lacks jurisdiction to try the second offense, (4) if the defense plea bargains over the prosecution's objection, and in still other situations.

- Double jeopardy protection also extends to sentencing increases.

Chapter Review

GOVERNMENT'S LAW-MAKING AUTHORITY AND GENERAL LIMITATIONS ON THE CRIMINAL LAW

Learning Objectives

- Explain how the separation of powers and federalism limit the government's law-making authority.
- Describe the principle of legality.
- Describe the principle of lenity.

Review Questions

1. How do the separation of powers and federalism place limitations on government's law-making authority? Be specific.
2. Explain the principle of legality.
3. What is lenity? How does it place limitations on the criminal law?

Key Terms

federalism
confederation
dual federalism

principle of legality
principle of lenity

CONSTITUTIONAL LIMITATIONS ON THE CRIMINAL LAW, PART 1

Learning Objectives

- Describe the Fourteenth Amendment's equal protection clause.
- Summarize the prohibition of *ex post facto* laws and bills of attainder.
- Summarize the void for vagueness principle.
- Explain the void for overbreadth doctrine.

Review Questions

1. What are the six constitutional limitations on the criminal law?
2. Explain how the Fourteenth Amendment's equal protection clause places limits on the criminal law.
3. What is an *ex post facto* law? Provide a specific example.
4. Provide an example of a law that could be considered "void for vagueness."
5. Provide an example of a law that could be considered "void for overbreadth."

Key Terms

equal protection clause
strict scrutiny
intermediate scrutiny
rational basis
ex post facto
bill of attainder

void for vagueness
libel
defamation
seditious speech
void for overbreadth

MODULE **2.3**   **CONSTITUTIONAL LIMITATIONS ON THE CRIMINAL LAW, PART 2**

Learning Objectives

- Describe the protections against cruel and unusual punishment.
- Explain the guarantee against double jeopardy.

Review Questions

1. What types of punishment are considered cruel and unusual?
2. Summarize the *Blockburger* Rule as it pertains to double jeopardy.
3. Explain the circumstances in which double jeopardy does not apply.

Key Terms

guided-discretion laws   *Blockburger* Rule
double jeopardy

Chapter Synthesis Questions

1. Is government's law-making authority sufficiently limited in the United States? Why or why not?
2. Is the "quantity" of criminal law in the United States insufficient, sufficient, or overreaching? Why?
3. Are the constitutional limitations on the criminal law too many or too few? Explain your answer.
4. Does the death penalty constitute cruel and unusual punishment in your view? Why or why not?
5. At what length in years (if any) should a prison sentence be considered cruel and unusual?
6. There are certain circumstances in which double jeopardy does not apply. Is this ideal? Why or why not?

3

THE ELEMENTS OF CRIMINAL LIABILITY

INTRODUCTION TO OFFENSE TYPES

Learning Objective

* **Explain the difference between conduct and result crimes.**

CORE CONCEPTS

general part of the criminal law Broad principles that apply to more than one crime.

special part of the criminal law The part of law that defines specific crimes.

There are many types of crimes, each with its own definition. Underlying each of them, however, are a series of basic elements. These basic elements form the foundation of the criminal law. We call these elements the **general part of the criminal law**. They are "general" because they are not unique to any one crime. For example, underlying every crime is a prohibited act or omission.

Much of the material presented in the last chapter, including the doctrines of legality and lenity, also fits within the general part of the criminal law. Why? Each principle we introduced applies to *all* crimes. The constitutional limitations we discussed apply to all offenses as well. In Chapter 9, we will look at defenses to criminal liability. They also fall into the general part of the criminal law, as the most popular criminal defenses are not limited to any specific criminal act. We will look later on in this book at accomplice liability, attempt, conspiracy, and solicitation. These also fall into the general part of the criminal law because they have "general applicability,"[1] meaning they apply in many different situations. For example, one can attempt to commit burglary, robbery, rape, murder, and so on. There is no requirement that attempt be linked to a specific type of crime.

Contrast this with the **special part of the criminal law**, that part of the law that defines specific crimes. The special part of the criminal law names the exact elements of a crime that must be proven in court. Assume, for example, that a person is charged with first-degree murder. The special part of the criminal law requires a prosecutor to prove beyond a reasonable doubt that the defendant intentionally killed another human being.

This chapter is intended to introduce the basics of criminal liability, the foundational elements of virtually every crime. First, it is necessary to explore the different types of criminal offenses.

Depending on what type of crime the defendant is charged with, all or only a few of the basic elements of criminal liability (*actus reus, mens rea*, concurrence, causation, and resulting harm—defined thoroughly later in this chapter) may need to be in place. There are two main crime types: conduct crimes and result crimes. It is critical to gain a grasp of the differences between each because each requires proof of a different set of elements.

---

[1]M. D. Dubber, *Criminal Law: Model Penal Code* (New York: Foundation Press, 2002), p. 142.

Conduct Crimes

conduct crimes Crimes that are complete when the criminal act and criminal intent concur. There is no requirement for resulting harm.

Conduct crimes are offenses for which engaging in a prohibited act constitutes the full offense. There is no requirement that any resulting harm occur, only that someone engaged in an action that was prohibited by law. An example is reckless driving. The law generally prohibits reckless driving out of concern that dangerous driver could cause harm to others, but there is no requirement that harm occur for one to be convicted of reckless driving. A more extreme example is the crime of burglary. By way of preview, burglary is basically the unlawful entry into a dwelling with intent to commit a felony inside. The crime is complete once the unlawful entry occurs. There is no requirement that a felony (such as grand theft) is actually committed.

Result Crimes

result crimes Crimes that require actual harm.

resulting harm An essential element of a result crime. For example, the resulting harm in homicide is the killing of a human being. Without the killing, it is not homicide.

Result crimes are offenses that are not complete without actual harm. The classic example is murder. A person cannot be convicted of murder without the killing of another. A person's death is the actual harm. Another example is arson, which usually entails the intentional destruction of another's property by burning. Without damage by fire, the crime of arson does not occur. Result crimes thus require that elements besides just criminal conduct are in place. This is known as **resulting harm**.

YOUR DECISION

1. The following is a state criminal statute: "Section 1.023(a): It shall be unlawful to trespass on the property of another without consent if the property suffers physical damage. Violators of this provision face up to six months of imprisonment and may be required to pay restitution to the property owner." Does this statute describe a result crime or a conduct crime? Why?
2. The following is another state criminal statute: "Section 4.073(a)(1): In order to be guilty of any crime within the state, the defendant must commit a criminal act. This act must be committed voluntarily and without duress. An involuntary act will generally not create criminal liability." Is this statute an example of the general or special part of criminal law? Explain.

Summary

- The general part of the criminal law is "general" because it is not unique to any one crime. For example, underlying every crime is a prohibited act or omission.
- The special part of the criminal law defines specific crimes and their elements.
- Conduct crimes are offenses for which engaging in a prohibited act constitutes the full offense.
- Result crimes are offenses that are not complete without actual harm. The classic example is murder.

THE CORE ELEMENTS OF CRIMINAL LIABILITY, PART 1: *ACTUS REUS*

Learning Objective

- **Explain *actus reus* and what constitutes a criminal act.**

CORE CONCEPTS

actus reus Latin term meaning "evil act" or criminal act. One of the core requirements of a crime.

There are three basic elements to criminal liability: *actus reus*, *mens rea*, and concurrence (see Figure 3.1). This module looks at *actus reus*. The next module looks at *mens rea* and concurrence. Module four then considers the two types of causation.

Actus reus, Latin for an "evil act," is the requirement that a crime contain some criminal act. There cannot be a crime without some action (or inaction, as we will also see) on the part of the defendant. For example, it is not a crime to fantasize about inflicting harm on someone else. Indeed, it is not even criminal for a person to *intend* to inflict harm on another. Intention must be coupled with an action. A simple example of *actus reus* is a defendant pulling the trigger of a gun and shooting a victim. The pulling of the trigger is a criminal act, or *actus reus*. This, in a nutshell, is the essence of the *actus reus*. But there is much more to it than meets the eye.

Voluntary Act

In general, a person cannot be guilty of a crime unless he or she commits a voluntary act. The issue of voluntariness is most often raised in the context of criminal defenses. If there is a chance the action in question is not voluntary, the defense bears the burden of proving as much. We will look in Chapter 9 at some so-called excuse defenses that raise the issue of voluntariness.

A criminal act is a physical movement. Such movement may be visible to the eye, such as when an assailant stabs a victim, but it could also be imperceptible. For example, someone could utter a word with minimal mouth movement and this could satisfy the *actus reus* requirement. The crime of solicitation, for example (see Chapter 5), can be completed with little more than words.

An act is considered *voluntary* when it is in some way willed by the actor. The act could be voluntary even if it is a result of habit or is inadvertent. As long as the actor had the option of acting differently, the act will be considered voluntary. Whether the action is a force of habit or a wholly deliberate act is important when it comes to gradations of offenses, but the *actus reus* requirement is satisfied in either case. Say Larry lights a cigarette, promptly falls asleep, drops the cigarette, catches the house on fire, and manages to wake up and escape before the fire consumes the house and kills his wife. As an alternative, say Larry went into his wife's room while she was asleep, poured gasoline around the bed, lit a cigarette, and set the room ablaze, killing his wife. Clearly his actions in both

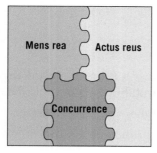

Figure 3.1
Basic Elements of Criminal Liability

scenarios were voluntary (he had the option of not lighting the cigarette in the first situation, for example), but it would be unreasonable to treat both acts in the same manner.

In most cases, it is safely assumed that the underlying act was voluntary, but ascertaining voluntariness can be difficult some of the time. Consider multiple personality disorder. In *State* v. *Grimsley*,[2] a woman drove a vehicle under the influence while she was disassociated from her primary personality. She claimed that her alternate personality was responsible for the crime, but the court disagreed, stating,

> There was only one person driving the car and only one person accused of drunken driving. It is immaterial whether she was in one state of consciousness or another, so long as in the personality then controlling her behavior, she was conscious and her actions were a product of her own volition.[3]

See the accompanying Court Decision for more on voluntariness in regards to *actus reus*. In it, we take a look at a classic case, *People* v. *Decina*, decided in 1956 by New York's highest court.

COURT DECISION

The Logic behind Voluntariness in *Actus Reus*

People of the State of New York v. Decina
138 N.E.2d 799 N.Y. App. (1956)

Decision: An individual who knowingly suffers from a medical condition can be found criminally liable if that condition occurs while driving a motor vehicle and injuries result.

Reason: (Decina was charged with criminal negligence in operating an automobile with knowledge that he was subject to epileptic seizures. His car struck a number of pedestrians, including a group of young schoolgirls and ultimately crashed through the brick wall of a grocery store. The Court of Appeals found the indictment to be sufficient.)

*** We turn first to the subject of defendant's cross appeal, namely, that his demurrer should have been sustained, since the indictment here does not charge a crime. The indictment states essentially that defendant, knowing "that he was subject to epileptic attacks or other disorder rendering him likely to lose consciousness for a considerable period of time," was culpably negligent "in that he consciously undertook to and did operate his Buick sedan on a public highway" (emphasis supplied) and "while so doing" suffered such an attack which caused said automobile "to travel at a fast and reckless rate of speed, jumping the curb and driving over the sidewalk" causing the death of 4 persons. In our opinion, this clearly states a violation of section 1053-a of the Penal Law. The statute does not require that a defendant must deliberately intend to kill a human being, for that would be murder. Nor does the statute require that he knowingly and consciously follow the precise path

(continued)

---

[2]*State* v. *Grimsley*, 444 N.E. 2d 1071 (Ohio Ct. App. 1982).
[3]Ibid., p. 267.

**COURT
DECISION**
(continued)

that leads to death and destruction. It is sufficient, we have said, when his conduct manifests a "disregard of the consequences which may ensue from the act, and indifference to the rights of others. No clearer definition, applicable to the hundreds of varying circumstances that may arise, can be given. Under a given state of facts, whether negligence is culpable is a question of judgment."

Assuming the truth of the indictment, as we must on a demurrer, this defendant knew he was subject to epileptic attacks and seizures that might strike at any time. He also knew that a moving motor vehicle uncontrolled on public highway is a highly dangerous instrumentality capable of unrestrained destruction. With this knowledge, and without anyone accompanying him, he deliberately took a chance by making a conscious choice of a course of action, in disregard of the consequences which he knew might follow from his conscious act, and which in this case did ensue. How can we say as a matter of law that this did not amount to culpable negligence within the meaning of section 1053-a?

To hold otherwise would be to say that a man may freely indulge himself in liquor in the same hope that it will not affect his driving, and if it later develops that ensuing intoxication causes dangerous and reckless driving resulting in death, his unconsciousness or involuntariness at that time would relieve him from prosecution under the statute. His awareness of a condition which he knows may produce such consequences as here, and his disregard of the consequences, renders him liable for culpable negligence, as the courts below have properly held. To have a sudden sleeping spell, an unexpected heart or other disabling attack, without any prior knowledge or warning thereof, is an altogether different situation, and there is simply no basis for comparing such cases with the flagrant disregard manifested here.

A related issue arises in the context of addiction. In *Robinson* v. *California*,[4] the U.S. Supreme Court was confronted with the question of whether a California statute that made it illegal for a person to "be addicted to the use of narcotics" was unconstitutional. The Court held that it was, arguing that the law

> is not one which punishes a person for the use of narcotics, for their purchase, sale or possession, or for antisocial or disorderly behavior resulting from their administration. It is not a law which even purports to provide or require medical treatment. Rather, we deal with a statute which makes the "status" of narcotic addiction a criminal offense, for which the offender may be prosecuted "at any time before he reforms". . . . It is unlikely that any State at this moment in history would attempt to make it a criminal offense for a person to be mentally ill, or a leper, or to be afflicted with a venereal disease. A State might determine that the general health and welfare require that the victims of these and other human afflictions be dealt with by compulsory treatment, involving quarantine, confinement, or sequestration. But, in the light of contemporary human knowledge, a law which made a criminal offense of such a disease would doubtless be universally thought to be an infliction of cruel and unusual punishment.[5]

[4]*Robinson* v. *California*, 370 U.S. 660 (1962).
[5]Ibid., p. 666.

A similar Supreme Court case dealt with Leroy Powell, a man who was charged with violating a Texas statute that prohibited "get[ting] drunk or be[ing] found in a state of intoxication."[6] Powell attempted to use his status as an alcoholic as a defense to the crime. Interestingly, the Court affirmed Powell's conviction, claiming that he "was convicted, not for being a chronic alcoholic, but for being in public while drunk on a particular occasion."[7]

The differences between *Robinson* and *Powell* are subtle but important. In *Powell*, the Court was concerned with *where* the conduct took place. Powell was held liable not just because he was drunk, but because he was *found* drunk in public. In *Robinson*, however, the crime in question was limited strictly to a person's status. Status alone is insufficient to satisfy *actus reus*. In other words, any law that punishes a person merely on the chance that he or she may act is unconstitutional.

Omission

omission The failure to act. In certain circumstances, an omission can satisfy the *actus reus* element of crime.

An **omission** is a failure to act. Certain omissions can satisfy the *actus reus* element of criminal liability, as well. The general rule is that, with a few exceptions, no person has a duty to act in a manner that prevents injury or loss of life to another. So, in *People* v. *Beardsley*,[8] when a man failed to come to the aid of his mistress who took a lethal dose of poison and died, he was not liable for her death. Some experts disagree with this rule, however. Graham Hughes argued, "In a civilized society, a man who finds himself with a helplessly ill person who has no other source of aid should be under a duty to summon help, whether the person is his wife, his mistress, a prostitute or a Chief Justice."[9] Others, however, feel it would be unrealistic to expect that everyone who is in a position to help should do so. In the famous Kitty Genovese case, some 38 people heard her get attacked and killed, yet none intervened—during the whole 30 minutes she cried out for help. This is surprising to say the least, but should all 38 people have been required to help? While it would be *morally* right to help, it is not *legally* required that the people intervene.

When can an omission satisfy the *actus reus* requirement? There are seven specific situations.

1. **Relationship.** When there is a status relationship between two parties, an omission can lead to criminal liability. For example, a woman who knew her children's father was abusing them and failed to act was guilty of child abuse by her omission.[10] Likewise, a parent who failed to seek treatment for a child, which then led to the child's death, was convicted of a homicide offense.[11]

Bad Samaritan laws Laws that make it a crime for someone to fail to come to the aid of another who is danger.

2. **Statute.** Many states have laws that require certain officials to report actions such as child abuse. Failure to report can lead to criminal liability by omission. Some states have gone so far as to enact so-called **Bad Samaritan laws**, which make it

---

[6]*Powell* v. *Texas*, 392 U.S. 514 (1968).
[7]Ibid., p. 532.
[8]*People* v. *Beardsley*, 113 N.W. 1128 (Mich. 1907).
[9]G. Hughes, "Criminal Omissions," *Yale Law Journal*, Vol. 67 (1958), pp. 590–637, 624.
[10]*State* v. *Williquette*, 385 N.W. 2d 145 (Wis. 1986).
[11]*State* v. *Williams*, 484 P.2d 1167 (Wash. Ct. App. 1971).

§ 519. Emergency Medical Care

(a) A person who knows that another is exposed to grave physical harm shall, to the extent that the same can be rendered without danger or peril to himself or without interference with important duties owed to others, give reasonable assistance to the exposed person unless that assistance or care is being provided by others.

(b) A person who provides reasonable assistance in compliance with subsection (a) of this section shall not be liable in civil damages unless his acts constitute gross negligence or unless he will receive or expects to receive remuneration. Nothing contained in this subsection shall alter existing law with respect to tort liability of a practitioner of the healing arts for acts committed in the ordinary course of his practice.

(c) A person who willfully violates subsection (a) of this section shall be fined not more than $100.00.

Figure 3.2

Vermont's Bad Samaritan Law (12 V.S.A. § 519)

criminal for someone to fail to come to the aid of another who is in peril.[12] See the text of Vermont's Bad Samaritan law in Figure 3.2. Bad Samaritan laws are distinctive from Good Samaritan laws, the latter of which are intended to protect people who come to the aid of those in need. For example, if Scott observes David collapse and stop breathing, attempts to perform CPR, and ends up doing more harm than good, killing David, then a Good Samaritan law would protect Scott from perhaps being sued by David's surviving family members.

3. **Contract.** If a contract sets up a special relationship between two parties and that contract is breached, criminal liability is possible. For example, if someone is contractually obligated to care for a physically disabled person but fails to do so, a crime may occur as a result of the inaction.[13]

4. **Voluntary Assumption of Care.** If a person voluntarily assumes care of another person (without a contract), that person may be held liable for failure to act. For example, in *People v. Oliver*,[14] a woman took an intoxicated man into her home and allowed him to use the bathroom, knowing his intent was to inject heroin (she even gave him a spoon to help prepare his injection). He emerged from the bathroom, collapsed, and was later dragged outside, where he died. The woman was found guilty of manslaughter.

5. **Creation of Peril.** If George pushes Gary, who cannot swim, into a lake, Gary struggles and cries out for help, and George fails to assist, George can be guilty of a crime. Something similar happened in *Jones v. State*.[15] A man raped a woman who escaped and, distraught, jumped into a creek and drowned. The man was convicted of murder.

6. **Duty to Control Conduct of Another.** Assume Larry, a business owner, knows that his delivery driver, Rick, is a reckless driver. Rick slams his delivery truck into a small car and kills the driver. Larry, through his omission (i.e., his failure to do anything about Rick's driving), may be held criminally liable.

---

[12]See, e.g., Vt. Stat. Ann. Tit. 12, Section 519(a) (2007).
[13]*Davis v. Commonwealth*, 335 S.E. 2d 375 (Va. 1985).
[14]*People v. Oliver*, 210 Cal. App. 3d 138 (Ct. App. 1989).
[15]*Jones v. State*, 43 N.E. 2d 1017 (Ind. 1942).

7. Landowner Duty. The owner of, say, a nightclub is required to perform certain functions, such as to ensure an adequate number of emergency exits. Failure to do so could lead to criminal liability in the event a fire occurs and one or more patrons die or are injured.

See the accompanying Court Decision for more on omission as a form of *actus reus*. In it, we take a look at *Commonwealth of Pennsylvania* v. *Julia Cardwell*, a case in which a mother was charged with endangering the welfare of her child.

COURT DECISION

The Logic behind Omission as a Form of *Actus Reus*

Commonwealth of Pennsylvania v. Julia Cardwell
515 A.2d 311 (Pa. Super. 1986)

Decision: A parent has an affirmative duty to protect their children from harm. Failure to prevent injury or maltreatment means the parent knowingly endangered the welfare of the child.

Reason: (Julia Cardwell was convicted of endangering the welfare of her child. The Superior Court of Pennsylvania affirmed her conviction. Julia's husband Clyde sexually abused her daughter, Alicia, for several years. Alicia became pregnant by Clyde twice in 1983 and had two abortions. Alicia specifically informed her mother of the abuse after the second abortion.)

Appellant's challenge to the sufficiency of the evidence is that the evidence adduced at trial was insufficient to prove beyond a reasonable doubt the intent element of the offense of endangering the welfare of a child. This challenge is in two parts. The first part concerns the intent required by the statute defining the offense and is a matter of statutory interpretation.

18 Pa.C.S.A. § 4304, Endangering the Welfare of Children, provides:

> A parent, guardian, or other person supervising the welfare of a child under 18 years of age commits a misdemeanor of the second degree if he knowingly endangers the welfare of the child by violating a duty of care, protection or support.

Appellant alleges that this statute requires a "knowing act" of endangering the welfare of a child, and appellant implies that an omission to act cannot satisfy the statute. We do not agree. The crime of endangering the welfare of a child is a specific intent offense. The intent element required by § 4303 is a knowing violation of a duty of care. We must, therefore, interpret when an accused knowingly violates his or her duty of care.

. . . Appellant's brief suggests that we must negate intent because Julia did "something." Therefore, the question is raised whether acts which are so feeble as to be ineffectual can negate intent. We find they cannot, and reject that argument. The affirmative performance required by § 4304 cannot be met simply by showing any step at all toward preventing harm, however incomplete or ineffectual. An act which will negate intent is not necessarily one which will provide a successful outcome. However, the person

(continued)

charged with the duty of care is required to take steps that are reasonably calculated to achieve success. Otherwise, the meaning of "duty of care" is eviscerated.

We conclude that a parent's duty to protect his or her child requires affirmative performance to prevent harm and that failure to act may mean that the parent "knowingly endangers the welfare of the child." 18 Pa.C.S.A. § 4304.

We hold that evidence is sufficient to prove the intent element of the offense of endangering the welfare of a child, 18 Pa.C.S.A. § 4304, when the accused is aware of his or her duty to protect the child; is aware that the child is in circumstances that threaten the child's physical or psychological welfare; and has either failed to act or has taken actions so lame or meager that such actions cannot reasonably be expected to be effective to protect the child's physical or psychological welfare.

Model Penal Code

The Model Penal Code limits criminal liability to conduct that "includes a voluntary act or the omission to perform an act of which he is physically capable."[16] Note that this definition contains the all-important term *includes*. This means that so long as there is at least one voluntary act in a chain of acts, *actus reus* is in place. For example, a person who shotguns six beers, immediately gets in a car, and after a short distance, runs a red light and kills a pedestrian, commits at least one voluntary act (getting in the car and driving). The killing may well be involuntary if the driver does not intend to hit the pedestrian.

The Model Penal Code goes on to define an *act* as a "bodily movement whether voluntary or involuntary."[17] Actions considered involuntary under the Model Penal Code include reflexes; convulsions; conduct committed during sleep, hypnosis, or while the actor is unconscious; and "a bodily movement that otherwise is not the product of the effort or determination of the actor, either conscious or unconscious."[18] And as we indicated earlier, involuntary actions (in the absence of any voluntary ones) cannot support a criminal conviction.

In closing, we should point out that the Model Penal Code—like many penal codes—also treats "possession" as an act. This is important because possession is a passive condition, not the same as, say, taking a step. In general, it is necessary that possession be "knowing," meaning that the person charged with possession is aware that what he or she possesses is contraband. Two classes of possession are also generally recognized: **actual possession** and **constructive possession**. Actual possession occurs when an individual has an item in their physical control, such as holding a marijuana joint in their hand. Alternatively, constructive possession occurs when an individual has the power or position to effectively control an item. For example, you constructively possess the items in your home while you are away at work, even if you are not physically touching them.

actual possession
Property that is either held by the individual or attached to them in some fashion.

constructive possession
Power or position to effectively control an item, even if it is not in immediate physical possession.

---

[16]Model Penal Code Section 2.01(1).
[17]Ibid., Section 1.13(2).
[18]Ibid., Section 2.01(2)(d).

YOUR DECISION

1. Jack is sitting in a crowded movie theater. Halfway through the movie, he jumps up and shouts, "Fire! We all have to get out of here! There's a fire!" In the pandemonium that ensues, several people are injured. It turns out there was no fire, however, and that Jack suffered from what is known as an "uncinate fit," a brief seizure in a part of the brain that can cause abnormal smell sensations. Is Jack guilty of a crime?

2. Joseph is a college junior rushing across campus to take his physics final exam. On his way to the classroom, Joseph passes another student passed out in the library parking lot. The student is unconscious and surrounded by a pool of blood. Joseph fears he will miss his final exam and fail the course if he stops to help, so he walks right by without intervening. The student later dies as a result of his injuries and doctors believe he would have survived if Joseph called for help. Can Joseph be charged with a crime? Why or why not?

Summary

- *Actus reus* is Latin for "evil act." There cannot be a crime without a criminal act.
- In general, a person cannot be guilty of a crime unless that person commits a voluntary act.
- An omission is a failure to act. Certain omissions can satisfy the *actus reus* element of criminal liability.
- An omission can satisfy *actus reus* when a special relationship is established.
- An omission can also lead to criminal liability in the case of statutory relationships, in contract situations, following a voluntary assumption of care, if an omission leads to the creation of peril, when there is a duty to control the conduct of another, and when a landowner duty exists.

MODULE

3.3

THE CORE ELEMENTS OF CRIMINAL LIABILITY, PART 2: *MENS REA* AND CONCURRENCE

Learning Objectives
- **Explain *mens rea* and the different types of intent.**
- **Distinguish between *mens rea* and motive.**
- **Identify strict liability offenses.**
- **Summarize concurrence.**

CORE CONCEPTS   *Mens rea*, Latin for "guilty mind," is the second critical component of criminal liability. With few exceptions, a person cannot be held criminally liability unless there

mens rea Latin term meaning "guilty mind." The mental state or criminal intent of the defendant.

was some degree of intention on that person's part to commit the crime. Even the defendant's simple "knowledge" that what he or she did was morally wrong can suffice—some of the time—to meet this requirement. *Mens rea*, like *actus reus*, is exceedingly complex, as there are many levels of intent. Indeed, one expert noted that "there is no term fraught with greater ambiguity than that venerable Latin phrase that haunts the Anglo-American criminal law: *mens rea*."[19]

At one point in history, *mens rea* was irrelevant. Under early English law, a person could be held criminally responsible regardless of his or her intent. Throughout the thirteenth century and onward to present, however, *mens rea* has become a deeply entrenched component of criminal liability. The Supreme Court once remarked that "[t]he contention that an injury can amount to a crime only when inflicted by [*mens rea*] is no provincial or transient notion. It is…universal and persistent in mature systems of law. . . ."[20] In other words, *mens rea* is a bedrock principle of criminal law.

Traditional and Statutory *Mens Rea*

It is useful to begin with a distinction between traditional *mens rea* and *statutory mens rea*.[21] Traditional *mens rea* is concerned with culpability, or an offender's level of blameworthiness for a crime.[22] Under this view, the offender is considered morally bankrupt, perhaps even a sinner. Terms like *wicked, evil*, and *vicious* were used throughout history to describe the *mens rea* of the crime. In contrast, statutory *mens rea* is the level of intent required by a specific statute, possibly independent of any notion of morality. Today, the traditional meaning of *mens rea* has been somewhat diluted and mostly replaced with legalistic rather than moral underpinnings. Unfortunately, statutes vary widely in the terms they include to capture the *mens rea* element of criminal liability. The Model Penal Code's drafters found 76 distinct terms for *mens rea* in federal statutes alone.[23]

The distinction between traditional and statutory *mens rea* is important, as it can bear on whether someone will be held criminally liable. What if, in order to get a conviction for drug possession, the prosecutor must show that the defendant "intentionally" carried an illegal substance on his or her person? And what if the defendant did not know the substance was illegal, only that he was carrying it? Under a statutory *mens rea* requirement, the defendant's knowledge about the substance being illegal would be irrelevant. Under a *traditional mens rea* requirement, it would be important to look at the defendant's awareness that he was doing something wrong. If he had no idea he was breaking the law, then can we say he was morally blameworthy? Was he "wicked" or "evil," even though he didn't know he was doing something wrong?

---

[19]G. P. Fletcher, *Rethinking Criminal Law* (New York: Oxford, 2000), p. 398.
[20]*Morissette v. United States*, 342 U.S. 246 (1952), p. 250.
[21]R. G. Singer and J. Q. LaFond, *Criminal Law: Examples and Explanations*, 4th ed. (New York: Wolters Kluwer, 2007), p. 53.
[22]J. Dressler, *Understanding Criminal Law*, 5th ed. (Newark, NJ: Lexis-Nexis, 2009), p. 118.
[23]Model Penal Code Section 2.02, commentary, p. 230, n. 3 (1980).

Common *Mens Rea* Terminology

Although *mens rea* defies a simple explanation, there are several terms that have appeared throughout the years in criminal codes, each of which captures its essence to some extent. The following subsections look at six of them.

Intent

direct intent Intent in which the consequences of a person's actions are desired.

Intent is perhaps the most straightforward conception of *mens rea*. A person who *intends* to commit a crime should be the one liable for it. When the consequences of a person's actions are desired, this is known as **direct intent**. But there are complications. What if the person intended to engage in criminal conduct but did not intend to cause harm? Say Fred pulled a gun on John, shot him, and John died. We can easily say Fred intended to pull the trigger, but did he intend for John to die? The answer is not completely clear. Maybe Fred thought the gun was empty. Maybe he knew the gun was loaded, but didn't think he would hit Fred. Maybe he just wanted to wound Fred. Maybe he meant to shoot someone else. And so on. To the extent Fred made a mistake, the law will treat his actions differently (see the Mistake section toward the end of this chapter). The other twists in this scenario present complications. For example, if Fred meant to shoot someone else, then we have a case of **transferred intent**. More than likely, however, the "intent follows the bullet,"[24] meaning that the requisite *mens rea* was in place for Fred's conviction.

transferred intent The defendant's intent to harm one person is transferred to the actual victim of the crime.

oblique intent Intent in which the consequences of a person's actions are not desired, but should have reasonably been foreseen.

If Fred only wanted to wound John, then we have an example of **oblique intent**. This means that while Fred did not *intend* for John to die, he had to know the outcome was almost certain to occur. Consider *Regina v. Cunningham*.[25] In that case, Cunningham broke into a house and stole the gas meter out of the basement, causing gas to escape. A person inhaled the gas and nearly died. Cunningham pleaded guilty to a burglary charge and was convicted at trial of attempted murder. An appellate court reversed his murder conviction because Cunningham lacked the required *mens rea*. Cunningham did not know the gas escaped and thus did not *intend* to kill anyone. As a general rule, intent exists if someone (1) desires to commit harm and (2) knows that the harm is almost certain to occur because of his actions.[26]

general intent The intent to commit the *actus reus* or criminal act of the crime only.

specific intent The intent to commit an act to achieve a specific criminal result.

Since we are on the subject of intent, it is important to point out the difference between **general intent** crimes and **specific intent** crimes. General intent crimes are those offenses that require only the intent to commit the *actus reus* of the crime without an additional *mens rea* component. General intent is doing an act prohibited by law, such as the crime of battery (discussed in Chapter 6). In a specific intent crime, however, the defendant must have the intent to commit an act to achieve a specific criminal result. Common law burglary, which is discussed in more detail in Chapter 7, is the classic example of a specific intent crime. In order to be guilty of burglary, the defendant must break and enter into the dwelling of another, in the nighttime, *with the intent to commit a felony inside*. The additional *mens rea* component requiring "the intent to commit a felony inside" distinguishes burglary as a specific intent crime.

---

[24]Singer and LaFond, *Criminal Law: Examples and Explanations*, p. 57.
[25]*Regina v. Cunningham*, 41 Crim. App. 155 (Ct. Crim. App. 1957).
[26]*Thornton v. State*, 919 A.2d 678 (Md. 2007), p. 691.

Knowledge

To *knowingly* commit a crime is not the same as *intentionally* committing one. In some cases, rather than *intending* to commit the harm, the defendant may only be required to *know* that the result is virtually certain. Some statutes even go so far as to add "knowing" or "knowingly" to the statute. For example, it is a federal offense to knowingly import any controlled substance into the United States.[27] The addition of "knowingly" thus satisfies the *mens rea* requirement.

What if someone doesn't *know* a crime is being committed, but he or she acts with "deliberate ignorance" or "willful blindness?"[28] In such situations, it is safe to say the defendant acts with knowledge. If the defendant is aware of a high probability that criminal activity is taking place and/or fails to make further inquiries as to whether criminal activity is taking place, then the defendant can be held liable. For example, if Lola agreed to drive Nancy's car from Mexico to the United States and was suspicious that drugs were hidden within it *and* failed to confirm whether her suspicions were correct, then she would most likely satisfy the *mens rea* component of the underlying offense and be found guilty.[29]

Negligence

negligence A type of *mens rea* or criminal intent in which the defendant unconsciously creates a risk of harm and does not act like a reasonable person under the circumstances.

Negligence is a common term in criminal law. Basically, it means that person has not foreseen any possibility that harm would result. Negligence is concerned with taking careless risks. This means negligence is a far cry from intent. Why? Instead of acting in a morally blameworthy state of mind, the actor instead *fails* to live up to some societal expectation.

For a person to be held criminally liable for negligent behavior, it may be necessary to show that the negligence was "wanton,"[30] very serious, or not how a "reasonable person" would have acted. Another court defined negligence as that behavior

> which is denominated as gross, and which constitutes such a departure from what would be the conduct of an ordinarily careful and prudent man. . . . as to furnish evidence of that indifference to consequences which in some offenses takes the place of criminal intent.[31]

Otherwise criminal negligence looks a lot like tort negligence, a different creature altogether. Under tort law, a person who breaches a duty of care to another acts negligently. But just because someone breaches a duty of care (e.g., a lifeguard fails to notice a person drowning) does not mean that person should be criminally convicted for it. Thus, *criminal* negligence is usually something more than ordinary tort negligence.[32]

More often than not, criminal negligence comes up in the homicide context, when someone dies because of another's careless—though not necessarily intentional—

---

[27]21 U.S.C. Section 952(a) (2008).
[28]See, e.g., *United States* v. *Lara-Velasquez*, 919 F.2d 946 (5th Cir. 1990); *United States* v. *Jewell*, 532 F.2d 697 (9th Cir. 1976); *State* v. *LaFreniere*, 481 N.W.2d 412 (Neb. 1992).
[29]See, e.g., *United States* v. *Jewell*, 532 F.2d 697 (9th Cir. 1976).
[30]*State* v. *Weiner*, 194 A.2d 467 (1964).
[31]*Fitzgerald* v. *State*, 20 So. 966 (1896).
[32]For an exception, see *United States* v. *Garrett*, 984 F.2d 1402 (5th Cir. 1993).

behavior. In Chapter 6, for example, we will distinguish murder from different forms of manslaughter, the latter of which are sometimes considered negligence. But negligence is not a culpability standard limited only to homicide.

Recklessness

recklessness A type of *mens rea* or criminal intent in which the defendant consciously creates a risk and chooses to act in disregard of that risk.

Recklessness takes negligence to the next level. It has been defined as "a conscious decision to ignore risk, of which the defendant is aware."[33] Put differently, an offender acts recklessly if he or she knows a harmful result is likely, yet proceeds anyway. Consider a dangerous driving example: If George drives his Corvette through a residential neighborhood at 90 miles per hour, he is certainly acting dangerously, maybe even negligently. He is only acting *recklessly*, however, if he acknowledges the risks he is posing to others *and* shrugs them off.

Williams v. *State* helps us gain a better sense of recklessness.[34] In that case, a woman left her two children with her boyfriend at his residence. Because the utilities were not working, a candle was lit in the children's room as they were put to sleep. At 1:00 A.M., the boyfriend woke to loud screams and saw that the room in which the children were sleeping was on fire. The children perished before they could be saved. The woman was convicted of injury to a child, but the Texas Court of Criminal Appeals reversed her conviction, concluding eloquently that

> there is legally insufficient evidence that appellant consciously disregarded a substantial or unjustifiable risk that her children would suffer serious bodily injury in a house fire if she took them from a house with utilities to one without utilities. Viewed objectively, this act [of] . . . leaving the girls in a room with a lit candle . . . does not involve a "substantial and unjustifiable" risk of serious bodily injury or death. There is nothing inherently dangerous about staying or sleeping in a structure that does not have utilities. Staying in a structure without utilities does not increase the likelihood of dying in a fire. . . . If taking children to spend the night in a structure without utilities is conduct that involves an extreme risk of danger for which one may be subject to criminal prosecution for injury to a child should harm befall that child, the backwoods campers of the world are in serious jeopardy. Any adult who lights a campfire that emits a spark that lands on a child's pajamas and severely burns the child can be prosecuted as a felon. Scoutmasters beware.[35]

Malice

malice The intent to commit a wrongful act without a legitimate cause or excuse.

Malice is the intent to commit a wrongful act without a legitimate cause or excuse. In *Martinez* v. *State*, a classic Texas case, malice was defined as "a condition of the mind which shows a heart regardless of social duty and fatally bent on mischief, the existence of which is inferred from the acts committed or words spoken."[36] For example, in one case, the defendant, who had been drinking heavily, swerved off the road as he was driving and hit and killed two children who were walking on the

---

[33]Singer and LaFond, *Criminal Law: Examples and Explanations*, p. 60.
[34]*Williams* v. *State*, 235 S.W.3d 742 (Tex. Crim. App. 2007).
[35]Ibid., pp. 757–758.
[36]*Martinez* v. *State*, 30 Tex.Ct.App. 129 (1891), p. 137.

shoulder. He was convicted of murder. In upholding his conviction, the Texas Court of Criminal Appeals noted that

> it seems to us that a person who had been proven to have taken five bottles of beer in about one hour just before the tragedy, who was admittedly not sober when he began drinking this beer, who drove out of town past city streets at sixty miles per hour, who swerved completely across a ninety foot highway to his left and crushed out the life of two innocent little boys, and then drove on away; who came back to find out what his acts had resulted in; who then spoke not a word but returned home by a circuitous route, releasing the wheel to another on the way, "turned the car over to his stepmother and went to bed,"—evidences a depraved nature, and such acts evidence wantonness and such a disregard for the rights of others, such a recklessness of action that the jury had the right there from to impute to his acts malice, and to punish him accordingly.[37]

The Role of Motive

motive The inducement or reason a defendant chooses to commit a crime.

Motive is sometimes likened to *mens rea*. Both are distinct, however. Think of motive as preceding *mens rea*. As such, it has been defined as "an idea, belief or emotion that impels or incites one to act in accordance with his state of mind or emotion."[38] Motive has also been defined as the "circumstance tending to establish the requisite *mens rea* for a criminal act and is the inducement which impels or leads the mind to indulge in a criminal act."[39] Notice how both these definitions put motive before *mens rea*. Importantly, motive is never a required element of any crime.

Motive is important in criminal law for three reasons. First, specific intent offenses (discussed in the earlier Intent section) often require proof of a specific motive. For example, in *Harrison v. Commonwealth*, a man was convicted of "willfully and *maliciously*" striking and wounding another man with a deadly weapon.[40] Motive is also important in the context of criminal defenses. Assume a defendant argues that she killed the victim out of self-defense. Self-defense is a motive that could bear heavily on whether she is convicted. She intended to kill the victim (the *mens rea*), but her motive was understandable. Finally, motive is important at the sentencing phase of the criminal process. Depending on sentencing practices in a particular jurisdiction, the judge may add or take time off a sentence based on motive. Hate crimes, for example, attach stiffer penalties for crimes committed with a particular motive.[41]

Proving *Mens Rea*

It is one thing for a person to have the *mens rea* to support a criminal conviction. It is quite another for a prosecutor to prove it in court. The problem is that it is practically impossible to prove what a person was thinking at the time of the crime. All the

---

[37]*Cockrell v. State*, 135 Tex.Crim. 218 (1938), p. 226.
[38]*People v. Gibson*, 128 Cal. Rptr. 302 (1976), p. 308.
[39]*State v. Segotta*, 100 N.M. 18 (1983), pp. 25–26.
[40]*Harrison v. Commonwealth*, 279 Ky. 510 (1939), p. 510.
[41]See, e.g., *Wisconsin v. Mitchell*, 508 U.S. 479 (1993).

prosecutor can do is present enough evidence for the jury to *infer* that the defendant acted with the required *mens rea*. This, along with *actus reus* and other elements, must be proven beyond a reasonable doubt. If jurors cannot infer *mens rea* from the defendant's actions and if they have a reasonable doubt that the defendant intended for the crime to occur, then they must acquit (or find the defendant guilty of a lesser offense if they are permitted to do so).

An example should help clarify. Assume Jack is a former military sniper and winner of numerous shooting contests. Assume further that he shot his wife and is now the defendant in a murder trial. Finally, assume he claims he did not know the gun was loaded. What is a juror to infer from this? At the least, Jack is an expert in handling guns, so his claim that the gun was unloaded may not hold much water. How would an expert shooter not know his gun was loaded? On the other hand, his argument may be convincing if there is plenty of other evidence to support his credibility. Either way, note that there is nothing the prosecutor—or anyone else—can do to give people a clear window into Jack's mental state at the time of the crime.

Model Penal Code Definitions

While there is a bewildering array of *mens rea* requirements in state statutes, the Model Penal Code keeps it simple. It names four mental states, from most to least culpable: purpose, knowledge, recklessness, and negligence (also see Figure 3.3).

1. **Purpose.** A person acts purposely when "it is his conscious object to engage in conduct" or cause a particular result.[42] Purpose, according to the Model Penal Code, is the most blameworthy state of mind.

2. **Knowledge.** A person acts knowingly if he is (a) "aware" that his conduct is criminal or (b) "aware that it is practically certain that his conduct will cause" a harmful result.[43] A person who acts knowingly is less culpable than one who acts with purpose.

3. **Recklessness.** The Model Penal Code defines recklessness as follows: "A person acts recklessly with respect to a material element of an offense when he consciously

Figure 3.3

Model Penal Code Levels of *Mens Rea* and Examples

> In all four situations, someone is killed. The *mens rea*, or criminal intent of the defendant, differs in each situation.
>
> - **Purpose:** "I have the specific intent to kill my neighbor."
> - **Knowledge:** "I am practically certain that if I fire multiple gunshots into a crowded room someone will be killed."
> - **Reckless:** "I know it is dangerous to drive under the influence of alcohol and drugs, but I do it anyway and cause a fatal car accident."
> - **Negligence:** "I didn't know the gun was loaded and dangerous, so I let my five-year old son play with it and he fatally shot himself."

---

[42]Model Penal Code 1:2, 229 (1985).
[43]Ibid.

disregards a substantial and unjustifiable risk that the material element exists or will result from his conduct. The risk must be of such a nature and degree."[44] For example, if Johnny knows that it is unsafe to drive 100 mph in a blizzard, but does it anyway—he has acted recklessly. Johnny is consciously aware of the substantial and unjustifiable risk but disregards it.

4. **Negligence.** The Model Penal Code defines *negligence*, the least culpable state, in this way: "A person acts negligently with respect to a material element of an offense when he should be aware of a substantial and unjustifiable risk that the material element exists or will result from his conduct. The risk must be of such a nature and degree that the actor's failure to perceive it, considering the nature and purpose of his conduct and the circumstances known to him, involves a gross deviation from the standard of care that a reasonable person would observe in the actor's situation."[45] Note that recklessness requires that the offender "consciously disregard" a risk. This requirement is not in place for negligence. Negligence only requires that the offender be "aware" of the substantial and unjustifiable risk.

Strict Liability

strict liability Crimes that do not require *mens rea* or criminal intent.

In some cases, a person can be held criminally liable in the complete absence of *mens rea*. Such is the case with **strict liability** offenses. An example of a strict liability offense is selling alcoholic beverages to a minor. If someone is charged with this offense, the state need only prove the crime occurred. Intent is irrelevant. Statutory rape (or rape of an underage person) is also a strict liability offense in many jurisdictions. Thus, when Mary Kay Letourneau, a 34-year-old Seattle school teacher, had intercourse with one of her 12-year-old students, she was guilty of statutory rape even though she claimed that the boy was a willing participant.

Driving while intoxicated is generally a strict liability crime, where no *mens rea* is required.

© Lisa F. Young/fotolia

---

[44]Ibid.
[45]Ibid.

Supporters cite several arguments in favor of strict liability. One is that there is a concern with promoting public safety and protecting people who cannot protect themselves. During the early days of the Industrial Revolution, strict liability laws were enacted in order to protect workers and the general public from unsafe conditions in the workplace and the community. Modern-day strict liability statutes are rooted in this tradition. Another pro-strict liability argument is that the penalties associated with strict liability laws are relatively mild. And this leads to another point—namely, that since the penalties are mild, the criminal stigma attached to it is minimal. Finally, supporters of strict liability laws feel they are beneficial in some instances because they make it difficult for crafty criminals to escape punishment by fooling juries with stories of their lack of intent.

Critics, however, claim that strict liability eliminates one of the fundamental principles of criminal liability, namely *mens rea*. And in the case of regulatory strict liability offenses (e.g., if a restaurant owner fails to conform to health standards), there is evidence that laws are not adequately enforced and, indeed, that those who the laws are intended to target routinely receive opportunities to correct their ways in advance of enforcement.[46]

Concurrence

concurrence The *actus rea* and *mens rea* existing simultaneously.

temporal concurrence The *mens rea* must accompany the *actus reus* in time.

motivational concurrence The *mens rea* must be linked to the *actus reus* it is intended to accompany.

Although it often goes without saying, there is also a requirement that the *actus reus* and the *mens rea* occur together. This is known as concurrence. There are two types of concurrence: temporal concurrence and motivational concurrence. Temporal concurrence means that the *mens rea* must accompany the *actus reus* in time. Assume, for example, that Bob intends on Tuesday to kill Fred. Assume further that Tuesday turns into Wednesday and Bob changes his mind. If Bob accidentally kills Fred in a hunting accident on Wednesday, he cannot be convicted of first-degree murder because he did not *intend* to kill Fred at that time. He may be guilty of another homicide offense (see Chapter 6), but not first-degree murder. What if Bob intends to kill Fred while they are hunting, Bob shoots Fred, but Fred manages to escape, get to hospital for treatment, only to die a few hours later from massive blood loss? Is there a concurrence problem? No, because the criminal act and the *mens rea* occurred together. Only the resulting harm (Fred's death) occurred at a later point.

Motivational concurrence requires that the *mens rea* be linked to the *actus reus* it is intended to accompany. In other words, if a person intends to commit Crime A but then ends up committing Crime B, motivational concurrence is absent. Return to the hunting example, but assume that Bob and Fred went hunting with their friend Hank. Furthermore, assume that Bob still intended to kill Fred that day, but accidentally shot and killed Hank. Bob could not be guilty of murder because he did not intend to kill Hank. This is all rather tedious, but in the end there is a simple point: For someone to be guilty of a particular crime, there can be no "mismatch" between the *mens rea* and the *actus reus*.

---

[46]G. Richardson, "Strict Liability for Regulatory Crime: The Empirical Record," *Criminal Law Review* (1987), p. 295.

YOUR DECISION

1. Jody Sweetana is from Honolulu, Hawaii, and recently moved to New Hampshire to attend college. Jody has never seen snow or driven in winter weather. While driving home from class one snowy afternoon, Jody mistakenly believes that it is safer to drive above the speed limit on the snow-covered roads. Eventually, Jody causes a major car accident and kills the driver of another vehicle. Jody has acted recklessly or negligently. Which is it?

2. Carrie recently learned that her husband, Brennan, is having an affair with his yoga instructor. Enraged, Carrie decides that she wants to kill Brennan and throw his body into the river. She even stays up late at night, writing in her journal and planning out his death. The next morning, Carrie has a change of heart. She decides she would rather divorce Brennan and try to get a large alimony check every month instead of committing murder. As she is pulling out of the garage on her way to work, however, she accidentally runs Brennan over as he is retrieving the morning paper. Brennan dies as a result of his injuries. Carrie is charged with first-degree murder, which requires a specific intent to kill. Is she guilty of first-degree murder? Why or why not?

Summary

- *Mens rea*, Latin for "guilty mind," is the second critical component of criminal liability.
- Traditional *mens rea* is concerned with culpability, or an offender's level of blameworthiness for a crime.
- Statutory *mens rea* is the level of intent required by a specific statute, possibly independent of any notion of morality.
- Common *mens rea* terms include intent (even transferred and oblique intent), knowledge, negligence, recklessness, and malice.
- General intent crimes are those offenses that contain no specific *mens rea* component.
- Specific intent crimes are those that *do* contain a specific *mens rea* component.
- Motive precedes *mens rea*.
- Motive has been defined as "an idea, belief or emotion that impels or incites one to act in accordance with his state of mind or emotion."
- Strict liability is criminal liability in the absence of *mens rea*.
- Strict liability offenses include selling alcohol to a minor and statutory rape, among many others.
- Concurrence is the requirement that the *actus reus* and the *mens rea* occur together.
- Temporal concurrence means that the *mens rea* must accompany the *actus reus* in time.
- Motivational concurrence requires that the *mens rea* be linked to the *actus reus* it is intended to accompany.

CAUSATION

Learning Objectives
- **Explain causation.**
- **Explain the difference between factual cause and legal cause.**

CORE CONCEPTS

causation The requirement that the defendant is responsible for the harm in result crimes.

To recap, the prosecutor must prove beyond a reasonable doubt that the defendant committed a criminal act with the required mental state. Concurrence between the *actus reus* and the *mens rea* is also necessary. Result crimes, however, also require the additional element of causation.

Causation, the requirement that the defendant is responsible for the harm, applies only to result crimes. In other words, the causation requirement does not exist in the case of conduct crimes because conduct crimes do not require a harmful result. What's more, causation inquiries usually only come up in homicide prosecutions, as more often than not it is clear who caused the harm in other result crimes (e.g., rape).

Requiring a causation element in certain crimes serves a protective function. Imagine a situation in which any person who was near a homicide could be prosecuted for it. This would certainly be unfair, especially if one person was responsible for the act. The causation requirement thus helps ensure that the actual offender is prosecuted and convicted, not some innocent passerby.

It is also important to note that causation can occur not just from an overt action, but also an omission. In some cases, failure to act can result in criminal liability because such failure can result in harm. Finally, there are two main types of causation: factual causation and legal causation. The next two subsections look at each in more detail.

Factual Causation

factual causation The requirement that the defendant's conduct was the cause in fact of the harm.

Factual causation (or "cause in fact") requires that there can be no criminal liability for a resulting harm "unless it can be shown that the defendant's conduct was the cause-in-fact of the prohibited result."[47] In order to determine factual causation, courts typically apply a "but-for," or "*sine qua non*" (Latin for "without which not") test. It requires answering a simple question: But for the defendant's actions, would the resulting harm have occurred? If the answer is no, then the defendant will be held liable. Consider this example: Sarah pulls a gun on Anne, shoots Anne in the chest, and Anne dies. We ask, "But for Sarah shooting the gun, would Anne have died?" The answer is most likely "no," which means Sarah was the factual cause of Anne's death.

---

[47]*Velazquez v. State*, 561 So.2d 347 (Fla. Dist. Ct. App. 1990), p. 350.

Another complication pertaining to factual causation arises if there are multiple actual causes of someone's death. Assume again that Sarah shot Anne, but that Anne survived for a time only to die from a botched medical procedure (say, for example, the emergency room anesthesiologist administered a lethal dose of drugs prior to Anne's surgery). Assume further, silly as it may sound, that a major earthquake struck at the precise moment the drugs were administered and that everyone in the emergency room, including Anne, was crushed to death. Who or what is the factual cause of Anne's death? We again ask the question, "But for Sarah's actions, would Anne have died when she did?" The answer is arguably yes, because of the emergency room mistake and the earthquake. In other words, it is plausible to assert that something besides Anne caused Sarah's death. In the event Anne was prosecuted for murder, the answer to the question could come down to medical testimony. The state would most likely call an expert who would argue that Anne's wounds were serious enough that she would have died regardless of whether surgery occurred. Sarah's defense attorney would probably call an expert to testify that Anne's wounds were not that serious and that the earthquake and/or anesthesiologist were responsible.

A similar issue came up in the case of *Oxendine* v. *State*.[48] Jeffrey Oxendine, Jr., a six-year-old, was killed after being the victim of two vicious attacks. In the first, his dad's girlfriend, Leotha Tyree, pushed Jeffrey, Jr. into a bathtub, causing tears in his intestines, or "peritonitis," a potentially lethal condition. The next day, Jeffrey, Jr.'s father, Jeffrey Oxendine, Sr., severely beat his son. Jeffrey, Jr. died later that day. Both Jeffrey, Sr. and Tyree were prosecuted for Jeffrey's death. Oxendine, Sr., was convicted of manslaughter, but he succeeded in having his conviction overturned because it was not clear exactly who was factually responsible for the boy's death. Why? At trial, two state medical experts offered conflicting testimony. One testified that he could not determine who was responsible for Jeffrey, Jr.'s death. The other testified that Tyree was responsible, but he didn't know for sure whether Jeffrey, Sr.'s actions accelerated Jeffrey, Jr.'s death.

Another complication arises with respect to the notion of concurrent causation. Return to the Sarah and Anne example. Assume Sarah and another friend, Sue, both shot Anne. Sarah shot Anne in the head and Sue shot Anne in the heart. Assume further that Anne died as a result of the wounds and that each wound was mortal. Who is the factual cause of Anne's death? In like situations, rare as they may be, the "but for" test has problems. We ask, first, "But for Sarah's conduct, would Anne have died?" The answer is yes—because of the fatal wound inflicted by Sue. Next we ask, "But for Sue's conduct, would Anne have died?" The answer is also yes, so in theory, neither Sarah nor Sue was the factual cause of Anne's death. Should Sarah and Sue escape prosecution and conviction? Of course not. To get around this problem, the courts may modify the "but for" test such that a different question is asked, namely, "But for either defendant's actions, would Anne's death have occurred 'when and as it did?'"[49] This question essentially redefines the harm in question, Anne's death. Instead of "Anne's death," the concern is with "Anne's death by two mortal wounds." With the resulting harm defined in this way, Anne could not have died as she did without the fatal shots from Sarah and Sue.[50]

---

[48]*Oxendine* v. *State*, 528 A.2d 870 (Del. 1987).
[49]*State* v. *Montoya*, 61 P.3d 793 (N.M. 2002), p. 797.
[50]For additional examples, see *State* v. *Munoz*, 126 N.M. 371 (1998); Dressler, *Understanding Criminal Law*, pp. 187–188.

Consider yet another, simpler, example. *People* v. *Arzon*[51] dealt with a man who, in an effort to keep warm, started a fire on the fifth floor of an abandoned building. Firefighters were called to the scene. Meanwhile, another person started a fire on the second floor, which trapped the firefighters after they arrived. One of the firefighters died from smoke inhalation. The man who started the fifth floor fire was indicted and moved to dismiss the indictment on the grounds that he was not the factual cause of the firefighter's death. The court disagreed, reasoning that

> the defendant's conduct need not be the sole and exclusive factor. . . . [A]n individual is criminally liable if his conduct was a sufficiently direct cause of the death, and the ultimate harm is something which should have been foreseen as being reasonably related to his acts. It is irrelevant that, in this instance, the fire which had erupted on the second floor intervened, thus contributing to the conditions that culminated in the death of [the fireman]. . . . Certainly, it was foreseeable that firemen would respond to the situation, thus exposing them, along with the persons already present in the vicinity, to a life-threatening danger. The fire set by the defendant was an indispensable link in the chain of events that resulted in the death. It continued to burn out of control, greatly adding to the problem of evacuating the building by blocking off one of the access routes. At the very least, the defendant's act . . . placed the deceased in a position where he was particularly vulnerable to the separate and independent force, in this instance, the fire on the second floor.[52]

Legal Causation

legal causation Also known as *proximate cause,* the primary act that sets a chain of events in motion. Focuses on whether it is fair to hold the defendant accountable for the resulting harm.

direct cause The defendant's actions are the direct causal agent that brings about the harm.

Intervening cause Another event besides the actions of the defendant that resulted in the harm after the defendant acted.

Factual causation, to recap, is concerned with identifying who or what (e.g., an earthquake) caused a harm. There could be many factual causes, as we saw in the preceding section. **Legal causation**, or "proximate" causation, is concerned with *who should be held criminally responsible*. We basically ask a simple question: Would it be *fair* to hold the defendant responsible for the crime? If the answer is "yes," then the defendant is the legal cause. In other words, the proximate cause of harm is the person who should be accountable for it.

A proximate cause is always the actual cause, but an actual cause is not necessarily the proximate cause. For example, a defendant could set in motion a chain of events that results in a victim's death ten years later. Would it be fair to hold the defendant responsible when many other events likely occurred during that period? Questions like this, as we will see momentarily, routinely arise when the proximate cause is not clear.

To make the distinction between factual and legal cause more clear, we also need to define what it means to be a **direct cause** and an **intervening cause**. In most cases, the defendant is the direct cause of the resulting harm. Direct causation occurs when the defendant—and only the defendant—is the causal agent that brings about a harm. An intervening cause, by contrast, is something else besides the actions of the defendant that resulted in the harm *after* the defendant acted. If there is an intervening cause that is responsible for a resulting harm, the defendant may not be the legal cause of the said injury. This is because the court determines that something else is a

---

[51]*People* v. *Arzon*, 92 Misc. 2d 739 (1978).
[52]Ibid., pp. 742–743.

superseding cause that had a bigger stake in the resulting injury than the defendant. Indeed, there are many considerations that come into play when deciding on matters of proximate causation. What follows are a few of them.

Foreseeability

dependent intervening cause A cause that is either intended or reasonably foreseen by the defendant.

A **dependent intervening cause** (sometimes called a "responsive intervening cause") is one that is either intended or reasonably foreseen by the defendant. For example, if a carjacker draws a gun on his victim and demands the keys but the victim hits the gas pedal and flees, only to be broadsided by a city bus and killed, the carjacker-now-defendant is arguably the one who should be held responsible for the victim's death. Why? The intervening cause—namely, the victim's flight from the scene—was *dependent* on the actions of the defendant. It is safe to assume that the victim would have been more cautious pulling out into traffic but for the attempted carjacking he or she endured.

independent intervening cause A cause that could not be intended or reasonably foreseen by the defendant.

In contrast, an **independent intervening cause** (sometimes called a "superseding cause") is, as you might guess, one that could not be intended or reasonably foreseen by the defendant. Say, for example, that Joe is stabbed by Larry. Larry inflicts only one minor injury before Joe flees. Joe then goes to the hospital for treatment. While Joe is waiting for treatment, a disgruntled former employee pulls a gun and begins shooting everyone in sight. Joe is killed. Would it be reasonable to conclude that Larry was the proximate cause of Joe's death? Probably not. He could not have reasonably foreseen that a crazed gunman would enter the hospital waiting room and begin shooting.

The Defendant's *Mens Rea*

The defendant's *mens rea* also deserves consideration in determining proximate causation. In *Regina* v. *Michael*,[53] a classic case, a woman wanted her child dead. She furnished poison to a nurse and told the nurse it was medicine. The nurse felt the child did not need the medicine and placed it on a mantel where, later, it was retrieved by another child and given to the intended victim who died from it. There were two intervening causes: (1) the nurse's negligent act of placing the medicine on the mantel and (2) the other child's act of giving the poison to the victim. The mother was deemed the proximate cause of her child's death because she *intended* to kill her child.

apparent safety doctrine A legal principle that states the defendant is not the legal cause of a resulting harm if the victim reaches a place of "apparent safety," at which point an intervening cause of harm comes into play.

Apparent Safety

The **apparent safety doctrine** holds that a defendant is not the legal cause of a resulting harm if the victim reaches a place of "apparent safety," at which point an intervening cause of harm comes into play. In *State* v. *Preslar*,[54] a man had an argument with his wife, beat her, and later drove her away from the home and left her close to her father's house. Instead of entering her father's house, the woman decided

---

[53]*Regina* v. *Michael*, 169 End. Rep. 48 (1840).
[54]*State* v. *Preslar*, 48 N.C. 421 (1856).

to sleep outside in the cold. She froze to death during the night. The husband was not held criminally liable. The court said,

> If, to avoid the rage of a brutal husband, a wife is compelled to expose herself, by wading through a swamp, or jumping into a river, the husband is responsible for the consequences; but, if she exposes herself thus, without necessity, and of her own accord, we know of no principle of law, by which he is held responsible, to the extent of forfeiting his life.[55]

Substantiality of the Intervening Cause

If an intervening cause is substantially more significant than the actual cause, the defendant may escape criminal liability. For example, if Bill shoots Alex with a .22 caliber pistol and he dies, but at the same time Colt shoots Alex with a .50 caliber sniper rifle, a much more lethal and higher velocity weapon, would it be fair to treat Bill as the proximate cause of Alex's death? Most likely not. The law will treat the *substantial* intervening case as the proximate cause, so Colt will be convicted of homicide, but Bill most likely won't be (perhaps he will be convicted of attempted murder or an analogous offense—an alternative we will consider in later chapters).

Voluntary Victim Intervention

Related to the apparent safety doctrine is the rule that an offender cannot be held liable if his or her victim acts in a free, voluntary, and informed manner that leads to the resulting harm. You may recall the Jack Kevorkian–assisted suicide case.[56] He

Jack Kevorkian and his suicide machine.

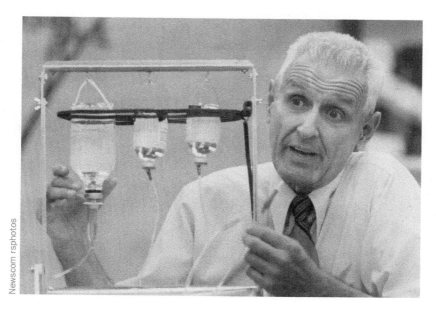

Newscom rsphotos

---

[55]Ibid., p. 428.
[56]*People v. Kevorkian*, 447 Mich. 436 (1994).
[57]*Stephenson v. State*, 205 Ind. 141 (1932).

made available a "suicide machine" that his patients could then use to kill themselves. The Michigan Supreme Court concluded that Dr. Kevorkian could not be liable for killing his patients because all he did was furnish the means for them to end their lives. (Dr. Kevorkian was eventually convicted of other crimes.) Contrast this with the case of a woman who was held against her will and sexually assaulted over a period of days. While being confined, she ingested a poisonous substance in an effort to commit suicide. She subsequently died from several causes, including ingestion of the poison. The defendant was deemed the proximate cause of the woman's death.[57] The court basically concluded that the woman was not of sound mind when she attempted to kill herself.

YOUR DECISION

1. John and Mark robbed a bank, wearing ski masks and armed with automatic weapons. While the robbery was taking place, the 60-year-old bank manager fainted and died of a heart attack. John and Mark were unaware that the bank manager had a history of heart disease. John and Mark never physically touched the bank manager. Are John and Mark the factual and legal cause of the bank manager's death? If not, why?

2. Brian convinces his friend Joe, who prefers to stay home and play video games all day, to go for a hike in the woods one sunny afternoon. During the hike, Brian jokingly pushes Joe and Joe falls over a ravine and suffers severe injuries. Feeling terrible, Brian carries Joe on his back all the way to the nearest hospital and leaves him in the emergency room. After Brian leaves, Joe enters the restroom under his own power and passes out. Joe eventually dies from internal bleeding in the emergency room bathroom. Is Brian the proximate cause of Joe's death? Why or why not? Explain what doctrine, if any, applies.

Summary

- Causation, the requirement that the defendant is responsible for the harm, applies only to result crimes.

- Factual causation (or "cause in fact") requires that there can be no criminal liability for a resulting harm "unless it can be shown that the defendant's conduct was the cause in fact of the prohibited result."

- Legal causation, or "proximate" causation, is concerned with *who should be held criminally responsible*.

- Direct causation occurs when the defendant—and only the defendant—is the causal agent that brings about a harm. An intervening cause, by contrast, is something else besides the actions of the defendant that resulted in the harm *after* the defendant acted.

- The apparent safety doctrine holds that a defendant is not the legal cause of a resulting harm if the victim reaches a place of apparent safety, at which point an intervening cause of harm comes into play.

3.5   IGNORANCE AND MISTAKE

Learning Objective

- **Distinguish between ignorance of the law and mistake.**

CORE CONCEPTS

Everyone makes mistakes. Suppose you engage in some action, thinking it is legal, only to find out later that it was not. Or, what if you just don't know whether a certain action is criminal and engage in it nevertheless? Should you be held criminally liable in both circumstances? Such is the essence of ignorance and mistake. In this section, we look at whether ignorance of the law is a defense. Then we consider the concept of "mistake" and distinguish it from ignorance. In doing so, we look at two types of mistake: mistake of law and mistake of fact. Finally, we consider situations in which ignorance and/or mistake can excuse a person from criminal liability.

Ignorance of the Law

Few rules of criminal law are as well known as *ignorantia lexis non exusat*, or "ignorance of the law is no excuse." Simply, people should know the law, and it is their responsibility to refrain from acting in certain situations without checking whether a law will be violated. In other words, everyone has a "duty to inquire" about the legality of their actions. Oliver Wendell Holmes once put it this way:

> The true explanation of the rule is the same as that which accounts for the law's indifference to a man's particular temperament, faculties, and so forth. Public policy sacrifices the individual to the general good. . . . It is no doubt true that there are many cases in which the criminal could not have known that he was breaking the law, but to admit the excuse at all would be to encourage ignorance . . . and justice to the individual is rightly outweighed by the larger interests on the other side of the scales.[58]

And it does not matter if a person's ignorance of the law is something short of intentional. If ignorance is reckless or even negligent, the criminal law does not care. Criminal liability will still attach.

Not everyone agrees with the general rule. For one thing, penal codes are *massive*. Not even seasoned lawyers can list—off the top of their heads and with certainty—what actions are legal and illegal. Also, many jurisdictions have antiquated and bizarre laws on the books, some of which seem to criminalize apparently legal behavior. For example, it is a misdemeanor in Washington State to go into public with a common cold, a communicable ailment.[59] Surely someone who has a cold and must

---

[58]O. W. Holmes, *The Common Law* (Boston: Little, Brown, and Company, 1881).
[59]RCW 70.54.050. Also see http://www.dumblaws.com for more unusual laws from state to state.

ride public transit to work is not as culpable as a murderer or rapist. Another problem is that the law is vague. Jerome Hall once remarked, in fact, that laws are so vague that we can "disagree indefinitely regarding the[ir] meaning."[60] Indeed, if the law was unambiguous, there would be no need for a book like this! But to defer to every person's subjective interpretation of the law would clearly cause problems.

Is it thus possible to reach a compromise? On the one hand, there are laws that everyone should know. On the other hand, it may be unreasonable to expect people to know about—much less be able to find and read up on—obscure laws that criminalize seemingly normal behaviors. The problem is no one could agree where the line should be drawn. It is just easier to maintain a rule that all people need to know the law. And besides, if the law is obscure, odd, disagreeable, or antiquated, it may not be enforced anyway. Just because a law criminalizes behavior does not mean prosecutors will use it!

Examples of Ignorance

It is important to distinguish between (1) a defendant who does not know there is a law applying to his or her activity and (2) a defendant who knows there is a relevant law, but is not sure whether it applies in the exact circumstances in question. The first defendant is demonstrating ignorance of the law. The second defendant is making a mistake. This section looks strictly at ignorance of the law.

Many "ignorance" cases involve aliens who are not familiar with a particular culture or its laws. For example, in *United States* v. *Moncini*,[61] the defendant, a citizen and resident of Italy, mailed child pornography to an undercover officer in the United States. Later on, when he entered the United States on unrelated business, he was arrested and convicted for a federal law violation. In challenging his conviction, he claimed that since the same conduct was not illegal in Italy, he should have been excused for his ignorance. The Ninth Circuit Court of Appeals disagreed, holding:

> Even assuming Moncini was ignorant of the law as he claims, he must bear the risk of the potential illegality of his conduct. . . . The child pornography laws are directly related to a commonly understood moral censure. The very nature of child pornography, which is commonly regulated throughout the world, should cause a reasonable person to investigate the laws of the United States before sending such material into this country. . . . This is not a case where due process prohibits convicting a defendant who has unwittingly broken the law through conduct which an ordinary person would not assume to be at least potentially criminal.[62]

In a more recent case, however, the Supreme Court moved away from this interpretation to some extent. In *Ratzlaf* v. *United States*,[63] a man owed a Reno casino over $100,000. He attempted to pay the debt in cash, but the casino reminded him that it would have to report the transaction to federal authorities (because the transaction was in an amount over $10,000). The casino then offered to drive the man around to various banks where he could obtain separate cashier's checks, each for

---

[60]J. Hall, *The General Principles of Criminal Law*, 2nd ed. (Indianapolis: Bobbs-Merrill, 1960), p. 382.

[61]*United States* v. *Moncini*, 882 F.2d 401 (9th Cir. 1989).

[62]Ibid., pp. 405–406.

[63]*Ratzlaf* v. *United States*, 510 U.S. 135 (1994).

less than $10,000, so as to avoid reporting requirements. He was charged with violating federal law and, despite claiming he was not aware that the conduct was criminal, convicted after the trial judge instructed the jury that ignorance was irrelevant. The Supreme Court disagreed, arguing that even though the defendant knew he was structuring a currency transaction to avoid reporting requirements, he didn't know this was illegal. The Court went on to note that "[b]ecause currency structuring is not inevitably nefarious, this Court is unpersuaded by the United States' argument that structuring is so obviously 'evil' or inherently 'bad' that the 'willfulness' requirement is satisfied irrespective of the defendant's knowledge of the illegality of structuring."[64]

This decision was echoed in *Lambert v. California*,[65] a case involving an ex-felon who was unaware of a requirement—per a local ordinance—that she register her presence in the city. The Supreme Court held that a due process violation occurred when the woman was prohibited from introducing evidence to the effect she was unaware of the ordinance. The moral of the story, then, between this and the last case is that, *some of the time*, ignorance can act as a defense. Successful ignorance defenses are *very* rare.

Allowing someone underage to enter a bar can potentially lead to a mistake of fact defense.

Mistake

In general, a mistake occurs when (1) a person knows what he or she is doing is wrong, but is not completely clear as to why, or (2) a person thinks what he or she is doing is legal, but is not correct in this knowledge. For example, assume Laura took her car to a mechanic who, in her view, charged an excessive amount for the repair.[66] She refused to pay, so the mechanic refused to give her the keys and kept the car. Laura returned after hours and, with a different set of keys, took her car. She was prosecuted for larceny. Laura made a mistake because, arguably, she knew that what she did was probably prohibited, but she may not have known that there was a state lien law that permitted the mechanic to keep her car until the bill was paid.

Or consider the case of Hank who went to the grocery store, selected 10 items from the shelves, and then visited a cashier who began scanning the items. Assume that Hank was talking on his cell phone and failed to notice that the cashier missed an item. Assume further that on leaving the store, a security guard noticed that Hank was leaving with an item that he had not paid for. Hank was prosecuted for theft. It

[64]Ibid., p. 135.
[65]*Lambert v. California*, 355 U.S. 255 (1957).
[66]*State v. Cude*, 383 P.2d 399 (Utah 1963).

mistake of law The defendant claims to misunderstand or misinterpret the law as it applies to the specific circumstances.

mistake of fact A misunderstanding or misinterpretation by the defendant about a relevant fact. Potentially used as a defense or to negate the *mens rea* requirement of a crime.

seems he made an honest mistake. We can safely assume he knew stealing was not acceptable, but he just failed to notice that the cashier missed something.

Both of these hypothetical scenarios illustrate two different types of mistake. Laura made what is known as a **mistake of law**. She knew larceny was a crime, but she was not aware of the state lien law. Hank, on the other hand, made a **mistake of fact**. He mistakenly left the store with an item he did not pay for. Unlike Laura, however, he will most likely be acquitted. Why? Because he did not form the requisite *mens rea* to support a criminal conviction. Had the crime he was prosecuted with contained no *mens rea* component, then his mistake might not have mattered and he could have been convicted.

See the accompanying Court Decision for more on mistake of fact. In it, we take a look at the case of *Tennessee* v. *Ballinger*, in which the defendant attempts to use the mistake of fact defense in regards to a statutory rape charge. This case illustrates the importance of jury instructions at trial.

COURT DECISION

The Logic behind Mistake of Fact

State of Tennessee v. Charles Arnold Ballinger
93 S.W.3d 881 (Tenn. App. 2001)

Decision: The defendant charged with statutory rape is entitled to a jury instruction on mistake of fact regarding the age of the alleged victim.

Reason: (Charles Ballinger was convicted of statutory rape and contributing to the delinquency of a minor for engaging in sexual intercourse with his 15-year-old neighbor. Defendant appealed claiming he was entitled to a jury instruction on the "mistake of fact" defense regarding the alleged victim's age. The Tennessee Court of Criminal Appeals reversed and remanded for a new trial.)

***The defendant complains that the trial court should have instructed the jury to consider the "mistake of fact" defense. . . The Tennessee Code defines mistake of fact as follows: "ignorance or mistake of fact is a defense to prosecution if such ignorance or mistake negates the culpable mental state of the charged offense." Tenn. Code Ann. § 39-11-502(a).

***We turn now to determine whether the jury should have been instructed to consider mistake of fact as a defense in this case. It is well-settled that the trial court has the duty of giving a correct and complete charge of the law applicable to the facts of the case, and that the defendant has the right to have every issue of fact raised by the evidence and material to the defense submitted to the jury upon proper instructions by the trial court. Mistake of fact is not an affirmative defense; it is merely a defense. Thus, if the evidence fairly raises mistake of fact, the trial court must instruct the jury to consider the defense and that any reasonable doubt on the existence of the defense requires acquittal. The statute defining mistake of fact provides that mistake of fact shall apply "[e]xcept in prosecutions for violations of §§ 39-13-504(a)(4) and 39-13-522 [aggravated sexual battery of a child

(continued)

**COURT
DECISION**
(continued)

and rape of a child, respectively]." Tenn.Code Ann. § 39-11-502(a). Thus, while the Legislature has specifically excluded the defense in certain situations, it has not excluded the defense in statutory rape cases.

In this case, although the defendant testified that he did not have sex with R.S., he also testified that he thought she was eighteen years old. Based upon the evidence, the jury could have found that the defendant had sex with R.S. but, under all the circumstances was reasonably mistaken about her age, thus negating the possibility of a conclusion that the defendant acted recklessly. Thus, based on the evidence adduced at trial, we find that the trial court should have instructed the jury to consider mistake of fact as a defense to statutory rape.

Accordingly, we REVERSE the judgment of the trial court and remand this case for a new trial.

When Ignorance or Mistake Can Serve as a Defense

There are three main situations in which ignorance or mistake can serve as a defense to criminal liability. First, in some circumstances, a person may be able to rely on an interpretation of the law that turns out later to be erroneous. This could include one's own reliance, reliance on an attorney's advice, or reliance on some other official's interpretation. *People* v. *Marrero*[67] offers an example of the self-reliance. In that case, a federal corrections officer was caught carrying a handgun without a permit. He cited a "peace officer" exemption in the state law he was charged with violating, which included any official or guard of "any state prison or of *any penal correctional institution.*" Although he was a federal corrections officer, he felt the state law with which he was charged should apply to him. The trial court sided with him in this regard, but the appellate court did not. As for relying on the advice of counsel, at least one court has decided that reliance on an attorney's mistaken interpretation of the law does not serve as an excuse for criminal liability.[68] While this decision was controversial, it helps avoid the problem of shady criminals seeking lawyerly advice from equally shady attorneys to support their own interpretations of the law.[69] If a person relies on an interpretation of the law made by an official or body charged with such tasks, that person will be excused from liability. The only way to succeed in this regard, however, is if the statute relied on is later ruled invalid[70] or the authorities in question are either the highest court in the jurisdiction[71] or a

---

[67] *People* v. *Marrero*, 507 N.E.2d 1068 (N.Y. 1987).
[68] *State* v. *Huff*, 36 A. 1000 (Me. 1897).
[69] See., e.g., M. Gur-Arye, "Reliance on a Lawyer's Mistaken Advice: Should It Be an Excuse from Criminal Liability?" *American Journal of Criminal Law*, Vol. 29 (2002), p. 455.
[70] See, e.g., *Brent* v. *State*, 43 Ala. 297 (1869).
[71] See, e.g., State v. *O'Neil*, 126 N.W. 454 (Iowa 1910).

public officer charged with interpreting and enforcing the law, typically an attorney general of the state.[72]

The second main situation in which a person may escape criminal liability because of ignorance or mistake concerns whether there was fair notice that the actions in question were criminal. Almost all the time, as we pointed out earlier, people are expected to know the law. In some situations, though, the law in question may be so obscure and unfamiliar that it would be unfair to hold someone liable for violating it. We return to the *Lambert* v. *California* case mentioned earlier in this section.[73] Recall that a convicted felon failed to register her whereabouts with local authorities. One point we did not raise earlier was that law required felons to register within five days of arriving in the city. The Supreme Court reversed the woman's conviction for violating the ordinance by pointing out the conduct in question was purely passive (i.e., failing to register). What the woman did, the Court felt, was not quite the same as an overt criminal act.

Finally, ignorance or mistake can—in *very* limited circumstances, mind you—excuse criminal liability if either manages to negate *mens rea*. Consider *Cheek* v. *United States*,[74] a case involving a "tax protestor" who did not file federal income tax returns for six years, even though he received income as a pilot during that time. He was charged with six counts of "willfully" failing to file a federal income tax return. Cheek testified at trial that he attended numerous "anti-tax" seminars where an attorney explained that capital gains, not wages, were considered income. In essence, he was relying on the advice of someone who, though mistaken, led Cheek to believe he was doing the right thing. Therefore, he argued that he did not "willfully" violate income tax laws. The trial judge instructed the jury that even a good faith misunderstanding like this could not serve as a defense to criminal liability, but the U.S. Supreme Court disapproved of this instruction and reversed Cheek's conviction. In essence the Court decided that Cheek's mistake *negated* the *mens rea* of the underlying offense. The Court made this argument:

> Willfulness, as construed by our prior decisions in criminal tax cases, requires the Government to prove that the law imposed a duty on the defendant, that the defendant knew of this duty, and that he voluntarily and intentionally violated that duty. . . . In this case, if Cheek asserted that he truly believed that the Internal Revenue Code did not purport to treat wages as income, and the jury believed him, the Government would not have carried its burden to prove willfulness, however unreasonable a court might deem such a belief.[75]

It cannot be overstated how rare it is for mistake or ignorance to successfully negate *mens rea*. If it were easier for this to occur, then every criminal defendant would claim ignorance and escape conviction. What makes the *Cheek* case unique is the government's failure to prove that he *willfully* committed the crime—and the trial court judge's instruction to the jury that it could not even consider this aspect of the offense.

---

[72]See, e.g., *Commonwealth* v. *Twitchwell*, 617 N.E. 2d 609 (Mass. 1993).
[73]*Lambert* v. *California*, 355 U.S. 225 (1957).
[74]*Cheek* v. *United States*, 498 U.S. 192 (1991).
[75]Ibid., pp. 201–202.

YOUR DECISION

1. Susan is returning from a spring break trip to Cancun, Mexico. While in Mexico, she decided to purchase cigars for her father. The cigars she ends up purchasing were actually manufactured in Miami, Florida. Believing that she has purchased authentic Cuban cigars that are illegal in the United States, Susan hides the cigars in her luggage and attempts to smuggle them through customs. The customs official searches her luggage and finds the cigars. Has Susan committed a crime? Why or why not?

2. Angie has just returned from a fantastic vacation to Costa Rica, and she is waiting for her luggage to arrive at the baggage claim. Angie's suitcase is black with a pink ribbon tied to the handle. While she is talking on her cell phone, excitedly discussing her trip with her mother, Angie picks up a black suitcase with a pink ribbon and begins to exit the terminal. Unbeknownst to Angie, she picked up the wrong suitcase. A police officer stops Angie at the exit after a drug sniffing dog showed interest in her suitcase. The suitcase is filled with illegal drugs and Angie is arrested. Does Angie have a defense to the drug charges? If so, what defense might be applicable to her case and why?

Summary

- Ignorance occurs when the defendant does not know there is a law applying to his or her activity.

- Mistake occurs when the defendant knows there a relevant law that applies to his or her conduct, but is not sure whether it applies in the circumstances at hand.

- In some circumstances, a person may be able to rely on an interpretation of the law that turns out later to be erroneous.

- If there was a lack of fair notice that the actions in question were criminal, a person may be able to successfully claim ignorance or mistake.

- Ignorance or mistake can—in *very* limited circumstances—excuse criminal liability if either manages to negate *mens rea*.

Chapter Review

MODULE **3.1**   **INTRODUCTION TO OFFENSE TYPES**

Learning Objective

- Explain the difference between conduct and result crimes.

Review Questions

1. What is the general part of the criminal law? Provide an example.
2. What is the special part of the criminal law? Provide an example.
3. Offer an example of a conduct crime *and* a result crime. Explain your answer.

Key Terms

general part of the criminal law	result crimes
special part of the criminal law	resulting harm
conduct crimes	

MODULE **3.2**   **THE CORE ELEMENTS OF CRIMINAL LIABILITY, PART 1: *ACTUS REUS***

Learning Objective

- Explain *actus reus* and what constitutes a criminal act.

Review Questions

1. When can an omission qualify as the *actus reus* of a crime?
2. What types of voluntary acts satisfy *actus reus*?

Key Terms

actus reus	actual possession
omission	constructive possession
Bad Samaritan laws	

MODULE **3.3**   **THE CORE ELEMENTS OF CRIMINAL LIABILITY, PART 2: *MENS REA* AND CONCURRENCE**

Learning Objectives

- Explain *mens rea* and the different types of intent.
- Distinguish between *mens rea* and motive.
- Identify strict liability offenses.
- Summarize concurrence.

Review Questions

1. Distinguish traditional from statutory *mens rea*.
2. Provide an example of both a general and specific intent crime. Explain your answer.

3. What is the role of motive in the *mens rea* context?

4. Explain strict liability and offer an example of two strict liability crimes.

Key Terms

mens rea	recklessness
direct intent	malice
transferred intent	motive
oblique intent	strict liability
general intent	concurrence
specific intent	temporal concurrence
negligence	motivational concurrence

MODULE **3.4**

CAUSATION

Learning Objectives

- Explain causation.

- Explain the difference between factual cause and legal cause.

Review Questions

1. Compare and contrast temporal and motivational concurrence.

2. Compare and contrast factual and legal causation.

Key Terms

causation	dependent intervening cause
factual causation	independent intervening cause
legal causation	apparent safety doctrine
direct cause	
intervening cause	

MODULE **3.5**

IGNORANCE AND MISTAKE

Learning Objective

- Distinguish between ignorance of the law and mistake.

Review Questions

1. Provide one example each for ignorance and mistake.

2. Can ignorance serve as a criminal law defense? If so, when?

3. Can mistake serve as a criminal law defense? If so, when?

Key Terms

mistake of law	mistake of fact

Chapter Synthesis Questions

1. Summarize the main elements of criminal liability, distinguishing between conduct and result crimes.

2. Which is more harmful to society, a conduct crime or a result crime? Why?

3. An omission can satisfy the criminal law's *actus reus* requirement in seven specific situations. Should there be more situations or fewer in which an omission can satisfy *actus reus*? Explain your answer.

4. What is the ideal *mens rea* terminology? If there is no one best "term," why do you feel this way?

5. It is sometimes said "ignorance is no defense." Is this a fair statement? Why or why not?

6. In what situations can ignorance and/or mistake serve as defenses to criminal liability?

4

COMPLICITY AND VICARIOUS LIABILITY

MODULE 4.1 INTRODUCTION TO ACCOMPLICE LIABILITY
Learning Objectives
- Distinguish between complicity and conspiracy.
- Identify the parties to crime, including principals, accomplices, and accessories.

MODULE 4.2 THE ELEMENTS OF COMPLICITY
Learning Objectives
- Explain the elements of complicity.
- Explain the elements of accessory liability.

MODULE 4.3 COMPLICITY ISSUES, LIMITATIONS, AND DEFENSES
Learning Objectives
- Discuss some of the issues that make complicity law complicated.
- Summarize the limitations of and defenses to accomplice liability.
- Explain the Model Penal Code approach to accomplice liability.

MODULE 4.4 VICARIOUS LIABILITY
Learning Objectives
- Explain the concept of vicarious liability.
- Distinguish between corporate and individual vicarious liability.

4.1 INTRODUCTION TO ACCOMPLICE LIABILITY

Learning Objectives

- **Distinguish between complicity and conspiracy.**
- **Identify the parties to crime, including principals, accomplices, and accessories.**

CORE CONCEPTS

complicity Involvement in a crime as an accomplice.

accomplice An individual who aids before or during the commission of a crime.

derivative liability When the defendant derives or obtains his criminal liability from the primary offender.

Complicity is defined as "a state of being an accomplice."[1] What is an accomplice? An **accomplice** is "one who knowingly, voluntarily and with common intent unites with the principal offender in the commission of a crime."[2] In the typical criminal scenarios we have presented thus far throughout the book, there has been one offender and one victim. With accomplice liability, our concern is with multiple offenders. Basically, if person B assists person A in the commission of a crime, then both can be held criminally liable. This is the essence of accomplice liability.

Complicity is a form of **derivative liability**, meaning that a second offender *derives* his or her liability from the primary individual with whom he or she associates.[3] Also, accomplice liability is generally limited to felonies. There are some exceptions, but most jurisdictions limit accomplice liability to the most serious offenses.

Common Law Parties to a Crime

The common law used four different terms to describe the parties to a crime involving two or more offenders: principal in the first degree, principal in the second degree, accessory before the fact, and accessory after the fact. While courts continue to refer to each in some of their modern-day decisions (and some statutes even use such language), the four-category approach has been basically abandoned in favor of a simpler scheme that we consider in the next section.

Principal in the First Degree

principal in the first degree Common law term used to describe the primary offender in a crime.

The **principal in the first degree** is the primary offender. More formally, the principal in the first degree is "one who actually commits a crime, either by his own hand, or by an inanimate agency, or by an innocent instrumentality."[4] A person who "pulls the trigger," for example, is a principal in the first degree." In other words, such an individual is "the criminal actor."[5]

---

[1]*Black's Law Dictionary*, 6th ed. (St. Paul, MN: West, 1990), p. 285.
[2]Ibid., p. 17.
[3]See, e.g., *People v. Perez*, 113 P.3d 100 (Cal. 2005), p. 104.
[4]*State v. Ward*, 284 Md. 189 (Md. Ct. App. 1978), p. 197.
[5]*State v. Burney*, 82 P.3d 164 (Or. App. 2003), p. 166.

Some of the terms in our definition require clarification. It is fairly clear what it means for an individual to offend "by his own hand." Clubbing someone over the head, shooting a person, and the like fit the bill. But what is "inanimate agency?" A booby trap is an example of inanimate agency. The principal in the first degree could set it, forget it, and yet still be guilty of a crime if it does what it is supposed to do. As for "innocent instrumentality," it is possible that an offender could dupe another person into committing a crime for which the latter has no *mens rea*. That individual would be exculpated, but the primary offender would be found guilty. Or assume, for example, that an adult convinces a child to commit a crime. Since the child cannot form the required criminal intent, she will not be guilty of a crime, but the adult who was pulling the strings will.[6]

Principal in the Second Degree

principal in the second degree Under common law, someone who intentionally assists the principal in the first degree with the commission of a crime and who is actually or constructively present at the time of the crime.

The **principal in the second degree** is someone who intentionally assists the principal in the first degree with the commission of a crime and who is actually or constructively present at the time of the crime. The individual is "actually present" if he or she is in close physical proximity to the principal in the first degree. For example, if Larry followed Keith into the bank that Keith robbed, with the intention of helping Keith carry bags of loot away, then Larry was "actually present." In contrast, if Larry sat in a "getaway car" and was prepared to quickly shuttle Keith away from the crime scene, then Larry was "constructively present."

Accessory before the Fact

accessory before the fact Under common law, someone solicits, encourages, or commands another to offend.

If someone solicits, encourages, or commands another to offend, then he is an **accessory before the fact**. Coercion cannot be used, however, because then the accessory before the fact would become the principal in the first degree, and the person who commits the act will be considered an innocent instrumentality. An example will clarify this point. Suppose Rocco, the local mob boss, orders a hit on a rival boss, Gino, in the next town over. His trusted hit man, Marco, does the deed. In this case, Rocco is an accessory before the fact because he ordered Marco to commit murder. Marco was arguably not "coerced" because he was the mob's hit man and presumably killed people on previous occasions. Suppose, in contrast, that Jim kidnaps and threatens to kill Tom's wife, Lynne, if Tom does not rob an armored truck. Tom, being coerced, is an innocent instrumentality. He could not be held criminally liable because he did not possess the required *mens rea* to commit the crime. Jim would then become a principal in the first degree, not an accessory before the fact.

Accessory after the Fact

accessory after the fact Under common law, a person who helps the principal after the criminal event takes place.

An **accessory after the fact** is a person who helps the principal after the criminal event takes place. For example, in one case, after causing a fatal traffic accident, the driver and his passenger fled the scene and were assisted by friends in dismantling

---

[6]See, e.g., *Queen v. Manley*, 1 Cox Crim. Cas. 104 (1844).

the car so that it could not be detected. Despite their efforts, the car was discovered and linked to the fatal accident. The friends were charged as accessories after the fact.[7] In another case, the passenger in a vehicle that was fleeing from the police threw full beer cans at the pursuing patrol car. He was charged as an accomplice for assisting with the driver's attempted escape.[8]

An accessory after the fact is often one who is involved in "aiding and abetting" a principal.[9] If Ted provides a place for Travis, who has recently murdered someone, to stay for the night, Ted may have been "aiding and abetting" in Travis's efforts to avoid apprehension. Under common law, Ted would have been subject to accomplice liability, but he probably would not have been punished as harshly as Travis. This is no longer the case. For example, federal law now provides that whoever ". . . aids, abets, counsels, commands, induces, or procures [a crime's] commission . . . is punishable as a principal."[10] This means that Ted would be punished as harshly as Travis, simply by providing him a place to stay.

Parties to a Crime Today

Why did the common law recognize four parties to a crime? At common law, all felons were subject to the death penalty. The stakes were thus much higher than they are in the case of some modern-day felonies, which is why there were distinctions between principals and accessories. The distinction spared accessories from the execution principals may have faced, but this created problems. Under common law, no accessory could be tried or convicted until the principal was both tried and convicted. What if, for example, the principal died? The accomplice would have escaped conviction. Once it was realized that some otherwise guilty accomplices were escaping conviction, the distinctions were largely abandoned. Because of these problems, today there are two main parties to a crime: accomplices and accessories. There are some exceptions to the general rules we list subsequently, but they are not the norm. See Figure 4.1 for a summary of the parties to a crime today compared to common law parties.

Accomplices

An accomplice, as we defined it earlier, is "one who knowingly, voluntarily and with common intent unites with the principal offender in the commission of a crime." Anyone,

Common Law Parties to a Crime	Parties to a Crime Today
Principal in the first degree	Accomplice
Principal in the second degree	Accessory
Accessory before the fact	
Accessory after the fact	

Figure 4.1
Parties to a Crime
Then and Now

[7]*People* v. *Cunningham*, 201 Mich. App. 720 (1993).
[8]*People* v. *Branch*, 202 Mich. App. 550 (1993).
[9]See, e.g., *People v. Robinson*, 715 N.W.2d 44 (Mich. 2006).
[10]18 U.S.C. 2(a).

other than the primary offender, who participates *before and during* the commission of a crime is thus an accomplice. Colorado's complicity statute offers an example:

> A person is legally accountable as principal for the behavior of another constituting a criminal offense if, with the intent to promote or facilitate the commission of the offense, he or she aids, abets, advises, or encourages the other person in planning or committing the offense.[11]

Accessories

accessory Modern term to describe someone who participates after the crime is already committed.

An **accessory** is typically a participant in a crime *after* it is committed. Again, there are some exceptions, but many states define accessories as such. Continuing with our Colorado example, an "accessory to a crime" is defined in this way:

> A person is an accessory to a crime if, with intent to hinder, delay, or prevent the discovery, detection, apprehension, prosecution, conviction, or punishment of another for the commission of a crime, he renders assistance to such person."[12]

Importantly, whereas the accomplice is usually charged with the underlying crime (e.g., murder or robbery), an accessory is generally charged with a less serious crime (potentially even a misdemeanor). Being an accomplice to murder can mean life in prison, while being an accessory can lead to a relatively minor punishment.

YOUR DECISION

1. Fred is extremely jealous that Justin was selected to be the varsity quarterback on the Happy Valley High School football team. He meets with his friends, Brian and Dan, after school one day to plan "revenge." Brian actively encourages Fred to kill Justin using a gun with a silencer. Brian even helps acquire the gun from his grandfather's basement. On the night of the shooting, only Dan accompanies Fred to Justin's home to carry out the killing. Dan serves as a lookout while Fred shoots and kills Justin in his kitchen. Using the traditional common law terms for complicity, identify the appropriate role, if any, for Fred, Brian, and Dan in the murder.
2. Don kidnapped his seven-year-old daughter, Brittany, after the family court refused to give him legal visitation rights. Don and Brittany are on the run and need a place to hide from authorities. Don arrives unannounced at the home of his childhood friend, Joe, and begs for help. Joe agrees to let Don and Brittany stay at his home for as long as necessary and does not notify the police. Using today's definitions for complicity, is Joe an accomplice or an accessory? Why or why not?

Summary

- Complicity and accomplice liability are one and the same.
- An accomplice is one who knowingly, voluntarily and with common intent unites with the principal offender in the commission of a crime.

---

[11]Colorado Revised Statutes 18-1-603 (2009).
[12]Colorado Revised Statutes 18-8-105 (2009).

- The common law used four different terms to describe the parties to a crime involving two or more offenders: principal in the first degree, principal in the second degree, accessory before the fact, and accessory after the fact.

- The principal in the first degree is the primary offender.

- The principal in the second degree is someone who intentionally assists the principal in the first degree with the commission of a crime and who is actually or constructively present at the time of the crime.

- If someone solicits, encourages, or commands another to offend, then he is an accessory before the fact.

- An accessory after the fact is a person who helps the principal after the criminal event takes place.

- Today there are two main parties to a crime: accomplices and accessories.

- An accessory is typically a participant in a crime *after* it is committed.

MODULE

MODULE
4.2 — THE ELEMENTS OF COMPLICITY

Learning Objectives
- **Explain the elements of complicity.**
- **Explain the elements of accessory liability.**

CORE CONCEPTS

The *actus reus* and *mens rea* for accomplice and accessory liability are distinct, so we will treat each one separately. We begin with the elements of accomplice liability, which require the most discussion. We wrap up with the elements of accessory liability.

Accomplice *Actus Reus*

The *actus reus* for accomplice liability is, at its most basic level, assistance. That is, a person who *assists* a principal in the commission of a crime has satisfied the *actus reus* of accomplice/accessory liability. According to Joshua Dressler, there are three means by which assistance is typically provided: "(1) assistance by physical conduct; (2) assistance by psychological influence; and (3) assistance by omission (assuming in this latter case that the omitter has a duty to act)."[13]

---

[13]J. Dressler, *Understanding Criminal Law*, 5th ed. (San Francisco, CA: Lexis-Nexis, 2009), p. 473.

Physical Conduct

Assistance by physical conduct is straightforward. For example, in *Hensel* v. *State*[14], the defendant, Hensel, aided in the commission of a felony by providing dynamite and fuses that were used to blow up a storage bunker. According to the court, for accomplice liability to attach, the *actus reus* component requires that the defendant "... aid, abet, assist, or facilitate the commission of the particular substantive crime for which the state seeks to hold the defendant liable as an accomplice."[15] Hensel indeed satisfied this requirement because, in the words of the court, he "... provided the codefendants with capped and fused dynamite knowing that they would return to the premises previously burglarized, plant the dynamite inside the bunkers, and explode the buildings."[16]

In another case, physical assistance came in the form of "casing" the crime scene in advance of a robbery. *Actus reus* was present because the defendant had been driving around with two other individuals while they planned a robbery. Moreover, "[t]he defendant was well aware of the potential for danger, yet remained with the group of would-be robbers in spite of his awareness, even though he had several opportunities to remove himself from the plan before the robbery was committed. For example, while defendant's cohorts argued about where to find the bullets for the rifle, he went into the store which he knew was to be robbed, but never attempted to abort the robbery by warning the owner."[17]

In yet another case, 14-year-old Mario Wall accompanied a man who had a shotgun into Elizabeth Turner's apartment to retrieve guns that she allegedly kept stored there. When Turner refused to tell them where the guns were, Wall's codefendant

At its most basic level, accomplice liability occurs when one person assists another in the commission of a crime.

DmitriMaruta/Shutterstock

---

[14]*Hensel* v. *State*, 604 P.2d 222 (Alaska 1979)
[15]Ibid., p. 238.
[16]Ibid., p. 239.
[17]*State* v. *Arillo*, 553 A.2d 281 (N.H. 1988), p. 298.
[18]*Commonwealth* v. *Hatchin*, 709 A.2d 405 (Pa. Super. Ct. 1998).

became upset. He told Wall to close the window and lock the door, presumably so Turner (and a friend who was also present) could not escape. He then shot Turner in the chest. She later died. He also shot Turner's friend in the arm. She survived. Wall was convicted of criminal homicide, even though he did not pull the trigger. An appellate court upheld his conviction because he ". . . clearly and directly aided his codefendant's criminal conduct."[18]

Psychological Influence

What is psychological influence? It generally requires a certain amount of coaxing, encouraging, persuading, or soliciting. Mere presence at the scene of the crime is not enough.[19] For example, here are the facts from a case in which Carl Pace appealed his conviction of being an accomplice in a robbery:

> . . . appellant, his wife and two infant children were in a car driving from South Bend to LaPorte. Eugene Rootes was riding with them. The appellant was driving with his wife and one child in the front seat. Rootes and appellant's other child were in the back seat. While in South Bend, appellant after asking his wife for permission stopped to pick up a hitchhiker, Mr. Reppert, who sat next to Rootes in the back seat with one of appellant's infant children. Later Rootes pulled a knife and took Reppert's wallet. After driving further, Reppert got out of the car, Rootes then took his watch. The appellant said nothing during the entire period and they continued driving to LaPorte. This is all of the evidence presented by the record which would have any bearing on the crime charged, i.e., accessory before the fact of robbery by placing in fear.[20]

The court decided that Pace was not an accomplice because "[w]hile he was driving the car, nothing was said nor did he act in any manner to indicate his approval or countenance of the robbery."[21] He passively acquiesced to the robbery and, therefore, could not be considered an accomplice.

Contrast the *Pace* case with one in which a woman, Constance Doody, was having arguments with her mother and, on more than one occasion, expressed a desire to have the woman killed. At one point, when Doody was with her husband, Michael, in their pickup truck, Michael opened the glove box and showed her a box of bullets. Doody reportedly said, "I won't give you any problem." When Michael subsequently killed her mother, Doody, along with Michael, was charged with murder under a theory of accomplice liability. An appellate court affirmed her conviction.[22] This case is interesting because Doody's conduct fell in the vast gray area between mere presence and outright encouragement. Doody was not present at the murder, nor did she expressly encourage or order her husband to kill her mother. However, she did seem to know what was going to happen and indicated that she would not get in the way. According to the court, her statement in the truck ". . . could be reasonably found by the trial court to imply an assurance to Michael that she would not interfere with his plans and that she approved of the proposed crime."[23]

---

[19]See, e.g., *State* v. *Vaillancourt*, 453 A.2d 1327 (N.H. 1982).
[20]*Pace* v. *State*, 224 N.E.2d 312 (Ind. 1967), p. 313.
[21]Ibid., p. 314.
[22]*State* v. *Doody*, 434 A.2d 523 (Me. 1981).
[23]Ibid., p. 530.

Omission

The *actus reus* of accomplice liability can also be satisfied by way of an omission. In the case of accomplice liability, an omission will only result in conviction if the omitter has a duty to intervene. For example, in *State v. Walden,*[24] a mother stood by and did not attempt to intervene (or call for help) while her child was being assaulted. She was convicted as an accomplice because a North Carolina statute requires that parents have an "affirmative duty" to protect their children. In a related case, a mother knew that two men who lived with her repeatedly raped and sexually assaulted her two daughters. The court noted that there was "no doubt" that the woman was aware of what was happening and did nothing to intervene or stop it.[25]

To illustrate the *lack* of a duty to intervene, consider the infamous 1983 gang rape of a young woman in Big Dan's bar in New Bedford, Massachusetts.[26] Several bar patrons witnessed the incident, but not one of them reported it. No one cheered on the rapists or encouraged them, but none intervened and none called the police. They just stood idly by and watched. As disturbing as that may sound, not one individual who witnessed the rapes had a *legal duty to act*. As such, none of them could be held criminally liable as accomplices to the rapes.

Accomplice *Mens Rea*

The *mens rea* requirement for accomplice liability is a little more tedious than the *mens rea* requirement for other crimes. For ordinary criminal liability, there is one type of *mens rea* (e.g., purpose, knowledge, etc.). For accomplice liability, there are *two* levels of *mens rea*. First, there must be some degree of intent or desire to aid the primary offender. Second, there must also be intent to commit the underlying offense.[27]

Consider the case of *State v. Harrison*.[28] Harrison drove two friends, Thompson and Carter, to a commuter parking lot where they stole a vehicle. Thompson and Carter attempted to rob a gas station attendant, but when unsuccessful, fled the crime scene and were later arrested. Harrison was also arrested and charged as an accessory to the robbery, even though he did not participate in the actual crime. He was convicted, but appealed his conviction, arguing that the judge's instructions to the jury were flawed. The judge instructed jurors as follows:

> The State does not have to offer evidence to prove that a man charged with a crime actually had a guilty intent. This is because a person is presumed to have intended to do the act which he did do. Accordingly, until some credible evidence comes into the case tending to prove that because in the light of the circumstances as he honestly and in good faith believed them to be, the act which he did would appear to be lawful, or because the act was an accident, until such credible evidence appears in the

---

[24]*State v. Walden*, 293 S.E.2d 780 (N.C. 1982).
[25]*Hutcheson v. State*, 213 S.W.3d 25 (Ark. App. 2005).
[26]For a detailed explanation of the events, see L.S. Chancer, "New Bedford, Massachusetts, March 6, 1983-March 22, 1984: The 'Before and after' of a Group Rape," *Gender and Society*, Vol. 1(1987), pp. 239–60.
[27]*State v. Harrison*, 425 A.2d 111 (Conn. 1979), p. 113.
[28]Ibid.

case, the State may rest upon the presumption that the accused intended to commit an act which he did commit. Until such evidence appears in the case, the jury must presume that the accused intended to commit such acts as the jury finds he did commit, and accordingly find that the requisite guilty intent was present if it is shown that the accused, [sic] done by the accused, was unlawful.[29]

Harrison further argued that this instruction put the burden on *him* to prove that he did or did not intend to see the robbery completed. As you will recall, however, this burden should fall on the prosecution. The Supreme Court of Connecticut agreed. Harrison's argument was successful and he was given a new trial.

Harrison's case dealt with the crime of robbery, for which intent to commit the crime was a specific element. But what if the *mens rea* requirement for the underlying offense involves something less than outright intent, such as recklessness or negligence? How does this affect the *mens rea* calculation for accomplice liability? *State v. Foster,*[30] another Connecticut case, offers an answer. Foster, who was convicted of being an accessory (ordinarily he would have been considered an accomplice, but some courts use both terms interchangeably) to criminally negligent homicide, argued in his appeal that there was no such crime because he could not *intend for an unintended death to occur* (negligent homicide, by way of preview, is a homicide that generally can be foreseen). While his argument was certainly plausible, the Connecticut Supreme Court disagreed:

> Contrary to the defendant's assertions, . . . liability does not require that a defendant act with the conscious objective to cause the result described by a statute . . . [The defendant] may be liable in aiding another if he acts intentionally, knowingly, recklessly or with criminal negligence toward the result, depending on the mental state required by the substantive crime. When a crime requires that a person act with criminal negligence, [the defendant] is liable if he acts "with respect to a result or to a circumstance described by a statute defining an offense when he fails to perceive a substantial and unjustifiable risk that such result will occur or that such circumstance exists."[31]

In other words, it is necessary to look at the specific statute to determine the *mens rea* for accomplice liability. Thus, an all-encompassing definition of accomplice *mens rea* is as follows:

1. The intent to assist the primary party to engage in the conduct that forms the basis of the offense; and

2. The mental state required for commission of the offense, as provided in the definition of the substantive crime.[32]

This means, first, that the accomplice must intend to assist. Second, assuming she intends to assist, then criminal liability will attach as long as her mental state meets with what the statute requires. If the statutory *mens rea* is defined in terms of negligence, then she will be held liable as an accomplice if she acted negligently. Similarly, if the statutory *mens rea* was defined in terms of knowledge, then she will be considered an accomplice if she acted with knowledge.

---

[29]Ibid., pp. 112–113.
[30]*State* v. *Foster*, 202 Conn. 520 (Conn. 1987).
[31]Ibid., pp. 529–531
[32]J. Dressler, *Understanding Criminal Law*, 5th ed. (San Francisco, CA: Lexis-Nexis, 2009), p. 478.

What if, to make matters a little more complicated, the accomplice *seems* to intend for the primary offender's crime to occur, but does not *really* intend for it to occur? *Wilson v. People*,[33] a classic case, offers an answer. Wilson accused Pierce of stealing his watch. The two eventually stopped arguing, but Wilson remained convinced that Pierce was guilty. Later, they agreed to break into a drug store. After Wilson boosted Pierce up so that he could break a window and enter the store, he left and called the police. For unknown reasons, he returned to the drug store and received several bottles of stolen liquor from Pierce as he passed them out the window. The police arrived and arrested both men. Wilson was convicted as an accomplice, but his conviction was overturned by the Colorado Supreme Court, which placed significant emphasis on Wilson's call to the police. While he certainly had the intent to assist Pierce in the theft, the court felt he did not have the intent to permanently deprive the drug store owner of his property.

In an analogous case from some years earlier,[34] Price accompanied two acquaintances, Moran and Lindohl, on a robbery. Price's gun, however, was not loaded because unbeknownst to the other two men, he had supposedly talked to both a constable and a justice of the peace about the planned crime the day before it was committed. He reported that his intent was to foil the crime and ensure that Moran and Lindohl were caught. The court recounted the events as follows:

> . . . the undisputed facts, as appears from the foregoing, are, that the accused, on the day of the attempted robbery, went deliberately to a constable of the town in which he lived and told him all about the contemplated crime, giving the true names of the parties, and telling him when and where it was to take place, and the name of the intended victim; that the attempt was made at the very time and place, and by the parties, stated by him, and that on the following morning he, in like manner, went to a justice of the peace and told him all about what had been done, and furnished him with the true names of the parties implicated, by means of which, on the same day, they were brought to trial, and were subsequently convicted of the crime. That a sane person, really guilty of committing so grave a crime as the one imputed to the accused, would thus act, is so inconsistent with all human experience as not to warrant the conviction of any one under the circumstances shown.[35]

Price was initially convicted, but his conviction was overturned. Again, he intended to help his codefendants, but the some *mens rea* component (mental state required for the commission of the crime of robbery) was lacking. To summarize, then, ". . . the accomplice must not only have the purpose that someone else engage in the conduct which constitutes the particular crime charged, . . . but the accomplice must also share in the same intent which is required for the substantive offense."[36]

Before concluding our look at *mens rea* in the complicity context, one more issue bears discussion. Assume Craig helps Victor plan a "home invasion" robbery. The two pick the residence of an elderly widow, Sandy, and proceed to commit the crime. Victor kicks in the front door, armed, and finds Sandy sitting in the living room. He points the gun at her and demands that she give him all her cash and jewels. Craig

---

[33] *Wilson v. People*, 87 P.2d 5 (Colo. 1989).
[34] *Price v. People*, 109 Ill. 109 (Ill. 1884).
[35] Ibid., pp. 115–116.
[36] *State v. Williams*, 718 A.2d 721 (Super Ct. of N.J. Law Div. 1998), p. 723.

sits in the car outside serving as a lookout, ready to drive away at a moment's notice. As Victor has the gun trained on Sandy, Jim steps out from a nearby corridor and surprises Victor who, startled, shoots and kills him. Victor then panics, binds and gags Sandy, and locks her in a closet while he quickly ransacks the house and exits. The two men flee the scene empty-handed. At the risk of putting the cart before the horse (we will look at specific crime types starting in Chapter 6), there are three crimes here: robbery, murder, and kidnapping. Clearly Craig could be considered an accomplice to the robbery, but what about the murder and kidnapping? The answer, which has common law origins and is still in use in many jurisdictions today is as follows:

> a person encouraging or facilitating the commission of a crime could be held criminally liable not only for that crime, but for any other offense that was a "natural and probable consequence" of the crime aided and abetted.[37]

natural and probable consequences doctrine
An individual encouraging or assisting a crime can be liable not only for the original crime, but for any other offenses that are the natural and probable consequences of the original crime.

This has come to be known as the **natural and probable consequences doctrine**. In our example, the resultant murder and kidnapping were natural and probable consequences of the home invasion robbery. Craig would likely be considered an accomplice in all three crimes because it is not uncommon for home invasion robberies to result in other (and potentially more serious) criminal acts.

Contrast the Craig and Victor example with *People* v. *Butts*,[38] an actual California case in which Butts encouraged Otwell to assault a third man, Barnard. Butts did not know, however, that Otwell would use a knife and kill, rather than assault, Barnard. The court ruled that the killing was not a natural and probable consequence of an assault.

See Figure 4.2 for a summary of accomplice liability presented in flowchart format.

Accessory *Actus Reus*

Recall from earlier that an accomplice most often assists before and during the crime, while the accessory typically helps after the fact. Being an accessory is not quite as serious as being an accomplice, as one who assists after the crime may engage in behaviors that are far more innocuous than helping with commission of the crime. Thus, it is common for accessories to felonies to only be convicted of a misdemeanor rather than a felony. Also, accessory liability is often limited to felonies; many states do not regard it possible for someone to act as an accessory in a misdemeanor crime. With those points made, the *actus reus* for accessorial liability happens when the accessory personally aids the person who committed the crime (e.g., by providing a place to "hide out"). For example, federal law defines the *actus reus* for an accessory after the fact as one who "... receives, relieves, comforts or assists the offender ..."[39]

See the accompanying Court Decision box for more on criminal liability as an accessory. In it we take a look at the case of *State* v. *Chism*, in which the defendant was charged as an accessory after the fact to murder.

---

[37] *People* v. *Prettyman*, 926 P.2d 1013 (Cal. 1996), p. 1019.
[38] *People* v. *Butts*, 236 Cal. App. 2d 817 (Court App. Ca. 1965).
[39] 18 U.S.C. Section 3.

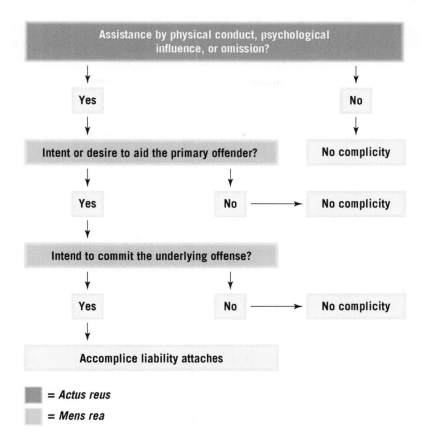

Figure 4.2
Accomplice Liability
(Complicity)

☐ = *Actus reus*

☐ = *Mens rea*

COURT DECISION

The Logic behind Targeting Accessories to Crime

State v. Chism
436 So.2d 464 (La. 1983)

Decision: Transporting and helping to dispose of a victim's body under no threat from the perpetrator gives rise to accessorial liability.

Reason: . . . On the evening of August 26, 1981, in Shreveport, Tony Duke gave the defendant, Brian Chism, a ride in his automobile. Brian Chism was impersonating a female, and Duke was apparently unaware of Chism's disguise . . . Chism's one-legged uncle, Ira Lloyd, joined them, and the three continued on their way, drinking as Duke drove the automobile. When Duke expressed a desire to have sexual relations with Chism, Lloyd announced that he wanted to find his ex-wife Gloria for the same purpose . . . As Ira Lloyd stood outside the car attempting to persuade Gloria to come with them, Chism and Duke hugged and kissed on the front seat as Duke sat behind the steering wheel.

(continued)

Gloria and Ira Lloyd got into an argument, and Ira stabbed Gloria with a knife several times in the stomach and once in the neck. Gloria's shouts attracted the attention of two neighbors, who unsuccessfully tried to prevent Ira from pushing Gloria into the front seat of the car alongside Chism and Duke. Ira Lloyd climbed into the front seat also, and Duke drove off . . .

Lloyd ordered Duke to drive to Willow Point, near Cross Lake. When they arrived Chism and Duke, under Lloyd's direction, removed Gloria from the vehicle and placed her on some high grass on the side of the roadway, near a wood line. Ira was unable to help the two because his wooden leg had come off. Afterwards, as Lloyd requested, the two drove off, leaving Gloria with him.

. . . Duke proceeded to drop Chism off at a friend's house, where he changed to male clothing. He placed the blood-stained women's clothes in a trash bin. Afterward, Chism went with his mother to the police station at 1:15 a.m. He gave the police a complete statement, and took the officers to the place where Gloria had been left with Ira Lloyd. The police found Gloria's body in some tall grass several feet from that spot.

. . . An accessory after the fact is any person, who, after the commission of a felony, shall harbor, conceal, or aid the offender, knowing or having reasonable ground to believe that he has committed the felony, and with the intent that he may avoid or escape from arrest, trial, conviction, or punishment. La.R.S. 14:25.

In this case we conclude that the evidence is sufficient to support an ultimate finding that the reasonable findings and inferences permitted by the evidence exclude every reasonable hypothesis of innocence. Despite evidence supporting some contrary inferences, a trier of fact reasonably could have found that Chism acted with at least a general intent to help Lloyd avoid arrest because: (1) Chism did not protest or attempt to leave the car when his uncle, Lloyd, shoved the mortally wounded victim inside; (2) he did not attempt to persuade Duke, his would-be lover, exit out the driver's side of the car and flee from his uncle, whom he knew to be one-legged and armed only with a knife; (3) he did not take any of these actions at any point during the considerable ride to Willow Point; (4) at their destination, he docilely complied with Lloyd's directions to remove the victim from the car and leave Lloyd with her, despite the fact that Lloyd made no threats and that his wooden leg had become detached; (5) after leaving Lloyd with the dying victim, he made no immediate effort to report the victim's whereabouts or to obtain emergency medical treatment for her; (6) before going home or reporting the victim's dire condition he went to a friend's house, changed clothing and discarded his own in a trash bin from which the police were unable to recover them as evidence; (7) he went home without reporting the victim's condition or location; (8) and he went to the police station to report the crime only after arriving home and discussing the matter with his mother.

. . . Therefore, we affirm the defendant's conviction . . .

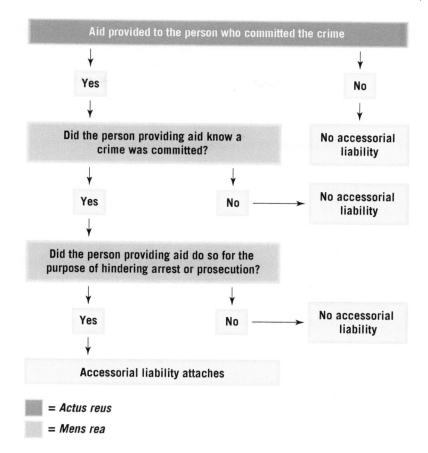

Figure 4.3
Accessorial Liability
(Complicity)

Accessory *Mens Rea*

There are two parts to the *mens rea* of accessorial liability. First, the accessory must have known that a crime was committed. Second, the individual must have aided the principal for the purpose of hindering arrest and prosecution. To again use a federal law example, an accessory after the fact satisfies the first *mens rea* requirement by ". . . knowing that an offense against the United States has been committed."[40] The second requirement is satisfied if the accessory provides assistance ". . . in order to hinder or prevent [the principal's] apprehension."[41]

See Figure 4.3 for a summary of accessorial liability presented in flowchart format.

YOUR DECISION

1. Jamie O'Connor is a second grade teacher in a rural area. She notices that one of her students, Bobby, consistently comes to school with bruises and cuts. When Jamie asked Bobby about the injuries, he stated, "My daddy hits me a lot." Not wanting to interfere in family business, Jamie does nothing. Two weeks later,

---

[40]Ibid.
[41]Ibid.

Bobby is beaten to death by his father. Can the prosecution charge Jamie as an accomplice to murder? Why or why not?

2. Joe discovers that his wife is having an affair after 20 years of marriage. Distraught, he goes to a local bar one evening to drink away his sorrows with a few friends. During the evening, Joe announces a plan to kill his wife and her lover. His friend Brian responds, "Sounds like a great idea. She deserves to die for what she did." Two days later, Joe fatally shoots his wife and her companion. Can Brian be charged as an accomplice? Why or why not?

Summary

- The *actus reus* for complicity is, at its most basic level, assistance.
- There are three means by which assistance is typically provided: (1) assistance by physical conduct; (2) assistance by psychological influence; and (3) assistance by omission (assuming in this latter case that the omitter has a duty to act).
- For accomplice liability, there are *two* levels of *mens rea*.
- First, there must be some degree of intent or desire to aid the primary offender.
- Second, there must also be intent to commit the underlying offense.
- An accomplice most often assists before and during the crime, while the accessory typically helps after the fact.
- The *actus reus* for accessorial liability happens when the accessory personally aids the person who committed the crime (e.g., by providing a place to "hide out").
- There are two parts to the *mens rea* of accessorial liability. First, the accessory must have known that a crime was committed. Second, the individual must have aided the principal for the purpose of hindering arrest and prosecution.

MODULE

4.3 COMPLICITY ISSUES, LIMITATIONS, AND DEFENSES

Learning Objectives

- **Discuss some of the issues that make complicity law complicated.**
- **Summarize the limitations of and defenses to accomplice liability.**
- **Explain the Model Penal Code approach to accomplice liability.**

CORE CONCEPTS   Complicity law is somewhat difficult to grasp because it involves multiple offenders. Likewise, the elements of accomplice liability make it a little more difficult to grasp than the types of criminal liability we introduced in earlier chapters. For example, as we just showed, there is more than one dimension to *mens rea*. What's more, the *actus reus* of accomplice liability can also take on more than one form. In this module, we begin by looking at issues that pose complications for complicity. Toward the end, we shift our attention to limitations and defenses. We wrap up with a review of the Model Penal Code's language concerning complicity.

Issues

Five issues complicate complicity law: (1) non-proxyable offenses, (2) the pretending principal, (3) the meaning of intent, (4) what happens if the primary party is acquitted, and (5) whether an accomplice can be "more guilty" than the primary party. Each is briefly reviewed in the following sections.

Non-proxyable Offenses

non-proxyable offense A crime that can only be committed by a specific person or class of individuals.

According to Dressler, a **non-proxyable offense** ". . . is one that, by definition, can only be perpetrated by a designated person or class of persons."[42] Such offenses introduce complications in the case of multiple offenders. For example, in *People v. Enfeld*,[43] a woman fraudulently induced a public official into issuing a false certificate, a crime that only a public official can commit. Because the official was fraudulently induced to commit the crime, criminal liability did not attach. Nor did it attach to the woman who obtained the false certificate! Why? She could not be an accomplice to a crime that only a public official could commit.

In another case, a male security guard was convicted of rape because he coerced a young couple into having intercourse.[44] His conviction was overturned, however, because he successfully argued that ". . . one element of rape is penetration of the female sexual organ by the sexual organ of the principal of the first degree."[45] Since the security guard did not participate in the sexual act himself, he could not be guilty as an "accomplice" to rape in this jurisdiction.

Some courts have taken a different approach, deciding that accomplices to such non-proxyable offenses should nevertheless be held liable for their actions. For example, in *People v. Hernandez*,[46] a woman, armed with a rifle, forced her husband to have intercourse with another woman. She was convicted of rape and appealed, but the reviewing court rejected her appeal, stating:

> It would be unreasonable to hold a woman immune from prosecution for rape committed by a man under her "threats or menaces sufficient to show that [he] had reasonable cause to and did believe [that his life] would be endangered if [he] refused." . . . If such were the law it would create a crime without a punishable perpetrator.[47]

In yet another case, this one involving perjury (i.e., lying under oath), a woman caused a man to (without his knowledge) testify falsely at trial.[48] Traditionally, only

---

[42]J. Dressler, *Understanding Criminal Law*, 5th ed. (San Francisco, CA: Lexis-Nexis, 2009), p. 469.
[43]*People v. Enfeld*, 518 N.Y.S.2d 536 (Sup. Ct. 1987).
[44]*Dusenbery v. Commonwealth*, 263 S.E.2d 392 (Va. 1980).
[45]Ibid., p. 394.
[46]*People v. Hernandez*, 18 Cal. App. 3d 651 (Ct. App. 1971).
[47]Ibid., p. 657.
[48]*United States v. Walser*, 3 F.3d 380 (11th Cir. 1993).

the person who lies under oath can be convicted of perjury, making it a non-proxy-able offense, but the woman in this case was convicted of perjury. An appeals court upheld her conviction, noting that even though she was not under oath, she caused an innocent party to unwittingly present false testimony.

The Pretending Principal

In the *mens rea* discussion earlier, we presented two cases in which an accomplice *feigned* involvement as such. What if we turn things around a bit and consider a case in which the *principal* pretends to work, with criminal intent, along with another individual to commit a crime? In a classic case,[49] two men, A and B, agreed to bur-glarize a C's store. Unknown to A, B was C's relative and before the burglary was to take place, but after the agreement was made, B obtained permission from C to enter the store so that A could be captured "in the act." On the night of the crime, A helped B enter the store through a window. B then passed goods out the window to A. As they were leaving the scene, A was arrested and convicted of burglary. His conviction was overturned, however, because B did not technically burglarize the store; he had permission from the owner. In other words, A's criminal liability could not derive from B's because B did not commit a crime.

Contrast this decision with *Vaden v. State*,[50] a case in which two hunting guides aided undercover agents in illegal hunting and fishing activities. The Alaska Supreme Court upheld the convictions against both guides, in part, because agents' actions were not justified—even though they were never prosecuted for their actions:

> We are not persuaded by [defendants'] argument that the charges in this case be dismissed solely because the government agents engaged in illegal hunting and fish-ing activity . . . the correct remedy when police go outside the scope of their duties is to "prosecute the police," not "free the equally culpable defendant."[51]

The Meaning of Intent

In our *mens rea* discussion earlier, it was noted that accomplice liability attaches when (1) there is intent to assist the primary party and (2) there is intent to commit the underlying offense. But what exactly does *intent* mean? Does intent mean delib-erate purpose to commit the act? Or could it mean something less, such as simple knowledge? These are important questions. Consider *United States v. Giovannetti*,[52] a case in which a man, Janis, rented one of his houses to some people who conducted illegal gambling activities within it, using it as a "wireroom." At Janis's trial, the judge gave jurors the so-called **ostrich instruction**, which read as follows:

> You may infer knowledge from a combination of suspicion and indifference to the truth. If you find that a person had a strong suspicion that things were not what they seemed or that someone had withheld some important facts, yet shut his eyes for fear that he would learn, you may conclude that he acted knowingly.[53]

ostrich instruction A jury instruction regarding the *mens rea* of accomplice liability that allows the jury to infer knowledge on the part of the defendant from indifference to finding the truth.

[49]*State* v. *Hayes*, 16 S.W. 514 (Mo. 1891).
[50]*Vaden* v. *State*, 768 P.2d 1102 (Alaska 1989).
[51]Ibid.
[52]*United States* v. *Giovannetti*, 919 F.2d 1223 (7th Cir. 1990).
[53]Ibid., p. 1226.

Even though two people commit a crime together, they may be treated differently by the courts depending on the circumstances.

Flirt/SuperStock

This is called the ostrich instruction because had Janis "stuck his head in the sand" and acted in a deliberately ignorant fashion, then he would be hard-pressed to argue he had no knowledge of what was occurring at his property.[54] The trial jury convicted Janis, concluding that he acted like an ostrich insofar as he was a gambler who regularly conversed with others as though he knew what was happening on his property.

The Seventh Circuit, however, disagreed, holding that more than just knowledge—or efforts to avoid such knowledge—was necessary. To be held criminally liable as an accomplice, Janis would have needed to "in some sort associate himself with the venture, that he participate in it as in something that he wishes to bring about, that he seek by his action to make it succeed."[55] As another court put it, a person cannot be considered an accomplice unless he "share[s] the criminal intent of the principal; there must be a community of purpose in the unlawful undertaking."[56] To summarize, then, the *intent* for accomplice liability is something much higher than mere knowledge.

What Happens if the Primary Party Is Acquitted?

As you know by now, there are many means by which a person can be acquitted. Suppose, then, that the primary party (or principal) is acquitted. What will become

---

[54] See, e.g., *United States v. Craig*, 178 F.3d 891 (7th Cir. 1999), p. 896.
[55] Citing *United States v. Peoni*, 100 F.2d 401 (2nd Cir. 1938), p. 402.
[56] *State v. Duran*, 526 P.2d 188 (N.M. Ct. App. 1974), p. 189.

of the accomplice? Should that individual be acquitted? These questions have come up in a number of cases. For example, in *United States* v. *Lopez,*[57] Ronald McIntosh, the accomplice, escaped prison and then stole and landed a helicopter at another prison, flying off with one Samantha Lopez, the principal. Lopez successfully asserted a necessity defense in her trial on escape charges, claiming that she faced repeated threats in prison and thus had no choice but to escape. McIntosh asserted a similar defense, but did not succeed. An appellate court affirmed his conviction, mainly because some of the conduct he was charged with (air piracy and use of a firearm) was not considered necessary in the eyes of the court.

The *Lopez* case dealt with an affirmative defense (necessity). What if, instead, the primary offender escapes conviction because the prosecution cannot prove *mens rea*? Should an accomplice then go free? *Regina* v. *Cogan and Leak,*[58] a classic case, offers some answers. In that case, Leak convinced Cogan to have intercourse with Leak's wife by falsely telling him she consented. Cogan was acquitted of rape because he lacked the *mens rea* (i.e., he thought she consented). Leak was convicted as an accomplice to the rape. His appeal was unsuccessful, as it should have been. As one source put it, ". . . courts will not allow individuals to hide behind their own legal incapacity to commit a crime if they use others to accomplish it."[59] To summarize, then, even if the principal is acquitted, the accomplice can still be held criminally responsible for participation in the crime.

Can an Accomplice Be "More Guilty" than the Principal?

Earlier on we pointed out the common law rule that no accessory could be tried or convicted until the principal was both tried and convicted. Again, this rule has been abandoned, as it should have been, but it raises a potential problem. Can an accomplice be "more guilty" than a principal? In other words, must both the accomplice and the principal be convicted of the same offense? Or, alternatively, can the accomplice be convicted of a more serious offense than the principal? To this latter question, the answer is yes.

In *Regina* v. *Richards,*[60] a wife hired two men to beat her husband severely enough that he would be hospitalized. However, they merely roughed him up. Interestingly, the court held that the wife could not be convicted of a more serious crime than the men who roughed up her husband.

A number of courts take a different approach today, paving the way for greater accomplice culpability. For example, in *People* v. *McCoy,*[61] the California Supreme Court ruled that an accomplice to murder can be found guilty of a more serious form of homicide than the primary offender. For example, if the accomplice premeditates the killing, while the principal does not, a more serious conviction is warranted for the accomplice (the distinctions between levels of homicide, again, will be covered in

---

[57] *United States* v. *Lopez,* 662 F.Supp. 1083 (N.D. Cal. 1987).
[58] *Regina* v. *Cogan and Leak,* 1 Q.B. 217 (Eng. 1976).
[59] R.G. Singer and J.Q. La Fond, *Criminal Law: Examples and Explanations,* 4th ed. (New York: Wolters Kluwer, 2007), p. 387.
[60] *Regina* v. *Richards,* Q.B. 776 (1974).
[61] *People* v. *McCoy,* 24 P.3d 1210 (Cal. 2001).

Chapter 6). The court in that case offered up the following hypothetical in support of its decision:

> . . . assume someone, let us call him Iago, falsely tells another person, whom we will call Othello, that Othello's wife, Desdemona, was having an affair, hoping that Othello would kill her in a fit of jealousy. Othello does so without Iago's further involvement. In that case, depending on the exact circumstances of the killing, Othello might be guilty of manslaughter, rather than murder, on a heat of passion theory. Othello's guilt of manslaughter, however, should not limit Iago's guilt if his own culpability were greater. Iago should be liable for his own acts as well Othello's, which he induced and encouraged. But Iago's criminal liability, as Othello's, would be based on his own personal *mens rea*. If, as our hypothetical suggests, Iago acted with malice, he would be guilty of murder even if Othello, who did the actual killing, was not.[62]

Limitations and Defenses

There are a few situations in which accomplice liability is a legal impossibility. Likewise, an accomplice can assert any number of defenses (see Chapter 9 for more on criminal defenses). To these we can add another, namely abandonment.

Abandonment

One who assists in the commission of a criminal act may choose to withdraw from the collaborative effort or otherwise abandon his or her intent to participate in the crime. To succeed, though, the individual must notify the principal and neutralize the effects of any assistance offered to that point. For example, if someone provides a weapon for the principal to use in the crime, he must get it back. As an alternative, had that person's assistance gone only so far as an expression, then he must neutralize its effect. A statement along the lines of "let's burglarize that house" could be neutralized by a statement to the effect that "let's not, I changed my mind."

Importantly, it is not enough for one who offers assistance before the commission of a crime to turn heel and leave as the crime is about to be committed. Again, there must be a bona fide effort to stop the crime or neutralize the assistance already provided. For example, in *State* v. *Thomas*,[63] a man, Thomas, expressed his desire to two acquaintances to "shoot the police." When one of them pulled a gun on an officer, Thomas left. The officer was shot and killed. Thomas was convicted of aiding and abetting in the murder, and he appealed unsuccessfully. The reviewing court held:

> Defendant's own testimony at trial, taken at face value, indicates that he simply left the roof when he saw Jennette take out his gun. Nothing in his testimony suggests that he communicated to Jennette that he was leaving or that he disapproved of the contemplated act, or that he otherwise sought to actively withdraw the support to the proposed event which his presence on the roof supplied. According to defendant, he merely left the scene within minutes before the shooting occurred. As a matter of

---

[62]Ibid., pp. 1216–1217.
[63]*State* v. *Thomas*, 356 A.2d 433 (N.J. Super. Ct. App. Div. 1976).

law, such a spontaneous, unannounced withdrawal, without more, only briefly before the commission of the offense which had been previously encouraged by defendant's presence or other support, is insufficient to insulate the defendant from criminal liability as an aider and abettor.[64]

Immunity from Conviction

Accomplice liability is not possible when on the parties to a crime is supposed to be protected by the applicable statute. The best example is statutory rape. Statutory rape laws make it a crime to have sexual intercourse with a minor. So assuming Clint, an 18-year-old, has sex with his 17-year-old girlfriend (and assuming the jurisdiction in which they are located treats 17-year-olds as juveniles), he has committed statutory rape. His girlfriend was a party to the crime, but she was also protected by the statutory rape law. Thus, she cannot be considered an accomplice to her own rape. If she were to be considered an accomplice, it would undermine the purpose of the law.

Consider *In re Meagan R.,*[65] a case involving a minor female who, along with her boyfriend, broke into a neighbor's house and used the bed for intercourse. The juvenile court entered a finding that Meagan committed burglary. Interestingly, the burglary conviction was not based on any intent on her part to burglarize the home. Rather, it was based on the theory that Meagan entered the house with intent to aid and abet in her own statutory rape. The reasoning behind this approach was not laid out in the case, but an appeals court nevertheless reversed the conviction, stating:

> . . . . although we grant Meagan was not the member of a protected class with regard to the burglary offense of which she was convicted, she was the intended and protected victim of the predicate felony used by the court to support the burglary finding. As such, she cannot harbor the culpable state of mind necessary to commit the burglary, because under any theory she cannot commit the crime of her own statutory rape. Consequently, the burglary true finding must be reversed.[66]

Next, consider an adultery case, *In re Cooper.*[67] An unmarried woman was charged with aiding and abetting in a married man's adulterous relationship. The case was decided in 1912 and concerned a California statute that made it a felony for two married persons to live together in a state of cohabitation and adultery. The woman could not be considered an accomplice to the crime of adultery because she was not married. Nor did the California Supreme Court agree with the state's argument that she would be considered the principal in the crime, as her conduct was neither criminal nor punishable by any statute—even though what she did may have been morally wrong.

The Model Penal Code and Complicity

The Model Penal Code does not use the common law terms *accessory* or *principal*. It simply defines an accomplice as one who "solicits" another to commit the offense,

---

[64]Ibid., p. 445.
[65]*In re Meagan R.*, 42 Cal. App. 4th 17 (Ct. App. 1996).
[66]Ibid., pp. 21–22.
[67]*In re Cooper*, 162 Cal. 81 (1912).

"aids or agrees or attempts" to aid another in the commission of the offense, or fails to perform a legal duty to prevent the offense.[68] As to the *mens rea* of complicity, the Model Penal Code provides:

> When causing a particular result is an element of an offense, an accomplice in the conduct causing such result is an accomplice in the commission of that offense if he acts with the kind of culpability, if any, with respect to that result that is sufficient for the commission of the offense.[69]

This is just a fancy way of saying that the accomplice's *mens rea* must match the *mens rea* of the underlying offense. The Model Penal Code's other complicity provisions closely resemble those we have already discussed above. For example, a person cannot be considered an accomplice if he abandons his complicity prior to the offense by warning authorities. Similarly, to be an accomplice according to the Model Penal Code, one must act with the "purpose of promoting or facilitating the commission of an offense."[70] Mere knowledge that illegal activity is about to take—or is taking—place is insufficient.

YOUR DECISION

1. Late one Sunday evening, Joe and Mark decide to burglarize their neighbor's house. The pair plans to hop the fence and break in through the back sliding glass door. As they are about to jump over the fence, they notice a very large Rottweiler in the back yard barking loudly. They also notice the next door neighbor watching them from her kitchen window and she appears to be dialing 911 on her telephone. The police arrest Joe and Mark. As their defense counsel, what defense, if any, can you raise? Why or why not?

2. Samantha has been physically and emotionally assaulted by her husband, Robbie, for over 15 years. She finally decides to kill Robbie and puts poison in his meatloaf one evening. She then calls her neighbor, Jodie, and asks for help disposing of the body. Jodie helps Samantha put Robbie's body in her minivan, drive it to the lake and dump it in the water. At trial, the evidence of the physical abuse Samantha suffered during her marriage overwhelms the jury. They engage in jury nullification and acquit Samantha. You are the prosecutor and you must decide how to handle the case against Jodie. What, if anything, can Jodie be tried with? How, if at all, will Samantha's acquittal impact Jodie's trial?

Summary

- Complicity cannot occur in the case of non-proxyable offenses, those that can only be committed by one individual or group.
- If the principal pretends to work, with criminal intent, along with another individual to commit a crime, he or she most likely will not be held liable.
- The *intent* for accomplice liability is something much higher than mere knowledge.

---

[68]Section 2.06(3).
[69]Section 2.06(4).
[70]Section 2.06(3)(a).

- If the principal is acquitted, an accomplice can still be held criminally liable.
- It is possible for an accomplice to be found guilty of a more serious offense than that committed by the primary offender.
- There are a few situations in which accomplice liability is a legal impossibility.
- One who abandons his or her intent to participate in the crime may not be considered an accomplice. To succeed, though, the individual must notify the principal and neutralize the effects of any assistance offered to that point.
- Accomplice liability is not possible when on the parties to a crime is supposed to be protected by the applicable statute. The crime of statutory rape serves as an example.
- The Model Penal Code does not use the common law terms *accessory* or *principal*.
- The Model Penal Code simply defines an accomplice as one who "solicits" another to commit the offense, "aids or agrees or attempts" to aid another in the commission of the offense, or fails to perform a legal duty to prevent the offense.
- Under the Model Penal Code approach, the accomplice's *mens rea* must match the *mens rea* of the underlying offense.

MODULE

4.4   VICARIOUS LIABILITY

Learning Objectives
- **Explain the concept of vicarious liability.**
- **Distinguish between corporate and individual vicarious liability.**

CORE CONCEPTS

vicarious liability
Criminal liability for the acts of another person.

With accomplice liability, as we mentioned earlier, the accomplice *derives* his or her liability from a primary offender. In other words, complicity is impossible without two or more people who act with criminal purpose. **Vicarious liability** occurs when one person is held liable for the actions of another—and perhaps when the former person has no idea what the latter person is up to.

Formally defined, vicarious liability is "[t]he imposition of liability on one person for the actionable conduct of another, based solely on a relationship between the two persons."[71] So while vicarious liability involves two or more parties, there are two conditions that make it different from accomplice liability: (1) it takes only one party's actions to trigger liability and (2) liability *transfers* from one of them to the other. For example, an employee may do something that is prohibited by law, but the *employer* will be held responsible for it.

It goes against most everything you have learned so far to hold one person responsible for the actions of another. After all, one of the key requirements of a

---

[71]*Black's Law Dictionary*, 6th ed. (St. Paul, MN: West, 1990), p. 1566.

criminal act is *mens rea*, the offender's mental state. Is it fair to hold, say, a business owner responsible if one of her employees commits a crime and she has absolutely no knowledge or awareness of it? Probably not, but just because liability can shift to another does not mean that other party is always innocent or ignorant. And sometimes, even if the other party *is* "innocent," liability can attach. The logic for this was laid out way back in 1787, in *Phile* v. *Ship Anna*:

> The law never punishes a man criminally but for his own act, yet it frequently punishes him in his pocket, for the act of another. Thus, if a wife commits an offence, the husband is not liable to the penalties; but if she obtains the property of another by any means not felonious, he must make the payment and amends.[72]

Modern-day vicarious liability works in a similar fashion.

There are many forms and theories of vicarious liability. Some are criminal; some are civil. In this section, we will introduce two of the more common forms: corporate vicarious liability and individual vicarious liability. Our focus is largely on criminal liability because, after all, this is a book on criminal law and criminal procedure. However, in some situations it is helpful to briefly consider developments in the realm of civil law, as they have implications for vicarious criminal liability.

Corporate Vicarious Liability

corporate vicarious liability Liability of a corporation for the actions of its agents and employees.

respondeat superior An employer is liable for the actions of its agents and employees while in the course of employment.

Corporate vicarious liability refers to the liability of a corporation, no matter its size, for the criminal conduct of its employees. Its origins can be traced to the medieval doctrine of *respondeat superior*, Latin for "let the master answer." Under *respondeat superior*, the master could be held to answer for the action of his agent. A number of nineteenth-century English court decisions also formed the basis for corporate vicarious criminal liability. However, the turning point in American history was the U.S. Supreme Court's decision in *New York Central & Hudson River Railroad* v. *United States*.[73] At issue was whether a corporation could be held criminally liable for the issuance of illegal rebates by its agents and officers. The Court held, in part, that "We see no valid objection in law, and every reason in public policy, why the corporation which profits by the transaction, and can only act through its agents and officers, shall be held punishable."[74] In a subsequent case, a steamship corporation was convicted of illegal dumping.[75] In the court's words, the corporation "failed to prevent the commission of a forbidden act."[76]

The general rule today is that a corporation is criminally liable for the actions of its agents when (1) those agents act in the official scope of their employment for (2) the benefit of the corporation. As one court put it, "An agent's knowledge is imputed to the corporation where the agent is acting within the scope of his authority and where the knowledge relates to matters within the scope of authority."[77] Needless to say,

---

[72]*Phile* v. *Ship Anna*, 1 U.S. 197 (1 Dall. 1787), p. 207.
[73]*New York Central & Hudson River Railroad* v. *United States*, 212 U.S. 481 (1909).
[74]Ibid., p. 495.
[75]*Dollar S.S. Co.* v. *United States*, 101 F.2d 638 (9th Cir. 1939).
[76]Ibid., p. 640.
[77]*In re Hellenic, Inc.*, 965 F.2d 311 (7th Cir. 1992).

then, if an employee exploits his or her position for personal gain (such as by stealing inventory and selling it on the side), the corporation will most likely not be held liable.

The second requirement, that the employee be acting with the corporation's interests at heart, is less clear. As one team of experts put it, it "is not necessary that the employee be primarily concerned with benefitting the corporation, because courts recognize that many employees act primarily for their own personal gain."[78] In fact, some corporations have been held criminally liable for the actions of low-ranking employees who may have little to no knowledge about the parent company's structure or motives.[79] And corporations have even been held criminally liable for their subordinates' actions after putting into place policies and procedures intended to prevent misconduct![80]

How exactly is a corporation prosecuted, convicted, and punished? In the typical criminal context, the defendant is a human being, someone who can be fined or confined. A corporation, however, is a legal entity, not a person. Obviously something that does not exist in a physical form cannot be incarcerated. It would be more than a little difficult to take an office building and everyone in it and put it in prison! The form of punishment for corporations whose employees' actions forms the basis of vicarious liability, then, is a fine. At the federal level, the amount of the fine depends on the victim's loss and/or the company's gain multiplied by some factor set in the U.S. Sentencing Guidelines.[81]

See the accompanying Court Decision for more on corporate vicarious liability. In it we examine the case of *U.S. v. Ionia Management*, where a corporation is criminally charged for its employees illegal dumping of oil waste.

COURT DECISION

The Logic behind Corporate Liability

United States v. Ionia Management
526 F.Supp.2d 319 (D. Conn. 2007)

Decision: A corporation is not relieved of its responsibility because an agent's act was illegal, contrary to its instructions, or against its general policies.

Reason: On September 6, 2007, at the conclusion of a jury trial, Defendant Ionia Management S.A. ("Ionia") was convicted on eighteen counts: thirteen counts of violating the Act to Prevent Pollution from Ships ("APPS") and associated regulations, 33 U.S.C. § 1908(a); three counts of falsifying records in connection with a federal investigation in violation of 18 U.S.C. § 1519; one count of obstructing

(continued)

---

[78]K. Drew and K.A. Clark, "Corporate Criminal Liability," *American Criminal Law Review*, Vol. 42 (2005), pp. 277–303, 282.
[79]See, e.g., A. Weissmann and D. Newman, "Rethinking Criminal Corporate Liability," *Indiana Law Journal*, Vol. 82(2007), pp. 411–451, n. 37.
[80]Ibid.
[81]K. Drew and K.A. Clark, "Corporate Criminal Liability," *American Criminal Law Review*, Vol. 42(2005), pp. 277–303, 287.

COURT DECISION
(continued)

justice in violation of 18 U.S.C. § 1505; and one count of conspiring to commit these offenses in violation of 18 U.S.C. § 371...

Ionia's position is that the actions of the Kriton's crew cannot be imputed to the company because they were acting illegally and violating company environmental policy without authorization. Moreover, Ionia contends that there was no actual benefit to be gained from illegally discharging oil waste, for the vessel's pollution prevention equipment obviated the need to make illegal discharges or shoreline disposals.

First, the Government introduced evidence that the putative agents of Ionia were acting under direct orders from their superiors. According to Second Engineer Edgardo Mercurio, Chief Engineer Efstratios Tsigonakis specifically instructed him not to use the oily water separator and to pump the oily waste overboard without utilizing the oil pollution prevention equipment; Tsigonakis and Mercurio then directed the engine room crew to connect the bypass hose and dispose of the waste directly into the ocean...

The jury could reasonably have concluded that the crew participated in the pump-outs and records falsification with the intention of, for example, (1) following orders and maintaining the chain of command aboard the Kriton; (2) saving Ionia the time and expense of properly maintaining and using the oil pollution prevention equipment; and (3) enabling the Kriton to continue to dock at U.S. ports despite having false records.

Finally, that Ionia had official policies prohibiting the conduct by the crew which formed the basis for this prosecution does not change the conclusion that imposing vicarious criminal liability was proper. As the Court explained in instructing the jury, the existence of contrary company policies is not by itself a defense to criminal liability; whether Ionia had an official position on the course of conduct undertaken by its agents is merely one factor to be considered by the jury when assessing whether to impose vicarious liability. In this case, reasonable jurors could have concluded that, notwithstanding company policies, training, and general instructions, the actions of the Kriton's crew attributable to Ionia were actions by agents of Ionia performed within the scope of their employment.

... a rational trier of fact could have found Ionia guilty beyond a reasonable doubt through the acts of its employees, and there is no basis for granting a new trial in the interest of justice. Insofar as Ionia's Motion for a Judgment of Acquittal, or in the Alternative, a New Trial rests on the jury's misapplication of agency principles, it is denied.

Deferred Prosecution Agreements

Since the 2001 demise of energy giant Enron, much has changed in the realm of corporate vicarious liability. Instead of jumping straight to criminal prosecutions, the government often enters into so-called **deferred prosecution agreements**. In exchange for facing criminal prosecution, corporations are given an opportunity to "correct their ways" before the criminal law is used. This often occurs with close

deferred prosecution agreement When corporations (and sometimes even individuals) are given an opportunity to "correct their ways" before the criminal law is used. Deferred prosecution is an alternative to adjudication, leaving the "threat" of criminal charges as an incentive for the defendant to engage in agreed-upon actions.

monitoring by federal officials in the U.S. Justice Department. Corporations appear quite willing to enter into these agreements:

> The willingness of corporations to enter into such deferred prosecution agreements is due in large measure to the vastly disproportionate power of the two sides. Prosecutors have enormous leverage due to the doctrine of vicarious liability. A single low-level employee's criminal conduct can be sufficient to trigger criminal liability on the part of the corporation.[82]

If a company rejects the government's offer for deferred prosecution, it can have dire consequences. You may recall that Arthur Anderson, one of the "big five" accounting firms, went under in 2002, in part because it handled much of the auditing for Enron. The company was given the opportunity to enter into a deferred prosecution agreement, but it rejected the offer. It was indicted and convicted of various crimes, including obstruction of justice. And while the conviction was later overturned,[83] the company has yet to return to normal operations.

Civil Law Developments

In the civil arena, numerous restrictions have been put in place that make it increasingly unlikely that corporations will be held liable for their employees' behaviors. We discuss two such restrictions: (1) limitations on corporate liability in of Title VII (shorthand for Title VII of the Civil Rights Act of 1964, which prohibits employer discrimination on the basis of race, color, religion, sex, or national origin) sexual harassment cases and (2) limitations on corporate punitive damages in vicarious criminal liability case. While these developments have occurred as a result of civil cases, they have interesting implications for corporate criminal liability.

In *Faragher* v. *City of Boca Raton*,[84] the Supreme Court dealt with a Title VII question of whether a city was responsible for sexual harassment by its supervisory lifeguards. The city argued that it had an antisexual harassment policy in place and thus could not be held civilly liable the actions of one of its employees. The Supreme Court sided with the city because the female subordinate lifeguard who alleged sexual harassment did not argue that any adverse action was taken against her (known as "quid pro quo" harassment). The practical result of the Court's decision is that cities are shielded to some extent from vicarious *civil* liability for employee sexual harassment so long as they have in place policies intended to discourage such behavior.[85] Why do we care? Recall from the previous section that no such rule exists for criminal liability. To this day, corporations can be held *criminally* liable for the actions of their subordinates even if they have policies in place intended to prevent such misconduct! Why is civil law so much more restrictive? This discrepancy will need to be resolved some day.

The Supreme Court has also placed restrictions on punitive damages (a dollar amount intended to "punish" those at fault) that corporations can be required to pay

---

[82]Ibid., pp. 425–426.
[83]*Arthur Anderson, LLP v. United States*, 544 U.S. 696 (2005).
[84]*Faragher* v. *City of Boca Raton*, 524 U.S. 775 (1998).
[85]See also *Burlington Industries, Inc.* v. *Ellerth*, 524 U.S. 742 (1998).

in civil vicarious liability cases. In *Kolstad* v. *American Dental Association*,[86] Carole Kolstad sued the American Dental Association, alleging that she was passed over for promotion because of sexual harassment. The Court held that ". . . in the punitive damages context, an employer may not be vicariously liable for the discriminatory employment decisions of managerial agents where these decisions are contrary to the employer's 'good-faith efforts to comply with Title VII.'"[87] Since the defendant had enacted policies intended to prevent employment discrimination, it was basically immune from punitive damages. This decision was significant because it placed limits on how much companies can be forced to pay as punishment for the actions of their subordinates. No such restriction has been put in place in the criminal context, where the sky remains the limit as far as what companies can be forced to pay.

Individual Vicarious Liability

With individual vicarious liability, one person (instead of a corporation) is held liable for another's behavior. For example, in some states, parents can be held criminally liable for their kids' illegal activities. So-called principals can also be held liable for the actions of their agents (an "agent" is one who acts on behalf of a principal).

Parental Liability for a Child's Behavior

There are two main types of statutes used to hold parents accountable for the actions of their children. First, every state penalizes "contributing to the delinquency of a minor."[88] Known as CDM statutes, these can be used against basically anyone who contributes to a child's delinquency, not just parents. Second, parents can be held criminally liable for endangering the welfare of a child. To illustrate, New York's "endangering the welfare of a child" statute provides:

> A person is guilty of endangering the welfare of a child when:
> 1. He knowingly acts in a manner likely to be injurious to the physical, mental or moral welfare of a child less than seventeen years old or directs or authorizes such child to engage in an occupation involving a substantial risk of danger to his life or health; or
> 2. Being a parent, guardian or other person legally charged with the care or custody of a child less than eighteen years old, he fails or refuses to exercise reasonable diligence in the control of such child to prevent him from becoming an "abused child," a "neglected child," a "juvenile delinquent" or a "person in need of supervision,". . . .
> Endangering the welfare of a child is a class A misdemeanor.[89]

Neither of these two offenses is new, nor does either create vicarious liability. In other words, parents who contribute to the delinquency of a minor or endanger the

---

[86]*Kolstad* v. *American Dental Association*, 527 U.S. 526 (1999).
[87]Ibid., p. 545.
[88]P.K. Graham, "Parental Responsibility Laws: Let the Punishment Fit the Crime," *Loyola Law Review*, Vol. 33(2000), p. 1719, 1729–1739.
[89]N.Y. Penal Law 260.10.

welfare of a child are punished for their own actions and not simply for their status as parents. This changed, however, with the introduction of certain parental responsibility laws establishing vicarious liability. Such laws make criminals out of parents simply because of their *status* as parents, not because of any particular act or omission.

To illustrate the reach of parental responsibility laws, consider the story of Alex Provenzino, a Detroit teenager who started getting into trouble when he began associating with older kids. He was first arrested for burglarizing his family's church. Later, he was arrested for assaulting his father. Three months later, he was arrested for a string of residential burglaries. His last arrest occurred after police found marijuana and a stolen handgun on his nightstand. A year later, Alex's parents were found guilty of a misdemeanor for failing to prevent their son from committing the burglaries. Theirs was the first case tried under the St. Clair Shores parental responsibility law. The law required that parents were:

1. To keep illegal drugs or illegal firearms out of the home and legal firearms locked in places that are inaccessible to the minor.

2. To know the Curfew Ordinance of the City of St. Clair Shores, and to require the minor to observe the Curfew ordinance. . .

3. To require the minor to attend regular school sessions and to forbid the minor to be absent from class without parental or school permission.

4. To arrange proper supervision for the minor when the parent must be absent.

5. To take the necessary precautions to prevent the minor from maliciously or willfully destroying real, personal, or mixed property which belongs to the City of St. Clair Shores, or is located in the City of St. Clair Shores.

6. To forbid the minor from keeping stolen property, illegally possessing firearms or illegal drugs, or associating with known juvenile delinquents, and to seek help from appropriate governmental authorities or private agencies in handling or controlling the minor, when necessary.[90]

The parents were ordered to pay $2,200 in fines and court costs plus $13,000 per year for their son's care in a youth detention home. An appeals court later overturned the verdict on a technicality,[91] but the case thrust the issue of parental responsibility laws into the limelight and is similar to many other such cases.

Principal-Agent Liability

Principal-agent liability is also commonplace. Once again, a principal is the individual who hires or is in charge of an agent; the agent acts on his or her behalf. Often the principal is the employer and the agent is the employee, but this need not always be the case. We will offer an example of each relationship. To illustrate an employer–employee relationship, in one case, an El Paso, Texas, bank hired a repossession company to recover Yvonne Sanchez's vehicle because she defaulted on her loan. Two men who were dispatched to Sanchez's home found the vehicle in the driveway. Sanchez confronted the men as they were hooking the vehicle to a tow truck. Just as

---

[90]St. Clair Shores, Mich., Parental Responsibility Ordinance 20.560-20.566 (July 26, 1994).
[91]*City of St. Clair Shores* v. *Provenzino*, No. 96-1483 AR (County of Macomb Cir. Ct. 1997).

the men were getting ready to tow the vehicle away, Sanchez jumped inside it, locked the doors, and refused to get out. The men then towed the vehicle away with Sanchez inside. They parked the car in a fenced lot and left Sanchez inside while a Doberman pinscher guard dog wandered about the lot. She was later rescued by her husband and police. An appeals court held that the bank had a duty to take precautions for safety and was responsible for the breach of peace committed by the repossession company agents.[92]

Let us use another Texas case to illustrate a principal–agent relationship that is not of the employer–employee variety. In *Marshall* v. *Allstate*, a 20-year-old college student, Wayne, had some friends over to his parents' house in Katy, Texas. At 10:30 P.M., his father told him to "wrap things up." Wayne and friends ignored the request and instead went into the garage, after having been drinking, and built a large wooden cross. Then they carried it across town and set it on fire in the front yard of an African-American family. The father was found vicariously liable for delegating authority over the family premises to his son (by simply saying, "wrap things up"). The Fifth Circuit, however, reversed the trial court's decision:

> Assuming arguendo that [Wayne] was [his father's] agent for the purpose of "wrapping things up" around the [home] on the night of the cross-burning, the record is devoid of facts suggesting Wayne acted within the scope of that authority when he participated in the cross-burning. [His father's] testimony clearly demonstrates that when he told Wayne to "wrap things up," he intended for Wayne to send his friends home. Any suggestion that [the father] gave Wayne authority to construct a large wooden cross [at the father's premises], transport that cross to the home of an African-American family and set it on fire is the height of absurdity. The fact that [the father] knew or should have known of his son's difficulties with alcohol does not alter this analysis; that [the father] may have been negligent in delegating authority over his property to an untrustworthy son does not serve to expand the scope of authority given to encompass unimaginable criminal conduct wholly unrelated to the task assigned.[93]

Not unlike corporations, then, individual principals can be liable (criminally and civilly) for the actions of their agents. And whether the principal is an employer or just an ordinary person is largely immaterial.

YOUR DECISION

1. Judy Smart is a 17-year-old high school junior. One Saturday night, she is drinking beer with a number of her high school friends in the basement of her home. Judy's parents, Bob and Mary Smart, are home at the time. They did not buy the beer the underage minors are consuming but they are aware of the party in their basement. Bob and Mary Smart do nothing to stop the party. On the way home, one intoxicated minor is killed when she drives her car into a ditch. Can Bob and Mary Smart be charged with a crime? Why or why not?

2. Jimmy owns a local liquor store that sells beer, wine, and hard liquor. He hired Gina to work the evening shift as a cashier. Jimmy repeatedly reminded Gina to

---

[92] *MBank El Paso* v. *Sanchez*, 836 S.W.2d 151 (Tex. 1992).
[93] *Ross* v. *Marshall*, 426 F.3d 745 (5th Cir. Tex. 2005), p. 764.

make sure that she asked for identification for anyone who looked to be younger than 30. Gina, however, never carded her customers in order to boost her sales. She was ultimately caught by the police one evening selling a bottle of Jack Daniels to an 18-year-old high school student. Can Jimmy be charged with a crime as a result of Gina's actions? Why or why not?

Summary

- Vicarious liability occurs when one person is held liable for the actions of another—and perhaps when the former person has no idea what the latter person is up to.
- There are two conditions that make vicarious liability different from accomplice liability: (1) it takes only one party's actions to trigger liability and (2) liability *transfers* from one of them to the other.
- Corporate vicarious liability refers to the liability of a corporation, no matter its size, for the criminal conduct of its employees.
- The general rule today is that a corporation is criminally liable for the actions of its agents when (1) those agents act in the official scope of their employment for (2) the benefit of the corporation.
- With individual vicarious liability, one person (instead of a corporation) is held liable for another's behavior. For example, in some states, parents can be held criminally liable for their kids' illegal activities.

Chapter Review

INTRODUCTION TO ACCOMPLICE LIABILITY

Learning Objectives

- Distinguish between complicity and conspiracy.
- Identify the parties to crime, including principals, accomplices, and accessories.

Review Questions

1. Explain how conspiracy differs from complicity.
2. Compare and contrast common law and modern-day parties to a crime.

Key Terms

complicity
accomplice
derivative liability
principal in the first degree

principal in the second degree
accessory before the fact
accessory after the fact
accessory

THE ELEMENTS OF COMPLICITY

Learning Objectives

- Explain the elements of complicity
- Explain the elements of accessory liability.

Review Questions

1. Compare and contrast three means by which assistance is provided in the complicity context.
2. Explain the two levels of *mens rea* for purposes of a complicity.
3. How do the elements of accessory liability differ from the elements of accomplice liability?

Key Terms

natural and probable consequences
   doctrine

COMPLICITY ISSUES, LIMITATIONS, AND DEFENSES

Learning Objectives

- Discuss some of the issues that make complicity law complicated.
- Summarize the limitations of and defenses to accomplice liability.
- Explain the Model Penal Code approach to accomplice liability.

Review Questions

1. What is a non-proxyable offense? Explain.
2. Offer an example of a prinicipal being acquitted and an accomplice being found guilty.
3. Identify two limitations on accomplice liability.
4. Summarize the Model Penal Code's approach to accomplice liability.

Key Terms

non-proxyable offense   ostrich instruction

MODULE **4.4**   ### VICARIOUS LIABILITY

Learning Objectives

- Explain the concept of vicarious liability.
- Distinguish between corporate and individual vicarious liability.

Review Questions

1. Compare and contrast vicarious and accomplice liability.
2. Compare and contrast the two main varieties of vicarious liability.

Key Terms

vicarious liability   *respondeat superior*
corporate vicarious liability   deferred prosecution agreement

Chapter Synthesizing Questions

1. Compare and contrast modern complicity law with the common law approach.
2. Identify and describe two factors that complicate complicity.
3. Explain the defenses to complicity.
4. Compare and contrast complicity and vicarious liability. Why are both presented in the same chapter?

INCHOATE CRIMES

INTRODUCTION TO INCHOATE CRIMES: ATTEMPT

Learning Objectives

- **Explain the concept of inchoate crimes.**
- **Explain the relationship of attempt to the substantive offense.**
- **Summarize what constitutes attempt.**
- **Summarize the defenses to charges of attempt.**

CORE CONCEPTS

inchoate crime A crime that has not been completed. The three inchoate offenses are attempt, conspiracy, and solicitation.

An **inchoate crime** is one that is "partial; unfinished; begun, but not completed."[1] Inchoate crimes are also considered "incipient," meaning they often lead to one or more other crimes. Yet even though they are "incomplete," inchoate crimes are offenses in themselves. In other words, a person can be convicted of an inchoate crime even if he does not actually complete the crime he intended to commit. One who *attempts* a robbery can be found guilty of attempted robbery. Likewise, one who attempts to kill another can be found guilty of attempted murder.

Why punish people for uncompleted crimes? There are several reasons:

- Untold numbers of crimes are started or set in motion, but never completed. But just because they are not completed, should we turn a blind eye?

- It would be unfair to let an otherwise guilty person go free simply because she failed to complete the intended crime.

- Penalizing "incomplete" crime allows the criminal justice system to be more proactive instead of reactive; without being able to prosecute certain offenders for what they *plan* or *try* to do, we would be forced to wait around until the damage was already done.

This module introduces the crime of attempt. The next module introduces conspiracy and solicitation. While attempt, conspiracy, and solicitation get most of the attention as far as inchoate crimes go, there are other crimes that we introduce in later chapters that can also be considered inchoate. Assault (Chapter 6) is a good example. Assault is a widely misunderstood offense because uninformed observers liken it to a physical attack. Assault, however, is anything but physical. It is *attempted* or *threatened* battery, the latter consisting of unlawful touching. Viewed this way, assault is an inchoate crime—at least some of the time. There are people who are content merely to threaten others, but often the objective is physical harm. When that is the case, assault is the incipient offense to battery.

---

[1]*Black's Law Dictionary*, 6th ed. (St. Paul, MN: West, 1990), 761.

Attempt

attempt An inchoate offense in which the defendant has the specific intent to commit the underlying offense and takes some action in furtherance of that intent, but is unsuccessful in completing the crime.

Attempt is the "intent to commit a crime coupled with an act taken toward committing the offense."[2] There are four elements of attempt to commit a crime:

- "... intent to commit it,
- an overt act toward its commission,
- failure of consummation,
- and the apparent possibility of commission."[3]

The first two elements are basically the *mens rea* and *actus reus* of attempt, respectively. We devote detailed treatment to each of them shortly. The last two elements—failure of consummation and the apparent possibility of commission—are self-explanatory. If the crime is consummated, or completed, then it is no longer just an attempt. "Apparent possibility" just refers to the possibility that the offender could have attempted the crime. If, for example, a defendant is charged with attempted burglary but was nowhere near the scene of the crime, then it is not apparent that he could have committed the offense. This is roughly analogous to an alibi defense. See Figure 5.1 for a summary of the elements of attempt.

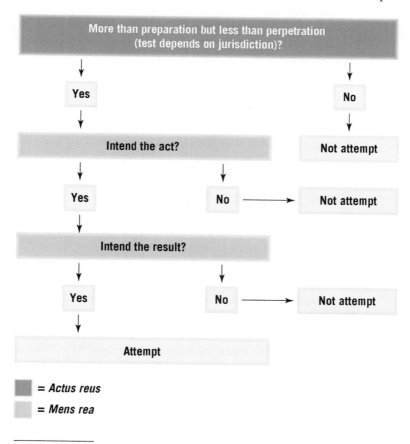

Figure 5.1

Attempt

---

[2]*Black's Law Dictionary*, p. 127.
[3]*State v. Stewart*, 537 S.W.2d 579 (Mo. App. 1976), p. 580.

The Relationship of Attempt to the Substantive Offense

Criminal attempt is, in most instances, "an adjunct crime; it cannot exist by itself, but only in connection with another crime."[4] This does not mean the other crime (e.g., robbery) must be completed, but rather that there is no crime of attempt that is not linked to some other substantive crime. To convict a person of attempt without reference to any other offense would leave one asking, "Attempted what?" If the offender successfully completes the target offense, then he also attempted to commit it. The reverse, of course, is not true; a person who takes a step toward the commission of a substantive offense may not "get there," which is why we have the crime of attempt. To keep it simple, in most jurisdictions a "person is guilty of a criminal attempt when, with intent to commit a crime, the person engages in conduct which constitutes a substantial step toward the commission of that crime whether or not his intention is accomplished."[5]

As a practical matter, one cannot be guilty of both attempt and the completed crime. For example, if a robbery is completed, then attempt is "absorbed" by the completed robbery. More technically, the attempted robbery would be the "lesser included offense" of robbery. If a jury were to convict an offender of both, the Fifth Amendment's double jeopardy provision would be violated because it is unconstitutional to punish a person twice for the same offense. For constitutional purposes, a completed robbery is viewed as the same offense (refer back to Chapter 2 for more on double jeopardy) as attempted robbery.

Jurors, however, can be given the option of convicting an offender of either robbery or attempted robbery. Assume the prosecutor fails to convince the jury that the defendant completed the robbery. In such an event, the jury could fall back on attempt and ensure that the defendant does not go free.

The *Mens Rea* of Attempt

Because an attempt is not a completed crime, it is more difficult to prove *mens rea*. There are two parts of the *mens rea* of attempt, namely to (1) intend the act and (2) intend the result. To intend the act means the offender must intend to commit some sort of overt act toward completion of the offense. As to intending the result, the defendant must also intend for the substantive crime to occur. So, for example, if Brian intends to shoot Larry in the knee but does not intend for Larry to die, Brian has not satisfied the *mens rea* of attempted murder. Brian will likely be convicted of some other crime, however, as he certainly did something illegal (e.g., battery).

Attempt is a specific intent offense (revisit the Chapter 3 discussion on the differences between specific and general intent offenses). This is so even if the target offense is of the general intent variety. For example, "breaking and entering" is a general intent offense; it has no specific *mens rea* requirement. Nevertheless, to be

---

[4]*Lane v. State*, 703 A.2d 180 (Md. 1997), p. 186.
[5]*Townes v. State*, 548 A.2d 832 (Md. 1988), p. 834.

found guilty of *attempted* breaking and entering, the defendant must specifically intend to break and enter. This adds yet another layer of complexity to the *mens rea* of attempt.

Result Crimes

Recall from Chapter 3 that result crimes require actual harm. Murder is the consummate example; without a death, the crime does not occur. Consider *State* v. *Hawkins*,[6] a case in which Gregory Thomas's Chevrolet Astrovan was rear-ended by another van driven by Darnell Hawkins. As soon as his van was hit, Thomas guided it into a nearby hotel parking lot. As he parked, he heard gunshots. He looked over his shoulder and observed Hawkins walking toward him and firing a gun in his direction. As Hawkins neared Thomas's van, Thomas opened the driver's door and raised his hands to show that he was unarmed. Hawkins reached into the van and, with a pistol in one hand, grabbed Thomas, put the pistol to his head and stated, "I'm going to kill you, mother f***er, I'm going to kill you!" Thomas then responded, "You can't kill me. I got three children to raise and my wife is dead, so you can't kill me." Thomas then pushed away Hawkins's hand, at which point Hawkins fired past him into the van. Once he emptied his clip, he returned to his own van to reload, at which point Thomas ran into the hotel lobby to hide. Hawkins then unloaded a second clip of ammunition into Thomas's van. Hawkins was soon apprehended, prosecuted for, and convicted of attempted second-degree murder. An appeals court reversed the conviction, however, noting,

> The evidence shows that the defendant had numerous opportunities to shoot the victim, but did not. He unloaded two clips of ammunition, one of those was while in close proximity to the victim. Although the defendant initially stated that he was going to kill the victim, he then chose to shoot bullets into and around the victim's van. This was indicative of his intent to damage the victim's property, not kill the victim. . . . The defendant held the gun to the victim's head, yet did not shoot, or attempt to shoot him. After the victim pushed away the defendant's hand, the defendant fired past him into the van. Such a firing is evidence of anger, but not an intent to kill someone who is standing less than three feet away. The victim, although shaken, remained unscathed. . . . Viewing the evidence in a light most favorable to the prosecution, no rational trier of fact could conclude that the State proved the essential elements of attempted second degree murder beyond a reasonable doubt.[7]

Hawkins was then found guilty of the lesser included offense of aggravated battery. Why? The *mens rea* was lacking for attempted second-degree murder. Hawkins clearly intended to discharge his weapon. And though he announced his intent to kill Thomas, it is doubtful, as the court noted, that it was his intent to do so.

A similar issue comes up in the context of felony murder. While we will define felony murder more fully in the next chapter, it bears mentioning here that if a person dies during the commission of some nonhomicide felony (e.g., robbery), the offender will be held liable for both crimes. This raises a question: "If a person is injured but not killed during the commission of a felony, can one be found guilty of

---

[6] *State* v. *Hawkins*, 631 So.2d 1288 (La. Ct. App. 1994).
[7] Ibid., p. 1290.

attempted felony murder?" Assume, for example, that George robs a convenience store and demands that the manager, Leroy, open the safe. Leroy swears he cannot get into the safe so George shoots his pistol at it a few times in an effort to force it open. A bullet ricochets off the safe and hits Leroy in the stomach, causing severe injury, but not killing him. Should George be convicted of attempted felony murder? Surely not, because there is no evidence that he *intended* to kill.[8] All but two states would take this approach, but Florida and Arkansas do not. In Florida, for example, attempted felony murder occurs when a person "commits, aids or abets an intentional act that is not an essential element of the felony and that could, but does not, cause the death of another."[9]

What about manslaughter? Although we give manslaughter more attention in the next chapter, we have to ask here, "Can one be convicted of attempted manslaughter?" In general, manslaughter consists of either an unintentional killing or a killing that takes place in the "heat of passion." Assume, for example, that a husband and wife have consumed several drinks and entered into a heated argument. Then assume the husband kills his wife during the course of the argument. This is arguably an example of manslaughter because even though the husband kills his wife, he did so in the heat of passion. In contrast, assume a speeding motorist accidentally hits and kills a pedestrian. The motorist would also be guilty of manslaughter, but the killing was unintentional. So which offender could be held liable for *attempted* manslaughter if the victim does not die? The husband could be held liable because his actions were voluntary.[10] The motorist, however, could not be convicted of attempted manslaughter if the pedestrian did not die. Why? It is safe to assume the motorist did not *intend* for the pedestrian to die, so to hold the motorist criminally liable for attempted manslaughter would mean that someone can intend to commit an involuntary act, which is a legal impossibility. This was further explained by the Florida Supreme Court in *Taylor* v. *State*:

> [T]here may be a crime of attempted manslaughter. We reiterate, however, that a verdict for attempted manslaughter can be rendered only if there is proof that the defendant had the requisite intent to commit an unlawful act. This holding necessitates that a distinction be made between the crimes of "manslaughter by act or procurement" and "manslaughter by culpable negligence." For the latter, there can be no corresponding attempt crime. This conclusion is mandated by the fact that there can be no intent to commit an unlawful act when the underlying conduct constitutes culpable negligence. On the other hand, when the underlying conduct constitutes an act or procurement, such as an aggravated assault, there is an intent to commit the act and, thus, there exists the requisite intent to support attempted manslaughter.[11]

To summarize, the *mens rea* for attempt in the result crime context must "match up" with the result. If, in our examples, there is no killing coupled with no intent to kill, then an attempted murder or manslaughter conviction is unlikely. The same would seem to extend to other crimes. If the defendant does not *intend* the result, then he or she cannot (with the possible exception of a failed manslaughter committed in the heat of passion) be convicted of attempting it.

---

[8]See, e.g., *State* v. *Robinson*, 883 P.2d 764 (Kan. 1994).
[9]Fla. Stat. ch. Section 782.051(1) (2008).
[10]See, e.g., *Cox* v. *State*, 534 A.2d 1333 (Md. 1988).
[11]*Taylor* v. *State*, 444 So.2d 931 (Fla. 1983), p. 934.

Conduct Crimes

Recall from Chapter 3 that conduct crimes do not require any end result, just the conduct in question. Presumably, it would be easier to hold someone liable for an attempted conduct crime because there is no requirement that the defendant desire some end result apart from the criminal act itself. As Dressler has argued, "[T]here is no logical reason why a person should not be convicted of an attempt to commit such a conduct crime, as long as she possesses the specific intent to engage in the conduct which, if performed, constitutes the substantive offense."[12]

The *Actus Reus* of Attempt

There is no uniformly accepted definition of *actus reus* for the crime of attempt. There are two reasons for this. First, the *actus reus* of attempt falls somewhere between "preparation" and "perpetration."[13] But deciding where preparation ends and perpetration begins is rather difficult, especially since no one crime is the same as the next. Second, there is a greater inclination to find intent when the substantive offense is of the serious variety. For example, if a murder fails, most would agree that holding the offender accountable for attempted murder is desirable. However, if a petty theft fails, would there be much point in going to the ends of the earth to convict someone of attempting the crime? Probably not.

The courts have formulated a number of tests for gauging the presence of *actus reus* in attempt crimes. They are not unlike the tests for insanity we will introduce in Chapter 9, each state is free to adopt whichever test they prefer. They are complex, they overlap to some extent, and they still leave unanswered the core question at hand: What is the *actus reus* of attempt? There simply is no clear answer; the tests merely offer some guidance. Dressler calls attention to six such tests: the "last act" test, the "physical proximity" test, the "dangerous proximity" test, the "indispensable element" test, the "probable desistance" test, and the "unequivocality" test.[14] Let's us briefly consider each one (See Figure 5.2 for a summary of the various tests).

The "Last Act" Test

According to the "last act" test, the *actus reus* of attempt is satisfied once the defendant has committed the last act necessary to complete the target crime. This test is advantageous because it is basically "black and white." Unfortunately, however, to wait until the very last moment undermines the intent of criminalizing attempt. As one court put it, "[T]he law of attempts would be largely without function if it could not be invoked until the trigger was pulled, the blow struck, or the money seized."[15] For this reason, there is a preference to move back in time from the completed crime to some earlier act.

---

[12]J. Dressler, *Understanding Criminal Law*, 5th ed. (San Francisco, CA: Lexis-Nexis, 2009), p. 394.
[13]Ibid., p. 396.
[14]Ibid., pp. 398–402.
[15]*People* v. *Dillon*, 668 P.2d 697 (Cal. 1983), p. 703.

In order to satisfy the *actus reus* of attempt, the defendant needs to cross the line from preparation to actually attempting to commit the crime.

Lisa S./Shutterstock

The "Physical Proximity" Test

According to this test, the *actus reus* of attempt is satisfied once the offender is *nearly able* to commit the target crime. Moreover, the offender must be physically close to the intended victim, hence the test's name. A few court decisions have offered explicit definitions of physical proximity. For example, the defendant's action "must go so far that it would result, or apparently result in the actual commission of the crime it was designed to effect, if not extrinsically hindered or frustrated by extraneous circumstances."[16]

There is a problem with the physical proximity test, however. It is possible for an attempt crime to occur when the defendant is nowhere close to the victim. For example, a person could use the Internet and attempt to take money from another's account without any requirement that the first person be in close physical proximity to the victim. A similar issue came up in *Commonwealth* v. *Kelley*,[17] a case in which two men, Kelley and Phillips, tricked a third man, Robinson, into taking $400 in cash out of his own bank account. Before the cash was taken out, an observant teller let Robinson know what was happening, so the crime was never completed. Importantly, Kelley and Phillips were not at Robinson's side as he tried to withdraw the money. They were subsequently arrested and convicted of attempted larceny. Interestingly, however, an appeals court reversed the convictions, highlighting the limitations of the physical proximity test. The court noted,

> Whether Kelley and Phillips intended by some method, at some time and at some place to secure possession of a part, if not all, of the $400.00 which Robinson intended to withdraw from his account may be assumed but it is a matter of pure conjecture. Conjecture is not a substitute for evidence and a conviction based thereon must be set aside.[18]

---

[16]*Commonwealth* v. *Kelley*, 58 A.2d 375 (Pa. Super. Ct. 1948), p. 377.
[17]Ibid.
[18]Ibid., p. 377.

Had a different test been relied on, one that did not require physical proximity of the offenders to the victim, a different result would have been likely.

The "Dangerous Proximity" Test

According to this test, the *actus reus* of intent is satisfied once the individual's conduct is in "dangerous proximity to success."[19] Alternatively, an attempt is said to occur when the act "is so near to the result that the danger of success is very great."[20] The dangerous proximity test does not require physical proximity, only a high degree of likelihood that the target offense will be completed. For example, in *People* v. *Rizzo*,[21] four men, two of whom were armed, rode about in their car looking for a fifth man, Charles Rao, who was carrying $1,200 in payroll cash that they intended to rob him of. Before they found Rao, two police officers were alerted to their behavior and began following them. The men never found Rao. Soon thereafter they were arrested and convicted of attempted robbery in the first degree. Applying the test, a New York appeals court reversed Rizzo's conviction and ordered a new trial. The court's logic was as follows:

> [T]hese defendants had planned to commit a crime and were looking around the city for an opportunity to commit it, but the opportunity fortunately never came. Men would not be guilty of an attempt at burglary if they had planned to break into a building and were arrested while they were hunting about the streets for the building not knowing where it was. Neither would a man be guilty of an attempt to commit murder if he armed himself and started out to find the person whom he had planned to kill but could not find him. So here these defendants were not guilty of an attempt to commit robbery in the first degree when they had not found or reached the presence of the person they intended to rob.[22]

Because the men were not in "dangerous proximity" to completing the crime, they were not guilty of attempt.

The "Indispensable Element" Test

The "indispensable element" test looks not at proximity to crime completion, but rather at what, if anything, is *lacking* such that the crime could not be completed. The test focuses on whether the defendant has control of everything that he or she needs to complete the crime. For example, in *State* v. *Addor*,[23] the defendants apparently intended to manufacture illegal liquor, but they lacked a still. Since the still was an indispensable element (liquor could not be made without it), the men were not guilty of attempting to manufacture illegal liquor.

The "Probable Desistance" Test

This test looks at the likelihood of the offender stopping once the wheels have been set in motion. The American Law Institute (which wrote the Model Penal Code)

---

[19] *Hyde* v. *United States*, 225 U.S. 347 (1912), p. 388.
[20] *People* v. *Rizzo*, 158 N.E. 888 (N.Y. 1927), p. 889.
[21] Ibid.
[22] Ibid., pp. 889–890.
[23] *State* v. *Addor*, 110 S.E. 650 (N.C. 1922).

came up with this test, noting that attempt occurs when "the actor…reached a point where it was unlikely that he would have voluntarily desisted from his effort to commit the crime."[24] Understood differently, the probable desistance test looks at the proverbial "point of no return." If the offender reaches it, but fails to complete the target offense, attempt occurs. The Wisconsin Supreme Court put it this way: "The defendant's conduct must pass that point where most men, holding such an intention as the defendant holds, would think better of their conduct and desist."[25] Unfortunately, it is difficult for juries to draw conclusions about the offender's subjective motivations. It is rarely clear to anyone exactly what is going on in the defendant's head, making this test somewhat limited.

The "Unequivocality" Test

Simply put, the unequivocality test (also called the *res ipsa loquiter* test, which is Latin for "the act speaks for itself") holds that attempt occurs when it is no longer ambiguous to an ordinary person what the would-be offender intends. That is, attempt occurs "when it becomes clear what the actor's intention is and when the acts done show that the perpetrator is actually putting his plan into action."[26] As with the rest of the tests, this one is also ambiguous. It may not always be clear when an individual intends to commit a crime.

The Model Penal Code "Substantial Step" Test

We summarize the Model Penal Code's approach to attempt later in this chapter, but its "substantial step" test is relevant here. For an attempt to occur, a substantial step must be undertaken and it must strongly corroborate the defendant's criminal purpose. Examples of a "substantial step" include "lying in wait," "enticing or seeking to entice" the intended victim to a particular location, and unlawfully entering a structure in which the intended crime is to occur.[27]

Last Act	The offender committed the last act necessary to complete the target crime
Physical Proximity	The offender is "nearly able" to complete the crime
Dangerous Proximity	The offender's conduct is in "dangerous proximity to success"
Indispensable Element	The offender has control of everything necessary to complete the crime
Probable Desistance	Unlikely the offender will stop his activities towards commission of the crime
Unequivocality	A normal law abiding citizen views the offender's actions as criminal
MPC Substantial Step	Offender takes a substantial step that corroborates the criminal purpose

Figure 5.2
Various Tests for the
Actus Reus of Attempt

[24]American Law Institute, Comment to Section 5.01.
[25]*Berry* v. *State*, 280 N.W.2d 204 (Wis. 1979), p. 209.
[26]*People* v. *Staples*, 6 Cal. App. 3d 61 (1970), p. 67.
[27]See Model Penal Code, Section 5.01(2)(a)-(d).

Defenses to Attempt

One who is charged with a crime of attempt can assert almost any criminal defense (which are outlined in Chapter 9). There are, however, two defenses that are unique to attempt: impossibility and abandonment. Both are similar to accomplice liability defenses that we discussed in the last chapter, but they operate somewhat differently in the attempt context.

Impossibility

In some situations, it is impossible for a defendant to have committed the attempt crime in question. For example, if an adult male enters an Internet chat room and carries on a discussion with someone who he thinks is an underage female but is actually a law enforcement officer, then he sends obscene photographs of himself to the undercover officer, can he be guilty of attempted distribution of obscene materials to a minor? The answer is not cut-and-dried, but clearly the person who received the images in our hypothetical was not a minor.[28] Such is the essence of the defense of impossibility.

factual impossibility Extraneous circumstances prevent the defendant from completing the intended crime.

legal impossibility A defense to the crime of attempt. The action the defendant intends to perform is not a crime, even if completed.

The courts recognize two types of impossibility. **Factual impossibility** occurs when "extraneous circumstances unknown to the actor or beyond his control prevent consummation of the intended crime."[29] A classic example of this is when a person reaches into the pocket of another to steal a wallet, but there is no wallet in the pocket.[30] **Legal impossibility** "is said to occur where the intended acts, even if completed, would not amount to a crime."[31] Legal impossibility exists when:

1. The motive, desire, and expectation are to perform an act in violation of the law;
2. There is intention to perform a physical act;
3. There is a performance of the intended physical act; and
4. The consequence resulting from the intended act does not amount to a crime.[32]

Some examples of legal impossibility include:

1. If a married man forcibly has intercourse with a woman whom he believes to be his wife's twin sister, but who in fact is his wife, he is not guilty of rape because his intent was to have intercourse with the woman he attacked, who was in fact his wife.

2. If A takes an umbrella which he believes to belong to B, but which in fact is his own, he does not have the intent to steal, his intent being to take the umbrella he grasps in his hand, which is his own umbrella.

3. If a man, mistaking a dummy in female dress for a woman, tries to ravish it, he does not have the intent to commit rape since the ravishment of an inanimate object cannot be rape.

---

[28]See, e.g., *People* v. *Thousand*, 631 N.W.2d 694 (Mich. 2001).
[29]*United States* v. *Berrigan*, 482 F.2d 171 (3rd Cir. 1973), p. 188.
[30]Ibid.
[31]Ibid.
[32]Ibid.

4. If a man mistakes a stump for his enemy and shoots at it, notwithstanding his desire and expectation to shoot his enemy, his intent is to shoot the object aimed at, which is the stump.[33]

Legal impossibility is often regarded as a defense to attempt, while factual impossibility is not. If, for example, a person commits an act thinking it is illegal when it is not, this is the textbook case of legal impossibility. Because there is no law criminalizing the act, it is *legally* impossible for it to occur. More difficult is the situation in which the intended result is a criminal act, but the actor's actions fall short. In an early case, *Wilson v. State*,[34] Wilson was prosecuted for and convicted of forgery because he added a "1" to the amount on a check written to him for $2.50, making it $12.50. However, he did not alter the *writing* on the check. Under existing law at the time, he altered an "immaterial" part of the check; for forgery to have occurred, he must have also altered the written part, changing it from "Two and 50/100" to "Twelve and 50/100"—or similar. As such, his conviction was overturned.

More difficult is what Dressler calls "hybrid legal impossibility."[35] This occurs when the accused makes a factual mistake about the legal status of some detail of the crime. The classic example is when a person shoots a corpse, thinking it is alive.[36] The *factual* mistake is thinking the corpse is a living, breathing person. The *legal* mistake is basically the same, because to be convicted of homicide, the key requirement is that a "human being" be killed. In cases like this, to keep things simple, courts will default to factual instead of legal impossibility and deny the defense. The reason should be clear. In our example, a person who shoots a corpse thinking it is a living person is someone who is intent on killing another person; to clear that person of any wrongdoing would undermine efforts to criminalize attempted wrongdoing.

Factual impossibility, on the other hand, is generally not regarded as a defense to the crime of attempt. For example, just because an abortionist (assuming abortion is illegal in the jurisdiction in question) attempts to remove the fetus from a nonpregnant woman, should we absolve that person of all guilt? Clearly there was intent to commit the crime.[37] Alternatively, if a would-be killer points a gun at his intended victim, pulls the trigger, and then realizes it is not loaded, should he cleared of any wrongdoing? Probably not, as he certainly had the intent—and tried—to kill.[38] What if, however, a would-be terrorist tries to bring down a skyscraper with a firecracker? Would it be sensible to find him guilty of an attempt crime? According to at least one state (Minnesota), the answer is no. Minnesota recognizes a defense of **inherent impossibility**, which is a form of factual impossibility. If the actor "uses means which a reasonable person would view as completely inappropriate to the objectives sought,"[39] that person can

Inherent impossibility A defense to a crime of attempt in which the means the defendant employs to complete the crime are completely implausible and inappropriate.

---

[33]Ibid., p. 35.
[34]*Wilson v. State*, 38 So. 46 (Miss. 1905).
[35]Dressler, *Understanding Criminal Law*, p. 408.
[36]*State v. Taylor*, 133 S.W.2d 336 (Mo. 1939).
[37]See, e.g., *State v. Moretti*, 244 A.2d 499 (N.J. 1968).
[38]See, e.g., *State v. Damms*, 100 N.W.2d 592 (Wis. 1960).
[39]*State v. Logan*, 656 P.2d 777 (Kan. 1983), p. 779.

successfully assert a factual impossibility defense. But the courts in every other state take the opposite approach, which the Nevada Supreme Court summarized in this way:

> [E]ven though the actual commission of the substantive crime is impossible because of circumstances unknown to the defendant, he is guilty of an attempt if he has the specific intent to commit the substantive offense, and under the circumstances, as he reasonably sees them, he does the acts necessary to consummate what would be the attempted crime. It is only when the results intended by the actor, if they happened as envisaged by him, would fail to consummate a crime, then and only then, would his actions fail to constitute an attempt.[40]

See the accompanying Court Decision for more on the defense of factual impossibility. In it we take a look at the case of *People* v. *Dlugash*. The central issue in the case concerns whether the victim was already dead when Defendant Dlugash shot him multiple times in the head and face.

COURT DECISION

The Logic behind the Defense of Factual Impossibility

People v. Dlugash
363 N.E.2d 1155 (N.Y. 1977)

Decision: Factual impossibility is not a defense to the charge of attempted murder. Dlugash may be convicted of attempted murder even though the victim may have already been dead by the hands of another when Dlugash fired the shots.

Reasoning: . . . The most intriguing attempt cases are those where the attempt to commit a crime was unsuccessful due to mistakes of fact or law on the part of the would-be criminal. A general rule developed in most American jurisdictions that legal impossibility is a good defense but factual impossibility is not. Thus, for example, it was held that defendants who shot at a stuffed deer did not attempt to take a deer out of season, even though they believed the dummy to be a live animal. The court stated that there was no criminal attempt because it was no crime to "take" a stuffed deer, and it is no crime to attempt to do that which is legal. State v. Guffey, 262 S.W.2d 152 (Mo.App.). These cases are illustrative of legal impossibility. A further example is Francis Wharton's classic hypothetical involving Lady Eldon and her French lace. Lady Eldon, traveling in Europe, purchased a quantity of French lace at a high price, intending to smuggle it into England without payment of the duty. When discovered in a customs search, the lace turned out to be of English origin, of little value and not subject to duty. The traditional view is that Lady Eldon is not liable for an attempt to smuggle.

On the other hand, factual impossibility was no defense. For example, a man was held liable for attempted murder when he shot into the room in which his target

(continued)

---

[40]*Darnell* v. *State*, 92 Nev. 680 (1976), pp. 681–682.

usually slept and, fortuitously, the target was sleeping elsewhere in the house that night. Although one bullet struck the target's customary pillow, attainment of the criminal objective was factually impossible. State v. Moretti, 52 N.J. 182, presents a similar instance of factual impossibility. The defendant agreed to perform an abortion, then a criminal act, upon a female undercover police investigator who was not, in fact, pregnant. The court sustained the conviction, ruling that "when the consequences sought by a defendant are forbidden by the law as criminal, it is no defense that the defendant could not succeed in reaching his goal because of circumstances unknown to him." On the same view, it was held that men who had sexual intercourse with a woman, with the belief that she was alive and did not consent to the intercourse, could be charged for attempted rape when the woman had, in fact, died from an unrelated ailment prior to the acts of intercourse. United States v. Thomas, 13 U.S.C.M.A. 278.

. . . In the belief that neither of the two branches of the traditional impossibility arguments detracts from the offender's moral culpability . . . . Thus, a person is guilty of an attempt when, with intent to commit a crime, he engages in conduct which tends to effect the commission of such crime. It is no defense that, under the attendant circumstances, the crime was factually or legally impossible of commission, "if such crime could have been committed had the attendant circumstances been as such person believed them to be." Penal Law, s 110.10. Thus, if defendant believed the victim to be alive at the time of the shooting, it is no defense to the charge of attempted murder that the victim may have been dead.

Turning to the facts of the case before us, we believe that there is sufficient evidence in the record from which the jury could conclude that the defendant believed Geller to be alive at the time defendant fired shots into Geller's head. Defendant admitted firing five shots at a most vital part of the victim's anatomy from virtually point blank range. Although defendant contended that the victim had already been grievously wounded by another, from the defendant's admitted actions, the jury could conclude that the defendant's purpose and intention was to administer the coup de grace . . . The Appellate Division erred in not modifying the judgment to reflect a conviction for the lesser included offense of attempted murder . . .

Abandonment

If a would-be offender abandons his attempt to commit a crime, should he be cleared of any wrongdoing? In general, the answer is no; most courts do not recognize a defense of abandonment in the attempt context. But there are exceptions. For example, if the defendant completely and voluntary has a change of heart, the defense may succeed. Consider the facts as explained by the court in *Pyle* v. *State*:

> At 1:15 p.m. on October 7, 1981, appellant arrived at a residence occupied by Mary McCoy and Sally Sower. Ms. McCoy was his former girlfriend. After he was

invited to enter, he pulled a gun on the women. He ordered Ms. McCoy to wrap and padlock chains around herself. Thereafter, he ordered Ms. McCoy to handcuff Ms. Sowers to a bannister. He then forced Ms. McCoy into his van and drove away with her. Ms. Sowers liberated herself fifteen minutes later and called the police. Meanwhile, appellant spent the next six hours driving to Defiance, Ohio and then back to Fort Wayne, Indiana. During the trip, he repeatedly told Ms. McCoy that if the police stopped the van he would empty six bullets into her head. Eventually, a police car signaled the van to stop. Consequently, appellant exclaimed "we're caught" and proceeded to pull over to the side of the road. Subsequently, he grabbed the gun, said "good bye Mary" and shot her in the chest. He then surrendered to the police.[41]

Mary did not die, but rather suffered a serious wound. The defendant was found guilty of attempted murder. He appealed, claiming that he did not intend, at the last minute, for Mary to die and only wanted to inflict a superficial wound. The court did not buy his argument and affirmed his conviction, noting that he evidenced no "rising revulsion for the harm intended."[42] Likewise, if a would-be offender abandons his attempted crime in the face of victim resistance, he will not succeed with an abandonment defense, as it is not voluntary.[43] For an abandonment claim to succeed, then, the offender must *genuinely and completely* withdraw from his or her efforts to break the law—and convince a jury of it.

YOUR DECISION

1. Joseph is a member of the notorious Crips gang, while Walter is a member of the Arian Brotherhood. These two organizations are often engaged in violent confrontations, often motivated by racial hatred. One evening, Joseph enters an area of the city within the control of the Arian Brotherhood and is attacked by Walter. Joseph survives the encounter but is severely beaten. Joseph suffers a broken nose, broken jaw, severe facial lacerations, and internal bleeding. The prosecutor wants to charge Walter with battery and attempted murder. Walter is challenging the attempted murder charge, claiming he only wanted "to teach Joseph a lesson" about trespassing on the Brotherhood's land and never intended to kill him. Is Walter guilty of attempted murder? Why or why not?

2. Tracie Reeves and Molly Coffman, 12-year-old middle school students, decided they wanted to kill their homeroom teacher, Janice Geiger. The girls were planning on poisoning Ms. Geiger with rat poison, stealing her car, and driving it to the Smoky Mountains. One morning, Molly Coffman brought a packet of rat poison to school and placed in on Ms. Geiger's desk next to her coffee cup. Ms. Geiger saw the girls at her desk and asked them to return to their seats. Tracie and Molly never put the poison in Ms. Geiger's coffee cup. Tracie and Molly are charged with attempted murder in a jurisdiction that

---

[41]*Pyle v. State*, 476 N.E.2d 124 (Ind. 1985), p. 125.
[42]Ibid., p. 126.
[43]See, e.g., *People v. Cross*, 466 N.W.2d 368 (Mich. Ct. App. 1991).

uses the Model Penal Code's "substantial step test." Are they guilty of attempted murder? Would your answer be the same in a jurisdiction that utilizes the "Last Act" test?

Summary

- An inchoate crime is one that is partial, unfinished, or begun and not completed.
- Inchoate crimes include attempt, conspiracy, and solicitation.
- Criminal attempt is an adjunct crime, meaning it cannot exist by itself.
- There is no crime of attempt that is not linked to some other substantive crime.
- There are two parts of the *mens rea* of attempt, namely to (1) intend the act and (2) intend the result.
- Attempt is a specific intent offense.
- The *mens rea* for attempt in the result crime context must "match up" with the result. For example, if there is no intent to kill, then an attempted murder conviction is unlikely.
- It would be easier to hold someone liable for an attempted conduct crime because there is no requirement that the defendant desire some end result apart from the criminal act itself.
- Multiple tests are used to determine the presence of *actus reus* in the attempt context.
- According to the "last act" test, the *actus reus* of attempt is satisfied once the defendant has committed the last act necessary to complete the target crime.
- According to the "physical proximity" test, the *actus reus* of attempt is satisfied once the offender is *nearly able* to commit the target crime.
- According to the "dangerous proximity" test, the *actus reus* of intent is satisfied once the individual's conduct is in "dangerous proximity to success."
- The "indispensable element" test looks not at proximity to crime completion, but rather at what, if anything, is *lacking* such that the crime could not be completed.
- The "probable desistance" test looks at the likelihood of the offender stopping once the wheels have been set in motion.
- The "unequivocality" test holds that attempt occurs when it is no longer ambiguous what the would-be offender intends.
- The Model Penal Code "substantial step" test holds that attempt occurs when the offender takes a substantial step toward completing the crime and the action strongly corroborates the criminal purpose.
- Legal impossibility is generally a defense to the crime of attempt, while factual impossibility is not.
- Abandonment is sometimes available as a defense in the attempt context. For example, if the defendant completely and voluntary has a change of heart, the defense may succeed.

5.2 CONSPIRACY AND SOLICITATION

Learning Objectives
- **Identify the elements and complications of conspiracy.**
- **Describe the defenses to conspiracy.**
- **Describe solicitation.**
- **Distinguish solicitation from other inchoate crimes.**

CORE CONCEPTS

Conspiracy, the next inchoate crime we consider, generally refers to the act of *planning but not completing* a crime. Conspiracies often involve two or more people and thus tend to resemble some of the accomplice liability situations we introduced in the previous chapter. The key difference, again, is that conspiracies are *plans* or *agreements* to commit one or more specific crimes. This is why conspiracies are considered inchoate crimes. The chapter then wraps up with the introduction to solicitation, another inchoate crime in which one person seeks to have another person commit a crime on his or her behalf.

Conspiracy

conspiracy An inchoate offense in which an agreement is reached to commit a crime.

Conspiracy is a type of inchoate crime, but it also closely resembles complicity because one person (or multiple people) can be held criminally liable for the actions of someone else. Under common law, a **conspiracy** was defined as an agreement between two or more persons to commit a criminal act. The common law's approach was "bilateral," in reference to the minimum requirement that two or more people be involved in the conspiracy. Thus, if one person entered into an agreement with an undercover police officer to break the law, there was no conspiracy because there were not two guilty parties. Modern statutes take a "unilateral" approach, which permits the conviction of *any* person who agrees with another to commit a crime, even if only one party to the agreement breaks the law.

overt act A voluntary action taken by the defendant in furtherance of the crime of conspiracy.

Under common law, nothing other than the agreement was necessary. Under modern statutes, however, it is often required that the prosecutor prove that those who entered into the agreement actually took some step in furtherance of the agreement—called an **overt act**. For example, if Susan and Margie agreed on a plan to kill Mike, this would be conspiracy under common law. If they went one step further and acquired a gun, then this is the "overt act" part of modern conspiracies. There are exceptions to the overt act requirement, however. On the one hand, the Supreme Court has held, with respect to federal drug laws, that an overt act is not necessary for a conspiracy to be completed.[44] On the other hand, some states require

---

[44]*United States v. Shabani*, 513 U.S. 10 (1994).

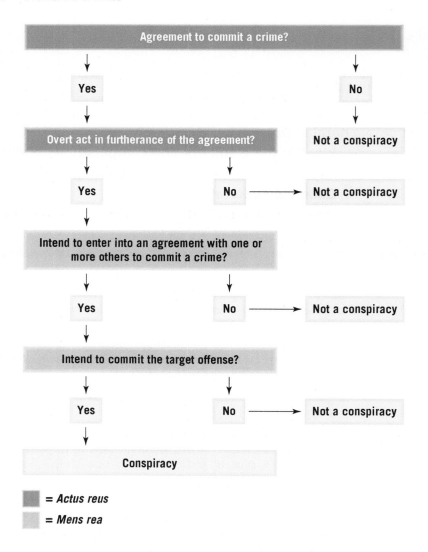

Figure 5.3
Conspiracy

a "substantial act," which is more significant than an "overt act." See Figure 5.3 for a summary of conspiracy.

Distinguishing Complicity from Conspiracy

Students are sometimes confused as to the relationship between complicity and conspiracy. Conspiracy is an inchoate (i.e., incomplete) crime. In other words, conspiracy is an *agreement* to commit a crime, typically combined with some overt act in furtherance of that agreement.

Complicity, by way of reminder, occurs when two or more offenders work together and actually commit a criminal act. A conspiracy could evolve into complicity, but it cannot work the other way around. For example, if Fred and Susan settle on a plan to kill John and then buy the gun they hope to use, they may be found guilty of conspiracy. They would not, however, be complicit, or accomplices in any crime because John has not been killed. If, however, Fred and Susan ultimately kill John, they would both be accomplices to murder regardless of who pulled the trigger (and they could also be convicted of conspiracy because the elements of that offense are satisfied). This is the key difference between complicity and conspiracy.

The rule that complicity (and other noncomplicity) cases are distinct from conspiracy cases is known as the *Pinkerton* **Rule**, from the Supreme Court's decision in *Pinkerton* v. *United States*.[45] In that case, two brothers who conspired to avoid paying taxes were convicted of both conspiracy and tax law violations. They argued that they should have been convicted of one underlying offense. The Supreme Court disagreed. Justice Douglas wrote, "It has been long and consistently recognized by the Court that the commission of the substantive offense of conspiracy to commit it are separate and distinct offenses."[46] The *Pinkerton* Rule is also relevant in conspiracy cases because it means that each party to a conspiracy (an agreement to commit a crime) can be held liable for any reasonably foreseeable crime committed by any coconspirator in furtherance of the agreement.

Pinkerton **Rule** A defendant can be charged both with the crime of conspiracy and the completed offense.

Advantages of Conspiracy Laws

Conspiracy laws exist primarily because criminals often act in collaboration with others. Indeed, there are special dangers associated with group criminality, especially in the realm of organized crime. As it was put in one Supreme Court case, "[T]he strength, opportunities, and resources of many is obviously more dangerous and more difficult to police than the efforts of a lone wrongdoer."[47] Also, conspiracy laws are advantageous in the same way the crime of "attempt" exists; some of the time, it is helpful for authorities to tackle crime without having to wait until the harm is done. Since a big part of conspiracy is an *agreement* to offend, such laws permit earlier intervention and the possibility of disrupting a crime before it is carried through to completion.

Conspiracy laws are also advantageous from a prosecutorial standpoint. The Sixth Amendment states that the accused has the right to trial "by an impartial jury of the state and district wherein the crime shall have been committed." Conspiracies are not necessarily limited to any single locale, so this affords prosecutors the option of choosing a venue for the trial. Also, since all parties to a conspiracy are viewed as having committed the same crime, their trials can be combined into one or very few, which saves resources. But this raises problems of guilt by association. Jurors may find all defendants guilty even if just one clearly is by virtue of their association with one another. In *Krulewitch* v. *United States*, Justice Jackson said this of the guilt by association problem:

> A co-defendant in a conspiracy trial occupies an uneasy seat. There generally will be evidence of wrongdoing by somebody. It is difficult for the individual to make his own case stand on its own merits in the minds of jurors who are ready to believe that birds of a feather are flocked together.[48]

[45]*Pinkerton* v. *United States*, 328 U.S. 640 (1946).
[46]Ibid., p. 643.
[47]*Krulewitch* v. *United States*, 336 U.S. 440 (1949), pp. 448–449.
[48]Ibid., p. 454.

hearsay An out-of-court statement offered as evidence for the truth of the matter asserted.

Conspiracy laws also give prosecutors the advantage of using hearsay evidence, which is typically inadmissible. **Hearsay** is an out-of-court statement offered as evidence for the truth of the matter asserted. The declarant is not on the witness stand; instead the statement is conveyed via someone else who *is* testifying. It is something that is "heard," then "said"—hence the name *hearsay*. Courts prefer to go to the "horse's mouth," which is why hearsay is generally inadmissible. Yet there are many exceptions to this hearsay rule. Conspiracy is one of them. Since each co-conspirator is presumably authorized by other parties to the conspiracy to act on their behalf, hearsay is admissible. But this creates a logical problem. What if hearsay is the only type of evidence available to prove the existence of a conspiracy? Should evidence that is admissible only if a conspiracy exists be used to prove that a conspiracy exists? This has been called **bootstrapping** (a term used in many contexts to refer to a circular self-sustaining process). The Supreme Court, however, resolved it somewhat in *Bourjaily v. United States*,[49] where it held that jurors may indeed use hearsay evidence to decide whether a conspiracy existed. So, despite some of the pitfalls in this area, prosecutors still enjoy considerable advantages by proceeding with conspiracy (rather than individual) charges in certain cases.

bootstrapping A circular, self-sustaining process.

Finally, conspiracy laws offer prosecutors something of a "double whammy." Offenders can be convicted of both conspiracy to commit a crime *and* the crime itself. This, again, is known as the *Pinkerton* Rule.

The core of the crime of conspiracy is an agreement between the parties.

© Old Visuals/Alamy

---

[49]*Bourjaily v. United States*, 483 U.S. 171 (1987).

The *Mens Rea* of Conspiracy

Under common law, conspiracy was a specific intent crime. Today, it is regarded in basically the same fashion. First, the defendant must intend to enter into an agreement with one or more others to commit a crime. Second, the defendant must have intended to commit the target offense. Note the similarity of conspiracy *mens rea* to complicity *mens rea*.

There is some question about what *intent* means. Is it the defendant's conscious objective to commit the target crime? Or is it sufficient if the defendant simply knows it is likely to happen? At the risk of casting too wide a net, courts typically prefer to equate intent with purpose. However, knowledge may suffice. For example, in *Direct Sales Co. v. United States*,[50] the defendant, a drug wholesaler, sold morphine to a physician in quantities 300 times higher than those that would have been required for lawful purposes. The U.S. Supreme Court affirmed his conviction. In another case, defendants who sold sugar to persons they knew were manufacturing illegal whiskey had their convictions affirmed.[51] So while the defendants in these cases may not have intended for customers to break the law, they surely knew what the buyers were doing.

Attendant Circumstances

There is some question about whether, in a conspiracy prosecution, the government must prove that the defendants intended the circumstantial elements (if any) of the targeted crime. This came up in *United States v. Feola*,[52] a case in which several defendants agreed to sell heroin. They then decided to sell powdered sugar to unwitting customers in an effort to boost their profits. And they also agreed that if a buyer caught on to their scam, they would take the individuals' money by force. Unfortunately for the defendants, the buyers were undercover federal law enforcement agents and during the course of the sale, two of the defendants attacked one of the agents. The defendants were convicted of assault on a federal officer and *conspiring* to do the same. The Supreme Court affirmed the first assault charges, as both defendants had the intent to commit the assaultive act. But could their conspiracy charges be affirmed? Could they have *conspired* to assault a federal officer, not knowing that the victim was indeed an officer? The Court answered this question with a surprising "yes":

> This interpretation poses no risk of unfairness to defendants. It is no snare for the unsuspecting. Although the perpetrator of a narcotics "ripoff," such as the one involved here, may be surprised to find that his intended victim is a federal officer in civilian apparel, he nonetheless knows from the very outset that his planned course of conduct is wrongful.[53]

This case was significant because the court decided that the federal conspiracy statute did not require any higher degree of proof toward the circumstantial element

---

[50]*Direct Sales Co. v. United States*, 319 U.S. 703 (1943).
[51]*United States v. Falcone*, 311 U.S. 205 (1940).
[52]*United States v. Feola*, 420 U.S. 671 (1975).
[53]Ibid., p. 685.

(the assault, not the sale) than that required for the underlying offense. That said, the case was not decided on constitutional grounds, meaning that states are still free to set the bar higher.

The "Corrupt Motives" Doctrine

In *People* v. *Powell*,[54] a classic case, county officials bought supplies for the poor without putting a request out for bid, in violation of the law. They took this approach knowingly and did so with the intent of saving the county money. Even so, they were charged with conspiring to commit official misconduct. Their subsequent convictions were reversed because they did not have the "corrupt motives" necessary to sustain the conviction. The court noted, "The agreement must have been entered into with an evil purpose, as distinguished from a purpose simply to do the act prohibited, in ignorance of the prohibition."[55] This **corrupt motives doctrine** is recognized in several states, though not all of them. Also, to the extent the issue of corrupt motives ever comes up, it is usually in the context of *malum prohibitum* rather than *malum in se* crimes. The latter are wrong in themselves, so "evil purpose" is inferred from the act itself.

corrupt motives doctrine
A requirement in some states that defendants have a corrupt motive in order to commit the crime of conspiracy.

The *Actus Reus* of Conspiracy

The *actus reus* of conspiracy consists of two parts. First, and most importantly, there must be an agreement to commit a crime. Second, in a number of states it is also necessary that the parties to the conspiracy commit an "overt act" in furtherance of the agreement. Once again, common law did not require this second *actus reus* element, but modern statutes frequently do.

The Agreement

The agreement to commit a crime between two or more people can take a number of forms. It may be an express agreement. Jim could say to John, "Let's kill Bob." It may also be an unspoken agreement. John could look at Jim, nod his head in Bob's direction, and then be present when Jim kills Bob. Indeed, John may be nowhere around and still be convicted of a crime because he gave an earlier order to Jim that he "take care of Bob." In this instance, a "conspiracy may exist even if a conspirator does not agree to commit or facilitate each and every part of the substantive offense."[56] Assume, for example, that Jim decides to hire his own "hit man" to kill Bob. Even though John is arguably not aware of this, he is a party to a conspiracy because of that simple order to "take care of Bob."

Most conspiracies are relatively secret, at least beyond the parties to the agreement. This, it would seem, could make it difficult for a prosecutor to prove the presence of a conspiracy. After all, how could a prosecutor *prove* the existence of something that no one besides the parties to the agreement knows? Fortunately, the courts are

---

[54]*People* v. *Powell*, 63 N.Y. 88 (1875).
[55]Ibid., p. 91.
[56]*Salinas* v. *United States*, 522 U.S. 52 (1997), p. 63.

quite flexible in terms of the evidence that can be used to prove the existence of an agreement to commit a crime. They have to be, as the alternative would make it exceedingly difficult to prove the presence of a conspiracy. As one court observed, "[B]ecause of the clandestine nature of a conspiracy and the foreseeable difficulty of the prosecution's burden of establishing the conspiracy by direct proof, the courts have permitted broad inferences to be drawn...from evidence of acts, conduct, and circumstances."[57] Hearsay, circumstantial evidence, and the like are admissible. Yet the government must also ensure that defendants' due process rights are not violated in its zeal to prove the presence of conspiratorial agreements.

An example will clarify. *United States* v. *Alvarez*[58] dealt with Manuel Juan Alvarez, a man who was convicted of joining with three other men in a conspiracy to import 110,000 pounds of marijuana into the United States by air from Columbia. He was an underling in the operation and only involved in loading and off-loading the plane used to carry the drugs. He knew why the plane left the United States for Columbia and also knew about the cargo it was going to pick up. Undercover agents who agreed to purchase the drugs even asked him if he would be around to help unload the plane, to which Alvarez nodded and said, "Yes." As soon as the plane was about to leave, Alvarez and two other men were arrested and charged with conspiracy to important illegal drugs into the United States. Alvarez's conviction was reversed by the Fifth Circuit, but later affirmed, noting that

> the aggregate of the evidence is sufficient to infer that Alvarez knew that criminal activity was afoot. It must also have been obvious to him that there was conspiracy to import the contraband because prior planning and concerted action would be required to load the marijuana in Colombia, fly it into this country, and unload it upon its arrival.[59]

All it took was Alvarez's knowledge of the illegal activity to support his conspiracy conviction.

Contrast *Alvarez* with *Commonwealth* v. *Cook*.[60] In that case, two brothers, Maurice and Dennis Cook, were drinking and smoking marijuana at a housing project when they met a 17-year-old woman. The two introduced themselves, engaged in small talk, and invited the woman to walk with them to a convenience store in order to buy cigarettes. While they were walking to the store through a secluded area, the woman tripped and fell, at which point Maurice jumped on top of her, covered her mouth, and took off his belt, handing it to Dennis. Maurice then raped her—and Dennis encouraged him as he was doing so. The victim lost consciousness during the attack, later awoke after the brothers were gone, and then went to a friend's house to report the incident. Both brothers were arrested. Maurice was convicted of rape. Dennis was convicted of conspiring to rape the woman and as an accomplice to rape. An appeals court affirmed his conviction as an accomplice, as it should have, but it reversed his conspiracy conviction:

> The circumstances under which the victim and the Cooks met and socialized were not indicative of a preconceived plan between the defendant and his brother to commit

---

[57]*People* v. *Persinger*, 363 N.E.2d 897 (Ill. App. Ct. 1977), p. 901.
[58]*United States* v. *Alvarez*, 610 F.2d 1250 (5th Cir. 1980), conviction affd., 625 F.2d 1196 (1980) (en banc).
[59]Ibid., p. 1198.
[60]*Commonwealth* v. *Cook*, 411 N.E.2d 1326 (Mass. App. Ct. 1980).

a sexual assault. Rather, the meeting and subsequent engagement were consistent with a chance social encounter common between young persons. The area where the group stayed prior to setting out for the store was used frequently as a gathering spot, and there was no evidence either that the Cooks attempted to conceal from others the fact that they were with the victim or that they consciously attempted to mislead her as to their identities. . . . While openness will not automatically sanitize a conspiracy, highly visible conduct has to be considered inconsistent with the shadowy environment which usually shrouds the crime. The purpose for leaving the area was on its face innocuous and was suggested by Maurice, not the defendant. While the route chosen was arguably suspicious, the evidence established that it also was selected by Maurice, not the defendant. There was evidence that the path provided a short, reasonably direct route to a gasoline station which was nearby, well-lighted, and visible from the crest of the hill. We do not think that the events up to the time the victim fell were sufficient to establish a criminal agreement or to warrant the jury in inferring the state of facts that the Commonwealth claims to have existed.[61]

This case differed from the *Alvarez* case because of the apparently spontaneous nature of the rape; there was no preconceived plan in place.

The Overt Act

The overt act requirement for the *actus reus* of conspiracy is relatively recent in its origins. Not every jurisdiction requires proof of an overt act, but logic for such a requirement is straightforward; it offers evidence that a conspiracy has moved beyond the "talk stage" and is actively being carried out.

There is no requirement that the overt act be illegal. Indeed, it can be perfectly legal. The example we offered at the outset of this section was purchasing a gun. Assuming there is no law against doing so (or the person is barred by law from buying a gun), there is nothing criminal about such an act. There is also no requirement that all parties to a conspiracy commit an overt act. If one party to a larger conspiracy commits the overt act, no other action is necessary.

What exactly is an overt act? In jurisdictions that require an overt act, any act will suffice. No matter how trivial the action, it will meet the overt act requirement. For example, assume Steve and Mary agree to kill Sandy. If Steve calls Sandy to see if she is home, he has committed an overt act taken in furtherance of the agreement. The phone call is far more innocuous than, say, buying a gun. Nevertheless, Steve did *something* in furtherance of the agreement, which is all it takes.

As mentioned at the outset of this section, some jurisdictions require a "substantial act" or a "substantial step" in lieu of an overt act.[62] For example, Washington State's conspiracy statute reads, in part, that "[a] person is guilty of criminal conspiracy when, with intent that conduct constituting a crime be performed, he or she agrees with one or more persons to engage in or cause the performance of such conduct, and any one of them takes a substantial step in pursuance of such agreement."[63]

---

[61]Ibid., p. 1329.
[62]See, e.g., Maine Rev. Stat. Ann. tit. 17-A (West 2006), Section 151.4; Wash. Rev. Code Ann. Section 9A.28.040 (West 2006).
[63]Wash. Rev. Code Ann. Section 9A.28.040 (West 2006), Section (1).

Just what, then, is a *substantial step*? One court defined it as conduct that is "strongly corroborative of the actor's criminal purpose."[64] Moreover, the substantial step "need not be the last proximate act prior to the consummation of the offense."[65] This definition is clearly subjective, meaning that courts decide what constitutes a substantial step on a case-by-case basis. For example, in *State v. Sunderland*, the defendant, who mistakenly believed that an off-duty police officer was the person who previously threatened him, pointed a shotgun in the officer's direction and threatened to "blow [his] head off." This action constituted a substantial step in furtherance of the crime.[66] On the other hand, some jurisdictions have deemed preparatory acts, such as casing a building, substantial steps.[67] Clearly there is much room for interpretation.

Conspiracy Complications

No one conspiracy is the same as the next, which can make prosecuting one more than a little interesting. Conspiracies can get rather complicated because of the number of people involved, the scope of the agreement, the length of the agreement, and the purpose of the conspiracy, among other issues. In this section, we briefly touch on some of the issues (and cases involving them) that complicate the identification and prosecution of conspiracies.

Types of Conspiracies

Two of the most difficult questions facing prosecutors are (1) who is involved in the conspiracy and (2) how many conspiracies are there? These questions are important because their answers can help prosecutors decide on the proper venue in which to try the case, whether joint trials are warranted, what offenses the parties can be liable for, and so on. On the one hand, there may be one conspiracy with multiple criminal objectives.[68] For example, three friends may agree to rob a bank each day for a week. On the other hand, there may be multiple agreements to commit a single crime. A and B might agree today to kill X two days from now. C and D may agree tomorrow to kill X the next day. There are two conspiracies but one criminal outcome. These examples are simple, but reality can get rather tedious.

In *Kotteakos v. United States*,[69] 32 defendants were charged and convicted of participating in a *single* conspiracy with Simon Brown to fraudulently obtain loans. The defendants argued that they had each formed separate conspiracies with Mr. Brown. Why? Under the government's approach, each defendant could be punished for participating in 32 separate criminal acts. Under their approach, each would be punished for a single conspiracy and be spared a considerable amount of prison

---

[64]*State v. Brooks*, 44 Ohio St. 3d 185 (1989), p. 191.
[65]Ibid.
[66]*State v. Sunderland* (Dec. 19, 1985), Cuyahoga App. No. 49950, unreported. For more details, see *State v. Brooks*, 44 Ohio St. 3d 185 (1989).
[67]See, e.g., *United States v. Permenter*, 969 F.2d 911 (10th Cir. 1992).
[68]*Braverman v. United States*, 317 U.S. 49 (1942).
[69]*Kotteakos v. United States*, 328 U.S. 750 (1946).

Figure 5.4

Example of Spoke and Wheel Conspiracy

spoke and wheel conspiracy A type of large-scale conspiracy in which one central actor (the hub) has control of all of the aspects of the conspiracy, while the other members of the conspiracy (the spokes) have control of only one aspect.

chain conspiracy A type of large-scale conspiracy in which the individuals at one end of the conspiracy are not aware of the individuals at the other end.

time. The Supreme Court sided with the defendants, concluding that although the crimes were similar, the defendants did not know one another and thus could not have conspired together to obtain the loans. Prosecutors hoped to prove that Brown's was a so-called **spoke and wheel conspiracy** (see Figure 5.4) because they viewed Brown as the hub, the spokes as each of the 32 defendants, and the rim as the connection between each spoke. The Supreme Court decided that the rim was absent because there was no connection between each defendant. Perhaps more aptly, this conspiracy should have been called a "hub and spoke" conspiracy.

Contrast *Kotteakos* with *Interstate Circuit, Inc. v. United States*.[70] In that case, the manager of a chain of theaters conspired with eight movie distributors to fix prices, in violation of the Sherman Antitrust Act. Each distributor was copied on the correspondence to the others so that each knew precisely what was happening. The Supreme Court upheld the convictions, concluding, "It is elementary that an unlawful conspiracy may be and often is formed without simultaneous action or *agreement* on the part of the conspirators."[71] The defendants in this case completed the wheel; the connection between each was analogous to the rim of a wheel. Each defendant was a spoke—and each of the eight spokes was connected via a rim (the awareness on the part of each what was happening).

Sometimes prosecutors are faced with a **chain conspiracy** (Figure 5.5). The hallmark of a chain conspiracy is a linear connection in time, which is typically seen in large-scale illegal drug cases. For example, A's criminal conduct precedes B's, which precedes C's. These are typically the easiest conspiracies for prosecutors to prove. In *Blumenthal* v. *United States*,[72] one person sent shipments of liquor to Weiss and

---

[70]*Interstate Circuit, Inc.* v. *United States*, 306 U.S. 208 (1939).
[71]Ibid., p. 227, emphasis added.
[72]*Blumenthal* v. *United States*, 332 U.S. 539 (1947).

Figure 5.5
Example of a Chain Conspiracy

wheel and chain conspiracy A type of large-scale conspiracy that has attributes of both the spoke and wheel and chain type conspiracies.

Goldsmith who, in turn, agreed with three other defendants to sell liquor to various taverns at inflated prices, in violation of price cap laws. The Supreme Court affirmed the conspiracy convictions of all six defendants. It likened each one of them to links in a chain. If, for example, Weiss and Goldsmith did not participate, the chain would have been broken.

Courts have also recognized more complex **wheel and chain conspiracies**, which contain elements of both wheels and chains. *United States* v. *Bruno*[73] dealt with four groups, one of which imported drugs into the country (Group 1) and sold them to middlemen (Group 2). The middlemen then distributed the drugs to two groups of retailers in New York (Group 3) and Louisiana (Group 4). Each group was regarded as a wheel yet also connected together in time via a chain (the distributors first sold to the middlemen, then the middlemen sold drugs to the retailers). The convictions were affirmed.

The Length of the Agreement

There is always a time dimension to conspiracies, which begs the question, "How long does a conspiracy last?" Under common law, a conspiracy ended when all of its objectives were accomplished. Even today, once all the objectives are completed, the clock starts ticking on the statute of limitations, meaning that if prosecutors do not move soon enough, they will not be able to secure conspiracy convictions. This has prompted some prosecutors to get rather creative in terms of *extending* the time frame over which a conspiracy presumably runs. In *Krulewitch* v. *United States*,[74] a case introduced earlier on in this chapter, the government argued that the parties to a conspiracy continually sought to conceal their identities, even after the conspiracy's criminal objectives were accomplished. They then sought to introduce hearsay evidence, the out-of-court statement of one conspirator, to convict another conspirator several months after the crime. The Supreme Court decided that such evidence is inadmissible because the conspiracy terminated with the commission of the criminal act. There are exceptions to this rule, but they are exceedingly rare.[75] The common law rule thus remains more or less intact.

The Purpose of the Conspiracy

Just as there can be some confusion over when a conspiracy begins and ends, or how many people or conspiracies are involved, there can be some confusion over the very purpose of a conspiracy. It is important to clear up any such confusion, as it bears directly on what punishments are available. Assume that, in one agreement, Alex and Brock decide to commit a robbery today and a burglary tomorrow. Then assume that, *as an alternative*, they agree to commit only the robbery, one today and one tomorrow. Does the ordering of events in either instance bear on whether they will

---

[73]*United States* v. *Bruno*, 105 F.2d 921 (2nd Cir.), revd. on other grounds, 308 U.S. 287 (1939).
[74]*Krulewitch* v. *United States*, 336 U.S. 440 (1949).
[75]See, e.g., *State* v. *Rivenbark*, 311 Md. 147 (1987).

be convicted for conspiracy? And does it matter whether one agreement resulted in multiple and distinct criminal acts or repeated counts of the same offense? The Supreme Court offered an answer to these questions in *Braverman* v. *United States*[76]:

> [T]he precise nature and extent of the conspiracy must be determined by reference to the agreement which embraces and defines its objects. Whether the object of a single agreement is to commit one or many crimes, it is in either case that agreement which constitutes the conspiracy which the statute punishes. The one agreement cannot be taken to be several agreements and hence several conspiracies because it envisages the violation of several statutes rather than one.[77]

In other words, it is basically immaterial whether two or more people agreed to break two laws or break one law multiple times. The lynchpin is the agreement. In our examples, there was one agreement. Had Alex and Brock entered into separate agreements, then they might have been guilty of more than one conspiracy. Consider these two agreements:

Agreement 1. Rob a person today, burglarize a house tomorrow.

Agreement 2. Rob a person today, rob another person tomorrow.

Assuming Alex and Brock entered into both of these agreements *separately* and one was not an alternative to another, then each is guilty of participation in two distinct conspiracies. Needless to say, deciding whether two or more agreements were made can be difficult for prosecutors. As a result, they often place emphasis on the first agreement and treat it as the one that *implicitly* incorporated any other criminal objectives.

Conspiracy Defenses

There are four defenses to conspiracy. As you will recall from earlier in the chapter, two of them—abandonment and impossibility—are also defenses to attempt. The others—withdrawal and Wharton's Rule—are somewhat unique to conspiracy. We briefly look at each in the following subsections.

Abandonment

Since the essence of conspiracy is an agreement, once the agreement is made, the proverbial horse has already left the barn. In other words, once a crime has been committed, it cannot be "undone."[78] For this reason, there is usually no abandonment defense to a conspiracy charge. This is true regardless of whether an overt act is a requirement for a conspiracy conviction. That said, abandonment *may* work as something of a defense to charges for subsequent crimes arising from a conspiratorial agreement; if one party to a conspiracy withdraws and then finds him or herself charged with conspiracy for crimes committed after such withdrawal, then the defense may succeed.

---

[76]*Braverman* v. *United States*, Ibid.
[77]Ibid., p. 53.
[78]*United States* v. *Rogers*, 102 F.3d 641 (1st Cir. 1996), p. 644.

The Model Penal Code calls this defense "renunciation."[79] For it to apply, two conditions must be met. First, the defendant must have "thwarted the success of the conspiracy." Second, the abandonment must have been "complete and voluntary." For example, if Larry is a party to a murder conspiracy with Frank and tells police that he can no longer "see it through," he may succeed with the defense if the police are able to prevent Frank (such as by arresting him) from committing the crime. If the agreement was for any other crime than murder, and if Larry's decision to contact police still did not stop the intended crime, then the clock on the statute of limitations would begin running for Larry, but not for Frank.

Withdrawal

Withdrawal is similar to abandonment, but it is not the same. First, abandonment requires that the defendant seek to defeat the conspiracy. There is no such requirement with withdrawal. Also, the withdrawal defense is more widely available than abandonment.[80] Withdrawal is similar to abandonment, however, as it starts the clock on the statute of limitations; the statute of limitations starts at the point of withdrawal, not at some subsequent point in time if another crime is committed that the defendant did not agree to or participate in. The Model Penal Code also contains a withdrawal defense, which requires that the defendant either advise his co-conspirators that he is no longer involved in it or inform police about the conspiracy.[81]

See the accompanying Court Decision for more on the defense of withdrawal. In it we examine the case of *United States* v. *Schiro*, which involved the prosecution of several members of a Chicago mafia family.

**COURT
DECISION**

The Logic behind the Defense of Withdrawal

United States v. Schiro, et. al
679 F.3d 521 (7th Cir. 2012)

Decision: Posting an advertisement in a newspaper does not amount to an effective withdrawal for the crime of conspiracy.

Reason: This long-running criminal case is before us for the second time. In the first appeal, two defendants, Frank J. Calabrese, Sr., and James Marcello, charged with violating RICO by conspiring to conduct an enterprise's affairs through a pattern of racketeering activity, 18 U.S.C. § 1962(d), appealed from the denial of their motions to dismiss the indictment. The indictment charged them, along with other members of the "Chicago Outfit"—the long-running lineal descendant of Al Capone's gang—with having conducted the Outfit's affairs through a pattern of racketeering activity that extended from the 1960s to 2005 and included a number of murders, along with extortion, obstruction of justice, and other crimes.

(continued)

---

[79]Model Penal Code, Section 5.03(6).
[80]See, e.g., *Hyde* v. *United States*, 225 U.S. 347 (1912).
[81]Model Penal Code, Section 5.03(7)(c).

COURT DECISION
(continued)

. . . Joseph Lombardo argues that he withdrew from the conspiracy in 1992, which if true means that the five-year statute of limitations had run by the time he was indicted in 2005. The principal evidence of withdrawal was an announcement that he placed in the Chicago Tribune and two other Chicago newspapers in which he said he'd just been released from federal prison on parole and that "if anyone hears my name used in connection with any criminal activity please notify the F.B.I., local police and my parole officer, Ron Kumke." The government describes the announcement as a "stunt," but whatever it was, it was not effective withdrawal.

One cannot avoid liability for conspiracy simply by ceasing to participate, hoping the conspiracy will continue undetected long enough to enable the statute of limitations to be pleaded successfully when one is finally prosecuted, the conspiracy having at last been detected. It is true that although the best evidence of withdrawal is reporting the conspiracy to the authorities with sufficient particularity to facilitate their efforts to thwart and prosecute it, a number of cases hold that an unequivocal statement of resignation communicated to one's conspirators can also constitute withdrawal. The rationale is that "by communicating his withdrawal to the other members of the conspiracy, a conspirator might so weaken the conspiracy, or so frighten his conspirators with the prospect that he might go to the authorities in an effort to reduce his own liability, as to undermine the conspiracy." *United States v. Paladino*, 401 F.3d 471, 479–80 (7th Cir.2005). This implies that a public announcement that is certain to be seen by one's coconspirators could do the trick, though we can't find any examples. No matter; Lombardo asked for a jury instruction on withdrawal and his request was granted. Doubtless the jury agreed with the prosecution that the Tribune ad was a stunt; and its rejection of the claim of withdrawal was reasonable and therefore binds us.

Impossibility

Although impossibility rarely comes up in a conspiracy context, it is a possible defense in certain contexts. Assume Jack and Jill just bought a new mattress to replace their tired, worn-out one. They notice on the side of the mattress a tag that says "Under penalty of law, this tag may not be removed." They decide to tear it off, thinking they have committed a crime. They fail to notice, however, that the tag also says, "except by the consumer." They have not committed a crime, even though they think they have. Such is the essence of impossibility—particularly *legal* impossibility.

It is also helpful to think of *factual* impossibility. Assume once again that Frank and Larry decide to commit murder. One of them buys a gun. They then agree to break into John's house in the middle of the night and shoot him. Unbeknownst to Frank and Larry, John died of a heart attack earlier that night while he was sleeping. Frank pulls the trigger and shoots John. It is impossible for him to murder John because John is already dead. This does not mean, however, that Frank and Larry will go free. If caught, they will likely face conspiracy charges for *attempted* murder.

Wharton's Rule

Wharton's Rule A conspiracy cannot occur when two persons are required for the commission of a crime.

Recall that one of the key purposes of conspiracy laws was to give authorities some extra tools to address the dangers of group criminality. Certain crimes, however, cannot be completed without two people. Adultery is one such (common law) crime; it cannot be completed without two people. A drug sale works in the same way; it requires a buyer and seller. Does it make sense to use conspiracy laws to target such crimes? In general, no, and **Wharton's Rule** offers some protection. The rule provides that a conspiracy cannot occur when two persons are required for the commission of a crime.

The intentions of Wharton's Rule are noble, but it also frustrates law enforcement. Why? Strictly applied, if two parties entered into an agreement for one to sell and the other to buy drugs, prosecutors could do nothing until the sale was attempted. Instead of being able to *prevent* the crime, the authorities would have to wait until it was nearly completed. For this reason, courts often limit Wharton's Rule to cases in which the intended crime has been completed or attempted.[82] So, in our example, both parties could be charged with conspiracy to sell drugs—even in the face of Wharton's Rule.

Wharton's Rule is also limited in other ways. First, if more than the minimum number of offenders is involved (e.g., a third person in our drug sale example), the rule will not apply. Likewise, if there are two parties to an agreement, but they are not the two parties necessary to complete the crime, then the rule does not apply. For example, if two men conspire for one of them sell drugs to a third person, then the rule does not apply because the buyer was not a party to the agreement. Finally, the Supreme Court has limited Wharton's Rule such that it is widely regarded as no more than a presumption in the absence of contrary legislative intent.[83] If, for example, a law permits a conspiracy charge in the context of a two-party crime, then the rule will be ignored.

Solicitation

solicitation An inchoate offense that occurs when a person entices, advises, incites, orders, or otherwise encourages someone else to commit a crime.

Solicitation occurs when a person entices, advises, incites, orders, or otherwise encourages someone else to commit a crime. There is no requirement that the crime actually be completed. Solicitation is typically limited to felonies or misdemeanors that involve either obstruction of justice or breach of peace. Under common law, solicitation was a misdemeanor. Under the Model Penal Code and many state statutes, it is a crime of the same grade and degree as the most serious crime solicited. Some states, however, still treat solicitation as less serious than the target offense.[84]

Elements of Solicitation

Under common law, solicitation was a specific intent crime, meaning that the solicitor must have intended for the "solicited" to commit a particular crime. Much the same holds true today. For example, if Leroy says to Bubba, "Wouldn't it be cool if you blew up Cletus's trailer?," he has merely *joked* about having Bubba commit a

---

[82]See, e.g., *State v. Miller*, 929 P.2d 372 (Wash. 1997), p. 378.
[83]*Iannelli v. United States*, 420 U.S. 770 (1975).
[84]See, e.g., *Commonwealth v. Barsell*, 678 N.E.2d 143 (Mass. 1997).

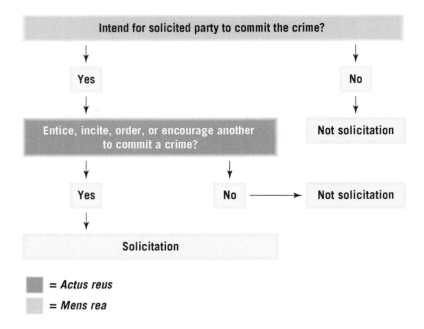

Figure 5.6
Solicitation

crime. He has not satisfied the *mens rea* element of solicitation. However, if Leroy offers Bubba $100 (although he is not obligated to offer money for solicitation to occur) and says, "I'll let you keep this if you blow up Cletus's trailer," then arguably he intends for a crime to be committed.

The *actus reus* of solicitation occurs when, as indicated earlier, another person entices, advises, incites, orders, or otherwise encourages another to commit a crime. The solicitor may *hire* someone to commit a crime, which is what we typically think of with respect to solicitation, but there is no requirement that money change hands. Also, there is no requirement that any steps be taken toward completion of the target crime. That is, there is no "overt act" requirement, as with conspiracy. A simple agreement between two people that one will commit the crime for the other suffices. This is true even if the solicited party refuses to commit the crime or *says* he or she will do so but does not really mean it.

One key limitation is that if the solicitor's message never reaches the solicited person (or if it cannot be known whether it reaches the solicited person), the *actus reus* requirement has not been satisfied. In *State* v. *Cotton*,[85] a prison inmate sent letters to his wife on the outside, soliciting various criminal activities. There was no evidence the letters actually reached his wife, so the inmate could not be convicted of solicitation. See Figure 5.6 for a summary of the crime of solicitation.

Distinguishing Solicitation from Other Crimes

"[T]he essence of criminal solicitation is an attempt [by the solicitor] to induce another to commit a criminal offense."[86] Moreover, it is a requirement that the

---

[85] *State* v. *Cotton*, 790 P.2d 1050 (N.M. 1990).
[86] *People* v. *Herman*, 97 Cal. App. 4th 1369 (2002), p. 1381.

solicitor intend to hide behind the solicited, or to "work behind the scenes."[87] Anything more than that may elevate a solicitation to something more significant, such as conspiracy or attempt.

Solicitation also does not occur if one person uses another as an "innocent instrumentality" in the commission of a crime. For example, if Leroy fraudulently tells Bubba that Cletus has his lawnmower and asks Bubba, "Will you go get it for me?," Leroy is an accomplice, not a solicitor. Why? Assuming Bubba believes Leroy and has no intent to steal the lawnmower, only to go get it for Leroy, then solicitation has not occurred. This issue was covered in the complicity section of the last chapter.

Solicitation is also distinguished from conspiracy. In general, solicitation is an attempted conspiracy. It consists of an *offer*. Usually conspiracy consists of an *agreement*—as well as an overt act. But a conspiracy need not be preceded by solicitation; conspiracy can occur at any time and without the requirement that one party solicit the other to commit a crime.

Finally, distinguish solicitation from the crime of attempt. Attempt is very similar to solicitation, but the former usually requires a "slight act" following the agreement[88] or that the solicitation be "proximate" to the intended crime—that is, in close temporal proximity to it.[89] For example, if Denise pays Jennifer to kill Patrick next week, she has solicited murder, but if she pays Jennifer to kill Patrick immediately, she may be guilty of attempted murder, too. A number of courts treat attempt and solicitation as fundamentally distinct, however, holding that "no matter what acts the solicitor commits, he cannot be guilty of attempt because it is not his purpose to commit the offense personally."[90] How attempt and solicitation are related to one another thus depends on the jurisdiction in question.

See the accompanying Court Decision for more on the crime of solicitation. In it we take a look at the case of *United States* v. *White*, where the defendant is charged with soliciting a crime via his Internet website. The First Amendment right of freedom of speech in relation to the potential crime of solicitation is also a key factor in the case.

COURT DECISION

The Logic behind the Crime of Solicitation

United States v. White
638 F.Supp.2d 935 (N.D. Ill. 2009)

Decision: The government charged defendant William White with violating 18 U.S.C. § 373 by soliciting another person to harm the foreperson of the federal jury that convicted white supremacist leader Matthew Hale. Defendant now moves to dismiss the indictment.

(continued)

---

[87]See, e.g., *People* v. *Kauten,* 755 N.E.2d 1016 (Ill. App. Ct. 2001).
[88]See, e.g., *People* v. *Decker,* 157 P.3d 1017 (Cal. 2007), p. 1022.
[89]See, e.g., *Mettler* v. *State,* 697 N.E.2d 502 (Ind. Ct. App. 1998).
[90]American Law Institute, Comment to Section 5.02.

COURT DECISION *(continued)*

Reason: . . . Specifically, the government alleged that on or about September 11, 2008, defendant displayed on the front page of his website a post entitled, "The Juror Who Convicted Matt Hale." The post read:

> Gay anti-racist [Juror A] was a juror who played a key role in convicting Matt Hale. Born [date], [he/she] lives at [address] with [his/her] gay black lover and [his/her] cat [name]. [His/Her] phone number is [phone number], cell phone [phone number], and [his/her] office is [phone number].

The post did not expressly advocate that Juror A be harmed.

. . . In order to state an offense under § 373, the indictment must allege that defendant intentionally solicited or endeavored to persuade another person to harm Juror A, under circumstances strongly corroborative of defendant's intent that the person commit a violent crime against Juror A. As stated, defendant's posts about Juror A do not expressly solicit or endeavor to persuade another person to harm him/her. Moreover, as discussed, defendant's posts about Juror A, in themselves, are protected by the First Amendment. Thus, the corroborating circumstances alleged must, consistent with the First Amendment, transform defendant's lawful statements about Juror A into a criminal solicitation. The corroborating circumstances alleged in the indictment fail to do so.

. . . This Court does not intend to minimize the real fear of harm and intimidation that law enforcement-related, corrections officer-related, and court-related employees, and their families, may experience. [J]udges and court employees are common targets of threats and harassment. However, we live in a democratic society founded on fundamental constitutional principles. In this society, we do not quash fear by increasing government power, proscribing those constitutional principles, and silencing those speakers of whom the majority disapproves . . . **THEREFORE, IT IS ORDERED** that defendant's motion to dismiss is **GRANTED.**

Solicitation under the Model Penal Code

In general, the Model Penal Code definition of solicitation requires that (a) a person "commands, encourages or requests" another person to engage in an illegal act with (b) the purpose to promote or facilitate it.[91] The Code treats solicitation as seriously as the target offense, and it does not limit solicitation to felonies. Even an attempted solicitation is considered solicitation under the Model Penal Code. However, the Model Penal Code does offer a defense of "renunciation." A person is not guilty of solicitation if he (a) completely and voluntarily renounces his criminal intent and (b) either persuades the other party not to offend or blocks the crime's commission.[92]

---

[91]Model Penal Code, Section 5.02(1).
[92]Model Penal Code, Section 5.02(3).

YOUR DECISION

1. The Bottoccellis, an Italian Mafia "family" in Chicago, are involved in a number of criminal enterprises. As part of tradition, it is generally understood that all relatives have an obligation to help the "family" whenever possible. Mario is the 18-year-old nephew of the Mafia boss. He has never discussed any illegal activity directly with his uncle or any other member of the family. One evening, however, a family member is arrested for dealing cocaine. In response, Mario bribes the arresting officer to release his relative and dispose of the evidence against him. The prosecutor believes Mario acted in agreement with other family members and wants to charge Mario both with bribery and conspiracy to commit bribery. Is Mario guilty of conspiracy? Why or why not?

2. George, a local delivery truck driver, is distraught to learn that his wife of 20 years is having an affair with her personal trainer, Fabio. George decides to drown his sorrows in beer at the local tavern with his friends. During the course of the evening, George states in a drunken rage, "I would pay a million dollars to anyone who kills Fabio and teaches him a lesson once and for all." An off-duty police officer is also in the bar and overhears the conversation. George is arrested and charged with solicitation to commit murder. Is he guilty of solicitation? Why or why not?

Summary

- Under common law, a conspiracy was defined as an agreement between two or more persons to commit a criminal act.

- Modern statutes take a "unilateral" approach, which permits the conviction of *any* person who agrees with another to commit a crime.

- Under common law, nothing other than the agreement was necessary.

- Under modern statutes, however, it is often required that the prosecutor prove that those who entered into the agreement actually took some step in furtherance of the agreement—called an *overt act*.

- Conspiracy is generally regarded as a specific intent crime.

- There are two parts to the *mens rea* of conspiracy. First, the defendant must intend to enter into an agreement with one or more others to commit a crime. Second, the defendant must have intent to commit the target offense.

- The courts typically equate intent with purpose.

- The *actus reus* of conspiracy consists of two parts. First, and most importantly, there must be an agreement to commit a crime. Second, more than likely it is necessary that the parties to the conspiracy commit an "overt act" in furtherance of the agreement.

- The agreement to commit a crime between two or more people can take a number of forms. It may be an express agreement, but it need not be.

- Not every jurisdiction requires proof of an overt act, but logic for such a requirement is straightforward; it offers evidence that a conspiracy has moved beyond the "talk stage" and is actively being carried out.

- It is often difficult for prosecutors to determine who is involved in the conspiracy and how many conspiracies there are. Making such determinations is important because they can help prosecutors decide on the proper venue in which to try the case, whether joint trials are warranted, what offenses the parties can be liable for, and so on.

- An abandonment defense *may* work as something of a defense to charges for subsequent crimes arising from a conspiratorial agreement; if one party to a conspiracy withdraws and then finds him- or herself charged with conspiracy for crimes committed after such withdrawal, then the defense may succeed.

- The withdrawal defense is more widely available for the crime of conspiracy than abandonment.

- Although impossibility rarely comes up in a conspiracy context, it is a possible defense in certain contexts.

- Wharton's Rule provides that a conspiracy cannot occur when two persons are required for the commission of a crime.

- Solicitation occurs when a person entices, advises, incites, orders, or otherwise encourages someone else to commit a crime.

- For solicitation, there is no requirement that the crime actually be completed.

- Solicitation is typically limited to felonies or misdemeanors that involve either obstruction of justice or breach of peace.

- Solicitation does not occur if one person uses another as an "innocent instrumentality" in the commission of a crime.

- Solicitation is distinguished from conspiracy. In general, solicitation is an attempted conspiracy.

- Attempt is very similar to solicitation, but the former usually requires a "slight act" (or something similar) following the agreement.

Chapter Review

INTRODUCTION TO INCHOATE CRIMES: ATTEMPT

Learning Objectives

- Explain the concept of inchoate crimes.
- Explain the relationship of attempt to the substantive offense.
- Summarize what constitutes attempt.
- Summarize the defenses to charges of attempt.

Review Questions

1. Compare and contrast attempt and the substantive offense.
2. Explain both components of the *mens rea* of attempt.
3. In your opinion, which is the best test for the *actus reus* of attempt? Defend your answer.

Key Terms

inchoate crime

attempt

factual impossibility

legal impossibility

inherent impossibility

CONSPIRACY AND SOLICITATION

Learning Objectives

- Identify the elements and complications of conspiracy.
- Describe the defenses to conspiracy.
- Describe solicitation.
- Distinguish solicitation from other inchoate crimes.

Review Questions

1. Compare and contrast conspiracy at common law and under modern-day statutes.
2. Briefly summarize the elements of conspiracy.
3. Explain the issues that pose complications for conspiracy prosecutions.
4. List and define the defenses to a conspiracy charge.
5. What is solicitation, and how does it differ from conspiracy?

Key Terms

conspiracy

overt act

Pinkerton Rule

hearsay

bootstrapping

corrupt motives doctrine

spoke and wheel conspiracy

chain conspiracy

wheel and chain conspiracy

Wharton's Rule

Solicitation

Chapter Synthesis Questions

1. Identify and describe an inchoate crime *other than* attempt, conspiracy, or solicitation.
2. Explain the logic for targeting inchoate crimes with the criminal law.
3. Which, in your opinion, is the most serious: attempt, conspiracy, or solicitation? Defend your answer.
4. Explain Wharton's Rule.

6

CRIMES AGAINST PERSONS

MODULE

6.1 HOMICIDE

Learning Objectives

- **Distinguish between first-degree murder and second-degree murder.**
- **Explain when the death penalty is an acceptable form of punishment for homicide.**
- **Summarize the elements of voluntary and involuntary manslaughter.**
- **Explain felony murder.**
- **Identify two types of "mercy killings."**
- **Explain corporation murder.**

CORE CONCEPTS

This chapter marks the beginning of our focus on specific crime types. We have occasionally referenced homicide, assault, and other offenses in previous chapters in order to make a point, but here is where we consider them in much more detail. This chapter focuses specifically on crimes against persons, where all of the offenses are against one or more live human beings. Homicide is arguably the most serious crime, which is why we focus on it first. We then shift our attention to a number of assaultive offenses, including rape, sexual assault, robbery, assault, battery, kidnapping, false imprisonment, and various "domestic" offenses (e.g., child abuse).

Homicide Defined

homicide The killing of a human being by another human being.

The common law defined **homicide** as the killing of a human being by another human being. All homicides were punishable by death under early common law, but that gradually changed. Homicide was eventually broken by judicial decisions and statutes into two categories: murder and manslaughter. Murder, in turn, was further broken down into subcategories, particularly first-degree and second-degree murder. In general, first-degree murderers could be executed; second-degree murderers could not. While the definition of *criminal homicide* seems straightforward on its face, there is some confusion and disagreement about what a *human being* is.

What Is a "Human Being?"

If homicide is the killing of another human being, then naturally we have to define the term *human being*. In most homicide situations, it is a nonissue, as it is clear that the victim was a living, breathing, human being. For example, when an otherwise healthy teenager is killed, there is little doubt that he or she was a "human being" within the meaning of applicable homicide statutes. It gets messy, however, near the beginning and end of life.

The Beginning of Life. When does life begin? Abortion proponents and opponents have been debating the answer to this question for generations. It is unlikely that we can achieve any resolution here. Fortunately, for purposes of homicide, there is some resolution. The common law defined the beginning of life as occurring when a fetus was born alive.[1] This definition has been carried forward into several modern court decisions. For example, in *Keeler v. Superior Court*,[2] the defendant purposely kicked his pregnant former wife in the stomach. The fetus died. The court held that the fetus was not a human being.

Contrast this decision with *Commonwealth v. Cass*,[3] a case in which a motorist crashed into another vehicle being driven by a woman who was nearly nine months pregnant. The fetus died as a result of injuries the woman sustained and was delivered by Caesarean section. An autopsy revealed that the fetus was viable at the time of the crash. The Supreme Judicial Court of Massachusetts rejected the common law definition of human being, noting,

> We think that the better rule is that infliction of prenatal injuries resulting in the death of a viable fetus, before or after it is born, is homicide. If a person were to commit violence against a pregnant woman and destroy the fetus within her, we would not want the death of the fetus to go unpunished. We believe that our criminal law should extend its protection to viable fetuses.[4]

Most jurisdictions continue to retain the common law definition of the beginning of life, but Massachusetts and several other states have begun to treat viable fetuses as human beings. In such states, it is possible for people to be convicted of the crime of **feticide**, causing the death of a fetus. Indeed, some states have gone even further than Massachusetts. California defines a human being as a fetus that has progressed beyond the embryonic stage of seven to eight weeks.[5] According to the California Supreme Court,

feticide Causing the death of an unborn fetus.

> The state's interest in protecting the 'potentiality of human life' includes protection of the unborn child, whether an embryo or a nonviable or viable fetus, and it protects, too, the woman's interest in her unborn child and her right to decide whether it shall be carried in utero. The interest of a criminal assailant in terminating a woman's pregnancy does not outweigh the woman's right to continue the pregnancy.[6]

The End of Life. Just as it can be difficult to decide when life begins, it can be difficult to decide when life ends. At what point is a person no longer considered a "human being?" The common law focused on whether the heart continued to beat;

---

[1] See, e.g., *Meadows v. State*, 722 S.W.2d 584 (Ark. 1987), p. 585.
[2] *Keeler v. Superior Court*, 2 Cal. 3d 619 (1970).
[3] *Commonwealth v. Cass*, 467 N.E.2d 1324 (Mass. 1984).
[4] Ibid., p. 1329.
[5] *People v. Davis*, 872 P.2d 591 (Cal. 1994).
[6] Ibid., p. 599.

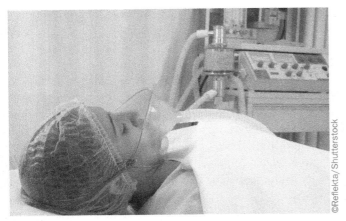

According to criminal law, life ends with brain death. A person can be kept alive on a ventilator, but until brain death occurs, he or she is still considered 'alive'.

©Reflekta/Shutterstock

if someone's heart stopped beating, that person was no longer considered a human being. Today, because of medical technologies, it is possible to preserve life even if a person's heart has stopped beating on its own. Thus, most courts now define *death* in terms of "brain death." That is, a person is no longer a human being if that person is "brain dead." Some states go further and define the cessation of life in terms of "whole brain death." Some states offer a broader definition of *death* that includes cessation of circulation, respiration, and/or brain function. According to the state of Kansas, for example,

An individual who has sustained either (1) irreversible cessation of circulatory and respiratory functions, or (2) irreversible cessation of all functions of the entire brain, including the brain stem, is dead.[7]

It may seem overly tedious to define *death* in such exact terms, but it is critically important from a homicide prosecution standpoint. And it is also important from the standpoint that all would-be killings do not necessarily result in death. Oftentimes the victim sustains serious injuries that require long-term hospitalization, but not death.

The common law's **year-and-a-day rule** provided that a person could not be prosecuted for homicide unless the victim died within a year and a day of the act that was responsible for the fatal injury. The rule can be traced to medieval times when the practice of medicine was far from an exact science. Doctors were not always able to ascertain the cause of death after a victim languished in a bed-ridden state for an extended period of time. Modern medicine, however, now affords the experts with a greater understanding of death's causes, even when death comes months or years after an injury was inflicted. For this reason, the common law year-and-a-day rule has been largely abandoned. One court called it "an outdated relic of the common law."[8] Today, most states have abandoned the rule and can prosecute killers for deaths that occur years after the crime was committed.

year-and-a-day rule A common law rule that stated that a person could not be prosecuted for homicide unless the victim died within a year and a day of the act that was responsible for the fatal injury.

Murder

murder The unlawful killing of another person with malice aforethought.

manslaughter The unlawful killing of another human being without malice aforethought.

Criminal homicides fall into two general categories: murder and manslaughter. The common law defined **murder** as "the killing of a human being by another human being with malice aforethought."[9] **Manslaughter** was the same as murder, but without the

---

[7]Kan. Stat. Ann. Section 77-205 (2008).
[8]*Rogers* v. *Tennessee*, 532 U.S. 451 (2001), p. 462.
[9]*United States* v. *Wharton*, 433 F.2d 451 (D.C. Cir. 1970), p. 454.

malice aforethought requirement. These definitions have been more or less retained over time, but now they are broken down further into different subtypes. Statutes often contain gradations, or levels of murder (first-degree, second-degree, etc.). Manslaughter, too, is typically broken down into subtypes.

As we go through the elements of homicide, bear in mind that most of our attention will focus on the *mens rea* of homicide rather than the *actus reus*. For homicide, the *actus reus* is rather simple—there must be a death. In other words, the death, rather than the killing, is the *actus reus*. What sets different types of homicide apart from one another is primarily the offender's mental state.

malice aforethought Killing another person without justification, excuse, or mitigating circumstances.

Without malice aforethought, a homicide is not murder. What, then, is *malice aforethought*? In general, if one person kills another person without justification, excuse, or any mitigating circumstances, that person is said to have killed with malice aforethought. There is no requirement that *aforethought* involve deliberate planning well in advance of a murder. Likewise, *malice* carries a particularly negative connotation, implying that it is someone's specific intent to kill another, but this is not a requirement. One person could decide to kill another on the spur of the moment and still display malice aforethought. *Malice aforethought* is thus a loosely defined term of art that can be manifested in a number of different ways.

Not all states grade murders by degree, but for ease of interpretation, we will do so here. There are usually two types of murder—first and second-degree. The former is eligible for the death penalty under certain circumstances; the latter is not.

First-Degree Murder

first-degree murder The deliberate, willful, and premeditated killing of another person.

Subject to some exceptions, first-degree murder is a murder that is willful, premeditated, and deliberated. The defendant *intends* for the killing to occur, *thinks* about his or her decision in advance of the killing, and *deliberates* it, perhaps thinking about the costs and benefits associated with killing another person. First-degree murder is set apart from other types of killings by the requirement that there must be *more than just intention to kill*. It is a "cold-blooded" killing, one that is arguably more "evil" than a spontaneous killing.

There is considerable variability across jurisdictions concerning the extent to which "willful," "premeditated," and "deliberate" are essential elements of first-degree murder. Some equate "deliberate" with "willful."[10] Others distinguish "deliberate" from "willful" by focusing on whether the defendant *weighed* the costs and benefits associated with a decision to kill.[11] Still others lump all three elements together, equating them with the specific intent to kill. Evidence of this latter view holds the following:

> There need be no appreciable space of time between the intention to kill and the act of killing. They may be as instantaneous as successive thoughts of mind. It is only necessary that the act of killing be preceded by a concurrence of will, deliberation, and premeditation on the part of the slayer, and, if such is the case, the killing is murder in the first degree.[12]

---

[10]See, e.g., *Commonwealth v. Carroll*, 194 A.2d 911 (Pa. 1963), p. 917.
[11]See, e.g., *People v. Morrin*, 187 N.W.2d 434 (Mich. Ct. App. 1971), p. 449.
[12]*Macias v. State*, 36 Ariz. 140 (1929), pp. 149–150.

At the risk of simplification, we can distinguish between the three terms in this way:

Willful: Intent to kill.

Deliberate: Acting with a cool mind and reflection.

Premeditated: A design to kill formed in the mind by the time of the killing.

Of these three terms, there is considerable disagreement over the precise meaning premeditation. While everyone can agree that premeditation is the same as thinking of something in advance, not everyone can agree on the *amount* of premeditation that is necessary—particularly the time it takes. According to one view, "[a]ny interval of time between the forming of the intent to kill and the execution of that intent, which is sufficient in duration for the accused to be fully conscious of what he intended" is sufficient.[13] According to another view, for a killing to become first-degree murder, the state must prove that "some appreciable time passed during which the consideration, planning, preparation, or determination . . . prior to the commission of the act took place."[14] Still other courts feel it is best to leave the decision to a jury:

> The law fixes upon no length of time as necessary to form the intention to kill, but leaves the existence of a fully formed intent as a fact to be determined by the jury, from all the facts and circumstances in the evidence.[15]

bifurcation Separating a trial into two parts. In first-degree murder cases, the defendant's guilt or innocence is decided first by the jury. Then, the penalty of life imprisonment or death is decided separately by the jury.

aggravating circumstances Circumstances that would lend toward a harsher penalty during sentencing.

mitigating circumstances Circumstances that would lend toward a lighter or reduced criminal penalty during sentencing.

The Death Penalty. Only certain first-degree murderers are eligible for the death penalty. Some states do not practice capital punishment and, as such, incarcerate murderers. And in those states that *do* practice capital punishment, just because someone is convicted of first-degree murder does not mean that person will be sentenced to death. The decision as to whether a first-degree murderer will be sentenced to death is usually made by a jury in a post-trial hearing. This is known as **bifurcation**. The jury will be asked to consider whether various **aggravating circumstances** were in place, which would call for execution. Aggravating circumstances are those factors that add to the seriousness or enormity of the offense. The jury will also consider whether **mitigating circumstances** existed. Mitigating circumstances serve to extenuate or reduce the degree of moral culpability.

The list of aggravating and mitigating circumstances that can make a first-degree murder eligible for the death penalty (or eligible for incarceration instead of death) varies by state. For example, here are some (though not all) of the aggravating factors that must be considered under Arizona law:

- The defendant has been or was previously convicted of a serious offense, whether preparatory or completed. Convictions for serious offenses committed on the same occasion as the homicide, or not committed on the same occasion but consolidated for trial with the homicide, shall be treated as a serious offense under this paragraph.

---

[13]*State v. Guthrie*, 461 S.E.2d 163 (W. Va. 1995), pp. 182–183.
[14]*State v. Moore*, 481 N.W.2d 355 (Minn. 1992), p. 361.
[15]*Commonwealth v. Drum*, WL 7210 (1868), p. 6.

- In the commission of the offense the defendant knowingly created a grave risk of death to another person or persons in addition to the person murdered during the commission of the offense.
- The defendant committed the offense in an especially heinous, cruel or depraved manner.
- The defendant has been convicted of one or more other homicides . . . that were committed during the commission of the offense.[16]

And here are some of the mitigating factors:

- The defendant's capacity to appreciate the wrongfulness of his conduct or to conform his conduct to the requirements of law was significantly impaired, but not so impaired as to constitute a defense to prosecution.
- The defendant was under unusual and substantial duress, although not such as to constitute a defense to prosecution.
- The defendant could not reasonably have foreseen that his conduct in the course of the commission of the offense for which the defendant was convicted would cause, or would create a grave risk of causing, death to another person.
- The defendant's age.[17]

To sentence a first-degree murderer to death, it is usually required that jurors (a) find at least one aggravating factor and (b) no mitigating circumstances.

Second-Degree Murder

States that grade murders by degree generally treat any murder that is not "willful, premeditated, and deliberate" as second-degree murder. In other words, second-degree murder is the default category. For a first-degree murder conviction to be secured, the prosecutor must prove the conditions for second-degree murder *plus* the added requirements discussed in the previous section. See Figure 6.1 distinguishing first-degree and second-degree murder.

In those states that grade murder by degrees, two types of killings constitute murder in the second degree. One occurs when the offender intends to cause grievous bodily injury and the result is death. Another occurs when the killer acts with a "depraved heart," which then leads to the death of another person.

Intent to Inflict Grievous Bodily Injury.
If a person intends to inflict grievous bodily injury (sometimes called *great bodily harm*, *great bodily injury*, *serious bodily harm*, or *serious bodily injury*) to another and death results, it is second-degree murder. This begs the question, "What is 'grievous bodily injury'?" One court defined it as "such injury as is grave and not trivial, and gives rise to apprehension of danger to life, health, or limb."[18] Tennessee's statutory definition is as follows: "substantial risk of death, protracted unconsciousness, extreme physical pain, protracted

---

[16]Ariz. Rev. Stat. Section 13-701(D).
[17]Ariz. Rev. Stat. Section 13-701(E).
[18]*State v. Bogenreif*, 465 N.W.2d 777 (S.D. 1991), p. 780.

or obvious disfigurement, protracted loss or substantial impairment of a function of a bodily member, organ, or mental faculty."[19] California's is more simplistic: "significant or substantial physical injury."[20]

None of these definitions are particularly helpful, as they fail to tell us exactly what kinds of actions can be said to amount to result in grievous or serious bodily injury. We must turn to some additional court decisions for clarification. For example, in *State* v. *Perry*,[21] a prison inmate beat and kicked another inmate and then put his belt around the other inmate's neck and began choking him. A trial court concluded that his actions resulted in serious bodily injury. In another case, the defendant kidnapped a woman, transported her across state lines, bound her, raped her, slashed her neck, and left her for dead.[22] Not surprisingly, his actions resulted in serious bodily injury. At the other end of the spectrum, were a person to slap another who then died of a heart attack, it is unlikely a court would conclude that serious bodily injury was inflicted.

It must be emphasized that this type of second-degree murder does *not require the intent to kill*, only the intent to inflict harm. If the victim then dies, a second-degree

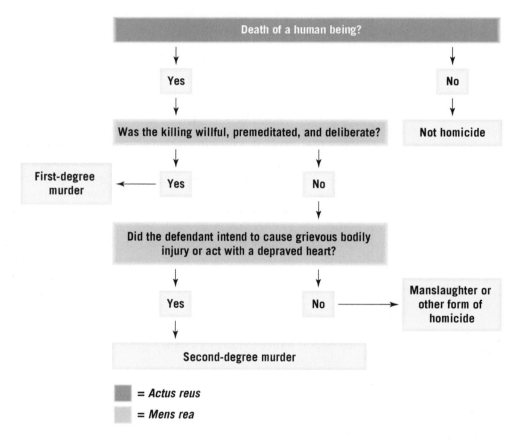

Figure 6.1

Distinguishing between First- and Second-Degree Murder

[19]Tenn. Code. Ann. Section 39-11-106(a)(34)(A)-(E) (2008).
[20]Cal. Penal Code Section 12022.7(f).
[21]*State* v. *Perry*, 426 P.2d 415 (Ariz. Ct. App. 1967), p. 418.
[22]*United States* v. *Rodriguez*, 581 F.3d 775 (8th Cir. 2009).

murder conviction is likely. If, on the other hand, the defendant sets out to kill the victim, then it is likely that it is first-, not second-,degree murder.

Depraved Heart Killings.
Depraved heart killings are also considered second-degree murders—again, in those states that grade murder by degrees. Simply, if a person acts with a "depraved heart,[23]" "an abandoned heart," or "an abandoned and malignant heart,[24]" and death results, it is second-degree murder. Depraved heart killings are also likened to killings based on "extreme recklessness" or "extreme indifference" to human life. Regardless of the terminology used, the key is that the accused does not *intend* to kill, but that death results because of, as one court put it, "wanton and willful disregard of the likelihood that the natural tendency of [the] defendant's behavior is to cause death or great bodily harm."[25]

Let's consider a couple of examples to get a sense of the meaning of *depraved heart*. In *State v. Robinson*,[26] the defendant, Robinson, hit the victim, Crowley, over the head with a golf club, killing him. Robinson was convicted of depraved heart murder and appealed, but the Kansas Supreme Court affirmed his conviction, noting that the following:

> The evidence was sufficient in this case for the jury to find that Robinson recklessly killed a person while manifesting an extreme indifference to the value of one specific human life—Crowley's life. The evidence indicated that Robinson swung a golf club at Crowley with great force, intending to hit Crowley.[27]

In Maryland, a *depraved heart murder* has been defined as a killing resulting from "the deliberate perpetration of a knowingly dangerous act with reckless and wanton unconcern and indifference as to whether anyone is harmed or not."[28] So, when Jacqueline Robinson shot her lover, Henry Garvey, in the leg, which caused the bullet to travel upward into his abdomen, where it lodged and eventually killed him, she arguably acted with a depraved heart.[29]

Throughout history, a number of depraved heart cases have turned on the issue of whether the defendant's indifference to human life be directed solely at the victim or at society at large. For example, in a classic case, *Darry v. People*,[30] the defendant beat his wife, who died as a result of the wounds she suffered. The New York Supreme Court decided that his actions did not amount to "recklessness and disregard of human life generally," which was required by statute at the time.[31] Likewise, in *Mitchell v. State*,[32] another classic case, the defendant struck another man with a stick, killing him. The Supreme Court of Alabama concluded that the universal malice required for a murder conviction was lacking. In other words, the defendant did not act with indifference to *all* life.

---

[23]See, e.g., *Windham v. State*, 602 So. 2d 798 (Miss. 1992), p. 800.
[24]See, e.g., Cal. Penal Code Section 188.
[25]*People v. Goecke*, 579 N.W.2d 868 (Mich. 1998), p. 879.
[26]*State v. Robinson*, 934 P.2d 38 (Kan. 1997).
[27]Ibid., pp. 49–50.
[28]*Robinson v. State*, 307 Md. 738 (1986), p. 744.
[29]Ibid.
[30]*Darry v. People*, 10 N.Y. 120 (1854).
[31]Ibid., p. 156.
[32]*Mitchell v. State*, 60 Ala. 26 (1877).

More recent decisions have abandoned any requirement that the defendant act with a depraved heart *generally*. Statutes have been amended, too, meaning that a person can now manifest extreme indifference to human life, even though such indifference is directed toward a single person.[33] Even Sir William Blackstone's classic commentaries suggested that a depraved heart could be directed at one person:

> Also, even if upon a sudden provocation one beats another in a cruel and unusual manner, so that he dies, though he did not intend his death, yet he is guilty of murder by express malice. . . . As when a park-keeper tied a boy, that was stealing wood, to a horse's tail, and dragged him along the park; when a master corrected his servant with an iron bar, and a schoolmaster stamped on his scholar's belly; so that each of the sufferers died; these were justly held to be murders, because the correction being excessive, and such as could not proceed but from a bad heart, it was equivalent to a deliberate act of slaughter. Neither shall he be guilty of a less crime, who kills another in consequence of such a willful act, as shows him to be an enemy to all mankind in general; as going deliberately with a horse used to strike, or discharging a gun, among a multitude of people. So if a man resolves to kill the next man he meets, and does kill him, it is murder, although he knew him not; for this is universal malice.[34]

Today, courts mostly focus on the issues of a depraved heart or extreme recklessness *without regard to the target of the behavior*. See the accompanying Court Decision for more on depraved heart murder. In it we take a look at the case of *People* v. *Roe*, where a 15-year-old plays a deadly game of Russian roulette.

COURT DECISION

The Logic behind Depraved Heart Murder

People v. Roe
542 N.E.2d 610 (N.Y. App. 1989)

Decision: A version of Russian roulette equates to depraved heart murder when the defendant's reckless conduct is imminently dangerous and presents a grave risk of death.

Reason: In defendant's appeal from his conviction for depraved indifference murder for the shooting death of a 13-year-old boy, the sole question we address is the legal sufficiency of the evidence. Defendant, a 15 1/2 -year-old high school student, deliberately loaded a mix of "live" and "dummy" shells at random into the magazine of a 12-gauge shotgun. He pumped a shell into the firing chamber not knowing whether it was a "dummy" or a "live" round. He raised the gun to his shoulder and pointed it directly at the victim, Darrin Seifert, who was standing approximately 10 feet away. As he did so, he exclaimed "Let's play Polish roulette" and asked "Who is first?". When he pulled the trigger, the gun discharged sending a "live" round into Darrin's chest. Darrin died as a result of the massive injuries.

(continued)

---

[33]See, e.g., *State* v. *Lowe*, 68 N.W. 1094 (Minn. 1896); *Hogan* v. *State*, 36 Wis. 226 (1874).
[34]4 Bl. Comm. 199-200 (1769, Facsimile ed. 1979).

COURT DECISION (*continued*)

. . . Before analyzing the evidence and its legal sufficiency, a brief examination of the crime of depraved indifference murder and its elements is instructive. Depraved indifference murder, like reckless manslaughter is a nonintentional homicide. It differs from manslaughter, however, in that it must be shown that the actor's reckless conduct is imminently dangerous and presents a grave risk of death; in manslaughter, the conduct need only present the lesser "substantial risk" of death. Whether the lesser risk sufficient for manslaughter is elevated into the very substantial risk present in murder depends upon the wantonness of defendant's acts—i.e., whether they were committed "[u]nder circumstances evincing a depraved indifference to human life." This is not a mens rea element which focuses "upon the subjective intent of the defendant, as it is with intentional murder"; rather it involves "an objective assessment of the degree of risk presented by defendant's reckless conduct." . . . Examples of conduct which have been held sufficient to justify a jury's finding of depraved indifference include: driving an automobile on a city sidewalk at excessive speeds and striking a pedestrian without applying the brakes; firing several bullets into a house; continually beating an infant over a five-day period; and playing "Russian roulette" with one "live" shell in a six-cylinder gun.

. . . The evidence of the objective circumstances surrounding defendant's point-blank discharge of the shotgun is, in our view, sufficient to support a finding of the very serious risk of death required for depraved indifference murder. Because the escalating factor—depraved indifference to human life—is based on an objective assessment of the circumstances surrounding the act of shooting and not the mens rea of the actor, the evidence stressed by the dissent concerning defendant's mens rea—his emotional condition in the aftermath of the killing is beside the point.

. . . The sheer enormity of the act—putting another's life at such grave peril in this fashion—is not diminished because the sponsor of the game is a youth of 15. . . . Accordingly, the order of the Appellate Division should be affirmed.

Manslaughter

Manslaughter is an unlawful homicide committed without the malice aforethought required for murder. As such, manslaughter can be voluntary and involuntary. At the risk of simplification, a voluntary manslaughter is the same as a "heat of passion" killing. An involuntary manslaughter is either a reckless or "criminally negligent" killing. See Figure 6.2 illustrating the difference between the two crimes. We look at each of these in more detail in the following subsections.

Voluntary Manslaughter

Under common law, a killing that was committed in the "sudden heat of passion" because of "adequate provocation" was considered less blameworthy than murder.[35]

---

[35]See, e.g., *Comber* v. *United States*, 584 A.2d 26 (D.C. Ct. App. 1990).

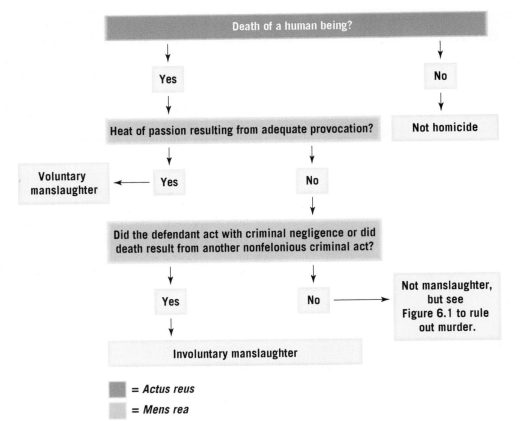

Figure 6.2
Distinguishing between
Voluntary and
Involuntary
Manslaughter

Note the three distinct elements here: (1) sudden heat of passion; (2) adequate provocation; and (3) causation, the requirement that the sudden heat of passion *resulted from* adequate provocation. Let's look at each of these in more detail.

Sudden Heat of Passion. The notion of heat of passion should be fairly self-explanatory. If a person acts when his or her emotions are running high, such actions are often undertaken in the heat of passion. So it goes with homicide. Blackstone put it this way:

> If upon a sudden quarrel two persons fight, and one of them kills the other, this is [voluntary] manslaughter. And, so it is, if they upon such an occasion go out and fight in a field, for this is one continued act of passion and the law pays that regard to human frailty, as not to put a hasty and a deliberate act upon the same footing with regard to guilty. So also a man be greatly provoked, as by pulling his nose, or other great indignity, and immediately kills the aggressor, though this is not excusable, since there is no absolute necessity for doing so to preserve himself, yet neither is it murder for there is no previous malice.[36]

So, the fight that erupted at the beginning of Blackstone's scenario is what prompted one party to act in the heat of passion. The killer in this instance arguably

---

[36]4 Bl. Comm. 191 (1769, Facsimile ed. 1979).

acted out of anger, but there is no requirement that "heat of passion" be likened to anger. Emotions ranging from jealousy[37] to desperation[38] can qualify.

For the heat of passion to exist, the accused must not have had time to cool off. In one classic case, the defendant killed a sodomist who victimized him some three weeks earlier while he was unconscious. An appellate court held that too much time had elapsed between the provocation and the killing to support a manslaughter conviction.[39] There are no hard and fast rules concerning the "cooling-off" period. Juries are usually tasked with making the decision.

Adequate Provocation. Under common law, a person was considered adequately provoked if what that person experienced or observed was sufficiently serious. Examples included assault, battery, mutual combat, witnessing a serious crime committed against someone else, and the like.[40] Actions that *did not*, according to the courts, provide adequate provocation to reduce a murder to manslaughter were insults, learning of spouse's adultery, or being a victim of minor battery, among others.[41]

As time has gone on, courts have abandoned their attempts to list all the circumstances that would be considered adequate provocation. More often than not, juries are left with making the decision. For example, it is not uncommon for someone to be prosecuted for murder, but the jury may be instructed that it can find the defendant guilty of manslaughter if the circumstances merit—that is, if it is confident that the crime was committed in the heat of passion and with sufficient provocation. As one court put it, if the circumstances "might render ordinary men, of fair average disposition, liable to act rashly or without due deliberation or reflection, and from passion, rather than judgment,"[42] then manslaughter is the appropriate verdict.

There is one exception to the modern rule that there is no agreed-upon list of circumstances that would be considered adequate provocation: Words alone are rarely sufficient. For example, in one case, an African-American man, Green, killed his white neighbor after the neighbor informed Green that he shot Green's dog the week earlier and that he had done so because "it was bad enough living around niggers, much less dogs."[43] The Supreme Court of Michigan declined to hear Green's appeal. We say "rarely" sufficient because there are exceptions. Minnesota, for example, defines first-degree (i.e., voluntary) manslaughter thusly:

> intentionally [causing] the death of another person in the heat of passion provided by *such words* or acts of another as would provoke a person of ordinary self-control under like circumstances, provided that the crying of a child does not constitute provocation.[44]

Causation. The third voluntary manslaughter requirement is, again, that adequate provocation must *cause* the heat of passion. Assume, for example, that Keith

---

[37]See, e.g., *People v. Berry*, 556 P.2d 777 (Cal. 1976).
[38]See, e.g., *People v. Borchers*, 325 P.2d 97 (Cal. 1958).
[39]*State v. Gounagias*, 153 P. 9 (Wash. 1915).
[40]See J. Dressler, *Understanding Criminal Law*, 5th ed. (Newark, NJ: Lexis-Nexis, 2009), p. 536.
[41]Ibid.
[42]*Maher v. People*, 10 Mich. 212 (1862), p. 220.
[43]*People v. Green*, 519 N.W.2d 853 (Mich. 1994), p. 856.
[44]Minnesota Criminal Code Section 609.20(1).

intends to kill his wife, Tammy, because, in his view, she was always "talking smack" about him behind his back. Further assume he comes home one afternoon, grabs his favorite gun, and when opening the bedroom door to find Tammy, sees her in bed with his best friend. Enraged, he kills her. Keith committed murder in this instance, not manslaughter. Why? He set out to kill Tammy in advance. Tammy's earlier words provoked him to engage in a planned killing. He was going to kill her anyway, so the fact that he observed his best friend sleeping with his wife was immaterial.

paramour rule A husband catching his wife in the act of adultery provides adequate provocation to reduce a charge for killing another from murder to manslaughter.

What if Keith hadn't planned to kill Tammy and instead killed her after witnessing her infidelity? Under common law, the **paramour rule** provided that a husband who caught his wife in an act of adultery had adequate provocation to kill (moving it from murder to manslaughter). Some states even sanctioned such killings. And over time the rule was modified such that wives could justifiably kill unfaithful husbands—or at least be found guilty of manslaughter rather than murder. These days, however, it is exceedingly rare for witnessing adultery to amount to adequate provocation. For example, in *Commonwealth v. Schnopps*,[45] the Supreme Judicial Court of Massachusetts upheld the first-degree murder conviction of a man who killed his wife, in part because of an affair she was having.

Also consider the case of John Patrick Dennis who killed his estranged wife, Robin, after witnessing her in an embrace with her boyfriend, Dantz, and after learning that she was doing drugs with Dantz in view of John and Robin's son. Dennis was convicted of first-degree murder, and his conviction was later affirmed:

> Antecedent events may be relevant in determining whether the triggering event in fact produced the hot blood necessary to rebut malice—they may support or detract from that nexus—but they do not suffice to give the triggering event a legal quality it does not otherwise have. Discovering one's spouse in an embrace with a paramour will not constitute adequate provocation because at some earlier time he or she committed adultery with that paramour. That is a matter for the divorce court; it does not reduce murder to some lesser offense.[46]

last straw rule An unlawful killing can be reduced from murder to manslaughter if it was caused by longstanding resentment or humiliation that triggered the crime.

The appeals court in this case basically rejected the so-called **last straw rule**. According to the rule, murder may be reduced to manslaughter in light of "a smoldering resentment or pent-up rage resulting from earlier insults or humiliating events culminating in a triggering event that, by itself, might be insufficient to provoke the deadly act."[47] The court felt that even though Dennis went through some trying times, including trying to support Robin and their son even in the face of Robin's infidelity and continued drug use, his tribulations were not sufficient to clear him of a murder conviction.

Involuntary Manslaughter

Involuntary manslaughter is typically an unintentional killing. Some states define involuntary manslaughter as a stand-alone offense. Others, like Minnesota, grade manslaughter by degree, usually defining first-degree manslaughters as voluntary

---

[45]*Commonwealth v. Schnopps*, 459 N.E.2d 98 (Mass. 1984).
[46]*Dennis v. State*, 105 Md. App. 687 (1995), p. 699.
[47]Ibid., p. 689.

and second-degree manslaughters as *in*voluntary. Regardless of the approach, there are typically two types of involuntary manslaughter: (1) criminal negligence manslaughter and (2) criminal act manslaughter.

Criminal Negligence Manslaughter. Involuntary criminal negligence manslaughter occurs when someone deviates substantially from the usual standard of care or behavior that we would expect of people in normal situations. It must be "so gross as to be deserving of punishment."[48] The defendant (1) creates a high degree of risk and (2) is aware that death or serious bodily injury could result, yet acts anyway.

Parental neglect is a classic example of behavior that can lead to an involuntary (criminal negligence) manslaughter conviction. An example would be a parent who ignores a child's need for food or medical care *and is unaware of the peril this places the child in*—the result is likely involuntary manslaughter.[49] On the other hand, if the parent *is* aware of the risk, then the child's death may be murder.[50]

Criminal Act Manslaughter. Criminal act manslaughter occurs when an unintentional death results from another *nonfelonious* criminal act. We discuss *felony* murder in the next section. Here we are interested in deaths that result during the commission of a separate offense or infraction that is less serious than a felony. For example, some states permit this sort of manslaughter conviction if a motorist runs a stop sign and kills another individual, such as a pedestrian crossing the street.[51] Some states take a more restrictive approach and limit (involuntary) criminal act manslaughter convictions to cases involving misdemeanors (as opposed to traffic law violations). If a person hits another person in the face and the latter dies, then arguably the result is involuntary manslaughter—provided that the person doing the hitting did not *intend* for the victim to die.[52]

Homicide under the Model Penal Code

The Model Penal Code references three types of criminal homicide: murder, manslaughter, and negligent homicide. Assuming there is no justification or excuse and/or no mitigating circumstances, a murder occurs when someone kills another person (1) purposely or knowingly or (2) recklessly, with extreme indifference to human life.[53] This differs from some of the other definitions of murder presented thus far, as the Model Penal Code does not grade the crime into levels. Nor does the Model Penal Code's definition of murder require malice aforethought, as was the case under common law.

Manslaughter occurs when someone either (1) recklessly kills someone else or (2) kills someone else under circumstances that would constitute murder, but the crime occurs as a result of "extreme mental or emotional disturbance" and for which

---

[48]*Hazelwood v. State*, 912 P.2d 1266 (Alaska Ct. App. 1996), p. 1279, n. 16.
[49]See, e.g., *State v. Williams*, 484 P.2d 1167 (Wash Ct. App. 1971).
[50]See, e.g., *People v. Burden*, 72 Cal. App. 3d 603 (Ct. App. 1977).
[51]See, e.g., *State v. Hupf*, 101 A.2d 355 (Del. 1953).
[52]*Comber v. United States*, 584 A.2d 26 (D.C. Ct. App. 1990).
[53]Model Penal Code, Section 210.2(1)(a)-(b).

there is a "reasonable explanation or excuse."[54] Reckless manslaughter is the lesser included offense of reckless murder, without the extreme indifference to the value of human life. As for "extreme mental or emotional disturbance," the Model Penal Code includes in it sudden heat of passion and diminished capacity. For example, a woman who finds her husband in bed with another woman and, enraged, kills him, would arguably be guilty of manslaughter under the Model Penal Code.

Finally, negligent homicide is the least serious form of homicide under the Model Penal Code. A person is guilty of the crime if that person kills another because of a "gross deviation" from the standard of care a reasonable person would exercise.[55] Assume a driver, texting, fails to see a child in the crosswalk in a school zone, hits the child, and kills him. The driver would likely be guilty of negligent homicide under the Model Penal Code.

Felony Murder

felony murder A person is guilty of murder when a death results during his or her commission of a violent felony.

The **felony murder** rule states that a person is guilty of murder when a death results during that person's commission of a felony. Nearly every state recognizes this rule, usually limiting it to certain listed (and serious) felonies. Examples include robbery, rape, arson, and burglary.

Assume, for example, that Bob burglarizes Jim's house. During the burglary, Jim grabs a gun and confronts Bob. Bob shoots Jim. Bob would be guilty of murder, as he intentionally shot Jim. What makes the felony murder rule even stricter than this, however, is that even if Jim's death was accidental, the rule would still apply. What if Jim died from fright instead of a gunshot wound? Bob would still be liable for murder. The felony murder rule thus establishes strict liability for *any* death that occurs during the commission of a felony.

Why maintain a felony murder rule? The primary logic behind it is deterrence. According to one court, the goal of the felony murder rule is

> to deter dangerous conduct by punishing as murder a homicide resulting from dangerous conduct in the perpetration of a felony. . . . If the felonious conduct, under all of the circumstances, made death a foreseeable consequence, it is reasonable for the law to infer . . . the malice that qualifies the homicide as murder.[56]

Felony Murder Limitations

Although the felony murder rule is far-reaching, there are limitations to it. One of them is that most states limit the rule to *inherently dangerous* felonies, those most likely to result in serious injury or loss of life. This includes any felony that "by its very nature, . . . cannot be committed without creating a substantial risk that someone will be killed."[57] For crimes like robbery and arson, this definition suffices. For some

---

[54]Model Penal Code, Section 210.3(1)(a)-(b).
[55]Model Penal Code, Section 210.4.
[56]*Fisher and Utley v. State*, 786 A.2d 706 (Md. 2001), p. 732.
[57]*People v. Burroughs*, 678 P.2d 894 (Cal. 1984), p. 900.

others, however, it may not. Thus courts will sometimes examine "the facts and the circumstances of the particular case to determine if such felony was inherently dangerous in the manner and circumstances in which it was committed."[58]

A second limitation placed on the felony murder rule is that the felony must be *independent of the homicide*. Assume Sarah negligently kills Michelle. Under most circumstances, such a killing (involuntary manslaughter) would be considered a felony. Since a death occurred here during the course of a felony (i.e., the involuntary manslaughter), then under the felony murder rule, the manslaughter would be murder. In other words, if the felony murder rule were strictly applied to situations like this, there could never be the crime of manslaughter, only murder. A harsher punishment could thus result—perhaps when it need not to.

So how do we determine if the felony is independent of the homicide? Here is how one court answered the question:

> [A] felony does not merge with a homicide where the act causing death was committed with a collateral and independent felonious design separate from the intent to inflict the injury that caused death.[59]

For example, if a kidnapping results in death, it will be considered distinct from homicide and the felony murder rule will apply.[60] The two offenses do not merge together into the same offense because the intent to kidnap is distinct from the intent to kill. Were the two offenses treated as the same, the felony murder rule could not serve its purpose, which is again to deter people from killing people during the commission of felonies.

The **res gestae** (Latin for "things done to commit") requirement places yet another limitation on the felony murder rule. Simply, the homicide must occur during the *res gestae* of the felony. There are three subcomponents to the *res gestae* requirement:

1. The felony and the homicide must accompany each other in close temporal proximity. On the one hand, if the homicide occurs first and is later followed by a separate felony, the felony murder rule will not apply. The temporal ordering should be reversed. On the other hand, when the homicide occurs post-felony, the felony murder rule applies. For example, if a suspect robs a bank and kills a security guard while fleeing the scene, felony murder results. The same would hold even if a police officer, in pursuit of the suspect across urban rooftops in the dark, falls into an air shaft and dies.[61] The felony murder rule would *not* apply, however, if the fleeing suspect runs a stop sign and kills another motorist hundreds of miles from the crime scene.[62]

2. The second component of the *res gestae* requirement is that there be a *cause* between the felony and the homicide. If the later is wholly independent of the former, the felony murder rule will not apply. This is not unlike the causation requirement introduced back in Chapter 3. Consider the case of Nelson King who, along

res gestae Latin term meaning "things done to commit." In regards to felony murder, the sequence of the felony from beginning to end.

---

[58] *State v. Stewart*, 663 A.2d 912 (R.I. 1995), p. 919.
[59] *People v. Hansen*, 885 P.2d 1022 (Cal. 1994), p. 1029.
[60] *People v. Escobar*, 48 Cal. App. 4th 999 (Ct. App. 1996), pp. 1012-13.
[61] *People v. Matos*, 634 N.E.2d 157 (N.Y. 1994).
[62] See *Doane v. Commonwealth*, 237 S.E.2d 797 (Va. 1977), p. 798.

with Mark Bailey, was flying a plane containing over 500 pounds of marijuana to a location in Virginia. The men encountered heavy cloud cover, became lost, and eventually crashed. Bailey was killed in the crash. The court in *King* v. *Commonwealth*[63] held that King was not guilty of felony murder because the crash could have occurred even if they were carrying legal cargo. In other words, the felony in this case (transporting the marijuana) did not *cause* Bailey's death.

3. The third component of the *res gestae* requirement focuses on the *who* of the killing. Simply, what if a killing occurs during the course of a felony, but at the hands of someone else? In general, the answer is that the felony murder rule "does not extend to a killing, although growing out of the commission of the felony, if directly attributable to the act of one other than the defendant or those associated with him in the unlawful enterprise." This means that if someone else other than the felon, even an adversary (such as a security guard who fires her gun at a bank robbery suspect and kills an innocent bystander), is responsible for the killing, the felony murder rule does not apply. So even though the felon sets the wheels in motion, he or she may not be properly held responsible for all harms that result from the felony he or she is responsible for. Not all courts agree with this approach. As one put it,

> [W]hen a felon's attempt to commit a forcible felony sets in motion a chain of events which were or should have been within his contemplation when the motion was initiated, he should have been responsible for any death which by direct and almost inevitable sequence results from the initial criminal act.[64]

Under this construction, it is still unclear whether a jury would find the defendant guilty of felony murder. The question is whether (to again use our security guard example) the death of an innocent at the hands of a security guard was a reasonable foreseeable consequence of the bank robbery.

Mercy Killings

physician-assisted suicide A patient seeks the assistance of a physician to end his or her life.

euthanasia Purposeful termination of life by someone other than the patient.

Most homicide victims are unwilling; they don't *want* to die. Some individuals, however, do want to die, either because they are in extreme pain, suffering from a debilitating condition, or both. From time to time, such individuals have sought the assistance of their physicians in ending their lives, a practice known as **physician-assisted suicide**. Others have sought **euthanasia**, a purposeful termination of life by someone other than the patient.

Emotions run high on these subjects. Supporters feel people should be able to chart their own destiny and end their lives if they see fit. Others feel it is morally wrong for anyone to prematurely end his or her own life. We cannot hope to settle the debate here. What we *can* do, however, is call attention to the legal implications of these practices. Is it a violation of the criminal law for a physician to assist a patient in ending his or her life? Likewise, is euthanasia criminal? We will look at each practice separately.

---

[63]*King* v. *Commonwealth*, 368 S.E.2d 704 (Va. Ct. App. 1988).
[64]*People* v. *Lowery*, 687 N.E.2d 973 (Ill. 1997), p. 976.

Physician-Assisted Suicide

On June 4, 1990, the American public learned that Dr. Jack Kevorkian helped Janet Adkins, a 54-year-old Alzheimer's patient, end her life.[65] He met Ms. Adkins in a van he had outfitted with a "suicide machine" that was set up to administer a lethal chemical cocktail via an intravenous line. Ms. Adkins pushed a lever that released the chemicals into her body, thus making her suicide physician assisted.

Jack Kevorkian's actions gained considerable publicity, thrusting the assisted suicide issue center stage (even though what Kevorkian did was not technically physician-assisted suicide, as we will see in the next subsection). It did so, in part, because what Kevorkian did was illegal in Michigan, but not in every state. For example, Washington State's "Death with Dignity Act," enacted in 2008, permits the practice, subject to certain restrictions.[66] It was patterned after Oregon's law that, like Washington's, came to pass by way of popular initiative (i.e., enough voter signatures were secured to put it on a statewide ballot). Washington's law contains these restrictions:

- The patient must be an adult (18 or over) resident of the state of Washington.
- The patient must be mentally competent, verified by two physicians (or referred to a mental health evaluation).
- The patient must be terminally ill with less than six months to live, verified by two physicians.
- The patient must make voluntary requests, without coercion, verified by two physicians.
- The patient must be informed of all other options including palliative and hospice care.
- There is a 15-day waiting period between the first oral request and a written request.
- There is a 48-hour waiting period between the written request and the writing of the prescription.
- The written request must be signed by two independent witnesses, at least one of whom is not related to the patient or employed by the health care facility.
- The patient is encouraged to discuss with family (not required because of confidentiality laws).
- The patient may change their mind at any time and rescind the request.[67]

In 1997, the Supreme Court upheld an earlier Washington statute (and a New York statute) that criminalized the practice of assisted suicide,[68] but the Court left open the possibility that states could opt to make the practice legal, which Washington and Oregon then did. Their laws continue to survive legal scrutiny.[69] Recently, the Georgia Supreme Court decided that a law aimed at controlling assisted suicides

---

[65]See *People v. Kevorkian*, 527 N.W.2d 714 (Mich. 1994).
[66]Revised Code of Washington Section 70.245.
[67]See http://apps.leg.wa.gov/RCW/default.aspx?cite=70.245 (accessed May 6, 2011).
[68]*Washington v. Glucksberg*, 521 U.S. 702 (1997).
[69]See, e.g., *Oregon v. Ashcroft*, 368 F.3d 1118 (9th Cir. 2004), aff'd., 546 U.S. 243 (2006).

was unconstitutional.[70] In particular, the court decided that Georgia's law violated free speech because it criminalized offers to assist people with suicide. The court said that a ban on assisted suicide *could* be legal, but not in the way the Georgia statute in question was written. Thirty-seven states criminalize assisted suicide, according to the Patients Rights Council.[71]

Over time, states have abolished their laws against suicide. While attempted suicide was a misdemeanor under common law, it no longer is. This trend suggests a certain measure of "tolerance" for the practice of suicide, which may be why some states have legalized physician-assisted suicide. Supporters view the practice as anything but homicide: "Assisted suicide is distinguished from murder by the individual's consent, the same principle that distinguishes sex from rape, exchange from theft, confession from duress, and a variety of other matters found throughout our legal system."[72]

Euthanasia

On September 17, 1998, Jack Kevorkian administered a lethal injection to Thomas Youk, then 52, who was in the final stages of amyotrophic lateral sclerosis (ALS). Although Youk consented, he did not actually press a lever to end his life, like Ms. Adkins did. Instead, Kevorkian administered the drug. Kevorkian thus *euthanized* Mr. Youk, which is distinct from helping him commit suicide. Kevorkian was prosecuted for murder and convicted by a Michigan jury of second-degree murder. He was paroled after spending just over eight years in prison.

Euthanasia is a form of intentional homicide, but with a motivation of mercy.[73] It is homicide because, though the victim may consent to the practice, he or she has no direct or active role in the killing. As such, euthanasia is considered a form of murder, even in the three states that sanction physician-assisted suicide. As one court put it, "Murder is no less murder because the homicide is committed at the desire of the victim."[74] At most, the defendant's or victim's intentions may serve as mitigating factors, thus reducing the punishment the defendant could receive. But euthanasia remains criminal in all 50 states.

Corporation Murder

Homicides are typically committed by one or more people against one or more other people. Can we extend this, then, to corporations? After all, corporations are made up of several people. The answer is yes, but it can be rather difficult for a prosecutor to secure a conviction.

---

[70]Kim Severson, "Georgia Court Rejects Law Aimed at Assisted Suicide," *New York Times*, February 6, 2012, http://www.nytimes.com/2012/02/07/us/assisted-suicide-law-is-overturned-by-georgia-supreme-court.html?_r=1 (accessed July 7, 2012).

[71]Ibid. See also http://www.patientsrightscouncil.org/site/assisted-suicide-state-laws/ (accessed July 7, 2012).

[72]E. Rubin, "Assisted Suicide, Morality, and Law: Why Prohibiting Assisted Suicide Violates the Establishment Clause," *Vanderbilt Law Review*, Vol. 63(2010), p. 811.

[73]N. M. Gorsuch, "The Right to Assisted Suicide and Euthanasia," *Harvard Journal of Law and Public Policy*, Vol. 23 (2000), pp. 599–710.

[74]*State* v. *Fuller*, 278 N.W.2d 756 (Neb. 1979), p. 761.

In 1978, the Ford Motor Company recalled the then-popular Pinto following allegations that a faulty fuel tank design was responsible for some motorists' deaths. The recall followed allegations that Ford was aware of the flaw and initially refused to redesign the fuel tanks, opting instead to settle lawsuits because the costs involved were lower. This claim, combined with other allegations, prompted the state of Indiana to bring reckless homicide charges against the company. In 1980, a jury returned "not guilty" verdicts on three counts that the Pinto's design flaw resulted in three women's deaths.[75] Although the verdict was a victory for the company, it signaled the possibility that a company could be held criminal liable for homicide.

In the 1980s, a Texas nursing home was prosecuted for murder when an 87-year-old woman died from apparent neglect.[76] The court granted a defense motion for a mistrial at the end of what is still the longest trial in Texas history (seven months). Even so, the case signaled the possibility that corporations, like individuals, can be criminally responsible for homicide. Such convictions are quite rare, however. Obvious questions remain. Who will be punished? A corporation, though it is made up of several people, is a legal construction, not flesh and bone. If it is not a physical being, it cannot be punished in the traditional sense (e.g., put in prison) but only through fines. Thus any resulting conviction, if not against the officers of the corporation, would be largely symbolic. No company would want a murder conviction to threaten its business!

YOUR DECISION

1. Elizabeth Harris and Paul Thibodeaux lived together with four children. Paul believed he was the biological father of all four children. One afternoon, however, Elizabeth informed Paul that she once had an affair and that he was not the biological father of the two-month-old baby girl. Devastated by the news, Paul took the infant, walked with her for about a mile, and then killed her. Paul is being charged with murder. He claims that he acted in the "heat of passion" and should only be charged with voluntary manslaughter. Is Paul guilty of murder or voluntary manslaughter? Was the provocation adequate to reduce the charges? Why or why not?

2. Joe and Jane Moyer were happily married for over 50 years. Tragically, in 2008 Jane was diagnosed with ALS, or Lou Gehrig's disease, and her health began to rapidly decline. Joe was heartbroken to see his wife suffer from such a terrible illness. One evening while Jane was asleep in their bedroom, Joe fatally shot her in the head. Joe claims he only killed Jane out of "mercy" to end her suffering. Can Joe be charged with some form of criminal homicide? If so, what type? Would you reach a different result in Montana, Washington, or Oregon? Why or why not?

[75] P. J. Becker, A. J. Jipson, and A. S. Bruce, "*State of Indiana v. Ford Motor Company* Revisited," *American Journal of Criminal Justice*, Vol. 26 (2002), pp. 181–202.
[76] *State of Texas* v. *Autumn Hills Convalescent Center, Inc.*, No. 85-CR-2625 (Dist. Ct. of Bexar Co., 187th Judicial District of Texas, March 25, 1986).

Summary

- *Homicide* is the killing of a human being by another human being.

- Most jurisdictions retain the common law definition of the beginning of life, namely that life begins when a fetus is born alive. There are exceptions to this definition.

- Most courts now define *death* as "brain death." A person is no longer considered alive if he or she is brain dead.

- *Murder* is homicide with malice aforethought.

- In general, if one person kills another person without justification, excuse, or any mitigating circumstances, that person is said to have killed with malice aforethought.

- In general, first-degree murder is murder that is willful, premeditated, and deliberated. It is a "cold-blooded" killing, one that is arguably more "evil" than a spontaneous killing.

- Any murder that is not "willful, premeditated, and deliberate" is considered second-degree murder.

- One form of second-degree murder occurs when the offender intends to cause grievous bodily injury and the result is death. Another occurs when the killer acts with a "depraved heart," which then leads to the death of another person.

- The death penalty may apply if aggravating circumstances, which add to the seriousness or enormity of the case, outweigh mitigating circumstances (factors that serve to extenuate or reduce the degree of moral culpability), if there even are any.

- Manslaughter is an unlawful homicide committed with the malice aforethought required for murder.

- At the risk of simplification, a voluntary manslaughter is the same as a "heat of passion" killing.

- An involuntary manslaughter is either a reckless or "criminally negligent" killing. There are typically two types of involuntary manslaughter: (1) criminal negligence manslaughter and (2) criminal act manslaughter.

- The Model Penal Code references three types of criminal homicide: murder, manslaughter, and negligent homicide.

- The felony murder rule states that a person is guilty of murder when a death results during that person's commission of a felony.

- Most states limit the felony murder rule to inherently dangerous felonies, those that are most likely to result in serious injury or loss of life.

- In physician-assisted suicide, a physician helps a person end his or her life (the person, not the physician, commits suicide).

- Euthanasia is a form of intentional homicide, with a motivation of mercy.

- Euthanasia is criminal in all 50 states; physician-assisted suicide is legal in 3 states (Washington, Oregon, and Montana).

- If a corporation is responsible for homicide, it can be found guilty of murder.

- Corporate murder convictions are exceptionally rare. Moreover, it is impossible to "punish" a corporation with a prison sentence.

Learning Objectives
- **Distinguish between rape and sexual assault.**
- **Summarize the nature and elements of the crime of rape.**
- **Summarize the laws pertaining to the crime of rape.**

CORE CONCEPTS

In this module, we begin our discussion on the wide array of what we call "assaultive offenses." We use the term *assaultive* for two reasons. First, the term loosely refers to criminal acts that involve physical harm—or the threat of physical harm—to others. If an assaultive act results in death, then the proper course of action is to treat the crime as a homicide, adhering the definitions we laid out in the previous module. Second, some states lump the offenses discussed in this chapter into a single penal code section. Texas offers an example. Its Penal Code combines rape, assault, and related offenses into a single chapter.

Comparing Rape and Sexual Assault

rape Sexual intercourse without the consent of the victim.

Rape and sexual assaults tend to evoke intense reactions because of their intimate and personal nature. At the risk of simplification, **rape** is "the taking of sexual intimacy with an unwilling person by force or without consent."[77] This definition is timeless, meaning that it incorporates both common law and current conceptions of rape. Early on, rape was a heterosexual crime, particularly male on female. At common law, a husband who forced his wife to engage in sexual intercourse was not guilty of rape, which is no longer the case in about half of the states.[78] Modern definitions of rape incorporate homosexual intercourse as well as forcible intercourse between married couples.

One of the reasons modern rape statutes are broader is that feminist criticisms prompted legislatures to abandon antiquated definitions of the crime that failed to account for some modern-day realities. Feminists argued, for example, that just because a man and woman are married does not mean that every act of sexual intercourse is voluntary. Some marriages are a loveless sham, held together only by a legal document, making a forcible sex act little different than one between strangers. Today, rape is regarded as "gender neutral," and the crime has been broadened to incorporate all forms of penetration.

---

[77]R. G. Singer and J. Q. LaFond, *Criminal Law: Examples and Explanations*, 4th ed. (New York: Wolters and Kluwer, 2007, p. 219).

[78]See M. J. Anderson, "Marital Immunity, Intimate Relationships, and Improper Inferences: A New Law on Sexual Offenses by Intimates," *Hastings Law Journal*, Vol. 54 (2003), pp. 1465–1574.

At many points throughout history, rape was treated as a capital offense. As recent as the mid-1920s, several states, the District of Columbia, and the federal government authorized capital punishment for rapists. In 1977, however, the U.S. Supreme Court decided that executing rapists, particularly males who raped adult females, constituted cruel and unusual punishment, in violation of the Eighth Amendment.[79] More recently, the Court outlawed the death penalty for offenders convicted of child rape.[80] Prison terms for rapists, however, can run from several years to life.[81]

Sexual Assault

sexual assault A general term that covers a range of nonconsensual sexual offenses against another person.

Sexual assault refers to an assault of a sexual nature. We define *assault* in detail later in this chapter (Module 4). For now, it is important to know, as we compare rape and sexual assault, that the former is a subtype of the latter. It is possible for a sexual assault to occur in the absence of intercourse. Inappropriate touching, forced kissing, indecent exposure, and a variety of other acts may constitute sexual assault. Definitions vary by jurisdiction. Because rape gets most of the attention, we limit our discussion primarily to it.

The term *sexual assault* is a bit of a misnomer. An assault does not require physical contact (see Module 4 for more details), but sexual assault is usually always likened with some form of physical contact. This is another reason why we limit our attention primarily to rape, as reconciling the meaning of *sexual assault* with a non-sexual assault can be rather difficult. Just know that some statutes use *sexual assault* to refer to a number of inappropriate actions of a sexual nature. Rape may be folded into a jurisdiction's sexual assault statute. It may also be a stand-alone offense.

Elements of Rape

In this section, we consider the elements of rape. The *mens rea* of rape is rather straightforward, as it is a general intent offense. The *actus reus* of rape can be a bit more complicated.

The *Mens Rea* of Rape

Recall from Chapter 3 that a general intent crime is one that contains no specific *mens rea* component. In most jurisdictions, rape is a general intent offense. This means that the defendant need not possess an intention that the rape is nonconsensual.[82] The act only need *be* nonconsensual, irrespective of what the offender was thinking.

On the other hand, if the defendant reasonably believed that the victim consented, then he (we will use *he* most of the time for consistency, realizing of course that rape is largely gender neutral these days) cannot be guilty of rape. As one court

---

[79]*Coker v. Georgia*, 433 U.S. 584 (1977).
[80]*Kennedy v. Louisiana*, 554 U.S. ___ (2008).
[81]See, e.g., Mich. Comp. Laws Section 750.520b (2008), authorizing life imprisonment for rapists.
[82]See, e.g., *Commonwealth v. Grant*, 464 N.E.2d 33 (Mass. 1984), p. 36.

put it, "The State must demonstrate either that [the] defendant did not actually believe that affirmative permission had been freely-given or that such a belief was unreasonable under all of the circumstances."[83] Not every jurisdiction takes this approach, however. For example, in Pennsylvania, the defendant's reasonable mistake as to the victim's lack of consent is not a defense to the crime of rape:

> The charge requested by the defendant [to inform jurors he believed the victim consented to his sexual advances] is not now and has never been the law of Pennsylvania. The crux of the offense of rape is force and lack of victim's consent. When one individual uses force or the threat thereof to have sexual relations with a person not his spouse and without the person's consent he has committed the crime of rape. If the element of the defendant's belief as to the victim's state of mind is to be established as a defense to the crime of rape, then it should be done by our legislature which has the power to define crimes and offenses. We refuse to create such a defense.[84]

This is a controversial decision—and it is not isolated. Other courts have taken a similar approach.[85] This begs some difficult questions: Is a defendant who mistakenly concludes that the victim consented to intercourse morally blameworthy? If not, should he then be found guilty of rape? As Joshua Dressler has observed, "The effect of dispensing with the reasonable-mistake-of-fact doctrine is, effectively, to convert rape, a felony carrying very severe penalties, into a strict liability offense."[86]

Even states that recognize a defendant can reasonably believe a victim consented are nervous about instructing jurors of the possibility. In California, this "reasonable mistake" instruction will not be given to jurors unless there is "substantial evidence of equivocal conduct [on the victim's part] that would have led a defendant to reasonably and in good faith believe consent existed where it did not."[87]

The Model Penal Code treats rape (in its section, Sex Offenses) as a specific intent offense, and since some state criminal codes emulate it, we cannot say that rape is *always* a general intent offense. Rape, according to the Model Penal Code, occurs when a male, acting purposely, knowingly, or recklessly, has sexual intercourse with a female under one or more of the following circumstances:

- the female is less than 10 years old
- the female is unconscious
- he compels the female to submit by force or threat of force (to her or others)
- he uses drugs or intoxicants such that the victim's ability to control her actions is compromised.[88]

Note that not only does the Model Penal Code regard rape as a specific intent offense, but the crime is also not gender neutral. Perhaps more interesting still, the Code does not define as rape nonconsensual intercourse between a husband and wife

---

[83]*State in the Interest of M.T.S.*, 609 A.2d 1266 (N.J. 1992), p. 1279.
[84]*Commonwealth v. Williams*, 439 A.2d 765 (Pa. Super. Ct. 1980), p. 769.
[85]See, e.g., *Commonwealth v. Ascolillo*, 541 N.E.2d 570 (Mass. 1989), p. 575; *Clifton v. Commonwealth*, 468 S.E.2d 155 (Va. Ct. App. 1996), p. 158.
[86]J. Dressler, *Understanding Criminal Law*, 5th ed. (Newark, NJ: Lexis-Nexis, 2009).
[87]*People v. Williams*, 841 P.2d 961 (Cal. 1992), p. 966.
[88]Model Penal Code, Section 213.1(1).

who live together. Why the apparently antiquated approach to rape? The Model Penal Code was drafted in the 1950s, then adopted by the American Law Institute in 1962, well before the feminist movement and the changes it imposed on rape statutes around the country. Critics of the Model Penal Code's rape definition claim Section 213 "should be pulled and replaced."[89]

The *Actus Reus* of Rape

The *actus reus* of rape varies somewhat, depending on whether the rape occurs in one or more of the following situations:

1. Force is used or threatened.
2. Deception is used.
3. The victim is asleep or unconscious.
4. The victim cannot give consent (e.g., is under the influence of drugs or is under age, as in the case of statutory rape).

Of these situations, forcible rape is most conventional. As such, we will devote most of our attention to it.

Forcible Rape.   What exactly is *forcible rape*? In general, it is rape that occurs when (1) the victim does not consent and (2) the sexual intercourse is secured by force or the threat of force. Both of these elements can be rather difficult to prove. What's more, there is a lack of agreement as to what each means. Let us begin with consent, then shift gears to force.

How is the determination made that a victim does not consent to intercourse? A verbal "no" may suffice, but for various reasons the victim may not externalize her preferences. For example, she may not want intercourse and yet fail to say as much. Should a defendant accused of rape in such a situation be guilty of the crime? Complicating the matter further is the fact that consent can be given and then withdrawn (or vice versa). What if the apparent victim consents initially and then withdraws consent once intercourse is underway? Unfortunately, there are no easy answers to questions like these[90]—and rape statutes rarely offer much clarification.

Consent is widely regarded as a self-evident term, but it may not be. Some courts have offered clarification by putting consent in terms of "affirmative and freely-given *permission* of the victim to the specific act of penetration (emphasis added)[91]," but even this definition is imperfect. What exactly constitutes permission? Often juries are left to decide whether consent was given, weighing the cases and testimony presented by both prosecution and defense.

As for the force dimension to rape, a little historical overview is necessary. Most people recognize force (or the threat thereof) when they see it. Yet force or threatened force was not always enough, even in the absence of consent, for a prosecutor

---

[89]D. W. Denno, "Why the Model Penal Code's Sexual Offense Provisions Should Be Pulled and Replaced," *Ohio State Journal of Criminal Law*, Vol. 1 (2003), pp. 207–218.
[90]See, e.g., *People v. John Z.*, 60 P.3d 183 (Cal. 2003); *State v. Siering*, 644 A.2d 958 (Conn. App. 1994).
[91]*State in the Interest of M.T.S.*, 609 A.2d 1266 (N.J. 1992), p. 1277.

to secure a rape conviction. At common law, the victim must also have *resisted*. Interestingly, this resistance requirement has carried forward into recent history. Even today, some courts require a lack of consent, force by the perpetrator, and resistance on the victim's part.

For example, in a 1962 Tennessee case, the state's supreme court required that the victim resist "the attack in every way possible and continue[] such resistance until she [is] overcome by force, [is] insensible through fright, or cease[s] resistance from exhaustion, fear of death or great bodily harm."[92] Some years later, in *Rusk* v. *State*,[93] a Maryland appeals court was confronted with the question of whether a man's rape conviction should be upheld after the victim said, once he put his hands lightly around her throat, "If I do what you want, will you let me go without killing me?" The court concluded that no rape occurred because the victim failed to resist, although it later reversed the decision, holding that the jury should have made that determination: The "reasonableness of [the victim's] apprehension of fear [and, thus, her justification for not physically resisting] was plainly a question of fact for the jury to determine."[94]

Much the same decision was reached in yet another case, this one involving a college student who was convicted of raping another student in her dorm room.[95] Although she said "no" several times, she did not resist after the male student locked the door, pushed her onto a bed, straddled her, and then had intercourse. The state supreme court affirmed a lower court's decision to overturn the conviction, pointing out that although consent was lacking, the victim's "testimony [was] devoid of any statement which clearly or adequately describes the use of force or the threat of force against her."[96] This decision was reached in 1992.

In recent years, courts, legislatures, and critics of traditional conceptions of rape have come to realize that the common law resistance requirement is unreasonable. Some rape victims become paralyzed with fear and thus do not physically resist. Should their rapists never be convicted? Of course not. And even if a victim resists, doing so can be rather dangerous. From a self-protection standpoint, there may be a compelling reason *not* to resist. In light of these realizations, a number of states have amended their rape statutes. Others have largely abandoned the resistance requirement through court decisions.

Courts have also reconceptualized force itself. Once regarded as a mostly violent act, one that causes physical harm, force is now viewed by some courts in more relaxed terms. For example, the California Supreme Court has stated that there is nothing "in the common usage definitions of the term 'force,' or in the express statutory language...that suggests force...actually means force '*substantially* different from or *substantially* greater than' the physical force normally inherent in an act of consensual sexual intercourse."[97] Another court put it this way:

> [T]he law of rape primarily guards the integrity of a woman's will and the privacy of her sexuality from an act of intercourse undertaken without her consent. Because the

---

[92]*King* v. *State*, 357 S.W.2d 42 (Tenn. 1962), p. 45.
[93]*Rusk* v. *State*, 406 A.2d 624 (Md. Ct. Spec. App. 1979), reversed, 424 A.2d 720 (Md. 1981).
[94]Ibid.
[95]*Commonwealth* v. *Berkowitz*, 609 A.2d 1338 (Pa. Super. Ct. 1992), aff'd, 641 A.2d 1161 (Pa. 1994).
[96]Ibid., 641 A.2d, p. 1164 (Pa. 1994).
[97]*People* v. *Griffin*, 94 P.2d 1089 (Cal. 2004), p. 1094.

fundamental wrong is the violation of a woman's will and sexuality, the law of rape does not require that "force" cause physical harm. Rather, . . ."force" plays merely a supporting evidentiary role, as necessary only to insure an act of intercourse has been undertaken against a victim's will.[98]

To summarize the *actus reus* forcible rape, then, the key *modern* ingredients are (1) a lack of consent on the victim's part and (2) sexual penetration. There is no requirement that injury result. Increasingly, there is no requirement that the victim resist in any manner (physical or verbal). Of course, there are some exceptions. And gray areas remain. For example, a key unresolved question is, "What level of consent, other than an express and verbally uttered 'yes' suffices?"

See the accompanying Court Decision for more on consent. In it we examine the case of *People* v. *Ireland*, where the defendant is charged with raping prostitutes who initially consented to sexual intercourse for money.

COURT DECISION

The Logic behind Consent in Rape Prosecutions

People v. Ireland
2010 WL 3489359 (Cal. App. 2010)

Decision: A prostitute can withdraw her consent to engage in sexual intercourse when threatened with a weapon.

Reason: Each of appellant's four convictions of forcible rape involved a different victim but a similar scenario. . . . In late October of 2007, V.B. was working as a prostitute on Motel Drive when appellant, in a four-door burgundy car, approached and asked her for a "date," which she described as an agreement to have sex for an agreed-upon amount of money. The two agreed on a price of $40. . . . They parked in a driveway near railroad tracks.

Appellant told V.B. to get into the back seat of the car, which she did. When appellant entered the back seat, V.B. felt a metal knife against her neck. V.B. began to cry and begged appellant "please don't hurt me." V.B. testified she was afraid and did not want to die. . . . Appellant then had vaginal intercourse with V.B., while holding the knife to her throat. V.B. described the knife as a big butcher knife with a seven-to nine-inch blade and a wooden handle. . . . V.B. had never met appellant prior to the incident. She did not consent to the sexual act as it happened, and she did not agree to the use of the knife when she got into the car. V.B. did not report the incident to the police at first, because she was a prostitute.

[Victim 2, Victim 3, A.H., and Victim 4, C.S. who was only 15-years old, had sexual intercourse under similar factual circumstances as the first count].

(continued)

---

[98]*People* v. *Cicero*, 157 Cal. App. 3d (Ct. App. 1984), p. 475.

COURT DECISION
(continued)

. . . Lack of consent is an element of the crime of rape. Consent is defined in section 261.6 as "positive cooperation in act or attitude pursuant to an exercise of free will. The person must act freely and voluntarily and have knowledge of the nature of the act or transaction involved." CALCRIM No. 1000, as given here, instructed that "[t]o consent, a woman must act freely and voluntarily and know the nature of the act."

. . . Appellant's argument is that each victim gave her consent to the sex act that was committed, that his use of the knife during the act did not automatically negate that consent, and that there was insufficient evidence that any of the victims communicated a withdrawal of consent to him. Respondent [State of California], on the other hand, contends the determinative question is not whether the victims communicated a withdrawal of consent. Instead, according to respondent, appellant's use of the knife, along with his express or implied threat to harm his victims if they did not cooperate, did automatically negate their previously given consent.

We agree with respondent's analysis. There is no doubt that, at the beginning of each encounter, each victim freely consented to intercourse. But as to each of the victims, appellant communicated the express or implied threat that, if they did not continue to cooperate even after he produced the knife and held it to their throats, he would do them harm. As to the victim V.B., the testimony was that appellant told her "just to cooperate" and she "won't get hurt." When the victim J.W. asked appellant what he was doing with the knife, he told her to "'shut up.'" She did, because she was afraid he would otherwise "slice [her] neck off." He told her not to scream or make any sudden movements and he would not use the knife. When the victim A.H. reacted to appellant putting the knife to her throat by saying "no," appellant responded by instructing her to put a condom on his penis, remove her pants, and get on her knees. She complied because she thought he would otherwise kill her. To the victim C.S., appellant said "do what I say and you won't get hurt." She cooperated out of fear.

. . . The essence of consent is that it is given out of free will. That is why it can be withdrawn. While there exists a defense to rape based on the defendant's actual and reasonable belief that the victim does consent, we do not require that victims communicate their lack of consent. We certainly do not require that victims resist. Yet this is what appellant proposes here. At the time of the offenses, appellant told his victims to cooperate or be hurt. Now he contends they were required to express to him their lack of cooperation. That cannot be the law. When appellant used the knife and expressly or impliedly threatened his victims, and in the absence of any conduct by the victims indicating that they continued to consent, the previously given consent no longer existed, either in fact or in law. . . . From all of this evidence, it is clear that these victims did not continue to consent when appellant put the knife to their throats and that appellant knew they did not continue to consent. Thus, if they were required to communicate a withdrawal of consent, they adequately did so.

Rape by Deception. At common law, rape by deception was not a crime. A man could use any method of trickery or deception to lure a woman into having intercourse. For example, in *Boro* v. *Superior Court*, a woman consented to sex after her doctor told her she contracted a dangerous disease that could only be cured through surgery or via intercourse with a male who was presumably injected with a serum.[99] She agreed to sex with the doctor. He was convicted of rape, but the conviction was overturned on appeal once it was clear that the "victim was aware of the nature of the act. . . ."[100] In contrast, as happened in an actual case, if a male doctor secures permission from his female patient to insert an instrument into her vagina while she is unconscious, he is guilty of rape if the instrument is his penis.[101]

Rape when the Victim Is Asleep or Unconscious. What if, in a situation similar to the one we just presented, a man has intercourse with a woman while she is asleep or unconscious? Typically, such an act will be considered rape, as consent is lacking. It is difficult to conceive of a situation in which a rape victim could have consented to sexual intercourse and then either fallen asleep or slipped into unconsciousness.

Rape when the Victim Cannot Give Consent. A victim may be incompetent to give consent in one of three situations. First, she is drugged and therefore not thinking rationally. It does not matter whether such intoxication was self-induced or attributable to another individual. Second, consent generally cannot be given if the

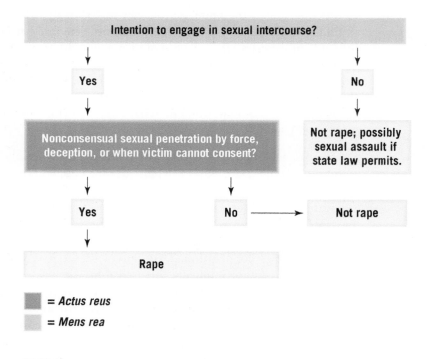

Figure 6.3
Rape

---

[99]See, e.g., *Boro* v. *Superior Court*, 163 Cal. App. 3d 1224 (Ct. App. 1985).
[100]Ibid., p. 1224.
[101]*Pomeroy* v. *State*, 94 Ind. 96 (1883).

statutory rape A strict liability crime in which the defendant has sexual intercourse with a minor under the age of consent.

victim is mentally disabled. Finally, if the victim is too young, consent cannot be given. This is known as **statutory rape**. Some states use the term *rape of a child* in place of statutory rape. In either case, the crime occurs when the victim is legally incapable of giving consent. The age at which a victim can legally give consent varies by state.[102] Likewise, the age of the offender may enter into the equation, but whether it does varies by state as well. Finally, most states also require that the two individuals have a certain "gap" of years between their ages, usually around four years. So, for example, an 18-year-old who has sex with a 17-year-old is generally not guilty of statutory rape in most states because there is an insufficient age gap.

See Figure 6.3 for a summary of rape.

Proving Rape

Recent developments in rape law have tipped the scales in favor of the prosecution. Rape prosecutions are not as difficult as they once were partly because of the disappearing corroboration requirement. Also, rape shield laws make it difficult for defense attorneys to call into question the victim's character.

The Disappearing Corroboration Requirement

At common law, there was no requirement that a rape victim have her testimony corroborated with physical evidence. Indeed, any crime other than perjury could be proven without physical evidence.[103] This made it rather easy to convict criminal defendants. As time went on, states began to add corroboration requirements, partly out of fear that false charges would be raised. Rape victims were required to show evidence such as bruises, ripped clothing, and evidence of physical struggle—or, in the extreme, to "display to honest men the injury done to her, the blood and her dress stained with blood, and the tearing of her dress."[104]

Recently, however, the vast majority of states have returned to the common law approach—at least so far as rape goes. Only three states (Ohio, New York, and Texas) retain any form of a corroboration requirement.[105] Critics of this progression raise arguments like this:

> Contrary to popular belief . . ., non-genital, physical injury from rape is uncommon. . . . Sixty-eight percent of . . . admitted emergency room rape victims suffered no non-genital physical injuries, 26 percent suffered mild non-genital physical injuries, only 5 percent suffered moderate non-genital physical injuries, and just 0.02 percent suffered severe non-genital physical injuries. . . . Even genital physical injuries are rare as most rape victims do not suffer the kind of genital trauma that hospital staffs can detect. . . .

---

[102]For an overview of statutory rape laws by state, see http://www.cga.ct.gov/2003/olrdata/jud/rpt/2003-r-0376.htm (accessed September 6, 2010).

[103]*United States* v. *Wiley*, 492 F.2d 547 (D.C. Cir. 1974).

[104]M. J. Anderson, "The Legacy of the Prompt Complaint Requirement, Corroboration Requirement, and Cautionary Instructions on Campus Sexual Assault," *Boston University Law Review*, Vol. 84 (2004), p. 947.

[105]See N.Y. Penal Law Section 130.16(2008); Tex. Crim. Proc. Ann. Section 38.07(a) (2007); Ohio Rev. Code Ann. 2907.06(B) (2004).

The other type of corroborative evidence courts will accept is torn clothing or other evidence of a serious physical battle between the assailant and the victim. Most rapes, however, do not involve a fight that would produce this kind of evidence. . . . Most rapists, particularly acquaintance rapists, are able to subdue their victims with verbal coercion and pinning and need not resort to overt physical violence. . . . Some women also become frozen with fear once an attack begins, preventing physical resistance of their assailants.[106]

Rape Shield Laws

Over the years, defense attorneys in rape prosecutions have raised a number of arguments. For example, they have argued in some instances that the victim consented to intercourse. They have also argued that the victim may have had prior consensual sexual relations with the accused, perhaps making the instant act consensual as well. And they have even gone so far as to argue that the victim was promiscuous, given to a lack of sexual discretion. While defense attorneys can and still do argue that consent existed, they are limited in the other two areas. Defense attorneys are now significantly limited in their abilities to attack the credibility of a suspected rape victim. Why? So-called **rape shield laws** have been enacted across the country.[107] They limit evidence about the victim's prior sexual history. In 1974, Michigan passed the first such law. It said,

rape shield laws Statutes that restrict the admissibility of the victim's past sexual history at trial.

> Evidence of specific instances of the victim's sexual conduct, opinion evidence of the victim's sexual conduct, and reputation evidence of the victim's sexual conduct shall not be admitted . . . unless and only to the extent that the judge finds that the following proposed evidence is material to a fact at issue in the case and that its inflammatory or prejudicial nature does not outweigh its probative value: (a) Evidence of the victim's past sexual conduct with the actor, (b) Evidence of specific instances of sexual activity showing the source or origin of semen, pregnancy, or disease.[108]

Consider *People* v. *Wilhelm*, a case in which the defendant sought to introduce evidence that the victim (both were in a bar at the same time, although not together) exposed her breasts to two men seated at her table, allowing them to fondle her breast. The court did not allow the evidence to be presented, however, noting that "we fail to see how a woman's consensual sexual conduct with another in public indicates to third parties that the woman would engage in similar behavior with them."[109] It fell back on the rape shield statute. Critics of rape shield laws claim that they threaten the Sixth Amendment right to confrontation, which gives defendants an opportunity to confront and cross-examine their accusers and adverse who testify against them.

---

[106]Anderson, "The Legacy of the Prompt Complaint," pp. 978–979.
[107]For an overview of such laws, see http://www.ndaa.org/pdf/ncpca_statutes_rapeshield_09.pdf (accessed September 6, 2010).
[108]Mich. Comp. Laws Section 750.520j (2009).
[109]*People* v. *Wilhelm*, 476 N.W.2d 753 (Mich. Ct. App. 1991), p. 759.

YOUR DECISION

1. Julie and her girlfriends are excited to attend their first college party at a campus fraternity. Before they head out to the party, the girls decide to do a few "pregame" shots of vodka in their dorm room. When they arrive at the party, Julie also drinks several glasses of a fruity purple punch. Unbeknownst to Julie, the punch is made with 80-proof grain alcohol. Julie soon finds herself intoxicated and passes out in the bedroom of one of the fraternity brothers, Roger. Julie and Roger have an astronomy class together and have been flirting the first week of school. When Roger returns to his room at 2:00 A.M. and finds Julie in his bed, he assumes she is there to pursue a sexual relationship. Roger and Julie engage in sexual intercourse. Julie's memory of the event is very "fuzzy." She does not recall whether she said anything to Roger while they were having sex. Can Roger be charged with rape? Why or why not?

2. Jim and Brenda dated for approximately 12 months before they finally ended their tumultuous relationship. One evening six months into the relationship, Brenda alleges that Jim forced her to engage in sexual intercourse against her will. Brenda suffered some injuries, and Jim drove her to a local hospital for medical treatment. Brenda did not report the incident to the police at that time and in fact continued to date Jim for another six months. Brenda reported the incident only after the two ended their relationship. Jim claims Brenda is just "bitter" that he dumped her and is trying to ruin his reputation. Assuming what Brenda says is true, can Jim be charged with rape? Why or why not?

Summary

- *Rape* is generally defined as the "taking of sexual intimacy with an unwilling person by force or without consent."
- Rape is usually intercourse; sexual assault is other sexual contact without consent.
- Rape is typically a general intent offense, meaning that as long as the act is not consensual, *mens rea* has been satisfied.
- The *actus reus* of rape varies somewhat, depending on whether the rape occurs by force, deception, the victim is asleep/unconscious, or the victim cannot give consent.
- In general, forcible rape occurs when (1) the victim does not consent and (2) the sexual intercourse is secured by force or the threat of force.
- A rape victim may not be able to give consent either because she is not thinking rationally (e.g., from intoxication) or because she cannot legally give consent (called *statutory rape*).
- Recent developments in rape law have tipped the scales in favor of the prosecution.
- Most states have abandoned the requirement that rape victims corroborate their allegations with physical evidence.
- Defense attorneys are now significantly limited in their abilities to attack the credibility of a suspected rape victim because of states' enactment of so-called rape shield laws.

MODULE

6.3

ROBBERY

Learning Objectives
- **Describe the crime of robbery.**
- **Distinguish armed robbery from other forms of robbery.**

CORE CONCEPTS

Like rape, robbery is a serious crime. The Federal Bureau of Investigation (FBI) classifies it as one of four serious crimes in the Uniform Crime Reports (the others are rape, homicide, and aggravated assault). Robbery is an assaultive offense, meaning that it involves threats and the potential for physical contact. It is also a crime of theft that occurs under circumstances in which the victim is in some way forced into submission.

Elements of Robbery

There are six traditional elements of robbery:

1. The taking
2. and carrying away
3. of the personal property
4. of another person
5. by violence or by putting the victim in fear
6. with intent to permanently deprive the owner of the property.[110]

Note that the first five parts of this definition constitute the *actus reus* of robbery; the last constitutes the *mens rea*. Not all states treat robbery as a specific intent offense, however. Let us look at each in more detail.

The *Actus Reus* of Robbery

The "taking" element of robbery is fairly self-explanatory. Early on, however, the "taking" element of robbery had to occur in a trespassory fashion, meaning from the person or in the victim's presence. Some jurisdictions have realized that this can make it difficult to convict a person of robbery in some circumstances. Sue Titus Reid presents these scenarios in which robbery occurs, but without the trespassory element:

- A person, wishing to steal property from a farmhouse, encounters the owner in the field, knocks him unconscious, and proceeds to the house to steal.

---

[110]A. A. Moenssens, R. J. Bacigal, G. G. Ashdown, and V. E. Hench, *Criminal Law: Cases and Concepts,* 8th ed. (New York: Foundation Press, 2008), p. 756.

- A person takes a victim at gunpoint and forces him to call his office and instruct an employee to remove money from the company safe and deliver it to a designated person.[111]

Note that were a trespassory taking required in either instance, a robbery would not have occurred because the crimes failed to occur in the victim's presence.

Or, as an alternative, consider this:

- . . . a bank teller receives a call from the defendant, who threatens to set off a bomb at the teller's home unless a large sum of money be delivered to a hidden location designated by the caller.[112]

Has a robbery occurred here? Again, were it not for abandoning the trespassory element of early robbery definitions, the answer would be "no."

Just as the "taking" component of robbery is fairly clear, so too is the "carrying away" part. For example, if Hank points a gun at Steve, demands that Steve hand over his wallet, and then waits patiently for police to arrive, Hank may not have committed robbery. Obviously no robber in his or her right mind would "stick around," but the point is that for robbery to formally occur, the offender must not only take the property, but also leave the scene.

Robbery is limited to *personal* property. In general, and exclusive of situations like the two we pointed out earlier, if the property sought is not in the actual possession or constructive possession of the victim and is taken, it is a crime of larceny, not robbery. As explained in Chapter 3, property is in a person's actual possession if he or she is holding it or it is attached to the victim in some fashion. Constructive possession means the victim has control over the property, usually because it is in close physical proximity to the victim.

While robbery is a crime against property, it is also a crime against a person—hence our decision to include it in the present chapter. If there is not a person as victim, then again the crime will be larceny. For example, if Bill steals Ted's lawnmower while Ted is sleeping, he has not "robbed" Ted because Ted was not present or in any way confronted (e.g., hit and knocked unconscious) prior to the commission of the crime.

Finally, the fifth element of the *actus reus* of robbery is violence or putting the victim in fear. Obviously, since Ted was sleeping in our previous example, he was not robbed because he was not put in fear. At the other extreme, the offender who threatens a victim with a knife has arguably done enough to put the victim in fear such that the *actus reus* of robbery is satisfied.

The *Mens Rea* of Robbery

In general, a robbery does not occur unless, along with the *actus reus* of the offense, the offender intends to permanently deprive the owner of the property. There are

---

[111]S. T. Reid, *Criminal Law*, 8th ed. (New York: Oxford University Press, 2010), p. 177.
[112]A. A. Moenssens, R. J. Bacigal, G. G. Ashdown, and V. E. Hench, *Criminal Law: Cases and Concepts*, 8th ed. (New York: Foundation Press, 2008), p. 769.

exceptions. For example, some statutes contain an implicit *mens rea* component. California defines robbery in this way:

> Robbery is the felonious taking of personal property in the possession of another, from his person or immediate presence, and against his will, accomplished by means of force or fear.[113]

The *felonious taking* language captures the *mens rea* of robbery in California. Usually *felonious taking* means the taking of property with intent to deprive.

Other states treat robbery as a general intent crime. In Kansas, robbery is simply "the taking of property from the person or presence of another by force or by threat of bodily harm to any person."[114] The norm, however, is to define robbery as a specific intent offense. But whether the required intent is (a) to permanently deprive the owner of the property or (b) to force a victim to give up property depends on the law. For example, New York's statute reads, in part,

> Robbery is forcible stealing. A person forcibly steals property and commits robbery when, in the course of committing a larceny, he uses or threatens the immediate use of physical force upon another person for the *purpose* of: (1) Preventing or overcoming resistance to the taking of the property or to the retention thereof immediately after the taking; or (2) Compelling the owner of such property or another person to deliver up the property or to engage in other conduct which aids in the commission of the larceny (emphasis added).[115]

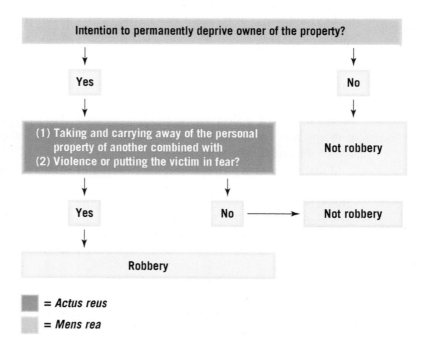

Figure 6.4

Robbery

[113]California Penal Code, Section 211 (2010).
[114]Kan. Stat. Ann. 21-3426 (2010); also see *State* v. *Thompson*, 558 P.2d 1079 (Kan. 1976).
[115]N.Y. Penal Law 160.00 (2010)

Note that the *mens rea* here is couched in terms of "purpose" and that there is no requirement imposed that the offender intend to permanently deprive.

Wisconsin's robbery statute emphasizes not just intent to commit the crime, but also the intent to steal:

> Whoever, with *intent to steal*, takes property from the person or presence of the owner by either of the following means is guilty of [robbery]: (a) By using force against the person of the owner with *intent* thereby to overcome his physical resistance or physical power of resistance to the taking or carrying away of property; or (b) By threatening the imminent use of force against the person of the owner or of another who is present with *intent* thereby to compel the owner to acquiesce in the taking or carrying away of property (emphasis added).[116]

See Figure 6.4 for a summary of robbery. Since there is no "one best" definition for the *mens rea* of robbery, we use the most common—namely, the intention to permanently deprive the owner of the property.

Armed Robbery

armed robbery The defendant is in possession of a weapon while committing the crime of robbery.

A robber who uses violence and/or puts the victim in fear need not use a weapon to do so. Indeed, many robbery statutes do not reference weapons. Some, however, do and thus define a more serious offense of **armed robbery**. In Illinois, for example, armed robbery requires that the offense be committed "while armed with a dangerous weapon."[117] Note the term *while*. It is not necessary that the weapon actually be *used* during commission of the offense.[118]

What qualifies as a deadly weapon? There are no easy answers. For example, what if a robbery suspect was carrying an unloaded pistol? Does doing so elevate the crime from robbery to armed robbery? According to a New York appeals court, the answer is "yes," partly because even an unloaded pistol can be used to bludgeon someone.[119] What about a toy gun? At least one court has decided that a toy gun, even one with a blocked barrel, can sustain a charge of robbery with a firearm.[120] Other jurisdictions have taken exception, especially if the gun in question is made out of lightweight plastic and could not be used as a bludgeon. To help other courts draw the line between deadly and nondeadly weapons, the Illinois Supreme Court adopted this fact-oriented test:

> [M]any objects, including guns, can be dangerous and cause serious injury, even when used in a fashion for which they were not intended. Most, if not all, unloaded real guns and many toy guns, because of their size and weight, could be used in deadly fashion as bludgeons. Since the robbery victim could be quite badly hurt or even killed by such weapons if used in that fashion, it seems to us they can properly be classified as dangerous weapons although they were not in fact used in that manner

---

[116]Wis. Stat. Ann. 943.32 (2010).
[117]Ill. Rev. Stats., Ch. 38, Section 18-2 (2010).
[118]See, e.g., *Commonwealth v. Blackburn*, 237 N.E.2d 35 (1968).
[119]*People v. Roden*, 235 N.E.2d 776 (1968).
[120]*Johnson v. Commonwealth*, 163 S.E.2d 570 (1968).

during the commission of the particular offense. It suffices that the potential for such use is present; the victim need not provoke its actual use in such manner.[121]

Some jurisdictions treat robbery with a firearm as two separate offenses, meaning that a person can be convicted of (a) robbery and (b) use of a firearm in the commission of a robbery. The latter crime is defined thusly:

> It shall be unlawful for any person to use or attempt to use any pistol, shotgun, rifle, or other firearm or display such weapon in a threatening manner while committing or attempting to commit murder, rape, forcible sodomy, inanimate or animate object sexual penetration. . . *robbery*, carjacking, burglary, malicious wounding . . ., or abduction.[122]

YOUR DECISION

1. Josh is an excellent pickpocket and manages to make a living lifting wallets from executives on Wall Street. Josh is generally so good that his victims do not even realize their wallets are being stolen right out of their back pockets. One afternoon, however, Josh's luck runs out. He accidentally trips and bumps into one his victims while trying to get the wallet. The victim realizes what is happening, knocks Josh to the ground, and calls the police. Can Josh be charged with robbery? Why or why not? Can Josh also be charged with robbery for the other jobs he completed where the victims were unaware of the encounter?

2. Joe and Janine are walking home from dinner and a movie one evening when Lucas suddenly pops out from behind a dumpster, points a gun at the couple, and demands they turn over all of their belongings. Joe tries to wrestle away the gun, but both Joe and Janine are fatally wounded. Only after the couple die from their gunshot wounds does Lucas take their money and jewelry. In addition to criminal homicide, can Lucas be charged with robbery? Why or why not? What if Lucas did not return until the next day to recover the belongings from the bodies? Would that be considered robbery?

Summary

- Robbery consists of (1) the taking (2) and carrying away (3) of the personal property (4) of another person (5) by violence or by putting the victim in fear (6) with intent to permanently deprive the owner of the property.

- At common law, the "taking" element of robbery must have been trespassory.

- Robbery is limited to *personal* property. If the property sought is not in the actual possession or constructive possession of the victim and is taken, it is a crime of larceny, not robbery.

- In general, a robbery does not occur unless, along with the *actus reus* of the offense, the offender intends to permanently deprive the owner of the property. There are exceptions.

---

[121]*People* v. *Skelton*, 414 N.E.2d 455 (1980), p. 458.
[122]Virginia Code Section 18.2-53.1 (2004).

- A robber who uses violence and/or puts the victim in fear need not use a weapon to do so.
- In addition to criminalizing robbery, some states also define a more serious offense of armed robbery.
- Armed robbery occurs when the offender commits robbery while armed with a dangerous weapon.

MODULE

6.4

ASSAULT AND BATTERY

Learning Objectives
- **Describe the crime of assault.**
- **Describe the crime of battery.**

CORE CONCEPTS

assault The threat or attempt of bodily harm to another person without physical contact.

battery Unlawful offensive touching of another without consent.

Assault and *battery* are among the most misused terms in criminal law. The mistake people typically make is to describe assault in terms of physical contact. Battery involves contact; assault falls just short of physical contact. We begin with battery, as it is difficult to understand assault without first understanding the meaning of battery.

Battery

Battery is unlawful touching, typically with injury. It occurs when one person makes violent physical contact with another person who does not consent to the contact, such as punching another person in the face. Not every statute requires injury, however. In addition, some courts have expanded the definition of *battery* and include actions that fall short of even physical contact. For example, if the law permits, it could be considered battery to spit in another person's face.[123]

Elements of Battery

Criminal statutes do not always spell out the *mens rea* of battery. For example, California defines the crime as nothing more than "willful and unlawful use of force or violence upon another."[124] In Florida, battery occurs when a person "actually and intentionally touches or strikes another person against the will of the other; or intentionally causes bodily harm to another person."[125] States that distinguish between

---

[123]*State v. Humphries*, 586 P.2d 130 (Wash. App. 1978).
[124]Cal. Penal Code Section 240 (2010).
[125]Fla. Stat. Section 784.03 (2010).

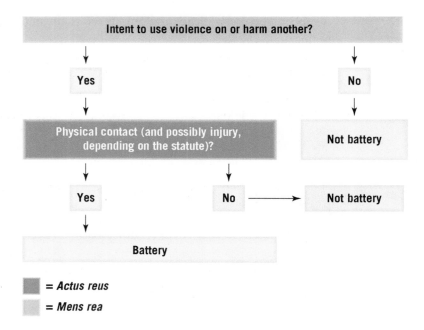

Figure 6.5
Battery

levels of intent (e.g., negligence vs. recklessness) for battery usually do so if they grade the offense by seriousness (e.g., first degree, second degree; felony, misdemeanor; etc.)

As for *actus reus*, as we mentioned earlier, battery is commonly associated with physical injury. This means that in some states battery does not occur unless there is physical injury. Yet in other states, such as Florida, all that is required is a "touch" or a "strike." Likewise, the California statute we quoted in the previous paragraph also falls short of requiring physical injury. Battery is summarized in Figure 6.5.

Many states go so far as to identify specific actions that are *not* considered battery. For example, Virginia law provides that various named school officials do not commit battery in any of the following instances while acting in their official capacities:

> (i) incidental, minor or reasonable physical contact or other actions designed to maintain order and control; (ii) reasonable and necessary force to quell a disturbance or remove a student from the scene of a disturbance that threatens physical injury to persons or damage to property; (iii) reasonable and necessary force to prevent a student from inflicting physical harm on himself; (iv) reasonable and necessary force for self-defense or the defense of others; or (v) reasonable and necessary force to obtain possession of weapons or other dangerous objects or controlled substances or associated paraphernalia that are upon the person of the student or within his control.[126]

Battery Classifications

It is relatively uncommon for states to maintain just one battery statute. Instead, the norm is to criminalize various types of battery, each with its own distinct elements.

---

[126]V.A. Code Section 18.2-57(F) (2010).

This accommodates the reality that there is no one "most common" type of battery, nor is there an ideal universal definition for the crime.

Some states define *battery* in terms of levels. Separate statutes may distinguish between, for example, simple battery and aggravated battery. To illustrate, aggravated battery occurs in Florida when the offender

> [i]ntentionally or knowingly causes great bodily harm, permanent disability, or permanent disfigurement; . . . uses a deadly weapon; [or] . . . if the person who was the victim of the battery was pregnant at the time of the offense and the offender knew or should have known that the victim was pregnant.[127]

In contrast, simple battery may be conduct that falls short of aggravated battery. Or it may be noninjurious yet nonconsensual insulting or harmful contact.

Other states reserve separate battery statutes for particular types of conduct, ranging from sexual battery to elder abuse. Florida is a state that does this—and also distinguishes between levels of battery (felony and aggravated). It reserves separate battery statutes for the following types of conduct, and several others:

- Domestic battery by strangulation
- Battery of law enforcement officers, firefighters, emergency medical care providers, public transit employees or agents, or other specified officers
- Battery on sexually violent predatory detention or commitment facility staff
- Battery on a juvenile probation officer
- Battery on health services personnel
- Battery on persons 65 years of age or older
- Battery on code inspectors
- Child battery[128]

Battery without Assault

Battery is usually regarded as a consummated assault. Yet there is no ironclad requirement that a battery be preceded by an assault.[129] And while we have not yet formally defined assault, suffice it to say for now that assault requires a measure of anticipation on the victim's part. So, if an irate student clubs an unsuspecting professor in the head from behind while she is writing on the whiteboard, the student has committed a battery without assault. Alternatively, assume Evan is at a fraternity party and thinks it would be neat to drop the glass "punch" bowl out a second-story window, above the sidewalk to the front door, just to hear it smash on the ground. If he drops the bowl and it hits a visitor in the head, he has committed battery with no assault. Whether this would happen is up for debate, but it illustrates a key point: Assault and battery are not necessarily tied together, nor are they one in the same offense.

---

[127]Fla. Stat. Section 784.045 (2010).
[128]Fla. Stat. Section 784 (2010).
[129]A. Reed, "Omission to Act Can Amount to an Assault or Battery," *Journal of Criminal Law*, Vol. 68 (2004), pp. 459–462.

A bar fight can be charged under the crime of battery, which is any unlawful offensive touching of another without consent.

Assault

Under common law, there were two kinds of assault: **threatened battery assault** and **attempted battery assault**. Threatened battery assault occurred when one person intentionally placed another person in anticipation of imminent battery.[130] Attempted battery assault occurred when one person attempted to commit the crime of battery with the intent to injure another. It is noteworthy that in an attempted battery assault, the victim did not need to be aware of the attempted battery. An attempted battery assault focused exclusively on the overt actions of the defendant.

threatened battery assault A type of assault in which the criminal intentionally places another person in fear of an imminent battery.

attempted battery assault A type of assault in which the criminal attempts to commit the crime of battery but is unsuccessful.

Some states do not distinguish these two types of assault. Others do not distinguish between assault and battery, either. Washington is one such state. It lumps all actions that would be considered assault and/or battery into a single category of assaults.[131] This likely contributes to some of the confusion concerning the use of the terms *assault* and *battery*.

Elements of Assault

The *mens rea* of threatened battery assault is the intention to cause another person to fear imminent battery. The *actus reus* is translating intent into action. For example, if one person aggressively lunges in the direction of another with the intention of scaring him or her, but stops short of physical contact, a threatened battery assault has occurred—so long as the victim is aware of the threat or reasonably fears imminent battery. In contrast, an attempted battery assault does not require that the victim be aware of the threat. Instead, the defendant must have the criminal intent to commit battery. For example, if the same victim was facing away from the offender and did not know about the aggressive lunge, then the result is attempted battery assault.

Prosecutions for assault (without battery) are relatively rare because of the absence of contact or injury. Why? The victimization is merely psychological. When an assault is carried through to completion and then results in battery, a prosecution is more likely because of the potential for physical injury. Assault is summarized in Figure 6.6.

See the accompanying Court Decision for more on using a deadly weapon in the commission of an assault and battery. In it we examine the case of *Commonwealth v. Fettes*, where the Appeals Court of Massachusetts examines whether a Pitt Bull Terrier can be a deadly weapon.

---

[130]See, e.g., *Carter* v. *Commonwealth*, 594 S.E.2d 284 (Va. Ct. App. 2004), p. 288.
[131]See Rev. Code Wash. Chapter 9A.36 (2010).

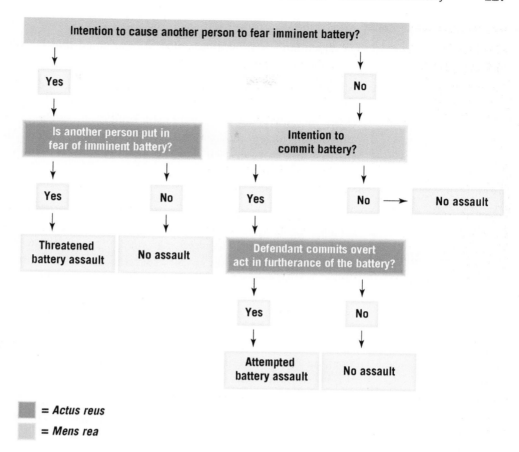

Figure 6.6
Assault

= *Actus reus*

= *Mens rea*

COURT DECISION

The Logic behind Use of a Deadly Weapon

Commonwealth v. Fettes
835 N.E.2d 639 (Mass. App. 2005)

Decision: A dog can be considered a "deadly weapon" for purposes of assault and battery.

Reason: . . . We relate the evidence in the light most favorable to the Commonwealth. On the day of the incident, the sixty-six year old victim went to an apartment building that she owned. Her purpose was to collect rents due her. There she saw a man . . . descending an exterior staircase of the building. The defendant was accompanied by a dog on a leash that was wrapped around his hand "very tightly by his side." As the victim and the defendant stood several feet apart from each other, she asked him whether he resided in the building. The defendant responded that he did not. At this time, the dog was standing by the defendant and was calm and well-behaved. The victim, admittedly "upset," then accused the defendant of allowing the dog to leave his droppings on the flat roof and yard of her building.

(continued)

**COURT
DECISION**
(continued)

The defendant then became agitated and denied that his dog was responsible for the alleged droppings.

As the victim then began to walk away from the defendant and the dog, she heard him speak a "short phrase" to the dog "[i]n a stern voice," and saw him partially release or unravel the leash while still holding it. As the defendant did so, the dog immediately lunged at the victim and bit her hand. The victim and the defendant, with his dog in tow, then fled the scene. The victim received medical attention (stitches, antibiotics, and tetanus and rabies shots) for the wound that caused her nerve damage.

. . . A dog can be a dangerous weapon. "A dangerous weapon is 'any instrument or instrumentality so constructed or so used as to be likely to produce death or great bodily harm.' *Commonwealth v. Farrell,* 322 Mass. 606, 614-615 (1948). There can be little doubt that a dog . . . used for the purpose of intimidation or attack falls within this definition." *Commonwealth v. Tarrant,* 2 Mass.App.Ct. 483, 486 (1974). The defendant does not argue to the contrary. Rather, he claims that he was entitled to a required finding of not guilty because the Commonwealth failed to show that the dog had been trained to attack, what the "stern words" used by the defendant were, or that the dog had been manipulated by the defendant to attack the victim. In short, he argues that the Commonwealth failed to show that the dog did not act of its own volition or that its actions were brought about through his reckless conduct.

We conclude that the Commonwealth's evidence was sufficient to allow the jury reasonably to infer that once the conversation between the defendant and the victim turned from casual to confrontational, the defendant either deliberately provoked the dog to attack the victim, or acted recklessly when he intentionally released his grip on the leash . . . *Judgment affirmed.*

Levels of Assault

Assaults are often lumped into two categories: simple and aggravated. For example, New Jersey defines simple assault as follows:

> A person commits a simple assault if he/she attempts to cause or purposely, knowingly or recklessly causes bodily injury to another.[132]

Note that this definition includes both the traditional definition of *assault* (an incomplete battery) and *battery*, or physical contact. Vermont takes a similar approach, defining simple assault in these terms:

a. A person is guilty of simple assault if he or she:
    1. attempts to cause or purposely, knowingly or recklessly causes bodily injury to another; or
    2. negligently causes bodily injury to another with a deadly weapon; or

---

[132]N.J.S.A. 2C:12-1a(1) (2010).

3. attempts by physical menace to put another in fear of imminent serious bodily injury.[133]

Note that (1) contains the traditional definition of *assault* and that (2) contains actual physical contact.

If the victim suffers serious bodily injury, the crime is more likely *aggravated assault.* The crime is aggravated in the sense that the victim is seriously injured or because the circumstances surrounding the assault demand that it be treated more harshly than a simple assault. The District of Columbia defines *aggravated assault* in this way:

a. A person commits the offense of aggravated assault if:
1. By any means, that person knowingly or purposely causes serious bodily injury to another person; or
2. Under circumstances manifesting extreme indifference to human life, that person intentionally or knowingly engages in conduct which creates a grave risk of serious bodily injury to another person, and thereby causes serious bodily injury.[134]

The Model Penal Code also identifies the crime of reckless assault, distinct from either simple or aggravated assault: "A person commits a misdemeanor if he recklessly engages in conduct which places or may place another person in danger of death or serious bodily injury."[135]

Some states opt to criminalize various *degrees* of assault. For example, Alaska recognizes four separate degrees of assault. *First-degree assault* is defined as follows:

a. A person commits the crime of assault in the first degree if
1. that person recklessly causes serious physical injury to another by means of a dangerous instrument;
2. with intent to cause serious physical injury to another, the person causes serious physical injury to any person;
3. the person knowingly engages in conduct that results in serious physical injury to another under circumstances manifesting extreme indifference to the value of human life; or
4. that person recklessly causes serious physical injury to another by repeated assaults using a dangerous instrument, even if each assault individually does not cause serious physical injury.[136]

On the other hand, *fourth-degree assault* occurs when

a. A person commits the crime of assault in the fourth degree if
1. that person recklessly causes physical injury to another person;
2. with criminal negligence that person causes physical injury to another person by means of a dangerous instrument; or
3. by words or other conduct that person recklessly places another person in fear of imminent physical injury.[137]

---

[133]13 V.S.A. Section 1023 (2010).
[134]D.C. Code, Title 22, Section 22-404.01 (2010).
[135]Model Penal Code, Section 211.2.
[136]Alaska Stat. 11.41.200 (2010).
[137]Alaska Stat. 11.41.230 (2010).

YOUR DECISION

1. Zach Schultz is the hottest new celebrity in Hollywood, starring in several successful films. One evening while Zach is on a dinner date, he is surrounded by paparazzi trying to get a photo for the weekly tabloids. Zach repeatedly asks the paparazzi to back off, but they continue to get more aggressive. Finally, Zach pushes a photographer, grabs his camera, and smashes it to the ground. You are the prosecutor in Los Angeles County. Can you charge Zach with battery or another crime? Explain.

2. Juliette is the top equestrian in the state and is out riding her horse, Biscuit, in preparation for an upcoming competition. Sarah is the second best equestrian in the state and really wants Juliette to "break a leg" so that she cannot compete in the state championships. While Juliette is riding, Sarah swings a large tree branch and hits Biscuit right in the chest. Juliette is not hit by the branch, but she is violently thrown off the horse and suffers several broken bones. Can Sarah be charged with battery? Why or why not?

Summary

- Battery is unlawful touching, typically with injury.
- Whether battery is a general or specific intent offense varies by state.
- Although the *actus reus* of battery usually requires injury, not all states impose this requirement.
- The norm in most states is to criminalize various types of battery, each with its own distinct elements.
- A *threatened battery assault* occurs when one person intentionally places another person in anticipation of imminent battery.
- An *attempted battery assault* occurs when the criminal attempts to commit the crime of battery but is unsuccessful.
- Assaults are often lumped into two categories: simple and aggravated. Aggravated assaults, which are counted in the FBI's crime index, are the most serious.

MODULE

6.5 OTHER ASSAULTIVE OFFENSES

Learning Objectives
- **Describe the crime of kidnapping.**
- **Describe the crime of false imprisonment.**
- **Define carjacking.**
- **Identify and define two domestic offenses.**
- **Differentiate between harassment and stalking.**

CORE CONCEPTS

As assaultive crimes, rape, robbery, assault, and battery get the lion's share of the attention. Yet there are many other such offenses that often get overlooked because crime statistics do not always tell us much about them. Examples include kidnapping, false imprisonment, carjacking, child abuse, domestic violence, harassment, and stalking. The FBI's crime index does not count any of these offenses, but it is difficult to argue that they are any less serious than the rest. We look at each in this section not because they are fundamentally similar to one another (they are not), but because they all contain an assaultive component.

Kidnapping

kidnapping The unlawful taking and carrying away of another person with the intent to deprive that person of his or her liberty.

asportation In regards to the crime of kidnapping, the taking and carrying away of another person.

Kidnapping is a bit of a misnomer, as there is no requirement that a "kid" be targeted. **Kidnapping** refers to the unlawful taking and carrying away of another person with the intent to deprive that person of his or her liberty. The *actus reus* is thus the seizing and carrying away (also called **asportation**) of another person. Although in many kidnapping cases the victim is often taken far away from the scene of the abduction, there is no specific distance requirement. In one case, the *actus reus* of kidnapping was satisfied once the victim was forced into a car just 22 feet away.[138] And although kidnappers sometimes demand ransoms, there is no requirement that any such demands be made to satisfy *actus reus*.

As for the *mens rea*, kidnapping statutes often require specific intent, such as intent to confine, restrain, or otherwise hold the victim in secret. Nevada's kidnapping statute illustrates the specific intent of kidnapping (although it does not *require* such intent):

1. A person who willfully seizes, confines, inveigles, entices, decoys, abducts, conceals, kidnaps or carries away a person by any means whatsoever with the *intent to hold or detain*, or who holds or detains, the person for ransom, or reward, or for the purpose of committing sexual assault, extortion or robbery upon or from the person, or for the purpose of killing the person or inflicting substantial bodily harm upon the person, or to exact from relatives, friends, or any other person any money or valuable thing for the return or disposition of the kidnapped person, and a person who leads, takes, entices, or carries away or detains any minor with the intent to keep, imprison, or confine the minor from his or her parents, guardians, or any other person having lawful custody of the minor, or with the intent to hold the minor to unlawful service, or perpetrate upon the person of the minor any unlawful act is guilty of kidnapping in the first degree. . . .

2. A person who willfully and without authority of law seizes, inveigles, takes, carries away or kidnaps another person with the intent to keep the person secretly imprisoned within the State, or for the purpose of conveying the person out of the State without authority of law, or in any manner held to service or detained against the person's will, is guilty of kidnapping in the second degree.[139]

Note the all-encompassing nature of Nevada's statute. It covers a wide range of motives for kidnapping. Also note the difference between first- and second-degree

---

[138]*People v. Chessman*, 238 P.2d 1001 (Cal. 1951).
[139]Nev. Rev. Stat. 200.310 (2010).

kidnapping. Second-degree kidnapping is more concerned with the act itself, whereas a first-degree kidnapping conviction is reserved for abductions with more nefarious motives.

False Imprisonment

false Imprisonment The unlawful detention or restraint of another person.

False imprisonment is similar to kidnapping, but is usually regarded as less serious because it lacks the "carrying away" element. It has been defined as forcing a person "to remain where he does not wish to remain."[140] For comparison's sake, let us once again consider the state of Nevada. There, *false imprisonment* is defined as "an unlawful violation of the personal liberty of another, and consists [of] confinement or detention without sufficient legal authority."[141] This definition contains no specific intent requirement, hence there is not much to the *mens rea*. The *actus reus* is also equally clear—confinement or detention of another without proper authority.

Some states call false imprisonment "unlawful restraint." And some states also require specific intent. Consider Texas' relatively concise statute: "A person commits an offense if he intentionally or knowingly restrains another person."[142] Note the requirement that the conduct be "intentional" or "knowing." This statute seems a bit far-reaching, however. What if a police officer wishes to apprehend a suspect? What if a private party wants to make a citizen's arrest? In either case, the same statute states, "It is no offense to detain or move another under this section when it is for the purpose of effecting a lawful arrest or detaining an individual lawfully arrested."[143]

Carjacking

carjacking Intentionally taking another person's occupied motor vehicle with the use of a deadly weapon, force and/ or intimidation.

Carjacking, another assaultive offense, combines elements of robbery with the motivation to take a person's vehicle. The *actus reus* usually contains two elements: (1) taking of another person's occupied motor vehicle (2) by use of a deadly weapon and/ or force or intimidation. Carjacking is a specific intent offense, meaning that the offender must intend for the crime to occur—or at least know that it is occurring. In Tennessee, carjacking is defined as "the intentional or knowing taking of a motor vehicle from the possession of another by use of: (1) a deadly weapon; or (2) force or intimidation."[144]

One of the key requirements for carjacking is taking possession from another. In other words, carjacking does not occur unless the offender takes possession of the vehicle from someone else (presumably its owner or someone legally authorized to drive it). Were it not for the presence of a victim, carjacking would be relegated to theft.

Domestic Offenses

Domestic violence and child abuse are both considered "domestic" offenses, as they typically occur in the home. Both, however, need not be stand-alone offenses, as traditional assault and statutes can be used to prosecute abusive intimate partners and adults to abuse child victims.

---

[140]*McKendree* v. *Christy*, 172 N.E.2d 380 (1961).
[141]Nev. Rev. Stat. 200.460 (2010).
[142]Texas Penal Code Section 20.02 (2010).
[143]Ibid.
[144]Tenn. Code Ann. Section 39-13-402 (2010).

Victims of domestic violence are sometimes reluctant to report the crime to police.

domestic violence
Assault, battery, or other abusive conduct committed against a family member or intimate partner.

wobbler A criminal offense that can be charged as either a felony or misdemeanor depending on the circumstances.

According to the National Center for Victims of Crime, **domestic violence** is defined as the "willful intimidation, assault, battery, sexual assault or other abusive behavior perpetrated by one family member, household member, or intimate partner against another."[145] California criminalizes domestic violence in two sections of its penal code. The felony domestic battery statute provides the following:

> Any person who willfully inflicts upon a person who is his or her spouse, former spouse, cohabitant, former cohabitant, or the mother or father of his or her child, corporal injury resulting in a traumatic condition, is guilty of a felony.[146]

California treats as a misdemeanor battery that which "is committed against a spouse, a person with whom the defendant is cohabiting, a person who is the parent of the defendant's child, former spouse, fiancé, or fiancée, or a person with whom the defendant currently has, or has previously had, a dating or engagement relationship."[147] Note the overlapping language between both statutes. What's a prosecutor to do? As defined in California, domestic violence is known as a **wobbler**, meaning that it is an offense that can be charged as either a felony or a misdemeanor depending on the circumstances.

To get a sense of the elements of domestic violence, look again at California's felony statute. The *mens rea* is straightforward—willful infliction of corporal injury. As for the *actus reus*, there is no requirement that physical injury result, only a "traumatic condition." Also note that California's statute is rather all-encompassing in terms of the relationships it covers. Domestic violence is not limited to spousal relationships, but also to many other current and former domestic relationships.

State child abuse statutes are worded similarly. For example, Florida law defines the crime as follows:

> any willful act or threatened act that results in any physical, mental, or sexual injury or harm that causes or is likely to cause the child's physical, mental, or emotional health to be significantly impaired. Abuse of a child includes acts or omissions. Corporal discipline of a child by a parent or legal custodian for disciplinary purposes does not in itself constitute abuse when it does not result in harm to the child.[148]

---

[145] http://www.ncvc.org/ncvc/main.aspx?dbName=DocumentViewer&DocumentID=32347#1 (accessed September 13, 2010).
[146] Cal. Penal Code Section 273.5 (2010).
[147] Cal. Penal Code Section 243(e)(1) (2010).
[148] Fla. Stat. Section 39.01(2) (2010).

Other states retain a variety of child abuse statutes, covering a wide range of abusive actions, including not just physical abuse, but also neglect, child exploitation, emotional abuse, parental substance abuse, and abandonment. The federal Child Abuse Prevention and Treatment Act (CAPTA) spells out minimum standards that, in order to receive financial assistance, states must incorporate into their child abuse laws. According to CAPTA, **child abuse** is defined as "any recent act or failure to act on the part of a parent or caretakers, which results in death, serious physical or emotional harm, sexual abuse, or exploitation, or an act or failure to act which presents an imminent risk of serious harm."[149]

child abuse The physical, sexual, or emotional abuse of a child through voluntary action or failure to act.

Domestic violence is an important offense not just because of its gravity, but because many states have enacted "mandatory arrest" laws intended to hold perpetrators accountable. This brings more and more cases before the courts, making domestic violence all the more serious and important.

Harassment and Stalking

Harassment and stalking are closely related assaultive offenses. According to federal law, **harassment** is defined as "a course of conduct directed at a specific person that causes substantial emotional distress in such person and serves no legitimate purpose."[150] **Stalking** is defined in almost the same way, but it usually adds an element of *following* the victim in some form or fashion. For example, Kansas law defines stalking as "an intentional, malicious, and repeated *following* or harassment of another person and making a credible threat with the intent to place such person in reasonable fear for such person's safety (emphasis added)".[151]

harassment Systematic conduct that intentionally annoys, threatens and/or intimidates another person.

stalking Intentionally frightening another person by following, harassing and/or terrorizing.

Note that under this definition, *harassment*, as we have defined it, and *stalking* are basically one in the same; one who harasses and does not necessarily *follow* a victim can be prosecuted as a stalker in Kansas.

Until recently, harassment and stalking took place either in the physical world or via written correspondence. With the integration of computers and the Internet into our daily lives, both crimes have moved into cyberspace. And while some states have been slow to respond to this development, others have already acted. For example, California recently amended its stalking law such that **cyberstalking**, or stalking via any electronic communication device, is now criminal. Stalking is now defined as

cyberstalking Committing the crime of stalking through electronic communication.

> a verbal or written threat, including that performed through the use of an electronic communication device, or a threat implied by a pattern of conduct or a combination of verbal, written, or electronically communicated statements and conduct made with the intent to place the person that is the target of the threat in reasonable fear for his or her safety or the safety of his or her family and made with the apparent ability to carry out the threat so as to cause the person who is the target of the threat to reasonably fear for

---

[149]42 U.S.C.A. Section 5106g(2) (2003).
[150]18 U.S.C.A. Section 1514(c)(1) (2010).
[151]K.S.A. Section 21-3438 (2010).

his or her safety or the safety of his or her family. It is not necessary to prove that the defendant had the intent to actually carry out the threat.[152]

Cyberstalking is no less serious than traditional stalking. As a U.S. Justice Department report observed:

> The fact that cyberstalking does not involve physical contact may create the misperception that it is more benign than physical stalking. This is not necessarily true. As the Internet becomes an ever more integral part of our personal and professional lives, stalkers can take advantage of the ease of communications as well as increased access to personal information. In addition, the ease of use and non-confrontational, impersonal, and sometimes anonymous nature of Internet communications may remove disincentives to cyberstalking. Put another way, whereas a potential stalker may be unwilling or unable to confront a victim in person or on the telephone, he or she may have little hesitation sending harassing or threatening electronic communications to a victim. Finally, as with physical stalking, online harassment and threats may be a prelude to more serious behavior, including physical violence.[153]

Cyberstalking also shares several characteristics with traditional stalking. Many stalkers, whether they are off-line or online, are motivated by the same objectives, such as the desire to exert control over their victims.[154] Evidence also shows that majority of stalkers, whether off-line or online, are males targeting female victims.[155] Finally, in many cases, the victims had prior relationships with the offenders.[156] See Figure 6.7 for a further comparison of traditional/off-line stalking and cyberstalking.

Figure 6.7

Comparison of Off-line and Online Stalking

Source: U.S. Department of Justice, 1999 Report on Cyberstalking: A New Challenge for Law Enforcement and Industry (Washington, DC: U.S. Department of Justice, 1999). Available at: http://preview.tinyurl.com/7bz3ewc (accessed July 19, 2012).

Major Similarities

Majority of cases involve stalking by former intimates, although stranger stalking occurs in the real world and in cyberspace.

Most victims are women; most stalkers are men.

Stalkers are generally motivated by the desire to control the victim.

Major Differences

Offline stalking generally requires the perpetrator and the victim to be located in the same geographic area; cyberstalkers may be located across the street or across the country.

Electronic communications technologies make it much easier for a cyberstalker to encourage third parties to harass and/or threaten a victim (e.g., impersonating the victim and posting inflammatory messages to bulletin boards and in chat rooms, causing viewers of that message to send threatening messages back to the victim "author.")

Electronic communications technologies also lower the barriers to harassment and threats; a cyberstalker does not need to physically confront the victim.

---

[152]Cal. Penal Code Section 646.9(g) (2010).
[153]U.S. Department of Justice, *1999 Report on Cyberstalking: A New Challenge for Law Enforcement and Industry* (Washington, DC: U.S. Department of Justice, 1999). Available at: http://www.justice.gov/criminal/cybercrime/cyberstalking.htm (accessed October 5, 2010).
[154]Ibid.
[155]Ibid.
[156]Ibid.

YOUR DECISION

1. Joey Bricker is a screenwriter for a famous Hollywood production company. Joey was thrilled to learn that one of the films he worked on, *Spiderman vs. the Hulk*, was nominated for an Academy Award. Joey and his wife Samantha arrived at the red carpet, ready to socialize with all the famous celebrities. Just as they began walking toward an entertainment news station for an interview, however, security guards at the Oscars ushered them off the red carpet to a small detention room. Joey and Samantha were held in the room for six hours and interrogated about how they managed to make their way onto the red carpet. Joey and Samantha contacted the police and would like to press charges. Can the Oscar security guards be charged with a crime? Why or why not?

2. Edward was devastated when Brittany ended their two-year relationship. Desperate for a way to win her back, Edward created a fictitious Facebook account under a different name. Brittany accepted the friend request unaware of Edward's disguise. Edward sent Brittany approximately 25 messages a day via this Facebook account. He even posted compromising photos and videos of Brittany he had obtained while they were dating. Brittany has contacted the police and would like to press charges for stalking. Can Edward be charged with stalking? Why or why not?

Summary

- *Kidnapping* refers to the unlawful taking and carrying away of another person with the intent to deprive that person of his or her liberty.

- The *actus reus* of kidnapping is the seizing and carrying away of another person. Kidnapping statutes often require specific intent, such as intent to confine, restrain, or otherwise hold the victim in secret.

- *False imprisonment* has been defined as forcing a person "to remain where he does not wish to remain."

- Carjacking, another assaultive offense, combines elements of robbery with the motivation to take a person's vehicle.

- The *actus reus* of carjacking usually contains two elements: (1) taking of another person's occupied motor vehicle (2) by use of a deadly weapon and/or force or intimidation.

- In terms of *mens rea*, carjacking is a specific intent offense, meaning that the offender must intend for the crime to occur—or at least know that it is occurring.

- *Domestic violence* is defined as the "willful intimidation, assault, battery, sexual assault or other abusive behavior perpetrated by one family member, household member, or intimate partner against another."

- *Child abuse* is defined as "any recent act or failure to act on the part of a parent or caretakers, which results in death, serious physical or emotional harm, sexual abuse, or exploitation, or an act or failure to act which presents an imminent risk of serious harm."

- Harassment and stalking are closely related assaultive offenses.
- According to federal law, *harassment* is defined as "a course of conduct directed at a specific person that causes substantial emotional distress in such person and serves no legitimate purpose."
- *Stalking* is defined in much the same way as *harassment*, but it usually adds an element of *following* the victim in some form or fashion.

Chapter Review

HOMICIDE

Learning Objectives

- Distinguish between first-degree murder and second-degree murder.
- Explain when the death penalty is an acceptable form of punishment for homicide.
- Summarize the elements of voluntary and involuntary manslaughter.
- Explain felony murder.
- Identify two types of "mercy killings."
- Explain corporation murder.

Review Questions

1. For purposes of defining homicide, when does life begin/end? Why?
2. When is a murder convict eligible for the death penalty, and how is the decision reached?
3. Explain the limitations that have been placed on the felony murder rule.
4. What is the difference between physician-assisted suicide and euthanasia? Which, if either, is criminal?
5. What is corporation murder? Can a corporation be found guilty of murder?

Key Terms

homicide	aggravating circumstances
feticide	mitigating circumstances
year-and-a-day rule	paramour rule
murder	last straw rule
manslaughter	felony murder
malice aforethought	*res gestae*
first-degree murder	physician-assisted suicide
bifurcation	euthanasia

RAPE AND SEXUAL ASSAULT

Learning Objectives

- Distinguish between rape and sexual assault.
- Summarize the nature and elements of the crime of rape.
- Summarize the laws pertaining to the crime of rape.

Review Questions

1. How does sexual assault compare to rape?
2. Explain the *mens rea* of rape.

3. In what ways does the *actus reus* of rape vary?

4. Explain forcible rape, and compare it to other types of rape.

5. What legislative developments have affected a prosecutor's ability to prove rape in court? Explain.

Key Terms

rape
sexual assault
statutory rape

rape shield laws

ROBBERY

Learning Objectives

· Describe the crime of robbery.

· Distinguish armed robbery from other forms of robbery.

Review Questions

1. Explain the five parts of the *actus reus* of robbery.

2. What is the *mens rea* of robbery?

3. Why do some states treat armed robbery different than other forms of robbery?

Key Term

armed robbery

ASSAULT AND BATTERY

Learning Objectives

· Describe the crime of assault.

· Describe the crime of battery.

Review Questions

1. What is battery, and how does it differ from assault?

2. Should assault and battery be defined separately in the penal code? Why or why not?

3. Can a person be a victim of battery without an assault? If so, explain.

Key Terms

assault
battery

threatened battery assault
attempted battery assault

MODULE **6.5**   **OTHER ASSAULTIVE OFFENSES**

Learning Objectives

· Describe the crime of kidnapping.

· Describe the crime of false imprisonment.

· Define carjacking.

· Identify and define two domestic offenses.

· Differentiate between harassment and stalking.

Review Questions

1. The term *kidnapping* is a misnomer. Why?
2. Compare and contrast kidnapping and false imprisonment.
3. Carjacking combines elements of what two offenses?
4. Distinguish between domestic violence and child abuse.
5. Compare and contrast harassment and stalking.

Key Terms

kidnapping	child abuse
asportation	wobbler
false imprisonment	harassment
carjacking	stalking
domestic violence	cyberstalking

Chapter Synthesizing Questions

1. Should homicide be graded into levels in all states? Why or why not?
2. Only some states treat the killing of an unborn fetus as murder. Why? What approach should be taken?
3. Who should be punished harsher, the person who kills an unarmed stranger or the mine corporation whose decision to cut corners leads to the deaths of ten employees? Why do you feel this way?
4. How are rape and sexual assault similar? How are they different?
5. Assault and battery are often lumped together in the same sentence. Why?
6. Which assaultive offense is most serious and why?
7. Look through your state's penal or criminal code, and identify two assaultive offenses not presented in this chapter. How are they similar or different?

7

PROPERTY DAMAGE AND INVASION

PROPERTY DAMAGE

Learning Objectives
- **Describe the crime of arson.**
- **Explain the elements of criminal mischief.**
- **Explain the elements of vandalism.**

CORE CONCEPTS

This chapter focuses on crimes against property, as opposed to crimes against persons. We look at the most serious property crimes, namely arson and burglary, both of which are reported in the FBI's crime index (arson became a reportable offense only some years after the launch of the Uniform Crime Reports in 1978). We also look at the lesser known but also fairly serious property crimes of criminal mischief, vandalism, and property damage/invasion with computers. In the last module, we turn our attention to theft and analogous offenses (e.g., larceny, embezzlement, forgery).

This module focuses on crimes that cause property *damage*. Arson is the most serious such offense, followed somewhat distantly by criminal mischief and vandalism. While criminal mischief and vandalism are chiefly concerned with damage to property, arson can also be damaging in terms of human life. For example, the intentional burning of an occupied dwelling that leads to loss of life could result not just in an arson prosecution, but also a homicide prosecution.

Arson

arson Intentionally setting a fire to burn a structure or other physical property.

Arson is defined, generally, as intentionally setting a fire. It is the leading cause of fires in the United States and results in hundreds of deaths and thousands of injuries each year.[1] William Blackstone, in his *Commentaries on the Laws of England*, once called it an "offense of very great malignity, and much more serious than simple theft." Why?

> Because, first, it is an offence against that right, of habitation, which is acquired by the law of nature as well as the laws of society. Next, because of the terror and confusion that necessarily attends it. And, lastly, because in simple theft the thing stolen only changes its master, but still remains in essence for the benefit of the public, whereas by burning the very substance is absolutely destroyed.[2]

---

[1]United States Fire Administration, *Topical Fire Research Series*, http://www.usfa.dhs.gov/downloads/pdf/tfrs/v1i8-508.pdf (accessed September 16, 2010).
[2]W. Blackstone, *Commentaries on the Laws of England*, IV (Oxford: Clarendon Press, 1769), p. 220.

Arson at Common Law

At common law, arson was limited to dwellings, requiring four elements:

1. The malicious
2. burning
3. of a dwelling
4. of another.[3]

Malicious did not need to mean intent per se, only the creation of great risk that something would burn. So, for example, a person who, on a hot, windy day, was burning scrap lumber next to an area full of dry brush and set the surrounding forest on fire created a great risk of fire, but did not *intend* for the damage to occur.

At common law, any burning of a dwelling sufficed for an arson conviction. There was no requirement that the property be totally destroyed, only that it be burned (as opposed to, say, discolored by smoke) to some degree. Yet arson was limited strictly to dwellings, defined as any structure used as a residence on either a permanent or part-time basis. Not limited to homes, arson could have occurred if any outbuilding, barn, or similar structure was burned, so long as it was used as a residence in some form or fashion.

The fourth common law element of arson limited the crime to the burning of *others'* property. It was not possible, therefore, to commit arson against one's own property. This was true even if a tenant set fire to his or her landlord's property. Even setting fire to one's own property for the purpose of collecting insurance money did not constitute common law arson.

Modern-Day Arson

Arson laws have undergone substantial changes over the years, in response to the dual realities that (1) a person can maliciously burn much more than a single dwelling, causing extensive damage and perhaps loss of life, and (2) insurance companies could not possibly stay in business if their insured could burn their homes with little fear of reprisal.

Arson (like some other crimes, including kidnapping) can be either a federal or state crime. Federal law provides, by way of summary, that it is a crime to "maliciously damage, by means of fire, any building used in interstate or foreign commerce or in any activity affecting interstate or foreign commerce."[4] To use a simple example, if a disgruntled former Walmart employee decided to set a distribution warehouse on fire, that employee would be subjected to federal prosecution because doing so would likely affect the company's ability to ship products around the country. However, in a 2000 case, the U.S. Supreme Court decided that the federal arson statute, codified as 18 U.S.C. Section 844(i), cannot be used to prosecute an individual for burning an owner-occupied property that is not used for commercial purposes.[5]

---

[3]A. A. Moenssens, R. J. Bacigal, G. G. Ashdown, and V. E. Hench, *Criminal Law: Cases and Comments*, 8th ed. (New York: Foundation Press, 2008), pp. 790–791.
[4]*Jones v. United States*, 529 U.S. 848 (2000), p. 850.
[5]Ibid.

State arson laws are typically reserved for prosecution of arsonists who do not fall within the federal law's interstate commerce limitation. Let us look closely at the *actus reus* and *mens rea* of state-level arson.

Actus Reus. The *actus reus* of modern-day arson is, typically, damage by fire or explosion. The meaning of *fire* and *explosion* are relatively straightforward, but *damage* is less clear. Everything from total destruction to visible charring satisfies the *actus reus* of arson.

What if there is no charring, just smoke damage or some soot left on the floor? This question arose in *Williams v. State*,[6] a case in which Tonyia Williams, a New Year's party guest, started a fire in the basement of the house she was visiting, after an argument. She was unsuccessful in setting the house on fire, but she managed to cause a measure of smoke and soot damage. She was convicted of arson, but argued that because there was no charring, she should not have been convicted. An appeals court disagreed, stating that "the smoke damage and the soot on the basement wall were enough to support a conviction for arson."[7] The Indiana statute used to support Williams's conviction provided, in part, that a person is guilty of arson if he or she "knowingly or intentionally *damages*...a dwelling of another person without his [or her] consent" (emphasis added).[8] The appeals court decided that a looser interpretation of *damage* was warranted than that which the common law suggested. In other words, the court disagreed with the common law definition of damage, namely,

> any charring of the wood of a building, so that the fiber of the wood was destroyed, was enough to constitute a sufficient burning to complete the crime of arson.[9]

The Model Penal Code avoids use of the word damage. Section 220.1 defines the *actus reus* of arson as, simply, starting a fire or causing an explosion. The Model Penal Code also defines as criminal the less serious offenses of "reckless burning or exploding" and "failure to control or report dangerous fire."

Mens Rea. The *mens rea* of arson varies by statute, but typically requires an element of intent or knowledge. The Indiana statute quoted earlier used both terms. Some states get very specific with their *mens rea* requirement. For example, the Texas arson statute reads, in part:

> A person commits an offense if the person starts a fire, regardless of whether the fire continues after ignition, or causes an explosion with intent to destroy or damage:
> 1. any vegetation, fence, or structure on open-space land; or
> 2. any building, habitation, or vehicle:
>   a. knowing that it is within the limits of an incorporated city or town;
>   b. knowing that it is insured against damage or destruction;
>   c. knowing that it is subject to a mortgage or other security interest;
>   d. knowing that it is located on property belonging to another;

---

[6] *Williams v. State*, 600 N.E.2d 962 (Ind. App. 1992).
[7] Ibid., p. 965.
[8] Ibid., p. 964.
[9] Ibid.

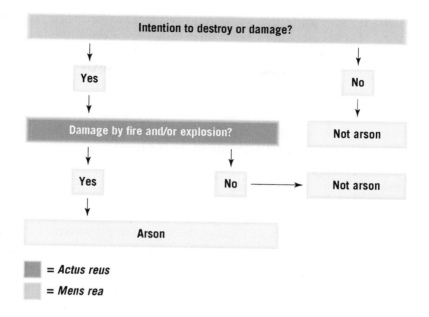

Figure 7.1
Arson

e. knowing that it has located within it property belonging to another; or
f. when the person is reckless about whether the burning or explosion will endanger the life of some individual or the safety of the property of another.[10]

Note that the *mens rea* in this statute appears in two places. First, the statute is limited to fires or explosions with which there is *intent* to destroy or damage. Second, elements A–F contain further *mens rea* requirements. Based on this statute, if Chad intends to burn an open field yet does not know it is part of an incorporated city or town (and further demonstrates no knowledge pertaining to B–E and does not act recklessly), he would not be guilty of arson under Texas law. One would be hard-pressed to come up with a real-life example of such a situation, however.

The *mens rea* of arson under the Model Penal Code is "purpose." Specifically, arson occurs if a person starts a fire or causes an explosion *"with the purpose of"* either "destroying a building or occupied structure of another" or "destroying or damaging any property, whether his own or another's, to collect insurance for such loss."[11] See Figure 7.1 for a summary of arson.

Criminal Mischief

criminal mischief
Intentionally damaging or destroying another's property.

Criminal mischief, once called *malicious mischief*, consists of intentionally damaging or destroying property. So long as it does not involve intentional burning or exploding, almost any form of damage, defacement, or destruction of property qualifies as criminal mischief. We will shift attention to vandalism in the next section, but

---

[10]Texas Penal Code Section 28.02 (2010).
[11]Model Penal Code Section 11.1(1).

for now know that some states criminalize under their "mischief" statutes conduct that would be considered vandalism, were a vandalism law on the books. Likewise, some state criminal mischief statutes cover conduct that could be considered arson. And depending on the offender's motivations, some states even maintain malicious *harassment* statutes, often reserved for conduct that does not necessarily lead to damage, but nonetheless amounts to harassment of the target.

Elements of Criminal Mischief

The *actus reus* of criminal mischief is usually satisfied by one or more of several behaviors. In Ohio, for example, the following actions constitute the *actus reus* of criminal mischief:

1. Defacement, damage, or destruction to property;
2. ". . . releasing a substance that is harmful or offensive to persons exposed or that tends to cause public alarm;"
3. Tampering with boundary markers, monuments, or survey stations;
4. Tampering with any safety device;
5. Setting fire to personal property outside and apart from any building or structure;
6. Impairing the function of a computer or computer system.[12]

Texas criminalizes much of the same conduct, but its criminal mischief statute also covers actions that could be considered vandalism: any "markings, including inscriptions, slogans, drawings, or paintings, on the tangible property of the owner."[13]

The *mens rea* of criminal mischief typically requires some level of intent. According to the Model Penal Code, criminal mischief includes damage to the tangible property of another person that is done "purposely, recklessly, or by negligence."[14] Some states use similar language; others do not. Texas requires "intent" or "knowledge."[15] The Ohio statute quoted above requires either knowledge or purpose depending on the specific conduct in question.

Former JetBlue flight attendant Steven Slater, who, in August 2010, allegedly "flipped out," opened a landed airplane's door, and exited it by way of an inflatable evacuation slide, was charged with criminal mischief for his actions—and also reckless endangerment. According to one article, "Cops must have been scratching their heads to come with the charges,"[16] as there are not too many statutes that target such actions.

See the accompanying Court Decision for more on criminal mischief. In it, we examine the case of *Marrero* v. *State*, where the Supreme Court of Florida is deciphering the difference between felony and misdemeanor criminal mischief charges.

---

[12]Ohio Rev. Code Section 2909.07 (2010).
[13]Texas Penal Code Section 28.03(a)(3) (2010).
[14]Model Penal Code Section 220.3.
[15]Texas Penal Code Section 28.03(a)(3) (2010).
[16]J. Molloy, "Slater Does What We All Dream of Doing," *New York Daily News*, http://tinyurl.com/237gtyw (accessed September 17, 2010).

COURT DECISION

The Logic behind Criminal Mischief

Marrero v. State
71. So.3d 881 (Fla. 2011)

Decision: Felony criminal mischief requires proof of the amount of damage caused by the defendant.

Reason: Marrero drove his Ford F150 pickup truck through the entrance of the Miccosukee Casino building located in Miami–Dade County. The entrance consisted of four impact-resistant glass doors, each of them sixteen or seventeen feet tall, each framed in special aluminum materials, and one of which was equipped with a handicap accessible automatic entry system. The crash required each of the four doors to be replaced and resulted in the injury of one casino patron. The State charged Marrero, as relevant here, with felony criminal mischief.

. . . Section 806.13, Florida Statutes (2006), provides, in part:

1. a. A person commits the offense of criminal mischief if he or she willfully and maliciously injures or damages by any means any real or personal property belonging to another, including, but not limited to, the placement of graffiti thereon or other acts of vandalism thereto.
   b. 1. If the damage to such property is $200 or less, it is a misdemeanor of the second degree, punishable as provided in s. 775.082 or s. 775.083.
      2. If the damage to such property is greater than $200 but less than $1,000, it is a misdemeanor of the first degree, punishable as provided in s. 775.082 or s. 775.083.
      3. *If the damage is $1,000 or greater, or if there is interruption or impairment of a business operation or public communication, transportation, supply of water, gas or power, or other public service which costs $1,000 or more in labor and supplies to restore, it is a felony of the third degree, punishable as provided in s. 775.082, s. 775.083, or s. 775.084.*

. . . Here, a plain reading of the criminal mischief statute reveals that the amount of damage is an essential element of the crime of *felony* criminal mischief. The *only* difference between second-degree misdemeanor mischief and third-degree felony mischief is the value of the damaged property. Felony criminal mischief requires proof of the amount of damage, whereas second-degree misdemeanor mischief does not. Absent proof of the amount of damage, an act of criminal mischief, as defined by the criminal mischief statute, is a *misdemeanor* of the second degree. The value of damage, therefore, is clearly an essential element of *felony* criminal mischief.

. . . A defendant can only be convicted of *felony* criminal mischief if the damage in question is $1,000 or greater. Absent evidence of the amount of damage, the State has failed to prove an essential element of the crime: the amount of damage . . . We remand for the trial court to reduce Petitioner's conviction of felony criminal mischief to the lesser offense of second-degree misdemeanor criminal mischief as defined in section 806.13(1)(b), Florida Statutes (2006).

Criminal Mischief without Damage

What if otherwise mischievous behavior fails to cause damage, but is nonetheless offensive or emotionally damaging? In some states, prosecutors may not press charges because no statute covers the conduct in question. In other states, laws have been enacted to address such limitations. Consider the Supreme Court's decision in *Virginia* v. *Black*,[17] a case addressing the constitutionality of Virginia's cross-burning statute. Two men were convicted, under Virginia's cross-burning statute, of burning crosses with intent to intimidate. They argued that the law was unconstitutional and violated their First Amendment rights to freely express themselves. The U.S. Supreme Court disagreed, however, siding with the state of Virginia:

> The First Amendment permits a state to outlaw cross-burnings done with the intent to intimidate because burning a cross is a particularly virulent form of intimidation. Instead of prohibiting all intimidating messages, a state may choose to regulate this subset of intimidating messages in light of cross-burning's long and pernicious history as a signal of impending violence. Thus, just as a state may regulate only that obscenity which is the most obscene due to its prurient content, so too may a state choose to prohibit only those forms of intimidation that are most likely to inspire fear of bodily harm. A ban on cross-burning carried out with the intent to intimidate is proscribable under the First Amendment.[18]

The state enacted the cross-burning statute partly because its criminal mischief statute would not otherwise permit prosecution of individuals who engage in mischievous conduct (in this case cross burning) but fail to cause physical damage.

Graffiti constitutes a type of vandalism and can affect neighborhood quality of life.

Stepanov/Fotolia

---

[17]*Virginia* v. *Black*, 538 U.S. 343 (2003).
[18]Ibid.

Vandalism

Vandalism, sometimes considered a form of criminal or malicious mischief, is usually defined as willful or malicious acts intended to damage property. This definition is quite similar to our earlier definition of criminal mischief, however. Whether it is a stand-alone offense depends on the laws of each state. For example, Pennsylvania includes within its criminal mischief statute "defacing or damaging property with graffiti."[19] At the other extreme, California maintains a vandalism statute, providing that:

> (a) Every person who maliciously commits any of the following acts with respect to any real or personal property not his or her own, in cases other than those specified by state law, is guilty of vandalism: (1) Defaces with graffiti or other inscribed material. (2) Damages. (3) Destroys.[20]

Tennessee takes yet another approach. Its *vandalism* statute includes actions that would be considered criminal mischief. Its law provides that "[a]ny person who knowingly causes damage to or the destruction of any real or personal property of another or of the state, the United States, any county, city, or town knowing that the person does not have the owner's consent is guilty of an offense under this section."[21] The offenses range from a misdemeanor to a serious felony (8–30 years in prison) depending on the monetary value assigned to the property damage.[22]

Vandalism is also frequently defined as such at the county or municipal level, usually in reference to graffiti and similar markings. For example, San Diego's municipal code makes it illegal to write graffiti on any building, fence, or structure, without the property owner's express permission.[23] A number of cities also criminalize the mere *possession* of graffiti-related tools. To illustrate, in Oklahoma City, "[n]o person under the age of 18 years may possess an aerosol spray paint container or broad-tipped indelible marker on any public property unless accompanied by a parent, guardian, employer, teacher, or other adult in any similar relationship and such possession is for a lawful purpose."[24]

YOUR DECISION

1. Just days before graduation, Jeremy Bates learns he failed his chemistry final and will not be graduating from high school. Determined to get "revenge," he plans to burn down the school. Jeremy's high school is constructed entirely of cinder block and cement and contains no wood or other flammable items; however, Jeremy does not realize that cinder block and cement will not burn. He starts a small fire with twigs in the corner of his science classroom, but obviously the wall and floor do not catch on fire. A small black residue remains on the wall and floor. Can Jeremy be charged with arson? Why or why not? Are there any other possible crimes to charge Jeremy with?

---

[19]42 Pa. Cons. Stat Section 3302 (2010).
[20]Cal. Penal Code Section 594 (2010).
[21]Tenn. Code Ann. Section 39-14-408 (2010).
[22]Ibid.
[23]San Diego Municipal Code Section 95.0127(c)(1),(2), (1992).
[24]Oklahoma City Mun. Code Section 35-201 (2010).

2. Stephanie, an amateur painter, lives in a rough inner city neighborhood with decaying buildings and littered streets. Stephanie decides she wants to "beautify" the neighborhood and make it a more pleasant place to live. One evening, she takes her painting supplies and creates a large mural of rainbows and flowers on the side of an abandoned tattoo parlor. Stephanie does not own the tattoo parlor. The next morning the police see Stephanie's "work." Can Stephanie be charged with a crime? If so, which crime or crimes?

Summary

- There were four common law elements of arson: (1) malicious (2) burning (3) of a dwelling (4) of another.
- The common law definition of *arson* was restrictive, mainly because it limited the crime to dwellings.
- At common law, setting fire to one's own property was not considered arson.
- The *actus reus* of arson today is damage by fire or explosion.
- Smoke damage, without visible charring, may satisfy the *actus reus* of arson.
- The *mens rea* of arson varies by statute, but typically requires intent or knowledge.
- Criminal mischief was called "malicious mischief" under common law.
- The *actus reus* of criminal mischief depends on the law in question, but usually consists of defacement, damage, or destruction of property.
- The *mens rea* of criminal mischief requires some level of intent, anything from "purpose" to simple "knowledge."
- The *actus reus* of vandalism is similar to that for criminal mischief, typically the damage to or defacement of property.
- The *mens rea* of vandalism is also similar to that for criminal mischief and arson: some degree of intent or knowledge.

MODULE

7.2   PROPERTY INVASION

Learning Objectives
- **Summarize the elements of trespassing.**
- **Describe the crime of burglary.**

CORE CONCEPTS   Property invasion crimes occur when the offender enters the private property of another individual. The two main property invasion crimes are trespassing and burglary. Trespassing is concerned primarily with illegal entry onto private property. Burglary combines trespassing with the intent to commit a felony.

Trespassing

trespassing Physical entry onto another person's property without consent.

The criminal law definition of **trespassing** is, simply, entry onto private property without the owner's consent. Odds are you have seen a "No Trespassing" sign at some time in your life. More often than not, property owners post such signs in an effort to protect their privacy, often without regard to whether the act of trespassing is criminal. But depending on the jurisdiction in question, trespassing may be a criminal offense.

Trespassing statutes offer prosecutors an alternative to criminal mischief or burglary statutes. We define *burglary* below, but for now it bears mentioning that if there is no intent to commit a felony (typically theft), burglary does not occur. Likewise, if a person's conduct does not amount to mischief, but that person nevertheless enters private land without permission, a trespassing conviction is possible.

Elements of Trespassing

The *actus reus* of trespassing is satisfied when a person either enters or remains on another's private property without permission. Trespassing is sometimes considered a general intent offense. In Texas, for example, it is defined as follows:

a. A person commits an offense if the person enters or remains on or in property of another, including residential land, agricultural land, a recreational vehicle park, a building, or an aircraft or other vehicle, without effective consent and the person:
   1. had notice that the entry was forbidden; or
   2. received notice to depart but failed to do so.[25]

There are a few noteworthy elements in this statute. First, note that trespassing in Texas is a general intent offense. There is no specific *mens rea* that the prosecutor is required to prove. If a person is given notice that entry is forbidden and enters anyway, then the *mens rea* is presumed. Second, note that trespassing extends to more than just real property. Finally, to find a person guilty of trespassing, it must be shown that he or she was given notice that entry was forbidden. According to Texas law, notice can include signs, fencing, and both oral and written communications. So, for example, if Ernest yells to Cletus, "Get off my land!," and Cletus fails to do so, he could be guilty of criminal trespass. Trespassing is considered a misdemeanor in Texas.

In Ohio, criminal trespass is considered a specific intent offense. The state defines criminal trespass thusly:

a. No person, without privilege to do so, shall do any of the following:
   1. Knowingly enter or remain on the land or premises of another;
   2. Knowingly enter or remain on the land or premises of another, the use of which is lawfully restricted to certain persons, purposes, modes, or hours, when the offender knows the offender is in violation of any such restriction or is reckless in that regard;

---

[25]Texas Penal Code Section 30.05(a) (2010).

3. Recklessly enter or remain on the land or premises of another, as to which notice against unauthorized access or presence is given by actual communication to the offender, or in a manner prescribed by law, or by posting in a manner reasonably calculated to come to the attention of potential intruders, or by fencing or other enclosure manifestly designed to restrict access;

4. Being on the land or premises of another, negligently fail or refuse to leave upon being notified by signage posted in a conspicuous place or otherwise being notified to do so by the owner or occupant, or the agent or servant of either.[26]

Note the use of the terms *knowingly*, *recklessly*, and *negligently* in this statute. To secure a trespassing conviction, prosecutors must prove the specific intent required for the criminal conduct being alleged (see Figure 7.2).

Both the Texas and Ohio statutes refer, generally, to others' private property. Some states add to their trespass statutes very specific types of property on which people cannot enter without permission—or outside of normal operating hours. For example, Maine's criminal trespass statute provides, in part, that a "person is guilty of criminal trespass if, knowing that that person is not licensed or privileged to do so, that person"[27]:

> Enters or remains in a cemetery or burial ground at any time between 1/2 hour after sunset and 1/2 hour before sunrise the following day, unless that person enters or remains during hours in which visitors are permitted to enter or remain by municipal ordinance or, in the case of a privately owned and operated cemetery, by posting.[28]

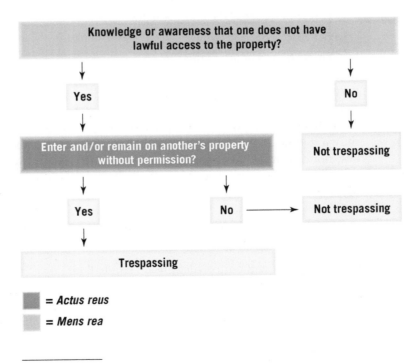

Figure 7.2
Tresspassing

---

[26]Ohio Rev. Code Section 2911.21 (2010).
[27]Maine Rev. Stat. 17-A Section 402(1) (2010).
[28]Ibid., Section 402(1)(F).

Burglary

burglary Breaking and entering into the dwelling or structure of another with the intent to commit a felony inside.

Burglary, like criminal trespassing, is concerned with property invasion. It is different from trespassing, however, because burglary typically adds to the invasion the *intent to commit a felony.*

Burglary is often viewed—inaccurately, mind you—as a crime of theft from a dwelling. A person who breaks into the home of another and steals the television is often described as a "burglar." Importantly, there is *no* requirement that a theft take place for the entry to become burglary. Even if no property is taken, a burglary may occur. The crime focuses on punishing the *invasion* of the home.

Burglary has long been considered a serious crime. This offense, along with homicide, rape, aggravated assault, and other serious crimes, is reported in the FBI's crime index, reinforcing its serious nature. As far back as 1769, Sir William Blackstone commented on the gravity of the offense:

> Burglary . . . has always been looked upon as a very heinous offense, not only because of the abundant terror that it naturally carries with it, but also as it is a forcible invasion and disturbance of that right of habitation, which every individual might acquire in a state of nature. . . . And the law of England has so particular and tender regard to the immunity of a man's house, that it styles it a castle and will never suffer it to be violated.[29]

Common Law Burglary

At common law, burglary elements were as follows:

1. Breaking and entering
2. of the dwelling of another
3. during the nighttime
4. with intent to commit a felony inside.

Breaking and entering is akin to trespassing. *Breaking* meant forcible entry, but simple *entering* also sufficed, say if the front door was unlocked. Also, like trespassing, "breaking and entering" assumes the person doing it does not have the owner's consent. Next, common law burglary was limited to dwellings—particularly "others" dwellings. This meant (and still means today) that a person could not burglarize his or her own dwelling. Next, *burglary* was defined at common law as a crime that was committed at night. Finally, common law burglary required that the intent to commit a felony was in place at the time of the breaking and entering. So, if a person forcibly entered the dwelling of another at night but had no intent to commit a felony inside, a burglary did not occur.

Burglary Today

Modern burglary statutes retain most of the common law elements, but the nighttime requirement has been largely abandoned. Since burglaries are largely crimes of

---

[29]Blackstone, *Commentaries on the Laws of England*, p. 223.

opportunity, they often occur during the daytime when people are not home, so it is sensible to relax the nighttime requirement. Several states have also eased up on both the "dwelling" and "intent to commit a felony" requirements. With respect to the former, many structures besides dwellings can now be burglarized. Likewise, many statutes permit burglary convictions if the defendant intends to commit a "crime," which of course includes felonies *and* misdemeanors. Pennsylvania's burglary statute captures several of these changes:

> A person is guilty of burglary if he enters a building or occupied structure, or separately secured or occupied portion thereof, with intent to commit a crime therein, unless the premises are at the time open to the public or the actor is licensed or privileged to enter.[30]

Note how the statute contains no nighttime requirement. Also note that it is not limited to intent to commit a "felony." Any crime suffices. The Pennsylvania statute *does* retain at least one common law element: the occupied dwelling requirement. Other states have extended the definition of burglary to much more than occupied structures. California's burglary statute offers one such example:

> Every person who enters any house, room, apartment, tenement, shop, warehouse, store, mull, barn, stable, outhouse or other building, tent, vessel, . . . floating home, . . . railroad car, locked or sealed cargo container, . . . trailer coach, . . .any house care, . . . inhabited camper, . . .aircraft, . . . or mine or any underground portion thereof, with intent to commit grand or petit larceny or any felony is guilty of burglary.[31]

This statute is very specific about the types of properties that can be burglarized. Also note, however, that its intent requirement is more restrictive than Pennsylvania's. Petit (or petty) larceny is the only misdemeanor that one can intend to commit and still have the unlawful entry amount to burglary. For example, if a person forcibly entered a railroad car for the purpose of marking it up with graffiti (a misdemeanor in most states), that person could not be found guilty of burglary.

The Model Penal Code definition of burglary is perhaps the most concise. To paraphrase, a burglary occurs if a person enters a building or occupied structure with the purpose to commit a crime inside.[32] Also, if the premises are open to the public, then entry does not constitute burglary.

Actus Reus of Burglary.

Burglary statutes are fairly specific in terms of the properties they seek to protect. Likewise, it is quite clear what constitutes entrance without permission. Some confusion surrounds the definition of *breaking*, however. And since the typical burglary that comes to mind is one premised on forcible entry, it behooves us to give this important term a little more thought. What exactly is *breaking*?

On the one hand, smashing a window in with a crowbar clearly constitutes breaking. But what if the defendant merely scales a fence? Does that constitute breaking? It depends on what the burglary statute requires. In a Nebraska case, the defendant scaled a fence and stole transmission parts from a secured storage yard.[33]

---

[30]18 Pa. Cons. Stat Section 3502(a)(b) (2010).
[31]California Penal Code Section 459 (2010).
[32]Model Penal Code Section 221.1.
[33]*State* v. *McDowell*, 522 N.W.2d 738 (Neb. 1994).

He was convicted of burglary, but later appealed, arguing that he did not forcibly enter the property, which the Nebraska burglary statute required. The statute defined *burglary* in this way:

> A person commits burglary if such person willfully, maliciously, and *forcibly* breaks and enters any real estate or any improvements erected thereon with intent to commit any felony or with intent to steal property of any value (emphasis added).[34]

McDowell, the appellant, argued that climbing a fence is not the same as forcible entry. The Nebraska Supreme Court agreed:

> Although it undoubtedly took McDowell some measure of force to climb or jump the fence in the instant case, no obstruction was removed. McDowell merely entered through the open space above the fence. Thus, as a matter of law there was no breaking, and therefore no burglary. McDowell's motion to dismiss should have been sustained with respect to the charge of burglary. McDowell's conviction for burglary is therefore, reversed.[35]

Just because McDowell's burglary conviction was reversed does not mean he went free. In all likelihood, he was convicted of a less serious larceny-related offense.

So breaking a window is forcible entry. Climbing a fence, at least in Nebraska, is not. What about the middle ground, say opening a closed, though unlocked, door? In case law from the same state, courts have repeatedly held that there is no requirement that a door be locked for a burglary conviction to stand: "The opening of a closed door to enter a building is 'breaking' within the definition of burglary."[36] If the door is both unlocked *and* open, then entrance through it is not considered breaking.[37] Note, again, that these decisions arose from Nebraska cases. Other states may take a more strict approach, while still others' approach may be more relaxed. For example, California's burglary statute (see earlier) does not contain any mention of "forcible"—thus the meaning of the term is something of a nonissue in that state.

Some statutes, and the Model Penal Code, extend the *actus reus* of burglary to the practice of **surreptitious remaining**. This occurs when a person has lawful access the property, but then remains until that person no longer does, and intends to commit a crime. Hiding in a department store bathroom until it closes with intent to steal merchandise is an example of behavior that would constitute surreptitious remaining.

surreptitious remaining
A person has lawful access the property, but then remains until he or she no longer does, and intends to commit a crime.

Mens Rea of Burglary.

Burglary is a specific intent offense because of the requirement that the prosecution prove the defendant's (a) intent of breaking, entering, or remaining, and (b) the intent to commit a crime once inside. Without such intent, there is no burglary. Again, burglary does not require that the intended crime (usually theft) be completed. All that is needed is intent. For example, if Dan breaks into Joe's house with the intent of stealing Joe's hunting rifle, but can't find it, he has still committed burglary even though he did not complete the crime.

---

[34]Neb. Rev. Stat. Ann. Section 28-507 (2010).
[35]*State v. McDowell*, 522 N.W.2d 738, p. 744.
[36]*State v. Sutton*, 368 N.W.2d 492 (Neb. 1985), p. 495.
[37]See, e.g., *Hayward v. State*, 149 N.W. 105 (1914).

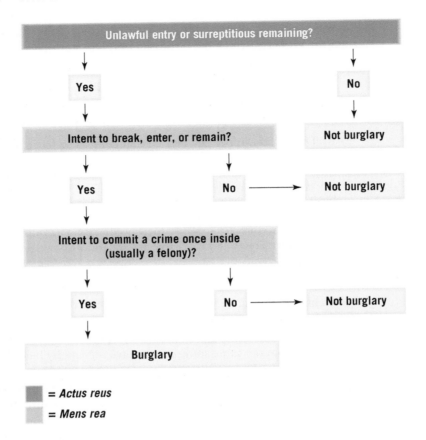

Figure 7.3
Burglary

If burglary can include this type of "attempted" theft, then what constitutes attempted burglary? Assume that Dan has a hard time breaking into Joe's house. Further assume that with a large crowbar, he tries for all he's worth to force open Joe's front door. And, finally, assume a police officer observes his actions and makes an arrest. Dan's actions in this situation amount to attempted burglary because he never successfully entered the property. See Figure 7.3 for a summary of burglary.

YOUR DECISION

1. Joey's family owns several acres of property in the Pocono Mountains. Joey often hunts, hikes, and rides snowmobiles throughout the family property. One snowy afternoon, Joey rides his snowmobile onto the neighbor's property. If Joey is unaware that he crossed onto his neighbor's property, can he be guilty of trespassing? What if an old "No Trespassing" sign was nailed to a tree?

2. One afternoon Dan notices that his neighbor's front door is wide open and no one appears to be home. Dan enters the front door to make sure that everything is OK inside. After he enters the foyer, however, Dan sees that the deliveryman left a brand new PlayStation 3, still in the box. Dan decides to take the box for himself, hoping that the neighbors will blame the missing PlayStation on a delivery error. Has Dan committed burglary? Why or why not?

Summary

- The *actus reus* of trespassing is entering or remaining on another person's property without permission.

- The *mens rea* of trespassing varies by statute, but in states with general intent trespassing laws, *mens rea* is presumed so long as the trespasser is given *notice* that access is not authorized. "Notice" can include signs, fencing, and oral or written communication.

- Burglary is not a crime of theft, contrary to popular belief.

- Common law burglary required (1) breaking and entering (2) of the dwelling of another (3) during the nighttime (4) with intent to commit a felony inside.

- Modern-day burglary has relaxed the second, third, and fourth common law elements.

- The *actus reus* of burglary occurs via "breaking" (which can include opening a closed yet unlocked door) or surreptitious remaining.

- Burglary is a specific intent offense, meaning that the prosecution must prove intent to commit a crime (usually a felony) inside.

MODULE 7.3
PROPERTY DAMAGE AND INVASION WITH COMPUTERS

Learning Objectives
- **Define and explain cybercrime.**
- **Identify laws aimed at controlling property invasion and damage with a computer.**

CORE CONCEPTS

cybercrime A criminal offense committed with the use of a computer or other electronic device.

It is difficult for the criminal law to "keep up" with technology. Before cybercrime statutes were enacted, prosecutors were forced to charge under traditional statutes, which posed difficulties. For example, if a traditional theft statute required the "carrying away" of items, how would that apply in the case of theft via computer? Unfortunately, criminals often continue to stay one step ahead of legislators, making it a continued struggle for prosecutors to target high-tech criminal activity.

Computer crime, or **cybercrime**, refers to any crime committed with the assistance of an electronic device, primarily a computer, but also smart phones and other devices. For our purposes, cybercrime falls into two separate yet closely related categories. The first is theft. Thieves use computers to steal a wide range of information from unsuspecting victims, ranging from ordinary citizens to powerful corporations. Computers are also used for the purpose of property invasion and destruction. Often criminals will try to gain access to sensitive data systems so that they can then steal information, which is why both types of activity are interrelated. Sometimes, however, they seek to gain access merely for the purpose of causing havoc and either overloading or shutting down valuable computer systems. Property damage and invasion are the focus of this module. We look at theft, including intellectual property theft and identity theft, in the next module.

Cybercrime

Most of us are at least somewhat familiar with computer crime through receipt of spam e-mail messages containing everything from appeals that we update our accounts (often in banks we are not customers of!) to requests that we become fiduciaries of some important person's fortune. Cybercrime can include everything from flagrant attacks through the use of viruses, Trojan horses, software piracy, and surreptitious installation of malware programs, to those annoying phishing e-mail messages that seek to acquire our personal information. Criminals often go further by posing as other individuals in an effort to obtain passwords and other privileged information, in a practice known as social engineering.

social engineering The practice of obtaining passwords or other sensitive information from individuals through the use of fraud or deception.

Kevin Mitnick, who was once the FBI's most wanted hacker, agrees. In an interview after his release from prison, Mitnick said that

> malicious hackers don't need to use stealth computer techniques to break into a network. . . . Often they just trick someone into giving them passwords and other information. . . . People are the weakest link. . . . You can have the best technology, firewalls, intrusion-detection systems, biometric devices . . . and somebody can call an unsuspecting employee . . . [and] they [get] everything.[38]

These and other computer crimes have taken on a transnational flavor, thus tying them in to some of the other problems we have discussed elsewhere in this chapter. Also, terrorists are increasingly exploiting computer technology to do everything from raising money through credit card fraud to communicating with each other. Figure 7.4 contains a list of specific cybercrimes, mostly those consisting of hacking, fraud, and Internet-related crime. It also presents a list of the federal agencies most likely to investigate such acts.

While these problems are most difficult for law enforcement officials to effectively target, these officials have certainly not been left behind. Technological advances have helped law enforcement, as well:

> Law enforcement access to high-technology investigative tools has produced enormous amounts of information on crimes and suspects, and the use of innovating investigative tools like DNA fingerprinting, keystroke captures, laser and night vision technologies, digital imaging, and thermography are beginning to shape many of the practical aspects of the twenty-first-century criminal justice system.[39]

The information suspected criminals voluntarily post on various social media sites, such as Twitter and Facebook, can also be valuable to law enforcement. See the

---

[38]E. Abreu, "Kevin Mitnick Bares All," *Industry Standard*. Web posted at http://www.networkworld.com/news/2000/0928mitnick.html (accessed June 27, 2007).

[39]F. Schmalleger, *Criminal Justice Today: An Introductory Text for the 21st Century*, 9th ed. (Upper Saddle River, NJ: Prentice-Hall, 2006), p. 712.

Type of Crime	Appropriate federal investigative law enforcement agencies
Computer intrusion (i.e. hacking)	• FBI local office • U.S. Secret Service • Internet Crime Complaint Center
Password trafficking	• FBI local office • U.S. Secret Service • Internet Crime Complaint Center
Counterfeiting of currency	• U.S. Secret Service • FBI local office
Child Pornography or Exploitation	• if imported, U.S. Immigration and Customs Enforcement • Internet Crime Complaint Center
Child Exploitation and Internet Fraud matters that have a mail nexus	• U.S. Postal Inspection Service • Internet Crime Complaint Center
Internet fraud and SPAM	• FBI local office • U.S. Secret Service (Financial Crimes Division) • Federal Trade Commission (online complaint) • if securities fraud or investment-related SPAM e-mails, Securities and Exchange Commission (online complaint) • The Internet Crime Complaint Center
Internet harassment	• FBI local office
Internet bomb threats	• FBI local office • ATF local office
Trafficking in explosive or incendiary devices or firearms over the Internet	• FBI local office • ATF local office

Figure 7.4

Primary Types of Computer Crime and Federal Agencies Tasked with Investigation
Source: http://www.justice.gov/criminal/cybercrime/reporting.html (accessed July 19, 2012).

accompanying Court Decision for more on the conflict over privacy rights and social media. In it we examine the case of *People* v. *Harris*, where the district attorney's office subpoenaed Twitter for information related to a criminal prosecution.

COURT DECISION

The Logic behind Social Media and Criminal Investigations

People v. *Harris*
2012 WL 1381238 (N.Y. Crim Ct.)

Decision: During a criminal investigation, the government can obtain information from third-party social media services, such as Twitter.

(continued)

**COURT
DECISION**
(continued)

Reason: The New York County District Attorney's Office seeks to obtain the Twitter records of @destructuremal using a subpoena. The defendant is alleged to have participated in a # OWS protest march on October 1, 2011. The defendant, Malcolm Harris, along with several hundred other protesters, were charged with Disorderly Conduct (P.L. § 240.20[5]) after allegedly marching on to the roadway of the Brooklyn Bridge. The defendant moved to quash that subpoena. That motion is denied.

. . . New York courts have yet to specifically address whether a criminal defendant has standing to quash a subpoena issued to a third-party online social networking service seeking to obtain the defendant's user information and postings. Nonetheless, an analogy may be drawn to the bank record cases where courts have consistently held that an individual has no right to challenge a subpoena issued against the third-party bank. New York law precludes an individual's motion to quash a subpoena seeking the production of the individual's bank records directly from the third-party bank as the defendant lacks standing. In *United States* v. *Miller*, the United States Supreme Court held that the bank records of a customer's accounts are "the business records of the banks," and that the customer "can assert neither ownership nor possession" of those records. In New York, the Appellate Division held that, "[b]ank records, although they reflect transactions between the bank and its customers, belong to the bank. The customer has no proprietary or possessory interests in them. Hence, he cannot preclude their production."

Here, the defendant has no proprietary interests in the @destructuremal account's user information and Tweets between September 15, 2011 and December 31, 2011. As briefly mentioned before, in order to use Twitter's services, the process of registering an account requires a user's agreement to Twitter's Terms. Under Twitter's Terms it states in part:

> By submitting, posting or displaying Content on or through the Services, you grant us a worldwide, non-exclusive, royalty-free license to use, copy, reproduce, process, adapt, modify, publish, transmit, display and distribute such Content in any and all media or distribution methods (now known or later developed). (See https://twitter.com/tos).

This court finds that defendant's contention that he has privacy interests in his Tweets to be understandable, but without merit... While a Twitter account's user information and Tweets contain a considerable amount of information about the user, Twitter does not guarantee any of its users complete privacy. Additionally, Twitter notifies its users that their Tweets, on default account settings, will be available for the whole world to see. Twitter also informs its users that any of their information that is posted will be Twitter's and it will use that information for any reason it may have. The @destructuremal account's Tweets were, by definition public. The defendant had knowledge that Twitter was to instantly distribute his Tweets to Twitter users and non-Twitter users, essentially anyone with Internet access. Indeed, that is the very nature and purpose of Twitter. Accordingly, this Court finds that the defendant has no standing to move to quash the subpoena.

The Jurisdiction Problem

Jurisdiction refers to the state's power to hear a criminal case and render a verdict. For example, if you commit a murder entirely in Texas, you cannot be prosecuted for the crime in Pennsylvania. Crimes committed *without* the assistance of computers usually have clear jurisdictional boundaries. This is at least true for the traditional types of serious crime with which we are most familiar—homicide, rape, robbery, and so on. Certain offenses, such as kidnapping, can cross jurisdictional boundaries, adding an interstate flavor and therefore complicating prosecution. Questions of cybercrime jurisdiction, however, can cause one's head to spin. Consider this scenario:

> A Web site in Germany caters to the adult market, and has done so happily for three years. Then, out of the blue, it finds itself indicted in Singapore because of spreading pornographic material in Singapore, even though the company has never done business with someone from Singapore. To make things worse, the Web site owners are ordered to appear in court in Belgium, because some of the adult pictures are considered to be of 17-year old minors, constituting the crime of child pornography (which, in Belgium, entails persons under 18 years of age; in Germany, the age limit is 14). The business is perfectly legal in Germany, but since it uses the Internet to conduct its business, it finds itself confronted with the criminal laws of all countries connected to the Internet—that is, all countries of the world.[40]

Clearly, a number of jurisdictional questions can arise. This is an area of continual development in the law, too. In the United States alone, there is a bewildering array of federal and state legislation that can be used to target cybercriminals. In general, however, if the federal government (or its interests) is the victim, federal prosecution is in order. If a state is the victim, then a state prosecution will likely occur. And if the victim is an individual, then depending on the conduct in question, the prosecution may occur at either the state or the federal level.

Computer Fraud and Abuse Act (CFAA) Federal legislation that criminalizes various types of cybercrime.

Federal cybercrime law continues to evolve and change with the times, but most of it is found in the so-called **Computer Fraud and Abuse Act (CFAA)**.[41] The types of actions criminalized in the CFAA as well as the penalties provided appear in Figure 7.5. State laws also continue to change as the needs arise.

Property Invasion with Computers

hacking Breaking into computer systems with the intent to alter or modify settings.

Hacking is the term used to describe breaking into computer systems, often with the intention to alter or modify settings. Hacking fits well within this chapter because it is similar in character to trespassing, criminal mischief, and vandalism. It is also similar to burglary if the offender is motivated to commit a more serious crime once he or she gains access. Every state has its own hacking, or

---

[40]S. W. Brenner and B. Koops, "Approaches to Cybercrime Jurisdiction," *Journal of High Tech Law*, Vol. 4 (2004), p. 3.
[41]18 U.S.C. Section 1030 (2010).

Figure 7.5

Summary of CFAA
Provisions

Source: S. Eltringham (Ed.),
Prosecuting Computer Crimes.
Washington, DC: United States
Department of Justice,
Computer Crime and
Intellectual Property Section,
2007. Available at: http://
www.justice.gov/criminal/
cybercrime/docs/ccmanual.pdf
(accessed July 19, 2012), p. 2.

Offense	Section	Sentence*
Obtaining National Security Information	(a)(1)	10 (20) years
Compromising the Confidentiality of a Computer	(a)(2)	1 or 5
Trespassing in a Government Computer	(a)(3)	1 (10)
Accessing a Computer to Defraud & Obtain Value	(a)(4)	5 (10)
Knowing Transmission and Intentional Damage	(a)(5)(A)(i)	10 (20 or life)
Intentional Access and Reckless Damage	(a)(5)(A)(ii)	5 (20)
Intentional Access and Damage	(a)(5)(A)(iii)	1 (10)
Trafficking in Passwords	(a)(6)	1 (10)
Extortion Involving Threats to Damage Computer	(a)(7)	5 (10)

* The maximum prison sentences for second convictions are noted in parentheses

"unauthorized access," law.[42] For example, New York's "computer trespass" statute reads as follows:

> A person is guilty of computer trespass when he or she knowingly uses, causes to be used, or accesses a computer, computer service, or computer network without authorization and:
> 1. he or she does so with an intent to commit or attempt to commit or further the commission of any felony; or
> 2. he or she thereby knowingly gains access to computer material.[43]

Note that there are two *mens rea* elements: knowledge that the individual is not authorized to access the data and either (1) intent to commit a crime once access is gained or (2) knowledge that the material sought is accessed. The *actus reus* is, simply, unauthorized access. New York also criminalizes a number of other access offenses, including unauthorized use, tampering, and unlawful duplication.

Some state laws, such as California's,[44] are considerably more elaborate and cannot be reprinted here because of space constraints. Other state laws are rather brief, yet encompass a wide range of actions. Texas's "breach of computer security" statute provides that "[a] person commits an offense if the person knowingly accesses a computer, computer network, or computer system without the effective consent of the owner."[45] Other state laws criminalize both access *and* tampering. We look at a few in the following section.

Property Damage with Computers

Cybercriminals sometimes access protected computer systems just to say they can do it. Other times their intentions are more insidious. They may seek to corrupt data; disrupt equipment; threaten system reliability; disseminate viruses, worms, or malware;

---

[42]For a state-by-state comparison, see http://www.ncsl.org/default.aspx?tabid=13494 (accessed September 27, 2010).
[43]N.Y. Penal Law Section 156.10 (2010).
[44]Cal. Penal Code Section 502 (2010).
[45]Texas Penal Code Section 33.02 (2010).

launch botnets (software running on a collection of compromised computers); steal sensitive information; and otherwise cause widespread havoc. In the worst case, terrorists may seek to use computers to launch attacks against their enemies.

Just as states have laws aimed at preventing hacking, they also have laws that prohibit tampering with computer systems. For example, Arizona's "computer tampering" law criminalizes not just unauthorized access, but also various forms of tampering and/or destruction once the offender gains access. The law reads, in part,

> A person who acts without authority or who exceeds authorization of use commits computer tampering by:
>
> 1. Accessing, altering, damaging or destroying any computer, computer system or network, or any part of a computer, computer system or network, with the intent to devise or execute any scheme or artifice to defraud or deceive, or to control property or services by means of false or fraudulent pretenses, representations or promises.
> 2. Knowingly altering, damaging, deleting or destroying computer programs or data.
> 3. Knowingly introducing a computer contaminant into any computer, computer system or network.
> 4. Recklessly disrupting or causing the disruption of computer, computer system or network services or denying or causing the denial of computer or network services to any authorized user of a computer, computer system or network.
> 5. Recklessly using a computer, computer system or network to engage in a scheme or course of conduct that is directed at another person and that seriously alarms, torments, threatens or terrorizes the person. . . .
> 6. Preventing a computer user from exiting a site, computer system or network-connected location in order to compel the user's computer to continue communicating with, connecting to or displaying the content of the service, site or system.
> 7. Knowingly obtaining any information that is required by law to be kept confidential or any records that are not public records by accessing any computer, computer system or network that is operated by this state, a political subdivision of this state or a medical institution. . . .
> 8. Knowingly accessing any computer, computer system or network or any computer software, program or data that is contained in a computer, computer system or network.[46]

Note how this statute criminalizes a variety of actions aimed at causing damage to computers, computer systems, networks, and the like. Also note that the *mens rea* varies by the conduct alleged.

cyberterrorism A politically motivated attack using computers or other technology.

Cyberterrorism

Of considerable concern these days is the threat of **cyberterrorism**. Defined as "politically motivated hacking operations intended to cause grave harm such as loss of life

---

[46]Ariz. Rev. Stat. Ann. Section 13-2316 (2010).

Computers can be used for a number of illicit purposes, including property damage, theft and cyberterrorism.

© Stephen Flint/Alamy

or severe economic damage,"[47] cyberterrorism combines elements of cybercrime and traditional terrorism. Computer security expert Dorothy Denning described the threat in this way:

> Cyberterrorism is the convergence of terrorism and cyberspace. It is generally understood to mean unlawful attacks and threats of attack against computers, networks, and the information stored therein when done to intimidate or coerce a government or its people in furtherance of political or social objectives. Further, to qualify as cyberterrorism, an attack should result in violence against persons or property, or at least cause enough harm to generate fear. Attacks that lead to death or bodily injury, explosions, plane crashes, water contamination, or severe economic loss would be examples. Serious attacks against critical infrastructures could be acts of cyberterrorism, depending on their impact. Attacks that disrupt nonessential services or that are mainly a costly nuisance would not.[48]

The United States has yet to see a large-scale cyberterrorism attack, but officials are still acknowledging the threat. As of this writing, one of the most significant attacks on record occurred in Estonia during 2007. A series of coordinated attacks caused a series of governmental websites to shut down for a period of time, blocking legitimate users and crippling not just government operations, but even banking.[49]

---

[47]D. Denning, "Activism, Hactivism, and Cyberterrorism: The Internet as a Tool for Influencing Foreign Policy," in J. Arquilla and D. Ronfeldt, eds., *Networks and Netwars* (Santa Monica, CA: Rand, 2001), p. 241.
[48]D. Denning, "Cyberterrorism," Testimony before the Special Oversight Panel of Terrorism, Committee on Armed Services, U.S. House of Representatives, May 23, 2000. Available at: http://www.cs.georgetown.edu/~denning/infosec/cyberterror.html (accessed September 28, 2010).
[49]C. Wilson, *Botnets, Cybercrime, and Cyberterrorism: Vulnerabilities and Policy Issues for Congress* (Washington, DC: Congressional Research Service, 2008), p. 6.

YOUR DECISION

1. Larry and Jeff are always playing practical jokes on each other at the office. One afternoon, Larry forgets to lock his computer while he goes to lunch. Jeff decides to log on to Larry's e-mail without permission and distribute a picture of child pornography to the entire office. Assume that the distribution of child pornography is a felony. Is Jeff guilty of any type of cybercrime? If so, which type?

2. Mark is a self-appointed computer science expert. He decides one day to challenge himself and see if he can hack into the U.S. Department of Defense website "just for kicks." Mark has no intention of stealing information or damaging the system. He just wants to prove to himself that he has the skill and ability to crack into such a secure computer system. Mark is finally successful, and does nothing with the information except to brag to his friends on Facebook. Has Mark committed a crime? If so, which one?

Summary

- Cybercrime refers to any crime committed with the assistance of a computer.
- Cybercrime often falls into two categories: theft and property damage/destruction.
- Hackers use computers for property invasion, which is similar to trespassing, criminal mischief, and vandalism.
- Hacking is also similar to burglary if the offender is motivated by the intent to steal.
- Computers are also used to cause property damage. For example, offenders may seek to corrupt data; disrupt equipment; threaten system reliability; disseminate viruses, worms, or malware; launch botnets; and steal sensitive information, among other actions.

MODULE

7.4 THEFT OFFENSES

Learning Objectives

- **Identify the elements of larceny.**
- **Describe the crime of receiving stolen property.**
- **Summarize the elements of extortion and embezzlement.**
- **Summarize the elements of false pretenses and forgery/uttering.**
- **Compare and contrast identity theft and theft of intellectual property.**

CORE CONCEPTS   We now turn our attention to theft offenses, which refers to a variety of ways a criminal can illegally take another's property. The specific facts and circumstances surrounding the taking dictate which crime actually takes place.

larceny The trespassory taking and carrying away of the person property of another with the intent to permanently deprive the owner of possession.

What we all know and recognize as *theft* or *stealing* is formally called **larceny**. Common law larceny consisted of four distinct elements:

1. The trespassory taking
2. and carrying away
3. of the personal property of another
4. with intent to permanently deprive the owner/possessor of the property.[50]

Note that the first three elements identified the *actus reus* of larceny and the fourth identified the *mens rea*. Also note that, as defined, larceny was a conduct crime, not a result crime. In other words, the offense was complete once a person took and carried away another's personal property. There was no requirement that the dispossessor (the person taking the property) put the property to his or her own use.

The common law distinguished between petit (petty) and grand larceny. The former involved theft of items beneath a certain value; the latter involved theft of items *above* a certain value. At common law, the amount that turned petty to grand larceny was "twelvepence," which equals less than ten cents in today's dollars.[51] Today, the cut-off point is somewhere in the neighborhood of $1,000, meaning that theft of items valued less than that is considered petty.

At common law, grand theft was punishable by death. Today, no theft conviction provides for capital punishment. Instead, grand theft is a felony and petty theft is a misdemeanor. That said, don't think for a moment that theft penalties are always light. California's three-strikes law provides for life in prison in the case of grand theft, provided the convicted individual has two "strikeable" felonies on his or her record beforehand.[52] Offenders have literally received life sentences for stealing items such as golf clubs.[53]

Elements of Larceny

Punishments for larceny have changed over time; however, the common law elements of the crime have remained more or less intact. We begin with the *actus reus*, then turn our attention to the *mens rea*.

Actus Reus

There are four elements to the *actus reus* of larceny. They are

1. Trespass
2. Taking
3. Carrying away
4. Personal property

---

[50]See, e.g., *Lee* v. *State*, 474 A.2d 537 (Md. Ct. Spec. App. 1984), p. 539.
[51]J. Dressler, *Understanding Criminal Law*, 5th ed. (Newark, NJ: Lexis-Nexis, 2009), p. 555.
[52]F. E. Zimring, G. Hawkins, and S. Kamin, *Punishment and Democracy: Three Strikes and You're Out in California* (New York: Oxford University Press, 2001).
[53]See *Ewing* v. *California*, 538 U.S. 11 (2003).

Trespass. Common law larceny required a "trespass." As noted in one early decision, "[t]here can be no larceny without a trespass, and there can be no trespass unless the property was in the possession of the one from whom it is charged to have been stolen."[54] The term *trespass,* however, took on a different meaning, distinct from the *crime* of trespassing. The trespass element of larceny stems from the Latin phrase *trespass be bonis asportatis,* which referred to a tort in which one party interfered with another's lawful possession of a chattel (i.e., movable personal property). The trespass of larceny was thus akin to taking possession of another's property. This remains true today.

Common law larceny also required that the trespass involved an element of stealth. The doctrine of *caveat emptor* (i.e., "let the buyer beware") applied, meaning that one who defrauded another of his or her property was not considered a thief. This, as you probably know by now, has changed with the times.[55] Indeed, as we will see later in this module, there are specific offenses aimed directly at those who would defraud people of their property.

Taking. The trespass element of larceny is straightforward enough, as we have seen. The *taking* element, however, is much more complicated. What does *taking* mean? What types of actions amount to "taking" another's property? There are a number of possible complications that make it difficult to arrive at any best answers to these questions.

In general, *taking* refers to the removing the property from the *possession* of another. This means that we have to define *possession.* The *actus reus* of Chapter 3 briefly distinguished between two types of possession: actual and constructive. To refresh your memory, property is in a person's actual possession if that person is holding it or it is attached to the victim in some fashion. In contrast, constructive possession means the owner has control over the property, usually because it is in close physical proximity to him or her, but also because the owner may have given custody (defined presently) of the property to someone else. As Dressler has observed, "[a]ll non-abandoned property is in the actual or constructive possession of some party at all times."[56]

Possession also has to be distinguished from custody. One who has property in his or her custody has control over it. However, just because one has custody over property does not mean the property is in that individual's possession. For example, a jewelry merchant who hands a ring to a customer who then tries it on transfers the custody of the ring *and* no longer has actual possession of it.[57] However, the merchant *does* retain constructive possession of the ring. Should the customer leave with the ring and not pay for it, larceny occurs.

Also consider the case of an employer who lends a company vehicle to an employee. The employee takes custody of the vehicle, but constructive possession remains with the owner. Thus, if the employee likes the vehicle and decides to keep it, he has committed larceny because he interfered with the employer's constructive

---

[54]*People* v. *Hoban,* 88 N.E. 806 (Ill. 1909), p. 807.
[55]The wheels were set in motion as early as 1779. See *King* v. *Pear,* 168 Eng. Rep. 208 (1779).
[56]Dressler, *Understanding Criminal Law,* p. 557.
[57]See, e.g., *Chisser's Case,* 83 Eng. Rep. 142 (1678).

possession of the vehicle.[58] Why do we care about these details? Again, larceny is a crime in which property is taken from the *possession* of another, not the custody of another. This distinction rarely comes up in practice, but it is still important. To summarize, taking is synonymous with dispossessing someone of property. In other words, one who removes property from the possession of another "takes" it.

Carrying Away (Asportation).

The carrying way (or asportation) of property is another essential—and time-honored—element of larceny. Significant movement is not necessary, however. For example, a shoplifter who has apparel in her possession and is moving toward the exit commits larceny, even though she has not yet "carried away" the property from the premises.[59]

It bears mentioning, however, that not all movement constitutes "carrying away." Assume a defendant removed a box from a high shelf and set it on the floor in order to steal the contents. Such action constitutes attempted larceny, but not larceny itself. Why? Because the purpose of moving the box was to make the contents more accessible; it was not the same as carrying it away.[60] Given the fine line between both types of movement, the Model Penal Code does not require proof of "carrying away."[61] Theft occurs simply if one person "unlawfully takes another's property."[62]

Personal Property of Another.

Personal property is distinct from real property, the latter of which is typically land. Since land cannot be picked up and carried away, it cannot be stolen—at least under a common law definition of larceny. The only ways to take possession of land are either to evict the owner from the property or obtain title to the land. Both actions, if illegal, are remedied by means other than larceny prosecution (there are legal means for taking land, such as eminent domain).

Even certain items *attached* to real property are considered the same as real property and thus cannot be stolen.[63] If items attached to real property are then removed, they become personal property and thus can be stolen. For example, if a Christmas tree farmer's trees are cut down without his permission and removed from the property, larceny has occurred.

What, then, is *personal property*? At the risk of simplification, *personal property* is anything other than real property that is also tangible (intangible property, such as intellectual property, is often covered in other statutes—see discussion later in this module). There were times in history when certain types of property that we would consider personal today were not. For example, at common law domesticated dogs were not considered personal property.[64] That has since changed. Modern larceny laws extend to nearly "anything of value."[65] Some even protect real property.[66]

---

[58]See, e.g., Dressler, *Understanding Criminal Law*, p. 558.

[59]See, e.g., *People* v. *Olivo*, 420 N.E.2d 40 (N.Y. 1981), p. 44.

[60]See, e.g., *Cherry's Case*, 168 Eng. Rep. 221 (1781).

[61]Model Penal Code Section 223.2(1).

[62]Ibid.

[63]See, e.g., *Parker* v. *State*, 352 So. 2d 1386 (Ala. Crim. App. 1977).

[64]Dressler, *Understanding Criminal Law*, p. 563.

[65]Model Penal Code Section 223.0(6).

[66]Ibid.

As mentioned earlier, the value of the stolen property is directly related to whether the defendant will be charged with a felony or a misdemeanor. Consequently, a number of courts consider the "value" of the property to constitute an additional element of certain types of larceny. See the accompanying Court Decision for more on this issue. In it we examine the case of *Foreman v. United States*, where the court is confronted with determining the value of an iPod and its downloaded contents.

COURT DECISION

Court Decision: The Logic behind the Value of Stolen Property

Foreman v. United States
988 A.2d 505 (D.C. App. 2010)

Decision: The prosecution must present evidence regarding the value of an iPod and its digital contents in order to convict a defendant of felony theft.

Reason: Appellant was charged with, among other things, armed robbery and possession of a firearm during a crime of violence, both arising from an incident in which, according to the indictment, he forcibly took an iPod from Marcus Curry while brandishing a handgun. The jury acquitted him of these charges but returned a guilty verdict on first-degree theft and hung on unarmed robbery . . .

We hold that the evidence was insufficient to permit appellant's conviction of first-degree theft, because the government presented no evidence from which a rational juror could infer that the combined value of the stolen iPod and its contents exceeded $250. Although the proof requirement for theft in the first degree that "the value of the property obtained" was "$250 or more" appears in a penalty statute, § 22-3212(a), not in the definition of "theft," § 22-3211, our decisions leave no doubt that the issue of value distinguishing first degree (or felony) theft from second degree (or misdemeanor) theft, implicates an element of the offense and must be submitted to the trier of fact. Our cases have further established that, "when the proof [at trial] indicates a value nearing [the] minimum" separating felony from misdemeanor theft, "such proof may need to be offered with greater precision" than when the issue is not a close one.

. . . Here, the government's proof of value exceeding the statutory amount of $250 was insufficient to rule out a verdict based on "surmise or conjecture." Perhaps understandably, in a case where the parties disagreed most strongly on whether appellant had forcibly assaulted (*i.e.*, robbed) Curry, and if so whether he had used a firearm, the evidence on the value of the iPod consisted of sparse testimony by Curry and his mother unelucidated by other evidence. Marcus Curry stated that his mother had bought the iPod for him in December 2006 as a Christmas gift (*i.e.*, some four months before the April 12, 2007 theft), and that he believed she had paid $300 for it. But Mrs. Curry corrected this by stating that she had paid "about $250" for the iPod, though with "tax and shipping it came up to about $300." Marcus Curry further testified that he had "movies and pictures of [himself] and [his] friends

(continued)

and . . . family" on the iPod, and had downloaded "about four hundred or more" songs onto the device. While he had "had to pay" to put the movies on the iPod, "some of [the] songs" were "free downloaded songs" and "some of them you had to pay for." That was the sum of the value evidence presented to the jury.

. . . Our decisions have also made clear, however, that electronic products of this nature have a tendency to depreciate rapidly as technology changes and old versions are replaced. Thus, since no contrary evidence was presented that iPods retain the market value reflected in their purchase price, only speculation allowed the jury to infer that Curry's device, by itself, was still worth $250 some four months after it was bought . . .

Consequently, appellant's conviction for theft in the first degree must be vacated for insufficient evidence. He asks us to remand with directions for the trial court to enter judgment on the lesser included offense of theft in the second degree, but the record does not tell us—nor could the parties at oral argument—whether the charge of robbery on which the jury hung is still pending and so subject to retrial. We leave these matters to be determined on remand.

Reversed and remanded with directions to enter judgment of acquittal on theft in the first degree.

Mens Rea

The *mens rea* of larceny requires intent to permanently deprive the owner/possessor of the property. More simply, it is *intent to steal*. Assume you test drive a vehicle at your local car dealership. If the salesperson lets you take the vehicle for a drive and you elect to keep it permanently, without paying for it, you commit larceny. If, instead, you keep it for a little longer than the usual test drive, just to take it for a "joy ride," then larceny has *not* occurred. This underscores the intent element of larceny. Again, there must be intent to permanently deprive the owner/possessor of the property.

What if the property in question is perishable? Perhaps Bill made off with Sarah's tasty-looking (and uncooked) rib eye steaks. If he gets distracted, fails to cook them, and the meat goes bad, is Bill guilty of larceny? As long as Bill's action was sufficient to "appropriate a major portion of its economic value," then the answer is "yes."[67] Since a rotten piece of meat would be worth less than a still-fresh one, then Bill has committed theft, so it is quite possible to be guilty of stealing perishable items.

Another issue that arises in the *mens rea* of larceny is whether the accused seeks to gain from the theft. In general, there is no requirement that the accused seek to gain from the theft. If the accused intends to deprive a woman of her priceless artwork by throwing it on a bonfire, then larceny still occurs. Figure 7.6 summarizes the elements of larceny discussed in this and previous subsections.

---

[67]American Law Institute, Comment to Section 223.3, p. 175.

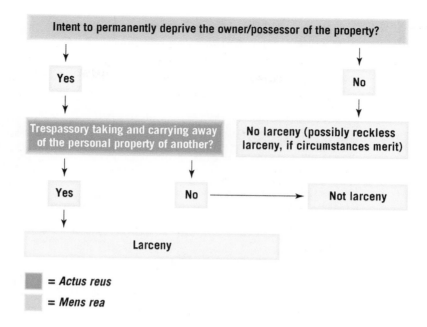

Figure 7.6
Larceny

Receiving Stolen Property

Closely tied to larceny are the crimes of receiving stolen property (not to be confused with *stealing* stolen property), extortion, and embezzlement. It is a crime for a person to receive stolen property, even if that person did not actually steal the property. Why criminalize the receipt of stolen property? It removes any possible benefit a person stands to gain a result of another person's theft. To prove receiving stolen property, the prosecution typically needs to show that the defendant knowingly received the property, the property was stolen, and the defendant knew the property had been stolen or believed it was. For example, New Jersey's receiving stolen property statute reads:

> A person is guilty of theft if he knowingly receives (or brings into this State) movable property of another knowing that it has been stolen, or believing that it has probably been stolen.[68]

Kentucky's statute is similar, but slightly more elaborate:

> A person is guilty of receiving stolen property when he receives, retains, or disposes of movable property of another knowing that it has been stolen, or having reason to believe that it has been stolen, unless the property is received, retained, or disposed of with intent to restore it to the owner.[69]

What if the defendant received stolen property, but only to return it to its rightful owner? He or she would not be convicted of the crime, as a receiving stolen property conviction requires an implied intent to keep the property. Also, most states do not require proof that the defendant knew the property was stolen. Knowledge is

---

[68]N.J.S.A. Section 2C:10-7a (2010).
[69]K.R.S. Section 514.110 (2010).

Purchasing products that "appear" to be stolen raises the potential for a receiving stolen property offense.

Peter Rayner/Axiom/Photographic/Newscom

often inferred, but some states, such as Texas, require proof that the defendant knew the property was stolen.[70] Finally, the crime of receiving stolen property is usually treated as a misdemeanor.

Extortion

extortion Also known as blackmail, taking property from another with threats of future harm.

Extortion, or blackmail, consists of taking another's property by threats of future harm. The key is *future* harm, otherwise extortion would be the same as robbery. A California appellate court distinguished between robbery and extortion thusly:

> The crime of extortion is related to and sometimes difficult to distinguish from the crime of robbery. . . . Both crimes have their roots in the common law crime of larceny. Both crimes share the element of an acquisition by means of force or fear. One distinction between robbery and extortion is that with robbery, property is taken from another by force or fear against the victim's will, while with extortion, property is taken from another by force or fear with the victim's consent. The two crimes, however, have other distinctions. Robbery requires a "felonious taking," which means a specific intent to permanently deprive the victim of the property. Robbery also requires the property to be taken from the victim's "person or immediate presence. . . . Extortion does not require proof of either of these elements. Extortion does, however, require the specific intent of inducing the victim to consent to part with his or her property.

Assume Susan knows that Jackie has a secret that could disgrace Jackie if it were revealed. If Susan demands money from Jackie in exchange for her silence, this is a classic instance of extortion. Extortion is a consensual crime, meaning that Jackie would have to consent (but not in the truest sense of the term) to pay Susan. If she

---

[70]See, e.g., *Sonnier* v. *State*, 849 S.W.2d 828 (Tex. App. 1992).

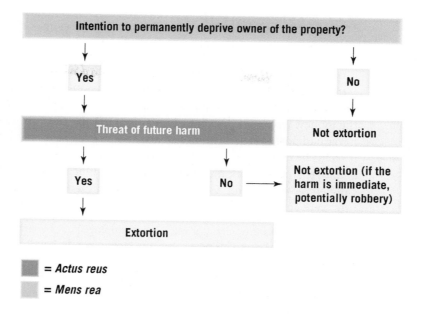

Figure 7.7
Extortion

did not consent and Susan still received the money, then she would most likely go about getting it via traditional larceny.

The *mens rea* of extortion is usually the general intent to take someone else's property by threats of harm or damage. The *actus reus* is actually doing so. Oregon's "theft by extortion" statute reveals each of these, including the many possible threats (also see Figure 7.7 for a summary):

1. A person commits theft by extortion when the person compels or induces another to deliver property to the person or to a third person by instilling in the other a fear that, if the property is not so delivered, the actor or a third person will in the future:
   a. Cause physical injury to some person;
   b. Cause damage to property;
   c. Engage in other conduct constituting a crime;
   d. Accuse some person of a crime or cause criminal charges to be instituted against the person;
   e. Expose a secret or publicize an asserted fact, whether true or false, tending to subject some person to hatred, contempt or ridicule;
   f. Cause or continue a strike, boycott or other collective action injurious to some person's business, except that such conduct is not considered extortion when the property is demanded or received for the benefit of the group in whose interest the actor purports to act;
   g. Testify or provide information or withhold testimony or information with respect to another's legal claim or defense;
   h. Use or abuse the position as a public servant by performing some act within or related to official duties, or by failing or refusing to perform an official duty, in such manner as to affect some person adversely; or
   i. Inflict any other harm that would not benefit the actor.[71]

---

[71]O.R.S. Section 164.075 (2009).

Embezzlement

embezzlement Someone in lawful possession of property retains or converts the property for his or her own use with the intent to steal or defraud the rightful owner.

Embezzlement is one of a few crimes that were not defined as such at common law; it is a relatively recent creation, partly because of what happened in the famous 1799 *Bazeley* case.[72] Bazeley, a bank teller, took a customer's deposit and pocketed it, rather than put it in the till. Bazeley was acquitted of larceny because he took possession of the money, which was given to him voluntarily by the customer. Moreover, the bank never had possession of the money because Bazeley never put it in the till. Even though it seems he committed larceny, he did not in the truest sense. Why? It was never in his employer's possession, much less its custody. Once it was realized that people (typically employees) could act dishonestly like this *and* escape larceny convictions, statutes were enacted to deal with the problem. For example, one early statute read:

> [I]f any servant or clerk, or any person employed . . . by virtue of such employment receive or take into his possession any money, goods, bond, bill, note, banker's draft, or other valuable security, or effects, for or in the name or on the account of his master or masters, or employer or employers, and shall fraudulently embezzle, secrete, or make away with the same, or any part thereof . . . [he] shall be deemed to have feloniously stolen the same.[73]

Modern-day embezzlement statutes are quite similar. Arizona's embezzlement statute reads as follows:

> Any bailee of any money, goods or property, who converts it to his or her own use, with the intent to steal it or to defraud the owner or owners thereof and any agent, manager or clerk of any person, corporation, association or partnership, or any person with whom any money, property or effects have been deposited or entrusted, who uses or appropriates the money, property or effects or any part thereof in any manner or for any other purpose than that for which they were deposited or entrusted, is guilty of embezzlement, and shall be punished in the manner prescribed by law for the stealing or larceny of property of the kind and name of the money, goods, property or effects so taken, converted, stolen, used or appropriated.[74]

bailee Person to whom goods or property are entrusted.

bailor The individual, usually an employer, who entrust the bailee with their property.

white-collar crime Various crimes typically committed by corporate executive or other employees in the course of their employment.

The *mens rea* of this statute is straightforward: "intent to steal it or to defraud. . . ." The *actus reus*, however, is a bit more complicated. Why? Embezzlement statutes have to cover every conceivable type of action by which a **bailee** (one to whom goods are entrusted) could benefit by *converting* the property of a **bailor** (the one, usually an employer, who entrusts the bailee with property).

Embezzlement is often regarded as a white-collar crime. **White-collar crime** is a term used to describe "various types of unlawful, nonviolent conduct committed by corporations and individuals including theft or fraud and other violations of trust committed in the course of the offender's occupation (e.g., embezzlement, commercial bribery, racketeering, anti-trust violations, price-fixing, stock manipulation, insider trading, and the like."[75] Embezzlement is typically an individual—as opposed to corporate—crime, meaning that no more than one person's actions are necessary to complete the offense.

---

[72]*King* v. *Bazeley*, 168 Eng. Rep. 517 (1799).
[73]39 Geo. III, C. 85 (1799).
[74]A.R.S. Section 205.300 (2010).
[75]*Black's Law Dictionary*, 6th ed. (St. Paul, MN: West, 1990), p. 1596.

False Pretenses

false pretenses
Obtaining the property of another through fraud or deception.

False pretenses is shorthand for "*obtaining property* by false pretenses" or, more simply, "deception." Obtaining property by false pretenses is different from embezzlement because the embezzler obtains the property lawfully at first, only to fraudulently convert it to his or her use later. In the crime of false pretenses, however, the victim *willingly* gives the property to the criminal. False pretenses also differs from larceny because it requires the additional elements of deception and false representation.[76]

The *core* element of false pretenses is false representation, or deception. Such deception can be manifested verbally, in writing, or even by conduct. An example of the latter occurred when one person obtained property from another by donning Oxford apparel, giving the (false) impression he was a student at the famous college.[77] In contrast, a person's *failure to disclose* important information (unless there is a legal obligation to do so) will not amount to false representation.

To get more specific, for something to amount to false representation, it must satisfy three criteria. First, it must in fact be false. If it is not false, there are no false pretenses. Second, opinions, even if expressed with intent to defraud another person, do not constitute false representation.[78] For example, if a car salesperson says "this is the best machine on four wheels" and it is not, it is not a case of false pretenses. Third, false pretenses applies to current, not future, conduct. That is, false pretenses are not the same as "false promises." A false promise would be a homebuyer's promise to repay a mortgage, only to stop making payments at some point in the future (even if that was the borrower's plan in the first place).

The *mens rea* of false pretenses is straightforward. It must be shown that the defendant intended to use the false information to secure property that he or she did not otherwise have a right to. This means that even if someone lies to obtain property to which she is entitled, there are no false pretenses.

To summarize, consider North Carolina's "obtaining property by false pretenses" statute. It succinctly captures both the *actus reus* and *mens rea* of the offense:

> If any person shall knowingly and designedly by means of any kind of false pretense whatsoever, whether the false pretense is of a past or subsisting fact or of a future fulfillment or event, obtain or attempt to obtain from any person within this State any money, goods, property, services, chose in action, or other thing of value with intent to cheat or defraud any person of such money, goods, property, services, chose in action or other thing of value, such person shall be guilty of a felony.[79]

Although North Carolina treats false pretenses as a felony, not all jurisdictions do. Such actions amounted to a misdemeanor at common law.

---

[76]See e.g., *Bell v. United States*, 462 U.S. 356 (1983), p. 359.
[77]*Rex v. Barnard*, 173 Eng. Rep. 342 (1837).
[78]See, e.g., *Regina v. Bryan*, 7 Cox. Crim. Cas. 312 (1857).
[79]N.C. Gen. Stat. Section 14-100 (2010).

Forgery/Uttering

forgery Materially altering a document with the intent to defraud.

uttering Passing a forged document to another with the intent to defraud.

Forgery is defined as "the false making or the material altering of a document with the intent to defraud."[80] **Uttering** refers to the act of passing a forged document on to someone else. Both are considered crimes. Obviously, however, the crime of forgery may well go undetected until someone actually attempts to use the forged document. Examples of forgery and uttering include

- Signing someone else's name on a legal document.
- Printing counterfeit tickets for a sporting event.
- Altering the amount of a check.
- Altering grades on a college transcript.

Many states have opted to criminalize forgery and uttering via a single statute. Arizona is one such state. Its forgery statute provides the following:

a. A person commits forgery if, with intent to defraud, the person:
   1. Falsely makes, completes or alters a written instrument; or
   2. Knowingly possesses a forged instrument; or
   3. Offers or presents, whether accepted or not, a forged instrument or one which contains false information.[81]

Note that the *mens rea* is "intent to defraud." Also note that the *actus reus* varies depending on the conduct in question. The "offers or presents" language is the uttering component of the statute.

Other jurisdictions have taken more elaborate measures to target forgery and uttering, having enacted separate statutes for a variety of specific offenses. For example, in West Virginia, there are eight statutes aimed at currency-related forgery alone.[82] This is not surprising given the scope of the counterfeit currency problem. All states and the federal government[83] maintain statutes aimed at discouraging counterfeiting as well. Much the same applies to misuse of credit cards, falsification of checks, and so on.

e-mail spoofing Altering an e-mail address so that it appears to come from a person other than the sender.

Recently, forgery has moved into cyberspace, particularly via **e-mail spoofing**, or "forging" key parts of an e-mail address to give the impression that a message comes from one person when in fact it comes from another.[84] This is often done as a means of shielding the identity of someone who sends "spam" e-mail. It is also done to trick recipients into divulging sensitive information. The recipient of such a spoof may get an:

- e-mail claiming to be from a system administrator requesting users to change their passwords to a specified string and threatening to suspend their account if they do not comply.
- e-mail claiming to be from a person in authority requesting users to send them a copy of a password file or other sensitive information.[85]

---

[80]*Black's Law Dictionary*, p. 650.
[81]Ariz. Rev. Stat. Section 13-2002 (2010).
[82]West Va. Code Sections 61-4-1-61-4-8 (2010).
[83]18 U.S.C. Section 471 (2010).
[84]See, e.g., S. Austria, "Forgery in Cyberspace: The Spoof Could Be on You!," *Pittsburgh Journal of Technology Law and Policy*, Vol. 4 (2004), p. 2.
[85]http://www.cert.org/tech_tips/email_spoofing.html (accessed July 22, 2011).

States have been slow to criminalize e-mail spoofing. Some have enacted antispam statutes aimed at deterring this high-tech form of forgery, but as of this writing, the majority of them have not.[86]

Identity Theft

Identity theft Utilizing personal information of another person to commit fraud or deception.

Recent data show that almost 8 million households in the United States experienced at least one form of identity theft in the past year.[87] From year to year, the number continues to grow. **Identity theft** (sometimes called "identity fraud") occurs "when someone uses or attempts to use the sensitive personal information of another person to commit fraud."[88] Common varieties of identity theft appear in Figure 7.8.

Identity theft is both a federal and state crime. Federal law provides, in part, that it is a felony to "knowingly transfer, possess or use, without lawful authority,

Account fraud: There are two basic forms of account fraud – the misuse of a victim's existing account, and the opening of a new account in the victim's name.

Blocking: Refers to a victim's right under §605B of the Fair Credit Reporting Act to prevent information that is the result of identity theft from appearing on her credit report.

Criminal Identity Theft: Criminal identity theft occurs when someone uses the victim's name and information as his own during an investigation, issuance of a ticket, or arrest by law enforcement.

Employment Identity Theft: Some identity thieves use a victim's Social Security number for employment. Identity thieves might use another person's identity if they have a criminal record that might prevent their being hired, or if they do not have legal status to work in this country.

Medical Identity Theft: In cases of medical identity theft, thieves use a victim's name, and possibly insurance information to obtain medical services or goods. The victim is then saddled with proving she is not responsible for costly medical bills, or may find that the thief has exhausted the victim's insurance coverage.

Synthetic Identity Theft: Each of the types of identity theft listed above involves the thief impersonating the victim to obtain benefits. In some cases the thief does not steal the victim's entire identity, but rather uses only the victim's Social Security number, in combination with another person's name and birth date, to create a new, fictitious identity.

Tax Fraud: In this type of fraud, an identity thief files a tax return in the victim's name in order to receive a refund or other payment, such as a stimulus check. If the thief files for the refund before the victim, the IRS may deny the victim's rightful refund or stimulus check.

Figure 7.8

Common Forms of Identity Theft

Source: President's Task Force on Identity Theft, *Guide for Assisting Identity Theft Victims*, http://www.idtheft.gov/probono/index.html (accessed July 19, 2012).

---

[86]Austria, "Forgery in Cyberspace," p. 2.

[87]L. Langton and K. Baum, *Identity Theft Reported by Households, 2007—Statistical Tables* (Washington, DC: U.S. Department of Justice, 2010).

[88]President's Task Force on Identity Theft, *Guide for Assisting Identity Theft Victims*, http://www.idtheft.gov/probono/index.html (accessed October 29, 2010).

a means of identification of another person with the intent to commit, or to aid or abet, any unlawful activity that constitutes a violation of Federal law, or that constitutes a felony under any applicable State or local law."[89] State laws vary in their intent and scope.[90] Some states maintain single identity theft/fraud statutes. Others criminalize identity theft/fraud through a wide range of statutes. Still others fit identity theft into their larceny statutes. As an example, Maryland law provides the following:

c. A person may not knowingly and willfully assume the identity of another:
1. to avoid identification, apprehension, or prosecution for a crime; or
2. with fraudulent intent to:
   i. get a benefit, credit, good, service, or other thing of value; or
   ii. avoid the payment of debt or other legal obligation.[91]

Note that the *mens rea* in this statute is "knowingly and willfully." The *actus reus* varies according to the defendant's intent. A recent Supreme Court case, *Flores-Figueroa v. United States*,[92] calls attention to the importance of *mens rea* in the identity theft context. In that case, a man presented to his employer counterfeit Social Security and alien registration cards, both of which contained numbers that had been assigned to other people. He was convicted in a federal district court of aggravated identity theft. The Eight Circuit affirmed, but the U.S. Supreme Court reversed, noting that the government had failed to prove, as applicable federal law[93] required, that the defendant "knowingly" assumed the identity of someone else. The Court's reasoning is rather informative:

[I]n the classic case of identity theft, intent is generally not difficult to prove. For example, where a defendant has used another person's identification information to get access to that person's bank account, the Government can prove knowledge with little difficulty. The same is true when the defendant has gone through someone else's trash to find discarded credit card and bank statements, or pretends to be from the victim's bank and requests personal identifying information. Indeed, the examples of identity theft in the legislative history (dumpster diving, computer hacking, and the like) are all examples of the types of classic identity theft where intent should be relatively easy to prove, and there will be no practical enforcement problem. For another thing, to the extent that Congress may have been concerned about criminalizing the conduct of a broader class of individuals, the concerns about practical enforceability are insufficient to outweigh the clarity of the text. . . . But had Congress placed conclusive weight upon practical enforcement, the statute would likely not read the way it now reads. Instead, Congress used the word "knowingly" followed by a list of offense elements. And we cannot find indications in statements of its purpose or in the practical problems of enforcement sufficient to overcome the ordinary meaning, in English or through ordinary interpretive practice, of the words that it wrote.[94]

---

[89] 18 U.S.C.A. Section 1028 (2010).
[90] For a list of the many state statutes, see http://www.ncsl.org/?tabid=12538 (accessed October 29, 2010).
[91] Md. Code Section 8-301 (2010).
[92] *Flores-Figueroa v. United States*, 129 S.Ct. 1886 (2009).
[93] 18 U.S.C. Section 1028(A)(a)(1).
[94] *Flores-Figueroa v. United States*, pp. 18–19.

Theft of Intellectual Property

Intellectual property
Intangible property that can be protected under federal law, such as copyrights, patents, and trademarks.

Thus far the crimes discussed in this module focused on taking tangible personal property or money. **Intellectual property** is a blanket term describing the many varieties of products attributable to human intellect. Examples include copyrights, patents, trademarks, and trade secrets. Since intellectual property can be quite valuable, it is no surprise that thieves target them. Patent infringement, copyright infringement, trademark counterfeiting, theft of trade secrets, and other crimes have become quite common and difficult to prevent and control.

"Copyrights" refer to the legal protection afforded to an author's original works. Examples include the lyrics of a popular song, books, and poetry. Federal law is the primary mechanism used for criminal prosecution of copyright infringement. The applicable statute reads:

> Any person who willfully infringes a copyright shall be punished as provided under section 2319 of title 18, if the infringement was committed—
> a. for purposes of commercial advantage or private financial gain;
> b. by the reproduction or distribution, including by electronic means, during any 180-day period, of 1 or more copies or phonorecords of 1 or more copyrighted works, which have a total retail value of more than $1,000; or
> c. by the distribution of a work being prepared for commercial distribution, by making it available on a computer network accessible to members of the public, if such person knew or should have known that the work was intended for commercial distribution.[95]

For example, if a student bought a copy of this textbook, made 100 copies of it, and sold it to friends for a cheap price, he or she would be violating federal law (note the "All Rights Reserved" provision in the book's opening pages).

A patent is a grant of right, from the federal government, to exclude others from producing or using a discovery or invention. Most inventions and discoveries that are not of an obvious nature apply for patent protection from the United States Patent and Trademark Office. The patent holder then benefits financially from marketing the product. Without patent law, there would be little incentive to invent, as competitors would take away sales from the inventor and possibly undercut the inventor in terms of price. Patent infringements are usually dealt with via civil process; however, the federal Patent Act provides for criminal prosecution in certain instances (beyond the scope of this book).

Trademarks, the distinctive words, phrases, and symbols used to identify products, are also protected intellectual property. The Trademark Counterfeiting Act of 1984 provides the following:

> Whoever intentionally traffics or attempts to traffic in goods or services and knowingly uses a counterfeit mark on or in connection with such goods or services shall, if an individual, be fined not more than $2,000,000 or imprisoned not more than 10 years, or both, and, if a person other than an individual, be fined not more than $5,000,000.[96]

---

[95] 18 U.S.C. Section 506(a) (2010).
[96] 18 U.S.C. Section 2320 (2010).

Generally, trademark infringement occurs when a competitor uses a phrase or symbol that is likely to cause confusion among consumers regarding the product. For example, if I sold counterfeit purses on the streets of New York City using the famous symbol of Louis Vuitton, I would be violating the Counterfeiting Act.

Finally, trade secrets are protected intellectual property. Examples include "all forms and types of financial, business, scientific, technical, economic, or engineering information . . . whether tangible or intangible, and whether or how stored, compiled, or memorialized physically, electronically, graphically, photographically, or in writing."[97] A customer list is a classic example of a trade secret, since it often takes businesses years to compile such sensitive and potentially lucrative information. In order for something to be legally considered a trade secret, however, the company must make reasonable efforts to keep that information private and secure from public view. Business is competitive, so there is often an incentive for one company to learn of another's secrets for the purpose of making it more profitable. Federal law criminalizes such activity, including even *attempting* to steal trade secrets.[98]

Consolidation of Theft Offenses

As time has gone on, theft law has become rather complicated. A number of states have dozens of theft-related statutes. To ease the burden on prosecutors, states have increasingly begun to consolidate their theft statutes into one all-encompassing law. Some have patterned their laws after the Model Penal Code's "theft" statute. The Model Penal Code's theft provision does not require "taking" or "asportation."[99] Nor does it require intent to permanently deprive. Trespass is not needed, either. And "anything of value, including real estate, tangible or intangible personal property, contract rights, choses-in-action [a form of intangible personal property] and other interests in or claims to wealth, admission or transportation tickets, captured or domestic animals, food and drink, electric or other power" are all possible targets of theft.[100] Theft, however, can be accomplished by a number of means under the Model Penal Code, including larceny, embezzlement, and false pretenses. California offers perhaps the most consolidated of all theft statutes, which reads in relevant part:

> Every person who shall feloniously steal, take, carry, lead, or drive away the personal property of another, or who shall fraudulently appropriate property which has been entrusted to him or her, or who shall knowingly and designedly, by any false or fraudulent representation or pretense, defraud any other person of money, labor or real or personal property, or who causes or procures others to report falsely of his or her wealth or mercantile character and by thus imposing upon any person, obtains credit and thereby fraudulently gets or obtains possession of money, or property or obtains the labor or service of another, is guilty of theft. . . .[101]

---

[97]18 U.S.C. Section 1839(3) (2010).
[98]18 U.S.C. Section 1832 (2010).
[99]Model Penal Code Section 223.
[100]Ibid.
[101]Cal. Penal Code Section 484.

Note the many different types of conduct referenced in this excerpt. California has not abolished all its other theft statutes, however, which has led to some confusion.[102] Nevertheless, the Penal Code section quoted earlier at least illustrates how a legislature can lump various theft-related offenses into a single statute.

YOUR DECISION

1. Joey offers to sell Melissa the latest version of a popular gaming system for only $25 cash, although in the store it generally costs over $200. The deal seems too good to be true and Melissa assumes that the gaming system is stolen. If Melissa purchases the item, is she guilty of receiving stolen property? What if Joey tells Melissa that the gaming system "fell off the back of a truck." Does that change Melissa's potential liability? Why or why not?

2. In the days following Hurricane Katrina, Steven Matthews established the website www.redcross-usa.org. Steven had no official affiliation with the Red Cross and was attempting to obtain donations from unwitting citizens following the natural disaster. In order to secure the online donations for himself, Steven created a number of PayPal accounts using the names, e-mail addresses and other personal information of third parties he obtained illegally. What crimes, if any, has Steven committed? Are any intellectual property rights implicated in this case?

Summary

- Common law larceny was defined as the trespassory taking and carrying away of the personal property of another with intent to permanently deprive the owner/possessor of the property.

- Larceny applies primarily to personal property, not real property. Personal property is anything other than real property that is also tangible.

- The *mens rea* of larceny, "intent to permanently deprive the owner/possessor of the property," is the same as intent to steal.

- It is a crime for a person to receive stolen property, even if that person did not actually steal the property.

- One who receives stolen property, but only to return the property to its rightful owner, does not commit a crime.

- Extortion (also called blackmail) consists of taking another person's property by threats of future harm. The key difference between extortion and robbery is the former's threat of *future* harm.

- Embezzlement occurs when, with intent to steal or defraud, a person in lawful possession of the property deprives an owner of his or her property for a permanent or indefinite period of time.

- "False pretenses" is shorthand for obtaining property by deception. It is distinct from larceny because of deception and/or false representation.

---

[102]See, e.g., S. A. Moore, "Nevada's Comprehensive Theft Statute: Consolidation or Confusion?," *Nevada Law Journal*, Vol. 8 (2008), pp. 672–697.

- The *mens rea* of false pretenses requires a showing that the defendant intended to use the false information to secure property that he or she did not otherwise have the right to.
- Forgery is the false making or material altering of a document with intent to defraud. Uttering refers to passing a forged document.
- E-mail spoofing is a form of forgery.
- Identity theft occurs when someone uses or attempts to use sensitive personal information of another person with intent to defraud.
- Intellectual property is a blanket term describing the many varieties of products attributable to human intellect. Examples include copyrights, patents, trademarks, and trade secrets, among many others. Theft of intellectual property is a crime.
- Given the complexity of theft laws (and the many varieties of theft), several states have increasingly begun to consolidate their theft statutes into one all-encompassing law.

Chapter Review

PROPERTY DAMAGE

Learning Objectives

- Describe the crime of arson.
- Explain the elements of criminal mischief.
- Explain the elements of vandalism.

Review Questions

1. Compare and contrast common law arson with modern-day arson.
2. Can criminal mischief occur without damage? If so, how?
3. Compare and contrast vandalism and criminal mischief.

Key Terms

arson   vandalism
criminal mischief

PROPERTY INVASION

Learning Objectives

- Summarize the elements of trespassing.
- Describe the crime of burglary.

Review Questions

1. A trespassing prosecution may be a "fallback" to other alternatives. Explain how.
2. Should the crime of trespassing have a more specific *mens rea* requirement? Why or why not?
3. Compare and contrast burglary and trespassing.

Key Terms

trespassing   surreptitious remaining
burglary

PROPERTY DAMAGE AND INVASION WITH COMPUTERS

Learning Objectives

- Define and explain cybercrime.
- Identify laws aimed at controlling property invasion and damage with a computer.

Review Questions

1. Which should we be more concerned with, traditional property damage and invasion or property damage and invasion with computers?
2. Explain social engineering.

3. Compare and contrast cybercrime and cyberterrorism.

4. In what way are cybercrime prosecutions compromised by jurisdictional problems?

Key Terms

cybercrime

social engineering

Computer Fraud and Abuse Act (CFAA)

hacking

cyberterrorism

MODULE **7.4**

THEFT OFFENSES

Learning Objectives

- Identify the elements of larceny.
- Describe the crime of receiving stolen property.
- Summarize the elements of extortion and embezzlement.
- Summarize the elements of false pretenses and forgery/uttering.
- Compare and contrast identity theft and theft of intellectual property.

Review Questions

1. Compare and contrast modern larceny with common law larceny.

2. Describe a situation in which someone who receives stolen property is not guilty of a crime.

3. Discuss some common forms of identity theft.

4. What, in your opinion, are the pros and cons of theft law consolidation?

Key Terms

larceny

extortion

embezzlement

bailee

bailor

white-collar crime

false pretenses

forgery

uttering

e-mail spoofing

identity theft

intellectual property

Chapter Synthesizing Questions

1. Compare and contrast trespassing and burglary.

2. Should officials be more or less concerned than they are with cybercrime and cyberterrorism? Explain your answer.

3. What could be done, if anything, to clear up the jurisdictional problems surrounding cybercrime prosecutions?

4. Which theft offense is most serious? Defend your answer.

5. Draft a consolidated theft statute that combines at least three distinct crimes covered in this chapter.

8

CRIMES AGAINST THE STATE AND PUBLIC ORDER

8.1

OFFENSES AGAINST PUBLIC ORDER

Learning Objectives

- **Identify three types of group criminality.**
- **Explain the difference between rioting and unlawful assembly.**
- **Summarize legislative approaches to criminalizing gang activity.**
- **Identify at least five offenses against the public order.**

CORE CONCEPTS   In this chapter, we present a variety of crimes that are committed against public order or the state—instead of against the usual individual victim. The first part of the chapter focuses on what we call public order, morality, and vice crimes. They are also referred to as "quality of life crimes" since they impact the quality of life of residents living in the neighborhoods where these offenses are committed. For example, a neighborhood filled with homeless individuals begging for money (the crimes of "vagrancy" and "panhandling") would, according to most people, have a lower quality of life than a neighborhood without homelessness. While quality of life crimes are still significant, the public and the law often regard them as "less serious" than the violent offenses, such as murder, rape, or robbery.

Offenses against public order can be committed by both individuals and groups. Riots, unlawful assembly, certain gang activity, resisting arrest, disorderly conduct, and other offenses fall into this category. Vice crimes include prostitution, gambling, and pornography/obscenity. Drug offenses focus on alcohol and other controlled substances. Finally, crimes against decency and morality cover a range of conduct, including incest, indecent exposure, bigamy, polygamy, and profanity.

This chapter does not cover every conceivable offense with a public order, morality, or vice dimension to it, but it certainly covers the more major ones. It is also important to note that some of the offenses we cover in one category could well fit in another. For example, we dedicate a specific section to alcohol and drug crimes, but many people feel the consumption of either is immoral.

In the latter half of the chapter, we turn attention to terrorism and offenses against the state. With respect to terrorism, we focus on definitions of the phenomenon, types of terrorism, and legal efforts to control and prevent terrorism. Other offenses against the state that we introduce include treason, sedition, espionage, sabotage, criminal syndicalism, and the like.

Group Criminality

Chapter 4 introduced complicity and vicarious liability. With complicity, an accomplice *derives* his or her criminal liability from a primary offender. With vicarious liability, one person is held liable for the actions of another based on their relationship. Both offense types require the involvement (whether knowing or not) of more than one person. Group criminality is similar in the sense that it involves more than one person. However, we distinguish this section's subject matter from complicity and vicarious liability because *many* offenders may be involved. Forms of group criminality that involve multiple offenders include riot, unlawful assembly, and certain types of gang activity. Although each necessarily requires multiple offenders, it is individuals who are held criminally liable for such actions (perhaps many will be prosecuted together).

riot A group of three or more people involved in a public disturbance of the peace.

Riot

According to the Federal Anti-Riot Act of 1968,

> . . . the term "riot" means a public disturbance involving (1) an act or acts of violence by one or more persons part of an assemblage of three or more persons, which act or acts shall constitute a clear and present danger of, or shall result in, damage or injury to the property of any other person or to the person of any other individual or (2) a threat or threats of the commission of an act or acts of violence by one or more persons part of an assemblage of three or more persons having, individually or collectively, the ability of immediate execution of such threat or threats, where the performance of the threatened act or acts of violence would constitute a clear and present danger of, or would result in, damage or injury to the property of any other person or to the person of any other individual.[1]

Various dimensions of rioting are criminalized at both the federal and state level. At the federal level, one who incites, encourages, participates in, and/or carries on a riot may be guilty of an offense—provided there is an interstate or foreign commerce dimension to the activities. For example, if a person mailed letters to other people in several states, encouraging them to riot against the government, his or her actions would violate federal law.

States have similar statutes that prohibit rioting within their jurisdictions. Oregon's riot statute provides that "a person commits the crime of riot if while participating with five or more other persons the person engages in tumultuous and violent conduct and thereby intentionally or recklessly creates a grave risk of causing public alarm."[2] Note that, as defined in Oregon, rioting is a specific intent offense, requiring either intentional or reckless action on the part of the defendant. The *actus reus* requires proof of three elements:

1. Five or more people who
2. engage in tumultuous or violent conduct [and]
3. create a grave risk of public alarm.

On their face, these elements may seem easy enough to prove. However, Oregon's law has been challenged more than once (albeit unsuccessfully) on the grounds that it is unconstitutionally vague.[3]

---

[1] 18 U.S.C. Section 2102(a) (2010).
[2] Or. Rev. Stat. Section 166.015 (2010).
[3] See, e.g., *State* v. *Chakerian*, 938 P.2d 756 (Or. 1997).

Unlawful Assembly

unlawful assembly A group of people publicly gather unlawfully or for an illegal purpose.

rout An unlawfully assembled groups takes a significant step toward rioting.

Riot closely parallels **unlawful assembly**, as each occurs when a group consisting of a certain number of people assemble unlawfully—or for an unlawful purpose. Both are distinct, however. The classic example of unlawful assembly is a protest. When a protest turns violent, then riot often occurs.

Some states also define a crime of **rout**, which occurs when an unlawfully assembled groups takes a significant step toward rioting. California's Penal Code provides that "[w]henever two or more persons, assembled and acting together, make any attempt or advance toward the commission of an act which would be a riot if actually committed, such an assembly is rout."[4] In other words, a riot is the culmination of both unlawful assembly and rout. Most states do not define rout as a crime and instead combine activities that would be considered rout with either their riot or unlawful assembly statutes.

Gang Activity

By definition, gang activity occurs in groups. And while gang affiliates who commit crimes are often prosecuted individually, a number of states—as well as the District of Columbia—have enacted statutes aimed at targeting gang assembly, participation, and membership.[5] The District of Columbia's controversial statute, which is undergoing challenge as of this writing, reads in part:

a. (1) It is unlawful for a person to solicit, invite, recruit, encourage, or otherwise cause, or attempt to cause, another individual to become a member of, remain in, or actively participate in what the person knows to be a criminal street gang . . .

b. (1) It is unlawful for any person who is a member of or actively participates in a criminal street gang to knowingly and willfully participate in any felony or violent misdemeanor committed for the benefit of, at the direction of, or in association with any other member or participant of that criminal street gang.[6]

A criminal street gang is defined as any association or group of six or more persons that either requires, as a condition of membership, the commission of a crime of violence or, as part of its purpose or frequent activities, violates the criminal laws of the District. The statute was written such that not only would the individual perpetrator be held liable for his or her criminal actions, but other members of the gang would, too.

Some states have also created "gang-free zones," making it a criminal offense for gang members to frequent particular locations, such as playgrounds, shopping malls, movie theaters, and schools.[7] And antigang legislation is by no means limited to assembly issues. Laws have been enacted to tackle every conceivable dimension of the gang problem. Judges have issued injunctions, barring known gang members from associating with one another. Most such approaches, unfortunately, are beyond the scope of this text.[8]

---

[4]Cal. Penal Code Section 406 (2010).
[5]For an overview, see http://www.nationalgangcenter.gov/Legislation (accessed November 4, 2010).
[6]D.C. Code Section 22-951 (2007).
[7]See, e.g., Tx. Penal Code Section 71.028 (2010).
[8]Again, see http://www.nationalgangcenter.gov/Legislation (accessed November 4, 2010).

Offenses against Public Order

A number of offenses are tied together by the theme that they threaten public order in some fashion. Within the category of crimes against public order certain quality of life crimes, including vagrancy and loitering. Some offenses considered later in this chapter, such as public intoxication, could also be said to threaten public order or quality of life, but we introduce those crimes alongside other very similar ones. The list of offenses discussed in this section is by no means exhaustive, but most people can agree that resisting arrest, disorderly conduct, breach of peace, vagrancy, loitering, and panhandling do their share to threaten public order. We consider each of these in no particular order of seriousness.

Resisting Arrest

It is a crime to resist a lawful arrest. To permit otherwise would seriously compromise law enforcement's effectiveness. At common law, it was not considered criminal to resist an *unlawful* arrest.[9] These days, however, it is generally unlawful to resist *any* kind of arrest.[10] New York's resisting arrest statute is illustrative:

> A person may not use physical force to resist an arrest, whether authorized or unauthorized, which is being effected or attempted by a police officer or peace officer when it would reasonably appear that the latter is a police officer or a peace officer.[11]

If the arresting officer uses excessive force to effect an otherwise lawful arrest, then the intended arrestee may usually use physical force in kind, but of a concern for protecting himself or herself, not just for the sake of resisting. As the Oregon Supreme Court argued,

> . . . if an officer making an arrest uses excessive force, the permissible use of physical force by the arrestee is limited to the use of such force as is reasonably necessary under the circumstances for self-defense against the excessive force being used by the arresting officer.[12]

If the arrest is unsupported by probable cause and excessive force is not used, resistance is typically criminal. Why? Probable cause is a bit of an amorphous concept. It would be unreasonable to let ordinary citizens decide when it is and is not present. Also, if an arrestee decides probable cause is absent and therefore resists, greatly increased is the possibility of injury to him or her. A "don't resist" rule protects against needless injury and/or loss of life.

Disorderly Conduct

disorderly conduct An individual causes a public disturbance, harm, or annoyance.

Disorderly conduct is roughly equivalent to an individual version of riot or unlawful assembly. According to the Model Penal Code, a person commits disorderly conduct

---

[9]See, e.g., *United States* v. *Heliczer*, 373 F.2d 241 (2nd Cir. 1967). Also see Chapter 4's "Resisting Unlawful Arrest" section.
[10]See, e.g., *Miller* v. *State*, 462 P.2d 421 (Alaska 1969).
[11]N.Y. Penal Law Section 35.27.
[12]*State* v. *Wright*, 799 P.2d 642 (Or. 1990), p. 645.

if, "with purpose to cause public inconvenience, annoyance or alarm, or recklessly creating a risk thereof, he:

a. engages in fighting or threatening, or in violent or tumultuous behavior; or

b. makes unreasonable noise or offensively coarse utterance, gesture or display, or addresses abusive language to any person present; or

c. creates a hazardous or physically offensive condition by any act which serves no legitimate purpose of the actor."[13]

State laws are relatively similar. For example, the Indiana Code provides that "(a) A person who recklessly, knowingly, or intentionally: (1) engages in fighting or in tumultuous conduct; (2) makes unreasonable noise and continues to do so after being asked to stop; or (3) disrupts a lawful assembly of persons . . ."[14] commits disorderly conduct. Also note the similarities in this statute and the above Model Penal Code excerpt to the rioting and unlawful assembly statutes introduced previously. The main difference between rioting, unlawful assembly, and disorderly conduct is that the latter focuses on "a person," as opposed to a group.

The key to a disorderly conduct conviction is *disorder*. A person who peacefully protests will not be guilty of the crime. For example, in a classic civil rights case, *Edwards* v. *South Carolina*,[15] the U.S. Supreme Court reviewed the convictions of several individuals who participated in a protest against the state's racial segregation laws. They gave speeches, sung songs, and clapped and stamped their feet, but they were no more disorderly than this. The Supreme Court concluded:

These petitioners were convicted of an offense as to be, in the words of the South Carolina Supreme Court, "not susceptible of exact definition." And they were convicted upon evidence which showed no more than that the opinions which they were peaceably expressing were sufficiently opposed to the views of the majority of the community to attract a crowd and necessitate police protection. The Fourteenth Amendment does not permit a State to make criminal the peaceful expression of unpopular views.[16]

The First Amendment rights to freedom of speech and assembly are also implicated in protest cases. See the accompanying Court Decision box for more on unlawful assembly and disorderly conduct. In it we examine the case of *Phelps-Roper* v. *Nixon*, which involves the highly publicized church group that protested at U.S. soldiers funerals.

COURT DECISION

The Logic behind Unlawful Assembly and the First Amendment

Phelps-Roper v. *Nixon*
545 F.3d 685 8th Cir. (2008)

Decision: Phelps-Roper is entitled to a preliminary injunction, temporarily stopping the enforcement of the Spec. Edward Lee Myers' Law, while a court determines if the statute violates the First Amendment to the U.S. Constitution.

(continued)

[13]Model Penal Code Section 250.2.
[14]Ind. Code Ann. Section 35-45-1-3 (2010).
[15]*Edwards v. South Carolina*, 372 U.S. 229 (1963).
[16]Ibid., p. 237.

COURT DECISION
(continued)

Reason: ***Phelps-Roper is a member of the Westboro Baptist Church (WBC) in Topeka, Kansas. Phelps alleges members of her church believe God is punishing America for what WBC considers the sin of homosexuality by killing Americans, including soldiers. As part of her religious duties, she believes she must protest and picket at certain funerals, including the funerals of United States soldiers, to publish the church's religious message: that God's promise of love and heaven for those who obey him in this life is counterbalanced by God's wrath and hell for those who do not. Phelps believes funerals are the only place where her religious message can be delivered in a timely and relevant manner.

On August 5, 2005, Phelps-Roper and other WBC members held a picket and protest near the location of the funeral of Army Spc. Edward Lee Myers in St. Joseph, Missouri. In direct response to the protest, Missouri enacted section 578.501, which criminalizes picketing "in front or about" a funeral location or procession, and section 578.502, which criminalizes picketing within 300 feet of a funeral location or procession, in the event section 578.501 is declared unconstitutional . . .

Phelps-Roper brought suit under 42 U.S.C. § 1983 alleging these laws invade her First Amendment rights . . . .

The district court found the state has a significant interest in preserving and protecting the sanctity and dignity of memorial and funeral services, as well as protecting the privacy of family and friends of the deceased during a time of mourning and distress . . . One other circuit court, which recently analyzed the constitutionality of similar funeral protest statutes, has . . . acknowledged the state has an interest in protecting mourners, which were found to be a captive audience, from unwanted speech during a burial or funeral.

We note our own opinion in Olmer v. Lincoln, 192 F.3d 1176, 1178 (8th Cir.1999), which affirmed a preliminary injunction enjoining the enforcement of an ordinance that "restrict[ed] to certain areas the 'focused picketing' of churches and other religious premises thirty minutes before, during, and thirty minutes after any scheduled religious activity" because it violated the First Amendment. In Olmer, we held the government has no compelling interest in protecting an individual from unwanted speech outside of the residential context . . .

Because of our holding in Olmer, we conclude Phelps-Roper is likely to prove any interest the state has in protecting funeral mourners from unwanted speech is outweighed by the First Amendment right to free speech . . .

Because we conclude Phelps-Roper has demonstrated a likelihood of prevailing on the merits of her claim, we find she will suffer irreparable injury if the preliminary injunction is not issued. The injunction will not cause substantial harm to others, and the public is served by the preservation of constitutional rights. The district court abused its discretion when it concluded the balance of harms weighed toward denying the motion for a preliminary injunction based on its erroneous determination as to Phelps-Roper being unlikely to succeed on the merits . . . We hold only that Phelps-Roper is entitled to a preliminary injunction while the constitutionality of section 578.501 is thoroughly reviewed. The contrary judgment of the district court is reversed.

In 2010, the Edward Lee Myers' Law addressed in the accompanying Court Decision was declared unconstitutional by the United States District Court for Western District of Missouri.[17] It is probably not the last we will hear of this issue.

Breach of Peace

breach of peace An unlawful act that disturbs the peace or harmony of the neighborhood.

Breach of peace, or, more formally, "breaching the peace" occurs in a number of ways. For example, in Connecticut, a breach of the peace in the *first degree* occurs when someone, ". . .with intent to cause inconvenience, annoyance or alarm, or recklessly creating a risk thereof, such person places a nonfunctional imitation of an explosive or incendiary device or an imitation of a hazardous substance in a public place or in a place or manner likely to be discovered by another person."[18] A *second degree* breach of the peace occurs when a person, "with intent to cause inconvenience, annoyance or alarm, or recklessly creating a risk thereof . . .:

1. Engages in fighting or in violent, tumultuous or threatening behavior in a public place; or

2. assaults or strikes another; or

3. threatens to commit any crime against another person or such other person's property; or

4. publicly exhibits, distributes, posts up or advertises any offensive, indecent or abusive matter concerning any person; or

5. in a public place, uses abusive or obscene language or makes an obscene gesture; or

6. creates a public and hazardous or physically offensive condition by any act which such person is not licensed or privileged to do."[19]

Some of these behaviors overlap with rioting and disorderly conduct, yet Connecticut criminalizes those behaviors under separate statutes. Breach of peace therefore acts, in some jurisdictions, as a "catch-all" statute that targets a variety of disruptive behaviors that do not always fit neatly into the categories of riot, unlawful assembly, and disorderly conduct.

Also note that, in Connecticut, fighting is a form of breaching the peace. Many states adopt this approach of criminalizing fighting under a disorderly conduct or breach of peace statute. Others retain stand-alone fighting statutes, especially for cases in which weapons may be used.

vagrancy Moving about with no visible means of financial support.

loitering The act of lingering aimlessly with no apparent purpose.

panhandling Public begging for food or money.

Vagrancy, Loitering, and Panhandling

Vagrancy refers to moving about with no visible means of financial support. Essentially, vagrancy laws can be viewed as criminalizing homelessness. **Loitering** is the act of lingering aimlessly or "hanging out" with no apparent purpose. Loitering statutes are often geared at groups of teenagers or young adults who tend to "hang out" on a particular street corner or area of the city. Finally, **panhandling** is the same as

---

[17]*Phelps-Roper v. Koster*, 734 F.Supp.2d 870 (2010).
[18]Conn. Code Section 53a-180aa (2005).
[19]Ibid., Section 53a-181.

begging. All three of these activities can have a dramatic effect on the "quality of life" of a particular neighborhood. Each action has been criminalized at various points in history and for various reasons, but defining them with precision has proven quite difficult. Vagrancy and loitering laws in particular have been subjected to constitutional challenge on multiple occasions (also see the "Void for Vagueness" discussion back in Chapter 2).

Consider *Papachristou* v. *City of Jacksonville*,[20] a case in which the Supreme Court declared unconstitutional a municipal ordinance that targeted "vagrants" and "rogues and vagabonds, or dissolute persons who go about begging . . . common drunkards, lewd, wanton and lascivious persons, . . . persons wandering or strolling around from place to place without any lawful purpose or object, habitual loafers, [and] disorderly persons."[21] The Court concluded that the ordinance provided "no standards governing the exercise of . . . discretion" and thereby "permit[ted] and encourage[d] an arbitrary and discriminatory enforcement of the law" and resulted "in a regime in which the poor and the unpopular are permitted to 'stand on the sidewalk . . . only at the whim of any police officer'."[22]

In a more recent case, *Kolender* v. *Lawson*,[23] the Supreme Court struck down another statute that made a misdemeanant of any person "[w]ho loiters or wanders upon the streets or from place to place without apparent reason or business and who refuses to identify himself and to account for his presence when requested by any peace officer to do so, if the surrounding circumstances are such as to indicate to a reasonable man that the public safety demands such identification."[24] The Court ruled that the statute was too vague because it "vests virtually complete discretion in the hands of the police to determine whether the suspect has satisfied the statute and must be permitted to go on his way in the absence of probable cause to arrest."[25]

States still retain vagrancy, loitering, and panhandling statutes, but they remain controversial due to definitional problems and the possibility of unequal enforcement by police officials. Statutes that withstand constitutional scrutiny are those that criminalize a person's *actions*, not their status. Even statutes that criminalize actions can prove flawed, however. The city of Akron, Ohio, once made it an offense to loiter "for the purpose of engaging in drug-related activity."[26] The ordinance listed several factors that police officers should consider in making that determination, including "looking like a drug user."[27] The ordinance was overturned because of its vague character.

Panhandling also potentially implicates the constitutional right to free speech under the First Amendment. Imagine you are walking down the street of a major metropolitan city. You see one individual with a sign that reads "The End of the World is Near" and he yells words or warning as you walk by. Generally, his speech would be protected under the First Amendment right to freedom of speech. What if, on the same street corner, you also see a man with a sign that reads, "Starving. Need

---

[20]*Papachristou* v. *City of Jacksonville*, 405 U.S. 156 (1972).
[21]Ibid., p. 157, n. 1.
[22]Ibid., p. 170.
[23]*Kolender* v. *Lawson*, 461 U.S. 352 (1983).
[24]Ibid., p. 354, n. 1.
[25]Ibid., p. 358.
[26]See *Akron v. Rowland*, 618 N.E.2d 138 (Ohio 1993).
[27]Ibid.

money for food," and as you walk by he asks you repeatedly for any spare change. Potentially, this second man has committed to the crime of panhandling. Shouldn't his "speech" also be protected by the First Amendment? The Supreme Court explained that states are permitted to regulate the time, place, and manner of speech to support governmental interests as long as they do not regulate the content of your speech (see Chapter 2 for further discussion).[28]

YOUR DECISION

1. A large group of young women, referred to as the Daughters of Anarchy, are standing on the corner of Main Street in front of the state capital. They are known in the area as a sort of female motorcycle gang. Their purpose is to protest a new law requiring motorcycle riders to wear helmets. They do not have a permit for the protest. Some members of the group are screaming profanity at lawmakers as they pass by. Other members are aggressively asking individuals on the street for monetary donations for their cause. Still others start a fight with a rival organization, Daughters of Peace. List all of the possible crimes, if any, committed by the Daughters of Anarchy.

2. The state legislature passes the following law: "It shall be illegal for any person to engage in aggressive panhandling in the evening within 100 feet of any major tourist attraction." You are a local civil rights attorney who represents a group of concerned homeless people who live in the area. These individuals rely on public begging for food and basic needs. What constitutional arguments, if any, can you make regarding this law?

Summary

- Forms of group criminality that involve multiple offenders include riot, unlawful assembly, and certain types of gang activity.

- Various dimensions of rioting are criminalized at both the federal and state level. At the federal level, one who incites, encourages, participates in, and/or carries on a riot may be guilty of an offense—provided there is an interstate or foreign commerce dimension to the activities. States have similar statutes that prohibit rioting within their jurisdictions.

- The classic example of unlawful assembly is a protest. When a protest turns violent, then riot often occurs.

- Some states also define a crime of rout, which occurs when an unlawfully assembled group takes a significant step toward rioting.

- A number of states—as well as the District of Columbia—have enacted statutes aimed at targeting gang assembly, participation, and membership.

- Some of the common offenses that threaten public order are resisting arrest, disorderly conduct, breach of peace, vagrancy, loitering, and panhandling.

- It is a crime to resist a lawful arrest. Today, it is usually a crime to resist both lawful *and* unlawful arrest.

---

[28] *R.A.V. v. City of St. Paul*, 505 U.S. 377 (1992).

- Disorderly conduct is roughly equivalent to an individual version of riot or unlawful assembly.
- Breach of peace occurs in a number of ways depending on state law. Examples include causing an inconvenience, creating a risk of harm to others, and even fighting.
- Vagrancy refers, generally, to moving about with no visible means of financial support. Loitering is the act of lingering aimlessly or "hanging out" with no apparent purpose. Finally, panhandling is the same as begging.

MODULE

8.2 VICE CRIMES AND DRUG OFFENSES

Learning Objectives
- **Identify a variety of vice crimes and their core elements.**
- **Distinguish between alcohol and drug offenses.**

vice Immoral conduct, practices, or habits.

Vice is loosely defined as immoral conduct, practices, or habits. Several of the crimes presented in this chapter could fit within that definition, but the most universally recognized crimes of vice are prostitution, gambling, and pornography/obscenity. Crimes involving drugs and alcohol are often said to fall into the category of vice, as well. The following sections look at each of these offenses.

Vice crimes are controversial because they are often based on moral considerations rather than objective harms. They are also referred to as "victimless crimes" since they lack the traditional victim seen in crimes like rape, murder, or robbery. It is often said, for example, that gambling, though criminal in many jurisdictions, does not cause harm in the sense that conventional street crimes do. Why, then, is it criminalized? For better or worse, the criminal law will continue to be premised to some extent on morals, beliefs, and values. Justice Byron White once remarked that "the law . . .is constantly based on notions of morality, and if all laws representing essentially moral choices are to be invalidated . . . ., the courts will be very busy indeed."[29]

Prostitution

prostitution Performing or agreeing to perform a sexual act for hire.

Often called the world's oldest profession, **prostitution** is defined as performing or agreeing to perform a sexual act for hire. It is criminalized in all states except Nevada, where a limited number of rural counties license legal brothels. Prostitution remains illegal in Las Vegas and other metropolitan areas throughout the state.

---

[29]*Bowers v. Hardwick*, 478 U.S. 186 (1986), p. 196.

Prostitution, the "world's oldest profession," consists of performing or agreeing to perform a sexual act for hire.

© David White/Alamy

In addition to criminalizing prostitution itself, every state does the same with solicitation, the act of securing a prostitute's (or a suspected prostitute's) agreement to participate in a sex act. Texas' prostitution law illustrates:

a. A person commits an offense if he knowingly:
   1. offers to engage, agrees to engage, or engages in sexual conduct for a fee; or
   2. solicits another in a public place to engage with him in sexual conduct for hire.[30]

The *mens rea* of prostitution is "knowingly." The *actus reus* is either the act itself or any effort to get to that point.

States also criminalize a number of activities related to prostitution, including:

- promotion of prostitution,
- compelling prostitution,
- child prostitution,
- running or residing in a house of prostitution, and/or
- receiving earning as or from a prostitute.

Gambling

gambling Making a bet involving monetary risk.

Gambling, the act of making a bet involving monetary risk, is criminalized in some form or fashion in nearly every state. Even so, people routinely gamble, even if it is illegal where they live. This is especially true for social gambling, or gambling in which no one individual profits by hosting the game.

---

[30]Tx. Penal Code Section 43.02 (2009).

Gambling laws are extraordinarily diverse and complex.[31] In Nevada, for example, gambling laws are relaxed, although the business of gambling is closely regulated by the state. At the extreme, some states ban nearly every conceivable form of gambling. To boot, Indian reservations often run casinos, which they are often entitled to do.

Idaho offers an interesting example of a restrictive gambling law. The state defines gambling rather thoroughly as:

> risking any money, credit, deposit or other thing of value for gain contingent in whole or in part upon lot, chance, the operation of a gambling device or the happening or outcome of an event, including a sporting event, the operation of casino gambling including, but not limited to, blackjack, craps, roulette, poker, bacarrat [baccarat] or keno . . .[32]

Even social gambling is illegal in Idaho. According to one review of state law, about half of all states sanction social gambling, so Idaho is not exactly in the minority.[33]

Pornography and Obscenity

The criminal law places a number of restrictions on pornography and obscenity. Before we can consider such restrictions, however, it is necessary to define both pornography and obscenity.

Definitions

pornography The depiction of sexual acts or behaviors intending to arouse sexual excitement.

obscenity Appealing to the prurient interest while lacking in scientific, artistic, or political merit.

What is pornographic? What is obscene? Answers to these questions have proven rather difficult to arrive at. At the risk of simplification, **pornography** is a form of **obscenity**. There is no requirement that obscenity be of a sexual nature. Anything foul, disgusting, or repulsive could be considered obscene, though not necessarily sexual. Most of the time, however, pornography and obscenity are used interchangeably to depictions and speech of a sexual or erotic nature.

Several decades ago, in *Roth* v. *United States*,[34] the Supreme Court announced that the test for identifying obscenity was "whether to the average person applying contemporary standards, the dominant theme of the material taken as a whole, appeals to the prurient interest."[35] "Prurient" refers, typically, to causing lust, desire, or sexual longing. Not long after that, Justice Potter Stewart famously remarked of obscenity that "I know it when I see it," but needless to say, he stopped short of a specific definition.[36]

In *Miller* v. *California*,[37] the Supreme Court refined its test, emphasizing that juries can make their judgments on what constitutes obscenity based on local standards:

> basic guidelines for the trier of fact must be: (1) whether "the average person, applying contemporary community standards" would find that the work, taken as a whole,

---

[31]See, e.g., http://www.gambling-law-us.com (accessed November 8, 2010).
[32]Idaho Stat. Section 18-3801.
[33]See, e.g., http://www.gambling-law-us.com (accessed November 8, 2010).
[34]*Roth* v. *United States*, 354 U.S. 476 (1957).
[35]Ibid., p. 489.
[36]*Jacobellis* v. *Ohio*, 378 U.S. 184 (1964), p. 197.
[37]*Miller* v. *California*, 413 U.S. 15 (1973).

appeals to the prurient interest; (b) whether the work depicts or describes, in a patently offensive way, sexual conduct specifically defined by the applicable state law; and (c) whether the work, taken as a whole, lacks serious literary, artistic, political, or scientific value.[38]

The Court interpreted "patently offensive" to mean "representations or descriptions of ultimate sexual acts, normal or perverted, actual or simulated . . . . , representations or descriptions of masturbation, excretory functions, and lewd exhibition of genitals."[39] Notice that Supreme Court essentially creates a special exception for items viewed as having "artistic value." For example, a play conducted entirely by nude actors would not be considered obscene under the *Miller* test.

In a later decision as to whether the popular 1970s movie *Carnal Knowledge* depicted obscenity under the *Miller* test, the Court offered further clarification, noting that the movie was not a "portrayal of hard core sexual conduct for its own sake, and for the ensuing commercial gain."[40] The "sexual conduct for its own sake" language sets the bar somewhat high; not just any depiction or description of a sex act will be considered obscene.

Although the Supreme Court defined obscenity, states are not obligated to follow its lead—at least as far as their pornography definitions go. Some have adopted rather relaxed obscenity standards. Others have gone the opposite route. An example of the former is the Oregon Supreme Court's interpretation that "any person can write, print, read, say, show or sell anything to a consenting adult even though that expression may be generally or universally condemned as 'obscene.'"[41]

Child Pornography

child pornography
Pornography which depicts actual minors in sexually explicit situations.

In *New York* v. *Ferber*,[42] the Supreme Court unanimously decided that **child pornography** is not protected by the First Amendment. In upholding a New York law that prohibited people from distributing materials depicting children engaged in sexual activity, the Court offered the following in defense of its position:

> (1) the legislative judgment that the use of children as subjects of pornographic materials is harmful to the physiological, emotional, and mental health of the child, easily passes muster under the First Amendment; (2) the standard of *Miller* v. *California* . . . . , for determining what is legally obscene is not a satisfactory solution to the child pornography problem; (3) the advertising and selling of child pornography provide an economic motive for and are thus an integral part of the production of such materials, an activity illegal throughout the Nation; (4) the value of permitting live performances and photographic reproductions of children engaged in lewd exhibitions is exceedingly modest, if not *de minimis*; and (5) . . .[w]hen a definable class of material, such as that covered by the New York statute, bears so heavily and pervasively on the welfare of children engaged in its production, the balance of competing interests is clearly struck, and it is permissible to consider these materials as without the First Amendment's protection.[43]

---

[38]Ibid., p. 24.
[39]Ibid., p. 25.
[40]*Jenkins v. Georgia*, 418 U.S. 153 (1974), p. 161.
[41]*State v. Henry*, 732 P.2d 9 (Or. 1987), p. 18.
[42]*New York v. Ferber*, 458 U.S. 747 (1982).
[43]Ibid., pp. 756–764.

Obscenity on the Internet

Were pornography and obscenity limited to verbal or print media, criminalization and enforcement would be difficult. The Internet, however, makes both nearly impossible. The government's effort to limit depictions of obscenity on the World Wide Web serves as a prime example. In *Reno v. American Civil Liberties Union*,[44] the Supreme Court struck down part of the Communications Decency Act of 1996 (CDA) that prohibited the knowing transmission of obscene material to people under the age of 18.

In 1998, Congress reacted by passing the Child Online Protection Act (COPA). In 2007, a federal judge struck down COPA, finding it unconstitutionally vague.[45] Not long after, the U.S. Court of Appeals for the Third Circuit upheld the judge's decision.[46] The U.S. Supreme Court then denied review, effectively ending COPA.[47]

In 2003, the so-called PROTECT Act (which stands for Prosecutorial Remedies and Other Tools to end the Exploitation of Children Today) passed.[48] Of particular relevance to the subject of Internet obscenity, the law prohibits "pandering" (i.e., offering or requesting to transfer, sell, or trade) child pornography. Moreover, it prohibits pandering "any material or purported material in a manner that reflects the belief, or that is intended to cause another to believe" that the material is illegal child pornography. In *United States v. Williams*,[49] the Supreme Court upheld the law, holding that there is no First Amendment protection for offers to engage in illegal behavior, nor is there protection for "the collateral speech that introduces such material into the child-pornography distribution network."[50] Williams, the man at the center of the case, used an Internet chat room to exchange child pornography with a Secret Service agent who posed as a person receptive to swapping images.

Although pandering can be accomplished by other means than the Internet, the law—and the Supreme Court's decision—bode well for the government's efforts to regulate online obscenity. Even so, there is the problem of hosting such material in other countries. The Internet knows no geographic boundaries. This makes it especially difficult to prosecute a person who resides in—and sends material from—somewhere outside the United States.

Sexting

sexting Transmitting sexually explicit images to another person via e-mail or cellular phone.

The increased use of cellular phones and other technological devices has led to the creation of a potentially new crime, **sexting**. A person is "sexting" if he or she transmits sexually explicit images to another person via a cellular phone or e-mail account. Among consenting adults, the practice would not violate any established criminal

---

[44] *Reno v. American Civil Liberties Union*, 521 U.S. 844 (1997).
[45] *American Civil Liberties Union v. Gonzales*, 478 F.Supp.2d 775 (E.D. Pa. 2007).
[46] *American Civil Liberties Uniion v. Mukasey*
[47] 129 S.Ct. 1032 (2009).
[48] Pub. L. 108-21.
[49] *United States v. Williams*, 553 U.S. 285 (2008).
[50] Ibid.

laws. When juveniles are involved, however, the practice can potentially rise to the level of child pornography. States are now struggling with how to charge defendants for these crimes. See the accompanying Court Decision for more on the crime of sexting. In it we examine the case of *State* v. *Canal*, where an 18-year-old man sends sexually explicit images to a 14-year-old high school student.

COURT DECISION

The Logic behind Criminalizing "Sexting"

State v. *Canal*
773 N.W.2d 528 (Iowa 2009)

Decision: Sexting, or sending obscene photos via text or e-mail, can result in a criminal conviction, in this cause under a statute prohibiting disseminating obscene material to a minor.

Reason: On May 15, 2005, C.E., a fourteen-year-old female attending high school, received two photographs via e-mail from Jorge Canal. Canal was eighteen years of age and attended the same school when this incident occurred. One of the photographs was of Canal's erect penis; the other was a photograph of his face. A text message attached to the photograph of his face said, "I love you.". . .

C.E.'s mother, who checked her daughter's e-mail and internet use, found the photographs and forwarded them to her husband. C.E.'s father then showed the photographs to a police officer . . . . The State charged Canal with violating Iowa Code section 728.2, for knowingly disseminating obscene material to a minor.

The case was tried to a jury. The jury found Canal guilty of knowingly disseminating obscene material to a minor. The court imposed a deferred judgment, a civil penalty of $250, and probation with the department of corrections for one year. The court also instructed Canal that he must register as a sex offender and ordered that an evaluation take place to determine if treatment was necessary as a condition of his probation. Canal received notification of the requirement to register as a sex offender on April 6, 2006 . . . .

Canal's sole contention regarding the sufficiency of the evidence is that the material he sent to C.E. was not obscene. The jury instruction defining obscenity incorporates the Supreme Court's definition of obscenity, but adds the phrase "with respect to what is suitable material for minors." In other words, the jury instruction recognizes that the obscenity test as to minors is different from the test as to adults . . .

Applying the jury instructions as given and reviewing the evidence in the light most favorable to the State, the question we must resolve is whether, under this record, a rational juror could find Canal guilty beyond a reasonable doubt of knowingly disseminating obscene material to a minor. Canal took one photograph of his face and one photograph of his erect penis. He e-mailed the photographs to C.E. separately. He attached a text message to the photograph of his face that said, "I love you."

(continued)

COURT DECISION
(continued)

Although Canal argued to the jury the material he sent C.E. only appealed to a natural interest in sex, under the instructions given the jury could find, by applying its own contemporary community standards with respect to what is suitable material for minors, that the material appealed to the prurient interest, was patently offensive, and lacked serious literary, scientific, political, or artistic value. On a sufficiency-of-the-evidence review, our task is not to refind the facts. Moreover, on this record we cannot conclude, as a matter of law, the materials Canal sent to C.E. were not obscene. Therefore, even though another jury in a different community may have found this material not to be obscene, the evidence in this record was sufficient for this jury to determine, under its own community standards, that the material Canal sent to C.E. was obscene.

Alcohol Offenses

driving under the influence Operating a motor vehicle with a blood or breath alcohol level over the legal limit of alcohol.

Alcohol and crime go hand-in-hand.[51] In some cases, however, alcohol itself is the key element of the crime. The leading stand-alone alcohol-related offenses are **driving under the influence** (DUI—also called driving while intoxicated, or DWI); minor in possession (MIP), or consumption of alcohol by a minor; and public intoxication. The following subsections take a brief look at each.

Driving under the Influence

According to the organization Mothers Against Drunk Driving, one person is injured every minute in an alcohol-related vehicular crash.[52] One person *dies* in an alcohol-related crash every 45 minutes.[53] Although fatalities have declined over the years (see Figure 8.1), drunk driving is a problem.

States currently maintain laws providing that a person is considered under the influence if he or she operates a motor vehicle with a blood or breath alcohol level of .08 or above. The point at which a person reaches this level depends on the quantity consumed, the percentage of alcohol in the drink, the person's weight, and the time spent drinking.[54] Some of the penalties include fines, community service, probation, imprisonment, impoundment of the driver's vehicle, or a mixture of each.

DUI laws are almost always of the strict liability variety (see Chapter 3). This means, by way of review, that there is no requirement that the prosecution prove a culpable mental state, only that the driver was indeed under the influence at the time of the crime. That DUI is considered a strict liability offense reinforces how seriously it is treated.

---

[51]See, e.g., J. Yu and W.R. Williford, "Alcohol, Other Drugs, and Criminality: A Structural Analysis," *The American Journal of Drug and Alcohol Abuse*, Vol. 20(1994), pp. 373–393.
[52]http://www.madd.org/statistics (accessed November 9, 2010).
[53]Ibid.
[54]To calculate blood alcohol level, visit http://www.bloodalcoholcalculator.org (accessed November 9, 2010).

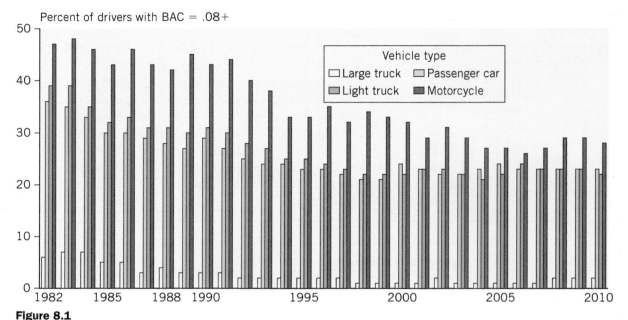

Figure 8.1

Proportion of Drivers Involved in Fatal Crashes with BAC = .08+ by Vehicle Type, 1982–2010

Source: U.S. Department of Transportation, National Highway Traffic Safety Administration, Traffic Safety Facts 2010 (Washington, DC: U.S. Department of Transportation, 2011), p. 37, Table 9; http://www-nrd.nhtsa.dot.gov/pubs/811659.pdf (accessed January 8, 2013).

Consumption/Possession by Minors

All states prohibit minors (those under the age of 21) from purchasing, possessing, and/or consuming alcohol. States are free to set their own drinking ages, but federal law requires the Secretary of Transportation to withhold otherwise allocable highway funds from states that set their drinking age below 21.[55] None have done so, as the Supreme Court has authorized the practice.[56]

Not only do states attempt to restrict underage drinking by setting age limits on purchase, they also put in place strict penalties for minors caught drinking (or in possession).[57] Despite the fact that alcohol cannot be legally purchased or consumed by those under 21 years of age, problems persist. For example, according to the Centers for Disease Control and Prevention, 42% of high school students report having drank alcohol in the past 30 days.[58] Other surveys indicate that nearly one-third of youth between 12 and 20 drink alcohol.[59] It seems no amount of legal deterrents is doing the job. In fact, approximately 100 college presidents from some of the nation's most respected universities recently called on lawmakers to lower the drinking age in an effort to control binge drinking on their campuses.[60] Not much has changed as of this writing.

---

[55]See 23 U.S.C. Section 158.

[56]*South Dakota v. Dole*, 483 U.S. 203 (1987).

[57]Texas Alcoholic Beverage Commission, *Underage Drinking Laws*. Available at: http://www.tabc.state.tx.us/laws/underage_drinking_laws.asp (accessed November 9, 2010).

[58]Centers for Disease Control and Prevention, *Fact Sheets: Underage Drinking*. Available at: http://www.cdc.gov/alcohol/fact-sheets/underage-drinking.htm (accessed November 9, 2010).

[59]Ibid.

[60]J. Pope, "College Presidents Want Lower Drinking Age," *Associated Press*, http://www.usatoday.com/news/education/2008-08-18-college-drinking_N.htm (accessed December 10, 2010).

Public Intoxication

public intoxication
Appearing in a public place while under the influence of alcohol or substances to a degree where the individual is likely to endanger himself, others, or property.

Public intoxication, or public drunkenness, is illegal in every state. For example, Kentucky law provides that:

> A person is guilty of public intoxication when he appears in a public place manifestly under the influence of a controlled substance, or other intoxicating substance, excluding alcohol (unless the alcohol is present in combination with any of the above), not therapeutically administered, to the degree that he may endanger himself or other persons or property, or unreasonably annoy persons in his vicinity.[61]

Public intoxication is usually treated as a misdemeanor. One of the problems with public intoxication laws is that they sometimes ensnare people with legitimate drinking problem who, without treatment, will be released from jail and arrested all over again. In light of this concern, some states have elected only to criminalize disorderly intoxication.[62]

Drug Offenses

Harrison Narcotics Tax Act A federal statute passed in 1914 that constituted the federal government's first effort to criminalize opium and cocaine.

Marijuana Tax Act A federal statute passed in 1937 that marked the federal government's first effort to regulate marijuana.

Controlled Substances Act Federal legislation that classifies illegal narcotics into five different schedules.

Alcohol is more ubiquitous than other drugs, but marijuana, cocaine, heroin, methamphetamine, and the like are often regarded as more serious and deserving of criminalization. Throughout American history, a number of laws have been enacted in an effort to criminalize the sale and possession of certain drugs. The **Harrison Narcotics Tax Act** of 1914[63] was the federal government's first effort to criminalize opium and cocaine. Although the Act purported to tax the production, importation, and distribution of opiates, it also created criminal penalties for those who failed to register and pay required taxes. The Act permitted doctors to prescribe opiates for legitimate medical reasons, but not to satisfy patients' addiction. The Harrison Act withstood challenge in the Supreme Court[64] and states soon went on to enact their own laws aimed at the control of opiates.

During Prohibition, many people turned to marijuana as a cheap alternative to alcohol. Once Prohibition ended, then states and the federal government turned their attention back to marijuana. By the late 1930s, the vast majority of states enacted laws criminalizing marijuana. In 1937, the **Marijuana Tax Act**[65] marked the federal government's first effort to control marijuana. Like the Harrison Act, it levied a tax against marijuana-related commerce, but did not criminalize it per se. This ran counter to most states' laws against marijuana, prompting the U.S. Supreme Court in 1969 to declare the Marijuana Tax Act unconstitutional.[66]

During the 1960s, the United States saw a surge in drug use, prompting further legislative action. Congress responded with the Drug Abuse and Prevention Control Act of 1970.[67] Also called the **Controlled Substances Act** (CSA), this legislation classified

---

[61]Ky. Rev. Stat. Section 525.100.
[62]Fl. Code Section 856.011.
[63]38 Stat. 785.
[64]*United States* v. *Doremus*, 249 U.S. 86 (1919).
[65]50 Stat. 551.
[66]*Leary* v. *United States*, 395 U.S. 6 (1969).
[67]84 Stat. 1236.

Schedule I
- The drug or other substance has a high potential for abuse.
- The drug or other substance has no currently accepted medical use in treatment in the United States.
- There is a lack of accepted safety for use of the drug or other substance under medical supervision.
- Examples of Schedule I substances include heroin, lysergic acid diethylamide (LSD), marijuana, and methaqualone.

Schedule II
- The drug or other substance has a high potential for abuse.
- The drug or other substance has a currently accepted medical use in treatment in the United States or a currently accepted medical use with severe restrictions.
- Abuse of the drug or other substance may lead to severe psychological or physical dependence.
- Examples of Schedule II substances include morphine, phencyclidine (PCP), cocaine, methadone, and methamphetamine.

Schedule III
- The drug or other substance has less potential for abuse than the drugs or other substances in schedules I and II.
- The drug or other substance has a currently accepted medical use in treatment in the United States.

- Abuse of the drug or other substance may lead to moderate or low physical dependence or high psychological dependence.
- Anabolic steroids, codeine and hydrocodone with aspirin or Tylenol®, and some barbiturates are examples of Schedule III substances.

Schedule IV
- The drug or other substance has a low potential for abuse relative to the drugs or other substances in Schedule III.
- The drug or other substance has a currently accepted medical use in treatment in the United States.
- Abuse of the drug or other substance may lead to limited physical dependence or psychological dependence relative to the drugs or other substances in Schedule III.
- Examples of drugs included in schedule IV are Darvon®, Talwin®, Equanil® ,Valium® and Xanax®.

Schedule V
- The drug or other substance has a low potential for abuse relative to the drugs or other substances in Schedule IV.
- The drug or other substance has a currently accepted medical use in treatment in the United States.
- Abuse of the drug or other substances may lead to limited physical dependence or psychological dependence relative to the drugs or other substances in Schedule IV.
- Cough medicines with codeine are examples of Schedule V drugs.

Figure 8.2
Controlled Substances Act Drug Schedules
Source: 21 U.S.C. Section 812.

Combat Methamphetamine Epidemic Act Federal legislation that primarily restricts access to precursor chemicals used in the manufacture of methamphetamines, particularly ephedrine, pseudoephedrine, and phenylpropanolamine.

drugs according to five different schedules (see Figure 8.2). The Drug Enforcement Administration and the Food and Drug Administration decide which drugs go in each schedule. So-called Schedule I drugs carry the highest potential for abuse and include heroin and marijuana, among others. The CSA provides penalties for the unlawful manufacture, distribution, and dispensing of controlled substances. See Figure 8.3 for a description of the penalties, by schedule, for trafficking in controlled substances. A number of other federal laws also establish penalties for a wide range of drug-related offenses, including simple possession and even possession of drug paraphernalia.

Federal law continues to evolve as new problems emerge. For example, in 2005, Congress passed the **Combat Methamphetamine Epidemic Act** in response to the increasing realization that methamphetamine (also called "crystal meth" or "crank") was becoming a serious public health threat. The legislation primarily restricts access to precursor chemicals used in the manufacture of the drug, particularly ephedrine, pseudoephedrine, and phenylpropanolamine.

Federal Trafficking Penalties

Drug Schedule	Quantity	1st Offense	2nd Offense	Quantity	1st Offense	2nd Offense
Methamphetamine Schedule II	5-49 gms pure or 50-499 gms mixture	Not less than 5 yrs and not more than 40 yrs. If death or serious injury, not less than 20 or more than life. Fine of not more than $2 million if an individual, $5 million if other than an individual.	Not less than 10 yrs and not more than life. If death or serious injury, not less than life or more than life. Fine of not more than $4 million if an individual, $10 million if other than an individual.	50 gms or more pure or 500 gms or more mixture	Not less than 10 yrs and not more than life. If death or serious injury, not less than 20 or more than life. Fine of not more than $4 million if an individual, $10 million if other than an individual.	Not less than 20 yrs and not more than life. If death or serious injury, not less than life. Fine of not more than $8 million if an individual, $20 million if other than an individual.
Heroin Schedule I	100-999 gms mixture			1 kg or more mixture		
Cocaine Schedule II	500-4,999 gms mixture			5 gms or more mixture		
Cocaine Base Schedule II	5-49 gms mixture			50 gms or more mixture		
PCP Schedule II	10-99 gms pure or 100-999 gms mixture			100 gms or more pure or 1 kg or more mixture		
LSD Schedule I	1-9 gms mixture			10 gms or more mixture	**3rd Offense or More**	
Fentanyl Schedule II	40-399 gms mixture			400 gms or more mixture	Life Imprisonment	
Fentanyl Analogue Schedule I	10-99 gms mixture			100 gms or more mixture		
Others Schedules I & II *(Includes 1 gm or more flunitrazepam and gamma hydroxybutyric acid)*	Any	Not more than 20 yrs. If death or serious injury, not less than 20 yrs, not more than life. Fine of $1 million if an individual, $5 million if other than an individual.	Not more than 30 yrs. If death or serious injury, life. Fine of $2 million if an individual, $10 million if other than an individual.			

		1st Offense		2nd Offense		
Others Schedules III *(Includes 30 mgs - 999 mgs flunitrazepam)*	Any	Not more than 5 yrs. Fine not more than $250,000 if an individual, $1 million if other than an individual.		Not more than 10 yrs. Fine not more than $500,000 if an individual, $2 million if other than an individual.		
Others* Schedules IV *(Includes less than 30 mgs flunitrazepam)*	Any	Not more than 3 yrs. Fine not more than $250,000 if an individual, $1 million if other than an individual.		Not more than 6 yrs. Fine not more than $500,000 if an individual, $2 million if other than an individual.		
All Schedules V	Any	Not more than 1 yr. Fine not more than $100,000 if an individual, $250,000 if other than an individual.		Not more than 2 yrs. Fine not more than $200,000 if an individual, $500,000 if other than an individual.		

*Although flunitrazepam is a Schedule IV controlled substance, quantities of 30 or more milligrams of flunitrazepam are subject to greater statutory maximum penalties than the above-referenced penalties for Schedule IV controlled substances. See 21 U.S.C. §841(b)(1)(C) and (D).

Figure 8.3

CSA Penalties for Drug Trafficking

Source: Drug Enforcement Administration, Federal Trafficking Penalties, www.justice.gov/dea/druginfo/ftp3.shtml (accessed December 14, 2012).

State Drug Laws

Uniform Controlled Substances Act A uniform acted drafted to standardize state drug laws. States must affirmatively adopt the act in order for the provisions to becoming binding law.

medical marijuana Marijuana legally available under state law by prescription. Available in 17 states as of this writing.

While the Controlled Substances Act was being drafted, so too was the **Uniform Controlled Substances Act**. Finalized in 1972, its purpose was to achieve uniformity in state laws concerning the criminalization and scheduling of drugs. It was later revised in 1990 and 1994. In neither version was it federal law. Rather, it was similar to the Model Penal Code—a suggested legal arrangement that states were encouraged to adopt in the interest of consistency and uniformity. Indeed, all states have since adopted one of the versions of the Uniform Controlled Substances Act.

While state drug laws are mostly aligned with federal law, such is not always the case, especially when it comes to marijuana. Marijuana has been made criminal by the CSA.[68] Yet a number of states (17 as of this writing[69]) have legalized **medical marijuana**, permitting doctors to prescribe the drug to select patients. This creates an obvious conflict between federal and state law. President Obama and Attorney General Eric Holder announced in 2009 that they would not pursue raids of medical marijuana dispensaries,[70] but it seems, as of this writing, that they may have gone back on that promise, such as by cracking down on several businesses in Colorado.[71] The federal government remains committed to the continued criminalization of marijuana.[72]

State drug laws are far too detailed and complex to summarize in this limited space. A number of resources are available, however, for those who are interested in exploring state-by-state differences in anti–drug policy. For example, the Office of National Drug Control Policy's *State and Local Resources* website[73] is a valuable resource, as is the website for the National Organization for the Reform of Marijuana Laws, which maintains an updated list of state marijuana laws.[74] State drug laws are more similar to federal law than they are different, however.

YOUR DECISION

1. Joseph is interested in child pornography and often searches the Internet for pictures of children engaged in sexual activity. One evening, Joseph downloads a piece of "virtual child pornography," which is completely computer generated and does not involve the use of child actors. Has Joseph committed a crime? Why or why not? What if the video involved 18-year-old actors who physically appeared to be only 14-year-olds?

2. George is suffering from a terrible cold at work one evening. To try and combat the symptoms, he drinks an entire bottle of a nighttime cold medicine before driving home. He is pulled over by the police for driving erratically and fails a

[68]And the Supreme Court has refused to acknowledge a "medical necessity exception" to the CSA. See *United States* v. *Oakland Cannibis Buyers' Cooperative*, 532 U.S. 483 (2001). Also see *Gonzales* v. *Raich*, 545 U.S. 1 (2005), which permitted the federal government, under the Commerce Clause, to prohibit mere possession of marijuana, even if solely for medical use.
[69]http://medicalmarijuana.procon.org/view.resource.php?resourceID=000881 (accessed June 19, 2012); http://www.huffingtonpost.com/2012/06/01/medical-marijuana-connecticut-17th-state_n_1563206.html (accessed June 19, 2012).
[70]D. Johnston, "Obama Administration to Stop Raids on Medical Marijuana Dispensers," *New York Times*, March 18, 2009. http://www.nytimes.com/2009/03/19/us/19holder.html (accessed November 15, 2010).
[71]See, e.g., http://www.huffingtonpost.com/2012/05/08/medical-marijuana_n_1498694.html (accessed June 19, 2012).
[72]See, e.g., http://www.whitehouse.gov/ondcp/marijuana (accessed June 19, 2012).
[73]http://www.whitehousedrugpolicy.gov/statelocal/index.html (accessed November 15, 2010).
[74]See http://norml.org/index.cfm?Group_ID=4516 (accessed November 15, 2010).

sobriety test. George assures the officer he has not been drinking, but is arrested. Is George guilty of driving under the influence? Is he guilty under the California statute described in the text? Why or why not?

Summary

- Vice is loosely defined as immoral conduct, practices, or habits. That said, the most universally recognized crimes of vice are prostitution, gambling, and pornography/obscenity.

- Vice crimes are controversial because they are often based on moral considerations rather than objective harms.

- Prostitution is defined as performing or agreeing to perform a sexual act for hire. It is criminalized in all states, except Nevada, where limited number of rural counties license legal brothels.

- In addition to criminalizing prostitution itself, every state does the same with solicitation, the act of securing a prostitute's (or a suspected prostitute's) agreement to participate in a sex act.

- Gambling, the act of making a bet involving monetary risk, is criminalized in some form or fashion in nearly every state.

- Social gambling, or gambling in which no one individual profits by hosting the game, is also illegal in a minority of states.

- Pornography is a form of obscenity. There is no requirement that obscenity be of a sexual nature.

- In *Roth* v. *United States*, the Supreme Court announced that the test for identifying obscenity was "whether to the average person applying contemporary standards, the dominant theme of the material taken as a whole, appeals to the prurient interest."

- Today, obscenity is defined in terms of the "portrayal of hard core sexual conduct for its own sake, and for the ensuing commercial gain."

- In *New York* v. *Ferber*, the Supreme Court unanimously decided that child pornography is not protected by the First Amendment.

- The control of pornography on the Internet has proven quite difficult. The Supreme Court has struck down several laws aimed at controlling Internet pornography because of its vague nature.

- Every state maintains a number of obscenity-related laws.

- The leading stand-alone alcohol-related offenses are driving under the influence (DUI—also called driving while intoxicated, or DWI); minor in possession (MIP), or consumption of alcohol by a minor; and public intoxication.

- Throughout American history, a number of laws have been enacted in an effort to criminalize the sale and possession of certain drugs. Examples include the Harrison Narcotics Tax Act, the Marijuana Tax Act, the Drug Abuse and Prevention Control Act of 1970, and more recently the Combat Methamphetamine Epidemic Act.

- Most state drug laws parallel federal law.

CRIMES AGAINST DECENCY AND/OR MORALITY

Learning Objectives

- **Summarize government efforts throughout history to criminalize morality.**
- **Describe modern-day crimes against decency and/or morality.**
- **Summarize the means by which the criminal law controls profanity.**

Some would argue that prostitution, drug use, alcohol consumption, and even gambling are immoral. In this section, though, we look at a hodge-podge of offenses that contain an element of indecency and/or immorality. The offenses that fall into this category include incest, indecent exposure, voyeurism, bigamy, and polygamy. Each of these crimes involves a sexual element (or at least has the *potential* to involve a sexual element, as in the case of bigamy or polygamy). To them we add another, non-sexual offense, namely profanity. Before looking at each offense in detail, some historical overview will be helpful.

Legislating Morality throughout History

fornication Sexual intercourse between unmarried persons.

adultery Sexual intercourse between a man and a woman, at least one of who is married to someone else.

sodomy Either oral or anal sex between humans or sexual intercourse between humans and animals.

The criminal law traditionally prohibited a wide range of consensual sexual acts, including fornication, adultery, sodomy, and others. **Fornication**, or sexual intercourse between unmarried persons, was regarded as immoral and was punished by the ecclesiastical courts of England. The same held true for **adultery**, or sexual intercourse between a man and a woman, at least one of who is married to someone else. Neither offense was considered a common law crime. Only if they were committed in the open were they treated as criminal.

Sodomy, usually defined as either oral or anal sex between humans or sexual intercourse between humans and animals (also called beastiality), *was* considered a crime under common law. Until fairly recently, most states had laws outlying sodomy in its various forms. That has since changed, however. As recently as 2003, in *Lawrence* v. *Texas*,[75] the U.S. Supreme Court struck down one of the country's last remaining sodomy laws. As police officers responded to a weapons disturbance, they entered a man's apartment and observed him engaging in anal intercourse with another man. The two men were arrested and prosecuted under a Texas statute that criminalized "deviate sexual intercourse." The Court held in part that "Their right to liberty under the Due Process Clause gives them the full right to engage in their conduct without

---

[75]*Lawrence* v. *Texas*, 539 U.S. 558 (2003).

intervention of the government.[76] Fornication, adultery, and sodomy, while perhaps frowned upon, are no longer considered criminal in most jurisdictions—or even deviant. Some states, however, still criminalize fornication and adultery.

Incest

Incest Sexual intercourse with certain relatives.

Incest refers to sexual intercourse with certain relatives. So-called "consanguineous" (i.e., close in kinship) relationships can produce deformed offspring, which is one of the primary reasons incest is taboo even today.[77] All states and the District of Columbia thus prohibit incest in some form or fashion. For example, Massachusetts law provides:

> Persons within degrees of consanguinity within which marriages are prohibited or declared by law to be incestuous and void, who intermarry or have sexual intercourse with each other, or who engage in sexual activities with each other, including but not limited to, oral or anal intercourse, fellatio, cunnilingus, or other penetration of a part of a person's body, or insertion of an object into the genital or anal opening of another person's body, or the manual manipulation of the genitalia of another person's body, shall be punished by imprisonment . . . .[78]

Massachusetts' law is rather sweeping. Other states limit the reach of their incest laws. New Jersey does not punish incest if it occurs between relatives over the age of 18.[79] Ohio targets only the acts of parental figures.[80]

Indecent Exposure and Voyeurism

indecent exposure Revealing your sexual genitalia to another person.

Indecent exposure, sometimes called "lewd and lascivious conduct," occurs when one displays his or her "private parts" in front of others—typically with their knowledge or awareness.[81] Indecent exposure laws are typically concerned with public exposure, but this need not always be the case. For example, in *People v. Neal*,[82] a Michigan appellate court upheld the conviction of a man who displayed his erect penis to a minor victim in a private residence.

Not every part one would consider "private" falls within the scope of indecent exposure laws. *Duvallon v. District of Columbia*[83] considered the indecent exposure conviction of a woman who protested in front of the U.S. Supreme Court building, wearing a cardboard sign around her neck that covered the front of her body but not the back. Her buttocks were in full view. The court concluded:

> Ms. Duvallon's actions offend individual senses of propriety, modesty and self-respect. But this court is not asked to decide whether or not Ms. Duvallon violated

---

[76]Ibid., pp. 525–526.

[77]There are many other reasons, too. See Harvard Law Review, "Inbred Obscurity: Improving Incest Laws in the Shadow of the 'Sexual Family'." *Harvard Law Review,* Vol. 119(2006), pp. 2464–2485.

[78]Mass. Gen. Laws Ann. 272 Section 17 (2005).

[79]N.J. Stat. Ann. Section 2C:14-2 (2005).

[80]Ohio Rev. Code Ann. Section 2907.03(A)(5) (1997).

[81]See, e.g., *State v. Werner*, 609 So.2d 585 (Fla. 1992); but see *State v. Bryan*, 130 P.3d 85 (Kan. 2006) for an opposing view.

[82]*People v. Neal*, 702 N.W.2d 696 (Mich. App. 2005).

[83]*Duvallon v. District of Columbia*, 515 A.2d 724 (D.C. App. 1986).

notions of personal modesty or propriety. Instead we are simply called upon to apply the rule of law and decide whether she broke the law. To answer this question, we search neither our own standards of morality nor standards of dress but rather the rule of law. An examination of decisional law, treatises, and basic principles of statutory construction leads inexorably to the conclusion that public exposure of the bare buttocks is not a violation of D.C. Code § 22-1112 (a).[84]

It would seem, then, that indecent exposure statutes are intended to control display of the genitalia. Also, for indecent exposure to be criminal, it must usually be done willfully and/or in an offensive manner.[85] One who experiences an embarrassing "wardrobe malfunction" will likely not be guilty of indecent exposure.

The subject of indecent exposure invariably brings up the question of nude dancing establishments. Typically nude dancing is a protected form of expression, but state and local governments are permitted to impose restrictions on what body parts can be exposed. For example, in *Barnes* v. *Glen Theatre, Inc.*,[86] the Supreme Court upheld an Indiana statute that required night club dancers to wear "pasties" over their breasts and G-string bottoms. A similar law was upheld in Erie, Pennsylvania.[87]

voyeurism The act of spying on the intimate activities of other people.

Voyeurism refers, in general, to the act of spying on the intimate activities of other people. So-called "Peeping Tom" laws (named for the legend of a man named Tom who watched Lady Godiva, an Anglo-Saxon noblewoman, ride naked through the streets of Coventry, England, in protests against taxation) criminalize voyeurism in nearly every state. Indiana defines the crime of voyeurism (or "peeping") as follows:

a. A person:
   1. who: (A) peeps; or (B) goes upon the land of another with the intent to peep; into an occupied dwelling of another person; or
   2. who peeps into an area where an occupant of the area reasonably can be expected to disrobe, including: (A) restrooms; (B) baths; (C) showers; and (D) dressing rooms; without the consent of the other person, commits voyeurism, a Class B misdemeanor.[88]

Some states fold voyeurism into other sexual deviance statutes and thus do not treat it as a stand-alone offense.

bigamy Marriage between two persons when one is married to another.

polygamy One person being married simultaneously to several others.

Bigamy and Polygamy

Bigamy, or marriage between two persons when one is married to another, is illegal in all American jurisdictions. The same is true for **polygamy**, or one person being married to several others. Religious arguments have been advanced in support of both practices, but the Supreme Court has decided bigamists and polygamists enjoy

---

[84]Ibid., p. 725.
[85]See, e.g., *People v. Randall*, 711 P.2d 689 (Colo. 1985).
[86]*Barnes v. Glen Theatre, Inc.*, 501 U.S. 560 (1991).
[87]*City of Erie v. Pap's A.M.*, 529 U.S. 277 (2000).
[88]Indiana Code Section 35-45-4-5

no First Amendment protection for their actions. In *Reynolds* v. *United States*,[89] the Court concluded:

> Polygamy has always been odious among the northern and western nations of Europe, and, until the establishment of the Mormon Church, was almost exclusively a feature of the life of Asiatic and of African people. At common law, the second marriage was always void, and from the earliest history of England polygamy has been treated as an offence against society . . . .
>
> From that day to this we think it may safely be said there never has been a time in any State of the Union when polygamy has not been an offence against society, cognizable by the civil courts and punishable with more or less severity. In the face of all this evidence, it is impossible to believe that the constitutional guaranty of religious freedom was intended to prohibit legislation in respect to this most important feature of social life.

In response to the Court's decision, the Mormon church renounced polygamy, but the practice continues in some "fundamentalist" Mormon communities. Prosecutions are rare, but they do occur from time to time.[90] For example, you may recall the widely publicized 2008 raid on the polygamist YFZ (Yearning for Zion) ranch in Eldorado, Texas. Several prosecutions followed.

Bigamy and polygamy statutes vary in their language, but all are remarkably similar. Several states criminalize both acts in a single statute because polygamy is a form of bigamy, albeit with multiple partners.[91]

Profanity

profanity Foul language or curse words generally deemed offensive.

Profanity was sometimes prohibited in dedicated state or local statutes, but that has changed. Most states now incorporate into their disorderly conduct (and similar) statutes various prohibitions against public profanity. Why? Normal prohibitions against profanity have a tendency to run afoul of First Amendment protections. In *Cohen* v. *California*,[92] for example, the Supreme Court invalidated the "offense conduct" conviction of a man who entered a courtroom wearing a jacket with "F*** the Draft" written across the front of it. Just Harlan wrote, "While the particular four-letter-word being litigated here is perhaps more distasteful than others of its genre, it is nevertheless often true that one man's vulgarity is another's lyric."[93]

Sanctions against the use of profanity remain for broadcasters who use it. In 2009, the Supreme Court ruled that the Federal Communications Commission (FCC) acts within its authority when it fines broadcasters for failing to shield viewers and/or listeners from profanity, especially during times when children may be watching/listening.[94] The case stemmed from a 2006 FCC decision to fine the Fox

---

[89] *Reynolds* v. *United States*, 98 U.S. 145 (1878).
[90] See, e.g., *State* v. *Green*, 99 P.3d 820 (Utah 2004).
[91] Texas Penal Code Section 25.01
[92] *Cohen* v. *California*, 403 U.S. 15 (1971).
[93] Ibid., p. 25.
[94] *Federal Communications Commission* v. *Fox Television Stations, Inc.*, 129 S.Ct. 1800 (2009).

television network for violating decency rules when singer Cher used profanity during the 2002 Billboard Music Awards and actress Nicole Richie did the same in the 2003 awards.

YOUR DECISION

1. John is part of a religious group that believes you should have multiple wives. However, since John realizes the United States criminalizes plural marriages, he only officially marries one woman at the local courthouse. While he has three other "wives," he never officially marries them in any formal ceremony. All of the women and their children live with John under one roof as a family. Since wives two, three, and four are technically considered "single mothers" in the eyes of the law, they apply for and receive food stamps, welfare, and other forms of government assistance. Have any crimes been committed by John and his family? Why or why not?

2. Judy was at the mall with her girlfriends trying on prom dresses at a local department store. Directly outside of the women's dressing rooms was a collection of large mirrors where the girls would stand to model and discuss the various dress choices. Edward, a 41-year-old man, sat outside the dressing room for over an hour watching the teenage girls model their dresses. Edward never entered the dressing room itself where the girls actually changed clothes. Upset by his presence, the girls contacted store security and Edward was ultimately arrested. Can he be charged with voyeurism? Why or why not? Apply the Indiana statute provided in the text to the scenario.

Summary

- Crimes against decency and/or morality include incest, indecent exposure, voyeurism, bigamy, polygamy, and, in some jurisdictions, profanity.

- The criminal law traditionally prohibited a wide range of consensual sexual acts, including fornication, adultery, and sodomy. These acts are no longer considered criminal.

- Incest refers to sexual intercourse with certain relatives. State incest laws vary considerably.

- Indecent exposure, sometimes called "lewd and lascivious conduct," occurs when one displays his or her "private parts" in front of others—typically with their knowledge or awareness.

- Voyeurism refers, in general, to the act of spying on the intimate activities of other people and is illegal in most jurisdictions.

- Bigamy, or marriage between two persons when one is married to another, is illegal in all American jurisdictions. The same is true for polygamy, or one person being married to several others.

- Profanity was sometimes prohibited in dedicated state or local statutes, but that has changed. Most states now incorporate into their disorderly conduct (and similar) statutes various prohibitions against public profanity.

TERRORISM

Learning Objectives
- **Define terrorism.**
- **Identify several types of terrorism.**
- **Explain how the criminal law controls terrorism.**

Terrorism is criminal activity not unlike the usual violent crimes that exist in almost all developed societies. Terrorists are murderers, exactly like the criminal who kills a victim during the course of a robbery. But terrorism also differs from the usual homicides we see all too often on the evening news because it tends to have religious and/ or political motivations, is often international in scope or origin, and is carried out with what the perpetrators consider to be noble (albeit delusional) goals.

Defining Terrorism

Most of us know terrorism when we see it; the 9/11 incidents were prime examples of terrorism. Even so, there is no single definition of terrorism. The Foreign Relations Authorization Act defines it in terms of four main characteristics: premeditation, political motivation, violence, and committed against noncombatants (e.g., innocent bystanders).[95] An alternative definition has been put forth by the FBI, which defines terrorism as:

> a violent act or an act dangerous to human life in violation of the criminal laws of the United States or of any state to intimidate or coerce a government, the civilian population, or any segment thereof, in furtherance of political or social objectives.[96]

These definitions are fairly concise. An even more detailed definition, this one from the Immigration and Nationality Act, appears in Figure 8.4.

Criminologist Gwynn Nettler proposes a definition of terrorism that consists of six characteristics:

1. **No rules.** There are no moral constraints or standards of what is considered acceptable. In other words, anything goes.

2. **No innocents.** Terrorists do not distinguish between innocents and noninnocents, or soldiers and civilians.

---

[95]In the words of the Act, "The term 'terrorism' means premeditated, political motivated violence perpetrated against noncombatant targets by subnational groups or clandestine agents." 22 U.S.C. 2656 f(d)(2).
[96]Federal Bureau of Investigation, *Counterterrorism Section, Terrorism in the United States, 1987* (Washington, DC: FBI, 1987).

The term "terrorist activity" means any activity which is unlawful under the laws of the place where it is committed (or which, if it had been committed in the United States, would be unlawful under the laws of the United States or any State) and which involves any of the following:

(I) The highjacking or sabotage of any conveyance (including an aircraft, vessel, or vehicle).

(II) The seizing or detaining, and threatening to kill, injure, or continue to detain, another individual in order to compel a third person (including a governmental organization) to do or abstain from doing any act as an explicit or implicit condition for the release of the individual seized or detained.

(III) A violent attack upon an internationally protected person (as defined in section 1116(b)(4) of title 18, United States Code) or upon the liberty of such a person.

(IV) An assassination.

(V) The use of any-
  (aa) biological agent, chemical agent, or nuclear weapon or device, or
  (bb) explosive, firearm, or other weapon or dangerous device (other than for mere personal monetary gain), with intent to endanger, directly or indirectly, the safety of one or more individuals or to cause substantial damage to property.

(VI) A threat, attempt, or conspiracy to do any of the foregoing.

Figure 8.4
Terrorism Defined
Source: Immigration and Nationality Act, Public Law 82-414 [Section 212(a)(3)(B)]

3. **Economy.** The concern is with inflicting as much damage as possible but at the same time scaring even more people (e.g., kill one person, terrify 10,000 more).

4. **Publicity.** All terrorist incidents are highly publicized. Terrorists seek publicity in an effort to heighten people's fear levels, weaken economies, and so forth.

5. **Meaning.** Violent acts and the infliction of mass casualties gives meaning to terrorists' lives.

6. **No clarity.** The long-term goals of terrorism are either delusion or impossible to implement (e.g., Islamic dominance).[97]

Types of Terrorism

domestic terrorism
Terrorism carried out by an individual or group based and operating within the United States in furtherance of a political or social objective.

International terrorism
The unlawful use of violence by a group or individual with some connection with a foreign power or group in furtherance of a political or social objective.

The two main types of terrorism are domestic and international. **Domestic terrorism** is homegrown terrorism, that is, terrorism carried out by an individual or group based and operating within this country. Moreover, domestic terrorism is not directed by international sources. The most notorious example of domestic terrorism is the infamous 1995 Oklahoma City federal building bombing by Timothy McVeigh. He was not only a homegrown terrorist, but he was also not directed by any foreign source.

International terrorism refers to the unlawful use of violence by a group or individual with some connection with a foreign power or group. International terrorism is sometimes mistakenly called "foreign terrorism," but "foreign" refers to

[97]G. Nettler, *Killing one another* (Cincinnati, OH: Anderson, 1982).

terrorism that takes place in another country, outside the United States. The most prominent example of international terrorism in recent years occurred at various American sites on September 11, 2001. While the acts took place within our borders, they clearly had international origins.

Other Forms of Terrorism

cyberterrorism The use of technology, including computers and the Internet, to carry our terroristic attacks.

narcoterrorism Terroristic activities that result from a collaboration between drug traffickers and traditional terrorist groups.

ecoterrorism Terroristic activities aimed at those perceived to be harming the environment.

The typical terrorist incident is international. Although there has not been much in the way of domestic terrorism to report in recent years, other, lesser-known forms of terrorism include **cyberterrorism**, **narcoterrorism**, and **ecoterrorism**.

Cyberterrorism uses high technology (computers and the Internet) to carry out attacks. Barry Collin, a senior research fellow at the California-based Institute for Security and Intelligence, first coined the term in the 1980s.[98] The term was later made popular in the report by the RAND Corporation where a warning of "new terrorism" was issued.[99] The FBI subsequently developed a definition of cyberterrorism as "the premeditated, politically motivated attack against information, computer systems, computer programs, and data which results in violence against noncombatant targets by subnational groups or clandestine agents."[100]

There have been no major cyberterrorist incidents to report, but it is easy to imagine some possibilities. An attack against the nation's air traffic control system, for example, could wreak havoc by leading planes to collide in midair. If power grids were successfully attacked, this could threaten the storage of valuable data, though technological advances have thus far kept these threats contained.

Narcoterrorism is concerned with collaboration between drug traffickers and terrorist groups. For example, during 2005, Afghan drug lord Bashir Noorzai was arrested in New York on charges that he attempted to smuggle $50 million worth of heroin into the United States. People have also used the term *narcoterrorism* to refer to attacks by drug traffickers against their governments and law enforcement authorities. These insurgent operations, like that of the Columbia-based 19th of April Movement (M-19), make enforcement of a nation's antinarcotics laws difficult, at best. The true extent of the problem remains unknown, due in part to the clandestine nature of the illicit drug trade. Narcoterrorism also raises a number of questions, such as those posed by noted drug researcher James Inciardi:

- What is the full threat posed by narcoterrorism?
- How should narcoterrorism be dealt with?
- Is narcoterrorism a law enforcement problem or a military one?
- How might narcoterrorism be affected by changes in official U.S. policy toward drugs and drug use?
- Is the international drug trade being used as a tool by anti-U.S. and other interests to undermine Western democracies in a calculated way?[101]

---

[98]B. Collin, "The Future of Cyberterrorism," *Crime and Justice International* (March 1997), pp.15–18.
[99]J. Arquilla and D. Ronfeldt, *The Advent of Netwar* (Santa Monica, CA: RAND Corporation, 1996).
[100]M.M. Pollitt, "Cyberterrorism: Fact or fancy?," in *Proceedings of the Twentieth National Information Systems Security Conference*, October 1997, pp. 285–289.
[101]J.A. Inciardi, "Narcoterrorism." Paper presented at the 1988 annual meeting of the Academy of Criminal Justice Sciences, San Francisco, p. 8.

While cyberterrorism and narcoterrorism can have a strong international component, this is less true of *ecoterrorism*. According to one source, "[e]coterrorism involves extremist views on environmental issues and animal rights, and is a fringe-issue form of terrorism aimed primarily at inflicting economic damage on those seen as profiting from the destruction and exploitation of the environment."[102] One well-known ecoterrorist group goes by the name Earth Liberation Front, or ELF. There is a website[103] that uses ELF's name but specifically disavows any connection to the unstructured organization states that ELF has no leadership, membership, or official spokesperson. The site describes ELF as an underground movement by autonomous and anonymous individuals who use sabotage and guerilla warfare to stop what it calls the "exploitation and destruction of the natural environment."

The 1998 arson attack against the Vail, Colorado, ski resort serves as an example of ecoterrorism. On December 15, 2006, Chelsea Dawn Gerlach and Stanilas Gregory Meyerhoff pleaded guilty to setting the fire (as well as several other fires in several western states) that led to some $12 million in damages. Readers may also note the irony inherent in destroying the earth to save the earth. Even Gerlach herself noted that the attacks that she and her colleagues in "the family" (a Eugene-based ELF cell) carried out probably did more harm than good. The ELF movement has by no means been quashed, and the group remains a significant concern to law enforcement officials.

Controlling Terrorism

The U.S. government has adopted a so-called "4D strategy" for combating terrorism: Defeat, Deny, Diminish, and Defend.[104] Defeat refers to defeating terrorists and their organizations. Deny refers to denial of "sponsorship, support, and sanctuary" to terrorists:

> The strategy to deny sponsorship, support, and sanctuary is three-fold. First, it focuses on the responsibilities of all states to fulfill their obligations to combat terrorism both within their borders and internationally. Second, it helps target U.S. assistance to those states who are willing to combat terrorism, but may not have the means. And finally, when states prove reluctant or unwilling to meet their international obligations to deny support and sanctuary to terrorists, the United States, in cooperation with friends and allies, or if necessary, acting independently, will take appropriate steps to convince them to change their policies.[105]

Diminish refers to altering the underlying conditions that terrorists use to justify their attacks. U.S. efforts to resolve regional disputes, foster development, and encourage democracy fall into this category. Defend refers to all strategies, both in the United States and abroad, to protect our country's interests. We will see shortly how some of this work is being carried out by federal, state, and local law enforcement officials. The military, intelligence agencies, and other entities also combine their efforts to round out the government's concern with defending the United States from (and preventing) future terrorist attacks.

---

[102]Accessed 6/20/2007 from: http://faculty.ncwc.edu/TOConnor/429/429lect16.htm.
[103]http://www.earthliberationfront.com/elf_news.htm.
[104]Ibid.
[105]Ibid.

The government has also taken many deliberate, particularly legislative, steps in addition to forming a national strategy to combat terrorism. In the wake of the 1995 Oklahoma City bombing, for example, the **Antiterrorism and Effective Death Penalty Act** (AEDPA) became law. The following lists the Act's key provisions:

Antiterrorism and Effective Death Penalty Act Federal legislation that defines specific terrorism crimes and penalties.

- Within the U.S., it bans fund-raising for and financial support of international terrorist organizations.
- It provided $1 billion for enhanced fighting of terrorism by federal and local officials.
- It allowed foreign terrorist suspects to be deported or to be kept out of the United States *without* disclosure of the evidence against them.
- It sanctioned use of the death penalty against anyone who commits an international terrorist incident within the United States.
- It made it a federal crime to use the United States as a base for planning terrorist attacks.
- It required that so-called "taggants," or chemical markers, be added to certain explosives during their manufacture.
- It ordered a feasibility study on marking other explosives (other than gun powder).[106]

Readers may be more familiar with the USA PATRIOT Act. Given its breadth relative to the AEDPA, we reserved a separate section for coverage of the Act. Now let's look more closely at the USA PATRIOT Act.

The USA PATRIOT Act

On September 14, 2001, in response to the 9/11 attacks on the World Trade Center, President George W. Bush declared a state of emergency, which permitted him to invoke certain presidential powers. These powers include the ability to summon reserve troops, marshal military units, and issue executive orders for the implementation of such things as military tribunals. Congress also took action to empower the Justice Department to respond to terrorism by passing the **USA PATRIOT Act** on October 26, 2001, which President Bush signed the Act into law the following day.

USA PATRIOT Act Federal legislation passed in response to the September 11, 2001 terrorist attacks, the Act includes expanded tools for law enforcement.

The Act's full title is the Uniting and Strengthening America by Providing Appropriate Tools Required to Intercept and Obstruct Terrorism. It is a very long and complex piece of legislation, consisting of 10 parts and over 300 single-spaced pages. Given its staggering size and breadth, the Act is a testament to the fact that Congress *can* move quickly when it must.

The USA PATRIOT Act made several important changes to past law and practice:

- It centralized federal law enforcement authority in the U.S. Department of Justice. For example, Section 808 of the Act reassigned the authority for investigating several federal crimes of violence from law enforcement agencies, such as the

---

[106]F. Schmalleger, *Criminal justice today: An introductory text for the 21st century*, 9th ed. (Upper Saddle River, NJ: Prentice-Hall, 2006), p. 684.

U.S. Secret Service and the Bureau of Alcohol, Tobacco, Firearms and Explosives to the U.S. Attorney General.

- It provided for CIA (Central Intelligence Agency) oversight of all domestic intelligence gathering. Prior to the USA PATRIOT Act, the CIA's role was primarily concerned with foreign intelligence gathering.

- It expanded the definition of the terms *terrorism* and *domestic terrorism* to include activities that: (A) involve acts dangerous to human life that are a violation of the criminal laws of the United States or of any state; (B) appear to be intended (i) to intimidate or coerce a civilian population; (ii) to influence the policy of a government by mass destruction, assassination, or kidnapping; or (iii) to effect the conduct of a government by mass destruction, assassination, or kidnapping; and (C) occur primarily within the territorial jurisdiction of the United States.[107]

There were also several noteworthy changes in criminal procedure attributable to the USA PATRIOT Act. Before describing these changes, some background will be informative. First, the U.S. Supreme Court has held that the Fifth and Sixth Amendment rights of due process and access to jury trials apply to all "persons," not just citizens of the United States.[108] In addition, the Court has held that all undocumented aliens living inside the U.S. borders are entitled to the protections enunciated in the Bill of Rights.[109] Specifically, the Court has stated that:

> the Fifth Amendment, as well as the Fourteenth Amendment, protects every one of these persons from deprivation of life, liberty, or property without due process of law. Even one whose presence in this country is unlawful, involuntary, or transitory is entitled to constitutional protection.[110]

These rights also apply to the exclusion of aliens from within the U.S. borders. That is, proceedings for the deportation of aliens must conform to constitutional requirements, especially due process.[111] In short, legal, illegal, resident, and temporary aliens have historically enjoyed the same constitutional protections as ordinary U.S. citizens. Why does all this matter? In several ways, the USA PATRIOT Act alters and even abolishes constitutional protections historically available to people under the jurisdiction of the United States, including aliens. Space constraints prevent full coverage of all the relevant changes (see Figure 8.5 for an overview of the Act's main sections), but we consider some of them here.

The USA PATRIOT Act also has implications for investigative detentions. Section 412 of the Act requires the U.S. Attorney General to take into custody any alien whom he has "reasonable grounds to believe" is "engaged in any other activity that endangers the national security of the United States."[112] The alien can

---

[107]USA PATRIOT Act 802, 115 Stat. at 376.
[108]*United States* v. *Verdugo-Urquidez*, 494 U.S. 259 (1990), pp. 264–266.
[109]*Mathews* v. *Diaz*, 426 U.S. 67 (1976), p. 77.
[110]Ibid.
[111]*Shaughnessy* v. *United States ex rel. Mezei*, 345 U.S. 206 (1953), p. 212.
[112]USA Patriot Act, Pub. L. No. 107-56, 412, 115 Stat. 272, 350 (2001).

TITLE I—ENHANCING DOMESTIC SECURITY AGAINST TERRORISM

TITLE II—ENHANCED SURVEILLANCE PROCEDURES

TITLE III—INTERNATIONAL MONEY LAUNDERING ABATEMENT AND ANTI-TERRORIST FINANCING ACT OF 2001

TITLE IV—PROTECTING THE BORDER

TITLE V—REMOVING OBSTACLES TO INVESTIGATING TERRORISM

TITLE VI —PROVIDING FOR VICTIMS OF TERRORISM, PUBLIC SAFETY OFFICERS, AND THEIR FAMILIES

TITLE VII—INCREASED INFORMATION SHARING FOR CRITICAL INFRASTRUCTURE PROTECTION

TITLE VIII—STRENGTHENING THE CRIMINAL LAWS AGAINST TERRORISM

TITLE IX—IMPROVED INTELLIGENCE

TITLE X—MISCELLANEOUS

Figure 8.5

Main Titles of the USA PATRIOT Act
Source: USA PATRIOT Act, Public Law 107-56.

then be held for seven days, at the end of which he or she must be released, charged criminally, or deported. Importantly, if an alien is detained for purposes related to immigration, rather than suspected criminal activity, he or she can be detained indefinitely. This has been one tool in the war on terrorism; authorities can indefinitely detain illegal immigrants, which obviously raises serious due process concerns.

The USA PATRIOT Act has also given enhanced authority to law enforcement in the name of intelligence gathering. For example, the Act modified portions of the Electronic Communications Privacy Act, which governs access to stored electronic communications, like e-mail correspondence and voice mail. Wiretap orders, which traditionally were difficult to secure, are now only required to intercept real-time phone communications. As another example of improved intelligence-gathering, Section 206 creates so-called roving wiretap authority. This basically abandons a previous requirement that a government eavesdropper make sure the target is actually using the device being monitored. This means that if a suspected terrorist switches cell phones, the government can continue to listen.

The Act also amended Title 18, Section 3103 of the U.S. Code to authorize courts to issue search warrants that delay notification of an impending search and that can be executed in the absence of the suspect. This is very different than the typical search warrant scenario, where an announcement is made before the warrant is served and the occupant is usually present during the search. These so-called "sneak and peak" warrants can be obtained, pursuant to the USA PATRIOT Act, if a court finds "reasonable cause" that by providing advance notification, even right before the search, an "adverse result" could occur. Several other such changes were authorized by the Act, all with a common theme of giving investigative authorities broader power to investigate terrorism and related forms of criminal activity.

Title VIII of the Act contains several provisions with relevance to criminal law. For example, it created a prohibition against harboring terrorists. It also eliminated

Amends the Federal criminal code to prohibit specific terrorist acts or otherwise destructive, disruptive, or violent acts against mass transportation vehicles, ferries, providers, employees, passengers, or operating systems.

(Sec. 802) Amends the Federal criminal code to: (1) revise the definition of "international terrorism" to include activities that appear to be intended to affect the conduct of government by mass destruction; and (2) define "domestic terrorism" as activities that occur primarily within U.S. jurisdiction, that involve criminal acts dangerous to human life, and that appear to be intended to intimidate or coerce a civilian population, to influence government policy by intimidation or coercion, or to affect government conduct by mass destruction, assassination, or kidnapping.

(Sec. 803) Prohibits harboring any person knowing or having reasonable grounds to believe that such person has committed or to be about to commit a terrorism offense.

(Sec. 804) Establishes Federal jurisdiction over crimes committed at U.S. facilities abroad.

(Sec. 805) Applies the prohibitions against providing material support for terrorism to offenses outside of the United States.

(Sec. 806) Subjects to civil forfeiture all assets, foreign or domestic, of terrorist organizations.

(Sec. 808) Expands: (1) the offenses over which the Attorney General shall have primary investigative jurisdiction under provisions governing acts of terrorism transcending national boundaries; and (2) the offenses included within the definition of the Federal crime of terrorism.

(Sec. 809) Provides that there shall be no statute of limitations for certain terrorism offenses if the commission of such an offense resulted in, or created a foreseeable risk of, death or serious bodily injury to another person.

(Sec. 810) Provides for alternative maximum penalties for specified terrorism crimes.

(Sec. 811) Makes: (1) the penalties for attempts and conspiracies the same as those for terrorism offenses; (2) the supervised release terms for offenses with terrorism predicates any term of years or life; and (3) specified terrorism crimes Racketeer Influenced and Corrupt Organizations statute predicates.

(Sec. 814) Revises prohibitions and penalties regarding fraud and related activity in connection with computers to include specified cyber-terrorism offenses.

(Sec. 816) Directs the Attorney General to establish regional computer forensic laboratories, and to support existing laboratories, to develop specified cyber-security capabilities.

(Sec. 817) Prescribes penalties for knowing possession in certain circumstances of biological agents, toxins, or delivery systems, especially by certain restricted persons.

Figure 8.6

Criminal Law Provisions of the PATRIOT Act

Source: http://www.govtrack.us/congress/bills/107/hr3162 (accessed December 14, 2012).

the statute of limitations for certain terrorist offenses and put in place new maximum penalties for terrorist offenses. A brief synopsis of these and other pertinent criminal law provisions in the PATRIOT Act appear in Figure 8.6.

A key provision of the PATRIOT ACT, Section 2339A, makes it a felony to "provide material support or resources" to terrorist organization. This crime, which was originally enacted as part of the AEDPA, is designed to target individual who provide crucial support to terrorist organization without actually participating in their illegal activities. The constitutionality of the material support provision has been challenged in court on void for vagueness and First Amendment grounds (see Chapter 2).[113]

The USA PATRIOT Act was set to expire at the end of 2005. In March 2006, President Bush signed into law a "renewal" of the Act that incorporated some changes. On the one hand, various civil liberties protections were written into the new version. On the other hand, the Act also expanded law enforcement, especially through the Combat Methamphetamine Epidemic Act of 2005.[114]

The PATRIOT Act has been amended under the Obama administration. For example, in early 2010, the president signed a one-year extension of several key provisions. The key activities President Obama reauthorized were "court-approved roving wiretaps that permit surveillance on multiple phones, . . . seizure of records and property in anti-terrorism operations, . . . [and] surveillance against a so-called lone wolf, a non-U.S. citizen engaged in terrorism who may not be part of a recognized terrorist group."[115]

Other Terrorism Legislation

A number of other federal laws are used to prosecute terrorists. The U.S. Justice Department classifies the available statutes as follows:

> **Category I** cases involve violations of federal statutes that are directly related to international terrorism and that are utilized regularly in international terrorism matters. These statutes prohibit, for example, terrorist acts abroad against United States nationals, the use of weapons of mass destruction, conspiracy to murder persons overseas, providing material support to terrorists or foreign terrorist organizations, receiving military style training from foreign terrorist organizations, and bombings of public places or government facilities . . .
>
> **Category II** cases include defendants charged with violating a variety of other statutes where the investigation involved an identified link to international terrorism. These Category II cases include offenses such as those involving fraud, immigration, firearms, drugs, false statements, perjury, and obstruction of justice, as well as general conspiracy charges under 18 U.S.C. § 371. Prosecuting terror-related targets using Category II offenses and others is often an effective method – and sometimes the only available method – of deterring and disrupting potential terrorist planning and support activities . . .[116]

Figure 8.7 contains a detailed listing of example offenses in each category.

---

[113]*Holder* v. *Humanitarian Law Project*, 130 S.Ct. 2705 (2010).

[114]http://www.whitehouse.gov/infocus/patriotact/.

[115]Associated Press, "Obama Signs Extension of Patriot Act," http://www.usatoday.com/news/washington/2010-02-27-Patriot-Act_N.htm (accessed January 3, 2011).

[116]U.S. Justice Department, http://www.justice.gov/cjs/docs/terrorism-convictions-statistics.pdf (accessed December 13, 2010).

Category I Offenses

- Aircraft Sabotage (18 U.S.C. § 32)
- Animal Enterprise Terrorism (18 U.S.C. § 43)
- Crimes Against Internationally Protected Persons (18 U.S.C. § § 112, 878, 1116, l201(a)(4))
- Use of Biological, Nuclear, Chemical or Other Weapons of Mass Destruction (18 U.S.C. §§ 175, 175b, 229, 831, 2332a)
- Production, Transfer, or Possession of Variola Virus (Smallpox) (18 U.S.C. § 175c)
- Participation in Nuclear and WMD Threats to the United States (18 U.S.C. § 832)
- Conspiracy Within the United States to Murder, Kidnap, or Maim Persons or to Damage Certain Property Overseas (18 U.S.C. § 956)
- Hostage Taking (18 U.S.C. § 1203)
- Terrorist Attacks Against Mass Transportation Systems (18 U.S.C. § 1993)
- Terrorist Acts Abroad Against United States Nationals (18 U.S.C. § 2332)
- Terrorism Transcending National Boundaries (18 U.S.C. § 2332b)
- Bombings of places of public use, Government facilities, public transportation systems and infrastructure facilities (18 U.S.C. § 2332f)
- Missile Systems designed to Destroy Aircraft (18 U.S.C. § 2332g)
- Production, Transfer, or Possession of Radiological Dispersal Devices (18 U.S.C. § 2332h) * Harboring Terrorists (18 U.S.C. § 2339)
- Providing Material Support to Terrorists (18 U.S.C. § 2339A) Providing Material Support to * Designated Terrorist Organizations (18 U.S.C. § 2339B)
- Prohibition Against Financing of Terrorism (18 U.S.C. § 2339C)
- Receiving Military-Type Training from an FTO (18 U.S.C. § 2339D)
- Narco-Terrorism (21 U.S.C. § 1010A)
- Sabotage of Nuclear Facilities or Fuel (42 U.S.C. § 2284)
- Aircraft Piracy (49 U.S.C. § 46502)
- Violations of IEEPA (50 U.S.C. § 1705(b)) involving E.O. 12947 (Terrorists Who Threaten to Disrupt the Middle East Peace Process); E.O. 13224 (Blocking Property and Prohibiting Transactions With Persons Who Commit, Threaten to Commit, or Support Terrorism or Global Terrorism List); and E.O. 13129 (Blocking Property and Prohibiting Transactions With the Taliban)

Examples of Category II Offenses

- Crimes Committed Within the Special Maritime and Territorial Jurisdiction of the United States (l8 U.S.C. §§ 7, 113, 114, 115, 1111, 1112, 1201, 2111)
- Violence at International Airports (18 U.S.C. § 37)
- Arsons and Bombings (18 U.S.C. §§ 842(m), 842(n), 844(f), 844(I))
- Killings in the Course of Attack on a Federal Facility (18 U.S.C. § 930(c))
- False Statements (18 U.S.C. § 1001)
- Protection of Computers (18 U.S.C. § 1030) False Information and Hoaxes (18 U.S.C. § 1038)
- Genocide (18 U.S.C. § 1091)
- Destruction of Communication Lines (18 U.S.C. § 1362) Sea Piracy (18 U.S.C. § 1651)
- Unlicensed Money Remitter Charges (18 U.S.C. § 1960)
- Wrecking Trains (18 U.S.C. § 1992)
- Destruction of National Defense Materials, Premises, or Utilities (18 U.S.C. § 2155)
- Violence against Maritime Navigation and Maritime Fixed Platforms (18 U.S.C. §§ 2280, 2281)
- Torture (18 U.S.C. § 2340A)
- War Crimes (18 U.S.C. § 2441)
- International Traffic in Arms Regulations (22 U.S.C. § 2778, and the rules and regulations promulgated thereunder, 22 C.F.R. § 121-130)
- Crimes in the Special Aircraft Jurisdiction other than Aircraft Piracy (49 U.S.C. §§ 46503-46507)
- Destruction of Interstate Gas or Hazardous Liquid Pipeline Facilities (49 U.S.C. § 60123(b))

Figure 8.7

Examples of Federal Statutes used to Prosecute Terrorists

Source: Federal of American Scientists, "Introduction to National Security Division Statistics on Unsealed International Terrorism and Terrorism-Related Convictions," http://www.fas.org/irp/agency/doj/doj032610-stats.pdf (accessed December 14, 2012).

YOUR DECISION

1. John Walker Lindh is an American citizen who was captured by the Northern Alliance on the battlefield in Afghanistan in November 2001. Known as "the American Taliban," Lindh attended a military training camp run by Harakut ul-Mujahideen in Pakistan before joining the Taliban in Afghanistan. Lindh allegedly told Taliban officials that he was an American and that he wanted to go to the front lines to fight, and received additional military training at an al Qaeda training camp. During his training, Lindh personally met Osama bin Laden who thanked him and other trainees for taking part in jihad. Lindh carried a weapon during his time fighting with the Taliban. What possible crimes has Lindh committed?

2. Judy Smith was just dumped by her boyfriend of five years, Stephen Myers. Stephen has found a new woman in his life and is about to take her on a seven-day Caribbean cruise. Jude is distraught at the thought of Stephen with another woman. She writes a letter threatening to blow up the entire cruise ship if Stephen does not take her back. Federal law enforcement learns of the threat to the cruise ship and uses the PATRIOT Act to investigate Judy. Has Judy committed a crime of terrorism? Why or why not? Should the PATRIOT Act be used to investigate this type of crime?

Summary

- An act is terrorism if it is premeditated, politically motivated, violent, and committed against noncombatants.
- Domestic terrorism is carried out by an individual or group that is based within and operates within this country. International terrorism refers to the unlawful use of violence by a group or individual having some connection with a foreign power or group.
- Cyberterrorism uses high technology, especially computers and the Internet, to carry out terrorist attacks. Narcoterrorism involves collaboration between drug traffickers and terrorist groups. Ecoterrorism involves extremist views on environmental issues and animal rights, and is a fringe-issue form of terrorism aimed primarily at inflicting economic damage on those seen as profiting from the destruction and exploitation of the environment.
- The U.S. government has adopted a so-called "4D strategy" for combating terrorism: Defeat, Deny, Diminish, and Defend.
- Legislative efforts to combat terrorism include the Antiterrorism and Effective Death Penalty Act (AEDPA), the USA PATRIOT Act, and dozens of other federal statutes.

MODULE

8.5 OTHER OFFENSES AGAINST THE STATE

Learning Objectives

- **Define treason.**
- **Distinguish between sedition, sabotage, criminal syndicalism, and espionage.**

Terrorism is perhaps the most visible and potentially destructive crime against the state. Yet there are several other offenses against the state that sometimes receive little attention. Examples include treason, sedition, sabotage, criminal syndicalism, and espionage. This module briefly introduces each. We conclude with a brief examination of the use of traditional criminal law offenses to target threats against the state.

Both the offenses discussed in this section *and* terrorism typically involve violations of federal law. As such, most cases are prosecuted in federal court. There are some exceptions, as in the case of criminal syndicalism, but to say an offense is "against the state" is almost always the same as saying it is against the federal government. For example, you would never see a county-level treason prosecution.

Treason

treason Levying war against the United States or providing aid and comfort to the enemies of the United States.

Treason is the only crime defined in the U.S. Constitution. Article III, Section 3 reads:

> Treason against the United States, shall consist only in levying War against them, or, in adhering to their Enemies, giving them Aid and Comfort. No Person shall be convicted of Treason unless on the Testimony of two Witnesses to the same overt Act, or on Confession in open Court.

The Constitution gave Congress the power to declare the punishment for treason, which it has since done. The U.S. Code contains the same language found in Article III of the Constitution, but also adds the punishment:

> Whoever, owing allegiance to the United States, levies war against them or adheres to their enemies, giving them aid and comfort within the United States or elsewhere, is guilty of treason and shall suffer death, or shall be imprisoned not less than five years and fined under this title but not less than $10,000; and shall be incapable of holding any office under the United States.[117]

Clearly treason is regarded as a serious offense. What, in simple terms, is treason? It is the betrayal of one's nation. Black's Law Dictionary defines it as "[a] breach of allegiance to one's government, usually committed through levying war against such government or by giving aid or comfort to the enemy."[118] Former Supreme Court Justice Robert Jackson defined treason even more specifically in *Cramer* v. *United States*:

> . . . the crime of treason consists of two elements: adherence to the enemy; and rendering him aid and comfort. A citizen intellectually or emotionally may favor the enemy and harbor sympathies or convictions disloyal to this country's policy or interest, but so long as he commits no act of aid and comfort to the enemy, there is no treason. On the other hand, a citizen may take actions, which do aid and comfort the enemy—making a speech critical of the government or opposing its measures, profiteering, striking in defense plants or essential work, and the hundred other things which impair our cohesion and diminish our strength—but if there is no adherence to the enemy in this, if there is no intent to betray, there is no treason.[119]

---

[117]18 U.S.C. Section 2381.
[118]Black's Law Dictionary, 6th ed. (St. Paul, MN: West, 1990), p. 1501.
[119]*Cramer* v. *United States*, 325 U.S. 1 (1945).

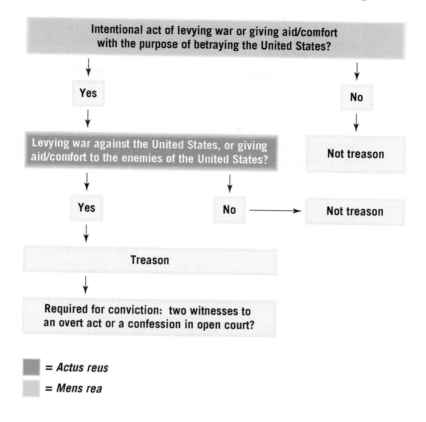

Figure 8.8
Treason

Also see Figure 8.8 for a summary of treason.

Treason is less of a concern today than it once was. The Founding Fathers realized that for the new republic to survive its formative years, the people would need to support and stand behind their government. Treason prosecutions have been exceptionally rare. Fewer than 40 individuals have been prosecuted for it since the Constitution was written.

The most recent treason indictment was against Adam Yahiye Gadahn, a U.S. citizen turned Al-Qaeda operative, who remains on the FBI's "Most Wanted" list. He was the first American charged with treason since Tomoya Kawakita in 1952. Kawakita was sentenced to death for treason in connection with World War II, but President John F. Kennedy pardoned him in 1963 on the condition that he be deported to Japan for the rest of his life.[120]

Sedition

It is also a crime—and it long has been—to incite rebellion against the government. More formally, **sedition** is:

> ... advocating, or with knowledge of its contents knowingly publishing, selling or distributing any document which advocates, or, with knowledge of its purpose, knowingly becoming a member of any organization which advocates the overthrow or reformation of the existing form of government ... by violence or unlawful means.[121]

sedition Advocating the violent overthrow of the U.S. government.

---

[120]See *Kawakita* v. *United States*, 343 U.S. 717 (1952).
[121]Black's Law Dictionary, 6th ed. (St. Paul, MN: West, 1990), p. 1357.

Today, the government relies on the federal seditious conspiracy statute to prosecute people for sedition. Title 18 of the U.S. Code defines the crime as follows:

> If two or more persons in any State or Territory, or in any place subject to the jurisdiction of the United States, conspire to overthrow, put down, or to destroy by force the Government of the United States, or to levy war against them, or to oppose by force the authority thereof, or by force to prevent, hinder, or delay the execution of any law of the United States, or by force to seize, take, or possess any property of the United States contrary to the authority thereof, they shall each be fined under this title or imprisoned not more than twenty years, or both.[122]

In *United States* v. *Rahman et al.,*[123] a fairly recent case, the Second Circuit heard an appeal involving ten defendants who were convicted of seditious conspiracy as part of a plot to conduct urban terrorism. According to the court, "[a]mong the activities of some or all of the defendants were rendering assistance to those who bombed the World Trade Center . . . , planning to bomb bridges and tunnels in New York City, murdering Rabbi Meir Kahane, and planning to murder the President of Egypt."[124] One argument raised in the appeal is that the federal statute threatened free speech under the First Amendment. The court was not convinced, noting:

> The evidence justifying Abdel Rahman's conviction . . . showed beyond a reasonable doubt that he crossed the line. His speeches were not simply the expression of ideas; in some instances they constituted the crime of conspiracy to wage war on the United States . . . and solicitation of attack on the United States . . .[125]

Sabotage

sabotage Damage to property of the United States or obstructing preparation for war or national defense.

Sabotage has a conventional meaning that need not be connected with the criminal law. The criminal offense of sabotage, however, is typically damage to property or obstructing preparation for war or national defense. The U.S. Code defines sabotage as follows:

> Whoever, when the United States is at war, or in times of national emergency as declared by the President or by the Congress, with intent to injure, interfere with, or obstruct the United States or any associate nation in preparing for or carrying on the war or defense activities, or, with reason to believe that his act may injure, interfere with, or obstruct the United States or any associate nation in preparing for or carrying on the war or defense activities, willfully injures, destroys, contaminates or infects, or attempts to so injure, destroy, contaminate or infect any war material, war premises, or war utilities, shall be fined under this title or imprisoned not more than thirty years, or both.[126]

It is also criminal, under federal law, to target certain installations, harbors, and other strategic assets.[127] In addition, it is an offense to intentionally produce defective war and national defense-related materials.[128]

---

[122]18 U.S.C. Section 2384.
[123]*United States* v. *Rahman et al.,* 189 F.3d 88 (2nd Cir. 1999).
[124]Ibid.
[125]Ibid.
[126]18 U.S.C. Section 2153.
[127]Ibid., Sections 2154 and 2155.
[128]Ibid., Section 2151.

Criminal Syndicalism

criminal syndicalism The use of unlawful means to accomplish economic or political reform.

Syndicalism is an alternative to capitalism, typically a cooperative economic system. Although such a system has never been realized, governments (especially America's) are naturally wary of any actions that could signal a movement in that direction. Criminal syndicalism is thus the use of unlawful means (sabotage, terrorism, etc.) to accomplish economic or political reform. Interestingly, there is no federal criminal syndicalism statute. Most states, however, have had them at one point or another. Utah's "advocating criminal syndicalism or sabotage" statute appears in Figure 8.9.

Several state syndicalism laws have been deemed unconstitutional because they run afoul of the First Amendment. For example, in *Brandenburg v. Ohio*,[129] the Supreme Court overturned the conviction of a Ku Klux Klan leader because of a speech he made that did not, the Court felt, incite lawless action. If not declared unconstitutional, some statutes have been severely criticized and discredited.[130] Still other state syndicalism statutes remain "on the books," but are rarely invoked.

Espionage

espionage Spying for the benefit of a foreign government.

Espionage, or spying, occurs when one gathers, transmits, and/or "loses" defense information to injure the United States or for the benefit of a foreign power. The

Figure 8.9
Criminal Syndicalism in Utah
Source: Utah Code, 76-8-902

Any person who by word of mouth or writing advocates, suggests, or teaches the duty, necessity, propriety, or expediency of crime, criminal syndicalism or sabotage, or who advocates, suggests or teaches the duty, necessity, propriety, or expediency or doing any act of violence, the destruction of or damage to any property, the bodily injury to any person, or the commission of any crime or unlawful act as a means of accomplishing or effecting any industrial or political ends, change or revolution, or who prints, publishes, edits, or issues, or knowingly circulates, sells, or distributes, or publicly displays, any books, pamphlets, paper, handbill, poster, document, or written or printed matter in any form whatsoever, containing, advocating, advising, suggesting, or teaching crime, criminal syndicalism, sabotage, the doing of any act of violence, the destruction of or damage to any property, the injury to any person, or the commission of any crime or unlawful act, as a means of accomplishing, effecting, or bringing about any industrial or political ends or change, or as a means of accomplishing, effecting, or bringing about any industrial or political revolution, or who openly or at all attempts to justify by word of mouth or writing the commission or the attempt to commit sabotage, any act of violence, the destruction of or damage to any property, the injury of any person, or the commission of any crime or unlawful act, with the intent to exemplify, spread, or teach or suggest criminal syndicalism, or organizes, or helps to organize, or becomes a member of, or voluntarily assembles with, any society or assemblage of persons formed to teach or advocate, or which teaches, advocates, or suggests the doctrine of criminal syndicalism or sabotage, or the necessity, propriety, or expediency of doing any act of violence or the commission of any crime or unlawful act as a means of accomplishing or effecting any industrial or political ends, change or revolution, is guilty of a felony of the third degree.

---

[129]*Brandenburg v. Ohio*, 395 U.S. 444 (1969).
[130]See, e.g., *Dennis v. United States*, 341 U.S. 494 (1951), p. 507.

Espionage Act of 1917,[131] now part of the U.S. Code, criminalizes espionage and breaks it into two categories: espionage during peace[132] and espionage during war.[133] Espionage during wartime is defined as follows:

> Whoever, with intent or reason to believe that it is to be used to the injury of the United States or to the advantage of a foreign nation, communicates, delivers, or transmits, or attempts to communicate, deliver, or transmit, to any foreign government, or to any faction or party or military or naval force within a foreign country, whether recognized or unrecognized by the United States, or to any representative, officer, agent, employee, subject, or citizen thereof, either directly or indirectly, any document, writing, code book, signal book, sketch, photograph, photographic negative, blueprint, plan, map, model, note, instrument, appliance, or information relating to the national defense, shall be punished by death or by imprisonment for any term of years or for life . . .[134]

Take note of the penalty. Espionage is a death penalty eligible offense (subject to certain restrictions), although the norm is to sentence offenders to lengthy prison terms. Ethel and Julius Rosenberg were, in 1953, the first (and only) civilians executed for espionage in connection with their passing of atomic bomb secrets to the Soviet Union. Executions of federal prisoners are fairly rare.[135] The military has executed approximately 160 soldiers for crimes they committed while in service to

U.S. officials continue to seek espionage charges against Julian Assange, the founder of WikiLeaks.

© Pawel Garski,/Alamy

---

[131]The Espionage Act of 1917 was upheld by the U.S. Supreme Court in *Schenck* v. *United States*, 249 U.S. 47 (1919).
[132]18 U.S.C. Section 794(a).
[133]18 U.S.C. Section 794(b).
[134]18 U.S.C. Section 794(a).
[135]For a list of executed federal prisoners, see http://www.bop.gov/about/history/execchart.jsp (accessed December 14, 2010).

the United States, but none were for espionage. Espionage prosecutions are also fairly rare. As of this writing, there is speculation that U.S. officials are considering charging Julian Assange, the founder of WikiLeaks, with espionage in connection with the publication of numerous classified diplomatic cables.[136]

YOUR DECISION

1. Geraldo is a newsman imbedded with an Army infantry unit in Afghanistan. In an effort to give his network the best coverage of the war on terror, Geraldo draws a map in the sand indicating where his unit is located in relation to the enemy. The U.S. intelligence community is aware that our enemies often watch U.S. television news stations to gain information. Has Geraldo committed a crime? If so, which crime? Does the media reveal too much information regarding our national defense?

2. Julian Assange is the founder of WikiLeaks, a nonprofit media organization that releases "leaked" information it receives from a variety of anonymous sources. In November 2010, WikiLeaks began releasing 251,287 leaked U.S. embassy cables to a variety of news outlets around the world. The cables were confidential and contained sensitive information regarding national security and relations with other countries. Although the exact source of the information is unknown, it is presumed Assange received the information from an individual who works for the U.S. government. Assange is not accused of directly accessing or stealing the information from the United States. What crimes, if any, has Assange committed?

Summary

*   Offenses against the state other than terrorism include sedition, sabotage, espionage, criminal syndicalism, and espionage.

*   Treason, or "[a] breach of allegiance to one's government, usually committed through levying war against such government or by giving aid or comfort to the enemy," is the only crime defined in the U.S. Constitution.

*   Sedition is akin to inciting rebellion against the government. The government relies primarily on seditious conspiracy statutes to prosecute people for sedition.

*   The criminal offense of sabotage is damage to property or obstruction the preparation for war or national defense.

*   Syndicalism is an alternative to capitalism, typically a cooperative economic system. Criminal syndicalism is thus the use of unlawful means (sabotage, terrorism, etc.) to accomplish economic or political reform. Interestingly, there is no federal criminal syndicalism statute.

*   Espionage, or spying, occurs when one gathers, transmits, and/or "loses" defense information to injure the United States or for the benefit of a foreign power.

---

[136]http://www.huffingtonpost.com/2012/06/19/julian-assange-seeks-asy_n_1609725.html, (accessed June 19, 2012).

Chapter Review

MODULE **8.1**   OFFENSES AGAINST PUBLIC ORDER

Learning Objectives

- Identify three types of group criminality.
- Explain the difference between rioting and unlawful assembly.
- Summarize legislative approaches to criminalizing gang activity.
- Identify at least five offenses against the public order.

Review Questions

1. Explain how group criminality differs from complicity and vicarious liability.
2. Explain the relationship between unlawful assembly, rout, and riot.
3. Compare and contrast at least three offenses against public order.

Key Terms

riot	breach of peace
unlawful assembly	vagrancy
rout	loitering
disorderly conduct	panhandling

MODULE **8.2**   VICE CRIMES AND DRUG OFFENSES

Learning Objectives

- Identify a variety of vice crimes and their core elements.
- Distinguish between alcohol and drug offenses.

Review Questions

1. Should prostitution be illegal? Why or why not?
2. Should gambling be illegal? What about social gambling? Defend your answer.
3. Has the Supreme Court adequately defined obscenity? Why or why not?
4. Should the drinking age be raised, lowered, or kept the same? Why?

Key Terms

vice	public intoxication
prostitution	Harrison Narcotics Tax Act
gambling	Marijuana Tax Act
pornography	Controlled Substances Act
obscenity	Combat Methamphetamine
child pornography	Epidemic Act
sexting	Uniform Controlled Substances Act
driving under the influence	medical marijuana

MODULE **8.3**   CRIMES AGAINST DECENCY AND/OR MORALITY

Learning Objectives

- Summarize government efforts throughout history to criminalize morality.
- Describe modern-day crimes against decency and/or morality.
- Summarize the means by which the criminal law controls profanity.

Review Questions

1. What is your opinion of government's efforts over the years to legislative morality?
2. At what point should indecent exposure be considered criminal? Why?
3. Should swearing be illegal? Why or why not?

Key Terms

fornication   voyeurism
adultery   bigamy
sodomy   polygamy
incest   profanity
indecent exposure

MODULE **8.4**   TERRORISM

Learning Objectives

- Define terrorism.
- Identify several types of terrorism.
- Explain how the criminal law controls terrorism.

Review Questions

1. Define terrorism.
2. Compare and contrast five types of terrorism.
3. Explain the U.S. government's "4D" strategy for combating terrorism.
4. What is the role of the PATRIOT Act in combating terrorism?

Key Terms

domestic terrorism   ecoterrorism
international terrorism   Antiterrorism and Effective Death
cyberterrorism   Penalty Act
narcoterrorism   USA PATRIOT Act

MODULE **8.5**   OTHER OFFENSES AGAINST THE STATE

Learning Objectives

- Define treason
- Distinguish between sedition, sabotage, criminal syndicalism, and espionage.

Review Questions

1. Compare and contrast treason, sedition, and sabotage.
2. Define criminal syndicalism. How is it similar to other offenses against the state?

Key Terms

treason
sedition
sabotage

criminal syndicalism
espionage

Chapter Synthesis Questions

1. Are dedicated antigang statutes necessary? Do they go too far or not far enough? Refer to specific statutory examples.
2. It is typically illegal to resist even an unlawful arrest. Is this good law? Why or why not?
3. Should loitering in and of itself be criminal? Why?
4. What can be done, if anything, to regulate pornography on the Internet? Should anything be done?
5. Should medical marijuana be legal? Why or why not?
6. Which is more important in the war on terror, the criminal law or military intervention? Why?
7. Does the criminal law do enough to control terrorism? Why or why not?

9

CRIMINAL DEFENSES

MODULE 9.1 **OVERVIEW OF DEFENSES**

Learning Objectives

- Distinguish between failure of proof, justification, and excuse defenses.
- Explain the differences between nonexculpatory defenses and offense modifications.
- Explain the difference between a perfect defense and an imperfect defense.

MODULE 9.2 **JUSTIFICATION DEFENSES**

Learning Objectives

- Summarize the defense of self-defense.
- Distinguish between defense of habitation and defense of property.
- Compare and contrast "make my day" laws and the castle doctrine.
- Explain the law enforcement defense.
- Describe the necessity defense.
- Explain the defense of consent.

MODULE 9.3 **EXCUSE DEFENSES**

Learning Objectives

- Summarize the conditions of the defense of duress.
- Describe the intoxication defense.
- Summarize what constitutes entrapment.
- Summarize defenses based on age/immaturity.
- Summarize methods by which some courts treat juveniles as adults.
- Describe the insanity defense and the controversy surrounding it.
- Distinguish between and offer examples of physiological, psychological, and sociological excuse defenses.

Learning Objectives

- **Distinguish between failure of proof, justification, and excuse defenses.**
- **Explain the differences between nonexculpatory defenses and offense modifications.**
- **Explain the difference between a perfect defense and an imperfect defense.**

CORE CONCEPTS

In a criminal trial, the prosecution bears the burden of proving beyond a reasonable doubt that the defendant committed the crime. This does not mean, however, that the defendant sits idly by and hopes the prosecution fails to meet its burden. Though they are not required to, most defendants usually present evidence at trial. For example, the defense attorney may cross-examine prosecution witnesses, attempting to call into question their credibility. The defendant may also assert any number of defenses, arguing why he or she should not be held liable for the crime. Such defenses are the focus of this chapter.

Defenses are broken into two general categories: justification and excuse defenses. There are some defenses, however, that do not fit neatly into either of these categories. We will introduce them briefly at the beginning of this chapter and elsewhere as needed.

We begin this chapter with some general background on criminal defenses, looking not just at the various types of defenses, but also at the differences between so-called perfect and imperfect defenses. After a foundation is put in place, we shift attention to the wide variety of justification and excuse defenses.

Criminal Defenses

Defenses almost always focus on the core elements of criminal liability—*actus reus*, *mens rea*, concurrence, causation, and resulting harm (the latter two applying, again, in only the result crime context). This is particularly true of justification and excuse defenses. Each attempts to make a case that the defendant should not be held liable. But these two defense types need to be put in context against a backdrop of other defense types—namely failure of proof defenses, various "special" defenses (also called "offense modifications)" and nonexculpatory defenses.[1]

---

[1] P. H. Robinson, "Criminal Law Defenses: A Systematic Analysis," *Columbia Law Review*, Vol. 82 (1982), p. 1999.

Failure of Proof

failure of proof defense
A defendant's acquittal is the result of the prosecution failing to prove one or more of the elements of a crime or leaving reasonable doubt in the mind of the jury.

If the prosecution fails to meet its burden of proving the various elements of an underlying offense beyond a reasonable doubt, then the result is essentially a failure of proof defense. That is, the prosecution's "failure to prove" one or more offense elements may result in the defendant's acquittal. Put differently, failure to prove one or more offense elements will leave "reasonable doubt" in the minds of the jury, thus meaning that the defendant could escape criminal liability, regardless of whether he or she is guilty.

A failure of proof defense *may* lead to the defendant's acquittal, but it may not. For example, assume that Fred shoots John, killing John. Fred is prosecuted for murder, but the prosecution fails to prove that Fred intended for John to die. This does not necessarily mean John will go free. John may well be convicted of a lesser homicide offense than murder (we looked at the many varieties in Chapter 6).

affirmative defense A defense formally raised by the defendant that requires the production of evidence.

A failure of proof defense is not the same as the other leading defenses we will look at in this chapter. Why? Because it is not an affirmative defense, or a defense formally raised at trial. The defense may not have to do *anything* and still benefit from a failure of proof. If the prosecution's evidence is weak, then the defense could just ride the trial out and wait for an acquittal. If the prosecution's evidence is modestly strong but dependent largely on witness testimony, then the defense may, at the cross-examination stage, challenge the prosecution's ability to prove the offense elements beyond a reasonable doubt.

Justification

justification defenses
A group of defenses in which the defendant claims that his actions were right or justified based on the circumstances.

With justification defenses, the defendant accepts responsibility for the act he or she is charged with, but argues that the act was permissible under the circumstances. More formally, conduct that is criminal but "which under the circumstances is socially acceptable and which deserves neither criminal liability nor even censure"[2] qualifies for a justification defense. It is often said that justification defenses focus on the *act* rather than the actor.

Self-defense is an example of a justification defense. There are two broad categories of justification defenses: those justified by necessity and those justified by consent. An example of justification by necessity is self-defense; consent is a common defense in rape cases when the defendant argues that the victim consented. There is common thread running throughout all justification defenses:

> All of the different kinds of justification defenses share the same basic internal structure and have the same integral components. In all situations allowing a justification defense, there is some adequate triggering condition that prompts the actor to violate the letter of the law. In order for the actor's responsive conduct to be justified, it must be both necessary and proportional, considering all of the circumstances.[3]

---

[2]P. D. W. Heberling, "Note: Justification: The Impact of the Model Penal Code on Statutory Reform," *Columbia Law Review*, Vol. 75 (1975), p. 916.
[3]E. R. Milhizer, "Justification and Excuse: What They Were, What They Are, and What They Ought to Be," *St. John's Law Review*, Vol. 78 (2004), pp. 812–813.

Excuse

excuse defenses A group of defenses in which the defendant admits what he did was wrong but claims he should be excused from criminal liability based on the circumstances.

With **excuse defenses**, the defendant admits that what he or she did was wrong but claims that he or she should not be held responsible for the crime. Excuse defenses focus on the *actor*, not the act. The common thread running throughout excuse defenses is an argument on the defendant's part that he or she was not "normal" at the time of the crime. Note that defenses such as these provide methods of avoiding, rather than dodging, criminal liability; dodging could include fleeing the country to avoid prosecution. Also, excuse defenses, like justification defenses, are affirmative defenses that are raised at trial.

Excuse defenses can be organized into three distinct categories: "involuntary actions, actions related to cognitive deficiencies, and actions related to volitional deficiencies."[4] Involuntary actions include unwilled bodily movements (e.g., reflex actions, convulsions, sleep walking). Cognitive deficiencies relate to the actor's ability to know certain things, such as whether the conduct in question was right or wrong. Volitional deficiencies refer to actions that are "willed" by someone or something else. For example, if Martians tell Frank to park his car in front of a fire hydrant, then Frank suffers from a volitional deficiency. The source in this case is internal (Frank's mind). Alternatively, if Bob threatens to shoot Frank if he doesn't park his car in front of the hydrant, then Frank also suffers from a volitional deficiency, but the difference is that it is external.

Offense Modifications

offense modifications A modification of a criminal offense that shields the defendant from criminal liability.

Excuse and justification defenses apply to most, but not necessarily all, types of criminal liability. For example, it would be nearly impossible to claim self-defense to the crime of burglary. One would be hard-pressed to claim that burglarizing a house serves a protective function in the sense that shooting a would-be murderer does. Instead, self-defense is claimed when a person has been threatened in such a fashion that it is necessary to take protective action.

Other so-called special defenses, or **offense modifications**, apply to a small handful of crime types. Consider criminal attempt (discussed in Chapter 5). Under the Model Penal Code, criminal attempt occurs when someone takes a significant step toward committing a criminal offense. However, the Model Penal Code says that a person is not guilty of attempt if he "abandons his effort to commit the crime or prevents it from being committed."[5] This is known as abandonment, or "renunciation." Abandonment is essentially a modification to the offense that shields the defendant from liability. Someone who takes a significant step toward committing a crime has satisfied the key elements of the crime, but the abandonment "modifies" that.

de minimus infraction defense A defense that prevents conviction if the defendant's actions were so trivial or minor in relation to the intent of the criminal law.

Another example is the *de minimus* **infraction defense**. Assume Dylan stole Alex's soccer ball, but almost immediately returned it because he found his own ball. Dylan could be convicted of larceny because he arguably intended to steal the ball and went so far as to do so, but it can also be argued that the infraction was so *de minimus* (or minor) that it "did not actually cause or threaten the harm or evil

---

[4]Ibid., p. 818.
[5]Model Penal Code, Section 20.06[G].

sought to be prevented by the law defining the offense or did so only to an extent too trivial to warrant the condemnation of conviction."[6]

Offense modifications operate very much like failure of proof defenses. But whereas failure of proof defenses usually focus on the prosecution's failure to prove *actus reus* and *mens rea*, offense modifications usually focus on other issues, such as whether a resulting harm occurred or whether the defendant shows that the statute does not apply to him or her. Sometimes offense modifications are even spelled out in the language of the statute. Consider these hypothetical statutes:

1. Unauthorized possession of A is a crime.
2. Possession of A is a crime. If the defendant shows authorization for the possession, there is no criminal liability.[7]

With Offense 1, the prosecution will most likely need to prove that the defendant possessed A and was unauthorized to do so. The prosecution may fail to meet this burden, in which case the defendant benefits from a failure of proof defense. With Offense 2, there is a clear "modification" in the language of the statute—namely, that the defendant will escape liability if he or she can prove authorized possession.

Nonexculpatory Defenses

nonexculpatory defense Defenses unrelated to the elements of the crime or the defendant's alleged fault or guilt.

statute of limitations The maximum amount of time allowed by law to seek prosecution for certain crimes or offenses.

Nonexculpatory defenses[8] are unrelated to the elements of the crime or the blameworthiness of the defendant. *Exculpatory* means "clearing or tending to clear from alleged fault or guilt."[9] So, *non*exculpatory defenses are those unrelated to the defendant's alleged fault or guilty. According to one expert, nonexculpatory defenses "reflect the proposition that society sometimes finds competing policy considerations to be weightier than its basic interest in convicting and punishing blameworthy defendants."[10] What are some examples? One is the **statute of limitations**, or the "maximum time periods during which certain actions can be brought or rights enforced."[11] Certain crimes have no statute of limitations, but of those that do, if the prosecution brings charges outside the defined period, then it does not matter whether the defendant committed the crime; he or she cannot be convicted.

We discussed double jeopardy in Chapter 2. It is relevant here, too, in the sense that it is also a nonexculpatory defense. If a defendant is twice prosecuted for the same offense, she cannot be convicted in the second prosecution, regardless of whether she actually committed the crime.[12] Alternatively, if the defendant is not competent to stand trial, a due process requirement, but understood what he was doing at the time of the crime, he cannot be convicted. In essence, incompetency

---

[6]Model Penal Code, Section 2.12(2).

[7]R. G. Singer and J. Q. LaFond, *Criminal Law: Examples and Explanations*, 4th ed. (Boston, MA: Wolters Kluwer, 2007), p. 407.

[8]P. H. Robinson, "Criminal Law Defenses: A Systematic Analysis," *Columbia Law Review*, Vol. 82 (1982), p. 1999.

[9]*Black's Law Dictionary*, 6th ed. (St. Paul, MN: West, 1990), p. 566.

[10]Milhizer, "Justification and Excuse," p. 810.

[11]*Black's Law Dictionary*, 6th ed. (St. Paul, MN: West, 1990), p. 927.

[12]See, e.g., *United States v. DiFrancesco*, 449 U.S. 117 (1980), pp. 127–131; *Green v. United States*, 355 U.S. 184 (1957), pp. 187–188.

Defense Type	What it Means
Failure of proof	Prosecution fails to meet its burden of proving the elements (*actus reus* and/or *mens rea*) of the underlying offense.
Justification	Defendant accepts responsibility for the act he or she is charged with, but argues it was permissible under the circumstances.
Excuse	Defendant admits that what he or she did was wrong, but claims that he or she should not be held responsible for the crime.
Offense Modification	Similar to failure of proof, but either alters the charge to something less serious or the statute fails to criminalize the defendant's action.
Nonexculpatory Defenses	Defenses that do not clear the defendant of guilt (e.g., the statute of limitations, double jeopardy).

Figure 9.1
Types of Defenses

serves as a nonexculpatory defense.[13] This is not to say, however, that the prosecution couldn't wait until the defendant is competent before pressing charges.

Nonexculpatory defenses are controversial because they can result in clearly guilty criminals going free. As Eugene Milhizer notes, "Provided that all the requirements of a nonexculpatory defense are satisfied, the defense will be allowed even if society suffers a net harm from the acquittal of a defendant in a particular case."[14] This is not unlike the operation of the exclusionary rule[15] in the criminal procedure context. If police violate the Fourth Amendment and seize evidence during an unwarranted search, the evidence will be inadmissible at trial and it may be impossible for the prosecution to meet its burden. In such a case, the defendant could well go free. See Figure 9.1 for a summary of the discussion thus far.

Perfect and Imperfect Defenses

perfect defenses
Defenses that result in the defendant being acquitted of the crime.

Some defenses are best viewed as **perfect defenses**. A perfect defense results in the acquittal of the defendant. For example, if the defendant was justified in committing a particular crime, he or she will almost always be acquitted. This often happens with the "law enforcement" defense, which we will consider later in this chapter; police officers who justifiably kill will escape criminal conviction.

imperfect defenses
Defenses that result in the defendant being convicted of a lesser crime, but do not result in an acquittal.

Contrast this with an **imperfect defense**. With an imperfect defense, the defendant will be found guilty, but of a lesser crime. Earlier on in this chapter, in the Failure of Proof section, we presented the hypothetical of Fred shooting John. If Fred did not intend to kill John, but nevertheless killed him, Fred's defense would

---

[13]*Pate* v. *Robinson*, 383 U.S. 375 (1966), pp. 386–387.
[14]Milhizer, "Justification and Excuse," p. 811.
[15]*Weeks* v. *United States*, 232 U.S. 383 (1914); Mapp v. *Ohio*, 367 U.S. 643 (1961).

be imperfect; he would most likely escape a first-degree murder conviction, but he would also likely be found guilty of some lesser homicide offense such as voluntary manslaughter.

Consider this example of a real—and successful—imperfect defense, from the state of California: Brian Robinson lived with his parents and his cousin, Charles Lambert. Late one night, as Robinson was coming home, he observed Randle emerging from Lambert's car with car stereo equipment. Robinson confronted Randle, saying he was going to "beat your ass." Randle pulled a .25-caliber pistol from his pocket and fired it several times, but Robinson was not hit. Randle and his cousin, Byron, who had helped him break into Lambert's car, fled on foot. Robinson woke Lambert and the two gave chase. They caught up with Byron, but Randle eluded them. Robinson then began beating Byron with his fists. He recovered the stolen stereo equipment and then continued beating Byron. As he was doing so, Randle returned, shot, and killed Robinson.

Randle later testified that he fired his gun to make Robinson stop beating his cousin, meaning he committed manslaughter, not murder. The trial court did not allow the jury to consider the possibility of an imperfect defense, and Robinson was found guilty of second-degree murder. The court of appeals reversed and the California Supreme Court affirmed, holding that the jury should have been able to convict on manslaughter if it felt Robinson's argument had merit.[16] In other words, the jury should have been allowed to consider the imperfect "defense of others."

It is difficult, if not impossible, to know what percentage of successful defenses are of the perfect versus imperfect variety. This much can be said, however: Of those defendants who successfully claim a defense, a significant percentage do not "go free." Instead, they often find themselves convicted, just of lesser crimes.

YOUR DECISION

1. An intruder broke into Gregory Mason's home at 3:00 A.M. on March 15, 2010, with the intent to steal his expensive and rare coin collection. Asleep upstairs when he heard the noises in the middle of the night, Gregory, armed with a baseball bat, proceeded to beat the intruder nearly to death. He was charged with the crime of aggravated battery and is awaiting trial. Gregory is considering what options, if any, he has as a defense to the crime. If you are Gregory's defense lawyer, what type of defense would you suggest and why?

2. Brian Jones was driving under the influence of alcohol and ran into a group of pedestrians walking down the sidewalk in New York City, killing two of them. Brian feels terrible about the incident, but insists it was an "accident" and that he did not intend to harm anyone. The prosecution is charging Brian with first-degree murder, a crime that requires that the defendant act with willful, deliberate, and premeditated action. Brian believes the prosecution will have difficulty proving the *mens rea* portion of its case. What possible defense, if any, can Brian claim?

---

[16]People v. *Randle*, 111 P.3d 987 (2005).

Summary

- If the prosecution fails to meet its burden of proving the various elements of an underlying offense beyond a reasonable doubt, then the result is essentially a failure of proof defense.
- With justification defenses, the defendant accepts responsibility for the act he or she is charged with, but argues that the act was permissible under the circumstances.
- With excuse defenses, the defendant admits that what he or she did was wrong but claims that he or she should not be held responsible for the crime.
- Offense modifications operate very much like failure of proof defenses. But whereas failure of proof defenses usually focus on the prosecution's failure to prove *actus reus* and *mens rea*, offense modifications usually focus on other issues, such as whether a resulting harm occurred.
- Nonexculpatory defenses are those unrelated to the defendant's alleged fault or guilt.
- A perfect defense results in the acquittal of the defendant.
- With an imperfect defense, the defendant will be found guilty, but of a lesser crime.

MODULE

9.2 JUSTIFICATION DEFENSES

Learning Objectives

- **Summarize the defense of self-defense.**
- **Distinguish between defense of habitation and defense of property.**
- **Compare and contrast "make my day" laws and the castle doctrine.**
- **Explain the law enforcement defense.**
- **Describe the necessity defense.**
- **Explain the defense of consent.**

CORE CONCEPTS We now shift our attention to justification defenses, where the defendants claim they were "justified" in taking particular action based on the circumstances. Several justification defenses focus on protecting someone or something from harm, such as self-defense, defense of others, and defense of property and habitation. For these defenses, the controversy generally centers on the amount of force permissible for each situation. The other justification defenses focus on the legitimate use of law enforcement authority, the need to act out of necessity and consensual encounters.

Reasons for Justification Defenses

Before getting into the specific varieties of justification defenses, it is important to further consider why they exist in the first place. What are the reasons for justification defenses? There are three main ones: public benefit, superior interest, and moral rights.

Certain otherwise criminal acts are beneficial to society. A law enforcement officer who shoots and kills a dangerous criminal is arguably *helping* the public by sparing it from further victimization. Some justification defenses are thus based on a **public benefit theory**. But there is a limitation to this public benefit. As Joshua Dressler has observed, "The benefit to society is not incidental to some self-interested goal of the actor; it is the underlying motivation for the actor's conduct."[17] In our police officer example, the rationale for "justifying" his conduct is not that he takes delight in killing criminals, but rather that he is motivated to *help society*.

Some justification defenses are also supported by a **superior interest theory**. Simply, if there is a superior interest that justifies criminal conduct, the "criminality" of said conduct will be overlooked. Dressler cites the example of a woman who trespasses by entering another person's home in order to avoid a tornado.[18] The superior interest in this instance is the preservation of human life; clearly a human life is more valuable than someone's privacy interest.

In some instances, otherwise criminal conduct is justified under a **moral rights theory**. If, for example, Julia shoots and kills Heather because Heather first tries to stab Julia, arguably Julia has a moral right to defend herself because of Heather's initial advance. This theory focuses on the threat that a criminal's conduct poses to an otherwise innocent person. A "moral rights" theory of justification essentially acts as a default, or base condition. That is, if a defendant successfully asserts a justification defense, if there is no superior interest, and if there is no public benefit, then the otherwise criminal act is justified on moral rights grounds.

public benefit theory A theory underlying justification defenses based on the idea that the allegedly criminal action benefits society.

superior interest theory A theory underlying justification defenses based on the idea that a superior interest justifies criminal conduct in some situations.

moral rights theory A theory underlying justification defenses based on the idea that an innocent person has the moral right to act for their own benefit in certain situations.

Self-Defense

self-defense A justification defense in which the defendant is permitted to act in order to prevent imminent death or bodily harm.

Self-defense is one of the more widely known criminal defenses. Self-defense is legal, in one form or another, in every state. And while courts have grappled with its exact meaning, they have yet to chip away at it significantly. Indeed, the right of a person to defend oneself was recently invigorated in the Supreme Court's controversial decision in *District of Columbia* v. *Heller*,[19] where the Court held that the U.S. Constitution's Second Amendment guarantees individuals the right to possess firearms, and to use such firearms for self-defense, among other activities. Similar rights are spelled out in nearly every state's constitution, underscoring the prominence of self-defense in the American system of criminal law.[20]

---

[17]J. Dressler, *Understanding Criminal Law*, 5th ed. (Newark, NJ: Lexis Nexis, 2009), p. 209.
[18]Ibid., p. 211.
[19]*District of Columbia* v. *Heller*, 554 U.S. ___ (2008).
[20]E. Volokh, "State Constitutional Rights of Self-Defense and Defense of Property," *Texas Review of Law and Politics*, Vol. 11(2007), p. 400.

Elements of Self-Defense

The claim of self-defense was first recognized under common law. The rule was that a nonaggressor was justified in using force against another if he or she reasonably believed that such force was necessary to prevent the unlawful use of force by an aggressor.[21] By extension, *deadly force* was authorized only if the unlawful force used by the aggressor was also of the deadly variety. Modern-day self-defense retains most of its common law origins, but with some twists and turns. There are four general requirements for a successful modern-day claim of self-defense: an unprovoked attack, imminent danger, absence of alternatives (also called "necessity"), and proportionality.

Before we get to each of these requirements, there is a particularly confusing aspect of self-defense that we must first address. Self-defense requires both a subjective and objective component. The subjective component is the *defendant's* belief that he or she is justified in using deadly force. The objective component is concerned with whether a *reasonable person* would belief the defendant's actions were justified under the circumstances. Self-defense will be available only when these two underlying "beliefs" are in place. Why? Consider this example: If Mary interpreted Steve's advance as a threat, when it was not, and killed him, Mary might otherwise be held liable for his death. However, if a reasonable person feels Mary did the right thing (e.g., she couldn't have known, perhaps in the heat of the moment, that Steve's advance was not threatening), then it makes sense that Mary escape criminal conviction. But just who is a "reasonable person"? Juries are usually called upon to make the determination, and many factors come into play.

Unprovoked Attack. Self-defense is only available in the case of an unprovoked attack. So, for example, if Bob attacks Sandy, but Sandy fights back, causing Bob to kill Sandy in self-defense, Bob will not succeed with a self-defense claim because he is the initial aggressor. He set the wheels in motion and thus should not escape criminal liability for actions that would not have occurred but for his initial attack. As one court eloquently put it, "[T]he law of self-defense is designed to afford protection to one who is beset by an aggressor and confronted by a necessity not of his own making."[22]

There is one key exception to the general rule that an aggressor cannot later claim self-defense. Simply, if the aggressor *withdraws* in some fashion and later uses force in self-defense, he or she may escape criminal liability. As Dressler puts it, "The initial aggressor in a conflict may purge himself of that status and regain the right of self-defense."[23] In order to succeed, however, the aggressor must not only withdraw but also communicate this fact, either "expressly or impliedly," to the intended victim.[24] Here is a simple example: Assume Trey points a 9mm pistol at David, but that David responds by pointing a .44 magnum at Trey. Seeing that he is outgunned, Trey says, "ok, you win," and sets his gun down. If David then chambers a round, Trey may be able to claim self-defense if he is able quickly grab his pistol and shoot David. This assumes, of course, that the other self-defense requirements are in place. For example, both Trey *and* a reasonable person would have to believe that the

---

[21]See, e.g., *State* v. *Gheen*, 41 S.W. 3d 598 (Mo. Ct. App. 2001), p. 606.
[22]*Bangs* v. *State*, 608 P.2d 1 (Alaska 1980), p. 5.
[23]Dressler, *Understanding Criminal Law*, p. 227.
[24]Ibid.

chambering of a round represented a sufficient threat to life such that Trey was entitled to respond with deadly force.

Imminent Danger.

A successful claim of self-defense can only be made in the face of an imminent threat. This was a requirement at common law and one that has carried forward to present day with little to no alterations.[25] A threat is considered imminent if it will occur "at the moment of . . . danger."[26] If a threat has subsided, then self-defense cannot be claimed.

The imminent danger requirement is sometimes likened to "necessity," the idea that force is *necessary* in order to protect one from a threat. In many situations involving an immediate threat, force is necessary, and self-defense can be reasonably claimed. If, again, David chambers a round in his .44 magnum, Trey may feel that quick action is necessary to save his life. But what if necessity and imminent danger don't match up? In other words, what if one precedes the other? Could it be necessary to use force to *prevent* an imminent attack? Some scholars certainly think so. According to Stephen Morse, "If death or serious bodily harm in the relatively near future is a virtual certainty *and* the future attack cannot be adequately defended against when it is imminent *and* if there really are *no* reasonable alternatives, traditional self-defense . . . ought to justify the pre-emptive strike."[27]

Absence of Alternatives.

Self-defense is typically justified when there are no alternatives and force is a necessity. Generally speaking, if the person threatened has the option not to use force in kind, that is the option that should be pursued. In *State* v. *Garrison*,[28] for example, the defendant disarmed a drunk man who was arguing with the defendant's sister. The drunk man then armed himself with a knife, made a threatening advance toward the defendant, at which point the defendant shot the man and killed him. An appeals court upheld his manslaughter conviction. Why? If the defendant could disarm his victim of a gun the first time, why was he so threatened by a knife the second time?

What if the would-be victim can retreat instead of use force in kind? Should he or she be required to do so? Self-defense is typically "measured against necessity,"[29] meaning that if force is not necessary, it shouldn't be used. And if there is so much as a shadow of a doubt in the defender's mind as to whether force is justified, he or she may do well to retreat, if retreat is possible, simply to avoid the possible legal ramifications that can follow even the most justifiable of self-defense actions. That said, the law in this area is complex and contradictory—and continually evolving. Most jurisdictions do *not* require retreat, and many have gone so far as to enact so-called **stand your ground laws.** Florida's law, enacted in 2005, says:

> A person who is not engaged in an unlawful activity and who is attacked in any . . . place where he has a right to be has no duty to retreat and has the right to stand his or her ground and meet force with force, including deadly force if he or she reasonably believes it is necessary to prevent death or great bodily harm to himself or another or to prevent the commission of a forcible felony.[30]

stand your ground laws A legal principle that does not require a person to retreat if they are the victim of an unprovoked attack.

---

[25]*Ha* v. *State*, 892 P.2d 184 (Alaska Ct. App. 1995), p. 191.
[26]*Sydnor* v. *State*, 776 A.2d 669 (Md. Ct. App. 2001), p. 675.
[27]S. J. Morse, "The 'New Syndrome Excuse Syndrome,'" *Criminal Justice Ethics*, Vol. 14 (1995), p. 3.
[28]*State* v. *Garrison*, 525 A.2d 498 (Conn. 1987).
[29]*State* v. *Abbott*, 174 A.2d 881 (N.J. 1961), p. 884.
[30]Fla. Stat. 776.013(3) (2008).

The 2012 shooting death of Trayvon Martin by George Zimmerman ignited significant controversy surrounding stand your ground laws in Florida and throughout the country. In light of the incident, Governor Rick Scott of Florida created a task force to review the continued necessity and validity of the State's law.[31] And in Georgia, a lawsuit was filed in federal court challenging the state's stand your ground rule as being unconstitutionally vague and applied disproportionately against minorities.[32] As of the writing of this text, the fate of these laws is still in dispute.

Some jurisdictions disagree with either the "no retreat" rule or stand your ground laws. This minority view is that all human life deserves protection and that force shouldn't be used simply because it can be. For example, Maryland courts have long required that it is the "duty of the defendant to retreat or avoid danger if such means were within his power and consistent with his safety,"[33] as have courts in other states.[34] Of the few jurisdictions that maintain a retreat requirement, they only require it when the nonaggressor can retreat to a place of *complete* safety: "Self-defense has not, by statute nor by judicial opinion, been distorted, by an unreasonable requirement of the duty to retreat, into self-destruction."[35]

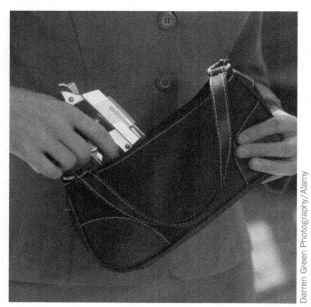

Self-defense is permissible usually only in cases of un-provoked attacks-and when danger is imminent. Use of force must be necessary and basically the last resort.

Proportionality. Subject to a few exceptions, for self-defense to apply, the nonaggressor must use no more force than is necessary to repel the aggressor. For example, if Margie (the defendant) is 5 feet 2 inches and weighs 110 pounds, and Mike (the aggressor) is 6 feet 3 inches tall and weighs 250 pounds, it may be "necessary" for Margie to use deadly force to repel Mike, even if Mike makes nothing more than an advance coupled with a threat to "tear Margie a new one." If the roles had been reversed, however, and Margie is the aggressor, then Mike would be hard-pressed to claim self-defense in the event he pulled a gun and fatally shot Margie.

Similar facts were observed in *State* v. *Wanrow*,[36] a case where the defendant was a small woman on crutches who shot and killed an unarmed drunk man who allegedly threatened to molest her child who was asleep a few feet away. Interestingly, Washington Supreme Court overturned the woman's conviction, partly because the jury was not allowed to hear a version of the argument that "women suffer from a

---

[31]Margie Menzel, "'Stand Your Ground' Panel Hears Emotional Testimony in Tallahassee," *Palm Beach Post*, http://www.palmbeachpost.com/news/news/crime-law/stand-your-ground-panel-hears-emotional-testimony/nPqkj/ (accessed July 18, 2012).
[32]Rhonda Cook, "Lawsuit Challenges Georgia's Stand Your Ground Law," *Atlanta Journal-Constitution*, http://www.ajc.com/news/georgia-government/lawsuit-challenges-georgias-stand-1411841.html (accessed July 18, 2012).
[33]*Bruce v. State*, 218 Md. 87 (1958), pp. 96–97.
[34]See, e.g., *People v. Riddle*, 649 N.W.2d 30 (Mich. 2002), p. 34.
[35]*State v. Gardner*, 104 N.W. 971 (Minn. 1905), p. 975.
[36]*State v. Wanrow*, 559 P.2d 548 (Wash. 1976).

conspicuous lack of access to training in and the means of developing those skills necessary to effectively repel a male assailant without resorting to the use of deadly weapons."[37] The court held that the trial judge should have instructed jurors of this "sex discrimination" because, if the judge had, they may have been inclined to sanction the woman's apparent overreaction.

Self-Defense Complications

A number of recent developments have complicated the law of self-defense. Many states retain "castle doctrine" laws that give people great latitude to take self-defense actions within their homes. Criminal defenses such as battered woman syndrome seem, on their face, counter to traditional self-defense rationales.

The "Castle Doctrine." A number of states, even those in which retreat is the preferable action to take when someone is threatened, recognize the so-called **castle doctrine**. Simply, the castle doctrine provides that a nonaggressor is not required to retreat from his or her own dwelling.[38] The logic is that "one should not be driven from the inviolate place of refuge that is the home."[39] In the typical situation, a dwelling is a person's place of residence, whether that be a house, a condominium, an apartment, a tent, and so on.[40] Courts have decided that even an attached porch represents a dwelling,[41] but that the common area in an apartment building does not.[42]

> **castle doctrine** A non-aggressor is not required to retreat from his or her home if attacked.

One of the problems with the castle doctrine is that killers and their victims know one another most of the time. This raises the question of whether a person who is related to or acquainted with—and maybe even lives with—a would-be killer should be able to fall back on the castle doctrine. Most of the activity in this area has revolved around domestic abuse. Courts are increasingly giving more deference to domestic violence victims, arguing, for example, that "imposing a duty to retreat from the home may adversely impact victims of domestic violence."[43] Basically, an innocent victim need not flee from a dwelling simply because the aggressor also lives there.[44]

Battered Woman Syndrome. Female victims of domestic violence who kill their partners often raise a battered woman syndrome defense. The typical situation is one in which the woman kills her partner in the heat of a fight or argument.[45] Sometimes such killings are clearly carried out in self-defense, in which case there is no need for a creative or novel claim other than straightforward self-defense. But in many situations, the traditional self-defense approach does not work because, for

---

[37]Ibid., p. 239.
[38]D. P. Boots, J. Bihari, and E. Elliott, "The State of the Castle: An Overview of Recent Trends in State Castle Doctrine Legislation and Public Policy," *Criminal Justice Review*, Vol. 34 (2009), pp. 515–535.
[39]*People v. Aiken*, 828 N.E.2d 74 (N.Y. 2005), p. 77.
[40]*State v. Marsh*, 593 N.E.2d 35 (Ohio Ct. App. 1990).
[41]*People v. Canales*, 624 N.W.2d 439 (Mich. Ct. App. 2002).
[42]*People v. Hernandez*, 774 N.E.2d 198 (N.Y. 2002).
[43]*Weiand v. State*, 732 So.2d 1044 (Fla. 1999), p. 1052.
[44]See, e.g., *State v. Glowacki*, 630 HN.W.2d 392 (Minn. 2001), p. 400.
[45]H. Maguigan, "Battered Women and Self-Defense: Myths and Misconceptions in Current Reform Proposals," *University of Pennsylvania Law Review*, Vol. 140 (1991), pp. 394–397.

example, the woman may shoot her husband for beating her, raising proportionality concerns. Should she then be convicted of homicide? Perhaps not. In order to address situations like this, female defendants have sought to introduce evidence of prior abuse in order to justify the actions.

In a minority of cases, female abuse victims kill their abusers while the abusers are asleep, passed out, or during periods of calm.[46] These situations are more complicated because they *really* run afoul of traditional self-defense concepts. Most notably, there is no imminent danger posed from an abuser who is asleep. But does this mean abuse victims must wait until their lives are threatened in order to take action? This is a tough question to answer. Courts often allow the defendant to introduce evidence of prior abuse, and some even permit expert witnesses to testify about battered woman syndrome, but there are no clear rules in this area. What's more, the caselaw is contradictory and confusing. Some courts have permitted juries to consider the possibility of self-defense in nonconfrontational killings.[47] Others have not.[48] In terms of likely verdicts, victims of domestic abuse are more likely to succeed with traditional self-defense claims in confrontational killings than they are with battered woman syndrome claims in nonconfrontational killings.

Defense of Others

defense of others A justification defense in which a person is justified using force to protect another from the unlawful use of force by an aggressor.

The criminal law also recognizes a **defense of others** claim. It is essentially an extension of the defense of self-defense we just introduced. The rule is that a person is justified using force to protect another from the unlawful use of force by an aggressor.[49] The typical defense of others claim involves a third party intervening on behalf of a crime victim who cannot defend him- or herself. Recently, however, we have seen some atypical arguments. For example, in *State* v. *Aguillard*,[50] abortion protestors argued that they were entitled to break the law under a defense of others theory because the unborn were unable to protect themselves. The court rejected the argument:

> The "defense of others" specifically limits the use of force or violence in protection of others to situations where the person attacked would have been justified in using such force or violence to protect himself. In view of *Roe* v. *Wade* and the provisions of the Louisiana abortion statute, defense of others as justification for the defendants' otherwise criminal conduct is not available in these cases. Since abortion is legal in Louisiana, the defendants had no legal right to protect the unborn by means not even available to the unborn themselves.[51]

See the accompanying Court Decision for more on the defense of others. In it we take a look at the case of *People* v. *Kurr*, where a mother argued that the defense of others also applied to the protection of unborn children.

---

[46]See, e.g., *State* v. *Norman*, 378 S.E.2d 8 (N.C. 1989).
[47]See, e.g., *State* v. *Leidholm*, 334 N.W.2d 811 (N.D. 1982).
[48]See, e.g., *State* v. *Stewart*, 763 P.2d 572 (Kan. 1988).
[49]*Commonwealth* v. *Martin*, 341 N.E.2d 885 (Mass. 1976).
[50]*State* v. *Aguillard*, 567 So.2d 674 (La. 1990).
[51]Ibid., p. 676.

**COURT
DECISION**

The Logic behind the Defense of Others

People v. Kurr
654 N.W.2d 651 (Mich. App. 2002)

Decision: The defense of others extends to a mother protecting her unborn fetus and failure to provide a jury instruction on the matter violates a defendant's constitutional rights.

Reason: . . . Defendant stabbed Pena on October 9, 1999. According to a Kalamazoo police officer, defendant told him that she and Pena had argued that day over Pena's cocaine use. Defendant told the officer that Pena subsequently punched her two times in the stomach and that she warned Pena not to hit her because she was carrying his babies. Defendant stated that when Pena came toward her again, she stabbed him in the chest. He died as a result of the stab wound.

. . . Defendant now argues that because the trial court did not instruct the jury on the defense of others theory, she was denied her constitutional right to present a defense. In order to determine whether the court should indeed have given the defense of others instruction, we must initially decide the purely legal question whether a nonviable fetus constitutes an "other" in the context of this defense. With certain restrictions, we conclude that it does.

"In Michigan, the killing of another person in self-defense is justifiable homicide if the defendant honestly and reasonably believes that his life is in imminent danger or that there is a threat of serious bodily harm." *People* v. *Heflin,* 434 Mich. 482 (1990). Deadly force may also be used "to repel an imminent forcible sexual penetration." *People* v. *Barker,* 437 Mich. 161, 163 (1991). Case law in Michigan also allows a person to use deadly force in defense of another . . .

We conclude that in this state, the defense should also extend to the protection of a fetus, viable or nonviable, from an assault against the mother, and we base this conclusion primarily on the fetal protection act adopted by the Legislature in 1998. This act punishes individuals who harm or kill fetuses or embryos under various circumstances. M.C.L. § 750.90a and 750.90b set forth penalties for harming a fetus or embryo during an intentional assault against a pregnant woman. M.C.L. § 750.90a punishes an individual for causing a miscarriage or stillbirth with malicious intent toward the fetus or embryo or for causing a miscarriage or stillbirth while acting "in wanton or willful disregard of the likelihood that the natural tendency of [his] conduct is to cause a miscarriage or stillbirth or great bodily harm to the embryo or fetus." M.C.L. § 750.90b punishes an individual for harming or killing a fetus or embryo during an intentional assault against a pregnant woman without regard to the individual's intent or recklessness concerning the fetus or embryo. M.C.L. § 750.90c punishes an individual for harming or killing a fetus or embryo during a grossly negligent act against a pregnant woman, again without regard to the individual's state of mind concerning the fetus or embryo.

(continued)

**COURT
DECISION**
(continued)

... Because the act reflects a public policy to protect even an embryo from unlawful assaultive or negligent conduct, we conclude that the defense of others concept does extend to the protection of a nonviable fetus from an assault against the mother. We emphasize, however, that the defense is available *solely* in the context of an assault against the mother. Indeed, the Legislature has *not* extended the protection of the criminal laws to embryos existing outside a woman's body, i.e., frozen embryos stored for future use, and we therefore *do not* extend the applicability of the defense of others theory to situations involving these embryos. ... Reversed and remanded.

Defense of Property and Habitation

The old saying that "a man's home is his castle" forms the foundation for defense of property. As the court in one classic case observed,

> The house of everyone is to him his castle and fortress, as well for his defense against injury and violence, as for his repose; and although the life of a man is a thing precious and favored in law . . . if thieves come to a man's house to rob him, or murder, and the owner or his servants kill any of the thieves in defense of himself and his house, it is not felony and he shall lose nothing.[52]

Property includes not just habitation, but anything a person can claim ownership to. We will discuss each in a separate subsection because, though they overlap to some extent, there are important differences in terms of what people can do to protect their property and protect themselves in their places of habitation.

Defense of Property

In general, a person is entitled to use *nondeadly* force to protect his or her possession of property. No more force may be used than is necessary to defend one's possessory interest in property. Also, other options should often be considered first. For example, it is advisable, if it is possible, to ask the would-be dispossessor to desist.[53]

Deadly force cannot be used in defense of property. Why? Because sanctioning as much would put property interests ahead of human life. One court offered this reasoning:

> When it is said that a man may rightfully use as much force as is necessary for the protection of his person and property, it should be recollected that this rule is subject to this most important modification, that he shall not, except in extreme cases, endanger human life or do great bodily harm. It is not every right of person, and still less of property, that can lawfully be asserted, or every wrong that may rightfully be redressed by extreme remedies. There is a recklessness—a wanton disregard of humanity and social duty in taking or endeavoring to take, the life of a fellow-being,

---

[52]*State v. Mitcheson*, 560 P.2d 1120 (Utah 1977), p. 1122.
[53]See, e.g., *State v. Elliot*, 11 N.H. 540 (1841), pp. 544–545.

in order to save one's self from a comparatively slight wrong, which is essentially wicked, and the law abhors. You may not kill, because you cannot otherwise effect your object, although the object sought to be effected is right.[54]

Even if deadly force is the *only* option available, it cannot be used in defense of property.[55] However, deadly force may be justifiable if a defense-of-property situation evolves into a self-defense or defense of others situations. For example, assume Tammy catches Keith in the act of stealing her lawnmower and yells, "Get out of here, that's not yours!" Then assume Keith pulls out a knife and runs toward Tammy. She would likely be able to claim self-defense if she drew her gun and shot Keith. In this situation, however, she is no longer defending the lawnmower, but rather herself.

Defense of Habitation

People are given considerably more latitude to protect their places of habitation—even with deadly force. At common law, people were permitted to use deadly force whenever it was necessary to prevent someone from unlawfully entering the dwelling.[56] The defense could be invoked even if the intruder was unarmed and posed no threat to the dweller. As time went on, restrictions were imposed governing the defense of habitation. One approach is to limit the use of deadly force to situations in which the intruder not only enters unlawfully but also intends to injure or harm an occupant, or commit a felony therein.[57] Some jurisdictions have restricted defense of habitation even further, limiting it to situations in which either the dweller's life is threatened or a *forcible* felony, not just any felony, is likely to be committed.[58] Forcible felonies include such offenses as "murder, robbery, burglary, rape or arson."[59]

Most defense of habitation statutes are aimed at giving people the authority to *prevent* unlawful access to their dwellings. But what if the intruder has already gained access? For example, assume you wake up to find a burglar already in your house. Can you use deadly force? It would seem so, but the courts are divided. Some states do not permit deadly force in this instance—for defense of habitation.[60] Only if the situation evolves into one in which self-defense can be claimed is deadly force authorized. In contrast, some states permit deadly force for defense of habitation after the intruder has accessed the property. Illinois allows such force "to prevent or terminate" another's unlawful entry.[61] The word *terminate* is important, as it suggests the unauthorized intruder has already entered the property.

make my day laws State laws that provide homeowners with considerable latitude to use force to defense their dwelling from unauthorized intruders.

"Make My Day" Laws. Needless to say, the law surrounding defense of habitation is somewhat muddy. The rules depend on where you live. Even the statutes within specific jurisdictions are not always entirely clear. To clear up the confusion, some states have enacted so-called **make my day laws,** named after the Clint Eastwood's

---

[54]*State* v. *Morgan,* 25 N.C. 186 (N.C. 2000), p. 193.
[55]*People* v. *Ceballos,* 526 P.2d 241 (Cal. 1974), p. 249.
[56]*State* v. *Reid,* 210 N.E.2d 142 (Ohio Ct. Ap. 1965).
[57]See, e.g., *State* v. *Pendleton,* 567 N.W.2d 265 (Minn. 1997).
[58]*Crawford* v. *State,* 190 A.2d 538 (Md. 1963), p. 542.
[59]Ibid.
[60]See, e.g., *State* v. *Brookshire,* 353 S.W.2d 681 (Mo. 1962).
[61]See N.C. Gen. Stat. Section 14-51.1 (2004); also see *People* v. *Stombaugh,* 284 N.E.2d 640 (Ill. 1992).

character, Dirty Harry Callahan, in the 1983 film *Sudden Impact*. These laws, which are similar in character to the "stand your ground" and "castle doctrine" laws discussed earlier in this chapter, give considerable latitude to people whose dwelling is entered by an unauthorized intruder. Colorado has perhaps the most "generous" statute of this sort. Its law provides:

1. The general assembly hereby recognizes that the citizens of Colorado have a right to expect absolute safety within their own homes.

2. . . . any occupant of a dwelling is justified in using any degree of physical force, including deadly physical force, against another person when that other person has made an unlawful entry into the dwelling, and when the occupant has a reasonable belief that such other person has committed a crime in the dwelling in addition to the uninvited entry, or is committing or intends to commit a crime against a person or property in addition to the uninvited entry, and when the occupant reasonably believes that such other person might use any physical force, no matter how slight, against any occupant.

3. Any occupant of a dwelling using physical force, including *deadly physical force*, in accordance with the provisions of subsection (2) of this section shall be immune from criminal prosecution for the use of such force.

4. Any occupant of a dwelling using physical force, including deadly physical force, in accordance with the provisions of subsection (2) of this section shall be immune from any civil liability for injuries or death resulting from the use of such force.[62]

Note that Colorado's make my day law is not unlike Florida's stand your ground law discussed earlier in the self-defense section. The difference is that make my day laws are premised on a defense of habitation theory, not a self-defense theory. Note the "uninvited entry" language in Colorado's statute, whereas Florida's stand your ground law referenced protection from "death or great bodily harm."

Spring Guns and Booby Traps. Many unauthorized entries occur in uninhabited dwellings. What, then, can a person do to protect her property while she is away? Certain standard steps, such as installation of a home security system, can be taken. But what about more extreme measures? For example, what if Caty lets her pet cobra have run of the house while she is away at work? If the snake bites an intruder, will Caty be able to claim defense of property? Probably not. This is a twist on a variety of spring gun cases. A spring gun is a gun that is set up to fire as someone attempts unlawful entry into a dwelling. In the simplest arrangement, the gun will be affixed to some sort of base and pointed toward an entry point, most likely a door. The trigger will be rigged to fire as soon as the door is opened. In general, people are not authorized to use spring guns or any other mechanical device of the sort because of the risks they pose.[63]

The most often-cited spring gun case is *People* v. *Ceballos*.[64] Don Ceballos was found guilty of assault with a deadly weapon after he aimed a .22-caliber pistol at

---

[62]Col. Rev. Stat. Section 18-1-704.5.
[63]*People* v. *Ceballos*, 526 P.2d 241 (Cal. 1974), p. 244.
[64]Ibid.

his garage door from the inside and set it to fire if the door opened several inches. A 16-year-old boy forced open the lock on the outside of the garage door and gained entry, only to be shot in the face by the Ceballos' spring gun. A California appellate court affirmed his conviction, as did the Supreme Court of California, which offered the following in support of its decision:

> Allowing persons, at their own risk, to employ deadly mechanical devices imperils the lives of children, firemen and policemen acting within the scope of their employment, and others. Where the actor is present, there is always the possibility he will realize that deadly force is not necessary, but deadly mechanical devices are without mercy or discretion. Such devices "are silent instrumentalities of death. They deal death and destruction to the innocent as well as the criminal intruder without the slightest warning. The taking of human life [or infliction of great bodily injury] by such means is brutally savage and inhuman."[65]

It is important to note that no one was home. Had the home been occupied, then the situation would have been different. Most likely, a self-defense or defense of habitation issues would have arisen.

Law Enforcement Defense

law enforcement defense
Defense available to police or other authorized agents for actions committed in the course of law enforcement.

The **law enforcement defense** extends only to those people tasked with and legally authorized to enforce laws. More often than not, those people are police officers or their equivalents. In some limited situations, private persons may be authorized to enforce the law—and thus benefit from a law enforcement defense if they succeed in doing so. For example, the common law authorizes people to make "citizen arrests" for certain crimes committed in their presence. In such instances, the arresting citizen may be charged with false imprisonment, but if he can convince a court that the arrest was justified under the circumstances, he will likely escape criminal liability.

Citizen enforcement activities have been somewhat curtailed over the years. Today, the right of citizens to use deadly force for crime prevention purposes—or to effect and arrest—is limited to forcible and otherwise "atrocious" felonies.[66] Why? Lawmakers are justifiably (no pun intended) concerned with "uncontrolled vigilantism and anarchistic actions . . . [and] the danger of death or injury of innocent persons at the hands of untrained volunteers using firearms."[67] Our concern here is mostly with the law enforcement defense as it is extended to sworn peace officers—federal, state, and local.

The law enforcement defense is different from other justification defenses. In self-defense situations, for example, the defendant goes on trial and claims self-defense at trial—prosecutors often default to criminal charges. In contrast, law enforcement officials who use nondeadly or deadly force rarely go on trial. When an officer discharges her gun, an internal departmental investigation most likely takes

---

[65]Ibid, p. 244; quoting *State* v. *Plumlee*, 149 So. 425 (La 1933), p. 430.
[66]See, e.g., *Laney* v. *State*, 361 S.E.2d 841 (Ga. Ct. App. 1987); *Holmes* v. *State*, 543 S.E.2d 688 (Ga. 2001).
[67]*Commonwealth* v. *Klein*, 363 N.E.2d 1313 (Mass. 1977), pp. 1317–1318.

place. Only in cases where it is fairly clear the officer was "in the wrong" will criminal charges be filed. Much of the discussion surrounding the law enforcement defense, then, hinges on the constitutionality of the officer's conduct. Two key Supreme Court decisions offer guidance.

Nondeadly Force

Law enforcement officials are authorized to use nondeadly force to prevent a crime, stop a crime while it is being committed, or make an arrest. The Supreme Court's 1989 decision in *Graham* v. *Connor*[68] set the standard for evaluating nondeadly force claims. The Court held that

> all claims that law enforcement officers have used excessive force—deadly or not—in the course of an arrest, investigatory stop, or other "seizure" of a free citizen should be analyzed under the Fourth Amendment and its "reasonableness" standard.

The Court also said that whether deadly force has been used appropriately should be judged from the perspective of a reasonable officer on the scene and not with the benefit of 20/20 hindsight. The justices wrote, "The calculus of reasonableness must embody allowance for the fact that police officers are often forced to make split-second judgments—in circumstances that are tense, uncertain, and rapidly evolving—about the amount of force that is necessary in a particular situation."[69]

In helping to decide what a reasonable police officer would do, courts need to consider three factors: the severity of the crime, whether the suspect poses a threat, and whether the suspect is resisting and/or attempting to flee the scene. Generally, if the crime in question is a serious one, and the suspect is dangerous or resists arrest, the suspect will have difficulty prevailing with an excessive force claim.

Depending on the circumstances, a police officer may be entitled to the law enforcement defense.

ivanfff/fotolia

---

[68]*Graham* v. *Connor*, 490 U.S. 386, 396–397 (1989).
[69]Ibid.

Deadly Force

The 1985 U.S. Supreme Court case of *Tennessee* v. *Garner*[70] specified the conditions under which deadly force could be used in the apprehension of suspected felons. Edward Garner, a 15-year-old suspected burglar, was shot to death by Memphis police after he refused their order to halt and attempted to climb over a chain-link fence. In an action initiated by Garner's father, who claimed that his son's constitutional rights had been violated, the Court held that the use of deadly force by the police to prevent the escape of a fleeing felon could be justified only where the suspect could reasonably be thought to represent a significant threat of serious injury or death to the public or to the officer and where deadly force is necessary to effect the arrest. In reaching its decision, the Court declared that "[t]he use of deadly force to prevent the escape of *all* felony suspects, whatever the circumstances, is constitutionally unreasonable."

More specifically, the U.S. Supreme Court ruled that deadly force may be used when two criteria are present: (1) It is necessary to prevent the suspect's escape, and (2) the officer has probable cause to believe the suspect poses a serious threat of death or serious physical injury to other people or police officers. Three justices dissented, noting that the statute struck down by the majority "assist[s] the police in apprehending suspected perpetrators of serious crimes and provide[s] notice that a lawful police order to stop and submit to arrest may not be ignored with impunity."[71]

Necessity

necessity (i.e., choice of evils) defense A justification defense in which the defendant commits a crime out of necessity or two avoid a greater evil.

In general, for a defense of **necessity (i.e., choice of evils) defense** to succeed, five conditions must be in place:

1. a threat of
2. imminent injury to [a] person or property
3. for which there are no (reasonable) alternatives except the commission of the crime;
4. the defendant's acts must prevent an equal or more serious harm; [and]
5. the defendant must not have created the conditions of his own [doing].[72]

A defense of necessity will likely succeed, for example, if a person drives on a suspended license, a relatively minor crime, to take a sick loved one to the hospital.[73] Note that the choice here is not a choice between *crimes*, as failure to take a loved one to the hospital is not necessarily criminal (although it could be, especially if there is a degree of negligence on the part of the loved one). Likewise, a woman who forges a check in order to obtain food out of economic necessity does not commit a crime

---

[70]*Tennessee* v. *Garner*, 471 U.S. 1 (1985).
[71]Ibid., p. 28.
[72]Singer and LaFond, *Criminal Law: Examples and Explanations*, p. 429.
[73]*State* v. *Baker*, 579 A.2d 479 (Vt. 1990).

if she goes without food. Yet some courts have noted that "economic necessity alone cannot support a choice of crime,"[74] so whether the defense will succeed depends heavily on the circumstances of the case.

Necessity and Homicide

Can homicide be justified on necessity grounds? In the movie *Outbreak*, starring Dustin Hoffman and Morgan Freeman, many residents of a small town were infected with a virulent strain of the Ebola virus. Military officials authorized a bomb drop that would have wiped out the town, thus ensuring the virus could not spread. Although the bombing was not ultimately carried out, assume that it had. Would the killing of a few have been justified on the grounds that millions, if not billions, of lives could have been saved? This may seem like the stuff of Hollywood, but similar dilemmas have arisen in some classic cases.

For example, in the 1884 case of *Regina* v. *Dudley* and *Stephens*,[75] three men and a boy were stranded at sea in a lifeboat. After the boy became ill from drinking seawater, and after assuming they would not be saved any time soon, the men killed the boy to eat his flesh so that they could survive. Four days later, they were saved. They raised a defense of necessity, but they were convicted of murder and sentenced to death; however, their sentences were ultimately reduced to six months' imprisonment. In another classic case, 14 passengers were thrown out of a lifeboat because it began to sink.[76] The survivors were prosecuted for murder, but ultimately convicted of manslaughter. Again, the necessity defense failed (at least as a perfect defense).

See the accompanying Court Decision for more on the defense of necessity. In it, we take a look at the case of *Commonwealth* v. *Leno* decided in 1993.

COURT DECISION

The Logic behind the Necessity Defense

Commonwealth v. *Harry W. Leno, Jr., et al.*
616 N.E.2d 453 (Mass. 1993)

Decision: The necessity defense is only available for the prevention of an imminent danger, not one that is "debatable or speculative." The possible spread of AIDS through drug use with dirty needles is not an imminent danger.

Reason: Massachusetts is one of ten States that prohibit distribution of hypodermic needles without a prescription. In the face of those statutes the defendants operated a needle exchange program in an effort to combat the spread of acquired immunodeficiency syndrome (AIDS). As a result, the defendants were charged with and convicted of (1) unauthorized possession of instruments to administer controlled

(continued)

---

[74]*People* v. *Fontes*, 89 P.3d 484 (Colo. App. 2003).
[75]*Regina* v. *Dudley and Stephens*, 14 Q.B.D. 273 (1884).
[76]*United States* v. *Holmes*, 26 F.Cas. 360 (C.C.E.D. Pa. 1842).

COURT DECISION
(continued)

substances, and (2) unlawful distribution of an instrument to administer controlled substances . . .

The defendants do not deny that they violated the provisions of the statutes restricting the possession and distribution of hypodermic needles; rather, they contend that the judge's refusal to instruct the jury on the defense of necessity was error. We disagree.

"[T]he application of the defense [of necessity] is limited to the following circumstances: (1) the defendant is faced with a clear and imminent danger, not one which is debatable or speculative; (2) the defendant can reasonably expect that his [or her] action will be effective as the direct cause of abating the danger; (3) there is [no] legal alternative which will be effective in abating the danger; and (4) the Legislature has not acted to preclude the defense by a clear and deliberate choice regarding the values at issue." *Commonwealth* v. *Schuchardt*, 408 Mass. 347, 349 (1990). "A defendant is entitled to an instruction on necessity 'only if there is evidence that would warrant a reasonable doubt whether [the defendants' actions were] justified as a choice between evils.'" *Schuchardt, supra* 408 Mass. at 349. We have emphasized that a person asserting the necessity defense must demonstrate that the danger motivating his or her unlawful conduct is imminent, and that he or she acted out of necessity at all times that he or she engaged in the unlawful conduct.

. . . The prevention of possible future harm does not excuse a current systematic violation of the law in anticipation of the eventual over-all benefit to the public. The defendants did not show that the danger they sought to avoid was clear and imminent, rather than debatable or speculative . . .

The defendants' argument is that, in their view, the prescription requirement for possession and distribution of hypodermic needles and syringes is both ineffective and dangerous. The Legislature, however, has determined that it wants to control the distribution of drug-related paraphernalia and their use in the consumption of illicit drugs. That public policy is entitled to deference by courts. Whether a statute is wise or effective is not within the province of courts. . . . Citizens who disagree with the Legislature's determination of policy are not without remedies. "[T]he popular initiative is coextensive with the Legislature's law-making power under Part II, c. 1, § 1 . . . ." *Paisner* v. *Attorney Gen.*, 390 Mass. 593, 601 (1983). Thus, the defendants did not meet the requirement that there be no legal alternative to abate the danger.

The defendants argue that the increasing number of AIDS cases constitutes a societal problem of great proportions, and that their actions were an effective means of reducing the magnitude of that problem; they assert that their possession, transportation and distribution of hypodermic needles eventually will produce an over-all reduction in the spread of HIV and in the future incidence of AIDS. The defendants' argument raises the issue of jury nullification, not the defense of necessity.

consent A justification defense in which the victim voluntarily agrees to physical contact with the defendant, such as in the case of rape.

Consent

The defendant's actions may be justified in certain circumstances if the victim consented to the activity or physical contact. **Consent** *may* serve as justification in four situations:

1. No serious injury results.
2. The injury happens in a sporting event.
3. The consenting party benefits from the conduct in question (e.g., a doctor performs surgery on a consenting patient).
4. The conduct is sexual.[77]

Importantly, consent can serve as a justification defense for these actions, but only if it is:

1. Given by someone who is legally competent to give consent (i.e., of proper age),
2. Fully understood (e.g., the person giving consent does not suffer from a mental disease or defect), and
3. Voluntary (not induced by force or deception).

Courts are hesitant to excuse criminal conduct with a successful consent defense. For example, in *State* v. *Hiott*,[78] Richard Hiott was convicted of third-degree assault after his friend, Jose, was hit in the eye while the two were shooting BB guns at each other. Hiott claimed that Jose consented, that the two were shooting guns at each other voluntarily, and that they were engaged in a legitimate game. An appellate court disagreed, holding that "[s]hooting BB guns at each other is not a generally accepted game or athletic contest; the activity has no generally accepted rules; and the activity is not characterized by the common use of protective devices or clothing."[79]

YOUR DECISION

1. Paul Matthews was a private security guard at the Quick-E-Mart grocery store in Compton, California. One afternoon while Paul was on duty, two armed men entered the store and demanded money from the cashier. Armed only with pepper spray, Paul was initially paralyzed with fear and unable to respond. As the criminals were fleeing from the store, however, they also decided to take Paul's new iPad. Fearing the criminals would escape with his iPad before the police arrived, Paul chased after the gunmen, sprayed them with pepper spray, wrestled one of the guns away, and shot both men. Can Paul use a law enforcement defense?
2. Kathy and Mark set off in late fall on a romantic camping trip on the Appalachian Trail. Mark, however, was not very skilled at camping and forgot to pack any type of tent or sleeping bag. As night fell, the two began to fear they would freeze to death without shelter. They stumbled upon a small cabin and broke a window to gain entry. Once inside, they started a fire, helped themselves to a few cans of SPAM and beans, and drank a bottle of fine aged scotch they found in the

---

[77] G. Fletcher, *Rethinking Criminal Law* (Boston, MA: Little, Brown, 1978), p. 770.
[78] *State* v. *Hiott*, 987 P.2d 135 (Wash. App. 1999).
[79] Ibid.

pantry. A neighbor noticed the smoke from the chimney and called the police. Mark and Kathy were charged with trespassing. Are they entitled to the choice of evils defense?

Summary

- There are three main reasons for justification defenses: public benefit, superior interest, and moral rights.
- There are four general requirements for a successful modern-day claim of self-defense: an unprovoked attack, imminent danger, absence of alternatives, and proportionality.
- Most jurisdictions do not require retreat, and many have gone so far as to enact so-called stand your ground laws.
- Castle doctrine laws, in the states that have them, provide that a nonaggressor is not required to retreat from his or her own dwelling before being able to use force in self-defense.
- Battered woman syndrome rarely succeeds as a defense when the abuser is killed when he poses no immediate danger (e.g., is passed out).
- The defense of others rule holds that a person is justified using force to protect another from the unlawful use of force by an aggressor.
- In general, a person is entitled to use *nondeadly* force to protect his or her possession of property. No more force may be used than is necessary to defend one's possessory interest in property. Deadly force cannot be used in defense of property.
- People are given considerably more latitude to protect their places of habitation—even with deadly force. Some states have enacted so-called make my day laws that sanction deadly force in protection of habitation.
- The law enforcement defense extends only those people tasked with and legally authorized to enforce laws. More often than not, those people are police officers or their equivalents.
- Today, the right of citizens to use deadly force for crime prevention purposes—or to effect and arrest—is limited to forcible and otherwise "atrocious" felonies.
- The 1985 U.S. Supreme Court case of *Tennessee* v. *Garner* prohibited the use of deadly force against unarmed fleeing felons.
- The necessity defense, also called the choice of evils defense, justifies certain types of criminal activity when it cannot be avoided.
- For a defense of necessity to succeed, five conditions must be in place: (1) a threat of (2) imminent injury to [a] person or property (3) for which there are no (reasonable) alternatives except the commission of the crime; (4) the defendant's acts must prevent an equal or more serious harm; [and] (5) the defendant must not have created the conditions of his own [doing].
- Claims of necessity generally fail in cases of homicide.
- A defendant's actions may be justified in certain circumstances if the victim consented to the activity or physical contact.

EXCUSE DEFENSES

Learning Objectives

- **Summarize the conditions of the defense of duress.**
- **Describe the intoxication defense.**
- **Summarize what constitutes entrapment.**
- **Summarize defenses based on age/immaturity.**
- **Summarize methods by which some courts treat juveniles as adults.**
- **Describe the insanity defense and the controversy surrounding it.**
- **Distinguish between and offer examples of physiological, psychological, and sociological excuse defenses.**

CORE CONCEPTS

In the last module, we introduced justification defenses, those in which the offender accepts responsibility, but argues that the commission of a crime was appropriate under the circumstances. Here we turn such thinking on its head. With excuse defenses, the offender argues that there was something "wrong" with him or her at the time of the crime. A defendant who asserts an excuse defense makes one of three claims: the action was involuntary, the action was the product of a cognitive deficiency (such as insanity), or the action resulted from a volitional deficiency, meaning that an outside force compelled the action.

Excuse defenses, while controversial, are essential. Consider the case of Daryl Renard Atkins who, armed with a handgun, abducted a man, robbed him of the money he was carrying, drove him to an ATM machine and forced him to withdraw cash at gunpoint, and then took him to an isolated location and shot him eight times, killing him. Most people would agree Atkins should have been held accountable for these cruel actions. Indeed, he was convicted of capital murder and sentenced to death. Case closed, right? Not so fast. It turns out Atkins had a full-scale IQ of 59. So struck it was by Atkins's case, the Supreme Court ruled that it would be cruel and unusual punishment to execute someone like him who is "mildly mentally retarded."[80] Atkins was not set free, but the Court's decision reaffirmed the important role that mental state plays in the criminal-law context.

Reasons for Excuse Defenses

There are three main reasons for excuse defenses.[81] The first is concerned with deterrence. Namely, if a person cannot be deterred, what is the point of punishing him or her? Returning to the earlier Atkins's case, would it have been sensible to execute

---

[80] *Atkins v. Virginia*, 536 U.S. 304 (2002).
[81] J. Dressler, *Understanding Criminal Law*, 5th ed. (San Francisco: Lexis-Nexis, 2009), pp. 211–214.

him if he could not "appreciate" his actions? More generally, if a person cannot grasp that what he or she did is wrong (not because of ignorance, but because of some deficiency), then no amount of criminal law or punishment will be capable of stopping that person. This requires weighing two competing sets of interests—those of society in catching and punishing lawbreakers and those of the undeterrable actor. In some cases, the pain inflicted on the undeterrable actor may deserve more weight than society's concern with catching criminals.

Another reason for excuse defenses is a lack of causation. Recall that causation is a core requirement in certain criminal offenses (particularly result crimes). If a defendant's conduct is *caused* by factors beyond her control, does it make sense to punish her for it? Perhaps you saw the first *Saw* movie. Jigsaw, the villain, rigged a "reverse bear trap" that would have killed the intended victim, Amanda, if she did not unlock it in time. The key, unfortunately, was in the stomach of a man lying on the floor nearby. Desperate, Amanda violently cut open the man's stomach, retrieved the key, freed herself from the trap, and presumably killed the man in the process. Would it have been fair to hold Amanda criminally responsible for his death? Almost certainly not. An argument could be made that Jigsaw forced her hand, leaving her no choice but to commit a homicide in order to save her own life.

The third reason for excuse defenses lies in the area of moral blameworthiness. Simply, if the offender is not a "bad character," one who *deserves* punishment for his actions, then the actions should be excused. In most situations, we simply infer character from one's actions; criminals are bad and should be punished. But as is clear by now, offenders are not created equal. Some simply cannot understand or appreciate what they do, meaning their character is "innocent" on some level. Consider the toddler who bites or hits his sister. Should he be charged with assault? Of course not. The child's "innocence" precludes a finding that he formulated the intent to hurt his sibling.

Duress

duress An excuse defense applicable when the defendant is forced to commit a crime by threat or force.

Duress is defined as compulsion by threat or force. Returning to the *Saw* example in the previous section, Amanda was arguably under duress because, had she not freed herself from the trap, she would have died—and violently. Her duress would have excused her from criminal liability. Thomas Hobbes put it this way:

> If a man, by the terror of present death, be compelled to do a fact against the law, he is totally excused, because no law can oblige a man to abandon his own preservation. And supposing such a law were obligatory, yet a man would reason thus: *If I do it not, I die presently; if I do it, I die afterwards; therefore by doing it, there is time of life gained* . . . .[82]

Duress versus Necessity

Duress is distinct from necessity, the latter of which was introduced in the last module. A necessity defense is raised in cases when the defendant argues that she chose between

[82]Thomas Hobbes, *Leviathan*, Pt. II, ch. 27 (1651).

the lesser of two evils. Duress basically takes the "choice" out of the equation; the defendant argues that she was *forced* by a coercer to engage in an unlawful act.

Another way to understand the difference between the two concerns *who* should be held responsible. In a necessity situation, there is no blameworthy actor if it turns out the defendant's choice was one society is prepared to accept. If Larry broke into John's isolated cabin in order to avoid freezing to death, no one other than Larry could potentially be held liable. If Larry did the right thing under the circumstances (the greater evil being death from freezing), then *no one* will be held to answer for his actions. In a duress situation, however, there is often some other actor who forced the defendant's hand. Returning once again to the *Saw* example, that person was Jigsaw, the villain.

Elements of the Defense

The elements of a duress defense depend on the crime in question. For all *nonhomicide* offenses, there are five general elements:

1. The defendant "acted under the compulsion or threat of imminent infliction of death or great bodily injury";
2. the defendant "reasonably believed that death or great bodily harm would have been inflicted upon him [or another] had he not acted as he did";
3. the compulsion or coercion was "imminent and impending and of such a nature as to induce a well-grounded apprehension of death or serious bodily harm if the act is not done";
4. there was "no reasonably opportunity to escape the compulsion without committing the crime"; and
5. the defendant must not have put him- or herself in a situation where it was "probable that he would have been subjected to compulsion or threat."[83]

Each of these requires a little clarification. First, for a duress defense to succeed, the threat must come from another human being. The duress defense will not be available if the defendant claims an animal, an inanimate object, or anything else coerced him or her to commit a crime. So what if Barbara commits criminal trespass by driving her vehicle into another person's carport in order to avoid impending hail damage? She will not be able to claim duress, but she could almost certainly claim necessity (see previous module).

Second, the threat must be directed at either the defendant or a member of his or her family. It is *possible* that the defense could extend to other individuals, but such cases are few and far between.[84] The typical duress situation is one in which the defendant fears for his or her life—or that of a family member, such as a child.

Third, it is important that the threat involve death or great bodily harm, not some lesser degree of force. For example, if Larry threatened to fire Dave if Dave does not dump hazardous waste down the drain, the duress defense will not be available.[85]

---

[83]*State* v. *Crawford*, 861 P.2d 791 (Kan. 1993), p. 797; see also *People* v. *Merhige*, 180 N.W. 418 (Mich. 1920), p. 422.
[84]See, e.g., *United States* v. *Haney*, 287 F.3d 1266 (10th Cir. 2002).
[85]See, e.g., *People* v. *Ricker*, 262 N.E.2d 456 (Ill. 1970).

Fourth, to say the threat is "imminent and impending" means that it must be operating on the actor *at the time of the crime*. This does not mean, however, that the threat and the crime take place at the same exact moment in time. The only requirement is that the threat be operating on the defendant's mind at the time of the crime.

Fifth, the possibility of escape should not be taken lightly. Consider *State* v. *Crawford*,[86] a case involving a drug-addicted defendant who asserted a duress defense after allegedly committing various crimes at the direction of his dealer (in order to pay his debts). The dealer was not present at the time the defendant committed the crime. An appeals court affirmed the defendant's conviction because it felt there was reasonable opportunity for the defendant to escape because he was out of sight of his dealer when he committed his crimes.

Finally, if the defendant puts himself in the situation and later claims duress, it is likely he will not succeed. Say, for example, that Leroy joins a white supremacist gang. The gang leader orders him to kill an African-American as part of his initiation. After being told he will be killed if he doesn't comply, Leroy identifies a target, kills the individual, and promptly gets caught and prosecuted for murder. Leroy will not likely succeed with a duress claim because it was his decision to join the gang in the first place.

Duress and Homicide

Duress is generally not a defense to intentional killing. Some states expressly forbid the defense in this context; some others treat it as an imperfect defense that could lead to a manslaughter conviction rather than a murder conviction. Why restrict the duress defense in this way? Why is it not an outright excuse? After all, if it is possible to claim duress in a situation where a victim was ordered to rob a bank or be killed, why would it be impermissible for the same victim to claim duress if he was ordered to take someone else's life? A California case, *People* v. *Anderson*,[87] offers at least one answer. Two men were charged with murder for killing a suspected child molester by beating her over the head with a rock. One of the men testified at trial that the other ordered him to retrieve a large rock or the other man would have "beat the shit out of him."[88] The man complied and, on appeal, claimed that he was under duress, fearing for his life because of his partner's threat. The California Supreme Court did not agree, stating,

> [W]hen confronted with an apparent kill-an-innocent-person-or-be-killed situation, a person can always choose to resist. As a practical matter, death will rarely, if ever, inevitably result from a choice not to kill.[89]

Some states, like we pointed out, recognize that duress can reduce culpability. For example, in *Wentworth* v. *State*,[90] Delores Taylor and her husband, David Wentworth, visited the home of another man, James Mosley. After having a few drinks, David accused James of having an adulterous affair with his wife Delores. At his

---

[86]Ibid.
[87]*People* v. *Anderson*, 50 P.3d 368 (Cal. 2002).
[88]Ibid., p. 370.
[89]Ibid., p. 371.
[90]*Wentworth* v. *State*, 349 A.2d 421 (Md. Ct. Spec. App. 1975).

request, Delores helped her husband find a gun and ammunition, which were located in the house. Delores then went outside and started the car once David said he was going to take both her and James for a ride. She even helped wipe fingerprints from surfaces she and her husband had touched. Soon, however, she developed second thoughts and fled to a neighbor's house. James's body was found the next day. Both husband and wife were prosecuted for murder, but Delores argued that she was under duress at the time she helped her husband and that he was "very paranoiac and was in another fit of rage" right before the killing. Even so, she was convicted of second-degree murder. She later appealed, arguing that her condition of duress could not have supported a murder conviction. The court agreed, reversed her conviction, and remanded the case for a new trial. This indicated that a manslaughter conviction may have been more appropriate under the circumstances.[91]

Intoxication

Intoxication An excuse defense applicable only if the intoxication through alcohol, drugs or other substances is involuntary.

Intoxication is formally defined as a "disturbance of mental or physical capacities resulting from the introduction of any substance into the body."[92] Note that this definition does not distinguish between alcohol and other drugs. Indeed, it is possible to become intoxicated from a substance that is neither alcohol nor a drug (e.g., paint), but we are—and most cases have been—concerned with alcohol- or drug-induced intoxication. That said, most of the popular intoxication cases referenced in criminal-law books focus on alcohol intoxication.

Intoxication is important in criminal law because it affects judgment. It is well known that controlled substances impair decision-making capabilities. For example, a person who is under the influence of alcohol may not be able to form the requisite *mens rea* to commit a crime (the person may act impulsively). And even if an intoxicated person *can* form intent, that person may not act the same way in a sober state.

Whether and how intoxication serves as a defense to criminal liability hinges on several factors. First, and most importantly, it is critical to determine whether the intoxication was voluntary or involuntary. A person who *voluntarily* becomes intoxicated will have a considerably harder time having his or her conduct "excused." Another factor is the role intoxication plays in the commission of a crime. Did it just negate *mens rea* or did it so affect the defendant to the extent he or she "blacked out" and did not even commit a voluntary act? Yet another factor is the type of offense. A strict liability crime, you will recall, requires no *mens rea*, so an intoxication defense may be impossible. In contrast, specific intent offenses are such that the defendant's intoxication can be rather important.

Voluntary Intoxication

In general, a person who voluntarily ingests an intoxicant will not succeed with a defense of intoxication. The reason is obvious: Why should a person who *chooses* to get drunk or stoned then be excused for actions committed in his or her altered

[91]Ibid., p. 428.
[92]*People* v. *Low*, 732 P.2d 622 (Colo. 1987), p. 627.

state? Even if a person voluntarily uses one substance and finds out later that it was laced or mixed with another, the defense will not succeed.

But wait, can someone then succeed with a voluntary intoxication defense if the substance used is alcohol? After all, one expects a certain amount of "purity" in a legally acquired product. Unfortunately, even voluntary alcohol intoxication almost never serves as a defense to criminal liability. We say *almost never* because a defendant can argue that intoxication weakened or eliminated the *mens rea* component of a specific intent offense. Say, for example, that an intoxicated man is arrested and charged with the specific intent offense of assault with intent to rape. He might be able to make a case that he did not *intend* to rape because of his intoxicated condition.[93] If the offense in question is of the general intent variety, then such an argument will not be permitted.[94]

Even allowing the mere argument that intoxication negates *mens rea*, however, is objectionable to some. As Supreme Court Justice Antonin Scalia once remarked,

> Disallowing consideration of voluntary intoxication has the effect of increasing the punishment for all unlawful acts ... and thereby deters drunkenness or irresponsible behavior while drunk. The rule also serves as a specific deterrent, ensuring that those who prove incapable of controlling violent impulses while voluntarily intoxicated go to prison.[95]

In the same case, Justice Sandra Day O'Connor argued, in dissent, that "where a subjective mental state [is] an element of the crime to be proved, the defense must be permitted to show, by reference to intoxication, the absence of that element."[96] But the majority in the same case upheld a Montana statute that expressly barred the introduction of intoxication evidence to disprove *mens rea*.[97] As part of its decision, the Court said, rather controversially, that "[t]he Due Process Clause does not bar States from making changes in their criminal law that have the effect of making it easier for the prosecution to obtain convictions."[98]

This case notwithstanding, some states permit evidence of intoxication, particularly in homicide cases, but only insofar as such evidence could reduce—not excuse—culpability. Intoxication *could* reduce, for example, what would otherwise be a first-degree murder conviction to one for second-degree murder.[99]

Involuntary Intoxication

A person is involuntarily intoxicated if he or she cannot be blamed for the intoxicated state. The court in *City of Minneapolis* v. *Altimus*[100] identified four circumstances in which a person is said to be involuntarily intoxicated:

1. The person is coerced to ingest an intoxicant.
2. The person accidentally ingests an intoxicant.

---

[93]See, e.g., *State* v. *Dwyer*, 757 A.2d 597 (Conn. Ct. App. 2000).
[94]See, e.g., *United States* v. *Sewell*, 252 F.3d 647 (2nd Cir. 2001).
[95]*Montana* v. *Egelhoff*, 518 U.S. 37 (1996), pp. 49–50.
[96]Ibid., p. 70.
[97]*Montana* v. *Egelhoff*, 518 U.S. 37 (1996).
[98]Ibid., p. 55.
[99]See, e.g., *State* v. *Ludlow*, 883 P.2d 1144 (Kan. 1994).
[100]*City of Minneapolis* v. *Altimus*, 238 N.W.2d 851 (Minn. 1976).

Intoxication is only a defense if it is involuntary. Voluntary intoxication, however, can potentially be used to negate the required *mens rea*.

© Aurora Photos / Alamy

3. The person becomes unexpectedly intoxicated from a prescribed medication.

4. The person suffers from "pathological intoxication," a "temporary psychotic reaction, often manifested by violence, which is triggered by consumption of alcohol by a person with a pre-disposing mental or physical condition."[101]

If a criminal defendant meets one of these conditions, he or she will be able to assert an involuntary intoxication defense and, if successful, will be entitled to full acquittal. The first three conditions are relatively straightforward; the fourth, however, is a bit complicated. To illustrate, in one case the defendant argued that he suffered from "undifferentiated schizophrenic disorder," which caused him to have adverse reactions to alcohol.[102] According to experts who testified on his behalf, "This condition lowers the tolerance level to alcohol so that not only does intoxication occur more readily but the results of intoxication are far more drastic than would normally be the case. Among such drastic reactions which may result from consumption of a relatively small amount of alcohol are confusion, amnesia, loss of perception to reality, and violent conduct."[103]

One exception to the rule that involuntary intoxication can serve as a defense lies in the realm of strict liability crimes. In *State v. Miller*,[104] the defendant drank coffee that, unbeknownst to him, was spiked with alcohol. He was subsequently convicted of driving under the influence of alcohol, a strict liability offense. The Oregon Supreme Court upheld his conviction, noting that because the crime required no proof of a culpable mental state, the defendant could not claim involuntary intoxication.

---

[101]Lawrence P. Tiffany and Mary Tiffany, "Nosologic Objections to the Criminal Defense of Pathological Intoxication: What Do the Doubters Doubt," *International Journal of Law and Psychiatry*, Vol. 13 (1990), p. 49.
[102]*Kane v. United States*, 399 F.2d 730 (9th Cir. 1968).
[103]Ibid., p. 735.
[104]*State v. Miller*, 788 P.2d 974 (Or. 1990).

Entrapment

entrapment An excuse defense applicable if the government is found to have manufactured or initiated a crime that would not have otherwise occurred.

The **entrapment** defense straddles the lines between criminal law and criminal procedure. It is a defense in the criminal-law sense, but it is one of the only defenses that calls into question law enforcement's role in the instigation of crime. Hence, it is almost always brought up in the realm of criminal procedure. Even so, entrapment is an affirmative defense, which means it can easily be raised at trial.

The entrapment defense is based on the belief that someone should not be convicted of a crime that the government instigated. In its simplest form, the entrapment defense arises when government officials "plant the seeds" of criminal intent. That is, if a person commits a crime that he or she otherwise would not have committed but for the government's conduct, that person will probably succeed with an entrapment defense.

The first Supreme Court case recognizing the entrapment defense was *Sorrells* v. *United States*.[105] In that case, Chief Justice Hughes stated, "We are unable to conclude that . . . [the] . . . processes of detection or enforcement should be abused by the instigation by government officials of an act on the part of persons otherwise innocent in order to lure them to its commission and to punish them."[106] This reasoning underlies the treatment of the entrapment defense in U.S. courts to this day. The Court further stated,

> The appropriate object of this permitted activity, frequently essential to the enforcement of the law, is to reveal the criminal design; to expose the illicit traffic, the prohibited publication, the fraudulent use of the mails, the illegal conspiracy, or other offenses, and thus to disclose the would-be violators of the law. A different question is presented when the criminal design originates with the officials of the Government, and they implant in the mind of an innocent person the disposition to commit the alleged offense and induce its commission in order that they may prosecute.[107]

Despite its apparent simplicity, the entrapment defense has been a contentious one. In particular, there has been some disagreement in the courts over the relevance of the offender's predisposition and how far the government can go to lure a person into criminal activity. When an entrapment decision is based on the offender's predisposition, this is known as a *subjective inquiry*. By contrast, a focus on the government conduct presumably responsible for someone's decision to commit a crime is known as an *objective inquiry*.

The Model Penal Code takes an objective approach with regard to the entrapment defense: If the government "employ[ed] methods of persuasion or inducement which create a substantial risk that such an offense will be committed by persons other than those who are ready to commit it,"[108] then the defense is available regardless of the offender's initial willingness to offend.

The Supreme Court, however, has opted to focus on the subjective predisposition of the offender instead the government's role in instigating the crime in question.[109] In *Sorrells*, discussed earlier, the defendant was charged with violating the National Prohibition Act.[110] After two unsuccessful attempts, a law enforcement agent convinced

---

[105]*Sorrells v. United States*, 287 U.S. 435 (1932).
[106]Ibid., p. 448
[107]Ibid., pp. 441–442.
[108]American Law Institute, *Model Penal Code* 2.13(1)(b)(1985).
[109]See, e.g., *Hampton v. United States*, 425 U.S. 484 (1976).
[110]Recall that during the Prohibition era, from 1920 to 1933, it was illegal to produce and sell alcohol in the United States.

the defendant to sell him whiskey. Chief Justice Hughes noted that "artifice and stratagem" are permissible methods of catching criminals, so entrapment did not occur. Instead, it was the defendant's predisposition to offend that was important.

Age

People who are below a certain age threshold cannot form, according to the law, the requisite intent to be convicted of a crime. Age thus serves to excuse criminal conduct in certain situations. Indeed, it may bar prosecution altogether.

The common law put children into three categories based on their capacity to commit crimes[111]:

1. Children under age 7 had no criminal capacity.
2. Children 7–14 had no criminal capacity, but this was a presumption that could be overcome.
3. Children over 14 had the same capacity to offend as adults.

Today, these exact categories have been abandoned to some extent, but there are exceptions. In general, children under the age of 18 (i.e., juveniles) are charged and adjudicated in the juvenile justice system. Those over 18 are prosecuted and tried in the adult system. Under the federal Juvenile Delinquency Act, a juvenile is a person who has not yet turned 18 years of age.[112] And while most states have followed the federal lead, several treat 17-, 16-, and even 15-year-olds as adults.[113]

See the accompanying Court Decision for more on the defense of age. In it we take a look at *State* v. *Guevara*, where a ten-year-old girl is charged with threatening to detonate a bomb at school.

COURT DECISION

The Logic behind the Defense of Age

State v. *Guevara*
2010 WL 961593 Court of Appeals of Washington

Decision: The ten-year-old defendant had sufficient capacity to understand the wrongfulness of her conduct when she committed the crime and, consequently, is not entitled to the age defense.

Reason: . . . Ten-year-old Esmeralda Guevara wrote a note on a stall in the girls' bathroom at a school in College Place, Washington, on the afternoon of Monday, November 5, 2007. The note read, "[B]omb set 20 mins were [sic] going to die." School administrators evacuated and closed the school to allow a bomb squad to search. The squad was unable to locate a bomb.

(continued)

---

[111]R. G. Singer and J. Q. La Fond, *Criminal Law: Examples and Explanations*, 4th ed. (New York: Wolters Kluwer, 2007), pp. 495–496.
[112]18 U.S.C., Section 5031.
[113]For more details, see the "Shifting Conceptions of Age" section later in this chapter.

COURT DECISION

(continued)

. . . A statutory presumption that children between 8 and 11 years old lack capacity to commit a crime applies in juvenile proceedings. To rebut this presumption, the State must convince the trial judge that the child had sufficient capacity to understand the act and to know that it was wrong. The court decides whether the State has rebutted the incapacity presumption by considering the following factors:

(1) the nature of the crime, (2) the child's age and maturity, (3) whether the child evidenced a desire for secrecy, (4) whether the child told the victim (if any) not to tell, (5) prior conduct similar to that charged, (6) any consequences that attached to that prior conduct, and (7) whether the child had made an acknowledgment that the behavior is wrong and could lead to detention. *State v. Ramer,* 151 Wash.2d 106, 114-15 (2004).

. . . The State, then, need not show, and the court need not find, that Esmeralda understood that her act would be punishable under the law. "The focus is on 'whether the child appreciated the quality of his or her acts at the time the act was committed,' rather than whether the child understood the legal consequences of the act." *Ramer,* 151 Wash.2d at 114 (quoting *State v. T.E.H.,* 91 Wash.App. 908, 913 (1998)).

. . . The juvenile court judge here considered and made appropriate findings on the seven factors outlined in *Ramer:*

Factor 1: The alleged crime is a Class B Felony and a serious offense. The language used threatens that people will die in a short passage of time. Considering the violent nature of our society, the recent history of violence in schools and the worldwide use by terrorists of bombs, school officials and law enforcement officers are supersensitive to threats of this nature.

Factor 2: The child, at the time of the incident, was approximately 10.5 years old. The child's appearance in court, her mother's testimony about the child and her activities and Officer Schneidmiller's testimony about his involvement with the child leads the Court to conclude Esmeralda is of at least average or above average maturity for a 10 year old . . .

Factor 3: The child did not tell anyone about her behavior that afternoon, or even early evening, when she was picked up by her mother after school was cancelled and when they returned to find the parent-teacher conferences were cancelled. She was secretive at that time.

Factor 4: There was no individual victim.

Factor 5: There is no history of prior similar conduct.

Factor 6: There were no prior consequences.

Factor 7: The child, when she told her mother later that evening, after awakening from nightmares, that she had written the threat, was at a minimum indirectly acknowledging the wrongfulness of her behavior. She also cried during the police interview.

. . . We conclude that this evidence supports the juvenile court judge's finding and that finding supports the conclusion that Esmeralda had the capacity to understand the wrongfulness of her actions. . . . We affirm the conviction.

Treating Juveniles as Adults

Juvenile courts have always had mechanisms in place for transferring, or waiving, juveniles to adult court. Whether a juvenile can be transferred to adult court varies by state. There are three main mechanisms for treating juveniles as adults: legislative exclusion, waivers, and concurrent jurisdiction. See Figure 9.2 for an overview.

legislative exclusion A statutory requirement that certain juveniles be treated as adults in the criminal justice system.

Legislative Exclusion. Legislative exclusion (also called *statutory exclusion*) refers to the fact that a statute excludes, or bars, a juvenile from being tried as a juvenile. In other words, legislative exclusion requires that certain juveniles be treated as adults; for example, Mississippi excludes all felonies committed by 17-year-olds,[114] whereas Arizona excludes any felony committed by a juvenile as young as 15 years old.[115]

juvenile waiver Trying juveniles as adults in the criminal justice system or waiving them into adult court.

Waiver. The term juvenile waiver refers to trying juveniles as adults, or waiving them to adult court. Waivers have been around for some time, and they have been used on occasion when a juvenile commits a particularly harsh crime and there is a desire to charge him or her in the adult justice system. Recent changes have made it easier to try juveniles as adult offenders, a significant departure from the original intent of having a separate juvenile justice system. There are three main types of waivers used with juveniles:

discretionary waiver The discretion of the juvenile court judge to waiver jurisdiction over a criminal case so that the minor can be tried as an adult.

1. **Discretionary waiver.** A discretionary waiver, as defined by several states, "gives juvenile court judges discretion to waive jurisdiction in individual cases involving minors, so as to allow prosecution in adult criminal courts. Terminology varies from State to State, but all transfer mechanisms in this category have the effect of authorizing but not requiring juvenile courts to designate appropriate cases for adult prosecution."[116]

presumptive waiver Waiver of a juvenile defendant from juvenile to adult court is presumed appropriate based on the age, offense or other factors.

2. **Presumptive waiver.** Several state statutes designate a category of cases called presumptive waiver, in which waiver to criminal court is presumed appropriate. "In such cases, the juvenile rather than the State bears the burden of proof in the waiver hearing; if a juvenile meeting age, offense, or other statutory criteria triggering the presumption fails to make an adequate argument against transfer, the juvenile court must send the case to criminal court."[117]

mandatory waiver Waiver of a juvenile defendant from juvenile to adult court is mandatory based on the age, offense or other factors.

3. **Mandatory waiver.** Several states use a mandatory waiver "in cases that meet certain age, offense, or other criteria. In these States, proceedings against the juvenile are initiated in juvenile court. However, the juvenile court has no role other than to confirm that the statutory requirements for mandatory waiver are met. Once it has done so, the juvenile court must send the case to a court of criminal jurisdiction."[118]

---

[114]Available at http://www.ncjj.org/stateprofiles/overviews/transfer4.asp (accessed February 29, 2008).
[115]Ibid.
[116]P. Griffin, P. Torbet, and L. Szymanski, *Trying Juveniles as Adults: An Analysis of State Transfer Provisions* (Washington, DC: U.S. Department of Justice, 1998). Available at http://ojjdp.ncjrs.org/pubs/tryingjuvasadult/transfer.html (accessed August 4, 2009).
[117]Ibid.
[118]Ibid.

Most states have multiple ways to impose adult sanctions on offenders of juvenile age

State	Judicial waiver Discretionary	Judicial waiver Presumptive	Judicial waiver Mandatory	Concurrent jurisdiction	Statutory exclusion	Reverse waiver	Once an adult/ always an adult	Blended sentencing Juvenile	Blended sentencing Criminal
Number of states	45	15	15	15	29	25	34	15	17
Alabama	■				■		■		
Alaska	■	■					■	■	
Arizona	■			■	■	■	■		
Arkansas	■			■		■		■	■
California	■	■		■		■	■		■
Colorado	■	■		■		■		■	■
Connecticut			■			■		■	
Delaware	■		■		■	■	■		
Dist. of Columbia	■	■		■		■	■		
Florida	■			■	■		■		■
Georgia	■		■	■	■	■			
Hawaii	■						■		
Idaho	■				■		■		■
Illinois	■	■	■		■	■	■	■	■
Indiana	■		■		■		■		
Iowa	■				■	■	■		■
Kansas	■	■					■	■	
Kentucky	■		■			■			■
Louisiana	■		■	■	■				
Maine	■	■					■		
Maryland	■				■	■	■		
Massachusetts					■			■	■
Michigan	■			■			■	■	■
Minnesota	■	■			■		■	■	
Mississippi	■				■	■	■		
Missouri	■						■		■
Montana				■	■	■		■	
Nebraska				■		■			■
Nevada	■	■			■	■	■		
New Hampshire	■	■					■		
New Jersey	■	■	■						
New Mexico					■			■	■
New York					■	■			
North Carolina	■		■				■		
North Dakota	■	■	■				■		
Ohio	■		■				■	■	
Oklahoma	■			■	■	■	■		■
Oregon	■				■	■	■		
Pennsylvania	■	■			■	■	■		
Rhode Island	■	■	■				■	■	
South Carolina	■		■		■				
South Dakota	■				■	■	■		
Tennessee	■					■	■		
Texas	■						■	■	
Utah	■	■			■		■		
Vermont	■			■	■	■		■	
Virginia	■		■	■		■	■		■
Washington	■				■		■		
West Virginia	■		■						■
Wisconsin	■				■	■	■		■
Wyoming	■			■		■			

■ In states with a combination of provisions for transferring juveniles to criminal court, the exclusion, mandatory waiver, or concurrent jurisdiction provisions generally target the oldest juveniles and/or those charged with the most serious offenses, whereas younger juveniles and/or those charged with relatively less serious offenses may be eligible for discretionary waiver.

Note: Table information is as of the end of the 2004 legislative session.

Source: Authors' adaptation of Griffin's National overviews. *State juvenile justice profiles.*

Figure 9.2

State Legal Arrangements Governing Treatment of Juveniles as Adults
Source: H.N. Snyder and M. Sickmund, *Juvenile Offenders and Victims: 2006 National Report* (Washington, DC: U.S. Department of Justice, Office of Justice Programs, Office of Juvenile Justice and Delinquency Prevention, 2006), Chap. 4, p. 111.

reverse waiver Waiver of a juvenile defendant from adult court to juvenile court for adjudication.

In a twist on these approaches to waiver, some states have a reverse waiver, which requires that certain cases initiated in adult court be sent to the juvenile court for an adjudicatory hearing.[119] In yet another twist, some state waiver laws have "once an adult, always an adult" provisions, requiring that once a juvenile is waived to adult court, all other offenses that juvenile commits are to be tried in adult court.[120]

concurrent jurisdiction Two courts, namely an adult and juvenile court, both have jurisdiction over a particular case. The prosecutor makes the decision regarding which court to initiate criminal proceedings.

Concurrent Jurisdiction. Concurrent jurisdiction means that certain cases can be tried in both juvenile and adult court, and the prosecutor makes a decision as to where the case should be tried. Concurrent jurisdiction sometimes occurs outside of the juvenile justice context, as well. For example, if both a federal and state court could try the same offense, it is said that each has concurrent jurisdiction.

Insanity

Hollywood loves to give the impression that crafty criminals routinely escape conviction by pleading insanity. Perhaps you recall the movie, *Primal Fear*, starring Edward Norton and Richard Gere. Norton played an abused altar boy who found himself charged with a priest's murder. He successfully feigned a split personality, which led to a mistrial and his confinement in a mental hospital. Though he did not "go free," he did escape conviction. And though his confinement to a mental hospital was somewhat realistic, it is exceedingly difficult for all but accomplished actors to feign insanity. As we will see, the tests to prove insanity set the bar rather high. Also, the defense itself is rarely raised, which moviemakers fail to tell us.

Competency to Stand Trial versus the Insanity Defense

The insanity defense is distinct from competency to stand trial. The latter deals with the defendant's ability to understand what is happening *at the time of trial* or a related criminal proceeding. The specific test to make such a determination is whether the defendant "has sufficient present ability to consult with his lawyer with a reasonable degree of rational understanding—and whether he has a rational as well as factual understanding of the proceedings against him."[121] The burden of proving incompetence falls on the defendant.[122] The insanity defense, in contrast, deals with the defendant's competence *at the time he or she committed the crime*.

The defendant's competence to stand trial is usually considered in a separate pretrial hearing. What happens to the defendant if he or she is declared incompetent to stand trial? Usually, the defendant will be hospitalized until his or her competency is restored, if it ever is. However, in *Jackson v. Indiana*,[123] the Supreme Court held that there are constitutional limitations on how long a defendant can be hospitalized

---

[119]H. N. Snyder and M. Sickmund, *Juvenile Offenders and Victims:2006 National Report* (Washington, DC: U.S. Department of Justice, Office of Justice Programs, Office of Juvenile Justice and Delinquency Prevention, 2006), Chap. 4, p. 111.

[120]Ibid.

[121]*Dusky v. United States*, 362 U.S. 402 (1960), p. 402.

[122]*Medina v. California*, 505 U.S. 437 (1992).

[123]*Jackson v. Indiana*, 406 U.S. 715 (1972).

for the purpose of restoring competency. That case dealt with a 27-year-old deaf-mute individual with the mental level of a preschooler, who was being hospitalized until the staff determined him sane. The Court concluded that it was likely the defendant's condition would *never* improve. Thus, the Court said,

> We hold . . . that a person charged by a State with a criminal offense who is committed [to an institution] solely on account of his incapacity to proceed to trial cannot be held more than the reasonable period of time necessary to determine whether there is a substantial probability that he will attain that capacity in the foreseeable future. If it is determined that this is not the case, then the State must either institute the customary civil commitment proceeding that would be required to commit indefinitely any other citizen, or release the defendant.[124]

Insanity versus Diminished Capacity

diminished capacity A failure of proof defense based on the defendant's inability to form the required criminal intent due to a medical disease or defect. It is a unique defense that is not equivalent to the insanity defense.

Insanity is not the same as **diminished capacity**, the latter of which is a failure of proof defense. By this we mean the defendant is permitted in most cases to introduce evidence that he or she suffered from a mental condition such that intent, or the *mens rea*, to commit the crime was lacking. Very importantly, this is independent of an insanity defense. Not all states permit the defense to present such an argument, but several do.[125] The Model Penal Code adopts the same approach, stating, "Evidence that the defendant suffered from a mental disease or defect is admissible whenever it is relevant to prove that the defendant did or did not have a state of mind that is an element of the offense."[126] The logic for permitting evidence of diminished capacity was explained by the Colorado Supreme Court in *Hendershott* v. *People*:

> Once we accept the basic principles that an accused is presumed innocent and that he cannot be adjudicated guilty unless the prosecution proves beyond a reasonable doubt the existence of the mental state required for the crime charged, it defies both logic and fundamental fairness to prohibit a defendant from presenting reliable and relevant evidence that, due to a mental impairment beyond his conscious control, he lacked the capacity to entertain the very culpability which is indispensible to his criminal responsibility in the first instance.[127]

Insanity Tests

Insanity An excuse defense to a criminal charge based on the defendant's mental condition at the time of the crime.

Black's Law Dictionary defines **insanity** as "a condition which renders the affected person unfit to enjoy liberty of action because of the unreliability of his behavior with concomitant danger to himself and others."[128] Unfortunately, it gets much more complex from here. For example, the insanity defense is a *legal* concept, so just because someone may be medically diagnosed as insane, he or she may not succeed with an insanity defense. Also, the courts use multiple tests to determine whether a person was insane at the time of the crime. Here we introduce five of them: (1) the

---

[124]Ibid., p. 738.
[125]Dressler, *Understanding Criminal Law*, p. 369.
[126]Model Penal Code, Section 4.02(1).
[127]*Hendershott* v. *People*, 653 P.2d 385 (Colo. 1982), pp. 393–394.
[128]*Black's Law Dictionary*, 6th ed. (St. Paul, MN: West, 1990), p. 794.

M'Naghten test, (2) the "irresistible impulse" test, (3) the Model Penal Code test, (4) the product test, and (5) the federal test. States can choose their own tests, combine two or more tests to suit their needs, or even have no insanity defense at all (see Figure 9.3).

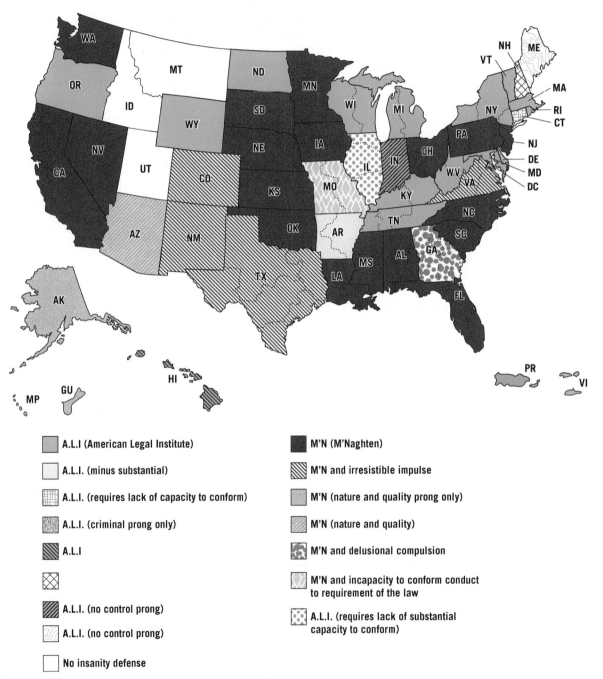

Figure 9.3

Insanity Tests by State

Source: D.B. Rottman and S.M. Strickland, *State Court Organization, 2004* (Washington, DC: Bureau of Justice Statistics, 2006), pp. 199–201. Available at: http://bjs.ojp.usdoj.gov/content/pub/pdf/sco04.pdf (accessed December 17, 2012)

The *M'Naghten* Test. In 1843, Daniel M'Naghten attempted to assassinate then-British Prime Minister Robert Peel. M'Naghten actually fired at Peel's secretary, Edward Drummond, and killed him. Realizing that M'Naghten was not of sound mind, the House of Lords asked a panel of judges to offer guidance in cases when a defendant pleads insanity, which M'Naghten did. In *M'Naghten's Case*, it was decided that in order to prove insanity, it must be clearly proved that, at the time of the crime, "the party accused was labouring [*sic*] under such a defect of reason, from disease of the mind, as not to know the nature and quality of the act he was doing; or, if he did know it, that he did not know he was doing what was wrong."[129] This has come to be known as the **M'Naghten Test**. According to recent data, 17 states and the federal government use this test.[130]

> **M'Naghten Test** An insanity test that focuses on the defendant's ability to appreciate the wrongfulness of his conduct based on a mental disease or defect.

While the *M'Naghten* test has survived time's test, it is not without problems. First, it fails to distinguish between levels of insanity; either a person is insane or she is not. In reality, there are *levels* of insanity. Second, critics have called the test antiquated because even though a person may know something is wrong, he or she may do it anyway because of something like a volitional deficiency, an inability to control movement.[131] Third, some of the terms that make up the test are confusing. An example is "know." What does it mean for an offender to "know" whether what he or she was doing was wrong? Does "know" mean the offender was aware of what he was doing? Or does it mean something more, like did the offender *appreciate* the gravity of what he did?

The "Irresistible Impulse" Test. To address some of the aforementioned *M'Naghten* deficiencies, some courts have added another element to the test. It has come to be known as the **Irresistible Impulse Test**. There are variations on the test, but there is a common theme to each. One holds that a person is insane if she "acted from an irresistible and uncontrollable impulse."[132] Another treats a person as insane if she "lost the *power to choose* between the right and wrong, and to avoid doing the act in question, as [her] free agency was at the time destroyed."[133] Yet another will result in a finding of insanity if the defendant's will "has been otherwise than voluntarily so completely destroyed that [his or her] actions are not subject to it, but are beyond [his or her] control."[134]

> **Irresistible Impulse Test** An insanity test that focuses on the defendant's ability to conform his conduct to the law.

The Model Penal Code Test. The Model Penal Code uses the following language for its insanity test: "A person is not responsible for criminal conduct if at the time of such conduct as a result of mental disease or defect he lacks substantial capacity either to appreciate the criminality [wrongfulness] of his conduct or to conform his conduct to the requirements of the law."[135] Notice the overlap with the *M'Naghten* test. Also notice that the word *appreciate* replaces the word *know* used in the *M'Naghten* test. Notice, further, how the Model Penal Code test contains a volitional component; if one cannot "conform" one's conduct to legal requirements, a not guilty (by reason of insanity) verdict may result.

---

[129]Ibid.
[130]*Clark* v. *Arizona*, 548 U.S. 735 (2006), pp. 750–751.
[131]See, e.g., *United States* v. *Pollard*, 171 F.Supp. 474 (E.D. Mich. 1959).
[132]*Commonwealth* v. *Rogers*, 48 Mass. 500 (1844), p. 502.
[133]*Parsons* v. *State*, 81 Ala. 577 (1886).
[134]*Davis* v. *United States*, 165 U.S. 373 (1897), p. 378.
[135]Model Penal Code, Section 4.01(1)

Product Test An insanity test that determines whether the criminal activity is the product of a mental disease or defect.

The Product Test.

The **Product Test** of insanity (also called the *Durham* test, after its namesake case), first developed in New Hampshire, provides that "an accused is not criminally responsible if his unlawful act was the product of mental disease or defect."[136] *Disease* refers to "a condition which is considered capable of either improving or deteriorating."[137] A defect is "a condition which is not considered capable of either improving or deteriorating and which may be either congenital, or the result of injury, or the residual effect of a physical or mental disease."[138] Under this test, the jury was asked to determine whether defendant suffered from a mental disease or defect and, if so, whether the mental disease or defect caused the defendant to commit the crime.

The product test is more general than some of the other tests introduced earlier because it leaves open the definition of "mental disease or defect." Critics, however, feel that the general nature of the test requires too much reliance on expert testimony to prove either mental disease or defect. Experts for the defense and prosecution make a case for and against insanity, respectively, and then jurors are forced to weigh their testimony and decide who to believe (or who is most persuasive). To this day, the product test is retained only by New Hampshire. For a time it was used in the District of Columbia, but it no longer is.[139]

The Federal Test.

Federal law treats insanity as a defense. Here is the specific statutory language:

> It is an affirmative defense to a prosecution under any Federal statute that, at the time of the commission of the acts constituting the offense, the defendant, as a result of a severe mental disease or defect, was unable to appreciate the nature and quality or the wrongfulness of his acts. Mental disease or defect does not otherwise constitute a defense.[140]

This definition of insanity also parallels some of others introduced earlier. For example, it retains the Model Penal Code's "appreciate" language. However, it adds the word *severe* to the equation, possibly making it more difficult for a federal defendant to succeed with an insanity defense.

The Real Effect of a Successful Insanity Defense

Not only are insanity defenses rarely invoked, but they rarely succeed. Moreover, even when they do succeed, they rarely result in an offender "going free." On one level, it is odd to even treat insanity as an excuse defense. It does not so much *excuse* criminal conduct as it does punish, or at least confine, someone with a lengthy term of confinement in a facility, just not a prison. As one team of researchers put it, "[T]he insanity defense is not a defense, it is a device for triggering indeterminate restraint."[141]

---

[136]*Durham* v. *United States*, 214 F.2d 862 (D.C. Cir. 1954, pp. 874–875); see *State v. Pike*, 49 N.H. 399 (1870), for the original.
[137]Ibid., p. 875.
[138]Ibid.
[139]*United States* v. *Brawner*, 471 F.2d 969 (D.C. Cir. 1972).
[140]18 U.S.C. Section 17(a).
[141]J. Goldstein and J. Katz, "Abolish the 'Insanity Defense'—Why Not?" *Yale Law Journal*, Vol. 72 (1963), p. 868.

Typically, a person who is found not guilty by reason of insanity (NGRI) is confined to an institution where that person can presumably be treated. Once an NGRI verdict is read, it is presumed that the person suffers from enough of a mental illness that instant confinement is necessary. In other words, there is no need for another hearing to make this determination.[142] Yet in some jurisdictions an individual found NGRI will be temporarily confined so experts can determine whether indefinite detention is warranted. Under federal law, for example, a postverdict commitment hearing must be held within a certain period of time.[143] In either case, if the convicted individual is mentally ill or a danger to herself or others (or both), she can be confined until which point she no longer is. The term of confinement is basically indefinite and is intended to last long enough to ensure the individual is fit for release.

Once a person found NGRI is successfully treated, release is considered. The mechanisms for release vary from one jurisdiction to the next, however. In some jurisdictions, the court that ordered the individual's commitment makes the determination. In others, the individual must petition for release, either to a court or a body charged with making such decisions. The burden of proof falls on the committed individual and varies, too, from one jurisdiction to the next.

Guilty but Mentally Ill

Since its inception, the insanity defense has met with a certain measure of opposition. Despite arguments in favor of the insanity defense, abolitionists have worked hard to remove it from the long list of criminal defenses. Prompted by the attempted assassination of Ronald Reagan in the 1980s, four states—Idaho, Kansas, Montana, and Utah—promptly abolished the defense.[144] These states permit the defendant to introduce evidence to rebut the prosecutor's argument that the defendant possessed the requisite mental state to commit the crime, but there is no express insanity defense recognized in their laws. And the Supreme Court, it seems, has no problem with this. In *Clark* v. *Arizona*, for example, it remarked, "We have never held that the Constitution mandates an insanity defense."[145]

guilty but mentally ill A verdict, short of finding insanity, in which the criminal defendant is mentally ill at the time of the crime.

A greater number of states have taken a more measured approach by, instead of abolishing the insanity defense, creating a guilty but mentally ill (GBMI; some states also use "guilty but insane," or GBI) verdict. The intent of GBMI is to address some of the (perceived) deficiencies associated with a traditional insanity defense. For example, a successful insanity defense followed by successful treatment can result in release. While this may be the intent of the insanity defense, some people resist to releasing even those who were insane at the time of their crimes. Returning to the attempted Reagan assassination, every attempt to grant outright release to John Hinckely, Jr., the man found not guilty by reason of insanity for making an attempt on the president's life, has been met with considerable resistance.[146]

---

[142]*Jones* v. *United States*, 463 U.S. 354 (1983).
[143]18 U.S.C. Section 4243(c).
[144]Dressler, *Understanding Criminal Law*, pp. 363–364.
[145]*Clark* v. *Arizona*, 548 U.S. 735 (2006), p. 752, n. 20.
[146]See, e.g., http://www.cnn.com/2009/CRIME/06/17/john.hinckley/index.html (accessed May 25, 2010).

Of the more than 20 states that have taken this approach, only two of them have abolished the insanity defense.[147] In GBMI states, jurors can choose between four verdicts rather than the usual three: guilty, not guilty, not guilty by reason of insanity, and guilty but mentally ill. In general, the GBMI verdict is reserved for individuals who are deemed (1) guilty of the crime, (2) sane at the time of the crime, and (3) "mentally ill" at the time of trial. An individual who is adjudicated GBMI will likely be sent to prison, but will also most likely receive treatment while there.

A problem with "guilty but mentally ill" is that it adds a layer of complexity to an already complex area of law. "Mentally ill" is not necessarily the same as "insanity," so how is a jury to distinguish between the two? Likewise, supporters of GBMI claim that the defense offers treatment to prisoners, but prisons can already offer treatment to mentally ill offenders, regardless of whether such a verdict is in place. Yet another problem is that the verdict generally is not possible unless the defendant first raises an insanity defense. Critics claim that this leads to more insanity pleas—and, by extension, more acquittals.[148] This has prompted at least one expert to call the verdict "an ill-conceived and ineffective overreaction to the problems associated with the insanity defense."[149]

Creative Excuses

The excuse defenses we already introduced are, for better or worse, fairly unsurprising and predictable. They are the "garden variety" excuses raised in countless criminal trials over many generations. Here we shift our attention to a variety of creative and relatively novel excuse defenses. Some have been recognized as stand-alone defenses; others are just arguments raised in the context of more traditional defenses, such as insanity. We organize them into three categories: excuses based on physiology, excuses based on psychology, and sociological excuses. Together, they are sometimes called "syndrome defenses."

Excuses Based on Physiology

Since Ceaseare Lombroso claimed he could predict a person's criminal tendency based on the shape of the head, criminologists have been looking for biological explanations for illegal behavior. At various points in history, biological explanations have fallen in and out of favor, but certain authorities have always been interested in whether some people are born predisposed to crime. It is not surprising, then, that some defenses to criminal liability pick up on this line of thinking.

One excuse based on physiology concerns the presence of an extra Y chromosome. Each fetus has two sex chromosomes. An X combined with an X yields a female. An X combined with a Y yields a male. Some males, however, are born with an extra Y chromosome. The thinking is that this extra Y chromosome makes the individual

---

[147]Dressler, *Understanding Criminal Law*, p. 365.
[148]See, e.g., C. Slobogin, "The Guilty But Mentally Ill Verdict: An Idea Whose Time Should Not Have Come," *George Washington Law Review*, Vol. 53 (1985), p. 516.
[149]Ibid., p. 527.

"hypermasculine" and even more disposed to crime than a male already is (recall that men, in general, are more likely to commit crime than women). Since no man can control his genetic makeup and since an extra Y chromosome may be a factor contributing to his criminal tendencies, shouldn't he be at least partially excused for any resulting criminal activity? In theory, perhaps, but the courts have answered with a resounding "no." Interestingly, the "XYY chromosome defect" is the only physiological or creative defense that has reached the appellate level in the United States (and thereby has been reported and published so that we can read the courts' logic for rejecting the defense). Multiple courts have rejected it, basing their decisions on the fact that there is no consensus with respect to the possibility of a "genetic criminal."[150]

Premenstrual syndrome (PMS) has also served as the basis for an excuse defense against criminal liability.[151] While many women experience cramps, nausea, and other discomforts during menstruation, some experience severe agony and sometimes even become violent. In 1994, the American Psychiatric Association (APA) added an extreme version of PMS, **Premenstrual Dysphoric Disorder (PMDD)**, to the list of depressive disorders in its *Diagnostic and Statistical Manual*, 4th edition (DMS-IV).[152] In light of these issues, it is not surprising that some female defendants have claimed that PMS or PMDD was responsible for their violent criminal behavior. The defense has been raised on multiple occasions in U.S. courts,[153] and despite the fact that it has yet to reach the appellate level, the defense has nevertheless succeeded. In June 1991, a Virginia court accepted the first criminal defense based on PMS.[154] Perhaps as many courts have rejected the defense, too.[155]

Although XYY and PMS defenses have garnered the most attention, a few other physiological excuse defenses are coming into the limelight. Examples include hypoglycemia, Alzheimer's disease, neurotoxic damage, and even testosterone overload.[156] It is unclear to what extent such defenses will gain a foothold.

Excuses Based on Psychology

Every criminal act contains a psychological element—namely *mens rea*. Many of the criminal defenses we have introduced already attempt to negate that element of intent. Some, however, go even further by raising creative claims of psychological causation and defense. One example is brainwashing. Singer and LaFond recount the story of Patty Hearst, heiress to the Hearst newspaper fortune:

> Ms. Hearst was kidnapped by a militant group of terrorists in California, who demanded that her father take certain social measures (such as distributing free

XYY chromosome defect A criminal defense based on the presence of an extra "Y" chromosome and hypermasculinity.

Premenstrual Dysphoric Disorder (PMDD) A medical condition creating extreme mental and emotional symptoms prior to menstruation that could potentially be used as a criminal defense to a crime.

---

[150]See, e.g., *People* v. *Tanner*, 91 Cal. Rptr. 656 (Cal. Ct. App. 1970); *Millard* v. *Maryland*, 261 A.2d 227 (Md. Ct. Spec. App. 1970); *People* v. *Yuki*, 372 N.Y.S.2d 313 (Sup. Ct. 1975).
[151]Colloquium, "Premenstrual Syndrome: The Debate Surrounding Criminal Defense," *Maryland Law Review*, Vol. 54 (1995), pp. 571–600.
[152]Ibid., p. 571.
[153]L. Taylor and K. Dalton, "Premenstrual Syndrome: A New Criminal Defense?" *California Western Law Review*, Vol. 19 (1983), pp. 269 and 276–277.
[154]M. Kasindorf, "Allowing Hormones to Take the Rap: Does the PMS Defense Help or Hinder Women?" *Newsday*, June 16, 1991, at 17.
[155]See, e.g., *Commonwealth* v. *Grass*, 595 A.2d 789 (1991), p. 792.
[156]See Singer and La Fond, *Criminal Law: Examples and Explanations*, p. 533.

food to thousands of hungry poor people in several California cities). Months later, Ms. Hearst appeared, dressed in black and carrying a machine gun, assisting the terrorists in robbing a California bank. She was arrested about a year later in San Francisco. When booked, she gave her name as Tanya, and her occupation as "revolutionary."[157]

At her trial, Hearst argued it was "Tanya," not she, who robbed the bank. She claimed the militants brainwashed her during captivity, indoctrinating her into their belief system. While the trial judge permitted the brainwashing argument, the jury did not buy it. Hearst was convicted and sentenced to 35 years in prison. Her sentence was later commuted to seven years—and commuted even further by then-President Jimmy Carter some years later. She was released on February 1, 1979, having served just 22 months.[158]

Some defendants have also claimed that a "mob mentality" was responsible for their criminal acts. In one incident, Damien Williams, an African-American and Los Angeles resident, joined a group of rioters who lashed out in response to the acquittal of several white police officers who were accused of beating Rodney King. The mob stopped a truck, pulled the white driver, Reginald Denny, from the cab, and began beating him (a video clip was broadcast across the country). Williams proceeded to hit Denny with a brick, severely injuring him. He survived, but Williams was arrested and charged with several crimes, including attempted murder. At his trial, Williams argued that he was "swept up" in the heat of the moment and had no intentions to hurt the innocent driver. The jury acquitted him of the most serious charges, but found him guilty of several misdemeanors.

Post-Traumatic Stress Disorder (PTSD) A potential defense to a crime based on psychological trauma the defendant suffered after experiencing a traumatic event.

Some defendants have also claimed that **Post-Traumatic Stress Disorder (PTSD)** led them to commit a crime. For example, in 2009, a Santa Clara County, California, jury found a former Army captain who was diagnosed with PTSD not guilty by reason of insanity for robbing a pharmacy of drugs at gunpoint.[159]

Post-traumatic stress disorder can potentially be a defense to a crime. Soldiers who served in combat zones have used the PTSD defense.

hurricane/Fotolia

---

[157]Ibid., p. 534.
[158]K. Dell and R. Myers, "The 10 Most Notorious Presidential Pardons," *Time*, http://www.time.com/time/2007/presidential_pardons/9.html (accessed May 27, 2010).
[159]See http://www.military.com/news/article/ptsd-tied-to-ex-gis-insanity-defense.html (accessed June 1, 2010).

Sociological Excuses

urban psychosis A criminal defense based on the defendant's traumatic upbringing in a violent area.

Many a defendant has also claimed that his or her background or surroundings contributed to a decision to break the law. One such defense is urban psychosis, a condition analogous to PTSD that results from a "traumatic childhood in a violent inner-city home and neighborhood."[160] A few defendants have asserted this defense, but it appears the most success they have had is in being convicted of lesser charges. Some defendants have also raised an urban survival syndrome defense. Although similar to urban psychosis, this defense suggests that crime results from heightened sense of fear and danger that results from living in a high-crime urban environment.

urban survival syndrome A criminal defense based on the heightened sense of fear the defendant experiences from being raised in a high-crime urban neighborhood.

Still other defendants have blamed television intoxication for their actions. In one case, 15-year-old Ronny Zamora and an accomplice broke into the home of an elderly neighbor. When the neighbor returned home, Zamora shot and killed her. At trial, his attorney claimed that he "had become involuntarily subliminally intoxicated by violent television programming."[161] Although the defense was couched in terms of insanity, it did not succeed. Zamora was sentenced to life imprisonment for murder.[162] He appealed on multiple occasions, and he and his family even sued three major television networks, but all these attempts failed. Zamora is not alone; others who have blamed television for their crimes have failed with the defense.[163] Efforts to blame violent conduct on watching too much pornography and listening to violent and/or "gangsta rap" music have also failed.[164]

black rage A criminal defense based on the defendant's past experience with racism that caused him to break the law.

Of the creative sociological excuses for criminal activity, black rage has been raised in perhaps the most cases,[165] although it is difficult to tell how often it has succeeded. Again, most trial court decisions are not published, meaning they cannot be uncovered by researchers. We are left to look at appellate decisions, which of course represent the tip of the proverbial iceberg. There are different variations of the black rage defense, but the common theme is that a defendant's experience with racism prompts him or her to break the law. "Experience" could be a perception of prolonged racism or simply a single racially motivated incident. In either case, the defendant claims that his or her mental state was "affected" by racism.

The black rage defense goes as far back as 1846 to the case of *Freeman* v. *People*. Freeman, accused of killing four white people, claimed that mistreatment by white society rendered him insane. The jury rejected his claim.[166] One such case went all the way to the Supreme Court. In *Fisher* v. *United States*,[167] the defendant was charged with murdering a white woman who uttered a racial epithet. While the Court upheld his conviction, it signaled the presence of a defense that does not fit neatly into traditional categories of insanity and diminished capacity.[168]

---

[160]P. J. Falk, "Novel Theories of Criminal Defense Based upon the Toxicity of the Social Environment: Urban Psychosis, Television Intoxication, and Black Rage," *North Carolina Law Review*, Vol. 74 (1996), p. 738.
[161]Ibid., p. 742.
[162]*Zamora* v. *State* (Dade County Cir. Ct. 1977), aff'd, 361 So. 2d 776 (Fla. Dist. Ct. App. 1978), cert denied, 372 So. 2d 472 (Fla. 1979).
[163]See, e.g., *State* v. *Molina*, No. 84-2314B (11th Judicial Dist., Fla. 1984); *State* v. *Quillen*, No. S87-08-0118, 1989 Del. Super. LEXIS 129 (Mar. 28, 1989).
[164]Falk, "Novel Theories of CriminalDefense," pp. 746–748.
[165]Ibid.
[166]*Freeman* v. *People*, 4 Denio 9 (N.Y. Sup. Ct. 1847).
[167]*Fisher* v. *United States*, 328 U.S. 463 (1946).
[168]For more cases invoking the black rage argument, see Falk, "Novel Theories of Criminal Defense," pp. 748–758.

YOUR DECISION

1. Scott Murphy is a freshman in college and recently decided to pledge the fraternity, Chi Gamma Omega. As a "pledge" of the fraternity, Scott is forced to participate in a number of initiation activities in order to become a brother of Chi Gamma Omega. Specifically, one night Scott was held down on the ground while other brothers poured shots of vodka into his mouth. Severely intoxicated by the initiation ritual, later that evening Scott broke into a female student's dorm room and sexually assaulted her. Scott is claiming he mistakenly believed he was entering the room of his girlfriend. Is Scott entitled to the defense of involuntary intoxication? Why or why not?

2. Jack Oberman is a pharmacist at a local drug store and has never engaged in any form of illegal activity. Local police officers received reports that the drug store was filling illegal prescriptions for OxyContin, a strong painkiller often sold on the streets. An undercover officer approached Jack on five separate occasions claiming that he had a daughter suffering from a terminal illness who was in severe pain and discomfort. The undercover officer claimed he could not afford medical treatment and asked Jack to illegally provide him with OxyContin for his daughter. Jack refused on the first four occasions, but finally consented after hearing the horrific stories of the young girl's suffering. Jack handed the undercover officer 10 OxyContin pills and was subsequently arrested. Is he entitled to the defense of entrapment? Would he be successful under both the objective and subjective tests?

Summary

- There are three main reasons for excuse defenses: possible lack of deterrence, possible lack of causation, and possible lack of moral blameworthiness.

- For all *nonhomicide* offenses, there are five general elements of duress: (1) The defendant "acted under the compulsion or threat of imminent infliction of death or great bodily injury"; (2) the defendant "reasonably believed that death or great bodily harm would have been inflicted upon him [or another] had he not acted as he did"; (3) the compulsion or coercion was "imminent and impending and of such a nature as to induce a well-grounded apprehension of death or serious bodily harm if the act is not done"; (4) there was "no reasonably opportunity to escape the compulsion without committing the crime"; and (5) the defendant must not have put him- or herself in a situation where it was "probable that he would have been subjected to compulsion or threat."

- Some states expressly forbid a duress defense in homicide cases; some others treat it as an imperfect defense that could lead to a manslaughter conviction rather than a murder conviction.

- In general, a person who voluntarily ingests an intoxicant will not succeed with a defense of intoxication.

- A person is involuntarily intoxicated if he or she cannot be blamed for the intoxicated states.

- The entrapment defense is based on the belief that someone should not be convicted of a crime that the government instigated.

- In its simplest form, the entrapment defense arises when government officials "plant the seeds."

- People who are below a certain age threshold cannot form, according to the law, the requisite intent to be convicted of a crime.

- In general, children under the age of 18 (i.e., juveniles) are charged and adjudicated in the juvenile justice system. Those over 18 are prosecuted and tried in the adult system.

- There are three main mechanisms for treating juveniles as adults: legislative exclusion, waivers, and concurrent jurisdiction.

- The insanity defense is distinct from competency to stand trial. The latter deals with the defendant's ability to understand what is happening at trial (as well as at pretrial hearings, etc.). The specific test to make such a determination is whether the defendant "has sufficient present ability to consult with his lawyer with a reasonable degree of rational understanding—and whether he has a rational as well as factual understanding of the proceedings against him."

- Insanity is not the same as diminished capacity, the latter of which is a failure of proof defense.

- Under the *M'Naghten* test, a defendant may escape liability if he "was labouring (sic) under such a defect of reason, from disease of the mind, as not to know the nature and quality of the act he was doing; or, if he did know it, that he did not know he was doing what was wrong."

- According to the irresistible impulse test, a person is insane if she "acted from an irresistible and uncontrollable impulse."

- The Model Penal Code test is as follows: "A person is not responsible for criminal conduct if at the time of such conduct as a result of mental disease or defect he lacks substantial capacity either to appreciate the criminality [wrongfulness] of his conduct or to conform his conduct to the requirements of the law."

- The product test of insanity, recognized only in New Hampshire, provides that "an accused is not criminally responsible if his unlawful act was the product of mental disease or defect."

- Federal law provides an affirmative defense of insanity that emphasizes a "mental disease or defect."

- Typically, a person who is found not guilty by reason of insanity (NGRI) is confined to an institution where that person can presumably be treated.

- There are three categories of creative excuse defenses: excuses based on physiology, excuses based on psychology, and sociological excuses.

- Examples of creative physiological excuse defenses include the XYY chromosome defect, premenstrual syndrome, and premenstrual dysphoric disorder.

- Examples of creative psychological excuse defenses include brainwashing and mob mentality.

- Examples of creative excuse defenses based on sociological factors include urban psychosis, urban survival syndrome, television intoxication, and black rage.

Chapter Review

OVERVIEW OF DEFENSES

Learning Objectives

- Distinguish between failure of proof, justification, and excuse defenses.
- Explain the differences between nonexculpatory defenses and offense modifications.
- Explain the difference between a perfect defense and an imperfect defense.

Review Questions

1. What is the difference between a justification defense and an excuse defense?
2. How does failure of proof differ from justification and excuse defenses?
3. What is the difference between a perfect and an imperfect defense?

Key Terms

failure of proof defense	statute of limitations
affirmative defense	perfect defenses
justification defenses	imperfect defenses
excuse defenses	public benefit theory
offense modifications	superior interest theory
de minimus infraction defense	moral rights theory
nonexculpatory defense	

JUSTIFICATION DEFENSES

Learning Objectives

- Summarize the defense of self-defense.
- Distinguish between defense of habitation and defense of property.
- Compare and contrast "make my day" laws and the castle doctrine.
- Explain the law enforcement defense.
- Describe the necessity defense.
- Explain the defense of consent.

Review Questions

1. What are the four elements of self-defense?
2. What is the castle doctrine? How is it relevant in the self-defense context?
3. How does defense of habitation differ from defense of property?
4. Is it ever legal to rig up a spring gun or a booby trap to prevent someone from breaking and entering?
5. Can an ordinary citizen use force and claim a law enforcement defense? If so, when? What about *deadly* force?
6. Can necessity ever justify homicide? Why or why not?

Key Terms

self-defense

stand your ground laws

castle doctrine

defense of others

make my day laws

law enforcement defense

necessity (i.e., choice of evils) defense

consent

MODULE **9.3**

EXCUSE DEFENSES

Learning Objectives

- Summarize the conditions of the defense of duress.
- Describe the intoxication defense.
- Summarize what constitutes entrapment.
- Summarize defenses based on age/immaturity.
- Summarize methods by which some courts treat juveniles as adults.
- Describe the insanity defense and the controversy surrounding it.
- Distinguish between and offer examples of physiological, psychological, and sociological excuse defenses.

Review Questions

1. Why can a duress defense rarely succeed in homicide cases? Should the courts and state legislatures relax their treatment of duress in homicide cases? Why or why not?

2. Should an intoxicated person be considered insane? Why or why not? What about a person who has been abusing alcohol for 20+ years?

3. Under what circumstances could voluntary intoxication serve as a defense? If none, should it result in conviction of a lesser crime? Why or why not?

4. What, in your opinion, is the appropriate age that a person should be tried in adult court?

5. Should the insanity defense be abolished? Why or why not?

6. Is "black rage" a legitimate excuse defense? Why or why not?

Key Terms

duress

intoxication

entrapment

legislative exclusion

juvenile waiver

discretionary waiver

presumptive waiver

mandatory waiver

reverse waiver

concurrent jurisdiction

diminished capacity

insanity

M'Naghten Test

Irresistible Impulse Test

Product Test

guilty but mentally ill

XYY chromosome defect

Premenstrual Dysphoric Disorder (PMDD)

Post-Traumatic Stress Disorder (PTSD)   urban survival syndrome
urban psychosis   black rage

Chapter Synthesis Questions

1. Which is more favorable—an excuse defense or a justification defense? Why?

2. Are people in the United States given enough latitude to be able to protect themselves and their property with force? Why or why not?

3. What justification is most important and why? If they are equally important, defend your answer with specifics.

4. Provide two examples of necessity and explain why they are justified.

5. What excuse defense is most difficult to prove? Why?

6. Should the insanity defense be available? Why or why not?

7. Creative excuse defenses are getting more and more popular. Is this beneficial? Why or why not?

INTRODUCTION TO CRIMINAL PROCEDURE

MODULE 10.1 **FOUNDATIONS OF CRIMINAL PROCEDURE**

Learning Objectives

- Summarize the constitutional basis for criminal procedure.
- Identify the rights of relevance in criminal procedure.

MODULE 10.2 **INTRODUCTION TO REMEDIES AND THE EXCLUSIONARY RULE**

Learning Objectives

- Explain the exclusionary rule and the exceptions to it.
- Summarize the fruit of the poisonous tree doctrine and the exceptions to it.

MODULE 10.3 **ALTERNATIVE REMEDIES**

Learning Objectives

- Explain how the criminal law can act as a remedy.
- Summarize the two key requirements for a successful Section 1983 lawsuit.
- Explain the defense of qualified immunity.
- Summarize three nonjudicial remedies.

MODULE 10.4 **JUSTIFICATION**

Learning Objectives

- Define probable cause.
- Identify several sources of information that a police officer can rely on to make the probable cause determination.
- Define reasonable suspicion and explain when it applies.
- Define administrative justification and explain when it applies.

10.1

FOUNDATIONS OF CRIMINAL PROCEDURE

Learning Objectives

- **Summarize the constitutional basis for criminal procedure.**
- **Identify the rights of relevance in criminal procedure.**

CORE CONCEPTS

American **criminal procedure** consists of a vast set of rules and guidelines that describe how suspected and accused criminals are to be handled and processed by the justice system. Of great significance is the relationship between the police and the people suspected of criminal activity. Criminal procedure arms the police with the knowledge necessary to preserve the rights of individuals who are seized, searched, arrested, and otherwise inconvenienced by law enforcement officials. It also arms other actors—such as judges, prosecutors, and defense attorneys—with the necessary information to preserve the rights of individuals accused of criminal activity. In short, criminal procedure begins when the police first contact a person and ends well after his or her conviction.

At least three important themes run throughout criminal procedure. First, there is a concern with the constitutional rights of accused persons, as interpreted by the courts. People enjoy a number of important rights in the United States, but the bulk of criminal procedure consists of *constitutional procedure* or what the U.S. Constitution says—usually through the interpretation of the U.S. Supreme Court (i.e., the Court)—with regard to the treatment of criminal suspects.

Second, criminal procedure contains an important historical dimension, one that defers regularly to how sensitive legal issues have been approached in the past. The role of *precedent*, or past decisions by the courts, cannot be overemphasized. At the same time, though, the world continues to evolve, and it is sometimes necessary to part ways with the past and decide novel legal issues.

Third, criminal procedure creates something of a collision between two different worlds: the world of the courts versus that of law enforcement. What the courts require and what law enforcement actually deals with do not always harmonize. That is, in the real world, the influence of the courts may not always be as significant or relevant as might be expected.

Emphasis on Constitutional Rights

The Preamble to the U.S. Constitution states:

> We the People of the United States, in Order to form a more perfect Union, establish Justice, insure domestic Tranquility, provide for the common defence, promote the general Welfare, and secure the Blessings of Liberty to ourselves and our Posterity, do ordain and establish this Constitution for the United States of America.

Of particular relevance to criminal procedure are the terms *justice* and *liberty*. The Constitution helps ensure these through both setting forth the various roles of government and protecting the rights of people within the nation's borders. Throughout the years, the courts have devoted a great amount of energy to interpreting the Constitution and to specifying what rights are important and when they apply. As discussed in detail later, criminal procedure focuses primarily on the Fourth, Fifth, Sixth, Eighth, and Fourteenth Amendments to the Constitution.

However, the Constitution is not the only source of rights; there are others worthy of consideration. In addition, some rights are more important than others, at least as far as criminal procedure goes. Finally, the two-tiered system of government in the United States creates a unique relationship between the federal and state levels. Criminal procedure cannot be understood without attention to the interplay between federal and states' rights.

Sources of Rights

In addition to the Constitution, important sources of rights include court decisions, statutes, and state constitutions. Most of the court decisions discussed in this section of the text are U.S. Supreme Court decisions.

Whenever the Supreme Court interprets the Constitution, it effectively makes an announcement concerning people's rights. For example, the Fourth Amendment states that unreasonable searches and seizures are impermissible. The term *unreasonable* is not self-explanatory, however, so the Court has taken steps to define it. One definition of *unreasonable* appears in the recent decision of *Wilson* v. *Layne*,[1] in which the Court held that it is unreasonable for the police to bring reporters along when serving a warrant, unless the reporters are there to serve a legitimate law enforcement objective.

Although the Constitution and the court decisions stemming from it reign supreme in criminal procedure, statutes also play an important role. Obviously, the Constitution and the courts cannot be expected to protect all of the interests that people represent. Statutes attempt to compensate for that shortcoming by establishing that certain rights exist. An example is Title VII of the 1964 Civil Rights Act. Among other things, it prohibits discrimination in employment. Another statute of relevance in criminal procedure (one that will be considered in some depth later in this chapter) is 42 U.S.C. Section 1983. It allows private citizens to sue local law enforcement officials for violations of federally protected rights.

In addition, each state has its own constitution, which can be considered an important source of rights. The supremacy clause of Article VI to the U.S. Constitution makes *it* the supreme law of the land and binds all states and the federal government to it. However, nothing in the U.S. Constitution precludes individual states from adopting stricter interpretations of the federal provisions. In general, if a state constitution gives *less* protection than the federal Constitution, such a limitation is unconstitutional. But a stricter interpretation of the federal Constitution is perfectly reasonable. For example, the Supreme Court has interpreted the Fifth Amendment in such a way that it requires police to advise a suspect of his or her so-called *Miranda*

---

[1] *Wilson v. Layne*, 526 U.S. 603 (1999).

rights when the suspect is subjected to custodial interrogation—an action that does not necessarily rise to the level of an arrest. A *state*, however, could require that *Miranda* rights be read whenever a person is arrested, regardless of whether he or she is interrogated.

Finally, although it is not a source of rights per se, the ***Federal Rules of Criminal Procedure*** are worth considering.[2] Excerpts from the *Federal Rules* are reprinted throughout this section of the text because they sometimes clarify important rulings handed down by the U.S. Supreme Court. In addition, the *Federal Rules* set forth the criminal procedure guidelines by which federal criminal justice practitioners are required to abide.

Fourth Amendment Part of the U.S. Constitution that protects against unreasonable searches and seizures, plus it spells out warrant requirements.

Rights of Relevance in Criminal Procedure

Of the many rights specified in the U.S. Constitution (which, incidentally, is reprinted in the Appendix), the rights stemming from five amendments are of special importance in criminal procedure. Four of these—the Fourth, Fifth, Sixth, and Eighth Amendments—can be found in the Bill of Rights. Beyond the Bill of Rights, the Fourteenth Amendment is of special relevance in criminal procedure. Sometimes the First Amendment, which protects assembly and speech, and the Second Amendment, which protects the right to bear arms, are relevant in criminal procedure, but only rarely.

The **Fourth Amendment** is perhaps the most well-known source of rights in criminal procedure. The Fourth Amendment states:

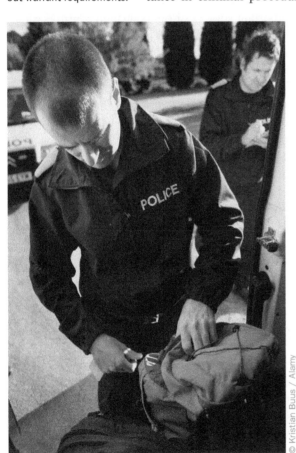

> The right of the people to be secure in their persons, houses, papers, and effects, against unreasonable searches and seizures, shall not be violated, and no Warrants shall issue, but upon probable cause, supported by Oath or affirmation and particularly describing the place to be searched, and the persons or things to be seized.

Several rights can be distinguished by reading the text of the Fourth Amendment. It refers to the right of people to be free from unreasonable searches and seizures, and it provides that specific requirements are to guide the warrant process. That is, a warrant must be issued by a magistrate or judge, supported under oath or affirmation by probable cause, and sufficiently specific as to what is to be searched and/or seized. Because of the complexity of the Fourth Amendment, this book devotes an entire chapter to its interpretation (see Chapter 11).

Searches are protected by the Fourth Amendment and must be reasonable, which generally means based on probable cause.

© Kristian Buus / Alamy

[2]*Federal Rules of Criminal Procedure*, http://www.law.cornell.edu/rules/frcrmp/ (accessed March 30, 2012).

The second constitutional amendment of special relevance to criminal procedure is the Fifth Amendment. It states:

> No person shall be held to answer for a capital, or otherwise infamous crime, unless on a presentment or indictment of a Grand Jury, except in cases arising in the land or naval forces, or in the Militia, when in actual service in time of War or public danger; nor shall any person be subject for the same offense to be twice put in jeopardy of life or limb; nor shall be compelled in any criminal case to be a witness against himself, nor be deprived of life, liberty, or property, without due process of law; nor shall private property be taken for public use, without just compensation.

This section of the text also examines the Fifth Amendment in detail, focusing in particular on the role of the grand jury, the statement that no one can be compelled "to be a witness against himself" (also known as the *self-incrimination* clause), and perhaps most important of all, the requirement that an individual cannot be deprived of life, liberty, or property without due process of law. The Fifth Amendment also contains the no-familiar double-jeopardy provision. We introduced this back in Chapter 2, as it applies in the criminal law context, too.

The Sixth Amendment is also of great importance in criminal procedure. It specifies:

> In all criminal prosecutions, the accused shall enjoy the right to a speedy and public trial, by an impartial jury of the State and district wherein the crime shall have been committed, which district shall have been previously ascertained by law, and to be informed of the nature and cause of the accusation; to be confronted with the witnesses against him; to have compulsory process for obtaining witnesses in his favor, and to have the Assistance of Counsel for his defence [sic].

Of relevance to criminal procedure is the Sixth Amendment's language concerning speedy and public trials, impartial juries, confrontation, and compulsory process. The Sixth Amendment also suggests that in addition to being public, trials should be open, not closed, proceedings. The Supreme Court has interpreted the Sixth Amendment as providing the right of the accused to be present at his or her trial and to be able to put on a defense.

The Eighth Amendment is relevant in criminal procedure but to a limited extent. It states:

> Excessive bail shall not be required, nor excessive fines imposed, nor cruel and unusual punishments inflicted.

The Eighth Amendment will be discussed in Module 15–2 in regards to sentencing criminal defendants who are either convicted of a crime or plead guilty.

The Fourteenth Amendment has an important home in criminal procedure. It is a fairly long amendment, however, and only a small portion is relevant to the handling and treatment of criminal suspects. That portion states:

> All persons born or naturalized in the United States, and subject to the jurisdiction thereof, are citizens of the United States and of the State wherein they reside. No State shall make or enforce any law which shall abridge the privileges or immunities of citizens of the United States, nor shall any State deprive any person of life, liberty, or property, without due process of law; nor deny to any person within its jurisdiction the equal protection of the laws.

Fifth Amendment Part of the U.S. Constitution that protects against compelled self-incrimination, plus spells out other important rights.

Sixth Amendment Part of the U.S. Constitution that provides the right to counsel, the right to jury trial, and other protections for the accused.

Eighth Amendment Part of the U.S. Constitution, which states: "Excessive bail shall not be required, nor excessive fines imposed, nor cruel and unusual punishments inflicted."

Fourteenth Amendment A part of the U.S. Constitution that has been used to incorporate various protections spelled out in the Bill of Rights, plus provides other protections, such as due process of law.

The due process language of the Fourteenth Amendment mirrors that of the Fifth Amendment. Nonetheless, because the Fifth Amendment is part of the Bill of Rights, it is only binding on the federal government. The Fourteenth Amendment, by contrast, has been used by the Supreme Court to *incorporate*, or make applicable to the states, several of the rights provided for in the Bill of Rights. (The following subsection introduces the so-called incorporation controversy.)

substantive due process
Protection from arbitrary and unreasonable action on the part of state officials.

procedural due process
Protection of significant life, liberty, or property interests, sometimes described as "procedural fairness."

The Fourteenth Amendment's due process clause has been interpreted to consist of two types of due process: (1) **substantive due process** and (2) **procedural due process**. The essence of substantive due process is protection from arbitrary and unreasonable action on the part of state officials. By contrast, a procedural due process violation is one in which a violation of a significant life, liberty, or property interest occurs.[3] Procedural due process is akin to procedural fairness.

Figure 10.1 lists the constitutional amendments that are of particular importance in criminal procedure. As the following section will describe, certain rights that are provided for in each amendment may not be binding on the states. Also, even though a particular amendment may provide a particular right, the Supreme Court may have interpreted that amendment to apply only in certain circumstances. Such circumstances will be discussed throughout the text.

The Incorporation Controversy

Incorporation The Supreme Court's practice of using the Fourteenth Amendment's due process clause, which holds that no state shall "deprive any person of life, liberty, or property, without due process of law," to make certain protections specified in the Bill of Rights applicable to the states.

The Bill of Rights, consisting of the first ten amendments to the U.S. Constitution, places limitations on the powers of the federal government. It does *not* limit the power of the states, however. In other words, the first ten amendments place no limitations on state and local governments and their agencies. Government power at the state and local levels is clearly limited by state constitutions.

Even though the Bill of Rights does not limit state and local governments, the Supreme Court has found a way to do so through the Fourteenth Amendment. In particular, the Court has used the Fourteenth Amendment's due process clause, which holds that no state shall "deprive any person of life, liberty, or property, without due process of law," to make certain protections specified in the Bill of Rights applicable to the states. This is known as **incorporation**.

The extent to which the Fourteenth Amendment should regulate state and local government power has been the subject of some disagreement—hence, the incorporation controversy. The basic question posed over the years has been "To what degree

Figure 10.1
Constitutional Amendments Important to Criminal Procedure and Their Relevant Provisions

- **Fourth Amendment:** Protects from unreasonable searches and seizures.
- **Fifth Amendment:** Provides protection from double jeopardy and self-incrimination and for grand jury indictment in serious crimes.
- **Sixth Amendment:** Provides for a speedy and public trial, impartial jury, confrontation, compulsory process, and assistance of counsel.
- **Eighth Amendment:** Protects from cruel and unusual punishment.
- **Fourteenth Amendment:** Includes the so-called due process clause, which has been used to incorporate various other rights described in the Bill of Rights.

---

[3]See, e.g., *Geddes* v. *Northwest Missouri State College*, 49 F.3d 426 (8th Cir. 1995).

Right	Deciding Case
First Amendment freedom of religion, speech, and assembly and the right to petition for redress of grievances	*Fiske v. Kamsas,* 274 U.S.380(1927)
Fourth Amendent prohibition of unreasonable searches and seizures	*Wolf v. Colorado,* 338 U.S.25(1949)
Fifth Amendment protection against compelled self-incrimination	*Malloy v. Hogan,* 378 U.S. 1(1964)
Fifth Amendment protection from double jeopardy	*Benton v. Maryland,* 395 U.S. 784(1969)
Sixth Amendment right to counsel	*Gideon v. Wainwright,* 372 U.S. 335(1963)
Sixth Amendment right to a speedy trial	*Klopfer v. North Carolina,* 386 U.S 213(1967)
Sixth Amendment right to public trial	*In re Oliver,* 333 U.S. 257(1948)
Sixth Amendment right to confrontation	*Pointer v. Texas,* 380 U.S. 400(1965)
Sixth amendment right to an impartial jury	*Duncan v. Louisiana,* 391 U.S. 145(1968)
Sixth Amendment right to compulsory process	*Washington v. Texas,* 388 U.S. 14(1967)
Eighth Amendment prohibition of cruel and unusual punishment	*Robinson v. California,* 370 U.S. 660(1962)

Figure 10.2
Rights Incorporated to the States

should the Fourteenth Amendment's due process clause incorporate the various provisions of the Bill of Rights so as to restrict state and local law enforcement in the same way federal law enforcement is restricted by the Bill of Rights?"

Figure 10.2 lists the rights that have been deemed fundamental by the Supreme Court and, as a result, incorporated to the states.[4] The Supreme Court cases responsible for these incorporation decisions are listed, as well.

YOUR DECISION

1. The First Amendment to the U.S. Constitution provides that "Congress shall make no law respecting an establishment of religion, or prohibiting the free exercise thereof; or abridging the freedom of speech, or of the press; or the right of the people peaceably to assemble, and to petition the Government for a redress of grievances." Given what you have read so far, is the First Amendment relevant to criminal procedure?

2. Assume federal agents have a trained dog sniff airline passengers' luggage on a baggage carousel in an airport. What constitutional amendment governs this activity, if any, and why?

Summary

- Criminal procedure is mostly about constitutional rights. What's more, it is about constitutional rights as primarily interpreted by the U.S. Supreme Court.

- The Fourth, Fifth, Sixth, Eighth, and portions of the Fourteenth Amendments are particularly relevant in criminal procedure.

---

[4]Some scholars believe that the Ninth Amendment to the U.S. Constitution (also referred to as the *penumbra clause*) implies that all of the rights not specifically spelled out in the Constitution are automatically protected nonetheless. But to demonstrate this, a court would have to recognize a particular right as fundamental in case law. Privacy could be considered one such right.

- Incorporation is concerned with the extent to which certain rights spelled out in the Bill of Rights (first ten amendments to the U.S. Constitution) are applicable to the states.

MODULE

10.2

INTRODUCTION TO REMEDIES AND THE EXCLUSIONARY RULE

Learning Objectives
- **Explain the exclusionary rule and the exceptions to it.**
- **Summarize the fruit of the poisonous tree doctrine and the exceptions to it.**

CORE CONCEPTS

remedy A method of rectifying wrongdoing.

extralegal remedies Remedies conducted outside the legal process, such as a personal vendetta.

legal remedies Remedies made available by the law, by a court decision, or by a police agency policy or procedure.

Criminal procedure cannot be fully appreciated without some discussion of remedies. A **remedy** provides a method of rectifying wrongdoing. That is, when a person believes he or she has been harmed in some way, he or she may seek to ease the pain, make the person who caused the harm "pay," or both. For example, if Sandy is unjustifiably assaulted by Jim, an on-duty police officer, she may opt to remedy the wrong inflicted on her. A remedy is the mechanism for enforcing violations of people's rights.

Remedies fall into two categories: (1) legal and (2) extralegal. **Extralegal remedies** are those conducted outside the legal process. A good example of an extralegal remedy is vigilantism. For example, if one man is assaulted by another, the assaulted individual may seek revenge and opt to solve the perceived injustice with his fists. Our focus here is on **legal remedies**—that is, remedies made available by the law, by a court decision, or by a police agency policy or procedure.

The most frequently discussed remedy in criminal procedure is the *exclusionary rule*. As such, the whole of this module is devoted to it. It is an example of a remedy made available because of court decisions; that is, it has no statutory basis. But in order to place the exclusionary rule in context, this chapter also focuses on other types of remedies, such as those provided in law and agency practice. These remedies are important because the exclusionary rule applies only in limited contexts. They are introduced in the third module.

The bulk of criminal procedure concerns *constitutional* procedure. It focuses on the various forms of government action permitted and not permitted by the U.S. Constitution. Accordingly, the bulk of the discussion in this and the next module is on remedies for constitutional rights violations—particularly the exclusionary rule and 42 U.S.C. Section 1983 (or, simply, Section 1983), a statute that provides people with an avenue for suing criminal justice officials. However, there are several situations in which neither the exclusionary rule nor 42 U.S.C. Section 1983 applies. Therefore, Module 3 also focuses on additional remedies that are available to people whose *constitutional* rights are not violated but whose *rights* are violated, nonetheless. These include disciplinary procedures, civilian review, mediation, and even the criminal law.

The Exclusionary Rule

exclusionary rule The Supreme Court-created rule requiring that evidence obtained in violation of the Constitution cannot be used in a criminal trial to prove guilt.

By far, the most significant remedy in criminal procedure is the exclusionary rule. It is, simply, a rule of exclusion. The exclusionary rule requires that evidence obtained in violation of the Constitution cannot be used in a criminal trial to prove guilt. It is a rule, as opposed to a constitutional provision, because nowhere in the Constitution does it say that illegally obtained evidence must be excluded at trial. In other words, the Supreme Court created the exclusionary rule through its case law.

History of the Exclusionary Rule

Somewhat surprisingly, the U.S. Constitution contains no provisions for enforcing the protections enunciated in the Bill of Rights. For example, even though people enjoy the right to be free from unreasonable searches and seizures, the Constitution does not specify how this right is to be enforced.

For a time, then, the Bill of Rights was more or less a sham, especially when it came to criminal procedure. Without a means for remedying an unlawful search, improperly obtained confession, or similar violation, evidence obtained in flagrant violation of the Constitution could be admissible at trial.

Weeks v. *United States*[5] was the first exclusionary rule case of major note. In that case, the Court held that papers seized following a search that was in violation of the Fourth Amendment should have been returned, rather than used in a criminal trial against the petitioner. *Weeks* was a federal case, however, meaning that states were not yet bound by it.

Elkins v. *United States*[6] took a step toward applying the exclusionary rule to the states. In that case, the Court denounced the so-called "silver platter" doctrine, which permitted the use of evidence in *federal* court that had been obtained illegally by *state* officials. For example, federal officials could not expect illegally obtained evidence to be admissible if they seized it (the decision in *Weeks*), but under the silver platter doctrine, they could ask state law enforcement officials to seize the evidence, even in violation of the Constitution, and it would be admissible in federal court. The silver platter doctrine, then, was a convenient means of circumventing the *Weeks* decision. The Court caught on to this practice and scrapped the doctrine.

"silver platter" doctrine A practice that permitted the use of evidence in *federal* court that had been obtained illegally by *state* officials.

The year 1961 marked a watershed in criminal procedure, as it was the year the Supreme Court decided the landmark case of *Mapp* v. *Ohio*.[7] Arguably, this was, and continues to be, the most significant criminal procedure case the Supreme Court has decided. In *Mapp*, the Court decided 5–4 that the exclusionary rule applies to the states. It concluded that other remedies, such as reliance on the due process clause to enforce Fourth Amendment violations, had proven "worthless and futile." Justice Clark, in a related case, stated that the exclusionary rule is the "imperative of judicial integrity," noting, "The criminal goes free, if he must, but it is the law that sets him free. Nothing can destroy a government more quickly than its failure to observe its own law, or worse, its disregard of the charter of its own existence."[8]

---

[5] *Weeks* v. *United States*, 232 U.S. 383 (1914).
[6] *Elkins* v. *United States*, 364 U.S. 206 (1960).
[7] *Mapp* v. *Ohio*, 367 U.S. 643 (1961).
[8] *Elkins* v. *United States*, 364 U.S. 206 (1960), p. 222.

The Logic behind Incorporating the Exclusionary Rule

Mapp v. *Ohio*
367 U.S. 643 (1961)

Decision: "All evidence obtained by searches and seizures in violation of the Federal Constitution is inadmissible in a criminal trial in a state court."

Reason: Some five years after *Wolf,* in answer to a plea made here Term after Term that we overturn its doctrine on applicability of the *Weeks* exclusionary rule, this Court indicated that such should not be done until the States had "adequate opportunity to adopt or reject the [*Weeks*] rule." . . .

And only last Term, after again carefully reexamining the *Wolf* doctrine in *Elkins* v. *United States,* . . ., the Court pointed out that "the controlling principles" as to search and seizure and the problem of admissibility "seemed clear" . . . until the announcement in *Wolf* "that the Due Process Clause of the Fourteenth Amendment does not itself require state courts to adopt the exclusionary rule" of the *Weeks* case. . . . At the same time, the Court pointed out,

"the underlying constitutional doctrine which *Wolf* established . . . that the Federal Constitution . . . prohibits unreasonable searches and seizures by state officers"

had undermined the "foundation upon which the admissibility of state-seized evidence in a federal trial originally rested . . ." . . . The Court concluded that it was therefore obliged to hold, although it chose the narrower ground on which to do so, that all evidence obtained by an unconstitutional search and seizure was inadmissible in a federal court regardless of its source. Today we once again examine *Wolf*'s constitutional documentation of the right to privacy free from unreasonable state intrusion, and, after its dozen years on our books, are led by it to close the only courtroom door remaining open to evidence secured by official lawlessness in flagrant abuse of that basic right, reserved to all persons as a specific guarantee against that very same unlawful conduct. We hold that all evidence obtained by searches and seizures in violation of the Constitution is, by that same authority, inadmissible in a state court.

Since the Fourth Amendment's right of privacy has been declared enforceable against the States through the Due Process Clause of the Fourteenth, it is enforceable against them by the same sanction of exclusion as is used against the Federal Government. Were it otherwise, then, just as without the *Weeks* rule the assurance against unreasonable federal searches and seizures would be "a form of words" valueless and undeserving of mention in a perpetual charter of inestimable human liberties, so too, without that rule, the freedom from state invasions of privacy would be so ephemeral and so neatly severed from its conceptual nexus with the freedom from all brutish means of coercing evidence as not to merit this Court's high regard as a freedom "implicit in the concept of ordered liberty." At the time that the Court held in *Wolf* [v. *Colorado*, 338 U.S. 25 (1949)] that the Amendment was applicable to the States through the Due Process Clause, the cases of this Court, as we have seen, had steadfastly held that as to federal officers the Fourth Amendment included the exclusion

(continued)

**COURT
DECISION**
(continued)

of the evidence seized in violation of its provisions. Even *Wolf* "stoutly adhered" to that proposition. The right to privacy, when conceded operatively enforceable against the States, was not susceptible of destruction by avulsion of the sanction upon which its protection and enjoyment had always been deemed dependent under the *Boyd, Weeks* and *Silverthorne* cases. Therefore, in extending the substantive protections of due process to all constitutionally unreasonable searches – state or federal – it was logically and constitutionally necessary that the exclusion doctrine – an essential part of the right to privacy – be also insisted upon as an essential ingredient of the right newly recognized by the *Wolf* case. In short, the admission of the new constitutional right by *Wolf* could not consistently tolerate denial of its most important constitutional privilege, namely, the exclusion of the evidence which an accused had been forced to give by reason of the unlawful seizure. To hold otherwise is to grant the right but, in reality, to withhold its privilege and enjoyment. Only last year, the Court itself recognized that the purpose of the exclusionary rule "is to deter – to compel respect for the constitutional guaranty in the only effectively available way – by removing the incentive to disregard it."

Exceptions to the Exclusionary Rule

Critics of the exclusionary rule routinely argue that it constitutes a loophole in the criminal justice process and is responsible for otherwise guilty criminals going free. On the whole, this argument is somewhat deceptive, in part because of the exceptions allowed to the exclusionary rule. Over the years, the Supreme Court has seen fit to *allow* evidence in light of honest mistakes as well as for other purposes. There are two key exceptions to the exclusionary rule: (1) the "good faith" exception and (2) the impeachment exception.

Good Faith Exception

"good faith" exception
An exception to the exclusionary rule providing that when an honest mistake is made during the course of a search or seizure, any subsequently obtained evidence will be considered admissible.

As a general rule, when an honest mistake is made during the course of a search or seizure, any subsequently obtained evidence will be considered admissible. Two cases decided together were responsible for this "good faith" exception: *United States* v. *Leon* and *Massachusetts* v. *Sheppard*.[9] In both *Leon* and *Sheppard*, the Supreme Court concluded that evidence obtained in reasonable (good faith) reliance on a defective warrant was admissible:

> [W]e cannot conclude that admitting evidence obtained pursuant to a warrant while at the same time declaring that the warrant was somehow defective will in any way reduce judicial officers' professional incentives to comply with the Fourth Amendment, encourage them to repeat their mistakes, or lead to the granting of all colorable warrant requests.[10]

---

[9]*United States* v. *Leon*, 468 U.S. 897 (1984) and *Massachusetts v. Sheppard*, 468 U.S. 981 (1984).
[10]*United States* v. *Leon*, 468 U.S. 897 (1984), p. 917.

The good faith exception enunciated in *Leon* and *Sheppard* is not unqualified, however. If, for example, a warrant is "so lacking in indicia of probable cause as to render official belief in its existence entirely unreasonable, then evidence obtained following its service will not be admissible."[11] Similarly, if a warrant is "so facially deficient—i.e., in failing to particularize the place to be searched or things to be seized—that the executing officers cannot reasonably presume it to be valid, then the exception does not apply."[12] Furthermore, if the judge issuing the warrant is deliberately misled by information in the affidavit, as when a police officer acts in *bad* faith, then the good faith exception will not apply.[13] Also, if the judge issues a search warrant without sufficient consideration, then good faith cannot later be asserted.

The good faith exception is not held in the highest regard by some. Critics believe that it gives police officers an incentive to "forum shop" or to find judges who will be quick to sign off on a warrant. Justice Brennan argued in opposition to the exception as follows:

> Creation of this new exception for good faith reliance upon a warrant implicitly tells magistrates that they need not take much care in reviewing warrant applications, since their mistakes will from now on have virtually no consequence: If their decision to issue a warrant is correct, the evidence will be admitted; if their decision was incorrect but [not "entirely unreasonable" and] the police rely in good faith on the warrant, the evidence will also be admitted. Inevitably, the care and attention devoted to such an inconsequential chore will dwindle.[14]

The good faith exception has been extended to other situations besides searches and seizures based on defective warrants. For instance, if a police officer acts in reasonable reliance on a statute that is later found to be unconstitutional, then the good faith exception will not apply.[15] In addition, if evidence is obtained following a search or seizure that is conducted in reasonable reliance on computer records that turn out to be inaccurate, then, again, the exception will not apply. In *Arizona* v. *Evans*,[16] for example, a defendant was arrested during a traffic stop because the officer's computer showed an outstanding warrant that, unknown to the officer, had been quashed 17 days earlier. Evidence obtained from a search of the vehicle was admissible because, according to the Court, "there is no basis for believing that application of the exclusionary rule in these circumstances will have a significant effect on court employees responsible for informing the police that a warrant has been quashed."[17] A similar decision was reached in a more recent case where the police arrested an individual and found contraband in a search incident to arrest, yet unbeknownst to the officers, the arrest warrant had been recalled months earlier.[18]

---

[11]*United States* v. *Hove*, 848 F.2d 137 (9th Cir. 1988), p. 139.
[12]*United States* v. *Leary*, 846 F.2d 592 (10th Cir. 1988), p. 607.
[13]*Lo-Ji* v. *State of New York*, 442 U.S. 319 (1979).
[14]*United States* v. *Leon*, 468 U.S. 897 (1984), p. 956.
[15]*Michigan* v. *DeFillippo*, 443 U.S. 31 (1979).
[16]*Arizona* v. *Evans*, 514 U.S. 1 (1995).
[17]Ibid., p. 15.
[18]*Herring* v. *United States*, 555 U.S. 135 (2009).

Impeachment Exception

impeachment exception An exception to the exclusionary rule providing that evidence considered inadmissible at one trial can be used in later trial to impeach (i.e., cast doubt on the credibility) the defendant.

The next leading exception to the exclusionary rule is the so-called impeachment exception. If an exception to the exclusionary rule does not apply, then the prosecution cannot use, as part of its case, evidence resulting from an illegal search or seizure. However, if the prosecution seeks to use such evidence for the purpose of impeaching (i.e., attacking the credibility of) a witness, then it will be considered admissible for that purpose. In *Walder v. United States*,[19] a narcotics case, the Supreme Court permitted the introduction of heroin that had been illegally seized from the defendant two years earlier (and excluded from the trial it was supposed to be used in) in order to attack his statement that he had never purchased, used, or sold drugs. An important restriction concerning the impeachment exception is that it applies only to criminal defendants, not other witnesses.[20] As a reminder, impeachment is not the same as introducing evidence to prove guilt. It is concerned solely with questioning the credibility of a witness, and the defendant can act as a witness if he or she takes the stand.

Good faith and impeachment are, again, the only two recognized exceptions to the exclusionary rule. Three additional exclusionary rule-type exceptions (i.e., inevitable discovery, independent source, and purged taint) are sometimes blended together with these two, but they should be kept separate. They are actually exceptions to the "fruit of poisonous tree" doctrine, to which the discussion turns now.

The "Fruit of the Poisonous Tree" Doctrine

"fruit of the poisonous tree" doctrine An extension of the exclusionary rule. The poisonous tree is the initial unconstitutional search or seizure. Anything obtained from the tree is considered forbidden fruit and is not admissible at trial.

The exclusionary rule has been expanded to other types of evidence. In *Silverthorne Lumber Co. v. United States*,[21] the Supreme Court created the "fruit of the poisonous tree" doctrine.[22] In that case, Silverthorne Lumber Company was convicted on contempt charges for failing to produce documents that were learned of during the course of an illegal search. The Court reversed the conviction, stating that forcing the company to produce documents that were learned of strictly because of an illegal search violated the Fourth Amendment. The *Silverthorne* holding was reaffirmed in the case of *Nardone v. United States*.[23] In it, the Court noted that it should be left to the discretion of "experienced trial judges" to determine whether "a substantial portion of the case against [the accused] was a fruit of the poisonous tree."[24]

The metaphor of the "fruit of the poisonous tree" can be traced to the biblical story of the Garden of Eden. As the story goes, Adam and Eve ate the apple, the forbidden fruit, from the tree, bringing original sin into the world. The poisonous tree, then, is the initial unconstitutional search or seizure. Anything obtained from the tree is considered forbidden fruit.

---

[19] *Walder v. United States*, 347 U.S. 62 (1954).
[20] *James v. Illinois*, 493 U.S. 307 (1990).
[21] *Silverthorne Lumber Co. v. United States*, 251 U.S. 385 (1920).
[22] Courts often use the term *derivative evidence* in lieu of "fruit of the poisonous tree." The former refers simply to evidence *derived* from a previous unconstitutional search or seizure.
[23] *Nardone v. United States*, 308 U.S. 338 (1939).
[24] Ibid., p. 341.

In short, the exclusionary rule applies not only to evidence obtained as a direct result of a constitutional rights violation but also to evidence *indirectly* derived from a constitutional rights violation. In many ways, the fruit of the poisonous tree doctrine resembles a "but for" test, in which the courts have to ask. But for the unconstitutional police conduct, would the evidence have been obtained regardless? If the answer is no, then the evidence will be excluded. If the answer is yes, then the issue becomes more complicated. The Supreme Court has carved out three important exceptions to the fruit of the poisonous tree doctrine.

Exceptions to Fruit of the Poisonous Tree

There are three main exceptions to the fruit of the poisonous tree doctrine. They are purged taint, independent source, and inevitable discovery. Each is briefly introduced in the following subsections.

Purged Taint

"purged taint" exception
An exception to the fruit of poisonous tree doctrine that permits the introduction of evidence if it has become attenuated to the extent that it dissipated the taint of the initial unconstitutional act.

The first exception to the fruit of the poisonous tree doctrine is known as the *attenuation*, or **"purged taint" exception**. In *Nardone*, Justice Frankfurter observed that in some cases, "sophisticated argument may prove a causal link obtained through [illegality] and the Government's proof. As a matter of good sense, however, such a connection may have become so attenuated as to dissipate the taint."[25] This observation was somewhat prophetic in the sense that the Court did not actually admit evidence because of attenuation. Several years later, in the case of *Wong Sun v. United States*,[26] however, the Court did admit evidence because of attenuation.

In making an attenuation analysis, the court must decide whether the derivative evidence was obtained by exploitation of the initial unconstitutional act or instead by other means that are purged of the primary taint. In *Wong Sun*, the Court determined that statements provided by a defendant who was illegally arrested and released but later returned to the police station on his own initiative were admissible because the statements did not result from the illegal arrest. Instead, the defendant decided to come back *later*, following his release. The Court noted that his statement had become attenuated to the extent that it dissipated the taint of the initial unconstitutional act.

In *Brown v. Illinois*,[27] the Supreme Court pointed to several factors that should be considered in determining whether the purged taint exception applies: (1) whether the *Miranda* warnings were given prior to a voluntary confession, (2) the "temporal proximity" of the illegal police conduct and verbal statements made by a suspect, (3) the presence of intervening events or circumstances, and (4) the "purpose and flagrancy of the official misconduct." Several later cases focused on these four factors to varying degrees.

---

[25] Ibid.
[26] *Wong Sun v. United States*, 371 U.S. 471 (1963).
[27] *Brown v. Illinois*, 422 U.S. 590 (1975).

For example, in *Dunaway* v. *New York*,[28] the Court chose to decide whether a confession obtained following a questionable stationhouse detention was admissible. The *Miranda* warnings had been given, but the Court still held that stationhouse detention intruded "so severely on interests protected by the Fourth Amendment as necessarily to trigger the traditional safeguards against illegal arrest."[29] The Court then held that despite the *Miranda* warnings, Dunaway's statements should not be admissible. To hold differently would allow "law enforcement officers to violate the Fourth Amendment with impunity, safe in the knowledge that they could wash their hands in the 'procedural safeguards' of the Fifth."[30]

In another case, *Taylor* v. *Alabama*,[31] the Court held that the purged taint exception should not apply even under these circumstances: (1) the defendant had been advised of his *Miranda* rights, (2) six hours had elapsed between the defendant's illegal arrest and confession, and (3) the defendant had been permitted to visit with friends before making his confession.

Contrast *Taylor* with *Rawlings* v. *Kentucky*,[32] in which the Court held that statements made 45 minutes after an illegal arrest *were* admissible because the defendant (1) had been advised of his *Miranda* rights just before making an incriminating statement, (2) had been in a house instead of a police station, and (3) had made spontaneous statements that did not result from direct questioning. Furthermore, the Court noted that the illegal arrest was not flagrant and that the defendant never argued that his admission was an involuntary product of police questioning.

Independent Source

independent source An exception to the fruit of the poisonous tree doctrine that permits the introduction of evidence if it has arrived via an independent source, such as a party disconnected from the case at hand.

The second exception to the fruit of the poisonous tree doctrine is the so-called **independent source** exception. The first case to affirmatively establish this type of exception was *Segura* v. *United States*.[33] There, the Court held that evidence found in an apartment pursuant to a valid search warrant was admissible, even though the police had entered the apartment illegally *prior* to serving the search warrant because the warrant was based on information totally disconnected with the initial illegal search. In other words, even though the police first entered the apartment illegally, the warrant they later served was based on information independent from that search.

Inevitable Discovery

inevitable discovery exception An exception to the fruit of the poisonous tree doctrine that permits the introduction of evidence if it would have been discovered anyway.

The third exception to the fruit of the poisonous tree doctrine is known as the **inevitable discovery exception**. Stated simply, if evidence would be found regardless of unconstitutional police conduct, then it is admissible. This exception was first recognized by the Supreme Court in *Nix* v. *Williams*.[34] In that case, the evidence was the body of a young girl, which was discovered after the police had illegally questioned

---

[28] *Dunaway* v. *New York*, 442 U.S. 200 (1979).
[29] Ibid., p. 216.
[30] Ibid., p. 219.
[31] *Taylor* v. *Alabama*, 457 U.S. 687 (1982).
[32] *Rawlings* v. *Kentucky*, 448 U.S. 98 (1980).
[33] *Segura* v. *United States*, 468 U.S. 796 (1984).
[34] *Nix* v. *Williams*, 467 U.S. 431 (1984).

the defendant concerning the body's whereabouts. Under ordinary circumstances, the body would not have been considered admissible, but the prosecution was able to prove that at the time of the illegal questioning, a search party looking for the girl's body had narrowed in on its target and would have "inevitably discovered" the body. The Iowa Supreme Court affirmed the lower court's decision to admit the body into evidence because "(1) the police did not act in bad faith for the purpose of hastening discovery of the evidence in question, and (2) . . . the evidence in question would have been discovered by lawful means."[35]

The inevitable discovery exception bears striking resemblance to the independent source exception. For all practical purposes, evidence that would be inevitably discovered comes from an independent source. The search that was underway in *Nix v. Williams*, for example, was totally disconnected from the questioning of the defendant. In light of the similarities between these two exceptions to the fruit of the poisonous tree doctrine, some courts have simply opted to call the inevitable discovery exception the *hypothetical independent source* exception.[36]

YOUR DECISION

1. Police Officer Wesson stopped a car that met the description of one supposedly driven away by two suspects from the scene of a burglary. He arrested both occupants and searched the car, finding illegal weapons in the trunk. It turns out the vehicle description was wrong and that Wesson arrested the wrong men. Nevertheless, should Officer Wesson's arrest come under the good faith exception to the exclusionary rule?

2. Suspecting that people were storing marijuana in a warehouse, several police officers entered the building without obtaining a warrant to do so. (Later, they argued that they had suspected that evidence would be destroyed or that the people would escape if they had waited to obtain a warrant.) In fact, the search revealed bales of marijuana but no people. The police then applied for a warrant to search the building, deliberately failing to mention their previous search. The warrant was granted, the search was conducted, and the police "discovered" the marijuana. Should the marijuana be considered admissible at trial?

Summary

- The exclusionary rule requires that evidence obtained in violation of certain constitutional amendments (notably the Fourth, Fifth, Sixth, and Fourteenth) be excluded from criminal trial.

- Exceptions to the exclusionary rule have been recognized in cases in which (1) the police acted in good faith but nonetheless violated the Constitution and (2) the prosecutor sought to impeach a witness at trial by pointing to contradictions in his or her out-of-court statements, even if such statements were obtained in an unconstitutional manner.

---

[35] *Iowa v. Williams*, 285 N.W.2d 248 (Iowa 1979), p. 260
[36] *Nix v. Williams*, 467 U.S. 431 (1984), p. 438.

- The exclusionary rule has been extended to require that derivative evidence obtained from a constitutional rights violation also be excluded. This is known as the "fruit of the poisonous tree" doctrine.
- Exceptions to the fruit of the poisonous tree doctrine include inevitable discovery, independent source, and purged taint.

MODULE 10.3

ALTERNATIVE REMEDIES

Learning Objectives

- **Explain how the criminal law can act as a remedy.**
- **Summarize the two key requirements for a successful Section 1983 lawsuit.**
- **Explain the defense of qualified immunity.**
- **Summarize three nonjudicial remedies.**

CORE CONCEPTS

When a person's constitutional or states rights are violated, the exclusionary rule is only one of the remedies available. As an alternative, the injured individual could "press charges" by seeking a criminal prosecution against the offending party. Or the person could initiate a civil lawsuit for monetary damages. Each of these remedies is introduced in detail in the present module.

Criminal Law

Various statutes at the federal and local levels provide criminal remedies for police misconduct, just like the exclusionary rule does. Some states make it criminal for police officers to trespass and/or to falsely arrest people. In fact, most criminal sanctions that apply to ordinary citizens also apply to police officers. Likewise, various statutes at the federal level make it not only improper but also criminal for police officers to engage in certain types of conduct.

The most common federal statute for holding police officers criminally liable is **18 U.S.C. Section 242**. It states:

18 U.S.C. Section 242 A federal statute used to hold police officers (and other government actors) criminally liable for actions that cause violations of people's constitutional or other federally protected rights.

> Whoever, under color of any law, statute, ordinance, regulation, or custom, willfully subjects any inhabitant of any State, Territory, or District to the deprivation of any rights, privileges, or immunities secured or protected by the Constitution or laws of the United States, or to different punishments, pains, or penalties, on account of such inhabitant being an alien, or by reason of his color, or race, than are prescribed for the punishment of citizens, shall be fined not more than $1,000 or imprisoned not more than one year, or both; and if death results shall be subject to imprisonment for any term of years or for life.

Although it is a federal statute, Section 242 can be used to prosecute either a state or a federal law enforcement officer. In other words, a state police officer who violates Section 242 can be charged criminally in federal court.

To be held liable under Section 242, a law enforcement officer must act with specific intent to deprive a person of important constitutional (or other federal) rights.[37] Also, for criminal liability under Section 242, a constitutional right must be clearly established.[38] Together, these restrictions have resulted in the filing of relatively few Section 242 cases. In fact, criminal liability under Section 242 is reserved for the most egregious forms of police misconduct.

Additional federal statutes make it a criminal act to unlawfully search and seize individuals,[39] although applications of this statute are rare, as well. Section 2235 of 18 U.S.C. makes it criminal to maliciously procure a warrant, and Section 2234 makes it criminal to exceed the authority of a warrant. Regardless of which criminal statute applies, an important distinction needs to be made between the various criminal statutes and 42 U.S.C. Section 1983 (discussed below). An officer who is held *criminally* liable will receive a criminal conviction and can even go to prison. Section 1983, by contrast, is *civil*, meaning that it is used independently of the criminal process. A successful Section 1983 lawsuit will never result in imprisonment of the defendant.

Some crimes are committed by police officers more often than other crimes. Birzer places such offenses into three categories: (1) violent and sex crimes, (2) drug crimes, and (3) other crimes.[40] With respect to violent crimes, the so-called Miami River Cops were charged with murdering drug smugglers. As for sex crimes, a police officer in Fort Myers, Florida, was charged with sexual assault against a 19-year-old female. These examples are not offered to suggest that police officers frequently engage in criminal activity but only that it happens. No one is above the law, even police officers.

Clearly, police officers also engage in many actions that would be crimes if performed by ordinary citizens. Police officers, however, enjoy immunity from criminal liability for these actions, if the actions are committed (justifiably) as part of their official duties. The so-called law enforcement to criminal liability is what shields police officers from criminal liability on most occasions. Assuming officers use deadly or nondeadly force properly, they will not be held criminally liable for their actions. Chapter 9 introduced this defense in more detail.

Beyond the realms of deadly and nondeadly force, police officers do not have much in the way of defense against criminal liability. If a police officer who committed burglary for his or her own personal gain attempted to assert a law enforcement defense, he or she would almost certainly fail. Similarly, if a police officer shoots and kills a person not for the purpose of preventing a crime or effecting an arrest but, say, for vengeance, that officer will almost certainly be convicted of some degree of homicide and probably sentenced to prison.

---

[37] *Screws v. United States*, 325 U.S. 91 (1945).
[38] *United States v. Lanier*, 520 U.S. 259 (1997).
[39] 18 U.S.C. Section 2236.
[40] M. L. Birzer, "Crimes Committed by Police Officers," in M. J. Palmiotto, ed., *Police Misconduct* (Upper Saddle River, NJ: Prentice Hall, 2001), pp. 171–178.

Civil Litigation

When a person's constitutional or other federal civil rights are violated, he or she can sue. Even if a person merely *believes* his or her rights have been violated, litigation is still an option. The worst (or best) that can happen is that the lawsuit will be dismissed. In this section, we look at one particular type of civil liability (casually referred to as "Section 1983"), but there are others, such as state tort liability, that are beyond the scope of this book. Before we continue, know that while civil liability may be an effective remedy for people whose rights are violated, litigation may come with a high price tag; it can be costly and time-consuming to sue.

civil litigation The same as a lawsuit.

What is the purpose of civil litigation? Aside from sometimes being the only remedy available, civil lawsuits are attractive because money can be awarded. A lawsuit in which one or more parties seek monetary compensation is called a damage suit. The *plaintiff*, or the person filing the lawsuit, seeks payment for injuries or perceived injuries suffered. In addition to damages, the plaintiff can also seek injunctive relief, which basically means he or she wants the court to bring the injurious or offensive action to a halt. Figure 10.3 provides an overview of the stages of a typical civil lawsuit.

damage suit A lawsuit in which one or more parties seek monetary compensation.

injunctive relief A court-ordered prohibition against a certain act or condition.

Why should we care about civil remedies in a book about criminal law and criminal procedure? One answer is that criminal remedies do not always apply. The exclusionary rule does not apply if there are no criminal charges. Likewise, criminal remedies made available by state and federal law generally apply in cases of the most egregious police misconduct. Another answer is that several important criminal procedure decisions began as civil lawsuits.

42 U.S.C. Section 1983 A federal statute that provides a remedy in federal court for the "deprivation of any rights ... secured by the Constitution and laws" of the United States. Also called "Section 1983."

42 U.S.C. Section 1983 provides a remedy in federal court for the "deprivation of any rights . . . secured by the Constitution and laws" of the United States. Section 1983 states:

> Every person who, under color of any statute, ordinance, regulation, custom, or usage, of any State or Territory, subjects, or causes to be subjected, any citizen of the United States or other persons within the jurisdiction thereof to the deprivation of any rights, privileges, or immunities secured by the Constitution and laws, shall be liable to the party injured in an action at law, suit in equity, or other proper proceeding for redress.

There are two key requirements for a Section 1983 lawsuit to succeed. First, the *defendant*, the person being sued, must have acted under "color of law." The Supreme Court has stated that someone acts under color of law when he or she acts in an official capacity.[41] For example, a police officer who is on duty acts under color of law. By contrast, someone acting in a private capacity, such as an ordinary citizen, cannot be said to have acted under color of law.

color of law One of two requirements for a successful Section 1983 lawsuit. An official acts under color of law when he or she acts in an official capacity.

Interestingly, plaintiffs *can* sue private parties under Section 1983 when private parties conspire with state officers. With regard to this point, the Supreme Court has held that "a state normally can be held responsible for a private decision only when it has exercised coercive power or has provided such significant encouragement, either overt or covert, that the choice must in law be deemed to be that of the state."[42]

---

[41]*Lugar* v. *Edmondson Oil Co.*, 457 U.S. 922 (1982).
[42]*Blum* v. *Yaretsky*, 457 U.S. 991 (1982), p. 1004.

1. *Citizen coplaint:* The first step in filing a lawsuit normally involves a citizen complaint. In citizen complaint, the aggrieved party can do one of two things: call attention to inappropriate police conduct *or* demand some form of remedial action (e.g., injunctive a relief or monetary damages). This latter form of citizen complaint is considered a *demand*.

2. *Demand:* If the complaint filed with the police by a citizen (the *complainant* requests some action on the part of the police, then the complainant will make a more or less informal demand of the police, who will then send a *response*. This may lead to informal discussions between the two sides. The complainant may retain the services of an attorney, but the procedure remains largely informal at this early juncture.

3. *Citizen complaint board:* In some jurisdictions (e.g., Spokane, WA), the complainant can further file a complaint with a local citizen complaint board if the police agency in question fails to take satisfactory action. Citizen complaint boards vary considerably in use, authority, and terminology, so they are only mentioned here in passing as one mechanism for dispute resolution. Other avenues of dispute resolution may well be in place.

4. *Lawyer's letter:* If the complainant and the police cannot work things out informally, the complainant usually brings in an attorney. The attorney will send a so-called lawyer's letter to the police agency, the officer(s) in question, and/or the city or county. While this letter may not have any legal significance, it usually gets a serious response.

5. *Prelitigation settlement discussion:* An informal prelitigation settlement discussion is often held, in which the police and/or their representatives and the complainant and/or his or her representatives work together to try to reach a settlement. If no settlement is reached, the complaint/demand will likely evolve into a full-blown lawsuit.

6. *Claim with city/county clerk:* Before being able to proceed with a lawsuit, the citizens in some states and countries are first required to file a claim with the city or country against which the complaint is made or to give the police agency a chance to respond to a formal complaint or a request for damages. This *claim* should be distinguished from a *citizen complaint*, discussed earlier. This claim is an explicit prerequisite that must be completed before a lawsuit can move forward; it is mandated by law. The purpose of such a claim is primarily to inform officials of what is about to transpire. Often, a lawsuit cannot be filed until the parties in question are given the opportunity to respond to a claim.

7. *Lawsuit:* A citizen complaint/demand evolves into a full-blown lawsuit when one of the informal proceedings discussed statisfy the complainant. To reach the stage of a lawsuit, two actions must occur: First, a *complaint* must be filed with the clerk of the court in which the lawsuit will be heard. (This complaint is a legal requirement and differs from the citizen complaint already filed.) Second, the court or an attorney must issue a *summons* to be served on the agencies or people named in the complaint. Sometimes, the summons is personally delivered; other times, it is sent by registered or certified mail. The parties named in the complaint (e.g., the police, their agencies, municipalities) are now known as the *defendants,* and the aggrieved party or parties filing the lawsuit are now known as the *plaintiffs*.

8. *Answer:* Once the defendants have been served with the summons, they must provide their formal answer within a prescribed timeframe. For obvious reasons, defendants in police civil liability cases rarely fail to acknowledge the summons.

9. *Discovery:* A lawsuit may involve pretrial discovery, in which one or both parties attempt to get evidence as to what happened in the alleged incident, perhaps by taking the testimony of witnesses or examining documents or physical evidence.

Figure 10.3

Stages of a Civil Lawsuit

10. *Motions:* In a lawsuit, either side may make motions to try to narrow the issues, to compel the other side to do something, or even to have the court decide the matter without actually conducting a trial. In police civil liability cases, two motions are commonly raised by the defendants: The first is the motion to *dismiss,* in which the defendants attempt to have the case thrown out on the grounds that it does not raise a question of law or other legitimate legal issue. Motions to dismiss are rarely granted. The second common type of motion calls for *Summary judgemnt,* in which the defendants ask the court to find in favor of the police without going to trial. The majority of these motions succeed, leaving only a few lawsuits that actually progress to the trial stage

11. *Pretrial conference:* Before the start of the trial the court will typically order a pretrial conference to narrow the issues still further and perhaps to get the parties to agree to a settlement. Again, the aim is to avoid a lengthy trial proceeding.

12. *Trial, judgment, and post-trial motions and appeals:* If a lawsuit progresses all the way to trial, it will be decided either by a judge alone or by a jury that decides the facts and a judge who decides the law. After the trial, the court will enter a judgment, in which the plaintiff, for example, might be entitled to fixed amount of money. Post-trial motions might also be raised, in which the losing party tries to convince the judge that some other judgment would be more appropriate (e.g., perhaps more money, added relief, or none at all) Finally, the losing party might appeal to a higher court.

13. *Collecting the judgment:* The party who wins the lawsuit may have received a judgment stating what he or she is entitled to recover. It is then his or her job to collect the judgment. This can be a difficult and time-consuming process, so it is typically put on hold unitill all relevant appeals have been exhausted.

Figure 10.3
(*Continued*)

The second requirement for a successful Section 1983 lawsuit is that a constitutional rights violation has taken place. In determining whether a constitutional rights violation has taken place, the plaintiff must establish that the defendant's conduct violated a specific constitutional provision, such as the Fourth Amendment. As noted in *Daniels* v. *Williams,* "[I]n any given Section 1983 suit, the plaintiff must still prove a violation of the underlying constitutional right."[43]

Defending against Wrongful Litigation

qualified immunity
Immunity from suit that applies some of the time and in certain situations. Sometimes qualified immunity serves as an "affirmative defense," meaning that it is raised at trial—if the case goes that far. If a criminal justice official acts on a reasonably mistaken belief, as gauged from the standpoint of a reasonable officer, then qualified immunity can be granted.

Officials who are sued under Section 1983 can assert a qualified immunity defense. Qualified immunity is a judicially created defense, just like the exclusionary rule is a court creation. In some cases, qualified immunity is more than a defense; it may afford immunity from suit.

Qualified immunity was developed to accommodate two conflicting policy concerns: effective crime control vis-à-vis the protection of people's civil liberties. While the Supreme Court has clearly intimated that Section 1983 should serve as a deterrent to official misconduct, the Court has also recognized that it is not fair to hold officials liable for lapses in judgment and honest mistakes. These issues were addressed in the seminal cases of *Harlow* v. *Fitzgerald* and *Wood* v. *Strickland.*[44]

[43] *Daniels* v. *Williams*, 474 U.S. 327 (1986), p. 330.
[44] *Harlow* v. *Fitzgerald*, 457 U.S. 800 (1982); *Wood* v. *Strickland*, 420 U.S. 308 (1975).

Similar to the Fourth Amendment's test for reasonableness, an objective reasonableness standard has been applied in order to determine if qualified immunity should be extended to criminal justice officials who are defendants. For the purposes of qualified immunity, a defendant is said to have acted in an objectively reasonable fashion if he or she does not violate clearly established rights about which a reasonable person would have known.[45] In some Section 1983 cases, defendants have benefited from qualified immunity even for violating clearly established constitutional rights, provided that the defendants' mistaken belief was objectively reasonable (i.e., acceptable in the eyes of a reasonable person).[46] Qualified immunity thus affords protection to defendant criminal justice officials for reasonably mistaken beliefs. In essence, it offers a defense for ignorance, provided that the ignorance in question is reasonable.

Nonjudicial Remedies

Nonjudicial remedies are available for situations where neither the exclusionary rule nor civil liability is a viable option. Consider the hypothetical case of a motorist who is stopped without proper justification. Assume the motorist is released. To be sure, he or she has suffered an inconvenience, but if no contraband was found and there was no egregious misconduct on the officer's part, what can this person do? About the only choice available is to file a written complaint. Depending on the particular jurisdiction, complaints may be reviewed internally, by a panel of citizens, or by both. We discuss each procedure later. An online feedback form from the federal Transportation Security Administration appears in Figure 10.4.

Mediation is also sometimes an option, depending on the situation. We wrap up this module with an introduction to mediation.

Internal Review

Internal review A nonjudicial remedy in which the police investigate on their own complaints against officers.

Internal review is the process by which a police department (or other criminal justice agency if one of its employees was responsible for alleged misconduct) investigates a complaint against one of its employees. In its model police misconduct policy, the Police Executive Research Forum listed three ways that the police themselves can implement effective complaint procedures:

> (1) [T]hrough the provision of meaningful and effective complaint procedures, citizen confidence in the integrity of police increases and this engenders community support and confidence in the police department; (2) through disciplinary procedures that permit police officials to monitor officers' compliance with departmental procedures; and (3) by clarifying rights and ensuring due process protection to citizens and officers alike.[47]

---

[45] *Harlow* v. *Fitzgerald*, 457 U.S. 800 (1982).
[46] See *Anderson* v. *Creighton*, 483 U.S. 635 (1987); *Malley* v. *Briggs*, 475 U.S. 335 (1988).
[47] Police Executive Research Forum, *Police Agency Handling of Officer Misconduct: A Model Policy Statement* (Washington, DC: Author, 1981), p. 1.

Please Complete this Form to Provide Feedback to TSA

(*Indicates required fields)

* State	Select One
* Airport	Select One
Date/Time of Travel	
Airline & Flight Number	
Checkpoint/Area of Airport	
TSA Employee (If Known)	
* Feedback Type	Select One
* Feedback Category	(Please select up to 2 items)
* Comment	

Rate your satisfaction	☆☆☆☆☆
Would you like a response?	No (If yes, then please provide an email address below)
Passenger Name	
Phone Number	(xxx-xxx-xxxx)
Email Address	

Submit

Collection of this information is made under 49 U.S.C.114(e) & (f). Providing this information is **voluntary**. TSA will used the information to improve customer service and may share it with airport operators for this purpose. For more information, please consult DHS/TSA 006 Correspondence and Matters Tracking Records. It should take no more than 5 minutes to complete this form. An agency may not conduct or sponsor, and a person is not required to respond to, a collection of information unless it displays a valid OMB control number. The control number assigned to this collection is OMB 1652-0030.

Figure 10.4

TSA Feedback Form

Source: https://apps.tsa.dhs.gov/talktotsa/ (accessed January 3, 2013)

Figure 10.5 shows the Claremont, California, Police Department's internal complaint review process, depicting one agency's approach to internal discipline.

Civilian Review

There has been a marked increase in the number of cities involving citizens at some stage of the police complaint process.[48] This has occurred because of the demand for some form of external input in the investigation process. It has also occurred due to some sentiments that citizens can investigate the police better than the police themselves:

> Citizen involvement in the complaint process will produce (1) more objective and more thorough investigations; (2) a higher rate of sustained complaints and more disciplinary actions against guilty officers; (3) greater deterrence of police misconduct (through both general and specific deterrence); and (4) higher levels of satisfaction on the part of both individual complainants and the general public.[49]

---

[48]S. Walker and V.W. Bumphus, *Civilian Review of the Police: A National Survey of the 50 Largest Cities* (Omaha: University of Nebraska at Omaha, 1992).

[49]S. Walker and B. Wright, "Varieties of Citizen Review: The Relationship of Mission, Structure, and Procedures to Police Accountability," in R. G. Dunham and G. P. Alpert, eds., *Critical Issues in Policing: Contemporary Readings*, 3rd ed. (Prospect Heights, IL: Waveland, 1997), pp. 319–336, p. 322.

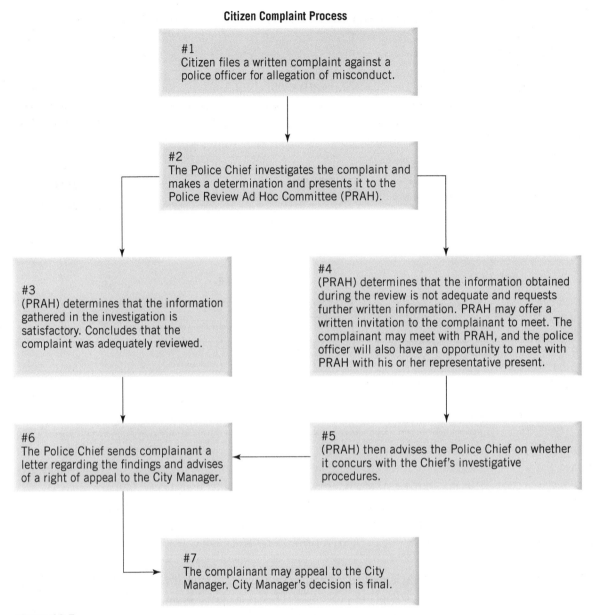

Figure 10.5

Citizen Complaint Process (Claremont, CA, Police Department)

Source: City of Claremont (California) Police Department. Reprinted by Permission. Available onilne: http://www.ci.claremont.ca.us/download.cfm?ID=18112 (accessed January 3, 2013)

civilian review The strongest method of citizen input in which a civilian panel investigates, adjudicates, and recommends punishment to the police chief.

West has identified three distinct forms of citizen review: (1) civilian review, (2) civilian input, and (3) civilian monitor.[50] Pure **civilian review** is the strongest form—a civilian panel investigates, adjudicates, and recommends punishment to the

---

[50]P. West, *Investigations of Complaints against the Police: Summary Findings* (Washington, DC: Police Executive Research Forum, 1987).

civilian input A method of citizen input into the complaint review process in which a civilian panel receives and investigates a complaint, leaving adjudication and discipline with the department itself.

civilian monitor The weakest method of citizen input that leaves investigation, adjudication, and discipline inside the department. A civilian is allowed to review the adequacy and impartiality of the process.

police chief. The second strongest form is civilian input; in this form, a civilian panel receives and investigates a complaint, leaving adjudication and discipline with the department itself. Finally, the civilian monitor form, the weakest of the three, leaves investigation, adjudication, and discipline inside the department; a civilian is allowed to review the adequacy and impartiality of the process. The research reported by West focused only on the first two forms: civilian review and civilian input. Both place investigative authority with an independent body and are arguably more satisfactory to disgruntled citizens than the third form, civilian monitor.

Critics of civilian review argue that such procedures suffer from a number of drawbacks:

- They ignore existing legal resources at citizens' disposal.
- It is difficult for people disconnected from the police department to have an adequate understanding of the internal operations of a civilian review board.
- Citizen review damages morale.
- Civilian review invites abdication of authority by line supervisors.
- Such boards weaken the ability of top management to achieve conformity through discipline.
- They are tantamount to admitting that the police are incapable of policing themselves.[51]

Mediation

mediation A method of alternative dispute resolution in which a neutral third party renders disciplinary decisions.

ombudsman A term used to describe the neutral third party who conducts mediation.

Some have argued that mediation, or relying on a neutral third party to render decisions, is a desirable approach to address the problem of police misconduct. In it, the decision of a neutral third party, or ombudsman (sometimes called a "mediator" or "arbitrator"), is sought.[52] As Whitebread and Slobogin observed:

> [Another] remedial system which, like the civilian review board, operates outside the judicial and internal police spheres, is the Scandanavian ombudsman system. The ombudsman is, most simply, an external critic of administration. His goal is improvement of administration rather than punishment of administrators or redress of individual grievances. Thus, instead of conducting formal hearings associated with adjudicating individual complaints, he relies primarily on his own investigations to gather information. On the basis of his findings, he may recommend corrective measure to the department, although he cannot compel an official to do anything.[53]

A key characteristic of the ombudsman system is that it is independent of the complainant and the person being complained against. The ombudsman should be a person to whom people may come with grievances connected with the government. The ombudsman stands between the citizen and the government, acting as something of an intermediary.

---

[51]W.A. Geller, *Police Leadership in America* (New York: Praeger, 1985), pp. 157–198.
[52]Technically there is a difference between arbitration and mediation, but for our purposes it is safe to treat them as more or less identical.
[53]C.H. Whitebread and C. Slobogin, *Criminal Procedure*, 4th ed. (New York: Foundation Press, 2000), p. 65.

YOUR DECISION

1. Officer Webster regularly patronized a bar. One night, while off duty, he got into a fight, drew his gun, and shot and killed James Ramos. Ramos's heirs filed a Section 1983 lawsuit against the city for which Webster worked, alleging that it failed to adequately train him as to whether and how to react during off-duty altercations. Furthermore, Ramos's heirs alleged that this failure caused Webster, acting under color of law, to deprive Ramos of his constitutional rights. Will this lawsuit succeed?

2. In a recent Supreme Court case, *Wilson v. Layne*,[54] the Supreme Court considered (1) whether law enforcement officers violated the Fourth Amendment by allowing members of the media to accompany them on the service of warrants and (2) whether the officers were nonetheless entitled to qualified immunity if such activity violates the Fourth Amendment. The Court decided that "a media 'ride-along' in a home violates the Fourth Amendment, but because the state of the law was not clearly established at the time the entry in this case took place, respondent officers are entitled to qualified immunity."[55] Do you see any problems with this decision?

Summary

- Both state and federal law enforcement officers can be held criminally liable for violating certain federal laws. Officers are also bound by the criminal law at the state level. They can, of course, engage in certain authorized public duties (e.g., to use deadly force in appropriate circumstances) that would be crimes if committed by regular citizens.

- Civil lawsuits against government officials—the police, mainly—can be filed when neither the exclusionary rule nor other criminal remedies apply.

- Section 1983 litigation requires the plaintiff to show that a constitutional rights violation was committed by an official acting under color of state law.

- Section 1983 lawsuits can be filed against individual police officers, supervisors, and municipalities/counties.

- Qualified immunity is a defense to Section 1983 litigation.

- Nonjudicial remedies include internal review, civilian review, and mediation.

- In the most common of these remedies, internal review, a police agency investigates its own for allegations of misconduct. Internal affairs divisions engage in this sort of activity.

- Civilian review occurs when citizens get involved in the investigation process; numerous varieties of citizen review are in place around the United States.

- A less common method of rectifying constitutional rights violations is mediation, in which a neutral third party decides on issues in dispute.

---

[54]*Wilson v. Layne*, 526 U.S. 603 (1999).
[55]Ibid., p. 603.

JUSTIFICATION

Learning Objectives
- **Define probable cause.**
- **Identify several sources of information that a police officer can rely on to make the probable cause determination.**
- **Define reasonable suspicion and explain when it applies.**
- **Define administrative justification and explain when it applies.**

CORE CONCEPTS

justification Also known as cause, justification is necessary for the police to engage in actions that trigger the Fourth Amendment. Examples of justification include probable cause and reasonable suspicion.

Put simply, the police need to have justification, or cause, before they can conduct a search or a seizure. Justification needs to be in place *a priori*—that is, before a person or evidence is sought in an area protected by the Fourth Amendment. The police cannot conduct an illegal search to obtain evidence and then argue *after the fact* that what they did was appropriate.

Although the language of the Fourth Amendment suggests that probable cause is the only important standard of justification, the Supreme Court has also focused on the amendment's reasonableness clause to carve out exceptions to the probable cause requirement. So-called *Terry* stops, for instance, do not require probable cause, but they are still required to be reasonable. (*Terry* stops are discussed in the next chapter.) At the other extreme, a quick reading of the Fourth Amendment would lead one to believe that the probable cause requirement is only necessary when a warrant is used. In actuality, however, the Supreme Court has held that the probable cause requirement applies in *warrantless* search-and-seizure situations, as well.[56]

Justification can be viewed as something of a sliding scale that hinges on the type of intrusion the police make. Generally, the more intrusive the police action, the higher the level of justification required. Conversely, the lower the level of intrusion, the lower the justification needed. Three primary levels of justification recognized by the courts will be considered throughout the remainder of this module: (1) probable cause, the standard for searches and seizures; (2) reasonable suspicion, the standard for stop-and-frisk; and (3) administrative justification, the standard for administrative searches.

Probable Cause

In principle, the definition of probable cause does not vary, regardless of the conduct in which the police engage. It was defined by the Supreme Court in *Beck* v. *Ohio* as more than bare suspicion; it exists when "the facts and circumstances within [the

---

[56]See, e.g., *Wong Sun* v. *United States*, 371 U.S. 471 (1963).

probable cause More than bare suspicion; it exists when "the facts and circumstances within [the officers'] knowledge and of which they [have] reasonably trustworthy information [are] sufficient to warrant a prudent man in believing that the [suspect] had committed or was committing an offense" (*Beck* v. *Ohio*, 379 U.S. 89 [1964], p. 91).

officers'] knowledge and of which they [have] reasonably trustworthy information [are] sufficient to warrant a prudent man in believing that the [suspect] had committed or was committing an offense."[57] In *Brinegar* v. *United States*, the Court added, "The substance of all the definitions of probable cause is a reasonable ground for belief of guilt."[58]

Unfortunately, these legal definitions are of little use to those on the frontlines of law enforcement. A more practical definition of probable cause is *more than 50% certainty*. As such, it exists somewhere below absolute certainty and proof beyond a reasonable doubt (the latter of which is necessary to obtain a criminal conviction) and somewhere above a hunch or reasonable suspicion (the latter of which is required to conduct a stop-and-frisk).

The notion of a *prudent man* is akin to the idea of objective reasonableness already discussed. Basically, it means that courts consider what the average person on the street would believe, not what a person who has received special training in the identification and apprehension of lawbreakers (e.g., police officer, judge, etc.) would believe. This is not to say, however, that the experience of a police officer is not relevant to a probable cause determination. On the contrary, in *United States* v. *Ortiz*, the Court ruled that "officers are entitled to draw reasonable inferences from these facts in light of their knowledge of the area and their prior experience with aliens and smugglers"[59] and, by extension, other people suspected of criminal activity.

Figure 10.6 lists a number of the ingredients in the "recipe" for probable cause as well as examples of each ingredient. Each in isolation is rarely, if ever, enough. Rather, a combination of the factors listed in Figure 10.6 is necessary for probable cause to be established.

Probable cause is always required in the following scenarios:

- arrests with warrants,
- arrests without warrants,
- searches and seizures of property with warrants, and
- searches and seizures of property without warrants.

When a warrant is required, the probable cause determination is made by the magistrate charged with issuing the warrant; when a warrant is not used, the police officer makes the probable cause determination. In general:

> Probable cause can be obtained from police radio bulletins, tips from "good citizen" informers who have happened by chance to see criminal activity, reports from victims, anonymous tips, and tips from "habitual" informers who mingle with people in the underworld and who themselves may [even] be criminals. Probable cause can be based on various combinations of these sources.[60]

When the police make an *arrest*, the probable cause determination concerns whether an offense has been committed and whether the suspect did, in fact, commit the

---

[57]*Beck* v. *Ohio*, 379 U.S. 89 (1964), p. 91.
[58]*Brinegar* v. *United States*, 338 U.S. 160 (1949), p. 175.
[59]*United States* v. *Ortiz*, 422 U.S. 891 (1975), p. 897.
[60]J.G. Miles, Jr., D.B. Richardson, and A.E. Scudellari, *The Law Officer's Pocket Manual* (Washington, DC: Bureau of National Affairs, 1988–1989), p. 6:4.

1. Prior record
   Example
   - prior conviction for same activity
   - offender known to have committed similar offense in the past
2. Flight from the scene
   Examples
   - suspect sees police and runs away
   - flight from an apartment known for drug dealing
3. Suspicious conduct
   Example
   - failure to make eye contact with officers
   - extreme inattention to police
   - suspect appears startled by police and truns quickly away
   - "casing" a jewelry store
4. Admissions
   Examples
   - *suspect tells informant that he committed a crime*
   - *officer overhears two men talking about their involvement in a crime*
   - *officer hears one suspect tell another, "I told you not to do it"*
5. Incriminating evidence
   Examples
   - *suspect found in possession of drug paraphernalia*
   - *burglary suspect found with pillowcase full of loot*
   - *sack of cash and ski mask in robbery suspect's car*
6. Unusual hour
   Examples
   - At 2:30 a.m., an officer sees a man depart a darkened property where valuables were kept
   - At 3:30 a.m., an officer observed two men walking in a business area who then fled at the sight of the officer
7. Suspect resembles the perpetrator
   Examples
   - *Suspect wears clothes similar to the perpetrator of a crime*
   - suspect is an occupant of the same car thought to flee the scene of a robbery
   - the number of suspects in the car is the same as the number of suspects reportedly involved in the crime
8. Evasive and untruthful responses to questions
   Examples
   - suspect caught in a lie about where she was coming from
   - suspect gives false name and/or identification
   - use of an alias
   - suspect denies owning a car that is registered to him
   - suspect gives vague and confusing answers to an officer's questions
9. Obvious attempt to hide something
   Example
   - officers hear a toilet flush when arriving to serve a search warrant
   - officer observes a suspect push something under the seat of his car
   - suspect is looking into the trunk of a vehicle but slams it quickly on seeing a police officer

Figure 10.6

Ingredients in the
Probable Cause Recipe

10. Presence in a high-crime area and/or near a crime scene
    Examples
    - officer observes a vehicle leave the scene of a burglary at which no other people or vehicles were located
    - the suspect is the only pedestrian near the scene of a burglary
    - officers observe an apparent drug transaction in an area known for narcotics activity
11. Furtive gestures
    Examples
    - officers observe the passenger in a vehicle duck from view
    - suspect makes a quick hand-to-mouth movement
    - suspect turns away from the officers when they announce their presence
    - the driver of a vehicle reaches under the seat
12. Knowing too much
    Example
    - suspect volunteers information that only perpetrator could possibly know

Figure 10.6
(*Continued*)

offense. In the case of a search, however, the probable cause issue concerns whether the items to be seized are connected with criminal activity and whether they can be found in the place to be searched. This means, then, that the courts sometimes treat the probable cause requirement differently, depending on the conduct in which the police engage.

One point needs to be underscored: Probable cause to search does not necessarily create probable cause to arrest, and, alternatively, probable cause to arrest does not necessarily create probable cause to search. With regard to the latter point, consider this hypothetical situation: Police officers pursue a drug suspect into her residence and, based on a hot-pursuit exigency, arrest her in her living room. Assuming probable cause was in place to pursue the suspect, the police do not possess unfettered latitude once in the house to search the place up and down. The courts have placed restrictions on what can be done in a situation such as this—that is, on how far the police can go with a search following (i.e., incident) to arrest. Searches incident to arrest will be covered in Chapter 11, but this example illustrates that the ingredients in the probable cause recipe are not always the same for arrests as they are for searches.

In several arrest cases, the courts have had the opportunity to decide what sources of information meet the probable cause burden. Three sources of information can be identified: (1) informants and other third parties; (2) firsthand knowledge; and (3) information that turns out, after the fact, to be mistaken but is reasonably relied on.[61] Other information may help establish the probable cause to arrest, but the courts have been most vocal about these three sources.

Informants and Other Third Parties

The police routinely rely on information supplied to them by a sophisticated network of *informants*. Informants are not necessarily shady characters connected to the criminal lifestyle; they can also be victims of crime, witnesses of crime, and other police officers.

---

[61]Whitebread and Slobogin, pp. 120–125.

As to the first type of informant, the courts have attempted to create tests to ensure that information supplied by informants is credible. In *Aguilar* v. *Texas*,[62] the Supreme Court ruled that an affidavit based on a tip from an informant must show (1) sufficient information to demonstrate how the informant reached his or her conclusion and (2) sufficient information to establish the reliability of the informant. Stated differently, the first prong asks, "Why should the police believe this person?" and the second prong asks, "How does the informant know what he or she claims to know?"

For both prongs of the *Aguilar* test to be satisfied, the police need to supply specific information in their affidavit. A statement to the effect that "this informant has provided reliable information in the past" is not enough. More appropriate is a statement such as "This informant has supplied information in the past that led to the conviction of John Doe."[63]

In *Spinelli* v. *United States*,[64] the Supreme Court clarified the meaning of the first prong. It concluded that insufficient knowledge about the details of the reported criminal activity can be overcome if "the tip describe[s] the accused's criminal activity in sufficient detail that the magistrate knows that he is relying on something more substantial than a casual rumor . . . or an accusation based merely on a individual's general reputation."[65] Similarly, in *Draper* v. *United States*,[66] the Court ruled that the first prong—the credibility prong—may also be satisfied when the informant implicates himself or herself in criminal activity, provided that such a statement is against self-interest. An example of a self-interested admission of criminal activity would be one in which the informant seeks to curry favor with the police and/or prosecutors in exchange for supplying information.[67]

The *Aguilar* and *Spinelli* tests were heavily modified in *Illinois* v. *Gates*,[68] when the Supreme Court basically abandoned the two-pronged probable cause analysis and replaced it with a *totality of circumstances* test. Thus, if "a particular informant is known for the unusual reliability of his predictions of certain types of criminal activities in a locality, his failure, in a particular case, to thoroughly set forth the basis of his knowledge surely should not serve as an absolute bar to a finding of probable cause based on his tip."[69] In other words, a deficiency in one prong can be compensated for with an abundant supply of information in the other.

Interestingly, *Aguilar*, *Spinelli*, and *Gates* were all search cases, which would seem to limit their applicability in the arrest context. Actually, the *Illinois* v. *Gates* totality of circumstances test is now used for determining probable cause based on information from informants in both the arrest and search/seizure contexts. However, relying on *Draper* v. *United States*, the courts will still give consideration to five factors in determining whether the totality of circumstances creates probable cause: (1) when the informant describes how he or she found out about the criminal activity, (2) when the informant gives a detailed description of that activity, (3) when evidence

---

[62]*Aguilar* v. *Texas*, 378 U.S. 108 (1964).
[63]Also see *United States* v. *Freitas*, 716 F.2d 1216 (9th Cir. 1983).
[64]*Spinelli* v. *United States*, 393 U.S. 410 (1969).
[65]Ibid., p. 416.
[66]*Draper* v. *United States*, 358 U.S. 307 (1959).
[67]see *United States* v. *Harris*, 403 U.S. 573 (1971); *United States* v. *Jackson*, 818 F.2d 345 (5th Cir. 1987).
[68]*Illinois* v. *Gates*, 462 U.S. 213 (1983).
[69]Ibid., p. 233.

for the informant's reliability exists, (4) when the informant predicts criminal activity that is later corroborated by the police, and (5) when the informant implicates himself or herself in criminal activity.

What happens when the informant is a victim or an eyewitness? In both situations, the Supreme Court has relaxed the *Aguilar/Spinelli/Gates* tests. For example, in *Jaben* v. *United States*, the Court held that "whereas some supporting information concerning the credibility of informants in narcotics cases or other common garden varieties of crime may be required, such information is not so necessary in the context of the case before us."[70] Similar rulings have been applied when the informants have been other police officers. For example, in *United States* v. *Ventresca*, the Supreme Court ruled that "[o]bservations of fellow officers of the Government engaged in a common investigation are plainly a reliable basis for a warrant applied for by one of their number."[71] Of course, probable cause is still required. When probable cause is found lacking, the arrest will most likely be deemed unconstitutional.[72]

Firsthand Knowledge

The second major category of probable cause to arrest cases hinges on information that results from *firsthand knowledge*. That is, when is probable cause established by someone other than a third party—namely, the arresting officer? The courts usually do not worry about the truthfulness or accuracy of the arresting officer's observations but, instead, whether probable cause to arrest was in place. In particular, the courts have required that probable cause *to* arrest must be determined independently from the arrest itself, meaning that probable cause to arrest must be required *before* the arrest. In *Sibron* v. *New York*, the Supreme Court stated, "It is axiomatic that an incident search may not precede an arrest and serve as part of its justification."[73] In simple terms, this means that police cannot search people and illegally seize evidence simply for the purpose of establishing probable cause to arrest. Stated differently, probable cause cannot be established in hindsight. It should be pointed out, though, that evidence encountered during law enforcement activity that does not constitute an arrest or a search (a patdown, for instance) can create or be used to establish probable cause to arrest or conduct a further search, depending on the circumstances.

In another case, *United States* v. *Di Re*,[74] the Supreme Court held that a suspect's proximity to criminal activity is not enough to establish probable cause to arrest. In that case, officers arrested Di Re from the front seat of a car on the grounds that there were two other men in the car passing counterfeit ration coupons between one another. The Court noted that had Di Re even seen the activity, "it would not follow that he knew they were ration coupons, and if he saw that they were ration coupons, it would not follow that he would know them to be counterfeit."[75] Simply put, then, proximity to criminal activity does not create probable cause to arrest.[76]

---

[70]*Jaben* v. *United States*, 381 U.S. 214 (1965), p. 224.
[71]*United States* v. *Ventresca*, 380 U.S. 102 (1965), p. 111.
[72]See *Whiteley* v. *Warden*, 401 U.S. 560 (1971).
[73]*Sibron* v. *New York*, 392 U.S. 40 (1968), p. 63.
[74]*United States* v. *Di Re*, 332 U.S. 581 (1948).
[75]Ibid., p. 593.
[76]Also see *Johnson* v. *United States*, 333 U.S. 10 (1948).

reasonable suspicion
Justification that falls below probable cause but above a hunch. Reasonable suspicion is Court-created justification; it is not mentioned in the Fourth Amendment. Reasonable suspicion is necessary for police to engage in stop-and-frisk activities.

In yet another case, one in which the police had a valid warrant authorizing them to search a tavern, the Court held that the search warrant did not give them permission to search the patrons of the bar, including the petitioner, because they were not named in the warrant.[77] If, however, the arresting officer were armed with additional information (from a third-party informant, for example), then probable cause would be easier to establish.[78] What is more, courts regularly defer to officers' judgments as to whether probable cause was in place.[79]

Reasonable Reliance on Mistaken Information

Interestingly, if information supplied by an informant or by an officer's firsthand observations later proves to be false, the courts will uphold the earlier action,[80] so long as the mistake was a reasonable one.[81] When such a mistake is deemed *unreasonable*, however, the courts will almost always reach a different conclusion. An example of unreasonable mistake exists in *Albright* v. *Oliver*,[82] in which the Supreme Court implied that it was unreasonable (and a violation of the Fourth Amendment) for a police officer to rely on an informant who had provided false information on 50 previous occasions.

When a police officer blocks a person's path, a seizure has likely taken place, meaning that proper justification is required for the stop.

© Steve Hamblin/Alamy

Reasonable Suspicion

To recap, the justification required to conduct a search or a seizure within the meaning of the Fourth Amendment is probable cause. But much police activity does not reach the level of intrusion that occurs when a search or seizure is carried out. For example, the police routinely have to confront people on the street in order to question them and to pull over automobiles to enforce traffic laws. If probable cause were required under such circumstances, the police could do little in terms of investigating suspicious activity.

Recognizing how essential these *lesser intrusions* are to the police mission, the Supreme Court established in *Terry* v. *Ohio*,[83] a different level of justification for such activities. The Court created the standard of **reasonable suspicion**—something below probable cause but above a hunch. *Terry* dealt with so-called

---

[77] *Ybarra* v. *Illinois*, 444 U.S. 85 (1979).
[78] See *Ker* v. *California*, 374 U.S. 23 (1963).
[79] See *Maryland* v. *Pringle*, 540 U.S. 366 (2003).
[80] See *Henry* v. *United States*, 361 U.S. 98 (1959); *United States* v. *Garofalo*, 496 F.2d 510 (8th Cir. 1974).
[81] *Franks* v. *Delaware*, 438 U.S. 154 (1978).
[82] *Albright* v. *Oliver*, 510 U.S. 266 (1994).
[83] *Terry* v. *Ohio*, 392 U.S. 1 (1968).

stop-and-frisk activities (covered more fully in the next chapter), but reasonable suspicion as a standard of justification permeates other arenas of criminal procedure (e.g., traffic stops).

In *Terry*, an officer's attention was drawn to two men on a street corner who appeared to the officer to be "casing" a store for a robbery. The officer approached the men and asked them to identify themselves. The officer then proceeded to pat down the men and found a gun on each one. The men were placed under arrest. They tried to suppress the guns, but the Supreme Court eventually held the officer's actions valid in the interest of "effective crime prevention and detection."[84] Balancing an intrusion that was arguably less serious than a search with the interests of society in apprehending lawbreakers, the Court held that a lower standard than probable cause was required because "street encounters between citizens and police officers are incredibly rich in diversity."[85]

COURT DECISION

The Logic behind Stop and Frisk

Terry v. *Ohio*
392 U.S. 1 (1968)

Decision: The Supreme Court decided that "Where a reasonably prudent officer is warranted in the circumstances of a given case in believing that his safety or that of others is endangered, he may make a reasonable search for weapons of the person believed by him to be armed and dangerous regardless of whether he has probable cause to arrest that individual for crime or the absolute certainty that the individual is armed."

Reason: If this case involved police conduct subject to the Warrant Clause of the Fourth Amendment, we would have to ascertain whether "probable cause" existed to justify the search and seizure which took place. However, that is not the case. We do not retreat from our holdings that the police must, whenever practicable, obtain advance judicial approval of searches and seizures through the warrant procedure . . ., or that, in most instances, failure to comply with the warrant requirement can only be excused by exigent circumstances. . . . But we deal here with an entire rubric of police conduct – necessarily swift action predicated upon the on-the-spot observations of the officer on the beat—which historically has not been, and, as a practical matter, could not be, subjected to the warrant procedure. Instead, the conduct involved in this case must be tested by the Fourth Amendment's general proscription against unreasonable searches and seizures . . .

We must now examine the conduct of Officer McFadden in this case to determine whether his search and seizure of petitioner were reasonable, both at their inception and as conducted. He had observed Terry, together with Chilton and another man, acting in a manner he took to be preface to a "stick-up." We think, on the facts and circumstances Officer McFadden detailed before the trial judge, a reasonably prudent

(continued)

---

[84]Ibid., p. 22.
[85]Ibid., p. 13.

man would have been warranted in believing petitioner was armed, and thus presented a threat to the officer's safety while he was investigating his suspicious behavior. The actions of Terry and Chilton were consistent with McFadden's hypothesis that these men were contemplating a daylight robbery -- which, it is reasonable to assume, would be likely to involve the use of weapons -- and nothing in their conduct from the time he first noticed them until the time he confronted them and identified himself as a police officer gave him sufficient reason to negate that hypothesis. Although the trio had departed the original scene, there was nothing to indicate abandonment of an intent to commit a robbery at some point. Thus, when Officer McFadden approached the three men gathered before the display window at Zucker's store, he had observed enough to make it quite reasonable to fear that they were armed, and nothing in their response to his hailing them, identifying himself as a police officer, and asking their names served to dispel that reasonable belief. We cannot say his decision at that point to seize Terry and pat his clothing for weapons was the product of a volatile or inventive imagination, or was undertaken simply as an act of harassment; the record evidences the tempered act of a policeman who, in the course of an investigation, had to make a quick decision as to how to protect himself and others from possible danger, and took limited steps to do so.

We conclude that the revolver seized from Terry was properly admitted in evidence against him. At the time he seized petitioner and searched him for weapons, Officer McFadden had reasonable grounds to believe that petitioner was armed and dangerous, and it was necessary for the protection of himself and others to take swift measures to discover the true facts and neutralize the threat of harm if it materialized. The policeman carefully restricted his search to what was appropriate to the discovery of the particular items which he sought. Each case of this sort will, of course, have to be decided on its own facts. We merely hold today that, where a police officer observes unusual conduct which leads him reasonably to conclude in light of his experience that criminal activity may be afoot and that the persons with whom he is dealing may be armed and presently dangerous, where, in the course of investigating this behavior, he identifies himself as a policeman and makes reasonable inquiries, and where nothing in the initial stages of the encounter serves to dispel his reasonable fear for his own or others' safety, he is entitled for the protection of himself and others in the area to conduct a carefully limited search of the outer clothing of such persons in an attempt to discover weapons which might be used to assault him. Such a search is a reasonable search under the Fourth Amendment, and any weapons seized may properly be introduced in evidence against the person from whom they were taken.

There is no clear definition of *reasonable suspicion*, just as there is no clear definition of *probable cause*. As stated in *United States* v. *Cortez*:

> Courts have used a variety of terms to capture the elusive concept of what cause is sufficient to authorize police to stop a person. Terms like "articulable reasons" and "founded suspicion" are not self-defining; they fall short of providing clear guidance dispositive of the myriad factual situations that arise. But the essence of all that has been written is that the totality of circumstances—the whole picture—must be taken

Factors That May Give Rise to Reasonable Suspicion	Factors That will Not Give Rise to Reasonable Suspicion
Suspect in high-crime area at unusual hour	Hunch
Suspect flees from officers	Rumor
Suspect appears to receive cash in exchange for two small envelopes	Intuition
Suspect puts television in the trunk of a car in an area where most businesses are closed	Instince
Suspect appears to be "casing" a convenience store	Curiosity

Figure 10.7

Factors That May and Will Not Give Rise to Reasonable Suspicion

into account. Based upon that whole picture the detaining officers must have a particularized and objective basis for suspecting the particular person stopped of criminal activity.[86]

As a level of justification lying below probable cause, then, reasonable suspicion is "considerably less than proof of wrongdoing by a preponderance of evidence"[87] but more than an unparticularized hunch. Figure 10.7 contains a list of specific factors that can contribute to reasonable suspicion—and some information that *cannot* give rise to reasonable suspicion.

Like probable cause, reasonable suspicion can be based on a number of different sources, including informants. But because the reasonable suspicion standard falls below that for probable cause, less information is required. In *Adams v. Williams*,[88] for example, the Supreme Court held that reasonable suspicion may be based on an anonymous telephone tip, so long as the police can corroborate certain details from the informant. In a similar case, *Alabama v. White*, the Supreme Court observed, "Reasonable suspicion is a less demanding standard than probable cause not only in the sense that reasonable suspicion can be established with information that is different but also in the sense that reasonable suspicion can arise from information that is less reliable than that required to show probable cause."[89]

In *United States v. Hensley*,[90] the Supreme Court unanimously held that the reasonable suspicion standard is satisfied when the police rely on "wanted" flyers, even those from other jurisdictions. A restriction on this ruling was that the flyer, regardless of its place of origin, must be based on articulable facts that connect the suspect to criminal activity. The key here is articulable facts. Articulable facts are events that are witnessed and can be explained. The opposite of articulable facts would be a gut reaction or a mere hunch.

The Court in *Hensley* also had to decide if a stop based on reasonable suspicion of *prior* criminal activity was permissible under the Fourth Amendment's reasonableness standard. All decisions up to that point had dealt with suspected criminal activity immediately before the officer's arrival or criminal activity likely to have occurred but for the officer's arrival. In *Hensley*, the police stopped a man 12 days

articulable facts Events that are witnessed and can be explained. Contrast articulable facts with hunches and guesses. Articulable facts are necessary for establishing probable cause.

---

[86]*United States v. Cortez*, 449 U.S. 411 (1981), p. 417.
[87]*United States v. Sokolow*, 490 U.S. 1 (1989), p. 7.
[88]*Adams v. Williams*, 407 U.S. 143 (1972).
[89]*Alabama v. White*, 496 U.S. 325 (1990), p. 330.
[90]*United States v. Hensley*, 469 U.S. 221 (1985).

after the commission of a robbery for which he was suspected. The Court upheld the police's action and stated that it "would not only hinder the investigation, but might also enable the suspect to flee in the interim and to remain at large."[91]

To further illustrate the meaning of reasonable suspicion, consider the case of *Sibron* v. *New York*. In that case, the Court held that talking to known addicts and reaching into their pockets does not produce reasonable suspicion that criminal activity is afoot. In yet another case, *Brown* v. *Texas*,[92] two police officers observed Brown and another man walking away from one another. One of the officers later testified that he thought the officers' arrival broke up some suspicious activity. Officer Venegas approached Brown and asked him to identify himself. Brown refused and was later convicted under a statute that made it illegal to refuse to give an officer one's name and address. According to the Court:

> There is no indication in the record that it was unusual for people to be in the alley. The fact that the appellant was in a neighborhood frequented by drug users, standing alone, is not a basis for concluding that the appellant himself was engaged in criminal conduct. In short, the appellant's activity was no different from the activity of other pedestrians in that neighborhood.[93]

Contrast *Brown* v. *Texas* with the Supreme Court's decision in *Illinois* v. *Wardlow*.[94] In that case, Chicago police officers were patrolling an area known for narcotics traffic. Upon seeing the officers, Wardlow ran and was chased down by the police. When he was patted down, the officers found a Colt .38 pistol and arrested him. Wardlow appealed his conviction, arguing that the stop-and-frisk was illegal because the officers did not have reasonable suspicion. The Court disagreed, noting that "a location's characteristics are relevant in determining whether the circumstances are sufficiently suspicious to warrant further investigation."[95] In addition, the Court noted that "it was Wardlow's unprovoked flight that aroused the officers' suspicion" and that "nervous, evasive behavior is another pertinent factor in determining reasonable suspicion, and headlong flight is the consummate act of evasion."[96] Thus, in the Court's view, the officers *did* have reasonable suspicion to stop and frisk Wardlow.

More recently, in *United States* v. *Arvizu*,[97] the Supreme Court highlighted the importance of the totality of circumstances as well as officers' experience in making a determination of reasonable suspicion. In that case, a border patrol agent in a remote part of Arizona became suspicious of a van that slowed upon seeing him. Also, the driver failed to acknowledge the agent. The agent stopped the van, and the Supreme Court upheld this decision. The Court stated the agent was "entitled to make an assessment of the situation in light of his specialized training and familiarity with the customs of the area's inhabitants."[98]

---

[91]Ibid., p. 229.
[92]*Brown* v. *Texas*, 443 U.S. 47 (1979).
[93]Ibid., p. 52.
[94]*Illinois* v. *Wardlow*, 528 U.S. 119 (2000).
[95]Ibid., p. 119.
[96]Ibid., p. 124.
[97]*United States* v. *Arvizu*, 534 U.S. 266 (2002).
[98]Ibid., p. 276.

Administrative Justification

A third level of justification has arisen by virtue of the fact that government entities occasionally conduct searches in circumstances other than criminal investigations. As noted earlier, a search-and-seizure aimed at obtaining evidence for use in a criminal proceeding cannot occur without appropriate justification. Noncriminal searches also occur, however, so the Supreme Court has created a different level of justification. Instead of being based on reasonableness, the **administrative justification** adopts a balancing approach, weighing the privacy interests of individuals with the interests of society in preserving public safety.

administrative justification A standard used to support certain regulatory and special needs searches. Created by the Supreme Court, it adopts a balancing approach, weighing the privacy interests of individuals with the interests of society in preserving public safety.

The first case creating an administrative form of justification was *Camara* v. *Municipal Court*,[99] which involved a health code inspection of residential dwelling units. The Supreme Court held that such inspections were subject to Fourth Amendment restrictions but rejected the argument that the appropriate level of justification was probable cause (or reasonable suspicion, for that matter). Invoking the Fourth Amendment's reasonableness clause, the Court balanced the public interest in enforcing safety codes with the "relatively limited invasion of the urban citizen's privacy," given that "the inspections are neither personal in nature nor aimed at the discovery of evidence of crime."[100] The Court further noted that such searches are permissible, so long as "reasonable legislative or administrative standards for conducting an area inspection are satisfied with respect to a particular dwelling."[101] In other words, administrative searches should not be conducted arbitrarily or with selective enforcement.

More recently, in *Colorado* v. *Bertine*, the Court stated that the "standard of probable cause is peculiarly related to criminal investigations, not routine, noncriminal procedures. . . . The probable-cause approach is unhelpful when analysis centers upon the reasonableness of routine administrative caretaking functions, particularly when no claim is made that the protective procedures are a subterfuge for criminal investigations."[102] Accordingly, the courts have required that administrative searches be conducted according to objective, standardized procedures. Also important, authorities cannot use an administrative search as a pretext for a full-blown search.

The administrative search rationale has been applied in a number of related situations. For example, the courts have been rather liberal in terms of upholding questionable searches of highly regulated business establishments. In *New York* v. *Burger*,[103] for instance, the Supreme Court authorized a warrantless search of an automobile junkyard. In *Donovan* v. *Dewey*,[104] the Court upheld the warrantless inspection of mines. The same logic carried over to a case involving the inspection of a gun dealership.[105] In support of its decisions, the Court argued that people who choose to conduct business in highly regulated environments enjoy a reduced expectation of privacy.

---

[99]*Camara* v. *Municipal Court*, 387 U.S. 523 (1967).
[100]Ibid., p. 537.
[101]Ibid., p. 538.
[102]*Colorado* v. *Bertine*, 479 U.S. 367 [1987], p. 317.
[103]*New York* v. *Burger*, 482 U.S. 691 (1987).
[104]*Donovan* v. *Dewey*, 452 U.S. 594 (1981).
[105]*United States* v. *Biswell*, 406 U.S. 311 (1972).

Other decisions have involved such varied enterprises as arson investigations[106]; border checkpoints to stop vehicles in an effort to detect illegal aliens[107]; searches of impounded vehicles (*Colorado* v. *Bertine*) and other personal items in need of inventorying[108]; and mandatory drug testing of public and private employees.[109] In *Skinner*, the Court observed:

> In light of the limited discretion exercised by the railroad employers under the [drug testing] regulations, the surpassing safety interest served by toxicological tests in this context, and the diminished expectation of privacy that attaches to information pertaining to the fitness of covered employees, we believe it is reasonable to conduct such tests in the absence of a warrant or reasonable suspicion that any particular employee may be impaired.[110]

It should be noted that the courts have placed significant restrictions on the scope of so-called administrative searches. For example, in *Marshall* v. *Barlow's, Inc.*, the Court ruled as unconstitutional searches based on the Occupational Safety and Health Act of businesses that had not been heavily regulated in the past. At the same time, however, administrative searches can give great latitude in terms of seizing contraband and evidence of a crime to whomever conducts the search. As stated in *New York* v. *Burger*, "The discovery of evidence of crimes in the course of an otherwise proper administrative inspection does not render that search illegal or the administrative scheme suspect."[111]

YOUR DECISION

1. Here are some facts from an actual case:

> . . . a Gulf service station in North Braddock, Pennsylvania, was robbed by two men, each of whom carried and displayed a gun. The robbers took the currency from the cash register; the service station attendant, one Stephen Kovacich, was directed to place the coins in his right-hand glove, which was then taken by the robbers. Two teenagers, who had earlier noticed a blue compact station wagon circling the block in the vicinity of the Gulf station, then saw the station wagon speed away from a parking lot close to the Gulf station. About the same time, they learned that the Gulf station had been robbed. They reported to police, who arrived immediately, that four men were in the station wagon and one was wearing a green sweater. Kovacich told the police that one of the men who robbed him was wearing a green sweater and the other was wearing a trench coat. A description of the car and the two robbers was broadcast over the police radio.[112]

A vehicle fitting the description was stopped. The occupants were arrested and the car was driven to the police station and searched. Was the stop justified? In other words, did the officers have probable cause to arrest the occupants of the car?

---

[106]*Michigan* v. *Clifford*, 464 U.S. 286 (1984); *Michigan* v. *Tyler*, 436 U.S. 499 (1978).
[107]See, e.g., *United States* v. *Martinez-Fuerte*, 428 U.S. 543 (1976).
[108]*Illinois* v. *Lafayette*, 462 U.S. 640 (1983).
[109]See, e.g., *National Treasury Employees Union* v. *Von Raab*, 489 U.S. 656 (1989); *Skinner* v. *Railway Labor Executives' Association*, 489 U.S. 602 (1989).
[110]*Skinner* v. *Railway Labor Executives' Association*, 489 U.S. 602 (1989), p. 602.
[111]*New York* v. *Burger*, 482 U.S. 691 (1987), p. 716.
[112]*Chambers* v. *Maroney*, 399 U.S. 42 (1970).

2. U.S. Customs and Border Protection agents used a drug dog to search the staterooms of ten passengers aboard the *Adventure of the Seas* cruise ship while it was in port in St. Thomas, a U.S. territory. One of the staterooms searched was that of James Whitted, a man to whom authorities were alerted because he purchased his ticket at the last minute, had traveled in and through various "source cities," and had a criminal record. During the stateroom search, the drug dog alerted to a bag. Nothing suspicious was found in the bag, so it was X-rayed. At that point, the agents noticed pebbles inside a shaving cream can. On further examination, the pebbles field-tested positive for heroin. Whitted was arrested and charged with possession with intent to distribute a controlled substance. He now moves to have the drugs excluded from his trial due to an alleged Fourth Amendment violation. Will he succeed?

Summary

- Justification requires that police must have cause before they can conduct a search or a seizure.
- There are three standards of justification necessary for searches in seizures: probable cause, reasonable suspicion, and administrative justification. Only one of them, probable cause, is spelled out in the Fourth Amendment.
- Probable cause falls between 51% and 100% certainty, and is required for arrests and searches with and without warrants.
- Reasonable suspicion, which falls below 51% certainty but above a hunch, is required for stops and investigative detentions that fall short of arrests.
- Administrative justification is required in administrative and "special needs beyond law enforcement" searches. The constitutionality of a search based on administrative justification is determined by balancing the interests of society with the privacy interests of the individual.
- Both reasonable suspicion and administrative justification are lower standards than probable cause.

Chapter Review

FOUNDATIONS OF CRIMINAL PROCEDURE

Learning Objectives

- Summarize the constitutional basis for criminal procedure.
- Identify the rights of relevance in criminal procedure.

Review Questions

1. Identify several sources of constitutional rights?
2. What is incorporation?
3. What rights have been incorporated?

Key Terms

Fourth Amendment	Fourteenth Amendment
Fifth Amendment	substantive due process
Sixth Amendment	procedural due process
Eighth Amendment	incorporation

INTRODUCTION TO REMEDIES AND THE EXCLUSIONARY RULE

Learning Objectives

- Explain the exclusionary rule and the exceptions to it.
- Summarize the fruit of the poisonous tree doctrine and the exceptions to it.

Review Questions

1. What is the exclusionary rule?
2. Compare and contrast the two key exceptions to the exclusionary rule.
3. Define the "fruit of the poisonous tree" doctrine and explain three exceptions to it.

Key Terms

remedy	impeachment exception
extralegal remedies	"fruit of the poisonous tree" doctrine
legal remedies	"purged taint" exception
exclusionary rule	independent source
"silver platter" doctrine	inevitable discovery exception
"good faith" exception	

ALTERNATIVE REMEDIES

Learning Objectives

- Explain how the criminal law can act as a remedy.
- Summarize the two key requirements for a successful Section 1983 lawsuit.

· Explain the defense of qualified immunity.

· Summarize three nonjudicial remedies.

Review Questions

1. How does the criminal law act as a remedy?

2. How does civil litigation act as a remedy?

3. What are the requirements of a successful Section 1983 lawsuit against an individual police officer?

4. Distinguish among three varieties of nonjudicial remedies.

Key Terms

18 U.S.C. Section 242	internal review
civil litigation	civilian review
damage suit	civilian input
injunctive relief	civilian monitor
42 U.S.C. Section 1983	mediation
color of law	ombudsman
qualified immunity	

MODULE 10.4   JUSTIFICATION

Learning Objectives

· Define probable cause.

· Identify several sources of information that a police officer can rely on to make the probable cause determination.

· Define reasonable suspicion and explain when it applies.

· Define administrative justification and explain when it applies.

Review Questions

1. What is justification and why is it important?

2. Explain probable cause as well as acceptable sources of information for the establishment of probable cause.

3. What is reasonable suspicion and when is it used?

4. What is administrative justification? Compare and contrast it with probable cause and reasonable suspicion.

Key Terms

justification	articulable facts
probable cause	administrative justification
reasonable suspicion	

Chapter Synthesis Questions

1. Which constitutional right is most relevant in the criminal procedure context and why?

2. Is the U.S. Constitution too strict, too generous, or just right when it comes to law enforcement investigation of criminal activity?

3. What are the arguments for and against the exclusionary rule?

4. Is the exclusionary rule a loophole through which guilty criminals escape justice? Why or why not?

5. What remedy discussed in this chapter is most effective and why?

6. Are the remedies introduced in this chapter sufficient to deter police misconduct? Why or why not? What other remedy, if any, would you propose?

11

SEARCH AND SEIZURE

MODULE 11.1 SEARCHES AND ARRESTS WITH WARRANTS

Learning Objectives

- Outline the components of search and arrest warrants.
- Explain when arrest warrants are required and how they should be served.
- Explain when search warrants are required and how they should be served.

MODULE 11.2 WARRANTLESS SEARCHES

Learning Objectives

- Summarize the issues involved in warrantless searches and seizures.
- Explain the search incident to arrest doctrine.
- Identify three types of exigent circumstances and explain how they operate as exceptions to the warrant requirement.
- Summarize the special issues involved in automobile searches.
- Summarize the plain view doctrine.
- Describe consent searches and issues associated with them.

MODULE 11.3 STOP AND FRISK

Learning Objectives

- Explain the Supreme Court's decision in *Terry v. Ohio*.
- Summarize the rules concerning a "stop" in the stop and frisk context.

- Summarize the rules concerning a "frisk" in the stop and frisk context.
- Explain the practice of conducting a protective sweep.

MODULE 11.4 SPECIAL NEEDS/REGULATORY SEARCHES

Learning Objectives

- Summarize the rules surrounding vehicle inventories.
- Distinguish between several types of inspections.
- Distinguish between legal and illegal checkpoints.
- Explain when school disciplinary searches are permissible.
- Explain when searches of government employees' offices are permissible.
- Summarize the Supreme Court's view on drug and alcohol testing.
- Summarize the Supreme Court's view on probation and parole searches.

MODULE

11.1 SEARCHES AND ARRESTS WITH WARRANTS

Learning Objectives

- Outline the components of search and arrest warrants.
- Explain when arrest warrants are required and how they should be served.
- Explain when search warrants are required and how they should be served.

CORE CONCEPTS

The Fourth Amendment seems fairly clear with respect to warrants: "and no Warrants shall issue, but upon probable cause, supported by Oath or affirmation, and particularly describing the place to be searched, and the persons or things to be seized." Despite this seemingly simple language, the Fourth Amendment's warrant requirement has been litigated extensively in the courts. And even though there are many cases involving searches and arrests with warrants, the law is actually very clear with respect to *when* a warrant is required. Generally, a search warrant is required for *any* type of search, regardless of where it is conducted, provided that (1) there are no exigent (i.e., emergency) circumstances and (2) the search is not one justified on so-called administrative grounds. Even searches pursuant to arrest and searches under the automobile

arrest warrant An order issued by a judge directing a law enforcement officer to arrest an individual identified as one who has committed a specific criminal offense.

search warrant An order issued by a judge directing a law enforcement officer to search a particular location for evidence connected with a specific criminal offense.

neutral and detached magistrate One of the three elements of a valid warrant, any judge who does not have a conflict of interest or pecuniary interest in the outcome of a particular case or decision.

exception are justified in terms of exigencies. Arrest warrants, by contrast, are required for arrests in private places, provided exigent circumstances are absent.

Warrant Components

An **arrest warrant** or a **search warrant** (see Figures 11.1 and 11.2 for examples) has three essential components. First, it must be issued by a neutral and detached magistrate. Second, a showing of probable cause is required. Finally, it must conform to the Fourth Amendment's particularity requirement. The first requirement—a neutral and detached magistrate—is the same regardless of the type of warrant. The probable cause and particularity requirements differ depending on the type of warrant in question. These requirements are considered in the following subsections.

Neutral and Detached Magistrate

The logic for requiring a **neutral and detached magistrate** in the issuance of an arrest or a search warrant was described by the Supreme Court over 50 years ago in *Johnson* v. *United States*:

> The point of the Fourth Amendment . . . is not that it denies law enforcement the support of the usual inferences reasonable men draw from evidence. Its protection consists in requiring that those inferences be drawn by a neutral and detached magistrate instead of being judged by the officer engaged in the often competitive enterprise of ferreting out crime.[1]

WARRANT OF ARREST ON COMPLAINT

(RCr 2.04, 2.06)
(Caption)

TO ALL PEACE OFFICERS
You are hereby commanded to arrest _____
                                 (Name of defendant)

and bring him forthwith before judge of the District Court (or, if he be absent or unable to act, before the nearest available magistrate) to answer a complaint made by _____ charging him with the offense of reckless driving.
Issued this _____ day of _____, 19 _____.

                          _____
                          Judge

(Indorsement as to bail)
The defendant may give bail in the amount of $ _____.

                          _____
                          Judge
(Amended October 14, 20___, effective January 1, 20 ____.)

Figure 11.1
Sample Arrest Warrant

---

[1]*Johnson* v. *United States*, 333 U.S. 10 (1948), pp. 13–14.

Example of a Search Warrant That Meets the Particularity Requirement

IN THE SUPERIOR COURT DISTRICT, EAST DESERT DIVISION
COUNTY OF SAN BERNARDINO, STATE OF CALIFORNIA

SEARCH WARRANT
(PENAL CODE 1529)

THE PEOPLE OF THE STATE OF CALIFORNIA: To any Sheriff, Constable, Peace Officer or Policeman in the County of San Bernardino:

Proof, by Affidavit, having been this day made before me by:

ROGER PEREZ
Deputy Sheriff
San Bernardino County Sheriff's Department
Morongo Basin Station

THAT THERE IS PROBABLE CAUSE FOR BELIEVING THAT:

There are narcotics, controlled substances and restricted substances records and documents which tend to show that a felony to wit, Transportation of Controlled Substances, in violation of Health and Safety Code Section 11379, Possession for Sales of Controlled Substances, in violation of Health and Safety Code Section 11378, Sales of Controlled Substances, in violation of Health and Safety Code Section 11379, is being committed in the County of San Bernardino, State of California.

YOU ARE THEREFORE COMMANDED at any time of the day or night _____ to make a search of:

PREMISES TO BE SEARCHED:

The premises located at:

2400 MAIN STREET, #12
TOWN OF PLEASANTVILLE
COUNTY OF SAN BERNARDINO
STATE OF CALIFORNIA

The location is further described as a multi-unit apartment complex located on the east side of Main Street south of Oak Dr. The complex consists of numerous two-story buildings with each building having multiple apartments. Apartment 12 is located in building "C", which is located at the northwest corner of the complex. The exterior is tan stucco with grayish/blue trim and a gray composite shingle roof. Apartment 12 has the numbers "12" which are black and approximately 4 inches tall, affixed to the wood trim to the right of the front door, which faces north.

And all rooms, attics, basements, cellars, safes, vaults, closed or locked containers, trash receptacles and other parts therein, surrounding grounds, garages, sheds, storage rooms, vehicles, campers, trailers and outbuildings of any kind located thereon.

And all persons located on or at the premises. And all vehicles belonging to or in the control of said persons.

And you are hereby authorized to answer all incoming telephone calls received at the premises and the vehicles to be searched and to further seize and record all the incoming

Figure 11.2

Sample Search Warrant
Source: Used courtesy of the San Bernardino Country Sheriff's Department.

telephonic pager numbers and messages received at the premises and the vehicles to be searched and to seize all telephonic "fax" messages received at the premises and the vehicles to be searched. And to determine if the aforementioned telephone calls, telephonic messages, or "faxed" messages are related to illegal activities.

FOR THE FOLLOWING PROPERTY:

Methamphetamine and paraphernalia commonly associated with the possession, packaging, and sale of methamphetamine such as scales, weighing devices and measuring devices; packaging materials including paper bindles, glass vials, plastic baggies, foil; processing materials including sifters, filters, screens and cutting agents; recordation of the purchase and/or sales of methamphetamine including ledgers, notebooks, pay/owe sheets, customer lists, video tapes and phone answering machine tape recordings, personal phone books; personal photographs which document the possession, sales and/or possession for sales of methamphetamine; and proceeds from the sales of methamphetamine consisting of currency.

Financial records including expenses incurred in obtaining chemicals and apparatus and income derived from sales of narcotics and other controlled substances as well as records showing legitimate income or the lack thereof and general living expenses.

Serial numbers, model numbers, identifying marks and descriptions of all personal property including, but not limited to, televisions, radios, stereo equipment, and other electrical devices, appliances, hand and power tools, firearms, bicycles, items of jewelry, silver, gold and coins which can be identified as stolen and/or evidence of the crime of Burglary and/or Possession of Stolen Property or property which is readily traded for narcotics in lieu of cash.

All articles of personal property which will identify persons in control of the premises, storage areas or containers where controlled substances may be found, including keys to those areas that may be locked, rental agreements and receipts, deeds of trust, documents or papers bearing names, canceled mail, paycheck stubs and other employment records, tax documents and personal identification.

AND IF YOU FIND THE SAME OR ANY PART THEREOF, to bring it forthwith before meat my courtroom

GIVEN UNDER MY HAND, and dated this 17th day of September 2002.

James D. Franklin
_____

Judge of the Superior Court
East Desert Division
County of San Bernardino
State of California

Figure 11.2
(Continued)

Most judges are considered neutral and detached. Even so, the Supreme Court has focused, in a number of cases, on this first critical warrant requirement. In *Coolidge* v. *New Hampshire*,[2] the Court declared that a state attorney general cannot issue a search warrant. State attorneys general are chief prosecutors and thus inclined to side with law enforcement officers. Similarly, in *United States* v. *United States District Court*,[3] the Court decided that the president, acting through the

_____

[2]*Coolidge* v. *New Hampshire*, 403 U.S. 443 (1971).
[3]*United States* v. *United States District Court*, 407 U.S. 297 (1972).

attorney general of the United States, cannot authorize electronic surveillance without judicial approval.

Probable Cause Showing

Probable cause was defined in Chapter 10. As such, there is no need to revisit the definition here, but it is important to point out that probable cause is required as a component of a valid warrant. Also, the meaning of probable cause—as opposed to the sources of information that give rise to it—differs, depending on whether an arrest or a search warrant is issued.

The showing of probable cause in an arrest warrant is not particularly complex. The officer applying for the warrant must simply show probable cause that the person to be arrested committed the crime. Acceptable sources of information for a probable cause showing were described in Chapter 10. When applying for an *arrest* warrant, the officer is not required to show probable cause that the suspect will be found at a particular location. In *Payton* v. *New York*, the majority stated, "If there is sufficient evidence of a citizen's participation in a felony to persuade a judicial officer that his arrest is justified, it is constitutionally reasonable to require him to open his doors to the officers of the law."[4]

The showing of probable cause in a search warrant is twofold. First, the officer applying for the search warrant must show probable cause that the items to be seized are connected with criminal activity. Second, the officer must show probable cause that the items to be seized are in the location to be searched. Note that this second requirement does not apply to an arrest warrant.

Particularity

The Fourth Amendment expressly provides that warrants particularly describe the "place to be searched, and the persons or things to be seized." Not surprisingly, the **particularity** requirement differs, depending on the type of warrant issued. For an arrest warrant, the particularity requirement is easily satisfied. The particularity requirement for a search warrant, however, is far more complex.

There are two ways to satisfy the Fourth Amendment's particularity requirement with regard to an arrest warrant. First, if the suspect's name is known, then simply supplying his or her name is enough to meet the particularity requirement. In some situations, however, the suspect's name is *not* known. Then, a specific description of the suspect is sufficient and a "John Doe" warrant will be issued. As long as other officers may locate the suspect with reasonable effort, the suspect's name is not required.

Arrest warrants are rarely issued without the suspect's name. This is not to suggest, however, that the police almost always know the suspect's name. Remember, there are many occasions involving warrantless arrests (e.g., after a suspect is caught fleeing the bank he or she just robbed) in which an arrest can be made without knowledge of the suspect's name. As long as probable cause is in place, the name of the suspect is not essential, regardless of whether a warrant is issued.

particularity The Fourth Amendment requirement that an arrest warrant name the person to be arrested (or provide a sufficiently detailed description) and that a search warrant describe the place to be searched and the things to be seized.

---

[4]*Payton* v. *New York*, 445 U.S. 573 (1980), pp. 602–603.

The particularity requirement for a search warrant is twofold. First, the warrant must specify the *place* to be searched. Next, the warrant must specify the *items* to be seized. Contrary to popular belief, a search warrant does not need to state with absolute precision the place to be searched. It "is enough if the description is such that the officer with a search warrant can, with reasonable effort, ascertain and identify the place intended."[5] However, the items mentioned in the warrant should be described with sufficient specificity that a reasonable officer would know where to look for them. As for the items to be seized, the warrant must clearly specify what the police wish to seize.

Arrest Warrants

arrest The act of taking an individual into custody for the purpose of charging the person with a criminal offense (or, in the case of a juvenile, a delinquent act).

An **arrest** is the act of taking an individual into custody for the purpose of charging the person with a criminal offense (or, in the case of a juvenile, a delinquent act). Sometimes a stop (as in "stop and frisk," or a vehicle stop) can evolve into a *de facto* arrest in a number of circumstances. The courts will give weight to four factors in making their decision: (1) the purpose of the stop (e.g., to question or interrogate a person), (2) the manner in which the stop takes place (e.g., stopped by one officer or several), (3) the location in which the stop takes place (e.g., stationhouse, street, or home), and (4) the duration of the stop. No single factor is necessarily determinative. If, however, a person is detained by several officers in a stationhouse for several days so as to be interrogated, then the court will almost certainly consider such police activity tantamount to an arrest.

Justice Powell once stated that "a search may cause only an annoyance and temporary inconvenience to the law-abiding citizen, assuming more serious dimensions only when it turns up evidence of criminality [but an] arrest . . . is a serious personal intrusion regardless of whether the person seized is guilty or innocent."[6] Even so, an unconstitutional arrest has little significance by itself in criminal procedure. The reason for this is that the remedy for an illegal arrest is simply a release from custody. It is possible that a person unlawfully arrested may sue, but little recourse is generally available to a person who is unlawfully arrested. Why, then, focus attention on the constitutionality of arrests? The answer is that the constitutionality of an arrest is frequently critical in determining whether seized evidence is admissible in court.

Consider this example: Assume that a police officer arrests a defendant without probable cause. Such an arrest is automatically unconstitutional. Assume also that the officer finds an illegal firearm on the defendant and turns it over to the prosecutor, who decides to use it against the defendant at his trial on firearm charges. The defendant will almost certainly seek to have the firearm excluded as evidence on the grounds that it resulted from an unlawful arrest. In other words, the defendant will argue that the firearm is "fruit of the poisonous tree," as discussed in Chapter 10.

When Arrest Warrants Are Required

Under common law, if an arresting officer had probable cause to believe that (1) a person was committing or had committed a felony or (2) a person was committing a

---

[5]*Steele* v. *United States*, 267 U.S. 498 (1925), p. 503.
[6]*United States* v. *Watson*, 423 U.S. 411 (1976), p. 428.

certain misdemeanor in the officer's presence, then an arrest warrant was not required. This held true regardless of where the arrest took place, even if it was effected in someone's private home.[7] The only real situation in which an arrest warrant *was* required was for a misdemeanor committed out of view of the arresting officer. The logic for this was set forth by the Supreme Court in *Carroll* v. *United States*:

> The reason for arrest for misdemeanors without warrant at common law was to promptly suppress breaches of the peace . . . while the reason for arrest without a warrant on a reliable report of a felony was because the public safety and the due apprehension of criminals charged with heinous offenses required that such arrests should be made at once without warrant.[8]

Since 1925, the Supreme Court has stuck to the rule set forth in *Carroll*, subject to two exceptions. First, an arrest in someone's private home cannot be made without a warrant, unless exigent circumstances are present. Second, an arrest in the home of a third party is impermissible without a warrant, again providing no exigent circumstances are in place. An example of a third-party situation is one in which the police seek to arrest a person who is visiting a friend's house.

In the landmark decision of *Payton* v. *New York*,[9] the Supreme Court held that the Fourth Amendment prohibits a warrantless, nonconsensual entry into a private home for the purpose of making an arrest. In that case, police officers, after two days of investigation, had assembled enough evidence to establish probable cause to believe that Payton had murdered the manager of a gas station. The officers went to Payton's apartment to arrest him. When no one answered the door, they used a crowbar to open the door and entered the apartment. They did not find Payton, but they did find, in plain view, a .30 caliber shell casing lying on the floor. They seized it and admitted it into evidence at Payton's trial. Payton ultimately surrendered to the police and was indicted for murder. The lower court admitted the shell casing into evidence, but the Supreme Court reversed, stating, "In terms that apply equally to seizures of property and to seizures of persons, the Fourth Amendment has drawn a firm line at the entrance to the house. Absent exigent circumstances, that threshold may not reasonably be crossed without a warrant."[10] Justice Stevens also stated, citing an earlier case (*United States* v. *United States District Court*), that "physical entry of the home is the chief evil against which the wording of the Fourth Amendment is directed."[11] In *Payton*, then, the Court handed down a bright-line rule: An arrest in the home must be accompanied by a warrant in the absence of exigent circumstances. This decision in *Kirk* v. *Louisiana* reaffirmed this.[12]

Not long after *Payton*, the Supreme Court decided *Steagald* v. *United States*.[13] Justice Marshall expressed concern that although an arrest warrant may protect a person "from an unreasonable seizure, it [does] absolutely nothing to protect [a third party's] privacy interest in being free from an unreasonable invasion and search of

---

[7]*Trupiano* v. *United States*, 334 U.S. 699 (1948).
[8]*Carroll* v. *United States*, 267 U.S. 132 (1925), p. 157.
[9]*Payton* v. *New York*, 445 U.S. 573 (1980).
[10]Ibid., p. 590.
[11]Ibid., p. 585.
[12]*Kirk* v. *Louisiana*, 536 U.S. 635 (2002).
[13]*Steagald* v. *United States*, 451 U.S. 204 (1981).

his home."[14] Accordingly, the Court decided that in such situations, the police must obtain not only an arrest warrant for the person they seek but also a *separate* warrant to search the third-party residence for the arrestee.

The facts in *Steagald* were as follows: Acting on an arrest warrant issued for a person by the name of Lyons, Drug Enforcement Administration (DEA) agents entered the home of Steagald. This entry was made without a warrant. While searching Steagald's home for Lyons, the agents found cocaine and other incriminating evidence, but they did not find Lyons. Steagald was arrested and convicted on federal drug charges. He appealed, and the Supreme Court eventually reversed Steagald's conviction.

The Court's decision in *Steagald* was not without opposition. Justices Rehnquist and White dissented, arguing that the police and judges "will, in their various capacities, have to weigh the time during which a suspect for whom there is an outstanding arrest warrant has been in the building, whether the dwelling is the suspect's home, how long he has lived there, whether he is likely to leave immediately, and a number of related and equally imponderable questions."[15] The majority countered by pointing out that if the police did not need warrants to enter third-party residences, "[a]rmed solely with an arrest warrant for a single person, [the police] . . . could search all the homes of that individual's friends and acquaintances."[16] Such a possibility would be controversial, indeed.

Thus, having an arrest warrant does *not* allow authorities to enter a third-party residence. A warrantless entry into a third-party residence violates the third party's rights. There are two exceptions to this rule, however. First, if the third party consents to a request by police, a search warrant won't be necessary (but the arrest warrant will still be necessary). Second, if there is an emergency, or "exigent circumstances," a warrant may not be required. See Figure 11.3 for a summary of situations in which an arrest warrant is required/not required.

Serving Arrest Warrants

Assuming a valid warrant is in place, the police cannot use any means available to effect the arrest. For example, they cannot kick in a door without having any reason to do so. Similarly, they cannot use deadly force unless absolutely necessary and for the most dangerous of criminal offenders. In almost all cases, the procedures for executing an arrest warrant are laid out in police department policy manuals.

Figure 11.3

Summary of Arrest Warrant Requirements

1. When an arrest warrant is required:
   a. in a home/residence absent exigent circumstances,
   b. in a third-party home; a separate search warrant is also required.
2. When an arrest warrant is not required:
   a. the arrest is made in public,
   b. exigent circumstances exist,
   c. consent is given.

---

[14]Ibid., p. 213.
[15]Ibid., p. 213.
[16]Ibid., p. 215.

The law generally requires that police officers announce their presence and state their authority (e.g., "Police officers! Search warrant!"). Doing so is important for several reasons: (1) It helps avoid needless destruction of property, (2) it helps prevent violence resulting from unnecessary surprise, and (3) it helps preserve people's dignity and privacy. Of course, in certain situations, these reasons for a "knock and announce rule" do not serve their intended purposes. In fact, the second reason can work opposite from what is intended: If the police are required to announce their presence for all manner of suspects, such an announcement could *result* in violence, rather than reduce the possibility for it. It is thus preferable for the police to announce their presence, but it is not constitutionally required, as was recently decided in *Hudson* v. *Michigan*.[17]

knock and announce rule The requirement that, before executing an arrest or search warrant, officers identify themselves and their intentions.

Search Warrants

Searches with warrants are subjected to many of the same restrictions that arrests with warrants are. However, because the purpose of obtaining a search warrant is to search for something, as opposed to seizing a person, the courts have placed significant restrictions on what the police can do when searching for evidence with warrants. Just because a warrant is obtained does not mean that the police can look anywhere and take unlimited time to search for the item(s) named in the warrant.

When Search Warrants Are Required

Search warrants are required any time the police seek to search for evidence in a manner that is not governed by one of the well-established exceptions to the Fourth Amendment's warrant requirement. Such warrantless searches (which have been sanctioned by the U.S. Supreme Court in very narrow and specific circumstances) are discussed at length in the next module. By way of preview, they include searches incident to arrest, hot pursuit, escape, endangerment, destruction of evidence, automobile searches, plain view searches, and when consent is obtained. In any other situation, a search warrant is necessary. Search warrants are also preferred any time they can be obtained, even if they are not formally *required*.

Serving Search Warrants

The knock and announce rules discussed earlier carry over to the service of search warrants. As indicated before, the police do not have to announce their presence if they have reasonable suspicion that exigent circumstances are present. Likewise, even if the police do not "knock and announce," evidence seized cannot be excluded per *Hudson* v. *Michigan*.

Use of force is rarely an issue that arises during the service of a search warrant because, strictly speaking, a search warrant authorizes the police to look for evidence. If a person gets in the way during the service of a search warrant, however, he or she may be arrested and force may be applied, if need be (i.e., subject to the restrictions discussed earlier).

---

[17]*Hudson* v. *Michigan*, 547 U.S. 586 (2006).

If the police mistakenly search the wrong residence, the search will not automatically be declared invalid. As long as the mistake is a reasonable one, any evidence seized during a search of the wrong residence will be admissible in a criminal trial. The key, however, is that the mistake must be an *objectively reasonable* one, gauged from the standpoint of a reasonable officer.

Two other issues are relevant to the service of a search warrant. These do not necessarily apply in the case of arrest warrants. They are: (1) time restrictions, both for when the warrant can be served and for how long the police can look for evidence, and (2) the scope and manner of the search.

There are three means by which the courts impose time constraints on the police when it comes to the service of search warrants. First, the service of a search warrant should take place promptly after its issuance. Second, judges commonly restrict the service of warrants to the daytime hours or at least favor daytime service.[18] The *Federal Rules of Criminal Procedure*, for example, restrict the service of warrants to daytime hours, unless the issuing judge specifically authorizes execution at another time. *Daytime hours*, according to the *Federal Rules*, are between the hours of 6:00 A.M. and 10:00 P.M. Finally, the general rule is that a search cannot last indefinitely. Once the item in the warrant has been discovered, the search must be terminated. If the police have difficulty finding the item or items named in the warrant, they can take as long as necessary to find them. If the police do not succeed in finding the evidence named in the warrant and then leave and come back later, they will be required to obtain another warrant. Steps should always be taken to avoid the appearance of arbitrariness, and people's Fourth Amendment privacy interests should always be respected.

Two additional restrictions with regard to the service of a search warrant concern the scope and manner of the search. *Scope* refers to where the police can look for evidence. *Manner* refers to the physical steps the police can take to find the evidence in question, including breaking down doors, forcibly opening locked cabinets, and so on. The scope of the search must be reasonable, based on the object of the search. In other words, the police are restricted in looking for evidence insofar as they can only look where the item could reasonably be found. For example, assume the evidence in question is a stolen diamond ring. Such an item is relatively small, so the police will be authorized to look almost anywhere for the ring. However, if the evidence in question is large in size—for example, a stolen big-screen television set—then the police cannot look in small places, where such an item could not possibly be found. The Supreme Court's statement in *Harris* v. *United States* provides further clarification: "[T]he same meticulous investigation which would be appropriate in a search for two small canceled checks could not be considered reasonable where agents are seeking a stolen automobile or an illegal still."[19]

YOUR DECISION

1. The police have in their possession the video from a security camera at a bank that was recently robbed. The suspect is a white male, 6 feet tall, and has a mustache, a bald head, a scar on his left cheek, and a tattoo of a skull and crossbones

---

[18] *Gooding* v. *United States*, 416 U.S. 430 (1974).
[19] *Harris* v. *United States*, 331 U.S. 145 (1947), p. 152.

on his neck. May the police apply for an arrest warrant based on this information, even if they never learned of the suspect's name prior to applying for the warrant?

2. On August 26, at approximately 7:30 P.M., the Sunny County Sheriff's Department executed a search warrant on the premises of 5678 Cherry Lane. The defendants later argued that the search warrant and its execution were defective because the warrant directed that it be executed during the *daytime*. In fact, the warrant was executed at approximately 7:30 P.M., and sunset occurred at 6:43 P.M., according to the National Weather Service. Given this, was the warrant therefore defective?

Summary

- A warrant has three required components: (1) a neutral and detached magistrate, (2) a showing of probable cause, and (3) particularity. The probable cause and particularity showings differ between search and arrest warrants.

- Arrest warrants are required in two situations: (1) arrests in the home and (2) arrests in third-party homes. Arrests in the public do not require warrants. During service of an arrest warrant, the police should announce their presence. Reasonable property damage is acceptable. Force can be used, but is subject to legal constraints.

- Search warrants are required unless the method by which the search is conducted is one the Supreme Court has permitted to occur without a warrant. Search warrants should be served in the same careful manner as arrest warrants. Additional limitations focus on time restrictions and the scope and manner of the search.

MODULE

11.2

WARRANTLESS SEARCHES

Learning Objectives

- **Summarize the issues involved in warrantless searches and seizures.**
- **Explain the search incident to arrest doctrine.**
- **Identify three types of exigent circumstances and explain how they operate as exceptions to the warrant requirement.**
- **Summarize the special issues involved in automobile searches.**
- **Summarize the plain view doctrine.**
- **Describe consent searches and issues associated with them.**

CORE CONCEPTS If it was not for exceptions to the warrant requirement, the Fourth Amendment would take substantially less effort to understand. At the same time, however, the many exceptions to the Fourth Amendment's warrant requirement are what make it

exceptions to the warrant requirement Law enforcement actions that do not require a warrant. Examples include searches incident to arrest, searches based on exigent circumstances, automobile searches, plain view searches, arrests based on exigent circumstances, and arrests in public places.

interesting. The so-called warrantless searches discussed in this module are based on Supreme Court decisions, in which it was believed that to require a warrant would constitute an undue burden on law enforcement officials. Still, though, a warrant is *always* preferable; whenever circumstances permit, one should be obtained.

Broadly, there are five types of warrantless searches that require probable cause. They are called **exceptions to the warrant requirement** because the actions at issue do not need to be supported by a search warrant. The five types of warrantless searches are (1) searches incident to (i.e., following) arrest, (2) searches in the presence of exigent circumstances, (3) searches involving automobiles, (4) searches based on the plain view doctrine and (5) consent searches.

Search Incident to Arrest

Imagine a situation in which a police officer has lawfully (i.e., with probable cause) arrested a suspect, is leading him away, and observes the suspect reach into his pocket.

A search incident to arrest is typical and constitutionally permissible provided the arrest is proper and based on probable cause.

What would be going through the police officer's mind as he or she observed this behavior? Scenarios like this illustrate the reasoning behind the **search incident to arrest** exception. Namely, police officers must be permitted to engage in a search of a suspect incident to arrest (i.e., following an arrest). It would be impractical, even dangerous, to wait for a warrant before conducting such a search incident to arrest.

The leading case in the area of incident searches is *Chimel v. California*.[20] As the Supreme Court stated, a search incident to arrest is permitted "to remove any weapons that the [arrestee] might seek to use in order to resist arrest or effect his escape" and to "seize any evidence on the arrestee's person in order to prevent its concealment or destruction."[21]

The most basic requirement concerning searches incident to arrest—and one that often goes overlooked—is that the arrest must be lawful. When the arrest itself is not lawful (i.e., when it is not based on probable cause), any search that follows is unlawful.[22]

Another important threshold issue with regard to searches incident to arrest concerns the nature of the offense. Courts have grappled with the question as to whether a search should be permitted when the offense on which the arrest is based is not serious. Because the rationale of the exception is to provide officer safety, then is officer safety likely to be compromised when a minor offense, as opposed to a serious offense, justifies the arrest?

---

[20]*Chimel v. California*, 395 U.S. 752 (1969).
[21]Ibid., p. 763.
[22]*Draper v. United States*, 358 U.S. 307 (1959).

search incident to arrest
An exception to the Fourth Amendment's warrant requirement that allows officers to search a suspect following his or her arrest.

Two important Supreme Court cases have sought to answer these questions. First, in *United States* v. *Robinson*,[23] the Court reversed a lower court's decision that only a patdown of the suspect's outer clothing was permissible following an arrest for driving with a revoked license. And in a companion case to *Robinson*, *Gustafson* v. *Florida*,[24] the Court upheld the search of a suspect after his arrest for failure to have his driver's license.

Thus, *any* arrest justifies a warrantless search incident to that arrest. A key restriction, however, is that the arrest must result in a person being *taken into custody*. This was the ruling from *Knowles* v. *Iowa*.[25] In that case, a police officer stopped a person for speeding, and rather than arresting him (which the officer had justification to do), the officer issued him a citation. Then, the officer conducted a search of the car and found a marijuana pipe. The Court noted that traffic stops rarely pose the same threat to officer safety as arrests. This is not to suggest, however, that police officers cannot search people incident to lawful arrest for minor vehicle-related infractions. If the authority to arrest is present, an incident search is permissible. The key restriction is that the person must actually be arrested and taken into custody. Otherwise, the search will not conform with the Fourth Amendment requirements.

Timing of the Search

A key restriction pertaining to searches incident to arrest has to do with the timing of the search. Probable cause to arrest must *precede* the warrantless search.[26] The reason for this is to restrict officers from engaging in "fishing expeditions," or searches based on less than probable cause that would presumably result in probable cause to make an arrest. Note, however, that if probable cause to arrest is in place, the officer is not required to formally arrest the suspect before engaging in the search.[27]

If the search follows an arrest, then it must take place *soon* after the arrest. In legal parlance, the search must be *contemporaneous* to the arrest. In *Preston* v. *United States*,[28] the case that established this rule, Justice Black observed that the "justifications [for the search incident to arrest] are absent where a search is remote in time or place from the arrest."[29] In *Preston*, police officers arrested the occupants of a car and took them to jail. After this, the officers searched the car, which had been towed to an impound lot. The Supreme Court noted that the possibilities of destruction of evidence and danger to the officers were no longer in place, as the suspects were no longer even present.[30]

Scope of the Search

The case of *United States* v. *Rabinowitz*[31] was the first to set limits on the scope of a search incident to arrest. In that case, the officers, armed with a valid arrest warrant,

---

[23] *United States* v. *Robinson*, 414 U.S. 218 (1973).
[24] *Gustafson* v. *Florida*, 414 U.S. 260 (1973).
[25] *Knowles* v. *Iowa*, 525 U.S. 113 (1998).
[26] *Sibron* v. *New York*, 392 U.S. 40 (1968).
[27] *Rawlings* v. *Kentucky*, 448 U.S. 98 (1980).
[28] *Preston* v. *United States*, 376 U.S. 364 (1964).
[29] Ibid., p. 367.
[30] See also *Chambers* v. *Maroney*, 399 U.S. 42 (1970).
[31] *United States* v. *Rabinowitz*, 339 U.S. 56 (1950).

arrested a man and then conducted a warrantless search of his one-room business, including the desk, safe, and file cabinets. The Supreme Court upheld the search because the room "was small and under the immediate and complete control of the respondent."[32]

Nearly 20 years after *Rabinowitz*, however, the Supreme Court voted to overturn its earlier decision. In the case of *Chimel* v. *California*, the Court argued that the *Rabinowitz* decision had been construed to mean that "a warrantless search 'incident to a lawful arrest' may generally extend to the area that is considered to be in the 'possession' or under the 'control' of the person arrested."[33] Furthermore, the Court noted that the *Rabinowitz* standard gave police "the opportunity to engage in searches not justified by probable cause, [but] by the simple expedient of arranging to arrest suspects at home rather than elsewhere."[34] To get around this problem, Justice Stewart argued in favor of a new **armspan rule**. In the Court's words, a search incident to arrest would now be limited to the area "within [the] immediate control" of the person arrested—that is, "the area from within which he might have obtained either a weapon or something that could have been used as evidence against him."[35]

What happens with a search incident to arrest during the course a vehicle stop? Probable cause to *arrest* (as opposed to search) does not authorize a full search of a vehicle, including the trunk, but it *can* authorize a search of the passenger compartment.[36] However, in *Arizona* v. *Gant*,[37] the Supreme Court restricted such searches. A man was arrested for driving on a suspended license. He was handcuffed and placed in a patrol car, then officers searched his car and found cocaine in the pocket of a jacket. He was convicted of drug offenses. The Supreme Court held that such a search is only permissible if it is reasonable to believe that the arrestee might access the vehicle at the time of the search or that the vehicle contains evidence of the offense of arrest. The *Gant* decision makes it somewhat difficult to determine whether a search is sanctioned. It forces officers to decide whether the vehicle contains evidence of the offense in question. The logic behind the *Gant* decision is explored more fully in the accompanying Court Decision box.

armspan rule Part of the search incident to arrest exception to the Fourth Amendment's warrant requirement that allows officers to search not only the suspect incident to arrest, but also his or her "grabbing area."

COURT DECISION

The Logic behind the Requirement that Vehicle Searches Incident to Arrest Must Be Related to the Offense of Arrest

Arizona v. *Gant*
556 U.S. 332 (2009)

Decision: A *Belton*-type automobile search is permissible "only if it is reasonable to believe that the arrestee might access the vehicle at the time of the search or that the vehicle contains evidence of the offense of arrest."

(continued)

---

[32]Ibid., p. 64.
[33]*Chimel* v. *California*, 395 U.S. 752 (1969), p. 759.
[34]Ibid., p. 767.
[35]Ibid., p. 768.
[36]*New York* v. *Belton*, 453 U.S. 454 (1981); *Thornton* v. *United States*, 541 U.S. 615 (2004).
[37]*Arizona* v. *Gant*, No. 07-542 (2009).

**COURT
DECISION**
(continued)

Reason: Although we have recognized that a motorist's privacy interest in his vehicle is less substantial than in his home . . . , the former interest is nevertheless important and deserving of constitutional protection. . . . It is particularly significant that [*New York* v.] *Belton* searches authorize police officers to search not just the passenger compartment but every purse, briefcase, or other container within that space. A rule that gives police the power to conduct such a search whenever an individual is caught committing a traffic offense, when there is no basis for believing evidence of the offense might be found in the vehicle, creates a serious and recurring threat to the privacy of countless individuals. Indeed, the character of that threat implicates the central concern underlying the Fourth Amendment—the concern about giving police officers unbridled discretion to rummage at will among a person's private effects . . .

Courts that have read *Belton* expansively are at odds regarding how close in time to the arrest and how proximate to the arrestee's vehicle an officer's first contact with the arrestee must be to bring the encounter within *Belton*'s purview . . . and whether a search is reasonable when it commences or continues after the arrestee has been removed from the scene. . . . The rule has thus generated a great deal of uncertainty, particularly for a rule touted as providing a "bright line." . . .

[A] broad reading of *Belton* is also unnecessary to protect law enforcement safety and evidentiary interests. Under our view, *Belton* and *Thornton* [v. *United States*] permit an officer to conduct a vehicle search when an arrestee is within reaching distance of the vehicle or it is reasonable to believe the vehicle contains evidence of the offense of arrest. Other established exceptions to the warrant requirement authorize a vehicle search under additional circumstances when safety or evidentiary concerns demand. For instance, *Michigan* v. *Long* . . . permits an officer to search a vehicle's passenger compartment when he has reasonable suspicion that an individual, whether or not the arrestee, is "dangerous" and might access the vehicle to "gain immediate control of weapons." . . . If there is probable cause to believe a vehicle contains evidence of criminal activity, *United States* v. *Ross* . . . authorizes a search of any area of the vehicle in which the evidence might be found. Unlike the searches permitted by Justice Scalia's opinion concurring in the judgment in *Thornton*, which we conclude today are reasonable for purposes of the Fourth Amendment, *Ross* allows searches for evidence relevant to offenses other than the offense of arrest, and the scope of the search authorized is broader. Finally, there may be still other circumstances in which safety or evidentiary interests would justify a search . . .

These exceptions together ensure that officers may search a vehicle when genuine safety or evidentiary concerns encountered during the arrest of a vehicle's recent occupant justify a search. Construing *Belton* broadly to allow vehicle searches incident to any arrest would serve no purpose except to provide a police entitlement, and it is anathema to the Fourth Amendment to permit a warrantless search on that basis. For these reasons, we are unpersuaded by the State's arguments that a broad reading of *Belton* would meaningfully further law enforcement interests and justify a substantial intrusion on individuals' privacy . . .

Not long after *Gant*, the Court decided *Davis* v. *United States*.[38] Davis was a passenger in a vehicle that was pulled over. He was arrested for giving police a false name. When he was seated in the back of the patrol car, officers searched the jacket he left in the vehicle. They found a gun, which Davis was not legally permitted to carry. Under *Gant*, the officers could not search the jacket because the search was not related to the arrest, but the Supreme Court sided with the police because at the time of the search (before the *Gant* decision was issued), their actions did not violate the Fourth Amendment. In other words, they acted in good faith.

Exigent Circumstances

exigent circumstances Emergency circumstances, including hot pursuit, the possibility of escape, or evanescent evidence. When exigent circumstances are present, the police do not need to abide by the Fourth Amendment's warrant requirement.

The exceptions to the search warrant requirement are premised on the impracticality of obtaining a warrant. Perhaps no exception illustrates this better than the exigent circumstances exception. Simply put, when the exigencies, or emergencies, of the situation require the police to act immediately at the risk of danger to themselves, danger to others, the destruction of evidence, or the escape of the suspect, it would be unreasonable to require the police to take time to obtain a warrant.

Generally, three types of exigencies are recognized by the courts as authorizing the police to act without a warrant: (1) hot pursuit, (2) likelihood of escape or danger to others absent hot pursuit, and (3) evanescent evidence. Despite the fact that these exceptions allow the police to act without a warrant, probable cause is still required. For example, probable cause that the person being pursued is the suspect is required before the police can enter a home or building without a warrant to arrest him or her.

Hot Pursuit

hot pursuit An exigent circumstance authorizing police to pursue criminal suspects without a warrant.

The Supreme Court first recognized the hot pursuit exception in the case of *Warden* v. *Hayden*,[39] in which the police were called by taxicab drivers who reported that their taxi company had been robbed. The police followed the suspect to a house, where they were granted entry by the suspect's wife. The suspect was upstairs in the house, pretending to be asleep. While searching the house for the suspect, the police found and seized clothing, a shotgun, and a pistol, all of which were used against the suspect at trial. The Court found the warrantless entry reasonable because the "exigencies of the situation made that course imperative."[40] Several reasons were offered for the decision. First, Justice Brennan stated that "[t]he Fourth Amendment does not require police officers to delay in the course of an investigation if to do so would gravely danger their lives or the lives of others."[41] Also, "[s]peed . . . was essential, and only a thorough search of the house for persons and weapons could have insured that Hayden was the only man present and that the police had control of all weapons which could be used against them or to effect an escape."[42]

---

[38]*Davis* v. *United States*, No. 09-11328 (2011).
[39]*Warden* v. *Hayden*, 387 U.S. 294 (1967).
[40]Ibid., p. 298.
[41]Ibid., pp. 298–299.
[42]Ibid., p. 299.

Despite the sweeping language from the *Hayden* decision, the Supreme Court has imposed several restrictions on searches and seizures premised on hot pursuit. In general, hot pursuit are constitutional only if the police have probable cause to believe (1) that the person they are pursuing has committed a serious offense, (2) that the person will be found on the premises the police seek to enter, and (3) that the suspect will escape or harm someone or that evidence will be lost or destroyed.

Escape and Endangerment to Others Absent Hot Pursuit

Hot pursuit is justified, as just discussed, when, among other things, the suspect may escape or inflict harm on police officers or others. In some situations, however, a suspect can potentially escape or inflict harm absent hot pursuit. In *Minnesota* v. *Olson*,[43] for example, the prosecution sought to justify a warrantless entry and arrest of a suspect in a duplex that the police had surrounded. There was probable cause to believe that Olson, the man in the duplex, had been the driver of a getaway car involved in a robbery/murder the day before. The Supreme Court ruled that the officers acted unconstitutionally under the circumstances because Olson was only the driver, not the murder suspect, and the weapon had been recovered, which diminished the urgency of the situation. In addition, it was unlikely Olson would escape because the building was surrounded. On its face, then, this case is not useful on this point. However, the Court seemed to suggest that had Olson *not* been the driver (i.e., had been the murderer), had the weapon *not* been recovered, and had the building *not* been fully surrounded, the warrantless action would have been lawful.

A more recent case, *Brigham City* v. *Stuart*,[44] brought clarification. Police were called to a house that received complaints about a loud party. On arriving at the scene, officers witnessed a fight involving four adults and one juvenile. One of the adults hit the juvenile. The officers announced their presence, but they couldn't be heard above the commotion inside, so they entered without a warrant. In a unanimous decision, the Supreme Court held that such warrantless entries are constitutionally permissible so long as the police have an objectively reasonable basis to believe that the occupant is "seriously injured or threatened with such injury."

Evanescent Evidence

evanescent evidence
Evidence that is likely to disappear. An example is alcohol in a person's bloodstream.

In situations in which the search incident to arrest or hot pursuit exceptions do not apply, the Court has recognized an additional exception to the warrant required, one that permits warrantless searches for **evanescent evidence** (i.e., disappearing evidence). This can include evidence inside a person or evidence that someone seeks or attempts to destroy.

Perhaps the best example of vanishing or disappearing evidence inside a person is alcohol in the blood. In *Breithaupt* v. *Abram*,[45] the Court upheld the warrantless intrusion (via a needle) into a man's body for the purpose of drawing blood to see if

---

[43] *Minnesota* v. *Olson*, 495 U.S. 91 (1990).
[44] *Brigham City* v. *Stuart*, 547 U.S. 398 (2006).
[45] *Breithaupt* v. *Abram*, 352 U.S. 432 (1957).

he had been drinking. The key in this case, however, was that medical personnel had conducted a *routine* blood test. The majority noted "that the indiscriminate taking of blood under different conditions or by those not competent to do so"[46] would not be allowed. (Indeed, this is why *Breithaupt v. Abram* is an isolated case; police officers rarely, if ever, draw blood from suspects. Breathalyzers usually provide sufficient evidence of intoxication.)

The *Breithaupt* decision also established that warrantless searches for evanescent evidence are permissible only when (1) there is no time to obtain a warrant, (2) there is a "clear indication" that the search will result in obtaining the evidence sought, and (3) the search is conducted in a "reasonable manner."

Recently, in *Kentucky v. King*,[47] the Supreme Court held that police can make a forcible warrantless entry into a private residence if they have reason to believe evidence is being destroyed. In that case, officers smelled marijuana outside an apartment, knocked loudly, and announced their presence. They then heard what they believed was the sound of evidence being destroyed. They announced their intent to enter, kicked in the door, and found drugs in plain view—and other evidence during the course of a protective sweep. The Supreme Court ruled that the evidence was admissible.

Automobile Searches

automobile exception An exception to the Fourth Amendment's warrant requirement that permits police to search a vehicle without a warrant, so long as they have probable cause to do so.

In the landmark case of *Carroll v. United States*,[48] the Supreme Court carved out an **automobile exception** to the Fourth Amendment's warrant requirement. The Court declared that the warrantless search of an automobile is permissible when (1) there is probable cause to believe that the vehicle contains evidence of a crime and (2) securing a warrant is impractical. *Carroll*, which was decided in 1925, resulted from the vehicle stop of a suspect who was known to have previously engaged in the sale of bootleg whiskey (i.e., during Prohibition). A warrantless search of the car revealed 68 bottles of illegal liquor. The Supreme Court upheld the warrantless search on the grounds that the evidence would be lost if the police had been required to take the time to secure a warrant. Note that *Carroll* deals with vehicle *searches*, not stops.

Automobile Search Requirements

Three general requirements must be met for a valid warrantless vehicle search: (1) The exception must only apply to automobiles; (2) with one exception, such a search must be premised on probable cause; and (3) it must be impractical to obtain a warrant (i.e., the vehicle stop must be such that it is impractical, burdensome, or risky to take time to obtain a warrant). The third requirement is unresolved, as the courts have relied on lesser expectation of privacy analysis rather than an exigency argument to support warrantless searches of automobiles.

So far, the term *automobile* has been tossed around with wild abandon. Note, though, that *automobile* has a very specific meaning. In other words, precise types of

---

[46]Ibid., p. 438.
[47]*Kentucky v. King*, No. 09-1272 (2011).
[48]*Carroll v. United States*, 267 U.S. 132 (1925).

vehicles are covered by the automobile exception. Cars, boats, and planes are all considered automobiles. However, what about the hybrid situation involving a vehicle serving the dual purpose of transportation and residence, such as a motor home or a tractor trailer with a sleeper cab? The Supreme Court was confronted with this question in the case of *California* v. *Carney*.[49] Unfortunately, it refused to define explicitly the types of automobiles covered by the automobile exception and held that the test of whether a vehicle serves a transportation or residence function requires looking at the *setting* in which the vehicle is located. If the setting "objectively indicates that the vehicle is being used for transportation,"[50] then the automobile exception applies.

In *Carroll*, the Court noted that "where seizure is impossible except without warrant, the seizing officer acts unlawfully and at his peril unless he can show the court probable cause."[51] Simply put, despite the fact that a vehicle search is permissible without a warrant, the search must still be based on probable cause. Note, however, that probable cause to *search* and probable cause to *arrest* are not one in the same. While probable cause to search may exist, this does not automatically create probable cause to arrest. In *Carroll*, for example, the police had probable cause to search the vehicle but not probable cause to arrest the occupants. This distinction is important because it can bear on the admissibility of seized evidence.

Scope of the Automobile Search

A number of court decisions have considered the scope of the search authorized under the automobile exception. Most of the decisions have focused on whether a container in an automobile can also be searched if probable cause to search the vehicle exists. In *Arkansas* v. *Sanders*,[52] the Court ruled that the warrantless search of a suitcase was not permissible when the police waited for the suitcase to be placed in the vehicle. Similarly, in *Robbins* v. *California*,[53] the Court held that a container discovered during a warrantless vehicle search can be seized but not searched until a warrant can be obtained.

Just one year after *Robbins*, the Court handed down its decision in *United States* v. *Ross*,[54] which overturned *Robbins*. The Court declared that as long as the police have justification to conduct a warrantless vehicle search, they may conduct a search "that is as thorough as a magistrate could authorize in a warrant."[55] The only limitation is "defined by the object of the search and the places in which there is probable cause to believe that it may be found."[56] Accordingly, if the contraband sought is small (e.g., a syringe), the scope of the vehicle search exception is almost limitless. The Supreme Court has even held that even passengers' personal belongings can be searched.[57] See Figure 11.4 for a summary of these rules.

---

[49]*California* v. *Carney*, 471 U.S. 386 (1985).
[50]Ibid., p. 386.
[51]Ibid., p. 156.
[52]*Arkansas* v. *Sanders*, 442 U.S. 753 (1979).
[53]*Robbins* v. *California*, 453 U.S. 420 (1981).
[54]*United States* v. *Ross*, 456 U.S. 798 (1982).
[55]Ibid., p. 800.
[56]Ibid., p. 824.
[57]*Wyoming* v. *Houghton*, 526 U.S. 295 (1999).

Level of Intrusion	Justification Required
Search of entire car, including containers	Probable cause to search
Search of passenger compartment and containers	Probable cause to arrest occupant
Weapons search of passenger compartment	Reasonable suspicion/fear for safety
Order occupants out of car	Reasonable suspicion to stop
Inventory search	Administrative

Figure 11.4
Levels of Justification for Automobile Searches

Plain View Searches

Untrained observers frequently suggest that "plain view" applies in situations in which evidence can be seen without having to search for it. While this may be a *literal* interpretation of what it means for something to be in plain view, it is not the interpretation the courts use. Plain view has a very specific meaning in criminal procedure, and the doctrine applies only in certain situations.

plain view doctrine An exception to the Fourth Amendment's warrant requirement that permits police to seize certain items in plain view.

The **plain view doctrine** first emerged in the Supreme Court's decision in *Coolidge* v. *New Hampshire*.[58] The issue in *Coolidge* was whether evidence seized during a search of cars belonging to Coolidge was admissible. The police had a warrant to search the cars, but it was later deemed invalid, so the state argued that the evidence should still be admissible because the cars were in plain view from a public street and from the house in which Coolidge was arrested. The Court did not accept this argument, pointing out that just because the police could *see* the cars from where they were not enough to permit seizure of the evidence in question. However, the Court did point out that had the police been *in* an area, such as a car or a house, evidence that was "immediately apparent as such" and was discovered "inadvertently" would have been admissible. In other words, part of the reason the evidence was not admissible in *Coolidge* was that the police officers were not lawfully in the cars when the evidence was seized.

To summarize, the Court decided in *Coolidge* that a plain view seizure is authorized when (1) the police are lawfully in the area where the evidence is located, (2) the items are immediately apparent as subject to seizure, and (3) the discovery of the evidence is inadvertent.

lawful access One of the requirements for a proper plain view seizure. The police must have lawful access to the item seized.

First, for the plain view doctrine to apply, the police must have **lawful access** to the object to be seized. Just because the police may *see* contraband does not necessarily mean they can *seize* it. If, for example, evidence is seen lying in a vacant lot or other public place, it may be seized. In such a situation, a search has not occurred. However, evidence that may be viewed from a public place but is, in fact, on private property cannot be seized unless a warrant is obtained or exigent circumstances are present. So, if a police officer on foot patrol observes a marijuana plant in the window of a private residence, he or she may not enter the premises and seize the plant, even though such observation establishes "the fullest possible measure of probable cause."

immediately apparent One of the requirements for a proper plain view seizure. The police must have probable cause that the item is subject to seizure.

In addition to the requirement that the police have lawful access to an object for the plain view doctrine to apply, it must also be **immediately apparent** that the object is subject to seizure. *Immediately apparent* means that the officer has probable

---

[58]*Coolidge* v. *New Hampshire*, 403 U.S. 443 (1971).

cause to seize the object. This was the decision reached in *Arizona* v. *Hicks*.[59] In that case, the police entered the defendant's apartment without a warrant because a bullet had been fired through his floor into the apartment below, injuring a person there. The warrantless entry was based on the exigency of looking for the shooter, for other potential victims, and for the weapon used in the incident. Once inside the apartment, the officer observed new stereo equipment that seemed out of place, given the surroundings. The officer suspected the stereo equipment was stolen but did not have probable cause to believe as such, so he picked up a turntable in order to obtain its serial number. He then called in the information and confirmed that it was stolen. The Court held that this warrantless action did not satisfy the plain view doctrine. It was not immediately apparent to the officer that the stereo equipment was stolen.

Finally, in *Horton* v. *California*, the Court declared that inadvertency, although a "characteristic of most legitimate 'plain view' seizures, . . . is not a necessary condition" of the doctrine.[60] The Court offered two reasons for abandoning the inadvertency requirement imposed in *Coolidge*. First, according to *Horton*, as long as a warrant particularly describes the places to be searched and the objects to be seized, the officer cannot expand the area of the search once the evidence has been found. In other words, it is unlikely that once officers have found the evidence listed in the warrant, they will go on a "fishing expedition," looking for evidence not listed in the warrant. According to the Court, the particularity requirement itself ensures that people's privacy is protected. Second, the Court noted that "evenhanded law enforcement is best achieved by the application of objective standards of conduct, rather than standards that depend upon the subjective state of mind of the officer."[61] An inadvertency requirement would force the courts to dwell on police officers' subjective motivations, which would be both time consuming and distracting. The Court went on to note that "[t]he fact that an officer is interested in an item of evidence and fully expects to find it in the course of a search should not invalidate its seizure if the search is confined in area and duration by the terms of the warrant or a valid exception to the warrant requirement."[62]

Consent Searches

The general rule is that validly obtained consent justifies a warrantless search, with or without probable cause. However, for consent to be valid, it must be voluntary. Consent cannot be "the result of duress or coercion, express or implied."[63] When does duress or coercion take place? There is no clear answer to this question. Instead, the Court has opted for a *totality of circumstances* test. This test requires looking at the *surrounding circumstances* of the consent, including whether a show of force was made; whether the person's age, mental condition, or intellectual capacities inhibited understanding; whether the person is or was in custody; and/or whether consent was granted "only after the official conducting the search [had] asserted that he possesses a warrant."[64]

---

[59]*Arizona* v. *Hicks*, 480 U.S. 321 (1987).
[60]*Horton* v. *California*, 496 U.S. 128 (1990), p. 130.
[61]Ibid., p. 138.
[62]*Horton* v. *California*, 496 U.S. 128 (1990).
[63]*Schneckloth* v. *Bustamonte*, 412 U.S. 218 (1973).
[64]*Bumper* v. *North Carolina*, 391 U.S. 543 (1968).

Importantly, consent to search may be valid even if the consenting party is unaware of the fact that he or she can refuse consent (*Schneckloth* v. *Bustamonte*). As the Court stated in *Ohio* v. *Robinette*, "[J]ust as it 'would be thoroughly impractical to impose on the normal consent search the detailed requirements of an effective warning,' so too would it be unrealistic to require police officers to always inform detainees that they are free to go before a consent to search may be deemed involuntary."[65] This view was reaffirmed in *United States* v. *Drayton*,[66] a case involving consent searches of bus passengers. Nevertheless, the issue of one's awareness of the right to refuse consent is still factored into the totality of circumstances analysis,[67] although ignorance of the right to refuse is not enough, in and of itself, to render consent involuntary.

Scope Limitations

The *scope* of a consent search is limited to the terms of the consent. In other words, the person giving consent delineates the scope. This was the decision reached in the case of *Florida* v. *Jimeno*.[68] For example, if a person tells the police "You may look around," it does not necessarily mean the police can look *anywhere* for evidence of criminal activity.

Another issue concerning the scope of a consent search is whether consent can be withdrawn once given. In *State* v. *Brochu*,[69] the Maine Supreme Court held that a defendant's consent to search his house for evidence of his wife's murder did not extend to another search carried out the day after he was arrested as a suspect. Thus, although the man did not expressly request that the search be terminated, the Maine court still decided that consent had been terminated. The Supreme Court has not directly decided whether consent can be withdrawn, however.

Third-Party Consent

A handful of Supreme Court cases have focused on whether a third party (the third party being someone other than the authority asking for consent to search and the individual whose property he or she hopes to search) can give consent to have another person's property searched (e.g., a landlord consenting to have a tenant's apartment searched; parents consenting to have their child's room searched). As far as the immediate family goes, there are several general rules: (1) Wives and husbands can give consent to have their partners' property searched and (2) parents can give consent to have their children's property searched, but (3) children cannot give consent to have their parents' property searched. The reason children cannot give consent is that they are considered incompetent to give voluntary consent, given their age.

---

[65]*Ohio* v. *Robinette*, 519 U.S. 33 (1996), pp. 39–40.
[66]*United States* v. *Drayton*, 536 U.S. 194 (2002).
[67]See, e.g., *United States* v. *Mendenhall*, 446 U.S. 544 (1980).
[68]*Florida* v. *Jimeno*, 500 U.S. 248 (1991).
[69]*State* v. *Brochu*, 237 A.2d 418 (Me. 1967).

More confusing is the situation of a roommate, former girlfriend, friend, or extended family member. Two important Supreme Court cases are relevant here. First, third-party consent can be given if (1) the third-party individual possesses "common authority" over the area to be searched and (2) the nonconsenting party (e.g., the roommate) is not present.[70] According to the Court, common authority rests on "mutual use of the property by persons generally having joint access or control for most purposes."[71] Thus, a third party could give consent to have a shared bathroom searched but not to have his or her roommate's bedroom searched. What happens, however, if the nonconsenting party is present and affirmatively objects to the search? The courts are divided on this issue.

There are some clear-cut situations, in which two people possess common authority over a particular area, but what happens when it is not clear to officers at the scene whether common authority exists? In response to this question, the Supreme Court has held that the warrantless entry of private premises by police officers is valid if based on the apparent authority doctrine. In other words, a warrantless entry of a residence is valid if it is based on the consent of a person whom the police reasonably believe has authority to grant consent, even if their beliefs are ultimately erroneous.[72] The test for reasonableness in this situation, according to the Court, is as follows: "[W]ould the facts available to the officer at the moment [of the entry] . . . warrant a man of reasonable caution in the belief that the consenting party had authority over the premises?"[73] *Rodriguez* involved consent given by a former girlfriend who possessed apparent authority to grant consent because she still had a key to her ex-boyfriend's apartment.

If two people who have common authority over the premises are present and one objects to the other's consent, then any subsequent search will be invalid without a warrant. Such was the Supreme Court's decision in *Georgia* v. *Randolph*, a case in which Randolph's wife gave consent to search the couple's property even though Mr. Randolph expressly objected to letting the police search without a warrant.[74]

---

common authority The "mutual use of the property by persons generally having joint access or control for most purposes" (*United States* v. *Matlock*, 415 U.S. 164 [1974], p. 172, n. 7).

apparent authority A person has apparent authority if the police *reasonably believe* he or she has authority to grant consent.

YOUR DECISION

1. A motor home that federal drug agents believed to contain a methamphetamine laboratory was parked in a secluded area near a river. The agents maintained visual surveillance throughout the afternoon. Around 4:00 P.M., one of the agents smelled chemicals "cooking." Shortly after that, the agents observed a man dash out of the motor home, gasping for air. In light of this incident, the agents decided to search the motor home. They ordered all of the occupants out of the motor home and placed them under arrest. The agents then entered the motor home to see if any other people were inside, to turn off any cooking apparatus, and to inventory the contents. They found a methamphetamine

---

[70] *United States* v. *Matlock*, 415 U.S. 164 (1974).
[71] Ibid., p. 172, n. 7.
[72] *Illinois* v. *Rodriguez*, 497 U.S. 177 (1990).
[73] Ibid., p. 179.
[74] *Georgia* v. *Randolph*, 547 U.S. 103 (2006).

laboratory behind a drawn curtain at the back of the motor home. Was this action justified?

2. Joan Lee was pulled over on Interstate 10 after a highway patrol officer observed her aggressively weaving from one lane to another. The officer had probable cause to search the vehicle for drugs. Accordingly, Lee opened the trunk, at which point the officer's attention was drawn to the spare tire. To the officer, it looked as though the spare was the wrong one for the vehicle. In addition, there appeared to be a white, powdery substance on the rubber. Based on his knowledge that narcotics are smuggled in such a fashion, the officer pulled the spare out of the vehicle, slashed it open with a knife, and found drugs inside. The drugs were seized and Lee was arrested. In terms of scope, was this search justified?

Summary

- The Supreme Court has carved out several exceptions to the Fourth Amendment's warrant requirement. While the exceptions vary considerably, a common thread runs through them: The Court has decided that it is not always practical to obtain a warrant.

- Searches incident to arrest are constitutionally permissible, but the arrest must, of course, be legal (i.e., based on probable cause). Also, the arrest must result in someone being taken into custody. Next, the search must follow the arrest closely in time. Finally, the search incident to arrest is limited to (1) the person arrested and any containers discovered from that search and (2) the arrestee's immediate grabbing area.

- Hot pursuit, threats to persons, and threats to evidence are exigent circumstances that also permit dispensing with the Fourth Amendment's warrant requirement.

- Warrantless searches and arrests based on hot pursuit are constitutional only if the police have probable cause to believe (1) that the person they are pursuing has committed a serious offense, (2) that the person will be found on the premises the police seek to enter, and (3) that the suspect will escape or harm someone or that evidence will be lost or destroyed.

- For an automobile search to be constitutional, it must be (1) directed at a vehicle ready to serve a transportation function, (2) premised on probable cause to believe the vehicle contains evidence of a crime, and (3) completed without unnecessary delay.

- Items in plain view can be seized if the police have lawful access to the items and if it is immediately apparent that the items are contraband. The discovery of such items does not have to be inadvertent.

- Consent searches are constitutional, but consent must be voluntary, as determined by the totality of circumstances. The scope of a consent search is defined by the person giving consent. Third parties can give consent if they have actual or apparent authority over the premises or property to be searched.

MODULE 11.3 STOP AND FRISK

Learning Objectives

- **Explain the Supreme Court's decision in *Terry v. Ohio*.**
- **Summarize the rules concerning a "stop" in the stop and frisk context.**
- **Summarize the rules concerning a "frisk" in the stop and frisk context.**
- **Explain the practice of conducting a protective sweep.**

CORE CONCEPTS

Chapter 10 introduced reasonable suspicion as the appropriate standard of justification required for a police officer to conduct a stop-and-frisk. Reasonable suspicion was defined as a lesser degree of certainty than probable cause but a greater degree of certainty than a hunch or unsupported belief.

The reason that the Court declared that certain confrontations between police and citizens can be based on reasonable suspicion is that crime control could not be accomplished without a lower standard than probable cause. If probable cause was always required, police officers would not even be able to question people about suspected involvement in criminal activity without a high degree of justification.

The law governing stop-and-frisk attempts to achieve a balance between due process and crime control. On the one hand, most people find it desirable for the police to control crime. If crime ran rampant, people would curtail their activities by, for example, not going out at night. On the other hand, the Constitution is a highly prized guarantor of personal freedoms. Many people, despite their desire to see crime decline, would object to aggressive search-and-seizure tactics by the police. Reasonable suspicion is something of a compromise between the conflicting goals of crime control and due process; it can be seen as achieving a balance between having unrestricted law enforcement and being able to apprehend lawbreakers.

Stop and Frisk: Two Separate Acts

A *stop* is separate from a *frisk*. A stop always precedes a frisk, but a stop *does not* give a police officer permission to conduct a frisk. Rather, the officer must have separate justification for each act. Reasonable suspicion is required to stop a person, and it is also required to frisk a person.

In *Terry v. Ohio*,[75] the Supreme Court ruled that in addition to the suspicion required to justify a stop, the officer must have reasonable suspicion that the person

---

[75]*Terry v. Ohio*, 392 U.S. 1 (1968).

stopped is *armed* and *dangerous* in order to conduct a frisk. In support of this position, the Court used a balancing test: Each intrusion by the government must be justified by a legitimate objective. In other words, no legitimate law enforcement objective is served when a police officer frisks a person whom the officer does not perceive as threatening.

For example, assume a police officer observes two men in an area with much drug traffic activity, whispering to each other and passing items back and forth. Arguably, the officer would have reasonable suspicion that criminal activity is afoot, thus permitting him or her to question the men. However, if the officer does not perceive that either suspect is armed and dangerous, then a frisk would be inappropriate.

The Stop

In many situations, it is clear when a police officer has stopped someone. For instance, when a patrol officer legally pulls a motorist over, it is safe to say that such activity constitutes a stop. Similarly, if a police officer handcuffs a suspect, that person has clearly been stopped (and arrested). But what about a simple confrontation between a foot patrol officer and a pedestrian? If the officer directs general questions—such as "What is your name?"—at the pedestrian, can this be considered a stop? Given that there are many situations such as this, the definition of a *stop* must be given special attention.

stop Sometimes called an "investigative stop" or an "investigative detention," a brief nonconsensual encounter between a law enforcement officer and a citizen that does not rise to the level of an arrest.

Generally speaking, a **stop** is the detention of a person by a law enforcement officer for the purpose of investigation. Why does the definition of a stop matter? Remember, if the police officer's activities do not amount to a stop, then the Fourth Amendment does not apply. This is because a stop is the same thing as a seizure of a person. As the Court observed in *Terry* v. *Ohio*, "[W]henever a police officer accosts an individual and restrains his freedom to walk away, he has 'seized' that person."[76]

In *Terry*, the Supreme Court stated that "obviously not all personal intercourse between policemen and citizens involves seizures of persons."[77] Instead, the Fourth Amendment applies only "when the officer, by means of physical force or show of authority, has in some way restrained the liberty of [a] citizen."[78] Thus, there is an important distinction to be drawn between (1) a forcible seizure or a stop and (2) a less intrusive type of confrontation in which, for example, the officer merely questions a person who is free to ignore the officer and leave. The seizure or stop requires reasonable suspicion (provided it is considered a *Terry* stop and not an arrest), but the simple questioning requires no justification. See Figure 11.5.

Duration of a Stop

What is the proper duration of a stop? Better yet, when does a stop evolve into an arrest because it takes too long? There are no easy answers. In *Florida* v. *Royer*,[79] the Supreme Court held that a 15-minute detention exceeded the bounds of a proper

[76]Ibid., p. 16.
[77]Ibid., p. 20, n. 16.
[78]Ibid., p. 20, n. 16.
[79]*Florida* v. *Royer*, 460 U.S. 491 (1983).

1. Threatening behavior on the part of officers
2. The presence of several officers
3. Display of a weapon by an officer
4. Physical touching of the person by the officer
5. The issuing of orders as opposed to requests
6. The use of intimidating language or tone of voice
7. A lengthy time period
8. Intrusive actions, such as a full-body search
9. Use of lights or sirens
10. The officer blocking the person's path
11. Coercive police behavior
12. Taking place out of public view

Figure 11.5

Factors Used to Distinguish between a Stop and a Consensual Encounter

stop—and became a *de facto* arrest. Yet, in certain exceptional circumstances, the Supreme Court has permitted detentions lasting much longer. For example, in *United States* v. *Sharpe*,[80] officers followed two vehicles suspected of involvement in drug trafficking. One vehicle was stopped and the driver was detained for 40 minutes while the officers sought and stopped the second car and its driver. The Court did not establish a bright-line rule for what time period is considered permissible, but it did state that "in evaluating whether an investigative detention is unreasonable, common sense and ordinary human experience must govern over rigid criteria."[81] Thus, the 40-minute detention of the driver of the first car was permissible.

In another case, *United States* v. *Montoya De Hernandez*,[82] a woman who was traveling from Colombia was detained for 16 hours in an airport because she was suspected of being a "balloon swallower" (i.e., a person who smuggles narcotics by hiding them in his or her alimentary canal). This was actually a very controversial case. The woman was given two options: (1) to return on the next available flight to Colombia or (2) to remain in detention until she was able to produce a monitored bowel movement. She chose the first option, but officials were unable to place her on the next flight, and she refused to use toilet facilities. Officials then obtained a court order to conduct a pregnancy test (she claimed to be pregnant), an X-ray exam, and a rectal exam. The exams revealed 88 cocaine-filled balloons in her alimentary canal. She was convicted of numerous federal drug offenses, but the court of appeals reversed that decision, holding that her detention violated the Fourth Amendment. The Supreme Court, in turn, reversed the court of appeals decision and ruled that the 16-hour detention was permissible. According to the Court, "The detention of a traveler at the border, beyond the scope of a routine customs search and inspection, is justified at its inception if customs agents, considering all the facts surrounding the traveler and her trip, reasonably suspect that the traveler is smuggling contraband in her alimentary canal."[83]

In another case, *Courson* v. *McMillian*,[84] the Eleventh Circuit Court ruled that an officer's act of stopping a car and holding the occupants at gunpoint for 30 minutes

---

[80]*United States* v. *Sharpe*, 470 U.S. 675 (1985).
[81]Ibid., p. 685.
[82]*United States* v. *Montoya De Hernandez*, 473 U.S. 531 (1985).
[83]Ibid., p. 541.
[84]*Courson* v. *McMillian*, 939 F.2d 1479 (11th Cir. 1991).

was not illegal because most of the time was spent waiting for backup to arrive. Citing *Adams* v. *Williams*, the court observed:

> The Fourth Amendment does not require a policeman who lacks the precise level of information necessary for probable cause to arrest to simply shrug his shoulders and allow a crime to occur or criminal to escape. On the contrary, *Terry* recognizes that it may be the essence of good police work to adopt an intermediate response. A brief stop of a suspicious individual, in order to determine his identity or to maintain the status quo momentarily while obtaining more information, may be most reasonable in light of the facts known to the officer at the time.[85]

Contrast the decision reached in *Courson* v. *McMillian* with that reached in *United States* v. *Luckett*.[86] In *Luckett*, the Second Circuit Court declared a jaywalker's detention invalid because it was based on a hunch that there was a warrant for the jaywalker's arrest. The court ruled that the stop effectively turned into an arrest, not just because of the duration of the stop but because there was no basis for an arrest at the time of the stop.

Are there any clear answers, then, as to what the appropriate duration of a stop is? Unfortunately, no, but the Supreme Court has stated that "the reasonableness of a stop turns on the facts and circumstances of each case." In particular, the Court has emphasized "(1) the public interest served by the seizure, (2) the nature and scope of the intrusion, and (3) the objective facts upon which the law enforcement officer relied in light of his knowledge and expertise."[87] Moreover, the Court has ruled that "the use of a particular method to restrain a person's freedom of movement does not necessarily make police action tantamount to an arrest" and that "police may take reasonable action, based upon the circumstances, to protect themselves . . . or to maintain the status quo."[88]

The Frisk

frisk A superficial examination by the officer of the person's body surface or clothing to discover weapons or items that could be used to cause harm.

As indicated, the additional step of frisking a suspect is a Fourth Amendment intrusion that requires justification apart from that required to stop the person. Specifically, in order to conduct a **frisk** (a superficial examination by the officer of the person's body surface or clothing to discover weapons or items that could be used to cause harm), the officer needs reasonable suspicion that the suspect is armed and dangerous. This is in addition to the reasonable suspicion required to stop the person for questioning.

Permissible Grounds for a Frisk

While *Terry* held that a frisk is permissible only when an officer reasonably fears for his or her safety, there is still considerable dispute over the situations in which a frisk is appropriate. What does it mean, in other words, to *fear for one's safety*? A number of court decisions have wrestled with this question.

---

[85] Ibid., pp. 145–6.
[86] *United States* v. *Luckett*, 484 F.2d 89 (9th Cir. 1973).
[87] *United States* v. *Mendenhall*, 446 U.S. 544 (1980), p. 561.
[88] *United States* v. *Kapperman*, 764 F.2d 786 (11th Cir. 1985), p. 790, n. 4.

For example, in *Pennsylvania* v. *Mimms*,[89] police officers observed a man driving a vehicle with expired plates. The officers stopped the vehicle in order to issue the man a traffic summons. When the officers asked the man to step out of the car, the officers observed a large bulge in the pocket of his jacket. Fearing that the bulge might be a weapon, one of the officers frisked the man. It turned out that the bulge was a .38 caliber revolver. The man claimed at his trial that the gun was seized illegally, but the Supreme Court upheld the frisk. Even though a bulge in one's pocket does not necessarily indicate he or she has a weapon, the Court granted some latitude in its decision to law enforcement personnel.

However, in *Ybarra* v. *Illinois*,[90] the Court ruled that officers did not have grounds to frisk 12 bar patrons during a search of the bar itself. Justice Stewart stated in *Ybarra* that "[t]he 'narrow scope' of the *Terry* exception does not permit a frisk for weapons on less than reasonable belief or suspicion directed at the person to be frisked, even though that person happens to be on premises where an authorized narcotics search is taking place."[91] Thus, just because someone happens to be in an area in which criminal activity is supposedly taking place does not make him or her eligible for a frisk.

Despite the limitations on frisks imposed by the *Ybarra* decision, the Court has since gone back somewhat on its decision in that case. In *Minnesota* v. *Dickerson*,[92] police officers observed a man leaving a "crack" house. As he approached and saw the officers, he turned and began walking in the opposite direction. The officers stopped and frisked him and found drugs on him. The frisk was conducted without reasonable suspicion or any other level of justification. The Court ruled that the police exceeded the bounds of a valid frisk when they found drugs on the man's person, but the Court did not rule that the *stop* was unconstitutional.

In *Arizona* v. *Johnson*,[93] the Court further expanded the frisk doctrine. In that case, gang task force officers were patrolling and stopped a vehicle for a traffic violation. The officers had no reason to suspect the vehicle's occupants of criminal activity, but they nevertheless ordered them out of the car. One of them was frisked and a weapon was found. The Court sanctioned this activity, noting that "a passenger's motivation to use violence during the stop to prevent apprehension for a crime more grave than a traffic violation is just as great as that of the driver."

So, are there any clear rules that establish when an officer can reasonably fear for his or her safety? The answer is no. Ultimately, the determination of a potential threat is a subjective one. Almost without exception, the courts will defer to the judgment of the officer, assuming that he or she is able to articulate some specific facts that contributed to reasonable suspicion that the suspect was armed and dangerous. Figure 11.6 summarizes the circumstances as to when a frisk is permissible.

Scope of a Frisk

A number of cases have focused specifically on the permissible scope of a frisk. Two issues have been raised: (1) the definition of a *frisk*—that is, what the officer can

---

[89]*Pennsylvania* v. *Mimms*m, 434 U.S. 106 (1977).
[90]*Ybarra* v. *Illinois*, 444 U.S. 85 (1979).
[91]Ibid., p. 94.
[92]*Minnesota* v. *Dickerson*, 508 U.S. 366 (1993).
[93]*Arizona* v. *Johnson*, No. 07-1122 (2009).

Figure 11.6

When a Frisk is Permissible

1. When the person has a reputation for dangerousness
2. When the person is suspected of having committed a dangerous felony
3. When visual cues suggest the presence of a weapon or similar dangerous instrument
4. When the suspect makes suggestive or furtive gestures

physically do to a person that does not rise to the level of a search; and (2) the items that can be felt for during the course of a frisk.

With regard to the first issue, the Supreme Court in *Terry* described a *frisk* as "a carefully limited search of the outer clothing . . . in an attempt to discover weapons which might be used to assault [a police officer]."[94] In *Sibron* v. *New York*, the Court offered additional clarification by declaring that the act of reaching into a suspect's pockets is impermissible when the officer makes "no attempt at an initial limited exploration for arms."[95] Generally, then, a frisk is little more than an open-handed patdown of someone's outer clothing. Only if the officer feels something that resembles a weapon can he or she then reach into the suspect's pocket (or other area used to conceal it) to determine what the item is. And as the Supreme Court observed in *United States* v. *Richardson*, "When actions by the police exceed the bounds permitted by reasonable suspicion, the seizure becomes an arrest and must be supported by probable cause."[96]

With regard to the second issue, or the items that can be felt for during the course of a frisk, the Supreme Court in *Ybarra* v. *Illinois* emphasized that frisks must be directed at discovering weapons, not criminal evidence. In *Ybarra*, one of the police officers had removed what he described as a "cigarette pack with objects in it" from the suspect. The Court basically decided that the officer's actions were too intrusive; the package could not have been considered a threat to the safety of the officers conducting the search. Significantly, the Court did not declare the seizure illegal because the officer was not looking for weapons but because the officer did not have reasonable suspicion to frisk every patron in the bar. Nevertheless, a frisk should not be used as a "fishing expedition" to see if some kind of usable evidence can be found on the person.

Two additional points concerning the scope of a frisk need to be underscored at this juncture. First, just because the Supreme Court has declared that a frisk should be conducted based on the motive to preserve officer safety, this does not mean the officer cannot seize contraband found during the course of a lawful frisk. If contraband, such as an illegal weapon, is found during a frisk, it can be seized.

Second, remember that a valid frisk can always evolve into a Fourth Amendment search, provided that probable cause develops along the way. For example, assume that a Chicago police officer frisks a suspect because she fears he may be carrying a gun. If it turns out that the suspect is carrying a pistol, which is illegal in the city of Chicago, she could arrest the suspect and conduct a full search incident to arrest. In this example, though, the object seized during the frisk (i.e., the gun) must be immediately apparent

---

[94]*Terry v. Ohio*, 392 U.S. 1 (1968), p. 30.
[95]*Sibron v. New York*, 392 U.S. 40 (1968), p. 65.
[96]*United States v. Richardson*, 949 F.2d 851 (6th Cir. 1991), p. 856.

to the officer for the seizure to be legal. As the Supreme Court stated in *Minnesota* v. *Dickerson*:

> Although the officer was lawfully in a position to feel the lump in respondent's pocket, because *Terry* entitled him to place his hands upon respondent's jacket, the court below determined that the incriminating character of the object was not immediately apparent to him. Rather, the officer determined that the item was contraband only after conducting a further search, one not authorized by *Terry* or by any other exception to the warrant requirement.[97]

In the example, then, had the seizure followed careful manipulation of the object by the officer, then a seizure based on the frisk would not conform to Fourth Amendment requirements. Figure 11.7 provides additional examples of proper and improper frisks.

Protective Sweeps

protective sweep A cursory visual inspection of those places in which a person might be hiding.

Another decision that essentially expands *Terry* is *Maryland* v. *Buie*.[98] If police lawfully make an arrest in a person's residence, a **protective sweep** of the home is permitted based on the *Terry* rationale. A *sweep* is when one or more officers disperse throughout the home with the intent of looking for other people who could pose a threat to the officers making the arrest. In the Court's words, a *protective sweep* is a "quick and limited search of the premises, incident to arrest, and conducted to protect the safety of police officers or others."[99] This protective sweep, which requires reasonable suspicion, should be distinguished from the automatic but more limited sweep that is permitted incident to a lawful arrest.

According to the Supreme Court, a sweep is permitted if the officer possesses "a reasonable belief based on specific and articulable facts that an area to be swept harbors an individual posing a danger to those at the arrest scene."[100] In addition, a sweep "may extend only to a cursory inspection of those spaces where a person may be found" and may last only as long as is necessary to eliminate the suspicion of danger. The case of *Maryland* v. *Buie* thus expands *Terry* in the sense that police officers can do more than just frisk a person who is arrested in a private residence. Note, however, that this case does not permit officers to *search* but only to *sweep* the area. A search would have to be supported by probable cause. However, items in plain view can be seized.

The Court's decision in *Maryland* v. *Buie* is not without its critics, however—the dissenters in the case being perhaps the most vocal. Consider Justice Brennan's observations in the dissent he wrote:

> *Terry* and its early progeny permitted only brief investigative stops and extremely limited searches based on reasonable suspicion . . . but this Court more recently has applied the rationale underlying *Terry* to a wide variety of more intrusive searches and

---

[97]*Minnesota* v. *Dickerson*, 508 U.S. 366 (1993), p. 379.
[98]*Maryland* v. *Buie*, 494 U.S. 325 (1990).
[99]Ibid., p. 325.
[100]Ibid., p. 337.

Proper: An officer notices a vehicle being driven erratically and stops it. The driver gives false identification, admits having done time for robbery, and is wearing a bulky jacket that he is having a hard time keeping his hands out of. The officer orders him out of the car, pats him down, and finds syringes in the suspect's jacked pockets (*People v. Autry,* 232 Cal. App. 3d 365 [1991]).

Proper: At 1:15 A.M., officers stop a vehicle for driving with its lights off. The driver gets out of the vehicle and heads toward the officers, leaving two other individuals in vehicle. When the officers asked for the driver's license, he says it is in his socks. Fearing for his safety, the officer quickly frisks the driver and finds a knife in the driver's sock (*People v. Barnes,* 141 Cal. App. 3d 854 [1983]).

Proper: Two officers observe a young man looking into two parked cars in a back alley where there have been several complaints of criminal activity. The suspect tries to stay out of view of the officers when he noticed them by hiding behind a dumpster. When the officers approach the suspect and ask questions, he becomes combative. They frisk him for weapons (*People v. Michael S.,* 141 Cal. App. 3d 814 [1933]).

Proper: An officer responds to a report of several suspicious individuals in a restaurant parking lot. On arriving at the scene, one of the suspects turns and walks away, whereupon the officer notices a large bulge in his pocket. The officer stops the man, frisks him, and finds a weapon (*People v. Miles,* 196 Cal. App. 3d 612 [1987]).

Proper: In response to a "panhandler" complaint, an officer frisks a man after observing a large bulge in the front waistband of his pants (*People v. Snyder,* 11 Cal. App. 4th 389 [1992]).

Proper: An officer is serving a search warrant and pats down a man who is sitting on the couch in the living room. The man is passive and nonthreatening—and the warrant did not authorize any searches of persons (*People v. Thurman,* 209 Cal. App. 3d 817 [1989]).

Proper: An officer responds to a reported "prowler" call and frisks two individuals who could produce no identification and speak only Spanish (*People v. Castaneda,* 35 Cal. App. 4th 1222 [1995]).

Proper: An officer encounters a suspect walking along a street, carrying a television set in an area known for excessive burglaries. He pats the suspect down, checking for weapons (*People V. Myles,* 50 Cal. App. 3d 1107 [1975]).

Proper: An officer is having a consensual encounter with a man on the street. The man reaches into his pocket, at which point the officer notices a bulge therein. The officer grabs the man's wrist to prevent him from reaching into the pocket (*People v. Rosales,* 211 Cal. App. 3d 325 [1989]).

Improper: An officer frisks a man who was sitting in a parked car, with the engine running, in the middle of a rural dirt road. The man had no identification or license and refused to the let the officer search the vehicle. He was also nervous (*People v. Dickey,* 21 Cal. App. 4th 952 [1994]).

Figure 11.7

Examples of Proper and Improper Frisks

Source: From *California Peace Officers Legal Sourcebook,* electronic edition, revision 113 (Sacramento, CA: California Department of Justice, Office of the Attorney General), section 2.20.

seizures prompting my continued criticism of the emerging tendency on the part of the Court to convert the *Terry* decision from a narrow exception into one that swallows the general rule that [searches] are reasonable only if based on probable cause.[101]

The exception Justice Brennan refers to is Terry's exception to the Fourth Amendment's requirement that reasonable searches be supported by probable cause. In a sense, *Terry* chipped away at the Fourth Amendment. Brennan's concern in this case, then, is that the Fourth Amendment continues to be weakened in cases that continue

---

[101]Ibid., p. 339.

to uphold police actions that would otherwise be considered searches, but for the Court's decision in *Terry* v. *Ohio*.

This is an important area of law about which to remain informed. No doubt, the Supreme Court will continue to decide cases that involve the relationship among probable cause, reasonable suspicion, and the police activities that each permits.

YOUR DECISION

1. On a Wednesday afternoon at 3:00 P.M., Officer Weber was on patrol in a neighborhood that had experienced several daytime burglaries. Her attention was drawn to a car in the driveway of one residence, which had its trunk open. In the trunk were several plastic trash bags of the type reportedly used by the burglar to carry away the loot. Weber pulled her cruiser into the driveway behind the vehicle, blocking its path. At that point, the driver of the car was closing the trunk and preparing to leave. The driver approached Weber, appearing quite nervous, and asked her to move the cruiser. Instead of doing so, Weber asked the driver for identification, which he produced. The identification indicated an address on the other side of town. Weber then frisked the driver, found a gun in his left coat pocket, and arrested him. No evidence connected the driver to the burglaries, but he was prosecuted for unlawfully carrying a concealed weapon. He moved to exclude the gun on the grounds that the initial stop was illegal and that the gun was the fruit of that illegal stop. What should the court decide?

2. Deputy Smith was on patrol in his police cruiser when he heard a report over the radio that a bank had just been robbed and that four male perpetrators had fled in a blue 1976 Ford pickup without license plates. Several minutes later, Smith observed a vehicle matching the description given over the radio except that it *had* license plates. He followed the truck and, after turning on his flashers, ordered the driver of the truck to pull over to the side of the road, which he did. Smith approached the truck and observed three men and a woman inside, each of whom appeared nervous and upset by the fact that they had been pulled over. After Smith ordered the occupants out of the car, he observed a bulge in the driver's pocket. He frisked the driver and found a weapon. Was Smith justified in stopping the vehicle and frisking the driver?

Summary

- A person can be stopped (defined as a brief detention) if an officer has reasonable suspicion that criminal activity is afoot and frisked if an officer has reasonable suspicion that the person is armed and dangerous.

- Frisks are limited. If one is authorized because the officer reasonably fears for his or her safety, it is limited to a patdown of the person's outer clothing. Above all else, the frisk must be motivated by an officer's concern for safety.

- A protective sweep, according to the Supreme Court, is a "quick and limited search of the premises, incident to arrest, and conducted to protect the safety of police officers or others."

SPECIAL NEEDS/REGULATORY SEARCHES

Learning Objectives

* **Summarize the rules surrounding vehicle inventories.**
* **Distinguish between several types of inspections.**
* **Distinguish between legal and illegal checkpoints.**
* **Explain when school disciplinary searches are permissible.**
* **Explain when searches of government employees' offices are permissible.**
* **Summarize the Supreme Court's view on drug and alcohol testing.**
* **Summarize the Supreme Court's view on probation and parole searches.**

CORE CONCEPTS

The Supreme Court has authorized numerous varieties of actions under the administrative justification exception to the Fourth Amendment's probable cause and warrant requirements. Sometimes they are described as *special needs beyond law enforcement searches*; other times, they are called *regulatory searches*. They include (1) inventories, (2) inspections, (3) checkpoints, (4) school discipline, (5) "searches" of government employees' offices, (6) drug and alcohol testing, and (7) parole and probation supervision. Note that when the term *search* appears in quotes, it is because while a particular action may look like a search, it is not the same as a true Fourth Amendment search.

Vehicle Inventories

vehicle inventory A procedure used to take record of a vehicle's contents after it has been lawfully impounded. Vehicle inventories do not invoke the Fourth Amendment and do not require probable cause.

A **vehicle inventory** occurs in a number of situations, usually after a car has been impounded for traffic or parking violations. In *South Dakota* v. *Opperman*,[102] the Supreme Court held that a warrantless inventory is permissible on administrative/regulatory grounds. However, it must (1) follow a *lawful* impoundment; (2) be of a routine nature, following standard operating procedures; and (3) not be a "pretext concealing an investigatory police motive." Thus, even though an inventory can be perceived as a fallback measure, which permits a search when probable cause is lacking, it cannot be used in lieu of a regular search requiring probable cause.

Why did the Court opt for another standard besides probable cause for the inventory, despite the fact that it is still a "search" in the conventional sense of the term? The Court noted that the probable cause requirement of the Fourth Amendment is

---

[102]*South Dakota* v. *Opperman*, 428 U.S. 364 (1976).

"unhelpful" in the context of administrative care-taking functions (e.g., inventories) because the concept of probable cause is linked to criminal investigations. Probable cause is irrelevant with this type of administrative action, "particularly when no claim is made that the protective procedures are a subterfuge for criminal investigations."[103]

Note that inventories include containers. That is, the police may examine *any* container discovered during the course of a vehicle inventory, but this should be mandated by departmental procedures. This was the decision reached in *Colorado v. Bertine*.[104] The decision also helped the police insofar as the Court refused to alter the vehicle inventory exception to the Fourth Amendment when secure impound facilities are accessible. As the Court stated, "[T]he security of the storage facility does not completely eliminate the need for inventorying; the police may still wish to protect themselves or the owners of the lot against false claims of theft or dangerous instrumentalities."[105]

Inspections

Inspection An exception to the Fourth Amendment's warrant requirement that permits certain authorities to inspect a closely regulated business.

A variety of **inspections** are permissible without a warrant or probable cause. For all practical purposes, they are "searches." Even so, the courts have continually stressed that the justification for such searches is the "invasion versus need" balancing act—that is, the benefits of some inspections outweigh the costs of inconveniencing certain segments of the population. Most of these exceptions to the warrant requirement are based on the Court's decision in *Camara v. Municipal Court*, where it was concluded that "there can be no ready test for determining reasonableness other than by balancing the need to search against the invasion which the search entails."[106]

Three types of home inspections have been addressed by the Supreme Court. In *Camara v. Municipal Court*,[107] the Supreme Court held that health and safety inspections of residence are unconstitutional. It noted that nonconsensual administrative inspections of private residences amount to a significant intrusion upon the interests protected by the Fourth Amendment. Today, a warrant is required for authorities to engage in a home inspection.

The Court has, however, sanctioned welfare inspections. In *Wyman v. James*,[108] it upheld the constitutionality of a statute that allowed welfare case workers to make warrantless visits to the homes of welfare recipients. The purpose of such inspections is to ensure that welfare recipients are conforming with applicable guidelines and rules. The Court declared that welfare inspections are not searches within the meaning of the Fourth Amendment, which means they can be conducted without a warrant *or* probable cause. Of course, such inspections should be based on neutral criteria and should not mask intentions to look for evidence of criminal activity.

In *Michigan v. Tyler*,[109] the Supreme Court authorized the warrantless inspection of a burned building/residence (i.e., fire inspection) immediately after the fire has been

---

[103]Ibid., p. 371.
[104]*Colorado v. Bertine*, 479 U.S. 367 (1987).
[105]Ibid., p. 373.
[106]*Camara v. Municipal Court*, 387 U.S. 523 (1967), pp. 536–537.
[107]*Camara v. Municipal Court*, 387 U.S. 523 (1967).
[108]*Wyman v. James*, 400 U.S. 309 (1971).
[109]*Michigan v. Tyler*, 436 U.S. 499 (1978).

put out. The key is that the inspection must be contemporaneous, not several days or weeks after the fire. The justification offered by the Court was that it is necessary to determine the cause of a fire as soon as possible after it has been extinguished. A warrant in such an instance, felt the Court, would be unduly burdensome. In a related case, *Michigan* v. *Clifford*,[110] the Court decided on the constitutionality of a warrantless arson-related inspection that was conducted five hours after the fire was extinguished. While the inspection began as just that, when evidence of arson was found, a more extensive search was conducted. The Court required a warrant because the officials engaging in the search admitted it was part of a criminal investigation.

Finally, the Supreme Court has permitted government officials to open incoming international mail. For example, in *United States* v. *Ramsey*,[111] customs agents opened mail that was coming into the United States from Thailand, a known source of drugs. Furthermore, the agents felt that a specific envelope was heavier than what would have been considered usual. Considering these factors, the Supreme Court upheld the warrantless search.

Checkpoints

checkpoint A brief detention that does not require probable cause or a warrant. Its purpose should *not* be to detect evidence of criminal conduct, such as narcotics trafficking. Examples include border checkpoints, illegal immigrant checkpoints, sobriety checkpoints, license and safety checkpoints, crime investigation checkpoints, and airport checkpoints.

Several types of **checkpoints** are constitutionally permissible without warrants. A checkpoint is a means of investigating a large number of people and should be distinguished from an inspection. Whereas an *inspection* targets particular homes and/or businesses, a *checkpoint* possesses an element of randomness—or total predictability. Either *everyone* is stopped or every *n*th person (e.g., every tenth person) is stopped. A checkpoint is similar to an investigation insofar as its purpose is not criminal in the sense that a typical search is. And to the extent that some checkpoints border on looking for evidence of crime (e.g., illegal immigrants), they are often justified because they are not based on individualized suspicion.

Border and Immigration Checkpoints

In *Carroll* v. *United States*,[112] the Supreme Court stated that brief border detentions are constitutionally permissible. Furthermore, it is in the interest of "national self protection" to permit government officials to require "one entering the country to identify himself as entitled to come in . . ."[113] More recently, in *United States* v. *Montoya de Hernandez*,[114] the Court reaffirmed the need for warrantless border inspections: "Routine searches of the persons and effects of entrants [at the border] are not subject to any requirement of reasonable suspicion, probable cause, or a warrant . . . [O]ne's expectation of privacy [is] less at the border."[115]

In *United States* v. *Martinez-Fuerte*,[116] the Court upheld the decision of the Immigration and Naturalization Service (INS—now called ICE, for Immigration and

---

[110]*Michigan* v. *Clifford*, 464 U.S. 287 (1984).
[111]*United States* v. *Ramsey*, 431 U.S. 606 (1977).
[112]*Carroll* v. *United States*, 267 U.S. 132 (1925).
[113]Ibid., p. 154.
[114]*United States* v. *Montoya de Hernandez*, 473 U.S. 531 (1985).
[115]Ibid., p. 538.
[116]*United States* v. *Martinez-Fuerte*, 428 U.S. 543 (1976).

Customs Enforcement) to establish roadblocks near the Mexican border for the purpose of discovering illegal aliens. The Court offered a number of reasons for its decision. First, "[t]he degree of intrusion upon privacy that may be occasioned by a search of a house hardly can be compared with the minor interference with privacy resulting from the mere stop for questioning as to residence."[117] Second, motorists could avoid the checkpoint if they so desired. Third, the Court noted that the traffic flow near the border was heavy, so individualized suspicion was not possible. Fourth, the location of the roadblock was not decided by the officers in the field "but by officials responsible for making overall decisions."[118] Finally, a requirement that such stops be based on probable cause "would largely eliminate any deterrent to the conduct of well-disguised smuggling operations, even though smugglers are known to use these highways regularly."[119] Importantly, law enforcement officers must have justification to examine the bags and personal effects of individuals who are stopped at immigration checkpoints (or during any immigration check).[120]

Sobriety Checkpoints

In *Michigan Dept. of State Police* v. *Sitz,*[121] the Court upheld a warrantless, suspicionless checkpoint designed to detect evidence of drunk-driving. In that case, police checkpoints were set up, at which all drivers were stopped and briefly (approximately 25 seconds) observed for signs of intoxication. If such signs were found, the driver was detained for sobriety testing, and if the indication was that the driver was intoxicated, an arrest

Warrantless, suspicionless drunk driving checkpoints were upheld in *Michigan Dept. of State Police* v. *Sitz.*

---

[117]Ibid., p. 565.
[118]Ibid., p. 559.
[119]Ibid., p. 557.
[120]*Bond* v. *United States*, 529 U.S. 334 (2000).
[121]*Michigan Dept. of State Police* v. *Sitz*, 496 U.S. 444 (1990).

was made. The Court weighed the magnitude of the governmental interest in eradicating the drunk-driving problem against the slight intrusion to motorists stopped briefly at such checkpoints. The key to the constitutionality of Michigan's checkpoint was two additional factors: (1) Evenhandedness was ensured because the locations of the checkpoints were chosen pursuant to written guidelines and every driver was stopped, and (2) the officers themselves were not given discretion to decide whom to stop. Significantly, the checkpoint was deemed constitutional even though motorists were *not* notified of the upcoming checkpoint *or* given an opportunity to turn around and go the other way.

License and Safety Checkpoints

In *Delaware* v. *Prouse*,[122] the Supreme Court held that law enforcement officials cannot randomly stop drivers for the purpose of checking their drivers' licenses. The Court's reasoning is interesting:

> An individual operating or traveling in an automobile does not lose all reasonable expectation of privacy simply because the automobile and its use are subject to government regulation. Automobile travel is a basic, pervasive, and often necessary mode of transportation to and from one's home, workplace, and leisure activities. Many people spend more hours each day traveling in cars than walking on the streets. Undoubtedly, many find a greater sense of security and privacy in traveling in an automobile than they do in exposing themselves by pedestrian or other modes of travel. Were the individual subject to unfettered governmental intrusion every time he entered an automobile, the security guaranteed by the Fourth Amendment would be seriously circumscribed. . . . Accordingly, we hold that except in those situations in which there is at least articulable and reasonable suspicion that a motorist is unlicensed or that an automobile is not registered, or that either the vehicle or an occupant is otherwise subject to seizure for violation of the law, stopping an automobile and detaining the driver in order to check his driver's license and the registration of the automobile are unreasonable under the Fourth Amendment.[123]

The Court did note, however, that "this holding does not preclude the State of Delaware or other States from developing methods for spot checks that involve less intrusion or that do not involve the unconstrained exercise of discretion."[124] In particular, "Questioning of all oncoming traffic at roadblock-type stops is one possible alternative."[125] If officers stopped every fifth, tenth, or twentieth vehicle, then this action would probably conform to the Court's requirement that roadblocks and checkpoints restrict individual officers' discretion to the fullest extent possible.

Crime Investigation Checkpoints

In *Illinois* v. *Lidster*,[126] the Supreme Court decided that checkpoints are also authorized for officers to ask questions related to crimes that had occurred earlier at the same area. The key in that case, however, was that officers asked questions about a crime that occurred *earlier*. They were not looking to detect criminal activity at that very moment.

---

[122]*Delaware* v. *Prouse*, 440 U.S. 648 (1979).
[123]Ibid., pp. 662–3.
[124]Ibid., p. 663.
[125]Ibid.
[126]*Illinois* v. *Lidster*, 540 U.S. 419 (2004).

Unconstitutional Checkpoints

The administrative rationale is *not* acceptable, by comparison, to detect evidence of criminal activity. This was the decision reached in *City of Indianapolis v. Edmond*,[127] a case in which the Supreme Court decided whether a city's suspicionless checkpoints for detecting illegal drugs were constitutional. Here is how the Supreme Court described the checkpoints:

> The city of Indianapolis operated a checkpoint program under which the police, acting without individualized suspicion, stopped a predetermined number of vehicles at roadblocks in various locations on city roads for the primary purpose of the discovery and interdiction of illegal narcotics. Under the program, at least one officer would (1) approach each vehicle, (2) advise the driver that he or she was being stopped briefly at a drug checkpoint, (3) ask the driver to produce a driver's license and the vehicle's registration, (4) look for signs of impairment, and (5) conduct an open-view examination of the vehicle from the outside. In addition, a narcotics-detection dog would walk around the outside of each stopped vehicle.[128]

The Court held that stops such as those conducted during Indianapolis's checkpoint operations require individualized suspicion. In addition, "because the checkpoint program's primary purpose [was] indistinguishable from the general interest in crime control,"[129] it was deemed violative of the Fourth Amendment.

School Discipline

Public school administrators and teachers may "search" a student without a warrant if they possess reasonable suspicion that the action will yield evidence that the student has violated the law or is violating the law or rules of the school. However, such school discipline "searches" must not be "excessively intrusive in light of the age and sex of the students and the nature of the infraction."[130] This was the decision reached in *New Jersey v. T.L.O.*[131] In *T.L.O.*, a high school student was caught smoking in a school bathroom (in violation of school policy) and was sent to the vice principal. When the vice principal searched the student's purse for cigarettes, he also found evidence implicating the student in the sale of marijuana. The Court held that the evidence was admissible because the administrator had sufficient justification to search the purse for evidence concerning the school's antismoking policy.

In support of its decision in *T.L.O.*, the Court noted that a warrant requirement "would unduly interfere with the maintenance of the swift and informal disciplinary procedures needed in the schools . . . [and] . . . the substantial need of teachers and administrators for freedom to maintain order in the schools."[132] The majority further stated that the reasonableness test for school disciplinary "searches" involves a twofold inquiry: "First, one must consider 'whether the . . . action was justified at its inception . . .' second, one must determine whether the search as actually conducted

---

[127]*City of Indianapolis v. Edmond*, 531 U.S. 32 (2000).
[128]Ibid., p. 32.
[129]Ibid., p. 44.
[130]*New Jersey v. T.L.O.*, 469 U.S. 325 (1985), p. 381.
[131]*New Jersey v. T.L.O.*, 469 U.S. 325 (1985).
[132]Ibid., p. 376.

'was reasonably related in scope to the circumstances which justified the interference in the first place.'"[133]

There are important limits on school discipline searches, especially in light of the Supreme Court's decision in *Safford Unified School District* v. *Redding*.[134] In that case, Savana Redding, an eighth grader, was "strip searched" by school officials on a belief that she was in possession of certain nonprescription medications, in violation of school policy. Writing for the majority, Justice Souter found that the search violated the Fourth Amendment because there was "indication of danger to the students from the power of the drugs or their quantity and any reason to suppose that (Redding) was carrying pills in her underwear." More than just reasonable suspicion is necessary, then, to support particularly intrusive searches of this nature—for school discipline, but also in the workplace.

"Searches" of Government Employee Offices

In a case very similar to *T.L.O.*, although not involving a public school student, the Court held that neither a warrant nor probable cause was required to "search" a government employee's office, but the "search" must be "a noninvestigatory work-related intrusion or an investigatory search for evidence of suspected work-related employee misfeasance."[135] Justice O'Connor summarized the Court's reasoning: "[T]he delay in correcting the employee misconduct caused by the need for probable cause rather than reasonable suspicion will be translated into tangible and often irreparable damage to the agency's work, and ultimately to the public interest."[136] It is important to note, however, that the Court was limiting its decision strictly to work-related matters: "[W]e do not address the appropriate standard when an employee is being investigated for criminal misconduct or breaches of other nonwork-related statutory or regulatory standards."[137] The Court further noted in *Ortega* that the appropriate standard by which to judge such "searches" is *reasonableness*.[138]

Recently, the Supreme Court was confronted with the question of whether a police officer's employer could examine the content of messages sent via a pager. Ontario, California police officers were given department-issued pagers. When some of them exceeded the number of allotted monthly messages, the department acquired transcripts of the officers' messages, learned that some of them were sexually explicit, and then disciplined the officers accordingly. They sued under Section 1983, alleging their Fourth Amendment rights were violated. The Supreme Court disagreed, holding that the department's "search" of the pager message contents was reasonable.[139]

At the risk of confusing matters, it should be pointed out that *reasonableness* in the context of public school student and government employee "searches" is not the same as *reasonable suspicion*. The latter refers to a certain level of suspicion, while the former focuses on the procedural aspects of the actions in question (e.g., Did authorities

---

[133]Ibid., p. 341.
[134]*Safford Unified School District* v. *Redding*, No. 08-479 (2009).
[135]*O'Connor v. Ortega*, 480 U.S. 709 (1987).
[136]Ibid., p. 724.
[137]Ibid., p. 729.
[138]Ibid., pp. 725–726.
[139]*City of Ontario v. Quon*, No. 08-1332 (2010).

go too far in looking for evidence?). The distinction between *reasonableness* and *reasonable suspicion* is a subtle but important one—hence, the reason for discussing disciplinary and work-related "searches" in the section on administrative justification.

Drug and Alcohol Testing

The Supreme Court has, especially recently, decided on the constitutionality of drug and alcohol testing programs. Three lines of cases can be discerned: (1) employee testing, (2) hospital patient testing, and (3) school student testing. Cases involving drug and alcohol testing of each of these three groups are reviewed in the following subsections.

Drug and Alcohol Testing of Employees

The Supreme Court has permitted warrantless, suspicionless drug and alcohol testing of employees. In *Skinner* v. *Railway Labor Executives' Association*[140] and *National Treasury Employees Union* v. *Von Raab*,[141] the Court upheld the constitutionality of certain regulations that permit drug and alcohol testing, citing two reasons for its decision. The first was deterrence; without suspicionless drug testing, there would be no deterrent to employees to stay off drugs. The second reason was that drug testing promotes businesses' interest in obtaining accurate information about accidents and who is responsible.

Two interesting limitations should be noted about both these cases. The first is that the Court did not decide whether warrantless, suspicionless drug testing could be used for *law enforcement* purposes. Rather, such testing was held to be constitutional for *regulatory* reasons. Second, both cases focused on federal regulations: Federal Railroad Administration guidelines in *Skinner* and U.S. Customs Service Policy in *National Treasury Employees Union*. Left open was the question of private business policy. Nevertheless, the courts have since upheld drug and alcohol testing of teachers, police officers, and several other groups.

Drug and Alcohol Testing of Hospital Patients

In a recent case, *Ferguson* v. *Charleston*,[142] the Supreme Court addressed the constitutionality of drug testing of hospital patients. In the fall of 1988, staff at the Charleston, South Carolina, public hospital became concerned over the apparent increase in the use of cocaine by patients who were receiving prenatal treatment. Staff at the hospital approached the city and agreed to cooperate in prosecuting pregnant mothers who tested positive for drugs. A task force was set up, consisting of hospital personnel, police, and other local officials. The task force formulated a policy for how to conduct the tests, preserve the evidence, and use it to prosecute those who tested positive. Several women tested positive for cocaine. The question before the Supreme Court was, "Is the Fourth Amendment violated when hospital personnel, working with the police, test pregnant mothers for drug use without their consent? Not surprisingly, the Court answered with a "yes."[143]

---

[140]*Skinner* v. *Railway Labor Executives' Association*, 489 U.S. 602 (1989).
[141]*National Treasury Employees Union* v. *Von Raab*, 489 U.S. 656 (1989).
[142]*Ferguson* v. *Charleston*, 532 U.S. 67 (2001).
[143]Ibid., pp. 77–78.

Drug and Alcohol Testing of School Students

The Supreme Court extended its drug testing decisions to include public school students. Specifically, in *Vernonia School District 47J* v. *Acton,*[144] the Court upheld a random drug testing program for school athletes. The program had been instituted because the district had been experiencing significant student drug use. Under the program, all students who wished to play sports were required to be tested at the beginning of the season and then retested randomly later in the season. The Court noted that athletes enjoy a lesser expectation of privacy, given the semipublic nature of locker rooms, which is where the testing took place. Also, athletes are often subject to other intrusions, including physical exams, so drug testing involved a "negligible" privacy intrusion, according to the Court.

More recently, the Supreme Court affirmed *Vernonia School District.* The case of *Board of Education* v. *Earls*[145] dealt with another student drug testing policy. The Student Activities Drug Testing Policy, implemented by the Board of Education of Independent School District no. 92 of Pottawatomie County, required students who participate in extracurricular activities to submit to random, suspicionless drug tests. Urine tests were intended to detect the use of illegal drugs. Together with their parents, two students, Lindsay Earls and Daniel James, brought a Section 1983 lawsuit against the school district, alleging that the drug testing policy violated the Fourth Amendment, as incorporated to the states through the due process clause of the Fourteenth Amendment. The district court found in favor of the school district, but the Tenth Circuit Court reversed the decision, holding that the policy violated the Fourth Amendment. It concluded that random, suspicionless drug tests would only be permissible if there were some identifiable drug abuse problem. However, the Supreme Court held that random, suspicionless drug testing of students who participate in extracurricular activities "is a reasonable means of furthering the School District's important interest in preventing and deterring drug use among its schoolchildren and does not violate the Fourth Amendment."[146]

Probation and Parole Supervision

A person on probation enjoys a lesser expectation of privacy than the typical citizen. In *Griffin* v. *Wisconsin,*[147] the Supreme Court held that a state law or agency rule permitting probation officers to search a probationer's home without a warrant and based on reasonable suspicion was constitutional. The majority (of only five justices) concluded that probation supervision "is a 'special need' of the State permitting a degree of impingement upon privacy that would not be constitutional if applied to the public at large."[148] See Figure 11.8 for a list of common federal probation conditions. Note in particular condition number 23, which pertains to searches.

---

[144]*Vernonia School District 47J* v. *Acton*, 515 U.S. 646 (1995).
[145]*Board of Education* v. *Earls*, 536 U.S. 822 (2002).
[146]Ibid., p. 822.
[147]*Griffin* v. *Wisconsin*, 483 U.S. 868 (1987).
[148]Ibid., p. 875.

(1) support his dependents and meet other family responsibilities;

(2) make restitution to a victim of the offense under section 3556 (but not subject to the limitation of section 3663 (a) or 3663A (c)(1)(A));

(3) give to the victims of the offense the notice ordered pursuant to the provisions of section 3555;

(4) work conscientiously at suitable employment or pursue conscientiously a course of study or vocational training that will equip him for suitable employment;

(5) refrain, in the case of an individual, from engaging in a specified occupation, business, or profession bearing a reasonably direct relationship to the conduct constituting the offense, or engage in such a specified occupation, business, or profession only to a stated degree or under stated circumstances;

(6) refrain from frequenting specified kinds of places or from associating unnecessarily with specified persons;

(7) refrain from excessive use of alcohol, or any use of a narcotic drug or other controlled substance, as defined in section 102 of the Controlled Substances Act (21 U.S.C. 802), without a prescription by a licensed medical practitioner;

(8) refrain from possessing a firearm, destructive device, or other dangerous weapon;

(9) undergo available medical, psychiatric, or psychological treatment, including treatment for drug or alcohol dependency, as specified by the court, and remain in a specified institution if required for that purpose;

(10) remain in the custody of the Bureau of Prisons during nights, weekends, or other intervals of time, totaling no more than the lesser of one year or the term of imprisonment authorized for the offense, during the first year of the term of probation or supervised release;

(11) reside at, or participate in the program of, a community corrections facility (including a facility maintained or under contract to the Bureau of Prisons) for all or part of the term of probation;

(12) work in community service as directed by the court;

(13) reside in a specified place or area, or refrain from residing in a specified place or area;

(14) remain within the jurisdiction of the court, unless granted permission to leave by the court or a probation officer;

(15) report to a probation officer as directed by the court or the probation officer;

(16) permit a probation officer to visit him at his home or elsewhere as specified by the court;

(17) answer inquiries by a probation officer and notify the probation officer promptly of any change in address or employment;

(18) notify the probation officer promptly if arrested or questioned by a law enforcement officer;

(19) remain at his place of residence during nonworking hours and, if the court finds it appropriate, that compliance with this condition be monitored by telephonic or electronic signaling devices, except that a condition under this paragraph may be imposed only as an alternative to incarceration;

(20) comply with the terms of any court order or order of an administrative process pursuant to the law of a State, the District of Columbia, or any other possession or territory of the United States, requiring payments by the defendant for the support and maintenance of a child or of a child and the parent with whom the child is living;

(21) be ordered deported by a United States district court, or United States magistrate judge, pursuant to a stipulation entered into by the defendant and the United States under section 238(d)(5) of the Immigration and Nationality Act, except that, in the absence of a stipulation, the United States district court or a United States magistrate judge, may order deportation as a condition of probation, if, after notice and hearing pursuant to such section, the Attorney General demonstrates by clear and convincing evidence that the alien is deportable;

(22) satisfy such other conditions as the court may impose or; [1]

(23) if required to register under the Sex Offender Registration and Notification Act, submit his person, and any property, house, residence, vehicle, papers, computer, other electronic communication or data storage devices or media, and effects to search at any time, with or without a warrant, by any law enforcement or probation officer with reasonable suspicion concerning a violation of a condition of probation or unlawful conduct by the person, and by any probation officer in the lawful discharge of the officer's supervision functions.

Figure 11.8

Common Federal Probation Conditions

Source: 18 U.S.C. Section 3563.

The Court has also ruled that evidence seized by parole officers during an illegal search and seizure need not be excluded at a parole revocation hearing.[149] This latter decision can be interpreted to mean that the exclusionary rule does not apply in parole revocation hearings. A warrant requirement, the Court noted, "would both hinder the function of state parole systems and alter the traditionally flexible, administrative nature of parole revocation proceedings."[150]

More recently, in *United States* v. *Knights*,[151] the Supreme Court held that warrantless searches of probationers are permissible not only for probation-related purposes (e.g., to ensure that probation conditions are being conformed with) but also for investigative purposes. In that case, a probationer was suspected of vandalizing utility company facilities. A police detective searched the probationer's residence and found incriminating evidence. The Supreme Court held that "[t]he warrantless search of Knights, supported by reasonable suspicion and authorized by a probation condition, satisfied the Fourth Amendment."[152]

In *Samson* v. *California*,[153] the Supreme Court extended its earlier probation decision to parole supervision. It held that "[t]he Fourth Amendment does not prohibit a police officer from conducting a suspicionless search of a parolee."[154] What was the Court's logic for this decision? It stated, "Parolees, who are on the 'continuum' of state-imposed punishments, have fewer expectations of privacy than probationers, because parole is more akin to imprisonment than probation is."[155]

YOUR DECISION

1. Komfortable Kitty Drug Company manufactures and packages veterinary drugs. Several times during a one-year period, the Federal Drug Administration (FDA) agents inspected the company's premises to ensure compliance with the Food, Drug, and Cosmetic Act (actual legislation). The agents cited Komfortable Kitty for several violations. Drugs that were allegedly in violation of the Act were seized pursuant to an *in rem* arrest warrant (i.e., a warrant authorizing the arrest of property). Altogether, over $100,000 worth of drugs and equipment were seized. Komfortable Kitty has contested the constitutionality of the seizure. Does the company have a valid case?

2. The school board approved a policy prohibiting a high school student from participating in any extracurricular activities or driving to and from school unless the student and his or her parent or guardian consented to and passed tests for drugs, alcohol, and tobacco in random, unannounced urinalysis examinations. (Extracurricular activities include not only athletic teams but also organizations such as the student council, foreign language clubs, and so on.) When consent for testing had been given and the individuals had taken and passed the tests, then participation in the extracurricular organizations or driving to and from school would be

---

[149]*Pennsylvania Board of Probation and Parole* v. *Scott*, 524 U.S. 357 (1998).
[150]Ibid., p. 364.
[151]*United States* v. *Knights*, 534 U.S. 112 (2001).
[152]Ibid., p. 112.
[153]*Samson* v. *California*, 547 U.S. 843 (2006).
[154]Ibid., p. 843.
[155]Ibid.

permitted. The testing was to be conducted by Acme Toxicology Services, which would collect the samples, and the local hospital's laboratory services division, which would perform the tests. Can this type of random, suspicionless drug testing be considered an administrative search?

Summary

- A vehicle inventory must follow a lawful impoundment, be of a routine nature, follow department policy, and not be used as a pretext concealing an investigative police motive.

- Four types of inspections have been recognized and sanctioned by the U.S. Supreme Court: welfare compliance inspections, closely-regulated business inspections, fire inspections, and international mail inspections.

- For a checkpoint to conform to constitutional requirements, it must be minimally intrusive, brief, and not directly tied to a criminal investigation. Examples of legal (i.e., constitutional) checkpoints are border checkpoints, illegal immigrant checkpoints, and sobriety checkpoints. Checkpoints conducted for the sole purpose of detecting criminal activity are unconstitutional.

- School disciplinary "searches" are constitutionally permissible, but they must be reasonable. Random, suspicionless locker inspections are permissible but only with ample notice to students.

- "Searches" of government employees' offices are permissible with neither a warrant nor probable cause but must amount to noninvestigatory work-related intrusions or investigatory searches for evidence of suspected work-related employee misconduct.

- Employees and public school students can be screened for substance use but only by properly trained individuals following appropriate policies (e.g., nurses). Hospital patients, however, cannot be subjected to drug and alcohol testing.

- Probation supervision permits warrantless searches premised on reasonable grounds. The same applies to parolee searches.

Chapter Review

SEARCHES AND ARRESTS WITH WARRANTS

Learning Objectives

- Outline the components of search and arrest warrants.
- Explain when arrest warrants are required and how they should be served.
- Explain when search warrants are required and how they should be served.

Review Questions

1. Explain the three components of a valid warrant.
2. How does the showing of probable cause differ for an arrest warrant versus a search warrant?
3. When can the knock and announce rule be dispensed with?
4. Briefly summarize the Supreme Court's view on time constraints for the service of a search warrant.
5. In what ways are the scope and manner of a search pursuant to a warrant restricted?

Key Terms

arrest warrant	particularity
search warrant	arrest
neutral and detached magistrate	knock and announce rule

WARRANTLESS SEARCHES

Learning Objectives

- Summarize the issues involved in warrantless searches and seizures.
- Explain the search incident to arrest doctrine.
- Identify three types of exigent circumstances and explain how they operate as exceptions to the warrant requirement.
- Summarize the special issues involved in automobile searches.
- Summarize the plain view doctrine.
- Describe consent searches and issues associated with them.

Review Questions

1. What are the main exceptions to the Fourth Amendment's warrant requirement?
2. What is the logic behind all the exceptions to the warrant requirement?
3. Summarize the requirements for a valid search incident to arrest.
4. What type of law enforcement activities fall under the banner of exigent circumstances?
5. When does the hot pursuit rule apply?

6. What are the requirements for a valid automobile search?

7. What does the term *automobile* mean in the automobile search context?

8. Why does the term *plain view* mean something different in criminal procedure than in everyday use?

9. Explain the role and importance of consent.

Key Terms

exceptions to the warrant requirement	automobile exception
search incident to arrest	plain view doctrine
armspan rule	lawful access
exigent circumstances	immediately apparent
hot pursuit	common authority
evanescent evidence	apparent authority

MODULE **11.3**

STOP AND FRISK

Learning Objectives

- Explain the Supreme Court's decision in *Terry* v. *Ohio*.
- Summarize the rules concerning a "stop" in the stop and frisk context.
- Summarize the rules concerning a "frisk" in the stop and frisk context.
- Explain the practice of conducting a protective sweep.

Review Questions

1. Why is it important to view stop and frisk as two separate acts?

2. Define stop.

3. Why is the duration of a stop important?

4. At what point does a stop evolve into an arrest?

5. Summarize the permissible grounds for a frisk.

6. What is the proper scope of a frisk?

7. Describe a situation in which a stop is justified but a frisk is not.

Key Terms

stop	protective sweep
frisk	

MODULE **11.4**

SPECIAL NEEDS/REGULATORY SEARCHES

Learning Objectives

- Summarize the rules surrounding vehicle inventories.
- Distinguish between several types of inspections.
- Distinguish between legal and illegal checkpoints.
- Explain when school disciplinary searches are permissible.
- Explain when searches of government employees' offices are permissible.

- Summarize the Supreme Court's view on drug and alcohol testing.
- Summarize the Supreme Court's view on probation and parole searches.

Review Questions

1. What interests are balanced in the administrative/regulatory/special needs search context?
2. How are vehicle inventories limited?
3. Explain the limitations on each type of constitutional inspection.
4. Distinguish between border checkpoints and illegal immigrant checkpoints.
5. What criteria make a checkpoint pass constitutional muster?
6. What justification, if any, is required for officials to conduct a school discipline search?
7. Under what circumstances are suspicionless searches of government employees' offices constitutional?
8. When does drug testing go too far? Cite specific case law.
9. Explain the Supreme Court's decision in *Griffin* v. *Wisconsin*.
10. Explain the Supreme Court's decision in *Samson* v. *California*.

Key Terms

vehicle inventory inspection

checkpoint

Chapter Synthesis Questions

1. Is the Fourth Amendment bane or boon for law enforcement? Explain.
2. Most Supreme Court cases pertaining to search and seizure involve actions that took place years ago. What are the implications of new technologies for the Fourth Amendment? Examples include GPS tracking, thermal imaging, and satellite imagery. Read the Supreme Court's decision in *United States* v. *Jones* (No. 10-1259 [2012]) to help with formulating your answer.
3. Which is preferable, an arrest or a stop? Why?
4. What is your opinion of the knock and announce rule? Defend your position.
5. Are there a sufficient number of warrantless searches that have been authorized by the Supreme Court? Why or why not?
6. Has the Supreme Court authorized a sufficient number of special needs/regulatory searches? Why or why not?

12

INTERROGATION AND IDENTIFICATION PROCEDURES

SIXTH AND FOURTEENTH AMENDMENT APPROACHES TO INTERROGATION

Learning Objectives

- **Describe why voluntariness is important in the confession/interrogation context.**
- **Summarize how the Sixth Amendment impacts interrogations and confessions.**

CORE CONCEPTS

confession When a person implicates himself or herself in criminal activity following police questioning and/or interrogation.

admission When a person can simply admit to involvement in a crime without any police encouragement.

A **confession** occurs when a person implicates himself or herself in criminal activity following police questioning and/or interrogation. An **admission**, by contrast, need not be preceded by police questioning; a person can simply admit to involvement in a crime without any police encouragement. Despite these differences, a confession and an admission will be treated synonymously throughout the remainder of this chapter.

Most of the law concerning confessions and admissions has arisen in the context of police interrogation. Whenever a suspect feels police interrogation procedures run afoul of the constitution, he or she may seek an audience in the courts. And indeed, the courts have listened. They have imposed a wide range of restrictions on what law enforcement officials can do in order to elicit incriminating statements from suspected criminals.

Confessions and admissions are protected primarily by the Fifth Amendment. The well-known and familiar "*Miranda* rights," which we touch on in Module 12.2, stem from the Fifth Amendment. However, confessions and admissions are also protected by the Fourteenth Amendment's due process clause as well as the Sixth Amendment's right to counsel clause. We thus begin this chapter with a focus on the Sixth and Fourteenth Amendment limitations on confessions and interrogations. After that, we turn attention to *Miranda*.

The very fact that *three* amendments place restrictions on what the government can do in order to obtain confessions suggests that the U.S. Constitution places a high degree of value on people's rights to be free from certain forms of questioning. In contrast, searches and seizures are limited by one constitutional amendment, namely the Fourth Amendment.

Sixth Amendment Right to Counsel

The Sixth Amendment places important restrictions on what the police can do to obtain confessions and admissions from criminal suspects. In particular, the Supreme Court's decision in *Massiah* v. *United States*[1] led to the rule that the Sixth Amendment's

---

[1] *Massiah v. United States*, 377 U.S. 201 (1964).

guarantee to counsel in all "formal criminal proceedings" is violated when the government "deliberately elicits" incriminating responses from a person. The two key elements to the Sixth Amendment approach are deliberate elicitation and formal criminal proceedings. The following subsections define each element.

Deliberate Elicitation

In the *Massiah* case, the defendant was released on bail pending a trial for violations of federal narcotics laws and subsequently made an incriminating statement in the car of a friend who had allowed the government to install a radio designed to eavesdrop on the conversation. Justice Stewart, writing for the majority, argued that if the Sixth Amendment's right to counsel is "to have any efficacy it must apply to indirect and surreptitious interrogations as well as those conducted in the jailhouse."[2] Furthermore, "Massiah [the defendant] was more seriously imposed upon . . . because he did not even know that he was under interrogation by a government agent."[3] These are issues of deliberate elicitation, in which police officers create a situation likely to induce a suspect into making an incriminating statement.

deliberate elicitation In the Sixth Amendment right to counsel context, deliberate elicitation occurs when police officers create a situation likely to induce a suspect into making an incriminating statement.

In another Sixth Amendment case, *Brewer* v. *Williams*,[4] a defendant was suspected of killing a ten-year-old girl. Before he was to be taken by police officers to another city, his attorneys advised him not to make any statements during the trip. The attorneys were also promised by the police officers that they would not question the defendant during the trip. Nevertheless, during the trip, one of the officers suggested that the girl deserved a "Christian burial." The officer further mentioned that an incoming snowstorm would make it difficult to find the girl's body. The officer then stated, "I do not want you to answer me. I don't want to discuss it further. Just think about it as we're riding down the road."[5] Shortly thereafter, the defendant admitted to killing the girl and directed the police to her body. The Court reversed the defendant's conviction, arguing that the officer had "deliberately and designedly set out to elicit information from Williams [the defendant] just as surely as—and perhaps more effectively than—if he had formally interrogated him."[6]

In a related case, *United States* v. *Henry*,[7] the Supreme Court focused on whether the officers "intentionally creat[ed] a situation likely to induce Henry [the defendant] to make incriminating statements without the assistance of counsel."[8] In that case, a man named Nichols, who was in jail with Henry, was enlisted by the police to be alert to any statements Henry made concerning a robbery. The police did not ask Nichols to start a *conversation* with Henry, only to be alert to what he said. The Supreme Court found that the officers created a situation likely to elicit an incriminating response but only because Nichols was a paid informant.

However, when law enforcement officers place an informant who is not paid but is working closely with the police in the same cell as the defendant, deliberate

---

[2]Ibid., p. 206.
[3]Ibid.
[4]*Brewer* v. *Williams*, 430 U.S. 387 (1977).
[5]Ibid., p. 432.
[6]Ibid., p. 399.
[7]*United States* v. *Henry*, 447 U.S. 264 (1980).
[8]Ibid., p. 274.

elicitation does not necessarily occur. This was the decision reached in *Kuhlmann* v. *Wilson*.[9] Kuhlmann, the informant, did not ask the defendant any questions concerning the crime for which the defendant was charged but instead listened to (and later reported on) the defendant's "spontaneous" and "unsolicited" statements. Clearly, the line between these two cases is thin. The only distinction appears to be that Nichols, the informant in *Henry*, had worked with the police in the past and was being paid.

Formal Criminal Proceedings

In order for the Sixth Amendment to apply to police interrogations, the second requirement is the initiation of "formal criminal proceedings" against the defendant. The Supreme Court has grappled with exactly when, in the process of a criminal investigation, arrest, and prosecution, the formal criminal proceedings officially begin.

A case closely related to *Massiah* (and decided shortly after it) is *Escobedo* v. *Illinois*.[10] Escobedo was arrested for murder, questioned, and released. Then, ten days later, an accomplice implicated Escobedo and he was rearrested. He requested to consult with his attorney, but that request was denied. Escobedo was convicted of murder, based partly on the statement provided by his accomplice. The Supreme Court reversed this decision, however:

> We hold . . . that where, as here, the investigation is no longer a general inquiry into an unsolved crime but has begun to focus on a particular suspect, the suspect has been taken into police custody, the police carry out a process of interrogations that lends itself to eliciting incriminating statements, the suspect has requested and been denied an opportunity to consult with his lawyer, and the police have not effectively warned him of his absolute constitutional right to remain silent, the accused has been denied "the Assistance of Counsel" in violation of the Sixth Amendment . . . and that no statement elicited by the police during the interrogation may be used against him at a criminal trial.[11]

Unfortunately, *Escobedo* was cause for some confusion. In *Massiah*, the Court held that the Sixth Amendment right to counsel applies once formal proceedings have begun (e.g., a preliminary hearing, trial, or anything in between). However, in *Escobedo*, the Court seemed to broaden the scope of the Sixth Amendment by holding that it also applies once the accused becomes the focus of an investigation by the police. This left a significant question unanswered: When does a person become an accused? That is, when do formal criminal proceedings commence?

Massiah was indicted, so many courts have concluded that formal criminal proceedings begin with indictment.[12] However, eight years after *Massiah* (and after *Miranda*), the Supreme Court decided *Kirby* v. *Illinois*.[13] In that case, the Court held that the Sixth Amendment is implicated whenever the "adverse positions of the government and defendant have solidified" so that "a defendant finds himself faced with

formal criminal proceedings In the Sixth Amendment right to counsel context, either a formal charge, a preliminary hearing, indictment, information, or arraignment.

---

[9]*Kuhlmann* v. *Wilson*, 477 U.S. 436 (1986).
[10]*Escobedo* v. *Illinois*, 378 U.S. 478 (1964).
[11]Ibid., pp. 490–1.
[12]See, e.g., *United States ex rel. Forella* v. *Follette*, 405 F.2d 680 (2nd Cir. 1969).
[13]*Kirby* v. *Illinois*, 406 U.S. 682 (1972).

the prosecutorial forces of organized society, and immersed in the intricacies of substantive and procedural criminal law."[14] Fortunately, the Court clarified this statement by noting that the Sixth Amendment applies "whether by way of *formal charge, preliminary hearing, indictment, information, or arraignment*."[15] This was echoed in *Rothgery* v. *Gillespie County*,[16] wherein the Court held that the Sixth Amendment right to counsel can attach at the initial appearance (see Chapter 13 for more on the initial appearance).

Massiah does not apply simply because a suspect or arrestee has retained the services of counsel. In *Moran* v. *Burbine*, the Supreme Court held that what is important in determining whether the Sixth Amendment right to counsel applies is whether "the government's role [has] shift[ed] from investigation to accusation."[17] Similarly, in *Maine* v. *Moulton*, the Court held that "to exclude evidence pertaining to charges as to which the Sixth Amendment right to counsel had not attached at the time the evidence was obtained, simply because other charges were pending at that time, would unnecessarily frustrate the public's interest in the investigation of criminal activities."[18]

It should be noted that the Sixth Amendment approach to interrogations and confessions is offense-specific. This was reiterated by the Supreme Court in *Texas* v. *Cobb*,[19] where it held that a man's confession to a crime with which he had not been charged did not violate the Sixth Amendment. In that case, the defendant was indicted for burglary and given access to counsel, which obviously prohibits deliberate elicitation of incriminating information. However, he confessed to murdering the woman and child who lived in the home he allegedly burglarized. He later sought to have his confession excluded, but the Supreme Court disagreed, in essence, finding that the burglary charge did not trigger the Sixth Amendment protection for the murder charge.

Waiver of the Sixth Amendment Right to Counsel (Confessions)

One's Sixth Amendment right to counsel can be waived in the confession context. In *Michigan* v. *Jackson*,[20] the Supreme Court held that once an accused individual has asserted his or her Sixth Amendment right to counsel, any statements obtained from subsequent questioning would be inadmissible at trial unless the accused initiated the communication.

This decision was recently overturned, however, in *Montejo* v. *Louisiana*.[21] Unbeknownst to police, Montejo had been appointed an attorney, but he was encouraged by a detective to write a letter of apology to the wife of the man he killed. Before doing so, he was advised of his *Miranda* rights (see the next module for details on *Miranda*), but again, he had been appointed counsel—it was just that the police

---

[14]Ibid., p. 689.
[15]Ibid., emphasis added.
[16]*Rothgery v. Gillespie County*, 554 U.S. 1 (2008).
[17]*Moran v. Burbine*, 475 U.S. 412 (1986), p. 430.
[18]*Maine v. Moulton*, 474 U.S. 159 (1985), p. 180.
[19]*Texas v. Cobb*, 531 U.S. 162 (2001).
[20]*Michigan v. Jackson*, (475 U.S. 625 (1986).
[21]*Montejo v. Louisiana*, No. 07-1529 (2009).

did not know this. The prosecution introduced the apology letter at trial. Montejo sought to have it excluded since, he felt, his attorney was not present when it was written. The Supreme Court disagreed. It felt that *Miranda* and other decisions offer sufficient protection. Also, had Montejo asserted his right to counsel, the outcome would have likely been different.

What is the practical meaning of the *Montejo* decision? Law enforcement is now allowed, after reading a suspect the *Miranda* rights and receiving a voluntary waiver of the right to counsel, to interrogate a suspect who has been appointed counsel, provided that the suspect (1) has not previously asserted *Miranda* protection or (2) has previously asserted *Miranda* protection and subsequently waived it. The decision is beneficial to law enforcement because it offers more opportunities for them to secure incriminating statements from criminal suspects.

Due Process Voluntariness

due process voluntariness approach
The requirement that any confession be voluntary under the "totality of circumstances."

The U.S. Constitution contains two distinct due process provisions—one in the Fifth Amendment for the federal government and one in the Fourteenth Amendment for the states. These provisions ensure that a criminal defendant will not be deprived of his rights or liberties without due process of the laws. Another approach to confessions and admissions relies on due process. We call it the **due process voluntariness approach**. In general, when a suspect makes an involuntary statement, his or her statement will not be admissible in a criminal trial (or, as indicated earlier, in any other criminal proceeding) to prove his or her guilt.

At one time, the Fifth and Sixth Amendments did not apply to the states. An illustrative case is *Brown* v. *Mississippi*.[22] Prior to the decision, police officers resorted to whippings and other brutal methods in order to obtain confessions from three African-American defendants who were later convicted based on their confessions alone. The Supreme Court analyzed this case under the Fourteenth Amendment's due process clause and found the convictions invalid because the interrogation techniques had been so offensive.

When, then, is a confession involuntary? As decided in *Fikes* v. *Alabama*, the answer is when, under the "totality of circumstances that preceded the confessions," the defendant is deprived of his or her "power of resistance."[23] This answer, unfortunately, does not provide any uniform criteria for determining voluntariness. Instead, the courts take a case-by-case approach to determining voluntariness. Usually, this requires focusing on two issues: (1) the police conduct in question and (2) the characteristics of the accused.

Police Conduct

The use of physical brutality to coerce a confession violates the Fourteenth Amendment. As Justice Douglas stated in *Williams* v. *United States*, "Where police take matters into their own hands, seize victims, and beat them until they confess, they

---

[22]*Brown* v. *Mississippi*, 297 U.S. 278 (1936).
[23]*Fikes* v. *Alabama*, 352 U.S. 191 (1957), p. 198.

deprive the victims of rights under the Constitution."[24] In many other situations, however, the police conduct in question may not rise to the level of torture but may still be questionable. For example, in *Rogers* v. *Richmond*,[25] a man confessed after the police told him they were going to take his wife into custody. And in *Lynumm* v. *Illinois*,[26] a defendant confessed after being promised leniency. Both confessions were found to be coerced. This is not to suggest that deception on the part of the police necessarily gives rise to an involuntary confession but only that it is one of several considerations in determining voluntariness.

It is safe to conclude that psychological pressures, promises of leniency, and deception are rarely *by themselves* enough to render a statement involuntary, but two or more such acts (especially if coupled with physical force) will more than likely result in an involuntary confession. Some illustrative cases are worth considering.

For example, in *Spano* v. *New York*,[27] detectives relied on a police officer who was a friend of the accused to question him. The officer falsely stated that his job would be in jeopardy if he did not get a statement from the accused. The Supreme Court concluded that the false statement, including the sympathy thereby obtained, was sufficient to render the accused's statement involuntary.

Next, in *Leyra* v. *Denno*,[28] police relied on a psychiatrist who posed as a doctor in order to give the accused relief from a sinus problem. The psychiatrist used subtle forms of questions and ultimately obtained a statement from the accused. The Court felt that the suspect was unable to resist the psychiatrist's subtle questioning.

Contrast *Spano* and *Denno* with *Frazier* v. *Cupp*.[29] There, the Supreme Court held that a police officer's false statement that a codefendant implicated the accused was not sufficient to produce an involuntary statement. However, if the accused is questioned far from home and denied access to friends and family for several days, his or her resulting statements will probably be deemed involuntary (see *Fikes* v. *Alabama*). Similarly, an overly lengthy period of questioning and/or a denial of basic amenities, such as food, may result in a determination of involuntariness.[30]

Characteristics of the Accused

As far as characteristics of the accused go, conditions such as disabilities and immaturity have resulted in excluded confessions. For example, in *Haley* v. *Ohio*,[31] the Supreme Court reversed a 15-year-old boy's confession. In the Court's words, "Mature men possibly might stand the ordeal from midnight to 5:00 A.M. but we cannot believe that a lad of tender years is a match for the police in such a contest."[32]

---

[24] *Williams* v. *United States*, 341 U.S. 97 (1951), p. 101.

[25] *Rogers* v. *Richmond*, 365 U.S. 534 (1963).

[26] *Lynumm* v. *Illinois*, 372 U.S. 528 (1963).

[27] *Spano* v. *New York*, 360 U.S. 315 (1959).

[28] *Leyra* v. *Denno*, 347 U.S. 556 (1954).

[29] *Frazier* v. *Cupp*, 394 U.S. 731 (1969).

[30] See, e.g., *Crooker* v. *California*, 357 U.S. 433 (1958); *Payne* v. *Arkansas*, 356 U.S. 560 (1958); *Ashcraft* v. *Tennessee*, 322 U.S. 143 (1944); *Chambers* v. *Florida*, 309 U.S. 227 (1940).

[31] *Haley* v. *Ohio*, 332 U.S. 596 (1948).

[32] Pp. 599–600. Note that *Haley* dealt with due process, not *Miranda*. The Court held in *Fare* v. *Michael C.* (442 U.S. 707 [1979]) that juveniles are not to be treated differently than adults in the *Miranda* context.

Police Behavior	Characteristics of the Suspect
• Psychological pressure by the police	• Disability
• Promises of leniency	• Immaturity
• Deception	• Intoxication
• Length of detention	• Fatigue
• Duration of questioning	• Pain
• Intensity of questioning	• Age
• Deprivation of access to family, friends, nourishment, and counsel	• Level of education
• Whether the suspect was advised of his or her right	• Familiarity with the criminal process

Figure 12.1
Factors Considered in Determining Voluntariness

In some instances, fatigue and pain (e.g., as the result of an injury) can also render an accused's statement involuntary; however, such a result usually requires some questionable conduct on the part of the officials engaged in questioning of the accused.[33]

As a general rule, voluntariness is overcome when (1) the police subject the suspect to coercive conduct and (2) the conduct is sufficient to overcome the will of the suspect. The second requirement requires looking at the totality of circumstances to determine if the suspect's vulnerabilities and condition, coupled with the police conduct, led to giving an involuntary confession.[34] See Figure 12.1 for a list of factors used to determine whether a confession is voluntary.

YOUR DECISION

1. A suspect was interrogated by five officers who, with their guns drawn, stood over him as he lay handcuffed on the ground, semiconscious from a gunshot he had received earlier (a wound that was not inflicted by the officers). The officers did not threaten to shoot the suspect if he failed to confess. Rather, they simply pointed their guns at him. Assuming the suspect confessed, would his confession be considered involuntary under the Fourteenth Amendment?

2. An arrest warrant was issued for Mark Eddie for the crime of burglary, following an indictment for his latest heist. A detective arrested Eddie, brought him to the stationhouse, and then interrogated him at length concerning the burglary without counsel present. The detective also interrogated Eddie about additional burglaries of which he was suspected of being involved in. While Eddie refused to talk about the most recent burglary (in which he made off with a substantial amount of money), he did admit to two prior burglaries. Was the questioning constitutional?

Summary

- Confessions are governed by the Sixth Amendment's right to counsel clause, but only when formal charges have been filed.

---

[33]See, e.g., *Ashcraft* v. *Tennessee*; *Mincey* v. *Arizona*, 437 U.S. 385 (1978); *Beecher* v. *Alabama*, 408 U.S. 234 (1972).
[34]See *Colorado* v. *Connelly*, 479 U.S. 157 (1986).

- If the police deliberately elicit information from a person after formal criminal proceedings have begun, the charged individual has the right to have counsel present during questioning.
- The Sixth Amendment right to counsel can be waived.
- An involuntarily obtained confession violates due process.
- Courts focus on police conduct and the characteristics of the accused in determining whether a confession was voluntary.

MODULE

12.2 *MIRANDA*

Learning Objectives

- **Explain *Miranda* v. *Arizona* and how it affects interrogations and confessions.**
- **Understand when unconstitutional confessions are admissible in court to prove guilt.**

CORE CONCEPTS

In a very important yet frequently overlooked case, *Malloy* v. *Hogan*,[35] the Supreme Court held that the Fifth Amendment's self-incrimination clause applies to the *states*. In announcing that ruling some 40 years ago, the Court said that "today the admissibility of a confession in a state criminal prosecution is tested by the same standard applied in federal prosecution since 1897."[36]

Not long after that decision, the Supreme Court moved beyond *Massiah*, *Escobedo*, and the due process voluntariness approaches to interrogation law, focusing instead on the Fifth Amendment. In *Miranda* v. *Arizona*, the Court announced the following important rule: "[T]he prosecution may not use statements, whether exculpatory or inculpatory, stemming from *custodial interrogation* of the defendant unless it demonstrates the use of procedural safeguards effective to secure the privilege against self-incrimination."[37] This wording clearly established that the Fifth Amendment should serve as the basis for determining the constitutionality of a confession.

Importantly, the Sixth and Fourteenth Amendments still apply to interrogations and confessions in certain situations. For example, if the police conduct in question is not a custodial interrogation (as in *Miranda*) but formal charges have been filed, the Sixth Amendment will apply. Similarly, if custody and interrogation do not take place *and* formal charges are not filed, the due process voluntariness test can still be relevant for the purpose of determining the constitutionality of a confession or

---

[35] *Malloy* v. *Hogan*, 378 U.S. 1 (1964).
[36] Ibid., p. 7.
[37] *Miranda* v. *Arizona*, 384 U.S. 436 (1966), p. 444, emphasis added.

Miranda **warnings** While there are some variations, the *Miranda* warnings contain four elements: (1) You have the right to remain silent; (2) anything you say can be used against you in court; (3) you have the right to talk to an attorney and to have the attorney with you during questioning; and (4) if you cannot afford an attorney, one will be provided for you.

admission. In fact, think of the Fourteenth Amendment's due process clause, in particular, as being something of a fallback. If no other constitutional protections apply, the guarantee of due process almost always does.

The *Miranda* warnings, which are most often read by police to an arrestee, often comprise a series of statements like this: "You have the right to remain silent. Anything you say can and will be used against you in a court of law. You also have the right to an attorney. If you cannot afford an attorney, one will be provided to you at no cost. Do you understand these rights as they have been read to you?"

The discussion will return to some Supreme Court cases addressing the substance and adequacy of these warnings, particularly when they are read differently. But for now, the concepts of custody and interrogation require attention. Since the Supreme Court limited its decision in *Miranda* to custodial interrogations, it is important to understand the definitions of these two important terms: *custody* and *interrogation*. They are also explored in the accompanying Court Decision box.

COURT DECISION

The Logic behind the Right to Counsel in Custodial Interrogation

Miranda v. *Arizona*
384 U.S. 436 (1966)

Decision: The prosecution may not use statements, whether exculpatory or inculpatory, stemming from questioning initiated by law enforcement officers after a person has been taken into custody or otherwise deprived of his freedom of action in any significant way, unless it demonstrates the use of procedural safeguards effective to secure the Fifth Amendment's privilege against self-incrimination.

Reason: At the outset, if a person in custody is to be subjected to interrogation, he must first be informed in clear and unequivocal terms that he has the right to remain silent. For those unaware of the privilege, the warning is needed simply to make them aware of it – the threshold requirement for an intelligent decision as to its exercise. More important, such a warning is an absolute prerequisite in overcoming the inherent pressures of the interrogation atmosphere. It is not just the subnormal or woefully ignorant who succumb to an interrogator's imprecations, whether implied or expressly stated, that the interrogation will continue until a confession is obtained or that silence in the face of accusation is itself damning, and will bode ill when presented to a jury . . . Further, the warning will show the individual that his interrogators are prepared to recognize his privilege should he choose to exercise it.

The Fifth Amendment privilege is so fundamental to our system of constitutional rule, and the expedient of giving an adequate warning as to the availability of the privilege so simple, we will not pause to inquire in individual cases whether the defendant was aware of his rights without a warning being given. Assessments of the knowledge the defendant possessed, based on information as to his age, education, intelligence, or prior contact with authorities, can never be more than speculation. . . .; a warning is a clear-cut fact. More important, whatever the background of the person interrogated, a

(continued)

**COURT
DECISION**
(continued)

warning at the time of the interrogation is indispensable to overcome its pressures and to insure that the individual knows he is free to exercise the privilege at that point in time.

The warning of the right to remain silent must be accompanied by the explanation that anything said can and will be used against the individual in court. This warning is needed in order to make him aware not only of the privilege, but also of the consequences of forgoing it. It is only through an awareness of these consequences that there can be any assurance of real understanding and intelligent exercise of the privilege. Moreover, this warning may serve to make the individual more acutely aware that he is faced with a phase of the adversary system – that he is not in the presence of persons acting solely in his interest.

The circumstances surrounding in-custody interrogation can operate very quickly to overbear the will of one merely made aware of his privilege by his interrogators. Therefore, the right to have counsel present at the interrogation is indispensable to the protection of the Fifth Amendment privilege under the system we delineate today. Our aim is to assure that the individual's right to choose between silence and speech remains unfettered throughout the interrogation process. A once-stated warning, delivered by those who will conduct the interrogation, cannot itself suffice to that end among those who most require knowledge of their rights. A mere warning given by the interrogators is not alone sufficient to accomplish that end. Prosecutors themselves claim that the admonishment of the right to remain silent, without more, "will benefit only the recidivist and the professional." . . . . Even preliminary advice given to the accused by his own attorney can be swiftly overcome by the secret interrogation process . . . Thus, the need for counsel to protect the Fifth Amendment privilege comprehends not merely a right to consult with counsel prior to questioning, but also to have counsel present during any questioning if the defendant so desires.

Custody

Many people believe that *Miranda* rights apply whenever the police begin to question a person. This is not the case; if the person being questioned is not in *custody*, *Miranda* rights do not apply. Simple police questioning, or even a full-blown interrogation, is not enough to trigger the protections afforded by the Fifth Amendment. The person subjected to such questioning must be in police custody.

custody Typically an arrest. Custody is important in the *Miranda* context because *Miranda* warnings do not need to be read if a person is not in custody.

What is **custody**? The Court announced that *Miranda* applies when "a person has been taken into custody or otherwise deprived of his freedom of action in any significant way." An arrest is a clear-cut case of police custody, but what about a lesser intrusion? Unfortunately, there is no easy answer to this question. Instead, the courts have chosen to focus on the circumstances surrounding each individual case. For example, in *J.D.B.* v. *North Carolina*[38] decision, the Supreme Court decided that the suspect's age properly informs the custody analysis; the younger that individual is, the more likely he or she will be considered in custody for *Miranda* purposes.

---

[38]*J.D.B.* v. *North Carolina*, No. 09-11121 (2011).

When interrogation occurs in a custodial situation, *Miranda* warnings are required.

© Marmaduke St. John/Alamy

In the absence of a full-blown arrest, the courts have focused on four types of police/citizen encounters in determining whether custody exists for purposes of *Miranda*: (1) traffic and field stops, (2) questioning in the home, (3) questioning at the police station or equivalent facility, and (4) questioning for minor crimes.

First, custody does not take place in the typical traffic stop. This was the decision reached in *Berkemer* v. *McCarty*.[39] There, a motorist was stopped for weaving in and out of traffic. After he admitted to drinking and smoking marijuana, the officer arrested him. The motorist argued that he should have been advised of his right to remain silent, but the Supreme Court disagreed, noting that vehicle stops are "presumptively temporary and brief" and sufficiently public to avoid the appearance of being coercive. The Court added, "From all that appears in the stipulation of facts, a single police officer asked [the defendant] a modest number of questions and requested him to perform a simple balancing test at a location visible to passing motorists"[40] and thus did not violate the Fifth Amendment.

The same applies to stops not involving vehicles. *Miranda* permits law enforcement officers to engage in "[g]eneral on-the-scene questioning as to facts surrounding a crime or other general questioning of citizens in the factfinding process."[41] With regard to *Terry* stops in particular, "[t]he comparatively non-threatening character of [investigative] detentions explains the absence of any suggestion in our opinions that *Terry* stops are subject to the dictates of *Miranda*."[42] But what if an investigative stop becomes more intrusive than a *Terry* stop, say, by taking place over a long period of time and/or in a private

---

[39]*Berkemer* v. *McCarty*, 468 U.S. 420 (1984).
[40]Ibid., p. 442.
[41]Ibid., p. 477.
[42]Ibid., p. 440.

setting? Then, the Fifth Amendment's self-incrimination clause, made known to suspects through the *Miranda* warnings, will usually apply. Likewise, if interrogation takes place behind closed doors at a school, and the suspect is a minor, custody occurs.[43]

Second, it is possible for questioning in one's home to rise to the level of custody. In *Orozco* v. *Texas,*[44] the Supreme Court declared that custody existed when four police officers woke a man in his own home and began questioning him. However, in contrast to *Orozco* is *Beckwith* v. *United States.*[45] There, Internal Revenue Service (IRS) agents interviewed a man in his home, an action that the Supreme Court declared noncustodial. The man argued that because he was the focus of a criminal investigation, he should have been advised of his right to remain silent. However, Chief Justice Burger noted that "*Miranda* specifically defined 'focus,' for its purposes, as 'questioning initiated by law enforcement officers *after* a person has been taken into custody or otherwise deprived of his freedom of action in any significant way.'"[46]

Third, questioning at the police station or an equivalent facility can also rise to the level of custody. However, not all stationhouse questioning can be considered custodial. Consider what the Supreme Court said in *Oregon* v. *Mathiason,*[47] a case involving a man who voluntarily agreed to meet officers at the police station for questioning. He admitted to involvement in a crime but later argued that his visit to the stationhouse was custodial because of its inherently coercive nature. The Court said:

> Any interview of one suspected of a crime by a police officer will have coercive aspects to it, simply by virtue of the fact that the police officer is part of a law enforcement system which may ultimately cause the suspect to be charged with a crime. But police officers are not required to administer *Miranda* warnings to everyone whom they question. Nor is the requirement of warnings to be imposed simply because the questioning takes place in the stationhouse, or because the questioned person is one whom the police suspect.[48]

In a later case, *California* v. *Beheler,*[49] the Court offered some clarification concerning its decision in *Mathiason*. It pointed out that *Miranda* is not implicated "if the suspect is not placed under arrest, voluntarily comes to the police station, and is allowed to leave unhindered by the police after a brief interview."[50]

Interestingly, the *Beheler* decision seems to hold even if a person is pressured to come to the police station for questioning.[51] For example, in *Minnesota* v. *Murphy*, a probationer was ordered to meet with his probation officer for questioning. During the meeting, the probationer confessed to a rape and a murder. He later argued that he should have been advised of his *Miranda* rights, but the Court disagreed, holding

---

[43]See, e.g., *J.D.B.* v. *North Carolina*, No. 09-11121 (2011).
[44]*Orozco* v. *Texas*, 394 U.S. 324 (1969).
[45]*Beckwith* v. *United States*, 425 U.S. 341 (1976).
[46]Ibid., p. 347.
[47]*Oregon* v. *Mathiason*, 429 U.S. 492 (1977).
[48]Ibid., p. 495.
[49]*California* v. *Beheler*, 463 U.S. 1121 (1983).
[50]Ibid., p. 1121.
[51]see, e.g., *Yarborough* v. *Alvarado*, 541 U.S. 652 (2004).

that Murphy's "freedom of movement [was] not restricted to the degree associated with formal arrest."[52] Furthermore, while "[c]ustodial arrest is said to convey to the suspect a message that he has no choice but to submit to the officers' will and to confess . . . [i]t is unlikely that a probation interview, arranged by appointment at a mutually convenient time, would give rise to a similar impression."[53] The Court commented further in *Murphy*:

> Many of the psychological ploys discussed in *Miranda* capitalize on the suspect's unfamiliarity with the officers and the environment. Murphy's regular meetings with his probation officer should have served to familiarize him with her and her office and to insulate him from psychological intimidation that might overbear his desire to claim the privilege. Finally, the coercion inherent in custodial interrogation derives in large measure from an interrogator's insinuation that the interrogation will continue until a confession is obtained. . . . Since Murphy was not physically restrained and could have left the office, any compulsion he might have felt from the possibility that terminating the meeting would have led to revocation of probation was not comparable to the pressure on a suspect who is painfully aware that he literally cannot escape a persistent custodial interrogator.[54]

Fourth, the Supreme Court has decided whether people can be considered in custody for minor offenses. Again, *Berkemer* was a case involving a traffic stop. The second issue before the Court in that case was whether an exception to *Miranda* should exist for relatively minor crimes, such as misdemeanors. The Court declared that no distinction should be drawn between types of crimes as far as *Miranda* goes. Instead, the only relevant issue is whether a person is in custody (and, of course, interrogated). Even for a misdemeanor, the incentive for the police to try to induce the defendant to incriminate himself or herself may well be significant.

It should be underscored before moving on that a key component of *Miranda* is that the questioning (and detention) must be conducted by government actors. If the people engaged in questioning cannot be considered government actors, then Fifth Amendment protections do not apply. However, when a private individual conducts a custodial interrogation as an agent of the police (i.e., working for the police), *Miranda* applies.[55] Figure 12.2 provides a list of factors that are used to distinguish custodial from noncustodial encounters.

Figure 12.2

Distinguishing between Custodial and Noncustodial Situations

Custodial Situation	Noncustodial Situation
Arrest	Typical traffic stop
Excessively lengthy confrontation	General on-the-scene questioning
Not free to leave	Free to leave
Involuntary encounter	Voluntary encounter
Private place, such as a police station	Public place, where movement is not restricted

---

[52]*Minnesota* v. *Murphy*, 465 U.S. 420 (1984), p. 430.
[53]Ibid., p. 433.
[54]Ibid.
[55]See, e.g., *Wilson* v. *O'Leary*, 895 F.2d 378 (7th Cir. 1990).

Interrogation

The second major component of *Miranda* is interrogation. Custody by itself is not enough to require that the *Miranda* warnings be given. For a person to be afforded Fifth Amendment protection—and particularly, to be advised of his or her right to remain silent—he or she must be subjected to interrogation.

Interrogation Express questioning (e.g., Where were you on the night of the crime?) or the functional equivalent of a question (see definition).

Miranda defined interrogation as "questioning initiated by law enforcement officers." Then, in *Rhode Island* v. *Innis*, the Court noted that interrogation "must reflect a measure of compulsion above and beyond that inherent in custody itself."[56] Thus, any questions that tend to incriminate—that is, those that are directed toward an individual about his or her suspected involvement in a crime—are considered interrogation.

Unfortunately, many *questions* are not readily identifiable as such. In *Innis*, the Supreme Court noted that in addition to "express questioning," the "functional equivalent" of a question is also possible. The functional equivalent of a question includes "any words or actions on the part of the police (other than those normally attendant to arrest and custody) that the police should know are reasonably likely to elicit an incriminating response from the suspect."[57]

functional equivalent of a question "[A]ny words or actions on the part of the police (other than those normally attendant to arrest and custody) that the police should know are reasonably likely to elicit an incriminating response from the suspect (*Rhode Island* v. *Innis*, 446 U.S. 291 [1980], p. 302, n. 8).

In *Innis*, while police officers were driving the defendant to the police station after his arrest for armed robbery, they engaged in a conversation about the danger the missing robbery weapon posed to schoolchildren with disabilities. Apparently in response to the conversation, the defendant directed the officers to the location of the weapon. Interestingly, though, the Supreme Court held that the officers' conversation did not constitute interrogation: It was "nothing more than a dialogue between the two officers to which no response from the respondent was invited."[58] The majority assumed implicitly that suspects will not respond to "indirect appeals to . . . humanitarian impulses," but Justice Stevens dissented and argued that such an assumption "is directly contrary to the teachings of police interrogation manuals, which recommend appealing to a suspect's sense of morality as a standard and often successful interrogation technique."[59]

Even though *Innis* did not ultimately involve the functional equivalent of a question, the Court essentially expanded the definition of *questioning*. Namely, a mere conversation between police officers designed to elicit an incriminating response—even if the conversation is not directed toward the suspect—can require giving the *Miranda* warnings. Of course, the person must also be in custody for the *Miranda* warnings to apply. Figure 12.3 lists some of the factors considered when distinguishing between interrogation and general questioning.

Figure 12.3

Distinguishing between Interrogation and General Questioning

Interrogation	General Questioning
Guilt-seeking questions	Information-gathering questions
Conversation intended to elicit a response	Conversation not intended to elicit a response

---

[56]*Rhode Island* v. *Innis*, 446 U.S. 291 (1980), p. 300.
[57]Ibid., p. 302, n. 8.
[58]Ibid., p. 315.
[59]Ibid.

Other *Miranda* Issues

A number of important Supreme Court cases have hinged on (1) the substance and adequacy of the *Miranda* warnings and (2) waivers of *Miranda*. If, for example, the *Miranda* warnings are not given adequately, then the police risk having a confession being thrown out of court. Also, like many rights, those provided by *Miranda* can be waived. That is, suspects can elect *not* to remain silent. Finally, suspects are not required to be advised of their *Miranda* rights when doing so could compromise public safety. These and other *Miranda* issues are considered in the four subsections that follow.

Substance and Adequacy of the Warnings

There is a long line of cases involving people who have sought to have their confessions excluded at trial because all or some of the *Miranda* warnings were not read adequately. For example, in *California* v. *Prysock*, the juvenile defendant was told, "You have the right to talk to a lawyer before you are questioned, have him present with you while you are being questioned, and all during the questioning."[60] The defendant was then told that he had the right to a court-appointed lawyer but not that one would be provided for him if he was indigent. The defendant challenged his conviction, but the Court concluded that the warnings given to him were sufficient and that "*Miranda* itself indicates that no talismanic incantation was required to satisfy its strictures."[61]

In another interesting case, *Duckworth* v. *Eagan*, the following warnings were given:

> Before we ask you any questions, you must understand your rights. You have the right to remain silent. Anything you say can be used against you in court. You have the right to talk to a lawyer for advice before we ask you any questions, and to have him with you during questioning. You have this right to the advice and presence of a lawyer even if you cannot afford to hire one. We have no way of giving you a lawyer, but one will be appointed for you, if you wish, if and when you go to court. If you wish to answer questions now without a lawyer present, you have the right to stop answering questions at any time. You also have the right to stop answering at any time until you've talked to a lawyer.[62]

Even though the warnings in this version suggested that counsel would only be provided at court, the Supreme Court held, in a 5–4 decision, that these warnings "touched all the bases required by *Miranda*."[63] Thus, as long as all the essential *Miranda* information is communicated, simple departures will not render a confession thereby obtained inadmissible in a criminal trial.

Another factor involving the substance and adequacy of the *Miranda* warnings concerns the role of additional, unnecessary information. If more information than the original *Miranda* warnings is provided to a suspect, will any subsequent confession

---

[60]*California* v. *Prysock*, 453 U.S. 355 (1981), p. 359.
[61]Ibid.
[62]*Duckworth* v. *Eagan*, 492 U.S. 192 (1989), p. 198.
[63]Ibid., p. 203.

be inadmissible? For example, must the defendant be advised of the consequences of deciding to answer questions? The case of *Colorado* v. *Spring*[64] is a useful point of departure. There, the defendant was arrested and questioned on suspicion of transporting stolen firearms. He was also questioned about a homicide. He admitted that he had been given his *Miranda* warnings and that he understood them; however, he argued that the statements he made about the homicide were not admissible because he had not been informed that he was going to be questioned about the homicide (i.e., he was arrested on suspicion of transporting stolen firearms). Unfortunately for the defendant, the majority held that "a suspect's awareness of all the possible subjects of questioning in advance of interrogation is not relevant to determining whether the suspect voluntarily, knowingly, and intelligently waived his Fifth Amendment privilege."[65] Unlike the Sixth Amendment right to counsel, the *Miranda* rights are not considered offense-specific.

A similar issue came up in *Florida* v. *Powell*,[66] a case in which the following was added to the *Miranda* warning: "You have the right to use any of these rights at any time you want during this interview." The Supreme Court held that advising a suspect that he or she has the right to talk with an attorney before answering any questions *and* that the suspect can invoke that right at any time during questions conformed with *Miranda*.

To ensure that the *Miranda* warnings are read properly, most police departments have a policy describing what that should entail. Figure 12.4 provides an example of one such policy from the San Bernardino, California, Police Department.

Waiver of *Miranda*

In *Miranda*, the Supreme Court stated that if a person talks after he or she has been read the warnings, "a heavy burden rests on the government to demonstrate that the defendant knowingly and intelligently waived his privilege against self-incrimination and his right to retained or appointed counsel."[67] Furthermore, "a valid waiver will not be presumed simply from the silence of the accused after warnings are given or simply from the fact that a confession was in fact eventually obtained."[68] According to the Supreme Court:

> Whatever the testimony of the authorities as to waiver of rights by an accused, the fact of lengthy interrogation or incommunicado incarceration before a statement is made is strong evidence that the accused did not validly waive his rights. In these circumstances the fact that the individual eventually made a statement is consistent with the conclusion that the compelling influence of the interrogation finally forced him to do so. It is inconsistent with any notion of a voluntary relinquishment of the privilege. Moreover, any evidence that the accused was threatened, tricked, or cajoled into a waiver will, of course, show that the defendant did not voluntarily waive his privilege.[69]

---

[64]*Colorado v. Spring*, 479 U.S. 564 (1987).
[65]Ibid., p. 577.
[66]*Florida v. Powell*, No. 08-1175 (2010).
[67]*Miranda*, p. 475.
[68]Ibid.
[69]Ibid., p. 476.

STANDARD OPERATING PROCEDURE   CHAPTER #15   PROCEDURE #1

PROCEDURE FOR *MIRANDA* ADVISEMENT   (Revised)   10-26-88

PURPOSE

To ensure uniformity when advising persons of their *Miranda* rights.

PROCEDURE

It is not necessary that the defendant sign a written waiver of his rights. The law only requires that the waiver be free, intelligent, and voluntary.

The *Miranda* warning should always be <u>read</u> to the suspect rather than relying on memory, using the following wording:

1. You have the right to remain silent.
2. Anything you say can and will be used against you in court.
3. You have the right to talk with an attorney and to have an attorney present before and during any questioning.
4. If you cannot afford an attorney, one will be appointed free of charge to represent you before and during any questioning.

After the warning and in order to secure a waiver, the following questions should be asked and an affirmative reply secured to each question. The officer should always make a record of the <u>exact words</u> used by the defendant when he answers each of the following questions.

1. Do you understand the rights I have just explained to you?
2. With these rights in mind, do you wish to talk to me/us now?

When the person being advised of his *Miranda* rights speaks only Spanish, the following waiver shall be read:

1. Usted tiene el derecho de no decir nada.
2. Cualquier cosa que usted diga puede usarse contra usted y se usara contra usted en una corte de leyes.
3. Usted tiene el derecho de hablar on un abogado, y de tener un abogado presente antes y durante cualquier interrogacion.
4. Si usted no puede pagarle a un abogado, uno le sera nombrado gratis para que le represente a usted antes ye durante la interrogacion.

Renucia

1. ¿ Entiende usted cada uno de los derechos que acabo de explicarle a usted? ¿Si o no?
2. ¿ Teniendo en cuenta estos derechos suyos, desea usted hablar on nosotros ahora? ¿ Si o no?

Figure 12.4

Miranda Advisement Policy (San Bernardino, CA, Police Department)
Source: Chapter 15, Procedure 1, "Use of Force," from *Standard Operating Procedure,* San Bernardino, California, Police Department (rev. December 22, 2004). Reprinted with permission.

In recent years, the courts have interpreted this language loosely. That is, whereas *Miranda* declared that a waiver should be viewed with considerable caution, later decisions have suggested that the burden of demonstrating a valid waiver is not difficult to meet. For example, in *Colorado* v. *Connelly*, the Court held that the government need only show the validity of a waiver by a "preponderance of evidence." And in *Fare* v. *Michael C.*, the Court held that the "totality of the circumstances approach is adequate to determine whether there has been a waiver."[70] This latter test is not

---

[70]*Fare* v. *Michael C.*, 442 U.S. 707 (1979), 725.

unlike the due process voluntariness test, discussed earlier in this chapter. It is used to assess juvenile waivers, as well.

Must the waiver be express? That is, must a person affirmatively state something to the effect that "I am willing to answer questions" for a waiver of *Miranda* to take place? The answer to this question is "no." In the past, the Court preferred an express waiver. But in *Miranda*, the Court noted that "a valid wavier will not be presumed." However, in *North Carolina* v. *Butler,*[71] the Court decided otherwise. According to Justice Stewart, "The question [of a waiver] is not one of form, but rather whether the defendant in fact knowingly and voluntarily waived his rights delineated in the *Miranda* case."[72] Furthermore, a "course of conduct indicating waiver" (such as the suspect deciding to converse with the police) is sufficient for a valid waiver to take place. Based on this decision, the current rule is that the government must show a valid waiver based on "the particular facts and circumstances surrounding [the] case, including the background, experience, and conduct of the accused."[73] In other words, the courts now take a case-by-case approach in determining whether *Miranda* waivers are obtained legally.

As was made clear in *Butler*, a valid *Miranda* waiver requires a showing that the waiver was knowing and intelligent. What, then, is a *knowing and intelligent waiver*? There is no clear answer to this question, but the Court has noted that a full and complete understanding of the *Miranda* warnings is not necessary for a valid waiver to take place. This was the decision reached in *Connecticut* v. *Barrett.*[74] In that case, the defendant refused to give the police any written statements before he talked to an attorney. He did state, however, that he had no problem *talking* to the police. As it turned out, the defendant thought that only written statements could be used against him in court. The Court called his actions "illogical" but nonetheless held that his oral statements were admissible. A similar conclusion was reached in *Berghuis* v. *Thompkins*, in which the Court held that "where the prosecution shows that a *Miranda* warning was given and that it was understood by the accused, an accused's uncoerced statement establishes an implied waiver of the right to remain silent."[75]

Two additional Supreme Court decisions focused on whether the police can use trickery to obtain a *Miranda* waiver and/or statement. In *Colorado* v. *Spring*, the Court held that trickery *had not* taken place when the police failed to advise the defendant that he would be questioned about a different crime than the one for which he was arrested. It did point out, however, that "any evidence that the accused was . . . tricked . . . into a waiver will, of course, show that the defendant did not voluntarily waive his privilege."[76]

In another interesting case, *Moran* v. *Burbine,*[77] the Supreme Court held that a confession was validly obtained even though the police questioned the defendant after assuring his attorney that he would not be questioned until the following day. In a 6–3 decision, the Court held that this action did not result in a coerced confession. As Justice O'Connor noted, "[T]he same defendant, armed with the same information

---

[71] *North Carolina* v. *Butler*, 441 U.S. 369 (1979).
[72] Ibid., p. 373.
[73] Ibid., pp. 374–5.
[74] *Connecticut* v. *Barrett*, 479 U.S. 523 (1987).
[75] *Berghuis* v. *Thompkins*, 08-1470 (2010).
[76] *Colorado* v. *Spring*, 479 U.S. 564 (1987), p. 575.
[77] *Moran* v. *Burbine*, 475 U.S. 412 (1986).

and confronted with precisely the same police conduct, would have knowingly waived his *Miranda* rights had a lawyer not telephoned the police station to inquire about his status."[78]

In light of these two cases, it seems somewhat difficult to determine what constitutes trickery. A general rule is this: If officials lead a defendant to believe that he or she has no right to remain silent, then trickery is taking place. However, if the police merely lead a defendant to believe there is no point to remaining silent (as in *Butler*, *Barrett*, *Fields*, *Spring*, and *Burbine*), then any subsequent incriminating statements that are made will probably be viewed as knowing and intelligent.

Before moving on, it is worth mentioning that in addition to the requirement that a valid *Miranda* waiver must be knowing and intelligent, it must also be voluntary. The test for voluntariness is similar to the due process voluntariness test discussed earlier in this chapter. Threats, physical force, and the like can lead to defendants issuing involuntary confessions. However, in *Fare* v. *Michael C.*, the Court held that the confession obtained from a 16-year-old was not involuntary. In a strongly worded dissent, Justice Powell argued that the juvenile in this case "was immature, emotional, and uneducated, and therefore was likely to be vulnerable to the skillful, two-on-one, repetitive style of interrogation to which he was subjected."[79] A safe rule is that the police must engage in seriously questionable conduct for the voluntariness requirement of a *Miranda* waiver to be violated.

Again, to be safe, many police departments require that each suspect completes a *Miranda* waiver before interrogation commences. Doing so helps ensure that the waiver is documented. An example of a *Miranda* waiver form, from the San Bernardino, California, Police Department, is reprinted in Figure 12.5.

In a recent twist on the notion of *Miranda* waivers,[80] the Supreme Court considered whether police officers' failure to complete the *Miranda* warnings—after the suspect interrupted midway through by saying, "I understand my rights"—violated

Figure 12.5

Miranda Waiver Form (San Bernardino, CA, Police Department)
Source: San Bernardino, California, Police Department. Reprinted with permission.

WAIVER

I have been advised that:

1. I have the absolute light to remain silent.
2. Anything i say can and will be used as evidence against me in court.
3. I have the right to be represented by an attorney and to consult with him before making any statement or answering any questions and I have the right to have an attorney present during any questioning.
4. If I cannot afford an attorney, one will be appointed by the court, free of charge, to represent me before any questioning, if I desire.

I understand these rights, these rights have been explained to me. With these rights in mind, I am willing to talk to officers about the charges against me.

Date _____   Signed _____
Witness _____   Witness _____

---

[78]Ibid., p. 422.
[79]*Fare* v. *Michael C.*, p. 733.
[80]*United States* v. *Patane*, 542 U.S. 630 (2004).

the Fifth Amendment. In that case, after the suspect had interrupted the reading of *Miranda* and said he understood his rights, he informed police of the location of a pistol. He was indicted for possession of a firearm by a convicted felon and sought suppression of the pistol, claiming his Fifth Amendment privilege was violated. The Supreme Court disagreed.

Questioning after Assertion of One's Right to Remain Silent

As a general rule, questioning must cease once the accused asserts his or her right to remain silent. According to the Supreme Court in *Miranda*:

> If the individual indicates in any manner, at any time prior to or during questioning, that he wishes to remain silent, the interrogation must cease. . . . Without the right to cut off questioning, the setting of in-custody interrogation operates on the individual to overcome free choice in producing a statement after the privilege has been once invoked. If the individual states that he wants an attorney, the interrogation must cease until an attorney is present. . . . If the individual cannot obtain an attorney and he indicates that he wants one before speaking to police, they must respect his decision to remain silent. . . . If authorities conclude that they will not provide counsel during a reasonable period of time in which investigation in the field is carried out, they may refrain from doing so without violating the person's Fifth Amendment privilege so long as they do not question him during that time.[81]

However, there is at least one circumstance in which the police can question a suspect after he or she has asserted the *Miranda* rights. In *Michigan* v. *Mosley*,[82] the Supreme Court permitted questioning after an assertion of *Miranda*. In that case, two hours after the defendant had stated that he did not want to talk, a different police officer confronted him in a different room about another crime and read him the *Miranda* rights for a second time. After this, the man made incriminating statements. In a 7–2 decision, the Court held that the suspect's *Miranda* rights had been "scrupulously honored." The Court said that the second officer's actions were acceptable because "the police here immediately ceased the interrogation, resumed questioning only after the passage of a significant period of time and the provision of a fresh set of warnings, and restricted the second interrogation to a crime that had not been a subject of the earlier interrogation."[83]

The key to *Michigan* v. *Mosley* was that the second set of questions concerned a *separate crime*. What if police had continued to ask questions about the same crime? Had they done so immediately, the questioning would have been inappropriate. But the issue is less than black and white according to the Supreme Court's recent decision in *Maryland* v. *Shatzer*.[84] In that case, police (albeit a different officer) resumed questioning about the same crime more than *two weeks* after the suspect was released following initial questioning. The suspect was re-read his *Miranda* rights, which he then waived. He confessed to various crimes of sex abuse. The Supreme Court

---

[81]*Miranda* v. *Arizona*, pp. 473–474.
[82]*Michigan* v. *Mosley*, 423 U.S. 96 (1975).
[83]Ibid., p. 106.
[84]*Maryland* v. *Shatzer*, 08-680 (2010).

decided that his confession was admissible, in part because "[h]is change of heart [was] . . . likely attributable to the fact that further deliberation in familiar surroundings [had] caused him to believe (rightly or wrongly) that cooperating with the investigation [was] in his interest."

The Public Safety Exception to *Miranda*

On some occasions, custodial interrogation is permissible without the *Miranda* warnings. Specifically, if public safety is in jeopardy, no warnings are required. This was the decision reached in *New York* v. *Quarles*.[85] There, the Court held that the warnings need not be given if the suspect could have endangered public safety.

The facts from *Quarles* are as follows: After receiving information that a man with a gun had just entered a supermarket, Officer Kraft, along with three other officers, entered the store. Kraft spotted the defendant, drew his gun, and ordered the man to stop and put his hands over his head. When the officers frisked the man, they found an empty shoulder holster on him. When they asked where the man had put the gun, he replied, "The gun is over there." Officer Kraft retrieved the revolver and then placed the man under arrest and read him the *Miranda* warnings. The trial court and the lower appellate courts excluded the gun on the grounds that it was obtained in violation of *Miranda* (i.e., the man had not been advised of his right to remain silent at the time the gun was found).

The Supreme Court disagreed. Justice Rehnquist wrote the majority opinion, arguing that rigid application of *Miranda* is not always warranted, particularly when public safety is a concern:

> [T]he need for answers to questions in a situation posing a threat to public safety outweighs the need for the prophylactic rule protecting the Fifth Amendment's privilege against self-incrimination. We decline to place officers such as Officer Kraft in the untenable position of having to consider, often in a matter of seconds, whether it best serves society for them to ask the necessary questions without the *Miranda* warnings and render whatever probative evidence they uncover inadmissible, or for them to give the warnings in order to preserve the admissibility of evidence they might uncover but possibly damage or destroy their ability to obtain that evidence and neutralize the volatile situation confronting them.[86]

The Court also made it clear that the appropriate test for determining whether a threat to public safety exists is an objective one—that is, one based on what a reasonable person in the same circumstances would believe: "[W]here spontaneity rather than adherence to a police manual is necessarily the order of the day, the application of the [public safety] exception . . . should not be made to depend on *post hoc* findings at a suppression hearing concerning the subjective motivation of the arresting officer."[87] The majority in *Quarles* apparently believed that an objective threat to public safety existed. Insofar as the officers did not know where the gun was located, not knowing "obviously posed more than one danger to the public safety: an accomplice might make use of it [or] a customer or employee might later come upon it."[88]

[85]*New York* v. *Quarles*, 467 U.S. 649 (1984).
[86]Ibid., pp. 657–658.
[87]Ibid., p. 656.
[88]Ibid., p. 657.

The *Quarles* decision is a controversial one. As Justice O'Connor noted in disagreement with the newly issued public safety exception to *Miranda* (though not with the majority's ultimate decision):

> *Miranda* has never been read to prohibit the police from asking questions to secure the public safety. Rather, the critical question *Miranda* addresses is who shall bear the cost of securing the public safety when such questions are asked and answered: the defendant or the state. *Miranda*, for better or worse, found the resolution of that question implicit in the prohibition against compulsory self-incrimination and placed the burden on the State.[89]

Quarles, by contrast, appears to place the burden on the defendant. It does so, in Justice O'Connor's view, not by ensuring that public safety is preserved but by creating a *Miranda* loophole that helps ensure that otherwise inadmissible evidence can be used against the defendant.

Challenging *Miranda*

18 U.S.C. Section 3501 A federal statute enacted in the wake of the *Miranda* decision providing that any confession "shall be admissible in evidence if it is voluntarily given." The statute was deemed unconstitutional in *Dickerson* v. *United States*.

The *Miranda* decision was not without controversy. In 1968, shortly after the decision was announced, Congress passed a Crime Control Act that, among other things, attempted to overrule the *Miranda* decision. The statute, codified as **18 U.S.C. Section 3501**, states that in any federal prosecution, a confession "shall be admissible in evidence if it is voluntarily given." Under the law, suspects are not required to be advised of their right to counsel, their right not to incriminate themselves, and so on.

For several years, Section 3501 remained dormant. The U.S. attorneys general have known that to utilize the statute would be to challenge the authority of the U.S. Supreme Court. But critics of *Miranda* were looking for an opportunity to bring Section 3501 before the Court. That opportunity arose in 2000: Charles Dickerson was indicted for bank robbery and related crimes. He moved to suppress a statement he made to Federal Bureau of Investigation (FBI) agents on the ground that he had not received his *Miranda* warnings. The district court granted Dickerson's motion to suppress but also noted that the confession was voluntary, despite the apparent *Miranda* violation.

Then, the Court of Appeals for the Fourth Circuit held (in a 2–1 decision) that "Congress, pursuant to its power to establish the rules of evidence and procedure in the federal courts, acted well within its authority in enacting Section 3501, [and] Section 3501, rather than *Miranda*, governs the admissibility of confession in federal court."[90] The case, *Dickerson* v. *United States*,[91] then went before the Supreme Court. In a 7–2 opinion, Chief Justice Rehnquist wrote for the Court:

> We hold that *Miranda*, being a constitutional decision of this Court, may not be in effect overruled by an Act of Congress, and we decline to overrule *Miranda* ourselves. We therefore hold that *Miranda* and its progeny in this Court govern the admissibility of statements made during custodial interrogation in both state and federal courts.[92]

[89]Ibid., p. 664.
[90]*United States* v. *Dickerson*, 166 F.3d 667 (4th Cir. 1999), p. 671.
[91]*Dickerson* v. *United States*, 530 U.S. 428 (2000).
[92]Ibid., p. 431.

The Court further noted:

> Whether or not we would agree with *Miranda's* reasoning and its resulting rule, were we addressing the issue in the first instance, the principles of *stare decisis* weigh heavily against overruling it now. . . . While *stare decisis* is not an inexorable command, particularly when we are interpreting the Constitution, even in constitutional cases, the doctrine carries such persuasive force that we have always required a departure from precedent to be supported by some special justification.
>
> We do not think there is such justification for overruling *Miranda. Miranda* has become embedded in routine police practice to the point where the warnings have become part of our national culture.[93]

Thus, according to the Supreme Court in *Dickerson*, Congress does not have the "final say" on matters of interrogations and confessions.

More Recent *Miranda* Decisions

In *Chavez* v. *Martinez*,[94] the Supreme Court seems to have shifted its view on *Miranda*. In that case, a police officer interrogated a man while he was receiving treatment for a gunshot wound. The man was *not* advised of his *Miranda* rights. He was never charged with a crime, but later sued under 42 U.S.C. Section 1983 (see Chapter 10), arguing that his constitutional rights were violated. The Supreme Court disagreed because the man was not compelled to be a "witness" against himself in a "criminal case." This decision would seem to suggest *Miranda* warnings are never required, unless statements obtained without the warnings are actually used against the accused in a criminal case.

In *Missouri* v. *Seibert*,[95] the Supreme Court made it clear that *Miranda* warnings must be given *before* interrogation commences. In that case, the accused was interrogated—without *Miranda* warnings having been read—and confessed. She was then advised of her *Miranda* rights and "re-confessed." The Supreme Court declared that the interrogating officer's pre-*Miranda* questioning was improper. The confession was deemed inadmissible at trial.

YOUR DECISION

1. Police officers lawfully executed a search warrant on Don Cheney's house. Cheney was not at home, but the officers were let into the house by his wife. When Cheney arrived at home, he was immediately arrested. He was then seated on the living room couch, and one of the officers brought in a potted marijuana plant and placed it on the coffee table in front of him. When Cheney saw the plant, he began crying and said, "OK, you got me. The plant is mine. As you probably know, there are plenty more where that came from." At trial, Cheney sought to have his statement suppressed on the grounds that a custodial interrogation without the *Miranda* warnings took place in his living room on the night of the search. How should the court decide?

2. William Wentworth was interrogated while in police custody. He wore an expensive suit, lavish jewelry, and otherwise exhibited an aura of financial success.

---

[93]Ibid., p. 443.
[94]*Chavez* v. *Martinez*, 538 U.S. 760 (2003).
[95]*Missouri* v. *Seibert*, 542 U.S. 600 (2004).

Before being interrogated, he was read the following rights: "You have the right to remain silent. Anything you say can and will be used against you in court. You have the right to talk with an attorney, either retained by you or appointed by the court, before giving a statement, and to have your attorney present when answering any questions." Wentworth made an incriminating statement during the interrogation and later moved to suppress it on the grounds that he was not informed that counsel would be provided if he was indigent. How should the court decide?

Summary

- A confession will be thrown out, as was the decision in *Miranda* v. *Arizona*, if a suspect's incriminating statement is a result of custodial interrogation in which the suspect was not advised of his or her constitutional right to have counsel present.

- Before custodial interrogation can commence, suspects must be advised of their so-called *Miranda* rights.

- If the *Miranda* warnings are not given adequately, then the police risk having a confession being thrown out of court.

- *Miranda* rights can be waived. This means the suspect agrees to talk.

- As a general rule, questioning must cease once the accused asserts his or her right to remain silent.

- Suspects are not required to be advised of their *Miranda* rights when doing so could compromise public safety.

- A summary of the relationship among *Miranda* and other approaches to confessions appears in Figure 12.6.

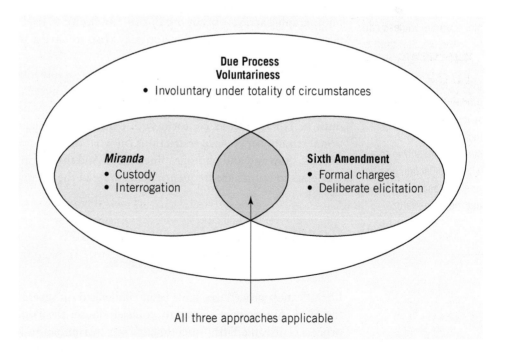

Figure 12.6

Relationship among the Various Approaches to Confession Law
Source: Adapted from R.M. Bloom and M.S. Brodin, Criminal Procedure: Examples and Explanations, 2nd ed. (New York: Little Brown, 1996)

MODULE 12.3   IDENTIFICATION PROCEDURES

Learning Objectives

- **Distinguish between three identification procedures.**
- **Summarize constitutional restrictions on identification procedures.**
- **Explain the problem of witness misidentification.**
- **Explain how the exclusionary rule operates in the identification context.**

CORE CONCEPTS

lineup An identification procedure in which the suspect is placed alongside several other people who resemble him or her.

showup An identification procedure in which the suspect is brought before the witness (or victim) alone, so the witness can be asked whether that person is the perpetrator.

photographic array A procedure in which several photographs, including one of the suspect, are shown to a witness or victim, and he or she is asked to pick out the perpetrator.

Identification procedures include those systems and activities that allow witnesses of crimes to identify suspected perpetrators. The three most common types of identification procedures are lineups, showups, and photographic arrays. In a lineup, the suspect is placed alongside several other people (sometimes called "fillers," "foils," or "distractors") who resemble him or her, and the witness (or victim) picks the suspect out of the lineup. The fillers may be jail inmates, actors, or volunteers. In a showup, the suspect is brought before the witness alone, so the witness can be asked whether that person is the perpetrator. Finally, in a photographic array (or photographic display), several photographs, including one of the suspect, are shown to a witness or victim, and he or she is asked to pick out the perpetrator.

Identification procedures fall into two broad categories: (1) out of court and (2) in court. The three identification procedures just described—lineups, showups, and photographic arrays—occur *out of court* and prior to trial. There are, however, many occasions in which the prosecution may wish to have a witness identify the suspect *in court* and during trial.

Naturally, it is in the prosecution's interest to introduce evidence that a witness or victim picked the perpetrator out of a lineup. However, it is not as simple as demonstrating that a witness identified the perpetrator. The identification procedure must be fair as well as conform with constitutional requirements. Those constitutional requirements place restrictions on what officials can do in terms of arranging lineups, showups, and photographic arrays. And these restrictions are critical because witnesses to crimes are frequently inaccurate in their descriptions.

Constitutional Restrictions on Identification Procedures

Identification procedures have been challenged on several grounds, stemming from the Sixth Amendment's right to counsel clause, the Fourteenth Amendment's due process clause, the Fifth Amendment's self-incrimination clause, and even on Fourth Amendment grounds. Each is introduced in the following subsections.

Lineups must be composed of individuals who look similar. Would this lineup conform to Constitutional requirements?

© Blend Images/Alamy

Right to Counsel

In *United States* v. *Wade,*[96] a defendant was placed in a police lineup, without his attorney present, *after* he had been indicted for a crime. The Supreme Court held that this violated the Sixth Amendment because a postindictment lineup is a "critical stage" in the criminal process. Furthermore, "the presence of counsel [at postindictment lineups] is necessary to preserve the defendant's basic right to a fair trial."[97] Indeed, the right to counsel extends well beyond the identification stage (see Chapter 15).

The key in *Wade* was that the lineup was postindictment—that is, conducted after charges had been filed. Had charges *not* been filed, a different decision would have probably resulted. Another important feature of the *Wade* decision was that it distinguished lineups from "various other preparatory steps, such as systematized or scientific analyzing of the accused's fingerprints, blood sample, clothing, hair and the like."[98] Counsel is not required for these types of activities because

> [k]nowledge of the techniques of science and technology is sufficiently available, and the variables in techniques few enough, that the accused has the opportunity for a meaningful confrontation of the Government's case at trial through the ordinary processes of cross-examination of the Government's expert witnesses and the presentation of the evidence of his own experts.[99]

The Supreme Court has extended the Sixth Amendment right to counsel to include other hearings, such as preliminary hearings and arraignments.[100] See the accompanying Court Decision box for more on the reasoning behind the *Wade* decision.

---

[96]*United States* v. *Wade*, 388 U.S. 218 (1967).
[97]Ibid., p. 227.
[98]Ibid.
[99]Ibid., pp. 227–228.
[100]See, e.g., *Kirby* v. *Illinois*, 406 U.S. 682 (1972).

**COURT
DECISION**

The Logic behind the Right to Counsel during Lineups

United States v. *Wade*
388 U.S. 218 (1967)

Decision: The post-indictment lineup (unlike such preparatory steps as analyzing fingerprints and blood samples) was a critical prosecutive stage at which respondent was entitled to the aid of counsel.

Reason: The fact that the lineup involved no violation of Wade's privilege against self-incrimination does not. . . . dispose of his contention that the courtroom identifications should have been excluded because the lineup was conducted without notice to, and in the absence of, his counsel . . .

The Framers of the Bill of Rights envisaged a broader role for counsel than under the practice then prevailing in England of merely advising his client in 'matters of law,' and eschewing any responsibility for 'matters of fact.' The constitutions in at least 11 of the 13 States expressly or impliedly abolished this distinction . . . 'Though the colonial provisions about counsel were in accord on few things, they agreed on the necessity of abolishing the facts-law distinction; the colonists appreciated that, if a defendant were forced to stand alone against the state, his case was foredoomed.'. . .

This background is reflected in the scope given by our decisions to the Sixth Amendment's guarantee to an accused of the assistance of counsel for his defense. When the Bill of Rights was adopted, there were no organized police forces as we know them today. The accused confronted the prosecutor and the witnesses against him, and the evidence was marshalled, largely at the trial itself. In contrast, today's law enforcement machinery involves critical confrontations of the accused by the prosecution at pretrial proceedings where the results might well settle the accused's fate and reduce the trial itself to a mere formality. In recognition of these realities of modern criminal prosecution, our cases have construed the Sixth Amendment guarantee to apply to 'critical' stages of the proceedings . . .

As early as *Powell* v. *Alabama* . . ., we recognized that the period from arraignment to trial was 'perhaps the most critical period of the proceedings . . .,' during which the accused 'requires the guiding hand of counsel . . .,' if the guarantee is not to prove an empty right. . . . The principle was also applied in *Massiah* v. *United States*, . . . where we held that incriminating statements of the defendant should have been excluded from evidence when it appeared that they were overheard by federal agents who, without notice to the defendant's lawyer, arranged a meeting between the defendant and an accomplice turned informant . . .

In *Escobedo* v. *Illinois*,. . . . we drew upon the rationale of *Hamilton* and *Massiah* in holding that the right to counsel was guaranteed at the point where the accused, prior to arraignment, was subjected to secret interrogation despite repeated requests to see his lawyer. We again noted the necessity of counsel's presence if the accused was to have a fair opportunity to present a defense at the trial itself . . . Finally, in

(continued)

**COURT
DECISION**
(continued)

Miranda v. *Arizona*, . . . the rules established for custodial interrogation included the right to the presence of counsel. The result was rested on our finding that this and the other rules were necessary to safeguard the privilege against self-incrimination from being jeopardized by such interrogation . . .

In sum, the principle of *Powell* v. *Alabama* and succeeding cases requires that we scrutinize any pretrial confrontation of the accused to determine whether the presence of his counsel is necessary to preserve the defendant's basic right to a fair trial as affected by his right meaningfully to cross-examine the witnesses against him and to have effective assistance of counsel at the trial itself. It calls upon us to analyze whether potential substantial prejudice to defendant's rights inheres in the particular confrontation and the ability of counsel to help avoid that prejudice.

Due Process

The Supreme Court has also clearly stated that the Fourteenth Amendment's due process clause bears on the constitutionality of identification procedures. For example, in *Stovall* v. *Denno*, the Court held that the accused is entitled to protection against procedures "so unnecessarily suggestive and conducive to irreparable mistaken identification"[101] as to amount to a due process violation. In general, for an identification procedure to satisfy the due process clause, it must be (1) reliable and (2) minimally suggestive.

Whether an identification procedure is *reliable* is determined in light of the facts and circumstances surrounding the case. Factors considered in determining whether an identification procedure is reliable include how much of an opportunity the victim/witness had to view the perpetrator, how confident he or she is in the identification, and the amount of time between the crime and the identification, among other factors. Indeed, the Supreme Court stated in *Neil* v. *Biggers*[102] that reliability is more important than *suggestiveness*. In the Court's words, it is "the likelihood of misidentification which violates a defendant's right to due process."[103] This position was reaffirmed in the case of *Manson* v. *Braithwaite*,[104] in which the Court held that the totality of circumstances determines whether an identification procedure is unreliable.

Suggestiveness has also been important in determining whether an identification procedure violates the due process clause. If the procedure is set up such that the witness or victim is almost guaranteed to pick the perpetrator, it is unnecessarily suggestive. If, for example, an offender is 6 feet tall and placed in a lineup with several others who are considerably shorter, then the procedure will be considered suggestive.

---

[101]*Stovall* v. *Denno*, 388 U.S. 293 (1967), p. 293.
[102]*Neil* v. *Biggers*, 409 U.S. 188 (1972).
[103]Ibid.
[104]*Manson* v. *Braithwaite*, 432 U.S. 98 (1977).

Self-Incrimination

The Fifth Amendment's self-incrimination clause has been invoked with regard to identification procedures. In particular, some defendants have argued that being forced to participate in a lineup or photographic array is itself incriminating and, as such, violates the Fifth Amendment. However, in *United States* v. *Wade*, the Court held that the privilege against self-incrimination does not limit the use of identification procedures.[105] The reason the Court offered is that even though incriminating information can result from identification procedures, such evidence is physical or real as opposed to testimonial. In *Wade*, the Court decided on the constitutionality of an identification procedure, in which the accused was required to utter words that were presumably uttered by the perpetrator. The Court concluded that this type of identification procedure was valid because the defendant's voice was used as an identifying characteristic, not as a means to get him to express his guilt. Thus, the Fifth Amendment does not apply to identification procedures.

The Fourth Amendment

Lastly, identification procedures have been challenged on Fourth Amendment grounds. Like the Fifth Amendment, the Fourth Amendment has yet to be successfully invoked with regard to identification procedures. According to the Supreme Court, no one enjoys a reasonable expectation of privacy in characteristics that are exposed to the public. For example, if an offender is viewed by a witness, the witness's identification of the offender will be admissible in court, even though the identification is incriminating. The offender/defendant may argue that the act of being viewed by the witness is incriminating, but the courts consider this sort of knowing exposure as beyond constitutional protection.

One of the leading cases in this area is *Schmerber* v. *California*.[106] There, a sample of the defendant's blood was taken by a doctor in a hospital following the defendant's arrest. The sample was used as evidence in the defendant's trial for drunk-driving. The defendant argued that the blood sample was incriminating and should be excluded from trial. The Supreme Court disagreed:

> Particularly in a case such as this, where time had to be taken to bring the accused to a hospital and to investigate the scene of the accident, there was no time to seek out a magistrate and secure a warrant. Given these special facts, we conclude that the attempt to secure evidence of blood-alcohol content in this case was an appropriate incident to petitioner's arrest.[107]

Obviously, if the police want to seize a person so as to obtain fingerprints, a voice exemplar, or some other form of evidence, they are bound by Fourth Amendment restrictions. As noted elsewhere in this book, probable cause is required before the police can seize a person. Assuming a seizure is justified, however, then any real or physical evidence obtained by the arrestee will be admissible.

---

[105]Note that the Fifth Amendment would apply if a defendant in a lineup was forced to answer questions from the police or witnesses.
[106]*Schmerber* v. *California*, 384 U.S. 757 (1966).
[107]Ibid., pp. 770–771.

- **Fourth Amendment:** The Fourth Amendment protects from an unlawful search or seizure conducted for the purpose of securing an identification. There is an exception, however: A witness can identify a suspect who is wrongfully seized if the identification is sufficiently independent of the illegal seizure.
- **Fifth Amendment:** Technically, the Fifth Amendment does not apply to identification procedures. This is true even if a suspect is asked to supply a voice exemplar, if this is done for the purpose of identification (and not a confession or admission).
- **Sixth Amendment:** The Sixth Amendment right to counsel exists in the context of making an identification but only in limited circumstances. First, the right to counsel only applies if formal adversarial charges have commenced. Second, a suspect in a photographic array does not enjoy Sixth Amendment protection, regardless of whether charges have been filed.
- **Fourteenth Amendment:** The Fourteenth Amendment's due process clause always applies to identification procedures. In particular, if an identification procedure is too suggestive, it will violate the Fourteenth Amendment.

Figure 12.7

Summary of Constitutional Issues in Identification Procedures

There is at least one exception to the Fourth Amendment's probable cause requirement as it pertains to identification procedures. In *Hayes* v. *Florida*, the Court stated:

> There is . . . support in our cases for the view that the Fourth Amendment would permit seizures for the purpose of fingerprinting, if there is reasonable suspicion that the suspect has committed a criminal act, if there is a reasonable basis for believing that fingerprinting will establish or negate the suspect's connection with that crime, and if the procedure is carried out with dispatch.[108]

However, if conducted in the home, such a seizure must be preceded by judicial authorization. See Figure 12.7 for a summary of constitutional issues in identification procedures.

Pretrial Identification Techniques

As described earlier, there are three types of pretrial identification techniques: lineups, showups, and photographic arrays. Each of these identification procedures is described in a following section, with particular focus on how the constitutional restrictions already discussed apply to it.

Lineups

Suspects can be forced to participate in lineups because lineups exhibit physical characteristics, not testimonial evidence. Indeed, suspects placed in lineups can also be required to supply voice exemplars but solely for identification purposes, not as a confession. If a suspect refuses to participate in a lineup, he or she can be cited with contempt,[109] and the prosecutor can comment at trial about the suspect's refusal to cooperate.[110]

---

[108]*Hayes v. Florida*, 470 U.S. 811 (1985), p. 817.
[109]See, e.g., *Doss v. United States*, 431 F.2d 601 (9th Cir. 1970).
[110]See, e.g., *United States v. Parhms*, 424 F.2d 152 (9th Cir. 1970).

suggestive lineup A flawed lineup that almost ensures the victim or witness will identify the suspect. For example, if the suspect is male and the other lineup participants are female, this would be a suggestive lineup.

Steps to Minimize Suggestiveness.

As noted earlier, the due process clause restricts identification procedures. In particular, an overly suggestive lineup violates due process. In *United States* v. *Wade*, the Supreme Court noted that a lineup becomes suggestive when, for instance,

> all in the lineup but the suspect were known to the identifying witness, . . . the other participants in a lineup were grossly dissimilar in appearance to the suspect, . . . only the suspect was required to wear distinctive clothing which the culprit allegedly wore, . . . the suspect is pointed out before or during a lineup, and . . . the participants in the lineup are asked to try on an article of clothing which fits only the suspect.[111]

There are several guidelines, or rules of thumb, for minimizing suggestiveness in a police lineup. They include:

- Including at least four people besides the suspect in the lineup.
- Ensuring persons in the lineup have similar physical characteristics.
- Let the suspect choose his or her place in line.
- Each lineup participant should be required to take whatever specialized action is required (e.g., to utter certain words).
- The persons in the lineup should be warned to conduct themselves such that the suspect does not stand out.
- A lineup should be photographed or videotaped.
- Everyone in the lineup should wear approximately the same clothing.
- The accused should be randomly placed in the lineup, so as not to stand out.
- For obvious reasons, persons known to the witness should not be placed in the lineup.
- Witnesses should view the lineup one at a time, so as to not unduly influence another in his or her identification of the perpetrator.
- Participants in the lineup should be instructed not to make any statements or comments unless ordered to do so.
- A written waiver of counsel should be obtained if the suspect waives his or her Sixth Amendment right to have counsel present at a *postindictment lineup*.

An important restriction concerning lineups is that people cannot be indiscriminately picked off the street for participation. If a person is *not* already in custody, the police must have reasonable suspicion that he or she has committed the crime in question. However, if the person *is* in custody prior to the lineup, then he or she can be forced to stand in a lineup without any judicial authorization.[112]

Showups

A *showup* is a one-on-one victim/offender confrontation, usually conducted outside the courtroom setting. Specifically, a showup is usually held when the suspect has been apprehended shortly after having committed the crime and the witness is still

---

[111]*United States* v. *Wade*, 388 U.S. 218 (1967), p. 233.
[112]*United States* v. *Anderson*, 490 F.2d 785 (D.C. Cir. 1974).

at or near the scene of the crime. A lineup is always preferable to a showup (because a lineup consists of several potential suspects); however, a showup is necessary under certain circumstances.

For example, when a witness is immobile and cannot be present at a lineup, a showup is an effective alternative. In *Stovall* v. *Denno*, the Supreme Court noted, "Faced with the responsibility for identifying the attacker, with the need for immediate action and with the knowledge that [the victim] could not visit the jail, the police followed the only feasible procedure and took [the accused] to the hospital room."[113] In a similar vein, a showup is preferable when the *suspect* is immobile.[114]

A showup is sometimes desirable to facilitate prompt identification when time is of the essence. If the witness is required to wait for a lineup, for instance, misidentification is more likely to result. A showup conducted more than 60 minutes after the crime, however, will usually not be upheld.[115] But in at least one case, the Supreme Court upheld a stationhouse showup in which no emergency existed. In *Neil* v. *Biggers*,[116] the Court sanctioned an arranged one-on-one showup, even though it took place well after the point at which the crime in question was committed. The Court noted, given the facts, that there was "no substantial likelihood of misidentification."[117] This was because the witness had an opportunity to view the suspect for almost 30 minutes, under good lighting, prior to the showup.

The same constitutional provisions that govern lineups also govern showups. Specifically, the Sixth Amendment right to counsel applies but only after adversarial proceedings have commenced.[118] Due process protections also exist. If the showup is unnecessarily suggestive under a totality of circumstances analysis, then any identification that comes from it will not be admissible in court.

In-Court Showups. What happens when a witness identifies the accused for the first time in *court*? This has happened on occasion and is best described as an **in-court showup**. The key feature of an in-court showup is that the witness has *not* identified the suspect, either in a lineup or related procedure, prior to trial. How do the courts deal with this? The answer is important because an in-court identification is highly suggestive. Namely, the suspect has already been identified by virtue of having been charged with the crime.

The leading case dealing with in-court showups is *Moore* v. *Illinois*, although the focus of the case was on the preliminary hearing, not the trial. The Court's decision would be expected to apply to criminal trials, as well as other adversarial proceedings, however. Here are the facts from that case, as described by the Supreme Court:

> After petitioner had been arrested for rape and related offenses, he was identified by the complaining witness as her assailant at the ensuing preliminary hearing, during which petitioner was not represented by counsel nor offered appointed counsel. The victim had been asked to make an identification after being told that she was going to view a suspect, after being told his name and having heard it called as he was led

in-court showup A procedure in which a witness identifies the perpetrator in court. This sometimes occurs when a prosecutor asks a testifying witness to point to the perpetrator.

---

[113]*Stovall* v. *Denno*, 388 U.S. 293 (1967), p. 295
[114]See, e.g., *Jackson* v. *United States*, 412 F.2d 149 (D.C. Cir. 1969).
[115]*United States* v. *Perry*, 449 F.2d 1026 (D.C. Cir. 1971).
[116]*Neil* v. *Biggers*, 409 U.S. 188 (1972).
[117]Ibid., p. 201.
[118]*Moore* v. *Illinois*, 434 U.S. 220 (1977).

before the bench, and after having heard the prosecutor recite the evidence believed to implicate petitioner. Subsequently, petitioner was indicted, and counsel was appointed, who moved to suppress the victim's identification of petitioner. The Illinois trial court denied the motion on the ground that the prosecution had shown an independent basis for the victim's identification. At trial, the victim testified on direct examination by the prosecution that she had identified petitioner as her assailant at the preliminary hearing, and there was certain other evidence linking petitioner to the crimes. He was convicted and the Illinois Supreme Court affirmed.[119]

Notwithstanding the clear violation of the Sixth Amendment in this case (which the Supreme Court also pointed out), the Court pointed to the suggestiveness that occurs when a witness identifies a suspect for the first time at a formal hearing:

> It is difficult to imagine a more suggestive manner in which to present a suspect to a witness for their critical first confrontation than was employed in this case. The victim who had seen her assailant for only 10 to 15 seconds, was asked to make her identification after she was told that she was going to view a suspect, after she was told his name and heard it called as he was led before the bench, and after she heard the prosecutor recite the evidence believed to implicate petitioner. Had petitioner been represented by counsel, some or all of this suggestiveness could have been avoided.[120]

What message is to be gleaned from *Moore* v. *Illinois*? In general, law enforcement officials should have witnesses identify suspects via lineups, showups, or photographic arrays *prior* to the point at which adversarial proceedings commence. Any of these identification procedures would result in a less suggestive identification than would be likely at trial. Clearly, though, lineups, showups, and photographic arrays can also be suggestive.

Photographic Identifications

The last type of identification procedure to be considered in this text is the photographic identification array. It involves displaying a picture of the suspect along with pictures of several other people to a victim or witness for the purpose of identification.

Photographic identification procedures approximate real-life lineups by including several people, but they are not subjected to the same constitutional restrictions that lineups are. In particular, there is no Sixth Amendment right to counsel during a photographic identification. However, due process protections *do* apply.

To minimize due process problems, several photographs of like individuals should be shown to the witness or victim so as to minimize unnecessary suggestiveness. In *Simmons* v. *United States*, the Supreme Court shed some light on the importance of a carefully constructed photographic array:

> Despite the hazards of initial identification by photograph, this procedure has been used widely and effectively in criminal law enforcement, from the standpoint both of apprehending offenders and of sparing innocent suspects the ignominy of arrest by allowing eyewitnesses to exonerate them through scrutiny of photographs. The danger that use of the technique may result in convictions based on misidentification may be

---

[119]Ibid., p. 220.
[120]Ibid., pp. 229–230.

substantially lessened by a course of cross-examination at trial which exposes to the jury the method's potential for error. We are unwilling to prohibit its employment, either in the exercise of our supervisory power or, still less, as a matter of constitutional requirement. Instead, we hold that each case must be considered on its own facts, and that convictions based on eyewitness identification at trial following a pretrial identification by photograph will be set aside on that ground only if the photographic identification procedure was so impermissibly suggestive as to give rise to a very substantial likelihood of irreparable misidentification.[121]

As indicated, to conform to due process requirements, multiple photographs of like individuals are ideal for a photographic array. However, in one case, the Supreme Court sanctioned a photographic array consisting of one picture. In *Manson v. Braithwaite*,[122] the Court sanctioned an in-court identification based on an earlier identification from a single photograph because it was reliable based on the totality of circumstances. The reasons the Court cited are illustrative. In particular, the Court described how Glover, the witness, who was also a police officer, arrived at his conclusion that the suspect (referred to later as the *vendor* of illegal drugs) in the photograph was, in fact, the perpetrator. Here are the criteria on which the Court focused:

- **The opportunity to view.** Glover testified that for two to three minutes he stood at the apartment door, within 2 feet of the respondent. The door opened twice, and each time the man stood at the door. The moments passed, the conversation took place, and payment was made. Glover looked directly at his vendor. It was near sunset, to be sure, but the sun had not yet set, so it was not dark or even dusk or twilight. Natural light from outside entered the hallway through a window. There was natural light, as well, from inside the apartment.

- **The degree of attention.** Glover was not a casual or passing observer, as is so often the case with eyewitness identification. Trooper Glover was a trained police officer on duty—and specialized and dangerous duty—when he called at the third floor of 201 Westland in Hartford on May 5, 1970. . . . It is true that Glover's duty was that of ferreting out narcotics offenders and that he would be expected in his work to produce results. But it is also true that, as a specially trained, assigned, and experienced officer, he could be expected to pay scrupulous attention to detail, for he knew that subsequently he would have to find and arrest his vendor. In addition, he knew that his claimed observations would be subject later to close scrutiny and examination at any trial.

- **The accuracy of the description.** Glover's description was given to D'Onofrio [a backup officer] within minutes after the transaction. It included the vendor's race, his height, his build, the color and style of his hair, and the high cheekbone facial feature. It also included clothing the vendor wore. No claim has been made that respondent did not possess the physical characteristics so described. D'Onofrio reacted positively at once. Two days later, when Glover was alone, he viewed the photograph D'Onofrio produced and identified its subject as the narcotics seller.

- **The witness's level of certainty.** There is no dispute that the photograph in question was that of respondent.

---

[121]*Simmons v. United States*, 390 U.S. 377 (1968), p. 384.
[122]*Manson v. Braithwaite*, 432 U.S. 98 (1977).

- **The time between the crime and the identification.** Glover's description of his vendor was given to D'Onofrio within minutes of the crime. The photographic identification took place only two days later. We do not have here the passage of weeks or months between the crime and the viewing of the photograph.[123]

Taken together, these five considerations led the Court to this conclusion:

> These indicators of Glover's ability to make an accurate identification are hardly outweighed by the corrupting effect of the challenged identification itself. Although identifications arising from single-photograph displays may be viewed in general with suspicion, see *Simmons* v. *United States*, 390 U.S., at 383, we find in the instant case little pressure on the witness to acquiesce in the suggestion that such a display entails. D'Onofrio had left the photograph at Glover's office and was not present when Glover first viewed it two days after the event. There thus was little urgency and Glover could view the photograph at his leisure. And since Glover examined the photograph alone, there was no coercive pressure to make an identification arising from the presence of another. The identification was made in circumstances allowing care and reflection.[124]

The *Manson* decision suggests that single-photograph arrays are constitutionally permissible, but understand that the witness in this case was a police officer and that the facts were somewhat unusual. It is doubtful that the Supreme Court would uphold a similar identification today. It is always preferable to place multiple pictures of like individuals in a photographic array.

Identification Procedures: Flaws and Fixes

Nearly every suspect identification procedure can be flawed in some fashion, some more than others. Consider showups. No matter what steps police take to ensure fairness, showups are prone to mistaken identification. And the consequences of mistaken identification can be serious:

> Billy Wayne Miller was asleep in a back bedroom of his father's modest Oak Cliff home when three Dallas police officers burst through the front door around 3 a.m., guns in hand, yelling another man's name. Still groggy and clad only in his underwear, Mr. Miller was taken to the front porch. There he spotted a woman in a squad car glance at him and nod to an officer seated beside her before the car drove away. That split-second, one-man lineup cost Mr. Miller 22 years of his life on a rape conviction that DNA evidence later invalidated.[125]

Stories like Billy Wayne Miller's could be less common if authorities relied exclusively on lineups and photographic identification procedures. However, even lineups can be flawed. And so can photographic arrays. The Innocence Project, an organization that works to exonerate wrongfully convicted inmates, claims that "eyewitness misidentification is the single greatest cause of wrongful convictions nationwide."[126]

---

[123]Ibid., pp. 114–116.

[124]Ibid., p. 116.

[125]http://www.thecrimereport.org/news/inside-criminal-justice/dallas-morning-news-case-study-overview-and-resources (accessed March 5, 2012).

[126]http://www.innocenceproject.org/understand/Eyewitness-Misidentification.php (accessed March 5, 2012).

The organization highlights some situations in which lineups and photographic procedures led to wrongful convictions:

- A witness in a rape case was shown a photo array where only one photo—of the person police suspected was the perpetrator—was marked with an "R."

- Witnesses substantially changed their description of a perpetrator (including key information such as height, weight, and presence of facial hair) after they learned more about a particular suspect.

- Witnesses only made an identification after multiple photo arrays or lineups—and then made hesitant identifications (saying they "thought" the person "might be" the perpetrator, for example), but at trial the jury was told the witnesses did not waver in identifying the suspect.[127]

Some might take issue with the Innocence Project's arguments, but many researchers have also found that identification procedures can be problematic, so much so that in May of 1998, then-U.S. Attorney General Janet Reno organized a working group of prosecutors, defense attorneys, police officers, and other experts who were tasked with creating a set of "best practices" for identification procedures. The working group's findings were echoed in an article published by a group of psychologists at around the same time. They identified "four simple rules of procedure that follow from the scientific literature that we argue could largely relieve the criminal justice system of its role in contributing to eyewitness identification problems."[128] The rules were:

- The person who conducts the lineup or photospread should not be aware of which member of the lineup or photospread is the suspect.

- Eyewitnesses should be told explicitly that the person in question might not be in the lineup or photospread and therefore should not feel that they must make an identification. They should also be told that the person administering the lineup does not know which person is the suspect in the case.

- The suspect should not stand out in the lineup or photospread as being different from the distractors based on the eyewitness's previous description of the culprit or based on other factors that would draw extra attention to the suspect.

- A clear statement should be taken from the eyewitness at the time of the identification and prior to any feedback as to his or her confidence that the identified person is the actual culprit.[129]

Double-Blind Lineups

When the investigator conducting a lineup knows who the suspect is, he or she can unintentionally (and even *in*tentionally) influence the witness and thereby taint the identification procedure. For example, the investigator may say to the witness, "Why

---

[127]Ibid.

[128]G. L. Wells, M. Small, S. Penrod, R. S. Malpass, S. M. Fulero, and C. A. E. Brimacombe, "Eyewitness Identification Procedures: Recommendations for Lineups and Photospreads," *Law and Human Behavior*, Vol. 22 (1998), pp. 603–647.

[129]Ibid., pp. 627–635.

don't you take another look at number three?" Assuming the suspect is in the number three position in a lineup, clearly this comment could sway the witness in the direction the investigatory prefers.

double-blind lineup A lineup procedure in which neither the witness nor the investigator staging the lineup knows who the suspect is.

A **double-blind lineup** is one in which the investigator conducting the lineup (or assembling a photo array) does not know who the suspect is. This helps ensure that the investigator will not lead the witness in a particular direction. Studies indeed show that double-blind procedures reduce the risks of mistaken identifications.[130] Here is a summary of the findings from one of the most recent studies in this area:

> Administrator knowledge had the greatest effect on identifications of the suspect for simultaneous photospreads paired with biased instructions, with single-blind administrations increasing identifications of the suspect. When biased instructions were given, single-blind administrations produced fewer foil identifications than double-blind administrations. Administrators exhibited a greater proportion of biasing behaviors during single-blind administrations than during double-blind administrations.[131]

Virtual Officer Lineups

A problem with double-blind lineups is that they are resource intensive. They require at least two investigators instead of the usual one—one to know the identity of the suspect and another to administer the lineup without knowing the suspect's real identity. One solution to this problem is to use a "virtual officer" to conduct the procedure.[132] One team of researchers has gone so far as to develop software in which a virtual officer (called "Officer Garcia") conducts a photographic display. Because the virtual officer does not know the identity of the suspect or his/her placement in the array, the procedure is not susceptible to investigator influence. A "YouTube" demonstration is available online.[133]

The Exclusionary Rule and Identifications

When identification procedures violate constitutional protections, the results from such procedures cannot be considered admissible in a criminal trial. Generally, there are two means by which identifications will be excluded: (1) when an in-court identification is tainted by an out-of-court identification and (2) when a suspect is searched and/or seized improperly and then identified by a witness.

---

[130]See, e.g., S. M. Greathouse and M. B. Kovera, "Instruction Bias and Lineup Presentation Moderate the Effects of Administrator Knowledge on Eyewitness Identification," *Law and Human Behavior*, Vol. 33(2009), pp. 70–82.; R. M. Haw and R. P. Fisher, "Effects of Administrator-Witness Contact on Eyewitness Identification Accuracy," *Journal of Applied Psychology*, Vol. 89 (2004), pp. 1106–1112; M. B. Russano, J. J. Dickinson, S. M. Greathouse, and M. B. Kovera, "Why Don't You Take Another Look at Number Three: Investigator Knowledge and Its Effects on Eyewitness Confidence and Identification Decisions," *Cardozo Public Law, Policy, and Ethics Journal*, Vol. 4 (2006), pp. 355–379.

[131]S. M. Greathouse and M. B. Kovera, p. 70.

[132]O. H. MacLin, L. A. Zimmerman, and R. S. Malpass, "PC-Eyewitness and the Sequential Superiority Effect: Computer-Based Lineup Administration," *Law and Human Behavior*, Vol. 29 (2005), pp. 303–321.

[133]http://www.youtube.com/watch?v=SEhcLQmwtjQ (accessed March 5, 2012).

Tainted Identifications

In-court identifications are viewed cautiously. In most such situations, the defendant is sitting in the courtroom, not surrounded by anyone else matching his or her description (as in a lineup), and sometimes looking sinister or even guilty (e.g., wearing prison coveralls). Furthermore, given the fact that the defendant has been identified—at least, for trial purposes—as the one suspected of having committed a crime, witnesses often jump to the conclusion that the defendant is the one who should be held responsible.

Nevertheless, courts routinely permit in-court identifications. But if an in-court identification is tainted by an out-of-court identification, it may be excluded. This is known as a **tainted identification**.

tainted identification An identification that would not have taken place but for some earlier unconstitutional activity.

Unfortunately, it is not always easy to decide whether an in-court identification is "fruit of the poisonous tree." In *United States* v. *Wade*, the Supreme Court held that an illegally conducted lineup does not invalidate later identifications resulting from an "independent source." The independent source in this context does not have to be another person. Instead, if the witness had plenty of time to view the perpetrator prior to the police lineup, showup, or photographic array, then his or her in-court identification may be admissible. Some factors that are considered include

> the prior opportunity to observe the alleged criminal act, the existence of any discrepancy between any pre-lineup description and the defendant's actual description, any identification prior to lineup of another person, the identification by picture of the defendant prior to the lineup, failure to identify the defendant on a prior occasion, and the lapse of time between the alleged act and the lineup identification.[134]

Also, if the witness did not experience intense anxiety or pressure during the criminal act (and thus had plenty of opportunity to absorb what was occurring), it is likely that his or her in-court identification will not be tainted by questionable police conduct during a lineup.[135]

Identifications Resulting from Illegal Searches and Seizures

What happens if a person is wrongfully arrested—say, based on less than probable cause—and then placed in a lineup and identified by a witness? Can the witness's identification be considered admissible in a criminal trial? What if, further, the lineup is nonsuggestive and otherwise abides by constitutional requirements? Unfortunately, the Supreme Court has offered few answers to these questions.

Davis v. Mississippi[136] is a worthwhile point of departure. In *Davis*, the fingerprint identification of a rape suspect was deemed inadmissible because it was the product of an illegal arrest. However, in *United States* v. *Crews*,[137] the Supreme Court decided otherwise. In that case, Crews was illegally arrested and photographed

---

[134]*United States* v. *Wade*, 388 U.S. 218 (1967), p. 241.
[135]see *United States* v. *Johnson*, 412 F.2d 753 (1st Cir. 1969), *cert. denied*, 397 U.S. 944 (1970).
[136]*Davis* v. *Mississippi*, 394 U.S. 721 (1969).
[137]*United States* v. *Crews*, 445 U.S. 463 (1980).

and then his photograph was shown to a witness, who identified him as the perpetrator. He was tried and convicted based, in part, on the witness's identification. The Supreme Court agreed with the trial court that the arrest was illegal but still upheld Crews's conviction. Three members of the majority justified this decision by arguing that the "fruit" was gathered at the point of the illegal arrest, as opposed to later, so the derivative evidence doctrine should not apply. The Court further noted that the identification had not "'been come at by exploitation' of the violation of the defendant's Fourth Amendment rights."[138]

Inasmuch as *Crews* was decided well after *Davis* v. *Mississippi*, it would seem that an identification resulting from an illegal search and/or seizure would be admissible. Think back, as well, to how the exclusionary rule applies in the *Miranda* context. The Supreme Court held in *United States* v. *Bayer*[139] that the "fruit of the poisonous tree" doctrine does not control the admissibility of physical evidence obtained from illegal confessions. These decisions, taken together, chip away at the exclusionary rule and reinforce the notion that the "fruit of the poisonous tree" doctrine applies in limited circumstances—primarily, when an illegal search and/or seizure (as opposed to an improper confession or identification) results in the subsequent seizure of tangible evidence.

YOUR DECISION

1. On December 24, the Toy Emporium was robbed. The suspect escaped before security guards and police could capture him, but store security cameras and several witnesses indicated that the crime was committed by a white male who was 6 feet, 3 inches tall, approximately 270 pounds, between 25 and 30 years of age, wearing a green trench coat, and having long hair. Two hours after the robbery, a man was arrested in a nearby town because he fit the general description of the robber. However, he was bald and wearing a brown trench coat. A lineup was conducted, in which the suspect was required to wear a wig resembling the long hair of the perpetrator. He was positively identified by several witnesses. Does the act of requiring the suspect to alter his appearance conform to constitutional requirements?

2. Janice Bolan, a rape victim, was examined at a hospital and a rape kit was collected. No sperm cells were identified in the first examination of the swabs. Bolan then gave police a description of her attacker, saying he was an African-American man between 25 and 30 years of age, approximately 6 feet tall, and had a beard. She then helped officers create a sketch of the perpetrator, which was circulated throughout the community. A week later, police received a call that a man fitting the description was working in a nearby grocery store. Police took Bolan by the store and asked if the man, Dean Cage, was her attacker. She answered yes. Police then conducted a lineup at the police station. Once again, Bolan identified Cage as her attacker. Cage was arrested and convicted in a bench trial, after she testified in court that she was "100 percent sure" Cage was the rapist—and pointed to him in court. Is there anything wrong with these events?

---

[138]Ibid., p. 471.
[139]*United States* v. *Bayer*, 331 U.S. 532 (1947).

Summary

- Identification procedures are of three types: (1) lineups, (2) showups, and (3) photographic identifications or arrays. All are bound by the Fourteenth Amendment's due process clause. That is, if they are too suggestive, they will be declared unconstitutional.

- Lineups and showups are also restricted by the Sixth Amendment's right to counsel clause, but this clause does not apply to photographic identifications.

- Identification procedures are not protected by the Fifth and Fourth Amendments because an identification is not considered testimony or a seizure.

- Witnesses are prone to mistaken identification, especially in show-up situations. Even lineups and photo arrays can result in mistaken identification.

- Various procedures have been developed to improve identification procedures. Two recent examples include double-blind lineups and virtual officer lineups.

- An identification, whether occurring during trial or prior to trial, can be excluded as evidence. First, if an in-court identification is tainted by an improper out-of-court identification, it will be inadmissible. Similarly, if an identification takes place following the illegal arrest and/or search of a suspect, it can be excluded, as well.

- Usually, if the identification is sufficiently divorced from any prior illegality, it will be admissible at trial.

Chapter Review

MODULE **12.1**   ### SIXTH AND FOURTEENTH AMENDMENT APPROACHES TO INTERROGATION

Learning Objectives

- Describe why voluntariness is important in the confession/interrogation context.
- Summarize how the Sixth Amendment impacts interrogations and confessions.

Review Questions

1. Summarize the due process voluntariness approach to interrogations and confessions.
2. What factors affect voluntariness?
3. Summarize the Sixth Amendment approach to interrogations and confessions.
4. Explain deliberate elicitation.
5. What are formal criminal proceedings, for purposes of the Sixth Amendment approach to interrogations and confessions?

Key Terms

confession
admission
deliberate elicitation

formal criminal proceedings
due process voluntariness approach

MODULE **12.2**   ### *MIRANDA*

Learning Objectives

- Explain *Miranda* v. *Arizona* and how it affects interrogations and confessions.
- Know when unconstitutionally obtained confessions are admissible in court to prove guilt.

Review Questions

1. When does *Miranda* apply?
2. Citing relevant cases, distinguish between custody and interrogation, for *Miranda* purposes.
3. Summarize the requirements for a valid *Miranda* waiver.
4. What is the public safety exception to *Miranda*?
5. How does the exclusionary rule operate in the context of confessions and interrogations?

Key Terms

Miranda warnings
custody
interrogation

functional equivalent of a question
18 U.S.C. Section 3501

MODULE **12.3**   **IDENTIFICATION PROCEDURES**

Learning Objectives

- Distinguish between three identification procedures.
- Summarize constitutional restrictions on identification procedures.
- Explain the problem of witness misidentification.
- Explain how the exclusionary rule operates in the identification context.

Review Questions

1. Explain how the Sixth Amendment right to counsel applies in the identification context.
2. Explain how due process applies in the identification context.
3. Why are the Fourth and Fifth Amendments not applicable in the identification context?
4. Explain the three types of pretrial identification procedures. How do they differ from one another?
5. What are some methods of reducing the suggestiveness of a lineup?
6. What is an in-court showup?
7. What does a constitutionally valid photographic array look like?

Key Terms

lineup
showup
photographic array
suggestive lineup

in-court showup
double-blind lineup
tainted identification

Chapter Synthesis Questions

1. Which constitutional approach to confessions and interrogations is most important and why? Which is the most far-reaching?
2. Is *Miranda* as relevant today as it was when it was decided? Why or why not?
3. Does the exclusionary rule work differently in the confessions context than in the Fourth Amendment context? Why or why not?
4. Witness misidentification is a serious problem in the criminal justice system. What, if anything, can be done about it?
5. How does the exclusionary rule work in the identification process vis-à-vis the confessions and Fourth Amendment context?

13

PRETRIAL PROCEDURE

MODULE

13.1

INITIAL APPEARANCE AND PROBABLE CAUSE HEARING

Learning Objectives

- **Explain the purpose and process of the initial appearance.**
- **Explain the purpose and process of the probable cause hearing.**

CORE CONCEPTS

The criminal process begins with one of two events: a warrantless arrest or a criminal complaint. If a person is arrested without a warrant—say, for committing a crime in the presence of a police officer—then the arresting officer will file a criminal complaint against the individual and the formal criminal process will commence. On the other hand, if a warrant is obtained before making an arrest, the warrant must be preceded by a criminal complaint. Basically, the would-be arresting officer needs to convince a judge that a crime has been committed before an arrest warrant will be issued. The complaint serves as a basis for issuing an arrest warrant. The same logic applies if a private party complains as to someone's presumed involvement in criminal activity. In such a situation, an officer will probably investigate the private party's complaint and, if it is meritorious, the officer will apply for a warrant.

booking The process by which an arrest is officially documented and the arrestee is placed into custody.

Once a person has been arrested, be it with or without a warrant, he or she will be booked at the arresting officer's police station or the sheriff's station (i.e., sheriffs usually run jails). **Booking** consists of filling out paperwork as to who was arrested, the time of the arrest, and the offense involved. Next, the arrestee's personal items will be inventoried. The arrestee may also be photographed and fingerprinted, depending on the offense and the jurisdiction involved. Finally, the arrestee will be placed in a holding cell, jail cell, or similar confinement facility and allowed to contact counsel, family, friends, and other individuals, as needed. (Contrary to popular depictions, more than one phone call is typically allowed.)

The Initial Appearance

initial appearance The first appearance of an accused person before a judge. Trial may occur for misdemeanors.

Once arrested and booked, the suspect is then brought before a magistrate or judge in what is known as the **initial appearance**. Not all jurisdictions require an initial appearance (also referred to as *presentment*), but for those that do, the suspect must be brought before a judge in a relatively short period of time. Delays of more than six hours are usually unacceptable; they may be necessary on occasion, however, if the time of arrest precludes appearance before a judge (e.g., 1 A.M. on Monday).

The initial appearance is designed to serve a number of purposes. In a misdemeanor case, such as minor in possession, the trial may take place at this stage. In a more serious case, however, the accused will be advised of

- the reason he or she is being detained (notification of formal charges often comes later at arraignment),

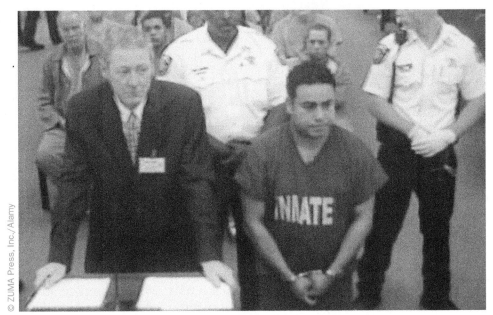

The key purpose of the initial appearance is for the accused to be notified of the charges against him or her.

- his or her protection against self-incrimination, and
- his or her right to appointed counsel, if need be.

The judge may also set bail at the initial appearance, but the bail determination often requires a separate hearing. For ease of exposition, this chapter treats the bail determination as its own hearing, independent of the initial appearance.

The initial appearance is usually swift and subject to few procedural constraints. In fact, only one Supreme Court decision has dealt explicitly with the initial appearance. In *Rothgery* v. *Gillespie County*,[1] the Court held that the Sixth Amendment right to counsel applies at the initial appearance. In contrast, the probable cause, bail, and preliminary hearings have received much more of the Court's attention.

The Probable Cause Hearing

probable cause hearing
A hearing in which a judge decides whether there was probable cause to arrest. If the arrest was with a warrant, the probable cause hearing is not necessary. Also called a *Gerstein* hearing (for the Supreme Court's decision in *Gerstein* v. *Pugh*).

In *Gerstein* v. *Pugh*,[2] the Supreme Court held that the Fourth Amendment requires a so-called **probable cause hearing** either before or promptly after arrest.[3] A probable cause hearing *before* an arrest usually results in an arrest warrant being issued. Recall that an arrest warrant is issued based on a judge's determination as to whether probable cause is in place. No hearing to determine probable cause after such an arrest is necessary because it would be redundant. However, when an arrest is made *without* a warrant, then a probable cause determination must often be made. The purpose of the probable cause hearing is, in essence, to determine whether there is probable cause to keep a person detained.

---

[1]*Rothgery* v. *Gillespie County*, 554 U.S. 191 (2008).
[2]*Gerstein* v. *Pugh*, 420 U.S. 103 (1975).
[3]Probable cause hearings are not required in certain jurisdictions.

The *Gerstein* decision challenged the preliminary hearing system in Florida. Probable cause was determined at preliminary hearings in that state, but those hearings were not required until 30 days after arrest. Basically, a person could be held following a warrantless arrest for 30 days, sometimes longer. The Court held that such a lengthy detention required a judicial determination of probable cause *early on*.[4] *Gerstein* is further explored in the accompanying Court Decision box.

COURT DECISION

The Logic behind Probable Cause Hearings

Gerstein v. Pugh
420 U.S. 103 (1975)

Decision: The Fourth Amendment requires a judicial determination of probable cause as a prerequisite to extended restraint of liberty following arrest. Accordingly, the Florida procedures challenged here whereby a person arrested without a warrant and charged by information may be jailed or subjected to other restraints pending trial without any opportunity for a probable cause determination, are unconstitutional.

Reason: . . . this case presents two issues: whether a person arrested and held for trial on an information is entitled to a judicial determination of probable cause for detention, and, if so, whether the adversary hearing ordered by the District Court and approved by the Court of Appeals is required by the Constitution . . .

Both the standards and procedures for arrest and detention have been derived from the Fourth Amendment and its common law antecedents...The standard for arrest is probable cause, defined in terms of facts and circumstances 'sufficient to warrant a prudent man in believing that the [suspect] had committed or was committing an offense.' . . . This standard, like those for searches and seizures, represents a necessary accommodation between the individual's right to liberty and the State's duty to control crime.

'These long-prevailing standards seek to safeguard citizens from rash and unreasonable interferences with privacy and from unfounded charges of crime. They also seek to give fair leeway for enforcing the law in the community's protection. Because many situations which confront officers in the course of executing their duties are more or less ambiguous, room must be allowed for some mistakes on their part. But the mistakes must be those of reasonable men, acting on facts leading sensibly to their conclusions of probability. The rule of probable cause is a practical, nontechnical conception affording the best compromise that has been found for accommodating these often opposing interests. Requiring more would unduly hamper law enforcement. To allow less would be to leave law-abiding citizens at the mercy of the officers' whim or caprice.' . . .

(continued)

---

[4]Ibid., p. 114.

COURT DECISION
(continued)

To implement the Fourth Amendment's protection against unfounded invasions of liberty and privacy, the Court has required that the existence of probable cause be decided by a neutral and detached magistrate whenever possible. The classic statement of this principle appears in Johnson v. United States . . .: 'The point of the Fourth Amendment, which often is not grasped by zealous officers, is not that it denies law enforcement the support of the usual inferences which reasonable men draw from evidence. Its protection consists in requiring that those inferences be drawn by a neutral and detached magistrate, instead of being judged by the officer engaged in the often competitive enterprise of ferreting out crime.' . . .

Maximum protection of individual rights could be assured by requiring a magistrate's review of the factual justification prior to any arrest, but such a requirement would constitute all intolerable handicap for legitimate law enforcement. Thus, while the Court has expressed a preference for the use of arrest warrants when feasible . . ., it has never invalidated an arrest supported by probable cause solely because the officers failed to secure a warrant . . .

Under this practical compromise, a policeman's on-the-scene assessment of probable cause provides legal justification for arresting a person suspected of crime, and for a brief period of detention to take the administrative steps incident to arrest. Once the suspect is in custody, however, the reasons that justify dispensing with the magistrate's neutral judgment evaporate. There no longer is any danger that the suspect will escape or commit further crimes while the police submit their evidence to a magistrate. And, while the State's reasons for taking summary action subside, the suspect's need for a neutral determination of probable cause increases significantly. The consequences of prolonged detention may be more serious than the interference occasioned by arrest. Pretrial confinement may imperil the suspect's job, interrupt his source of income, and impair his family relationships . . . Even pretrial release may be accompanied by burdensome conditions that effect a significant restraint of liberty . . . When the stakes are this high, the detached judgment of a neutral magistrate is essential if the Fourth Amendment is to furnish meaningful protection from unfounded interference with liberty. Accordingly, we hold that the Fourth Amendment requires a judicial determination of probable cause as a prerequisite to extended restraint of liberty following arrest.

The Court decided, in essence, that the prosecutor's decision to charge is not in itself enough to satisfy the probable cause requirement. However, the Court also noted that a probable cause hearing is *not* required after every arrest. An arrest with a warrant, as noted, need not be followed by a probable cause hearing. Likewise, when an arrest is based on a grand jury indictment, a probable cause hearing is not required, either. The logic for this is that the grand jury performs an investigative function, makes its probable cause determination, and then issues its indictment. Finally, if the detention in question is relatively short, such as when a preliminary hearing follows shortly after arrest, a probable cause hearing will not be required.

Procedural Issues Surrounding the Hearing

The lower court's decisions leading up to the Supreme Court's decision in *Gerstein* required that a probable cause hearing resemble an adversarial trial, complete with counsel, compulsory process, and the like. The Supreme Court reversed the lower courts' decisions as to these issues, declaring that the probable cause hearing is not a "critical stage" of the criminal process. In support of its decision, the Court observed:

> Criminal justice is already overburdened by the volume of cases and the complexities of our system. The processing of misdemeanors, in particular, and the early stages of prosecution generally are marked by delays that can seriously affect the quality of justice. A constitutional doctrine requiring adversary hearings for all persons detained pending trial could exacerbate the problem of pretrial delay.[5]

Thus, a probable cause hearing is generally much shorter than a preliminary hearing or a trial. It is primarily a procedural safeguard.

Timing of the Hearing

The Court, in *Gerstein*, required that if it is to be held, the probable cause hearing must take place "promptly after arrest." It did not define what was meant by *promptly*, but in *Riverside County v. McLaughlin*,[6] the Court offered some clarification. In a 5 to 4 decision, the Court held that a hearing that takes place within 48 hours of arrest conforms with Fourth Amendment requirements:

> In order to satisfy *Gerstein*'s promptness requirement, a jurisdiction that chooses to combine probable cause determinations with other pretrial proceedings must do so as soon as is reasonably feasible, but in no event later than 48 hours after arrest. Providing a probable cause determination within that time frame will, as a general matter, immunize such a jurisdiction from systemic challenges. Although a hearing within 48 hours may nonetheless violate *Gerstein* if the arrested individual can prove that his or her probable cause determination was delayed unreasonably, courts evaluating the reasonableness of a delay must allow a substantial degree of flexibility, taking into account the practical realities of pretrial procedures. Where an arrested individual does not receive a probable cause determination within 48 hours, the burden of proof shifts to the government to demonstrate the existence of a bona fide emergency or other extraordinary circumstance, which cannot include intervening weekends or the fact that in a particular case it may take longer to consolidate pretrial proceedings.[7]

Acceptable excuses for delay include "unavoidable delays in transporting arrested persons from one facility to another, handling late-night bookings where no magistrate is readily available, [and] obtaining the presence of an arresting officer who may be busy processing other suspects or securing the premises of an arrest."[8] Unacceptable reasons for delay, by contrast, include the need to gather additional evidence to support the arrest in hindsight and issues of bad faith, such as to inconvenience an individual and make him or her wait for no legitimate reason.

---

[5]Ibid., p. 122, n. 3.
[6]*Riverside County* v. *McLaughlin*, 500 U.S. 44 (1991).
[7]Ibid., p. 44.
[8]Ibid., p. 57.

YOUR DECISION

1. Conner Case was arrested for robbery. He was taken to the police station, booked, and placed in detention. The police department maintains a policy that arrestees may be detained in the city detention facility at the request of an investigatory officer without having formal charges filed against them. Persons who are so detained are said to be "on hold." The main reason for doing so is to stage a lineup, in which a witness or a complainant can view and identify the suspect. If the arrestee is suspected of committing multiple offenses, the police department will hold several lineups, extending the period of detention longer than usual. The average time for investigative hold is 26 hours if no charges are filed and 35 hours if charges are filed. Case was held for 35 hours. He is now suing pursuant to 42 U.S.C. Section 1983, claiming that the police violated his Fourth Amendment rights and denied him a prompt probable cause hearing. In particular, he claims that the only valid reasons for delaying a probable cause hearing are those associated with transporting arrestees to the police station, booking them into the jail, and filing charges. How should the court rule?

2. With probable cause, Officer Jones arrested three men for impersonating police officers. The men were brought to the police station at 4:30 A.M. and subsequently fingerprinted, photographed, and given breathalyzer tests. The test results showed that all three men were legally intoxicated, with blood-alcohol levels well above the legal limit. The police department maintains a policy that arrestees with blood-alcohol levels of over 0.05 cannot be interviewed until they are sober, so the three men were placed into custody. Eighteen hours later, after sobering up, they were interviewed. All charges against them were dropped following the interviews. The three men sued Officer Jones under Section 1983, arguing that they were denied a prompt probable cause hearing. How should the court rule?

Summary

- The pretrial process differs substantially across the United States. Some jurisdictions follow the procedures outlined in this chapter, in the order presented. Others follow the same basic procedures but in a different order. Still others combine various hearings into a single hearing or do not require them at all.

- The pretrial process always begins with an initial appearance. This is where, at a minimum, the accused is advised of the charges against him or her.

- In a misdemeanor case, the trial may take place at the initial appearance. Also, the accused may be advised of his or her privilege against self-incrimination as well as the right to appointed counsel, if he or she is indigent.

- If the defendant is arrested without a warrant, a separate court hearing may be held to determine whether probable cause to arrest existed. This determination can be made independent of any other hearing. The probable cause hearing, if required, needs to be held promptly after arrest, usually within 48 hours.

13.2   PRETRIAL RELEASE

Learning Objectives

- **Summarize bail and other types of pretrial release.**
- **Describe the criteria considered for pretrial release.**

CORE CONCEPTS

pretrial release One of several methods to release a defendant prior to his or her trial date.

bail A process by which a defendant pays a certain amount of money in order to be released from jail prior to his or her trial date.

Once a person has been arrested, the question as to whether he or she should be temporarily released while awaiting additional court proceedings (either via bail or on his or her own recognizance) invariably comes up. On the one hand, if the arrestee does not pose a significant risk of flight and has been arrested for a relatively minor offense, pretrial release seems a sensible approach. On the other hand, if the arrestee is likely to fail to appear in later proceedings, he or she should probably be jailed pending additional court proceedings.

A common mechanism for pretrial release is bail. Bail is a process by which a defendant pays a certain amount of money in order to be released from jail prior to his or her trial date. Defendants who appear for trial receive their money back. Those who fail to appear for trial forfeit the bail amount.

Criminal defendants do not have an absolute constitutional right to bail or any other type of pretrial release. The Eighth Amendment only states "Excessive bail shall not be required." This simply means that bail cannot be set ridiculously high. In capital cases, for example, bail has always been denied. Consider what the Supreme Court stated in *Carlson* v. *Landon*: "In England, [the Bail] clause has never been thought to accord a right to bail in all cases, but merely to provide that bail shall not be excessive in those cases where it is proper to grant bail. When this clause was carried over into our Bill of Rights, nothing was said that indicated any different concept."[9]

Critics of some courts' decisions to deny bail have argued that because the U.S. criminal justice system presumes innocence, everyone should be released. After all, a defendant cannot be considered guilty until the state proves his or her guilt beyond a reasonable doubt. However, in *Bell* v. *Wolfish*, the Supreme Court stated that the presumption of innocence is merely "a doctrine that allocates the burden of proof in criminal trials."[10]

It is also important to point out that the Eighth Amendment prohibition against excessive bail *has not* been incorporated to the states. For example, in *Murphy* v. *Hunt*,[11] a detainee sued under Section 1983 (see Chapter 10), claiming that his Eighth Amendment right was violated. The Supreme Court held that his suit was moot because he was convicted in Nebraska state court. This important decision,

---

[9]*Carlson* v. *Landon*, 342 U.S. 524 (1952), p. 545.

[10]*Bell* v. *Wolfish*, 441 U.S. 520 (1979), p. 533. Note that some states have preset bail schedules for low-level offenses. For these states, some of the following discussion is not applicable.

[11]*Murphy* v. *Hunt*, 455 U.S. 478 (1982).

coupled with the realization that the Eighth Amendment's excessive bail provision has not been incorporated, explains some of the discrepancies in bail decisions.

The Pretrial Release Hearing

The Constitution does not specify whether bail or another form of pretrial release should be set in a separate hearing, but numerous Court decisions seem to suggest a separate hearing is warranted. For example, in *Stack* v. *Boyle*, the Court stated that as part of the bail determination, the judge should consider "the nature and circumstances of the offense charged, the weight of the evidence against [the accused], [and] the financial ability of the defendant to give bail and the character of the defendant."[12] The Court also stated:

> Since the function of bail is limited, the fixing of bail for any individual defendant must be based upon standards relevant to the purpose of assuring the presence of that defendant. The traditional standards as expressed in the Federal Rules of Criminal Procedure ... are to be applied in each case to each defendant....It is not denied that bail for each petitioner has been fixed in a sum much higher than that usually imposed for offenses with like penalties and yet there has been no factual showing to justify such action in this case. The Government asks the courts to depart from the norm by assuming, without the introduction of evidence, that each petitioner is a pawn in a conspiracy and will, in obedience to a superior, flee the jurisdiction. To infer from the fact of indictment alone a need for bail in an unusually high amount is an arbitrary act. Such conduct would inject into our own system of government the very principles of totalitarianism which Congress was seeking to guard against in passing the statute under which petitioners have been indicted.[13]

Assuming a pretrial release hearing is required, it is also not clear whether a simple probable cause–type hearing is all that is needed or if a more adversarial proceeding is necessary. Since bail is set once charges have already been filed, it would seem that, at a minimum, counsel should be provided. In fact, in *United States* v. *Salerno*,[14] the Court concluded that a federal preventive detention statute that provided for counsel, evidence presentation, and cross-examination was acceptable, but it did not state whether such rights should be afforded to the accused in every pretrial release hearing. Thus, the question of what type of pretrial release hearing is required, if any, remains unanswered. In some situations (and in certain jurisdictions), the release decision is made during another hearing, such as the initial appearance.

The Pretrial Release Decision

The pretrial release decision has traditionally taken one of three forms. The first, and most common, results in release on bail. This is when the court collects a deposit from the individual being released in order to ensure that he or she will appear for

---

[12]*Stack* v. *Boyle*, 342 U.S. 1 (1951), p. 6, n. 3.
[13]Ibid., pp. 5–6.
[14]*United States* v. *Salerno*, 481 U.S. 739 (1987).

later hearings. Second, some arrestees are released on their own recognizance, which means they simply promise to show up when required. Finally, in recent years, the courts have adopted a policy of preventive detention for certain individuals, which involves a calculation as to the arrestee's level of dangerousness and flight risk. Release is denied to those individuals who are likely to pose a threat to others or not likely to appear at their scheduled hearings.

Release on Bail

Pretrial release with bail is a common practice. Indeed, 18 U.S.C. Section 3142 provides that "upon all arrests in criminal cases, bail shall be admitted, except where the punishment may be death." Most states have adopted similar language in their constitutions. California's constitution, for example, provides that "all persons shall be bailable by sufficient sureties, unless for capital offenses when the proof is evidence or the presumption great."[15] There is variability from state to state, however, because, once again, the Eighth Amendment's excessive bail provision has not been incorporated to the states through the due process clause of the Fourteenth Amendment.

The bail decision is sometimes problematic. More often than not, a judge sets bail according to the nature of the offense in question, not according to the accused's ability to pay.[16] The frequent result of this is that indigent defendants—no matter what they are accused of—languish in jail cells until their court dates because they cannot afford to post bail.

bail bond agent A professional who posts the defendant's bail in exchange for a fee.

In response to many defendants' inability to post bail, the professional bail bond agent has stepped in.[17] These individuals collect a fee from the accused, usually a percentage of bail, and then post a bond so the accused can be released. If the accused shows up at trial, the agent collects his or her fee and gets his or her money back from the court. If the accused fails to show up, then the agent loses the amount posted. In order to avoid such an eventuality, bail bonds agents employ *bounty hunters*, whose job is to catch the accused and bring him or her before the court. There is a misperception, however, that bail bonds agents can with impunity do whatever it takes to apprehend those who "skip" bail. Indeed, in response to concerns that such agents have been given too much

When defendants "jump bail", bail bond agents employ bounty hunters to retrieve the accused.

© Peter Jordan/Alamy

---

[15]Cal. Const. Art. I, Section 6.
[16]See, for example, M. Paulsen, "Pre-Trial Release in the United States," *Columbia Law Review*, Vol. 66 (1966), pp. 109–125, 113.
[17]Not all states have bail bonds agents.

(a) Any [bail bond agent], desiring to [apprehend] his [bond recipient] and after notifying the [bond recipient's] attorney, if the [bond recipient] is represented by an attorney, in a manner provided by Rule 21a, Texas Rules of Civil Procedure, of the [bail bond agent's] intention to surrender the [bond recipient], may file an affidavit of such intention before the court or magistrate before which the prosecution is pending. The affidavit must state:

(1) the court and cause number of the case;

(2) the name of the defendant;

(3) the offense with which the defendant is charged;

(4) the date of the bond;

(5) the cause for the [apprehension]; and

(6) that notice of the [bail bond agent's] intention to surrender the [bond recipient] has been given as required by this subsection.

(b) If the court or magistrate finds that there is cause for the [bail bond agent] to [apprehend] his [bond recipient], the court shall issue a warrant of arrest for the [bond recipient]. It is an affirmative defense to any liability on the bond that:

(1) the court or magistrate refused to issue a warrant of arrest for the principal; and

(2) after the refusal to issue the warrant the [bond recipient] failed to appear.

(c) If the court or magistrate before whom the prosecution is pending is not available, the [bail bond agent] may deliver the affidavit to any other magistrate in the county and that magistrate, on a finding of cause for the [bail bond agent] to [apprehend] his [bond recipient], shall issue a warrant of arrest for the [bond recipient].

(d) An arrest warrant issued under this article shall be issued to the sheriff of the county in which the case is pending, and a copy of the warrant shall be issued to the [bail bond agent] or his agent.

(e) An arrest warrant issued under this article may be executed by a peace officer, a security officer, or a private investigator licensed in this state.

Figure 13.1

Example of Bail Bonds Agent Rearrest Procedures

Source: Adapted from Texas Code of Criminal Procedures, Chapter 17, Article 17.19 (2002).

authority, some states have adopted legislation to restrict their activities. Texas is perhaps most restrictive. Figure 13.1 reprints a Texas statute that sets forth the procedures bail bonds agents must follow to rearrest those who skip bail.

It is important to note an important flaw inherent in the bail bonds agent system. The problem is that the agents, not the courts, gain a certain degree of power. Regardless of what amount the court sets as bail, bonds agents can then decide who gets released or who stays in jail based on the accused's ability to pay. Those who can pay the fee effectively buy their freedom, if only temporarily. Those who cannot pay stay in jail. The courts sit on the sidelines, essentially, while the whole bail bonds process plays out. As described in the decision for *Pannell* v. *United States*:

Certainly the professional bondsman system as used in this District is odious at best. The effect of such a system is that the professional bondsmen hold the keys to the jail in their pockets. They determine for whom they will act as surety—who in their judgment is a good risk. The bad risks, in the bondsmen's judgment, and the ones who are unable to pay the bondsmen's fees, remain in jail. The court and the commissioner are relegated to the relatively unimportant chore of fixing the amount of bail. The result of this system in the District of Columbia is that most defendants, for months on end, languish in jail unable to make bond awaiting disposition of their cases. Instead of being allowed the opportunity of obtaining worthwhile employment to support their families, and perhaps to pay at least in part for their defense, almost 90 per cent of the defendants proceed in forma pauperis, thus casting an unfair burden on the members of the bar of this community who are required to represent these defendants without pay.[18]

Release on One's Own Recognizance

release on recognizance (ROR) The accused is released with the assumption that he or she will show up for scheduled court hearings.

Even though release on bail is the most common form of pretrial release, the courts have experimented with releasing people on their own recognizance. **Release on recognizance (ROR)** means that the accused is released with the assumption that he or she will show up for scheduled court hearings. Naturally, then, this method of pretrial release is reserved for those individuals who pose a minimal risk of flight.

New York City's Manhattan Bail Project was the first significant effort to explore the possibilities of ROR. This program, administered by the Vera Institute, focused on indigent defendants who, according to carefully set criteria, posed a minimal flight risk. Among the criteria considered were previous convictions, the nature of the offense, whether the accused was employed, and whether the accused had roots in the community (e.g., a family to go back to). The program was a resounding success: Only 1.6% of those individuals recommended for ROR intentionally failed to appear at court.

The results of the Manhattan Bail Project prompted other cities around the United States to adopt similar programs. And in 1984, Congress passed the federal Bail Reform Act, which provided that any person charged with a noncapital offense "be ordered released pending trial on his personal recognizance or upon the execution of an unsecured appearance bond in an amount specified by the judicial officer, unless the officer determines . . . that such a release will not reasonably assure the appearance of the person as required."[19]

An important feature of this new legislation was that bail was to be considered only as one of many options to ensure the accused's appearance at trial. Among the other options were restrictions on travel and association, along with other conditions that would ensure the appearance of the accused.[20] The Bail Reform Act also provided that when bail was to be used, the money should be deposited with the court, not with a bail bonds agent.

The Bail Reform Act further provided that

> the judge shall...take into account the available information concerning: the nature and the circumstances of the offense charged, the weight of evidence against the accused, the accused's family ties, employment, financial resources, character and mental condition, the length of his residence in the community, his record of convictions, and his record of appearances at court proceedings or of flight to avoid prosecution or failure to appear at court proceedings.[21]

This is in stark contrast to the notion that judges simply consider the nature of the offense in setting bail.

While the federal government and many states still release people on their own recognizance, this practice is not regularly relied on for serious offenses. In fact,

---

[18]*Pannell* v. *United States*, 320 F.2d 698 (D.C.Cir. 1963), p. 699.
[19]18 U.S.C. Sections 3146–3152.
[20]18 U.S.C. Section 3146(a).
[21]18 U.S.C Section 3146(b).

when the offense in question is serious and the accused presents a significant risk of flight, bail may be altogether denied, as the following subsection attests.

Preventive Detention: Denying Pretrial Release

preventive detention The act of denying bail to certain defendants who are either dangerous or pose a high flight risk.

Growing concern over crimes committed by defendants out on pretrial release prompted some reforms. In 1970, for example, the District of Columbia passed the first **preventive detention** statute, which authorized denial of bail to dangerous persons charged with certain offenses for up to 60 days.[22] Then, Congress passed the federal Bail Reform Act of 1984,[23] which authorized judges to revoke pretrial release for firearms possession, failure to comply with curfew, and failure to comply with other conditions of release. The act also permitted detention for up to ten days of an individual who "may flee or pose a danger to any other person or the community."[24]

Somewhat controversially, the Bail Reform Act of 1984 permitted pretrial detention for *more than* ten days of certain individuals. Thus, according to the act, if it is deemed that no pretrial release condition "will reasonably assure the appearance of the person as required and the safety of any other person and the community," then indefinite detention is acceptable. For a detention of this nature to conform to Fourth and Eighth Amendment restrictions, a hearing must be held to determine whether the case "involves a serious risk that the person will flee; [or] a serious risk that the person will obstruct or attempt to obstruct justice, or threaten, injure, or intimidate, a prospective witness or jury."[25]

Criteria for Release

As indicated already, the Constitution does not guarantee the right to bail. Some people are denied bail, and others are granted bail. What criteria influence a judge's decision? Three factors are typically considered: (1) the accused's flight risk, (2) the level of dangerousness of the accused, and (3) the accused's financial status.

Flight Risk

In *Stack* v. *Boyle*, the Supreme Court declared that the purpose of bail is to ensure the accused's appearance at trial:

> Like the ancient practice of securing the oaths of responsible persons to stand as sureties for the accused, the modern practice of requiring a bail bond or the deposit of a sum of money subject to forfeiture serves as additional assurance of the presence of an accused. . . . Since the function of bail is limited, the fixing of bail for any individual defendant must be based upon standards relevant to the purpose of assuring the presence of that defendant.[26]

---

[22]D.C. Code 1970 Section 23-1322.
[23]18 U.S.C. Sections 3141–3150.
[24]18 U.S.C. Section 3142(d).
[25]18 U.S.C. Section 3142(f).
[26]*Stack* v. *Boyle*, 342 U.S. 1 (1951), p. 5.

This does not mean, though, that a judge can set an unrealistic bail amount, in light of the Eighth Amendment's admonition:

> Admission to bail always involves a risk that the accused will take flight. That is a calculated risk which the law takes as the price of our system of justice. . . . In allowance of bail, the duty of the judge is to reduce the risk by fixing an amount reasonably calculated to hold the accused available for trial and its consequence. But the judge is not free to make the sky the limit, because the Eighth Amendment to the Constitution says: "Excessive bail shall not be required."[27]

In short, a delicate balance needs to be struck to ensure the accused's appearance at trial. Bail should be set at an amount designed to minimize the risk of flight, yet the amount set should not be so much that the accused cannot reasonably afford to pay it, either by cash or by bond.

Dangerousness

Aside from the obvious risk of flight, some defendants are particularly dangerous individuals. Thus, the courts sometimes see fit either to deny bail or to set the amount relatively high because of perceived dangerousness. In *United States* v. *Salerno*, the Supreme Court dealt with a challenge to the Bail Reform Act of 1984 that, among other things, dangerousness cannot be considered. In the Court's words:

> Nothing in the text of the Bail Clause [of the Eighth Amendment] limits permissible government considerations solely to questions of flight. The only arguable substantive limitation of the Bail Clause is that the Government's proposed conditions of release or detention not be "excessive" in light of the perceived evil. . . . [W]hen the government has admitted that its only interest is in preventing flight, bail must be set by a court at a sum designed to ensure that goal, and no more. . . . We believe that when Congress has mandated detention on the basis of a compelling interest other than prevention of flight, as it has here, the Eighth Amendment does not require release on bail.[28]

The issue of dangerousness, as it pertains to the bail decision, also came up in the case of *Schall* v. *Martin*.[29] There, the Supreme Court upheld a statute that provided for detention of a juvenile who posed a serious risk of committing a crime while on release. The statute was criticized as essentially amounting to punishment without trial, but the Court decided that *punishment* only exists when the government's *intent* is to punish. And since the purpose of the state's detention policy was not to punish but rather to protect the community from a dangerous individual, it was deemed constitutional. Of course, given the problems inherent in predicting criminal behavior, the Court's argument is somewhat specious.

Financial Status

The courts usually take into account the accused's financial status in making a bail decision. Failure to do so can lead to irrational bail determinations. For example, if

---

[27]Ibid., p. 8.
[28]*United States* v. *Salerno*, 481 U.S. 739 (1987), p. 754.
[29]*Schall* v. *Martin*, 467 U.S. 253 (1984).

bail is set at a fixed amount, a poor individual will have a considerably more difficult time coming up with the required funds than a wealthy individual. Perhaps more important, if the wealthy individual views the amount as a "drop in the bucket," then he or she may not be motivated to show up for trial.

Surprisingly, bail can be denied simply because the accused is unable to pay it. In *Schilb* v. *Kuebel*,[30] the Supreme Court took it upon itself to decide on the constitutionality of a state statute that provided that a criminal defendant who was not released on his or her own recognizance could (1) deposit 10% of the amount of set bail with the court, 10% of which would be forfeited to the court as *bail bonds costs*, or (2) pay the full amount of bail, all of which would be refunded if the accused showed up at court. The defendant argued that the statute unfairly targeted indigent individuals because they were forced to choose the first option. However, the Supreme Court upheld the statute because "[i]t should be obvious that the poor man's real hope and avenue for relief is the personal recognizance provision."[31] Furthermore, in the words of the Court, "[I]t is by no means clear that [the second option, paying the full amount,] is more attractive to the affluent defendant."[32]

Treatment of Pretrial Detainees

The Supreme Court has dealt with several cases alleging unconstitutional conditions at pretrial detention facilities. For example, in *Bell* v. *Wolfish*,[33] the Court upheld several of the rules promulgated by New York City's Metropolitan Correctional Center (MCC), including rules prohibiting inmates from receiving books from entities other than publishers, bookstores, and book clubs, as well as outside packages. The Court also upheld unannounced searches of living quarters but was careful to state that when such prohibitions are intended to punish (i.e., instead of to serve some legitimate governmental purpose, such as to ensure the safety and security of inmates), they can violate due process. Quoting the Court:

> [If] a particular condition or restriction of pretrial detention is reasonably related to a legitimate governmental objective, it does not, without more, amount to "punishment." Conversely, if a restriction or condition is not reasonably related to a legitimate goal—if it is arbitrary or purposeless—a court permissibly may infer that the purpose of the governmental action is punishment that may not constitutionally be inflicted upon detainees *qua* detainees.[34]

In one case, a pretrial detainee argued that unannounced searches of his cell violated the Fourth Amendment. The Court concluded, however, in *Hudson* v. *Palmer*, that prisoners do not enjoy a reasonable expectation of privacy in their cells:

> A prisoner has no reasonable expectation of privacy in his prison cell entitling him to the protection of the Fourth Amendment against unreasonable searches. While prisoners enjoy many protections of the Constitution that are not fundamentally inconsistent with imprisonment itself or incompatible with the objectives of incarceration,

[30]*Schilb* v. *Kuebel*, 404 U.S. 357 (1971).
[31]Ibid., p. 369.
[32]Ibid., p. 370.
[33]*Bell* v. *Wolfish*, 441 U.S. 520 (1979).
[34]Ibid., p. 539.

imprisonment carries with it the circumscription or loss of many rights as being necessary to accommodate the institutional needs and objectives of prison facilities, particularly internal security and safety. It would be impossible to accomplish the prison objectives of preventing the introduction of weapons, drugs, and other contraband into the premises if inmates retained a right of privacy in their cells. The unpredictability that attends random searches of cells renders such searches perhaps the most effective weapon of the prison administrator in the fight against the proliferation of weapons, drugs, and other contraband. A requirement that random searches be conducted pursuant to an established plan would seriously undermine the effectiveness of this weapon.[35]

Furthermore, "society would insist that the prisoner's expectation of privacy always yield to what must be considered the paramount interest in institutional security."[36] Prison guards, then, can seize "any articles which, in their view, disserve legitimate institutional interests."[37]

YOUR DECISION

1. The Bail Reform Act of 1984 provided that judges can deny bail to certain individuals charged with specific crimes and after finding that "no condition or combination of conditions [attaching to release] will reasonably assure the appearance of the person as required and the safety of any other person and the community" (18 U.S.C. Section 3142[e]). Marty Corelli is a drug kingpin charged with serious narcotics offenses and is presumed to be a significant flight risk. Accordingly, the judge denies bail to Corelli, thereby requiring him to remain in jail until his trial. Is this action constitutional?

2. Several pretrial detainees at the county jail brought a class action in federal district court against the county sheriff and other officials, claiming that the jail's policy of denying pretrial detainees contact visits with their spouses, relatives, children, and friends violates due process. Should pretrial detainees be constitutionally entitled to contact visits of this nature? If so, why?

Summary

- After the probable cause hearing (if applicable) is the pretrial release determination. The accused may be released on bail, in which case he or she deposits a certain amount of money with the court (possibly through a bail bonds agent) as an incentive to show up for later hearings.
- Failure to show up will result in, among other things, forfeiture of the bail money.
- A defendant can also be released on his or her own recognizance (ROR).
- At the other extreme, a defendant who is presumed to pose a significant risk of flight may be held without bail. This tactic is known as preventive detention.
- Three different criteria are considered in making the pretrial release determination: the accused's (1) flight risk, (2) level of dangerousness, and (3) financial status.

---

[35] *Hudson v. Palmer*, 468 U.S. 517 (1984), p. 517.
[36] Ibid., p. 528.
[37] Ibid., p. 528, n. 8.

MODULE

13.3   PRELIMINARY HEARING AND ARRAIGNMENT

Learning Objectives

- **Explain the purpose and process of the preliminary hearing.**
- **Explain the purpose and the process of arraignment.**

CORE CONCEPTS

preliminary hearing A hearing that serves as a check on the prosecutor's charging decision.

The **preliminary hearing** is to be distinguished from the initial appearance, the probable cause hearing, and the pretrial release hearing. It almost always takes place after one of these hearings as well as after the charging decision. The preliminary hearing is designed as a screening mechanism to eliminate criminal cases without a significant factual and legal basis. According to the decision in *Thies* v. *State*, the preliminary hearing is intended to prevent "hasty, malicious, improvident, and oppressive prosecutions" and to ensure that "there are substantial grounds upon which a prosecution may be based."[38] Finally, the preliminary hearing resembles a criminal trial in that it is usually adversarial.

Preliminary Hearing Rules

Just as the Constitution does not require a pretrial release hearing, neither is a preliminary hearing required. This was the decision reached in *Lem Woon* v. *Oregon*[39] and reaffirmed in *Gerstein* v. *Pugh*.[40] Thus, it is up to each state to determine if such a hearing is warranted.

Fortunately, most states, as well as the federal government, require preliminary hearings, at least to a certain extent. Whether a preliminary hearing is required typically depends on a jurisdiction's method of filing criminal charges. In grand jury indictment jurisdictions (i.e., those that *require* that charges be filed in the form of a grand jury indictment), if the prosecutor secures an indictment within a specified time period, no preliminary hearing is required. However, if a prosecutor proceeds by **information**, then the defendant will usually be entitled to a preliminary hearing before the charges are filed.

information The prosecutor's formal charging document, and the alternative to a grand jury indictment, that informs the defendant of what crime he or she is being charged with.

Whether a jurisdiction proceeds by indictment or information has important implications concerning the defendant's rights. As discussed further in Chapter 14, the defendant does *not* enjoy the right to counsel during a grand jury proceeding. The defendant does not even enjoy the right to challenge the state's case. In a preliminary hearing, however, both rights exist. Thus, a zealous prosecutor in a jurisdiction that provides for either an indictment or an information-charging decision may

---

[38]*Thies* v. *State* (178 Wis. 98 [1922]), p. 103.
[39]*Lem Woon* v. *Oregon* (229 U.S. 586 [1913]).
[40]*Gerstein* v. *Pugh*, 420 U.S. 103 (1975).

opt for indictment because the accused will enjoy fewer rights. Of course, this issue may be moot because accused individuals can and often do waive their right to a preliminary hearing.

The Probable Cause Requirement

Assuming a preliminary hearing is required, the prosecutor has the burden of proving that the case should be *bound over* (i.e., handed over) to a grand jury or go to trial. The standard of proof is *probable cause*. Invariably, this step is confused with the probable cause hearing. The two hearings can be distinguished as follows: A probable cause hearing dwells on the justification to arrest, whereas a preliminary hearing dwells on whether probable cause exists to proceed with a trial. This is a critical distinction and is often responsible for holding separate probable cause and preliminary hearings in certain states.

The reason for setting probable cause as the appropriate standard for a preliminary hearing is that setting a *higher* standard would essentially make trial pointless. To require proof beyond a reasonable doubt, for example, would make holding a later criminal trial redundant. On the other hand, some people favor having more proof than probable cause because once a probable cause hearing has taken place, the preliminary hearing seems somewhat redundant. To minimize some of the confusion, one court observed that "probable cause to arrest does not automatically mean that the Commonwealth has sufficient competent legal evidence to justify the costs both to the defendant and to the Commonwealth of a full trial."[41]

Basically, the prosecutor needs to convince the judge that there is enough evidence to proceed with a trial. More specifically, there must be enough evidence to make a judge or jury contemplate which case is more convincing: that of the prosecution or the defense. If it is clear that the state has no case but perhaps had probable cause for arrest, the court will order that the would-be defendant be released.

Procedural Issues

Since a preliminary hearing is adversarial in nature, it seems sensible that the right to counsel should apply. According to the Supreme Court, in *Coleman* v. *Alabama*,[42] it does, and the state must provide counsel if the accused is indigent. The Court declared that the preliminary hearing is a critical stage of the criminal process: "Plainly the guiding hand of counsel at the preliminary hearing is essential to protect the indigent accused against an erroneous and improper prosecution."[43]

Evidence procedures in a preliminary hearing are markedly different than those in a criminal trial. First, the *Federal Rules of Criminal Procedure* allow hearsay evidence in preliminary hearings, though not explicitly.[44] By contrast, *hearsay evidence* (i.e., what one person previously heard and then repeats while testifying in court) is

---

[41]*Myers* v. *Commonwealth*, 363 Mass. 843 [1973], p. 849.
[42]*Coleman* v. *Alabama* (399 U.S. 1 [1970]).
[43]Ibid., p. 9.
[44]The hearsay language was removed from the *Federal Rules* in 2002, but the Advisory Committee notes make it clear that hearsay can still be admitted. See http://www.law.cornell.edu/rules/frcrmp/NRule5_1.htm (accessed November 5, 2008).

restricted in a criminal trial. Also, the exclusionary rule does not technically apply in preliminary hearings. Actually, it is not so much that the rule does not apply but rather that the preliminary hearing is an inappropriate stage of the criminal process in which to object to evidence. As the *Federal Rules of Criminal Procedure* also state, the defendant "may not object to evidence on the ground that it was unlawfully acquired."[45] (Note that the *Federal Rules of Criminal Procedure* apply to federal courts, not state courts. So some states may maintain different procedures.)

Another procedural matter in the preliminary hearing concerns the right to cross-examine witnesses as well as to use compulsory process to require their appearance. While these rights exist at criminal trials, preliminary hearings restrict them somewhat. In fact, the Supreme Court stated that there is no constitutional right to cross-examine at the preliminary hearing.[46] The court has discretion over the extent of cross-examination, but the bulk of it is reserved for trial.

Some have expressed concern that too much cross-examination at a preliminary hearing may turn it into a full-blown criminal trial. But one court has stated that "past experience indicates that trial strategy usually prevents such a result as both the prosecution and the defense wish to withhold as much of their case as possible."[47] Furthermore, "defense tactics usually mitigate against putting the defendant on the stand or presenting exculpatory testimony at the preliminary hearing unless defense counsel believes this evidence is compelling enough to overcome the prosecution's case."[48]

The Arraignment

Once a person has been formally charged, he or she will be arraigned. The purpose of the **arraignment** is to formally notify the defendant of the charge lodged against him or her. Also at the arraignment, the defendant enters one of three pleas: (1) **guilty**, (2) **not guilty**, or (3) *nolo contendere*. A plea of guilty is an admission by the defendant of every allegation in the indictment or information. Such a plea may be entered for a number of reasons. For example, the defendant may simply elect to be honest and admit responsibility. The defendant may also plead guilty after having made a plea agreement with the prosecution. (Plea bargaining is covered in Chapter 14.)

A plea of not guilty is fairly self-explanatory. The defendant formally contends that he or she did not commit the crime in question. A plea of not guilty will result in a full-blown criminal trial, especially for a serious crime. Finally, a plea of *nolo contendere* means "I do not desire to contest the action." It resembles a guilty plea but is different in the sense that it may not be used against the defendant in any later civil litigation that arises from the acts that led to the criminal charge. Also, in some jurisdictions, if the defendant enters a plea of *nolo contendere*, the court may not ask the defendant whether he or she committed the crime in question. But with a guilty plea, the defendant is required to allocute. **Allocution** is when the defendant explains

arraignment A hearing in which the defendant is formally notified of the charge lodged against him or her. The defendant also enters on of three pleas: (1) guilty, (2) not guilty, or (3) *nolo contendere.*

guilty A plea in which the defendant claims responsibility for the crime with which he or she has been charged.

not guilty A plea in which the defendant does not claim responsibility for the crime with which he or she has been charged. A not guilty plea is not the same as a plea of innocent. There is no plea of innocent.

nolo contendere A plea similar to guilty with a literal meaning of "I do not desire to contest the action."

allocution When the defendant explains to the judge exactly what he or she did and why. The defendant is usually required to allocate when he or she pleads guilty.

---

[45] *Federal Rules of Criminal Procedure*, Rule 5.1(e).
[46] *Goldsby* v. *United States*, 160 U.S. 70 (1895).
[47] *Myers* v. *Commonwealth*, 363 Mass. 843 (1973).
[48] Ibid., pp. 856–857.

to the judge exactly what he or she did and why. The allocution is documented in court records and can be used against the defendant in related civil proceedings.

Summary of Pretrial Proceedings

So far, the discussion has distinguished among five potential pretrial proceedings: (1) the initial appearance, (2) the probable cause hearing, (3) the pretrial release hearing, (4) the preliminary hearing, and (5) the arraignment. The initial appearance usually always takes place, regardless of the method of arrest or even of the charges in question, but it is not constitutionally required. Indeed, for a misdemeanor, the trial may take place at this stage.

The probable cause hearing is also not *required* by the Constitution, unless a warrantless arrest occurs, in which case a judge must make the probable cause determination. Nevertheless, a probable cause determination needs to be made at some stage of the criminal process. If the arrest is by warrant, the hearing is not necessary. If the arrest is warrantless, then a probable cause hearing is necessary but only if a preliminary hearing is not set to take place immediately. Also, if the arrest is premised on a grand jury indictment, a probable cause hearing will not be necessary. In short, the purpose of the probable cause hearing is to avoid unnecessarily lengthy detention unsupported by probable cause.

A few court decisions seem to suggest that a separate pretrial release hearing is required, but the Supreme Court has offered no clarification on this matter. And as a practical matter, it is sometimes worthwhile to make the bail decision in another hearing, such as the initial appearance. Today, whether a pretrial release hearing is required hinges on the jurisdiction in question and the nature of the offense.

Finally, the preliminary hearing is required but only in limited circumstances and for certain offenses—usually felonies. If a prosecutor obtains a grand jury indictment within a short period of time, a preliminary hearing may not be necessary. On the other hand, if the prosecutor proceeds with information, then a preliminary hearing may be required. Once a person has been charged with a crime, he or she will be arraigned. At the arraignment, the defendant will be notified of the charges against him or her and be allowed to enter a formal plea of guilty, not guilty, or *nolo contendere*.

YOUR DECISION

1. Assume that a jurisdiction maintains a policy that people charged with misdemeanors will not be given preliminary hearings. Is such a restriction constitutional?
2. A reporter announces on the evening news that John Smith, who was charged with murdering his wife and their young daughter, pleaded innocent to the charges. What, if anything, is wrong with this statement?

Summary

- The preliminary hearing differs from the other hearings already discussed in that it is intended to be a check on the prosecution's charging decision.
- The standard of proof for a preliminary hearing is probable cause, not proof beyond a reasonable doubt as required in a criminal trial.

- A preliminary hearing is generally not required if (1) the defendant waives it or (2) the prosecutor proceeds by indictment. In the latter instance, the grand jury essentially serves as an appropriate check on the charging decision.

- After the preliminary hearing (or grand jury indictment), the arraignment is held. At this stage, the defendant is formally notified of the charges against him or her. In addition, he or she enters a plea of guilty, not guilty, or *nolo contendere*.

MODULE

13.4   DISCOVERY

Learning Objectives
- **Summarize the discovery process.**
- **Explain the prosecution's duty to preserve evidence.**

CORE CONCEPTS

Contrary to the story Hollywood tells, it is rarely the case that prosecutors and defense attorneys are mortal enemies or that one side springs surprise evidence on the other side. Instead, criminal (as well as civil) trials in the United States are carefully choreographed events with few unpredictable twists and turns. In fact, as many a litigator will attest, criminal trials are relatively boring and predictable. Even the most celebrated of criminal trial can put the most attentive of observers to sleep at times.

Trials in this country are rarely exciting for several reasons. First, most prosecutors and defense attorneys are not great orators. They are *portrayed* as such in the movies and on television, but reality is much different. Prosecutors and defense attorneys are, for the most part, normal people doing difficult jobs for what many would describe as less than stellar pay. And second, given the process of *discovery*, each side *knows* what evidence the other side will present, with few exceptions.

discovery The process by which each party to a case learns of the evidence that the opposition will present.

Discovery is the process by which each party to a case learns of the evidence that the opposition will present. The *Federal Rules of Criminal Procedure* provide that the defendant may, upon request, *discover* from the prosecution (1) any written statements or transcriptions of oral statements made by the defendant that are in the prosecution's possession; (2) the defendant's prior criminal record; and (3) documents, photographs, tangible items, results from physical and mental evaluations, and other forms of real evidence considered *material* to the prosecution's case.[49] Evidence is considered *material* if it is consequential to the case or, more simply, capable of influencing the outcome of the case. If the defense requests items in the second or third categories, then the prosecution will be granted *reciprocal discovery*, where it learns of the defense's evidence. Relevant portions of Rule 16 are reprinted in Figure 13.2.

---

[49] *Federal Rules of Criminal Procedure*, Rule 16.

(a) **Government's Disclosure.**

   (1) Information Subject to Disclosure.

      (A) *Defendant's Oral Statement.*

         Upon a defendant's request, the government must disclose lo the defendant the substance of any relevant oral statement made by the defendant, before or after arrest, in response to interrogation by a person the defendant knew was a government agent if the government intends to use the statement at trial.

      (B) *Defendant's Written or Recorded Statement.*

         Upon a defendant's request, the government must disclose to the defendant, and make available for inspection, copying, or photographing, all of the following:

           (i) any relevant written or recorded statement by the defendant if:

              • the statement is within the government's possession, custody, or control; and

              • the attorney for the government knows—or through due diligence could know—that the statement exists;

           (ii) the portion of any written record containing the substance of any relevant oral statement made before or after arrest if the defendant made the statement in response to interrogation by a person the defendant knew was a government agent; and

           (iii) the defendant's recorded testimony before a grand jury relating to the charged offense.

      (C) *Organizational Defendant.*

         Upon a defendant's request, if the defendant is an organization, the government must disclose to the defendant any statement described in Rule 16(a)(1)(A) and (B) if the government contends that the person making the statement:

           (i) was legally able to bind the defendant regarding the subject of the statement because of that person's position as the defendant's director, officer, employee, or agent; or

           (ii) was personally involved in the alleged conduct constituting the offense and was legally able to bind the defendant regarding that conduct because of that person's position as the defendant's director, officer, employee, or agent.

      (D) *Defendant's Prior Record.*

         Upon a defendant's request, the government must furnish the defendant with a copy of the defendant's prior criminal record that is within the government's possession, custody, or control if the attorney for the government knows—or through due diligence could know—that the record exists.

      (E) *Documents and Objects.*

         Upon a defendant's request, the government must permit the defendant to inspect and to copy or photograph books, papers, documents, data, photographs, tangible objects, buildings or places, or copies or portions of any of these items, if the item is within the government's possession, custody, or control and:

           (i) the item is material to preparing the defense;

           (ii) the government intends to use the item in its case-in-chief at trial; or

           (iii) the item was obtained from or belongs to the defendant.

      (F) *Reports of Examinations and Tests.*

         Upon a defendant's request, the government must permit a defendant to inspect and to copy or photograph the results or reports of any physical or mental examination and of any scientific test or experiment if:

           (i) the item is within the government's possession, custody, or control;

           (ii) the attorney for the government knows—or through due diligence could know—that the item exists; and

           (iii) the item is material to preparing the defense or the government intends to use the item in its case-in-chief at trial.

      (G) *Expert Witnesses.*

         At the defendant's request, the government must give to the defendant a written summary of any testimony that the government intends to use under Rules 702, 703, or 705 of the Federal Rules of

Figure 13.2

Types of Discovery under Rule 16

Source: Federal Rules of Criminal Procedure, Rule 16. Available online: http://www.law.cornell.edu/rules/frcrmp/Rule16.htm (accessed February 16, 2011).

Evidence during its case-in-chief at trial. If the government requests discovery under subdivision (b)(1)(C) (ii) and the defendant complies, the government must, at the defendant's request, give to the defendant a written summary of testimony that the government intends to use under Rules 702, 703, or 705 of the Federal Rules of Evidence as evidence at trial on the issue of the defendant's mental condition. The summary provided under this subparagraph must describe the witness's opinions, the bases and reasons for those opinions, and the witness's qualifications.

(b) **Defendant's Disclosure.**

(1) *Information Subject to Disclosure.*

(A) *Documents and Objects.*

If a defendant requests disclosure under <u>Rule 16(a)(1)(E)</u> and the government complies, then the defendant must permit the government, upon request, to inspect and to copy or photograph books, papers, documents, data, photographs, tangible objects, buildings or places, or copies or portions of any of these items if:

(i) the item is within the defendant's possession, custody, or control; and

(ii) the defendant intends to use the item in the defendant's case-in-chief at trial.

(B) *Reports of Examinations and Tests.*

If a defendant requests disclosure under <u>Rule 16(a)(1)(F)</u> and the government complies, the defendant must permit the government, upon request, to inspect and to copy or photograph the results or reports of any physical or mental examination and of any scientific test or experiment if:

(i) the item is within the defendant's possession, custody, or control; and

(ii) the defendant intends to use the item in the defendant's case-in-chief at trial, or intends to call the witness who prepared the report and the report relates to the witness's testimony.

(C) *Expert Witnesses.*

The defendant musts, at the government's request, give to the government a written summary of any testimony that the defendant intends to use under Rules 702, 703, or 705 of the Federal Rules of Evidence as evidence at trail, if:

(i) the defendant requests disclosure under subdivision (a)(1)(G) and the government complies; or

(ii) the defendant has given notice under Rule <u>12.2(b)</u> if an intent to present expert testimony on the defendant's mental condition.

This summary must describe the witness's opinions, the bases ands reasons for those opinions, and the witness's qualifications[.]

(c) **Continuing Duty to Disclose.**

A party who discovers additional evidence or material before or during trial must promptly disclose its existence to the other party or the court if:

(1) the evidence or material is subject to discovery or inspection under this rule; and

(2) the other party previously requested, or the court ordered, its production.

Figure 13.2

(Continued)

Rule 16 of the *Federal Rules of Criminal Procedure* seems to permit a great deal of discovery, but it is actually restrictive. Several states permit even more discovery, such as the names and addresses of all persons known to have any information concerning the case. This means that the prosecution must provide the defense with a list of *all* individuals likely to give testimony at trial—and vice versa.

Discovery ends where strategy begins. That is, while both sides are given great latitude in terms of learning what evidence the opposition intends to use, strategy does not need to be shared. For example, the method of argument that the prosecution wishes to use in order to convince the jury of a particular fact is not subject to discovery. Similarly, the order in which the defense seeks to call witnesses need not be communicated to the prosecution. Strategy is also referred to as *work product*. Work product is not part of the discovery process.

The sections that follow focus on discovery by the prosecution, discovery by the defense, and constitutional issues raised in the discovery process. Be reminded that, consistent with the title of this chapter, discovery is part of the *pretrial process*. It takes place in the hours and days leading up to the criminal trial. But if, for example, a new witness becomes available during the course of a trial, then discovery can take place later in the criminal process, as well.

Discovery by the Prosecution

Discovery by the prosecution is relatively limited because of the constitutional rights enjoyed by criminal defendants. For example, the defense cannot be compelled to provide the prosecution with incriminating information, particularly in the form of statements and admissions. The scope of prosecutorial discovery has been addressed repeatedly in the courts via the Fifth and Sixth Amendments.

Fifth Amendment Restrictions

What if the defense wishes to present an alibi at trial or to assert a defense to criminal liability? Should the prosecutor be permitted to discover this information? The Supreme Court faced the alibi issue in *Williams v. Florida*.[50] Florida had a *notice of alibi statute*, which provided that the defendant had to permit discovery of alibi defenses coupled with a list of witnesses who would support them. The Court found that this type of discovery does not violate the Fifth Amendment because it is not self-incriminating. In fact, the purpose of an alibi defense is to exculpate (i.e., clear) the defendant. According to the Court, "Nothing in the Fifth Amendment privilege entitles a defendant as a matter of constitutional right to await the end of the State's case before announcing the nature of his defense, any more than it entitles him to await the jury's verdict on the State's case-in-chief before deciding whether or not to take the stand himself."[51]

The *Williams* decision extends to other defenses, as well. For example, if the defense intends to argue that the defendant is not guilty by reason of insanity, then the prosecutor needs to be notified in advance of this intention. Additionally, if the defense intends to argue that the defendant acted in self-defense, then the prosecution should be notified. The reason for requiring this notification is that it provides the prosecutor with an opportunity to plan its argument to the contrary.

The defense often has to supply the prosecution with a witness list and it must contain, at a minimum, the names of all the witnesses. Often, the defense also must provide the prosecution with information about how the witnesses will be testifying. Some people believe that compelling the defense to supply a witness list to the prosecution is incriminatory, but in fact, the prosecution would eventually discover the names and identities of the witnesses, as well as their testimony, at trial anyway.

---

[50]*Williams v. Florida*, 399 U.S. 78 (1970).
[51]Ibid., p. 85.

One item concerning witnesses that the defense is *not* required to share with the prosecutor is whether the defendant will testify. In *Brooks* v. *Tennessee*,[52] the Supreme Court declared unconstitutional a state statute that required the defendant, if he or she was to testify, to do so immediately after the prosecution rested its case. The Court held that the statute violated the Fifth Amendment's privilege against self-incrimination and diminished the defense counsel's ability to make such determinations as to when certain witnesses will testify. In reaching its decision, the Court cited *United States* v. *Shipp*:

> If the man charged with a crime takes the witness stand in his own behalf, any and every arrest and conviction, even for lesser felonies, can be brought before the jury by the prosecutor, and such evidence may have devastating and deadly effect, although unrelated to the offense charged. The decision as to whether the defendant in a criminal case shall take the stand is, therefore, often of utmost importance, and counsel must, in many cases, meticulously balance the advantages and disadvantages of the prisoner's becoming a witness in his own behalf. Why, then, should a court insist that the accused must testify before any other evidence is introduced in his behalf, or be completely foreclosed from testifying thereafter? . . . This savors of judicial whim, even though sanctioned by some authorities; and the cause of justice and a fair trial cannot be subjected to such a whimsicality of criminal procedure.[53]

It may prove useful, for example, to let the defendant take the stand at the *end* of the defense case if it is believed (1) that the defense's case was not particularly persuasive and (2) the defendant can offer testimony likely to sway the jury to support his or her version of events.

So far, the discussion has focused on Fifth Amendment restrictions to discovery in terms of defenses and witnesses. Of course, discovery extends beyond these areas to real evidence (e.g., a murder weapon) as well as documentary evidence (e.g., a falsified tax return). In general, the Fifth Amendment is not violated when the defense is compelled to disclose real and documentary evidence that will be introduced at trial. The reason for this should, by now, be clear: The Fifth Amendment's protection against self-incrimination is a personal right—that is, it applies to *people*, not to real or documentary evidence. However, the defense *cannot* be compelled to disclose evidence that will *not* be used at trial because of attorney/client privilege.

In summary, the Fifth Amendment is *not* violated when the defense is forced to provide the prosecution, in advance of trial, any of the following: (1) an alibi or other affirmative defense that will be raised at trial; (2) notice of witnesses who are to testify, including their statements; or (3) real or documentary evidence concerning the crime in question. By contrast, the Fifth Amendment *is* violated when the defense is compelled to (1) notify the prosecution as to whether the defendant intends to testify, (2) identify witnesses who will not testify at trial, or (3) disclose evidence that will not be introduced at trial.

Sixth Amendment Restrictions

The Sixth Amendment provides, in relevant part, that the accused enjoys the right "to have compulsory process for obtaining witnesses in his favor." As such, some constitutional challenges to the discovery process have been raised on these grounds.

---

[52]*Brooks* v. *Tennessee*, 406 U.S. 605 (1972).
[53]*United States* v. *Shipp*, 359 F.2d 185 (1966), pp. 190–1.

For example, in *United States* v. *Nobles,*[54] the defense attempted to call a private investigator to the stand whose testimony would have cast doubt on the prosecution's case. The trial judge ruled that the investigator could not testify until the prosecution received portions of the investigator's pretrial investigative report. The Supreme Court upheld this decision. The defense argued that this decision infringed on the accused's right to compulsory process—namely, to call the investigator to the stand. But according to the Court, "The Sixth Amendment does not confer the right to present testimony free from the legitimate demands of the adversarial system; one cannot invoke the Sixth Amendment as a justification for presenting what might have been a half-truth."[55] The defense further argued that being forced to supply information from the investigator's report violated attorney/client privilege, but the Court countered by concluding that attorney/client privilege was basically waived when the defense decided to have the investigator testify about the contents of his report.

A second Sixth Amendment issue that has been raised with regard to discovery is whether the testimony can be excluded of a witness whom the defense does not inform the prosecution will testify. In *Taylor* v. *Illinois,*[56] the defense called a witness who had not been on a witness list supplied to the prosecution before trial. The trial court excluded the witness's testimony, citing a violation of discovery procedure. The defendant appealed, arguing that exclusion of the witness's testimony violated the compulsory process clause of the Sixth Amendment. However, the Supreme Court ruled that exclusion of the testimony was appropriate and did not violate the Sixth Amendment. The purpose of discovery, the Court noted, is to "minimize the risk that fabricated testimony will be believed."[57]

In summary, *Nobles* and *Taylor* suggest that it is relatively difficult to infringe on a defendant's Sixth Amendment rights, as far as discovery goes. If the defense takes steps to secure a tactical advantage over the prosecution, either by failing to supply a complete list of witnesses or the documents about which witnesses will testify, then the Sixth Amendment right to compulsory process will not be violated. Thus, this particular Sixth Amendment right is a qualified one. Compulsory process must be preceded by granting the prosecution appropriate discovery.

Discovery by the Defense

Naturally, discovery should benefit the *defense* more than the *prosecution.* After all, the prosecution presents the state's case against the defendant; it is only sensible that the defense should learn the nature of the prosecution's case. Generally, though, the prosecution has more information because it has to prove *beyond* a reasonable doubt that the defendant committed the crime. The defense, by contrast, only needs to raise reasonable doubt in the minds of the jurors that the defendant did *not* commit the crime.

---

[54]*United States* v. *Nobles,* 422 U.S. 225 (1975).
[55]Ibid., p. 241.
[56]*Taylor* v. *Illinois,* 484 U.S. 400 (1988).
[57]Ibid., p. 413.

In *Wardius* v. *Oregon*,[58] the Supreme Court held that the prosecution must provide the defense with a list of witnesses who will testify in rebuttal to the defendant's alibi or defense:

> [I]n the absence of a strong showing of state interests to the contrary, discovery must be a two-way street. The State may not insist that trial be run as a "search for truth" so far as defense witnesses are concerned, while maintaining "poker game" secrecy for its own witnesses. It is fundamentally unfair to require a defendant to divulge the details of his own case while at the same time subjecting him to the hazard of surprise concerning refutation of the very pieces of evidence which he disclosed to the State.[59]

There are limitations. The prosecution is not required to share *everything* with the defense. For example, in *United States* v. *Armstrong*, the Supreme Court held that the prosecution need only supply the defense with evidence that is "material to the preparation of the defendant's case."[60] Basically, if the evidence the defense wants to discover is a "shield," or used to refute the state's case, access will be granted. If, by contrast, the evidence is a "sword," or intended to challenge prosecutorial conduct, access will not be granted.

In *State* v. *Eads*,[61] one court summarized the restrictions on defense discovery even for "shield" purposes. If a *state interest* is likely to be compromised, then the prosecution is not required to disclose evidence to the defense, even if such evidence is intended to be used by the defense to challenge or refute the state's case. State interest precludes discovery by the defense under these circumstances:

> (1) It would afford the defendant increased opportunity to produce perjured testimony and to fabricate evidence to meet the State's case; (2) witnesses would be subject to bribe, threat and intimidation; (3) since the State cannot compel the defendant to disclose . . . evidence [protected by the Fifth Amendment], disclosure by the State would afford the defendant an unreasonable advantage at trial; and (4) disclosure is unnecessary in any event because of the other sources of information which defendant has under existing law.[62]

In the wake of *Eads*, several states have imposed restrictions on defense discovery when certain state interests have been called into question. For example, many states prohibit discovery of the identities of prosecution witnesses until after they have testified so as to prevent defense tampering with (or threatening of) prosecution witnesses.

Nonreciprocal Discovery

With few exceptions, discovery is a two-way street: The defense must supply the prosecution with certain information and vice versa. For example, as already indicated, when the defense wants to assert an alibi, it must supply the prosecution with that alibi; the prosecution must, in turn, supply the defense with a list of witnesses who will testify in rebuttal to the alibi.

The restrictions on discovery discussed in the previous section, although controversial, do not leave the defense at a disadvantage. In fact, in some circumstances, the

---

[58]*Wardius v. Oregon*, 412 U.S. 470 (1973).
[59]Ibid., pp. 475–476.
[60]*United States v. Armstrong*, 517 U.S. 456 (1996), p. 462.
[61]*State v. Eads*, 166 N.W.2d 766 (Iowa 1969).
[62]Ibid., p. 769.

exculpatory evidence
Evidence that casts doubt on the defendant's involvement in a crime.

prosecution is required to supply information to the defense but *not* vice versa. Specifically, the prosecution has a constitutional duty to disclose exculpatory evidence to the defense. This is significant because, typically, the prosecution is interested in gaining a conviction. A requirement to disclose exculpatory evidence—including evidence that would otherwise not be admitted at trial—would seem to damage the state's case, especially since the defense is not required to disclose evidence that *it* will not use at trial. But the Supreme Court disagrees with this position.

Second, the prosecution has a constitutional duty to preserve evidence, but the defense does not. These two methods of so-called nonreciprocal discovery are discussed in the two subsections that follow.

The Prosecution's Duty to Disclose Exculpatory Evidence

As a matter of due process, the prosecution has a constitutional duty to reveal exculpatory evidence to the defense. Simply put, if the prosecution obtains evidence suggesting that the defendant is not guilty, it needs to inform the defense of this fact either before or well into the trial. Numerous Supreme Court cases have supported this important requirement. However, if the evidence clearly establishes factual innocence, it should be disclosed before the trial.[63]

First, in *Mooney* v. *Holohan*,[64] the prosecution allegedly used perjured testimony to convict the defendant. The Court held that due process is violated when the prosecution "has contrived a conviction through the pretense of a trial which in truth is but used as a means of depriving a defendant of liberty through a deliberate deception of court and jury by the presentation of testimony known to be perjured."[65] The key in *Mooney* was that the prosecution *arranged* to have a witness give false testimony. If perjured testimony is *not* arranged by the prosecution but, rather, given by a witness on his or her own volition, and if the prosecution learns of this, it will still be bound to notify the defense.[66]

Next, in *Napue* v. *Illinois*,[67] the Supreme Court held that falsification concerning the credibility of a witness constitutes a due process violation. In that case, a witness testified falsely that the prosecution had not promised him leniency for his willingness to cooperate. Since the prosecutor knew the witness's testimony was false and did nothing to correct it, the defendant's conviction was reversed, since "[t]he jury's estimate of the truthfulness and reliability of a given witness may well be determinative of guilt or innocence, and it is upon such subtle factors as the possible interest of the witness in testifying falsely that a defendant's life or liberty may depend."[68] In a related case, *Giglio* v. *United States*,[69] the promise of leniency was offered by a different prosecutor but the Court still required reversal, citing a due process violation.

In *Brady* v. *Maryland*,[70] perhaps the most important case in this area of law, the Supreme Court drastically altered its previous decisions concerning the prosecution's

---

[63]*Unites States* v. *Ruiz*, 536 U.S. 622 (2002).
[64]*Mooney* v. *Holohan*, 294 U.S. 103 (1935).
[65]Ibid., p. 112.
[66]*Alcorta* v. *Texas*, 355 U.S. 28 (1957).
[67]*Napue* v. *Illinois*, 360 U.S. 264 (1959).
[68]Ibid., p. 269.
[69]*Giglio* v. *United States*, 405 U.S. 150 (1972).
[70]*Brady* v. *Maryland*, 373 U.S. 83 (1963).

duty to disclose exculpatory evidence. The Court held that "the suppression by the prosecution of evidence favorable to an accused upon request violates due process where the evidence is *material either to guilt or to punishment*, irrespective of the good faith or bad faith of the prosecution."[71] The reasoning behind the *Brady* decision is also explored in the accompanying Court Decision box.

COURT DECISION

The Logic behind Revealing Exculpatory Evidence

Brady v. Maryland
373 U.S. 83 (1963)

Decision: The Court held that "suppression by the prosecution of evidence favorable to an accused who has requested it violates due process where the evidence is material either to guilt or to punishment, irrespective of the good faith or bad faith of the prosecution."

Reason: In separate trials in a Maryland Court, where the jury is the judge of both the law and the facts but the court passes on the admissibility of the evidence, petitioner and a companion were convicted of first-degree murder and sentenced to death. At his trial, petitioner admitted participating in the crime, but claimed that his companion did the actual killing. In his summation to the jury, petitioner's counsel conceded that petitioner was guilty of murder in the first degree, and asked only that the jury return that verdict "without capital punishment." Prior to the trial, petitioner's counsel had requested the prosecution to allow him to examine the companion's extrajudicial statements. Several of these were shown to him, but one in which the companion admitted the actual killing was withheld by the prosecution, and did not come to petitioner's notice until after he had been tried, convicted and sentenced, and after his conviction had been affirmed by the Maryland Court of Appeals. In a post-conviction proceeding, the Maryland Court of Appeals held that suppression of the evidence by the prosecutor denied petitioner due process of law, and it remanded the case for a new trial of the question of punishment, but not the question of guilt, since it was of the opinion that nothing in the suppressed confession 'could have reduced [petitioner's] offense below murder in the first degree.'

We agree with the Court of Appeals that suppression of this confession was a violation of the Due Process Clause of the Fourteenth Amendment...Society wins not only when the guilty are convicted but when criminal trials are fair; our system of the administration of justice suffers when any accused is treated unfairly. An inscription on the walls of the Department of Justice states the proposition candidly for the federal domain: 'The United States wins its point whenever justice is done its citizens in the courts.' . . . A prosecution that withholds evidence on demand of an accused which, if made available, would tend to exculpate him or reduce the penalty helps shape a trial that bears heavily on the defendant. That casts the prosecutor in the role of an architect of a proceeding that does not comport with standards of justice, even though, as in the present case, his action is not 'the result of guile'.

---

[71]Ibid., p. 87; emphasis added.

Whether evidence is *material* is not entirely clear, but in *United States* v. *Agurs,*[72] the Supreme Court offered some clarification. In that case, the defendant stabbed and killed another man with the man's knife. She claimed self-defense but was nevertheless found guilty. The defense argued that because the prosecution had not disclosed that the victim had a prior criminal record, the conviction should be reversed. The Court disagreed, stating that the victim's prior criminal record was not material enough to the question of guilt or innocence. Important to this decision is the fact that the defense did not request information about the victim's prior criminal record at trial, only on appeal. Had the defense explicitly requested such information at trial, a different decision probably would have resulted.

An obvious problem is posed by the *Agurs* decision: If the defense does not know what exculpatory evidence the prosecution has, it cannot request that evidence. Does this mean that the defense should be denied access to exculpatory evidence if it does not request it? In *United States* v. *Bagley,*[73] the Court sought to answer this question but, unfortunately, offered little clarification. In that case, the defense posed a broad request to the prosecution for discovery of "any deals, promises or inducements made to [prosecution] witnesses in exchange for their testimony."[74] The prosecution failed to disclose some of the requested information, but on appeal, the Supreme Court held that this action did not constitute a due process violation. According to the Court, there was no "reasonable probability" that the exculpatory evidence would have influenced the outcome of the case.

What amounts to a *reasonable probability* that the outcome of the case may be altered by failure to disclose exculpatory evidence? In *Kyles* v. *Whitley,*[75] the Court sought to answer this question. Justice Souter's opinion in that case cited four elements of the reasonable probability standard that should be considered. First, reasonable probability does not mean a preponderance of evidence but something less. Second, when exculpatory evidence is included, the reasonable probability standard does not require the defense to show that the other evidence presented by the prosecution is insufficient to prove guilt. Third, once the defense demonstrates a reasonable probability of a different outcome, its job is done. Moreover, the appellate court cannot decide that the prosecution's failure to disclose evidence amounted to a harmless error. Finally, while the prosecution is not required to present every shred of evidence that may prove helpful to the defense, it "must be assigned the consequent responsibility to gauge the likely net effect of all such evidence and make disclosure when the point of 'reasonable probability' is reached."[76]

In summary, the prosecution's constitutional duty to disclose exculpatory evidence hinges on whether such evidence would have a reasonable probability of changing the outcome of the case. The *Brady* decision, which created the reasonable

---

[72]*United States* v. *Agurs*, 427 U.S. 97 (1976).
[73]*United States* v. *Bagley*, 473 U.S. 667 (1985).
[74]Ibid., pp. 669–670.
[75]*Kyles* v. *Whitley*, 514 U.S. 419 (1995).
[76]Ibid., p. 437.

probability standard, suggests that some of the Court's previous decisions in this area may have been altered. For example, it is possible that failure on the part of the prosecution to disclose that a witness presented perjured testimony (i.e., as in *Mooney*) may not amount to a due process violation if the exculpatory evidence does not have a reasonable probability of influencing the jury's decision. Thus, the purpose of *Brady*, *Kyles*, and the cases that followed is not to correct or deter prosecutorial misconduct but only to ensure that due process protections are not violated.[77]

Who makes the decision as to what constitutes a reasonable probability that the outcome of a case will be changed if exculpatory evidence is not disclosed? Depending on the case, it is usually the judge (i.e., court) or prosecutor who makes the decision. If the defense can show that the prosecution possesses exculpatory evidence, then a hearing to determine the reasonable probability issue may be required.[78] However, if the defense has no knowledge of specific evidence possessed by the prosecution that may prove exculpatory, the prosecution can make the decision. In *Pennsylvania* v. *Ritchie*, for example, the Supreme Court held that the "defendant's right to discover exculpatory evidence does not include the unsupervised authority to search through the Commonwealth's files."[79]

In *District Attorney* v. *Osborne*,[80] the Court was confronted with the question of whether the due process clause requires the state to turn over DNA evidence to those found guilty of criminal activity. It decided that there is no such duty and that legislatures are the proper forum to set appropriate rules governing the release of DNA evidence. This decision makes clear, then, that there is no constitutional duty to disclose possibly exculpatory evidence *after* trial. However, "after trial" means post-sentencing. If a prosecutor withholds evidence that could affect the defendant's sentence, then a due process violation occurs.[81]

In a recent and related case, *Skinner* v. *Switzer*,[82] the Supreme Court decided that convicted individuals can file federal civil rights lawsuits to access DNA evidence rather than be forced to pursue *habeas corpus* review, which is considerably more difficult. Whereas *Osborne* seemed to close the door to DNA access, the *Switzer* case opened it slightly.

The Prosecution's Duty to Preserve Evidence

The prosecution is also constitutionally bound to *preserve* evidence. Simply put, the prosecution cannot destroy exculpatory evidence in an effort to gain a conviction. To do so would be a violation of due process. For the defense to convince the court that the prosecution has destroyed exculpatory evidence, it must demonstrate three facts: (1) that the evidence was expected to "play a significant role in the suspect's defense," (2) that the evidence was of "such a nature that the defendant would be unable to

---

[77] see, e.g., *Smith* v. *Phillips*, 455 U.S. 209 (1982).

[78] see *DeMarco* v. *United States*, 415 U.S. 449 (1974).

[79] *Pennsylvania* v. *Ritchie*, 480 U.S. 39 (1987), p. 59.

[80] *District Attorney* v. *Osborne*, No. 08-6 (2009).

[81] see, e.g., *Cone* v. *Bell*, No. 07-1114 (2009).

[82] *Skinner* v. *Switzer*, No. 09-9000 (2011).

obtain comparable evidence by other reasonably available means," and (3) that the destruction of the evidence was a result of "official animus toward [the defendant] or . . . a conscious effort to suppress exculpatory evidence."[83] Note that the third requirement departs from the *Brady* decision discussed in the previous section. *Brady* did not consider the prosecution's state of mind relevant.

A case that offers some clarification concerning these three requirements is *Arizona* v. *Youngblood*.[84] In it, the Supreme Court stated that "unless a criminal defendant can show bad faith on the part of the police [or prosecution], failure to preserve potentially useful evidence does not constitute due process of law."[85]

Not only must prosecutors preserve evidence but so, too, must police. Without a proper **chain of custody** (and sometimes even with one), the defense will allege that the evidence was tampered with or tainted in such away that it cannot prove the defendant's involvement in a crime. As such, prosecutors' offices and police departments are very concerned with maintaining a proper chain of custody.

> **chain of custody** A chronological documentation (or paper trail) showing how seized evidence has been preserved, transferred, analyzed, and disposed of.

YOUR DECISION

1. Anne Tator, the local prosecutor, learns from defendant Fred Lyons that he has a list of potential witnesses who will testify on his behalf. Tator learns further that Lyons will not call at least half of the potential witnesses. Nevertheless, Tator demands that Lyons supply her with the full names of everyone on the list, even the names of those who will not testify. Is Tator constitutionally entitled to discover the identities of witnesses whom the defense will not call to testify?

2. Leonard Baum was convicted of first-degree murder and sentenced to death. In preparing an appeal, Baum's attorney learned that the state never disclosed certain evidence favorable to Baum. That evidence included eyewitness statements taken by the police following the murder; statements made to the police by an informant who was never called to testify; and a list of the license numbers of cars parked at the crime scene on the night of the murder, which did not include Baum's car. Baum argues that had this evidence been disclosed at his trial, there would have been a reasonable probability that he would not have been found guilty. Should Baum be granted a new trial?

Summary

- The last stage of the pretrial process discussed in this chapter is discovery. In actuality, however, discovery can take place early on, perhaps prior to a preliminary hearing, or well into a trial.

- Discovery is the process whereby the prosecution advises the defense of the evidence it will use to secure a conviction.

---

[83]*California* v. *Trombetta*, 467 U.S. 479 (1984).
[84]*Arizona* v. *Youngblood*, 488 U.S. 51 (1988).
[85]Ibid., p. 58.

- The defense must also disclose the evidence it intends to use to exonerate the defendant.
- The prosecution has a duty to disclose the defendant's statements in its possession, tangible evidence that will be introduced at trial, test results that are material to the case, and a list of witnesses who will testify for the prosecution as well as the substance of their testimony.
- The defense, by contrast, must supply the defense with its intended alibi or other defense as well as a list of witnesses (and their statements) who will testify in support of the defense.
- The due process clause of the Fourteenth Amendment requires the prosecution to disclose exculpatory evidence to the defense *and* to preserve said evidence while in its custody.

Chapter Review

INITIAL APPEARANCE AND PROBABLE CAUSE HEARING

Learning Objectives

- Explain the purpose and process of the initial appearance.
- Explain the purpose and process of the probable cause hearing.

Review Questions

1. What is booking?
2. What is the initial appearance? What is its purpose?
3. What is the probable cause hearing? What is its purpose? When is it required?
4. How soon after arrest must the probable cause hearing be held?

Key Terms

booking
initial appearance

probable cause hearing

PRETRIAL RELEASE

Learning Objectives

- Summarize bail and other types of pretrial release.
- Describe the criteria considered for pretrial release.

Review Questions

1. What methods of pretrial release are available? Define each.
2. What are the criteria for pretrial release? How have they been used in court decisions?
3. Summarize key cases dealing with the treatment of pretrial detainees.

Key Terms

pretrial release
bail
bail bond agent

release on recognizance (ROR)
preventive detention

PRELIMINARY HEARING AND ARRAIGNMENT

Learning Objectives

- Explain the purpose and process of the preliminary hearing.
- Explain the purpose and the process of arraignment.

Review Questions

1. What is the preliminary hearing? What is its purpose? When is it required?
2. What rights does the defendant enjoy during the preliminary hearing?

Key Terms

preliminary hearing
information
arraignment
guilty

not guilty
nolo contendere
allocution

MODULE **13.4**   DISCOVERY

Learning Objectives

· Summarize the discovery process.
· Explain the prosecution's duty to preserve evidence.

Review Questions

1. What is discovery?
2. Citing cases, what are the restrictions on discovery by the prosecution?
3. Citing cases, what are the restrictions on discovery by the defense?
4. What is nonreciprocal discovery?

Key Terms

discovery
exculpatory evidence

chain of custody

Chapter Synthesis Questions

1. Compare the pretrial process in your jurisdiction to the pretrial process explained in this chapter.
2. Does the accused enjoy sufficient protection at the pretrial phase? Why or why not?
3. What is your opinion of bail bond agents? Defend your position.
4. Having read this chapter, how does your understanding of discovery compare to what is often portrayed in the movies and on television. Explain.
5. What is your opinion of the *District Attorney* v. *Osborne* and *Skinner* v. *Switzer* DNA cases?

14

CHARGING AND PLEADING

MODULE 14.4 GUILTY PLEAS

Learning Objectives
- Outline the elements of a valid guilty plea.
- Explain the process for contesting a guilty plea.

MODULE

14.1 THE PROSECUTOR

Learning Objectives
- **Understand the considerations going into the prosecutor's charging decision.**
- **Summarize restrictions that apply to the prosecutor's charging decision.**
- **Explain the concept of joinder and the reasons for it.**

CORE CONCEPTS

The prosecutor performs a valuable function in reinforcing the notion that a crime is an offense against the state. In fact, Article II, Section 3, of the U.S. Constitution states that the executive branch of the federal government "shall take Care that the Laws be faithfully executed." This constitutionally mandated duty to execute the law usually falls on prosecutors. Of course, police officers, as part of the executive branch, do their part to execute the laws, but a strong argument can be made that prosecutors possess even more authority because of their ability to decide whether to bring formal charges against suspected criminals.

Just as police officers have the discretion to decide whether to make an arrest, so, too, do prosecutors have enormous discretion. As the Supreme Court noted in *Bordenkircher* v. *Hayes*, "[S]o long as the prosecutor has probable cause to believe that the accused committed an offense defined by statute, the decision whether or not to prosecute, and what charge to file or bring before a grand jury, generally rests entirely on his discretion."[1] Figure 14.1 presents portions of a federal prosecutor's charging document (a.k.a., "information").

Prosecutors do not have *unlimited* discretion, however. There are important restrictions on their decision to charge. Some stem from the Constitution, while others stem from statutes and other related sources.

---

[1]*Bordenkircher* v. *Hayes*, 434 U.S. 357 (1978), p. 364.

Figure 14.1

Portions of a Federal Prosecutor's Charging Document
Source: http://www.usdoj.gov/usao/iln/pr/chicago/2008/pr0619_01i.pdf (accessed January 4, 2013).

United States District Court
Northern District Of Illinois
Eastern Division

UNITED STATES OF AMERICA	)	
	)	
v.	)	No. _____
	)	
ANTHONY MATTHEWS	)	Violations: Title 18. United States Code,
	)	Section 1343

COUNT ONE

The UNITED STATES ATTORNEY charges:

1. At times material to this information:
   a. Defendant ANTHONY MATTHEWS owned and controlled Express Mortgage, a licensed Illinois mortgage brokerage located on Wabash Street and on Western Boulevard in Chicago, Illinois.
   b. Bank One was a financial institution, the deposits of which were insured by the Federal Deposit Insurance Corporation ("FDIC"). Wells Fargo Home Mortgage was a subsidiary of Wells Fargo Bank.
   c. MIT Lending and St. Francis Mortgage were mortgage companies engaged in the business of issuing mortgage loans for die purchase of residential property.
2. Beginning no later than 2003 and continuing through at least 2006, at Chicago, in the Northern District of Illinois, Eastern Division, and elsewhere,

ANTHONY MATTHEWS,

defendant herein, together with other co-schemers known to the United States Attorney, devised, intended to devise, and participated in a scheme to defraud and to obtain money by means of materially false and fraudulent pretenses, representations, and promises, which scheme affected financial institutions. More specifically, defendant schemed to fraudulently obtain over $1 million in mortgage loan proceeds from various banks and mortgage lending institutions, including Bank One, Wells Fargo Bank. MIT Lending. St. Francis Mortgage and Wells Fargo Home Mortgage, among others (hereinafter referred to collectively as "lenders"), as described below.

The Charging Decision

prosecutorial discretion

A prosecutor's authority to decide whether to proceed with criminal charges against a particular suspect.

The prosecutor generally has the authority to decide whether to proceed with criminal charges. This is known as **prosecutorial discretion**. He or she can elect not to charge for a number of reasons, even over strenuous objection on the part of the complainant or victim. The prosecutor's discretion can be further manifested by the act of *plea bargaining* (discussed later in this chapter); that is, he or she can accept a guilty plea for a lesser offense than the one charged. Finally, prosecutors sometimes have to answer to authorities that mandate, or at least strongly encourage, prosecution.

Recall from Chapter 13 that the prosecutor's charging mechanism is the information. However, grand jury indictment is a possibility instead of information depending on the jurisdiction and the offense.

Deciding Not to Prosecute

The most obvious reason for nonprosecution is the lack of evidence. The prosecutor may determine that, based on the evidence presented to him or her by the police, the suspect is innocent. In such an event, there would be no point in proceeding to trial on the slight chance that a conviction would be obtained. Even if the prosecutor *believes* the suspect is guilty, if there is not enough *evidence* to obtain a conviction, then he or she will likely elect not to prosecute.

There are other reasons not to prosecute, as well. For example, even if the state's case is strong, there may be an incentive not to prosecute. In particular, if it appears the defense's case is *stronger*, then it may behoove the prosecutor to proceed with charges against a different individual.

Nonetheless, prosecutors are human and, as such, can be influenced by the facts of a particular case. Say, for instance, that a law mandates life in prison for growing in excess of 1,000 marijuana plants. Assume further that a suspect apprehended for violating such a law has a spotless record, is married, and has four children. Would life in prison be the best punishment for such an individual, or would a fine community service or other sanction be more appropriate? This decision is up to the prosecutor, and depending on the nature of the case, he or she may elect not to proceed with charges.

As another example, California's "three strikes" law requires life in prison for third-time felons. The first two felonies that qualify as "strikeable" under California's law can only be of certain varieties; typically, they are serious offenses. However, the third felony can be of *any* type. Critics of California's "three strikes" law often point to the man who was sentenced to prison for life for stealing a slice of pizza. Had the prosecutor who charged this individual been more sensible in exercising his or her discretion, then public outcry may not have been so significant.

Another reason for not charging traces to economic concerns. Simply put, it is not possible, given the resource restrictions that exist in most public agencies (prosecutors' offices included), to proceed with charges against every suspect. Not having the time to build a case because of a high caseload may effectively force a prosecutor to be lenient with certain individuals.

Challenging the Decision Not to Prosecute

A prosecutor's decision not to press charges is rarely challenged, but on occasion, higher authorities may get involved when they disagree with a prosecutor's decision. Failure to press charges can sometimes be questioned by a court, which can provide relief to individuals who disagree with the prosecutor's decision.[2] Other times, a prosecutor's supervisor or other high-ranking official may step in. According to one source, "Many states by statute confer upon the attorney general the power to initiate prosecution in cases where the local prosecutor has failed to act. In practice, however, attorneys general have seldom exercised much control over local prosecuting attorneys."[3]

Another way of preventing prosecutors from abusing their discretion (i.e., by failing to act) is to require them to abide by standards of conduct. These standards

---

[2]E.g., *NAACP* v. *Levi*, 418 F. Supp. 1109 (D.C. 1976).
[3]Y. Kamisar, W. LaFave, and J. Israel, *Modern Criminal Procedure*, 9th ed. (St. Paul, MN: West, 1999), p. 894.

help prosecutors decide which cases are worthy of prosecution as well as what charges to pursue, all the while ensuring that they act in accordance with the law.

Some U.S. jurisdictions require court approval of a prosecutor's decision not to pursue charges. The prosecutor is typically required to explain to the court in writing his or her reasons for failing to prosecute. While this approach may seem sensible on its face, the Supreme Court has been somewhat critical of judicial review of prosecutorial decisions. In *Wayte* v. *United States*, the Court gave this reason for avoiding judicial oversight: "Such factors as the strength of the case, the prosecution's general deterrence value, the Government's overall enforcement plan are not readily susceptible to the kind of analysis the courts are competent to make."[4]

In general, if the prosecutor's decision not to press charges stems from legitimate factors, such as lack of evidence or case backlog, then the decision should be honored. The prosecutor's decision should be honored even if he or she agrees to dismiss criminal charges if the defendant agrees not to file a civil suit.

Restrictions on Bringing Charges

This section turns to situations in which charges are filed but for inappropriate reasons. In other words, whereas the previous sections considered situations in which the prosecutor *fails* to bring charges, this section considers situations in which the prosecutor *cannot* bring charges.

There are two primary reasons a prosecutor cannot bring charges against an accused individual: (1) if the prosecution is unfair and selective (i.e., targets a certain individual unfairly) and (2) if the prosecution is pursued for vindictive reasons. The following subsections focus in detail on these situations.

Before going ahead, it is important to point out that prosecutors may occasionally bring charges, say, for vindictive reasons. Assuming such conduct comes to the attention of someone in a higher position of authority, the prosecuting decision will essentially be overruled. That is, the charges against the accused will be dropped, or in the event that the person is charged and convicted, his or her conviction will be overturned. However, if a prosecutor brings charges for inappropriate reasons and this decision goes uncontested, then the charges will most likely stand.

Unfair and Selective Prosecution

If the prosecutor's decision to press charges is *discriminatory* in nature, the Fourteenth Amendment's equal protection clause can be violated. For example, in *Yick Wo* v. *Hopkins*, the Supreme Court stated:

> Though the law itself be fair on its face and impartial in appearance, yet, if it is applied and administered by public authority with an evil eye and an unequal hand, so as practically to make unjust and illegal discriminations between persons in similar circumstances, material to their rights, the denial of equal justice is still within the prohibition of the Constitution.[5]

---

[4] *Wayte* v. *United States*, 470 U.S. 598 (1985), p. 606.
[5] *Yick Wo* v. *Hopkins*, 118 U.S. 356 (1886), pp. 373–374.

selective prosecution

When an individual is
targeted for prosecution
merely because he or she
falls into a certain group
(e.g., a minority group).

Simply put, if an individual is targeted for prosecution merely because he or she falls into a certain group (e.g., a minority group), then his or her constitutional rights will be violated. This is known as **selective prosecution**.

Since *Yick Wo*, the Court has become more specific as to what constitutes selective prosecution. In *Oyler v. Boles*,[6] the Court held that prosecution becomes selective and in violation of the equal protection clause only when it is intentional and is intended to target "a certain class of cases . . . or specific persons." In that case, the defendant presented evidence that he was the only individual of six sentenced under a particular statute. The Court held that this was not discriminatory because the defendant was unable to demonstrate intent by the prosecutor or provide evidence that he fit the group targeted for prosecution. In fact, the Court noted:

> The conscious exercise of some selectivity in enforcement is not in itself a federal constitutional violation. Even though the statistics in this case might imply a policy of selective enforcement, it was not stated that the selection was deliberately based upon an unjustifiable standard such as race, religion, or other arbitrary classification.[7]

Since the *Oyler* decision, the courts have imposed a three-pronged test for determining whether prosecution violates equal protection. It must be shown that (1) similarly situated individuals were not prosecuted, (2) the prosecutor intended for this to happen, and (3) the decision resulted from an arbitrary, rather than rational, classification scheme. An *arbitrary* classification scheme would be based on, for example, race or sex. A *rational* classification scheme would be one that considers the evidence against each individual without regard to the color of his or her skin, country of origin, religious preference, sex, or other such criterion.

Filing charges for discriminatory reasons is not the only type of unfair prosecution. Sometimes, prosecutors aggressively pursue *conspicuous individuals* and open themselves to criticism. This is not to say that highly public lawbreakers cannot be charged, however. Indeed, the courts have justified prosecution on the highest charge of certain individuals for the sole purpose of discouraging other people from committing the same offense. As one court noted, "Selective enforcement may . . . be justified when a striking example or a few examples are sought in order to deter other violators."[8]

In addition to being criticized for prosecuting high-profile offenders, prosecutors can also get into trouble for targeting the most *significant offender* in a group of offenders. To clarify, think of the conspicuous person cases discussed in the previous paragraphs, in which prosecutors opted to charge one offender instead of another, even though both were suspected of having committed the same offense. When a group of individuals is suspected of having committed various degrees of the same offense, why does the prosecutor only pursue the individual suspected of having committed the most serious offense?

An example of a case illustrating this practice is *State* v. *McCollum*.[9] In that case, the court dismissed prostitution charges against nude female dancers. In its

---

[6]*Oyler v. Boles*, 368 U.S. 448 (1968).
[7]Ibid., p. 456.
[8]*People v. Utica Daw's Drug Co.*, 16 A.D.2d 12 (1962), p. 21
[9]*State v. McCollum*, 159 Wis.2d 184 (App. 1990).

decision, the court pointed out that the male patrons of these dancers were not charged, even though Wisconsin law criminalized their behavior, as well. See the accompanying Court Decision box for more details on this case.

COURT DECISION

The Logic behind Prohibiting Selective Prosecution

State v. *McCollum*
159 Wis.2d 184 (App. 1990)

Decision: Prostitution charges against female dancers were dropped because their male patrons were not arrested.

Reason: The state contends that two important governmental objectives were served by a policy of arresting only the women: (1) the women represented the smallest, most manageable group of violators and thus it was reasonable to use limited police resources to arrest only that group; and (2) the prosecution of the women would result in maximum deterrence. We address each claim of governmental interest in turn.

First, the state points to a decision where the Georgia Supreme Court upheld the arrest of only a portion of some 200 people involved in a demonstration because the arrestees represented the smallest, most manageable group of violators, which made it reasonable to use limited police resources to arrest only that group. *Sabel v. State*, 300 S.E.2d 663 (Ga. 1983), *overruled on other grounds, Massey v. Meadows*, 321 S.E.2d 703, 704 (Ga. 1984). Also, the state urges that it was faced with "proof problems" in any case against a male patron, because the officers involved in the investigation could not identify any of the male patrons. It further argues that because one-half to one-fourth of the male patrons in the establishment did not have any sexual contact, and it would be difficult to differentiate these "innocent" patrons from others outside the tavern in the dark, it made sense to arrest only the women.

We reject these arguments and note that the reason the officers could not identify any of the male patrons, according to their own testimony, was because they understood the focus of the investigation to be on the female dancers. The state cannot legitimately discriminate against two groups of violators in the investigation phase, and then argue that they should be allowed to arrest only one because they did not have sufficient proof to arrest the other.

We further note that *Sabel* is factually distinguishable from the case before us. In *Sabel*, a small group of Communist party members who were demonstrating at an apartment complex attempted to gain entry to a tenant's apartment and prevented the tenant from closing her front door to shut them out. They were surrounded by a large group of angry tenants who were openly hostile to the Communist party members. In such a case, the *Sabel* court ruled, there is no selective prosecution when the police act to arrest the smaller group to prevent a riot. . . . No such emergency situation confronted the police in this case.

(continued)

Neither does the existence of some innocent male patrons among the crowd outside the tavern justify the discriminatory treatment. There was also one innocent female performer, who was not arrested or charged. Had the observing officers attempted to identify the male offenders, they could have used that information to select between those males who violated the statute and those who did not.

Second, the state argues that the prosecution of the women would result in maximum deterrence. It cites a decision where the North Carolina Court of Appeals held that the state could legitimately focus its attention on the providers of illegal sexual services because prosecutions of those individuals would provide the greatest public benefit. *State* v. *Evans*, 326 S.E.2d 303 (N.C. Ct. App. 1985). *Evans* involved a North Carolina statute different from ours, under which the customers of a prostitute could not be seen to be "loitering for the purposes of prostitution . . ." The *Evans* court stated that "*it is well within the power of the legislature* to punish the prostitute and provider of sexual services and not the customer . . .". (emphasis added).

While this differential punishment may be within the power of the legislature, it is precisely what the Wisconsin legislature did not choose to do in adopting sec. 944.30, Stats. As we previously indicated, the plain language of that statute criminalized the behavior of both the payor and the payee involved in a prostitution arrangement. Further, it is persuasive that the goals of both general and specific deterrence in this case would have been better served by the arrest of some of the large number of local citizens involved in illicit behavior than by the arrest of a small number of out-of-towners.

Here, the police intentionally focused their investigation on, and made their arrests of, only the female violators . . . There is no important governmental objective substantially related to this enforcement scheme. As such, the state selectively prosecuted the four women in violation of the equal protection clause, and therefore the trial court properly dismissed the charges.

pretextual prosecution
When the prosecutor lacks the evidence to charge someone with a particular crime and so charges him or her with a lesser crime.

A fourth method by which prosecutors can open themselves to allegations of unfair and selective prosecution is through what is known as pretextual prosecution. This occurs when the prosecutor lacks the evidence to charge someone with a particular crime and so charges him or her with a lesser crime. However, prosecutors are rarely chastised for this type of conduct. For example, in *United States* v. *Sacco*,[10] a court noted that allowing a prosecutor to pursue lesser charges when the evidence to mount a more serious charge does not exist is perfectly acceptable.

The Supreme Court recently decided a case dealing with alleged discriminatory prosecution. Specifically, in *United States* v. *Bass*,[11] the Court considered a defendant's request for discovery of the Department of Justice's charging practices in capital cases. He alleged that blacks were disproportionately charged in such cases and that he was charged because of his race. His argument did not succeed, however.

---

[10]*United States* v. *Sacco*, 428 F.2d 164 (9th Cir. 1970).
[11]*United States* v. *Bass*, 536 U.S. 862 (2002).

Vindictive Prosecution

If a prosecutor's charging decision is motivated by revenge, then the resulting charge violates the due process clause of the Fourteenth Amendment. Specifically, if a prosecutor charges an individual simply because he or she is exercising his or her constitutional rights, such charges will not be allowed. This is known as vindictive prosecution.

vindictive prosecution Prosecution based on revenge.

This was the decision reached in *Blackledge* v. *Perry*.[12] In that case, the defendant was convicted in a lower court for misdemeanor assault with a deadly weapon. After the defendant filed an appeal with the county superior court, the prosecutor obtained an indictment charging the offender with *felony* assault for the same conduct. The defendant pleaded guilty to this offense and was sentenced to five to seven years. Notwithstanding the obvious double-jeopardy concerns (covered earlier in Chapter 2) raised by the prosecutor's conduct in this case, the Supreme Court concluded that "vindictiveness against a defendant for having successfully attacked his first conviction must play no part in the sentence he receives after a new trial."[13] The Court concluded further that such punishment after the fact must be overturned, unless the prosecutor can explain the increase in charges.

The Supreme Court's decision in *Blackledge* applies only in limited contexts, a point that cannot be overemphasized. Namely, it applies only after (1) the charged individual exercises his or her legal rights and (2) the prosecutor increases the charges after the first trial. With regard to the latter restriction, this means that if the prosecutor threatens the defendant with more serious charges during the pretrial phase, the Fourteenth Amendment will not be violated. New evidence could come along during this phase, which may legitimately warrant a more serious charge.

However, in *United States* v. *Goodwin*,[14] the Supreme Court noted that it is possible for a prosecutor to act vengefully during the pretrial phase. It is possible, the Court noted, that "a defendant in an appropriate case might prove objectively that the prosecutor's [pretrial] charging decision was motivated by a desire to punish him for doing something that the law plainly allowed him to do."[15] Furthermore, while "the defendant is free to tender evidence to the court to support a claim that enhanced charges are a direct and unjustifiable penalty for the exercise of a procedural right . . . only in rare cases [will] a defendant be able to overcome the presumptive validity of the prosecutor's actions through such a demonstration."[16] In other words, if the more serious charging decision is made prior to trial, it is presumed that the prosecutor is not acting in a vindictive fashion, and the defendant must prove otherwise.

joinder When the prosecutor either (1) brings multiple charges against the same individual in the same trial or (2) brings charges against multiple individuals in the same trial.

Joinder

Joinder refers to a situation in which the prosecutor either (1) brings multiple charges against the same individual in the same trial or (2) brings charges against multiple individuals in the same trial. In determining whether either is appropriate, two questions

---

[12]*Blackledge* v. *Perry*, 417 U.S. 21 (1974).
[13]Ibid., p. 33.
[14]*United States* v. *Goodwin*, 457 U.S. 368 (1982).
[15]Ibid., p. 384.
[16]Ibid.

must be asked: First, based on the jurisdiction in question, is joinder appropriate? Second, if joinder is appropriate, will it be unfairly prejudicial? An answer of no to the first question and yes to the second requires what is known as a **severance**.

severance The opposite of joinder. For example, severance occurs when separate trials are held for different charges against the same defendant.

The question of whether joinder is appropriate is best resolved prior to trial, but sometimes joinder is not addressed until *after* trial. Assume, for example, that a single defendant is charged in the same trial for assault and robbery. Assume further that he is convicted on both counts. If he later claims that joinder was inappropriate (which, incidentally, means the burden of proof falls on him) and succeeds with this argument, what will the result be? According to the Supreme Court in *United States* v. *Lane*, if this joinder has "a substantial and injurious effect or influence in determining the jury's verdict,"[17] then new and separate trials must be held.

Multiple Charges against the Same Individual

According to the *Federal Rules of Criminal Procedure*, multiple charges can be brought against the same individual under the following circumstances: when the charges arise out of (1) the same criminal event (e.g., robbery of a convenience store and assault when fleeing the scene); (2) two separate criminal acts that are tied together in some fashion (e.g., a convenience store robbery to obtain cash to buy and sell illegal drugs); or (3) two criminal acts that are the same or similar in character.[18] This latter circumstance is somewhat vague, but an example should clarify: If a serial killer uses the same *modus operandi* against his victims, he may be tried for several homicides in the same criminal trial.

When the defense argues against joinder, there are a number of motivating concerns. First, there is the concern that the jury (or the judge, if a bench trial is held) will not consider the criminal acts for which the accused is charged separately. Another concern is that the jury will view all the evidence against the accused in a cumulative, rather than separate, fashion. Say, for example, that the prosecution presents eyewitness testimony against a defendant accused of robbery. Also assume that the prosecution presents a murder weapon allegedly used by the defendant on the victim of the robbery. The jury may consider together the eyewitness testimony and the murder weapon and arrive at the conclusion that the accused is guilty. But if the robbery and homicide were tried separately, the jury may not arrive at this conclusion so easily. Finally, another defense argument against joinder is that by trying an individual on several charges in the same trial, he or she will have difficulty asserting separate defenses to the criminal acts at issue.

An obvious problem with joinder is the possibility of double jeopardy. When a prosecutor tries a person on several related crimes in the same trial, he or she must do so carefully. In short, the criminal acts alleged must be similar but not identical. An example may prove helpful: If the prosecutor charges an individual for first-degree as well as second-degree murder of the same victim in the same trial and the individual is convicted of both offenses, then it will be deemed unconstitutional.

---

[17]*United States* v. *Lane*, 474 U.S. 438 (1986), p. 449.
[18]*Federal Rules of Criminal Procedure*, Rule 8.

Charges against Multiple Defendants

The second form of joinder is when multiple defendants are charged in the same criminal trial. The *Federal Rules of Criminal Procedure* state, "Two or more defendants may be charged in the same indictment or information if they are alleged to have participated in the same act or transaction or in the same series of acts or transactions constituting an offense or offenses."[19] In other words, joinder of defendants is reserved in most instances for crimes of conspiracy (i.e., crimes where two or more individuals plot during a criminal act).

As with joinder of *charges*, joinder of *defendants* raises a number of concerns. For instance, the jury may get confused as to who, if anyone, is guilty and simply convict all of the defendants. Or the jury may convict one defendant who is perhaps less guilty than another defendant who is clearly guilty simply because they associated together. Also, it is conceivable that one defendant may testify against another but then refuse to answer questions on cross-examination, citing self-incrimination concerns.

There are clearly arguments against joinder, concerning both charges and defendants. However, there is one clear argument in favor of joinder—namely, efficiency. Allowing prosecutors to join charges and defendants reduces court backlog and speeds up the administration of justice.

YOUR DECISION

1. The district attorney (D.A.) suspects that Corinne Dwyer is running a call-girl service out of her suburban home. The D.A. does not have enough evidence to prosecute Dwyer for her prostitution activities, but he does have sufficient evidence to prosecute Dwyer for abandoning an appliance. Dwyer had put a refrigerator at the end of her driveway with a "Free" sign on it, in violation of a statute that provides that "any person who discards or abandons or leaves in any place accessible to children, any refrigerator, icebox, deep freeze locker, . . . which is no longer in use, and which has not had the door removed or the hinges and such portion of the latch mechanism removed to prevent latching or locking of the door, is guilty of a misdemeanor." (This is an actual offense under the California Penal Code, Section 402b.) Dwyer is thus charged and argues that she has been unfairly targeted for pretextual prosecution, in violation of her Fourteenth Amendment right to equal protection. What should the court decide?

2. Cesar Fresco was arrested for uttering (i.e., giving, offering, cashing, or passing or attempting to pass) a forged document, which is a felony punishable by a prison term of two to ten years. He has an extensive criminal history and has committed forgery in the past. The prosecutor offers a plea bargain to Fresco, giving him two choices: (1) He can plead guilty to the crime and the prosecutor will recommend a five-year sentence; or (2) he can reject the plea, be prosecuted under the habitual offender statute, and face a potential life term. The prosecutor tells Fresco, "If you do not accept this agreement, I will prosecute you as a habitual offender and you will go to prison for the rest of your life." Fresco rejects the plea and is convicted. Later, he sues, claiming that the prosecution was vindictive. Will he succeed?

---

[19]Ibid.

Summary

- A prosecutor's decision whether to charge is rarely challenged.
- Reasons for nonprosecution include a lack of evidence and too much court backlog.
- A prosecutor's decision not to press charges *can* be challenged. On rare occasions, a court can effectively overrule a prosecutor's decision not to charge someone. Also, a prosecutor's superior can demand that charges be brought.
- Prosecutors' charging decisions are subject to certain constitutional restrictions. Unfair and selective prosecutions are inappropriate and violate the equal protection clause of the Fourteenth Amendment. Vindictive prosecutions violate due process.
- Joinder refers either to (1) bringing several charges against the same individual in the same trial or (2) bringing charges against multiple defendants in the same trial.
- Both methods of joinder are generally considered appropriate, but if the crimes (or defendants) in question are only tied together because they are similar, separate trials may be warranted.
- Assuming the court permits joinder, then for separate trials to be held, the defendant must prove that his or her interests will be prejudiced in some fashion by a joint trial.

MODULE

14.2   THE GRAND JURY

Learning Objectives

- **Summarize the rules surrounding grand jury composition.**
- **Explain why secrecy in grand jury proceedings is important.**
- **Summarize the rights of grand jury witnesses and the targets of grand jury investigations.**
- **Describe the investigative powers of the grand jury.**
- **Explain the rules for challenging a grand jury indictment.**

CORE CONCEPTS

grand jury A body of people selected to hear evidence against an accused person (or persons) and determine whether there is sufficient evidence to bring the case to trial.

According to the Fifth Amendment, "No person shall be held to answer for a capital, or otherwise infamous crime, unless on a presentment or indictment of a grand jury." This part of the Fifth Amendment cannot be fully appreciated without considering the time in which it was written. The framers favored grand jury indictments in certain situations for fear that the prosecutor, a representative of government, could become too powerful in terms of making charging decisions. Indeed, the framers shared a clear sentiment that government should be kept in check, and the grand jury was one method of ensuring this.

A grand jury room at the District Courthouse in Albuquerque, NM.

© ZUMA Press, Inc./Alamy

Despite that intent, the grand jury is no longer so independent. Instead, the grand jury is now highly dependent on the actions of the prosecutor. Grand juries still perform important investigative functions, and they are quite powerful in terms of, for instance, being able to subpoena witnesses and records. But their role today is tied closely to the prosecutor. In fact, almost every state makes the prosecutor the main legal adviser of the grand jury and requires him or her to be present during all grand jury sessions. However, in some states, the grand jury functions independently of the prosecutor.

Even though the Fifth Amendment suggests that indictment by grand jury is guaranteed for certain offenses, this right has not been incorporated to the states. In the 1884 decision of *Hurtado* v. *California*,[20] the Supreme Court stated that indictment by a grand jury is not a right guaranteed by the due process clause of the Fourteenth Amendment. The Court stated:

> [W]e are unable to say that the substitution for a presentment or indictment by a grand jury of [a] proceeding by information after examination and commitment by a magistrate, certifying to the probable guilt of the defendant, with the right on his part to the aid of counsel, and to the cross-examination of the witnesses produced for the prosecution, is not due process of law.[21]

It should be emphasized that just because the right to grand jury indictment has not been incorporated to the states, this does not mean that states do not require this method of prosecution. Several states do require that, for the most part, felonies are to be prosecuted only by grand jury indictment. The same is true for the federal system. Most states, however, permit prosecution by indictment or information. See Figure 14.2 for an overview of the mechanisms for filing serious charges in each state.

---

[20]*Hurtado* v. *California*, 110 U.S. 516 (1884).
[21]Ibid., p. 538.

Figure 14.2

Charging Methods for Serious Crimes by State

Source: D.B. Rottman and S.M. Strickland, *State Court Organization,* 2004 (Washington, DC: National Center for State Courts, 2004).

So, since most states permit indictment or information, under what circumstances is one or the other method used? Typically, grand jury indictment will be the charging mechanism of choice when (1) the case is of great public and/or political significance; (2) the investigative power of the grand jury is useful; (3) the grand jury may be able to issue an indictment more quickly compared to holding a preliminary hearing and then issuing an information indictment; or (4) one or more witnesses is hesitant to speak in open court, preferring the secrecy surrounding grand jury proceedings.

How a Grand Jury Is Constructed

A grand jury can be *impaneled* either by the court or the prosecutor. Usually, the court has this responsibility, but prosecutors are becoming increasingly able to decide whether a grand jury is necessary.

The term *grand jury* should not be construed as singular; in larger jurisdictions, several grand juries may be acting at the same time. One or more could be performing investigative functions, and one or more others could be working on specific cases.

Duration

Once a grand jury has been convened, its members serve for a specified period of time. A term can last from one to three months but sometimes less, if the court or prosecutor believes that further deliberation is unnecessary. Under the *Federal Rules of Criminal Procedure*, a regular grand jury cannot serve for a period longer than 18 months, unless the court extends the service "upon a determination that such extension is in the public interest."[22] Fortunately, people selected for grand juries do not have to meet every day; usually, a grand jury meets several days a month.

Size

Grand juries are larger than ordinary trial juries. In the past, grand juries consisting of 24 or so people were not uncommon. Today, grand juries are usually smaller, or in the neighborhood of 16–20 people. One state, Tennessee, permits a grand jury of 13 individuals, but the voting requirements in that state are fairly restrictive. See Figure 14.3 for an illustration of grand jury size requirements by state.

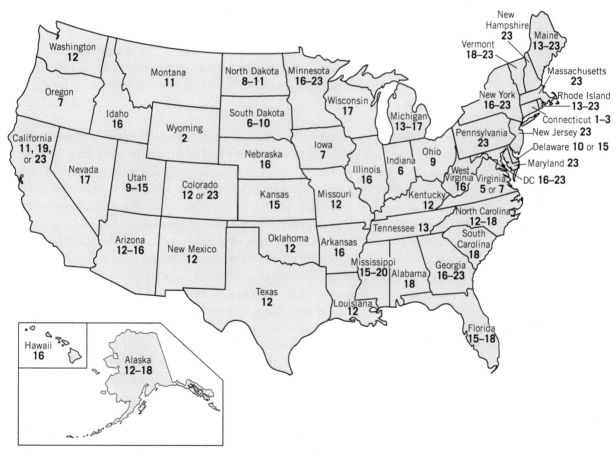

Figure 14.3

Grand Jury Size Requirements by State

Source: www.udayton.edu/~grandjur/stategj/sizegj.htm (accessed December 26, 2012).

---

[22]*Federal Rules of Criminal Procedure*, Rule 6.

Voting Requirements

true bill The grand jury's endorsement that it found sufficient evidence to warrant a criminal charge.

Grand jury voting requirements also vary by state. The most common voting requirement is that 12 grand jury members must agree on an indictment. However, one state, Virginia, requires only four votes for issuance of a true bill, which is the endorsement made by a grand jury when it finds sufficient evidence to warrant a criminal charge. Texas requires a vote of 9 out of 12. As with a *petit jury* (i.e., that used in criminal trials), a grand jury is headed by a foreperson, who is charged with, among other duties, signing the indictment and keeping track of the votes of each member.

Selection of Members

People are selected for a grand jury in the same way they are selected for an ordinary trial (i.e., petit) jury: They are subpoenaed. In some states, grand jury members are selected from a list of eligible voters. In others, they are selected from a list of licensed drivers. Still other states select grand jury members from a list of tax returns, telephone directories, and so on. Most people do not get the opportunity to serve on a grand jury because grand juries are not convened that frequently.

The grand jury selection process usually involves two stages. First, a list of potential grand jury members is compiled by any of the methods (or others) just described. This list of grand jury members is known as the *venire*. Next, people are selected from the list to serve on the grand jury. At both stages, constitutional complications can arise.

First, special steps need to be taken to ensure that the list of potential grand jurors, like that for a typical petit jury, is fair and impartial. In particular, the defendant can raise constitutional challenges to the grand jury selection process if it is *not* fair and impartial. One such challenge is based on the *equal protection clause*. This requires showing that there is a significant disparity between a group's representation in the community and its representation on the grand jury.[23]

Another constitutional challenge against the composition of the grand jury pool stems from the *fair cross-section requirement* announced in *Taylor* v. *Louisiana*.[24] In that case, the Court held that "systematic exclusion" of a "large distinct group" from the pool from which the (petit) jury is chosen violates the Sixth Amendment. The same logic carries over to the grand jury. If, for example, a grand jury consists of all white members and 40% of the community is black, the fair cross-section requirement will have been violated. By contrast, if the grand jury does not contain a snake handler, a militant feminist, a rabbi, or some such specific type of individual, the fair cross-section requirement will not have been violated because these and other individuals do not constitute large, distinct groups.

As for the selection of grand jury members from the pool, similar constitutional concerns can be raised. If, for instance, the grand jury pool is representative of a fair cross-section of the community, it is still possible that people could be excluded from the jury on a systematic basis. In *Rose* v. *Mitchell*, the Court held that the

---

[23]*Casteneda* v. *Partida*, 430 U.S. 482 (1977).
[24]*Taylor* v. *Louisiana*, 419 U.S. 522 (1975).

"right to equal protection of the laws [is] denied when [the defendant] is indicted from a grand jury from which members of a racial group purposefully have been excluded."[25] The final composition of the grand jury can also be challenged on due process grounds.[26]

Secrecy of Grand Jury Proceedings

Grand jury proceedings are intensely secret. In *United States* v. *Rose*, the Third Circuit Court of Appeals announced several reasons for this:

> (1) [T]o prevent the escape of those whose indictment may be contemplated; (2) to insure the utmost freedom to the grand jury in its deliberations, and to prevent persons subject to indictment or their friends from importuning the grand jurors; (3) to prevent subornation of perjury or tampering with the witnesses who may testify before the grand jury and later appear at the trial of those indicted by it; (4) to encourage free and untrammeled disclosures by persons who have information with respect to the commission of crimes; [and] (5) to protect the innocent accused who is exonerated from disclosure of the fact that he has been under investigation, and from the expense of standing trial where there was no probability of guilt.[27]

Notwithstanding these concerns, there are two categories of case law concerning grand jury secrecy: (1) Cases addressing whether grand jury witness testimony should be supplied to the defense and (2) cases addressing the extent to which grand jury witnesses can share their testimony with other parties, such as other government officials.

Disclosure of Witness Testimony to the Defense

According to the *Federal Rules of Criminal Procedure*, grand jury proceedings can be shared with the defense when the defendant makes "a showing that grounds may exist for a motion to dismiss the indictment because of matters occurring before the grand jury."[28] This type of disclosure is exceedingly rare and generally limited to situations in which there is evidence that prosecutorial misconduct occurred before the grand jury proceedings commenced. Indeed, as we discuss below, the defense is generally not even permitted to attend grand jury proceedings.

Disclosure of Witness Testimony to Other Parties

In *Butterworth* v. *Smith*,[29] the Supreme Court declared that the First Amendment may provide an exception to the grand jury secrecy requirement. In that case, the Court held that a Florida statute that prohibited grand jury witnesses from recounting their own testimony violated freedom of speech.

---

[25] *Rose* v. *Mitchell*, 443 U.S. 545 (1979), p. 556.
[26] *Beck* v. *Washington*, 369 U.S. 541 (1962).
[27] *United States* v. *Rose*, 215 F.2d 617 (1954), pp. 628–629.
[28] Ibid.
[29] *Butterworth* v. *Smith*, 494 U.S. 624 (1990).

Butterworth dealt with a defendant who wanted to share his testimony with third parties. However, many more cases deal with the issue of whether other third parties (i.e., besides the defense) should be able to access the records of grand jury proceedings. One such case is *Douglas Oil Co. of California v. Petrol Stops Northwest*.[30] In that case, the Supreme Court held that parties seeking access to grand jury records "must show that the material they seek is needed to avoid a possible injustice to another judicial proceeding, that the need for disclosure is greater than the need for continued secrecy, and that their request is structured to cover only material so needed."[31]

A third party that has traditionally been given greater latitude in terms of access to grand jury proceedings is the government. In fact, the *Federal Rules of Criminal Procedure* provide that no showing of "particularized need" is necessary in order to disclose information to other government attorneys who are assisting in prosecution.[32] However, when disclosure is sought by government officials who are *not* assisting in the prosecution, the Supreme Court has held that a showing of need *does* have to be made.[33]

Rights of Witnesses Testifying before Grand Juries

Grand juries rely heavily on witness testimony, but the rights afforded to grand jury witnesses differ significantly from those afforded to witnesses in other settings (e.g., at trial). Also, the rights afforded to the individuals targeted by grand jury investigations differ from those afforded to criminal defendants.

The cases in this area revolve around three issues: (1) the right of the individual targeted by a grand jury investigation to testify, (2) whether grand jury witnesses are required to be advised of their right not to testify, and (3) the right to counsel as applied in grand jury proceedings.

Right to Testify

It is well known that the defendant in a criminal trial has a constitutional right to testify or not testify in his or her own defense. In contrast, someone who is the target of a grand jury investigation usually *does not* enjoy the right to testify. Indeed, several states do not even grant the target of a grand jury investigation the right to be present. This restriction is justified on the same secrecy grounds discussed earlier. Also, since many grand jury proceedings are investigative, there may not be a specific target until the proceedings have reached a close. In such a situation, it would be cumbersome to allow all potential targets to be present in order to give testimony in their defense.

---

[30]*Douglas Oil Co. of California v. Petrol Stops Northwest*, 441 U.S. 211 (1979).
[31]Ibid., p. 222.
[32]Ibid.
[33]*United States v. Sells Engineering, Inc.*, 463 U.S. 418 (1983).

Being Advised of the Right Not to Testify

When witnesses appear before grand juries, they enjoy the Fifth Amendment's privilege against self-incrimination. This is no different than in a criminal trial. However, a question has arisen in the courts over whether grand jury witnesses must be *told* that they can remain silent. In other words, the courts have grappled with whether the *Miranda* warnings should apply in the grand jury context.

As noted earlier in this book, the *Miranda* warnings are only required during custodial interrogation. Therefore, the question must be asked, "Are grand jury proceedings akin to custodial interrogations?" At least one decision suggests that *Miranda* does not apply in the grand jury context because the proceedings are not as "inherently coercive" as traditional custodial interrogations.[34] However, some states require by law that the targets of grand jury investigations, as well as grand jury witnesses, be advised of their right not to testify. The Supreme Court has yet to rule on this issue.

Right to Counsel

We review the right to counsel for criminal defendants more fully in the next chapter, but for now, should grand jury witnesses and the targets of grand jury investigations be provided with counsel? The Supreme Court has answered no to this question in at least two cases.[35] A person who has already been charged may have a right to counsel before a grand jury proceeding, but such an individual is rarely the target of such a proceeding.[36] The typical grand jury witness is someone called upon to shed light on a particular case. Such witnesses do not enjoy the right to counsel in grand jury proceedings, but they can of course assert Fifth Amendment protection and refuse to incriminate themselves. As we will see shortly, though, the grand jury may offer a grant of immunity in exchange for a witness's testimony.

The Supreme Court has stated that grand jury proceedings take place before the initiation of adversarial criminal proceedings and, as such, are outside the scope of the Sixth Amendment's right to counsel. There are also several additional reasons for not allowing counsel to be present during grand jury proceedings: (1) the investigation could be delayed if the witness repeatedly confers with his or her attorney; (2) the investigation could be disrupted if the witness raises objections and arguments; and, of course, (3) secrecy could be compromised.

Investigative Powers of the Grand Jury

One of the main duties of a grand jury is to investigate alleged wrongdoing in order to determine whether an indictment should be issued. Because of this function, a grand jury has a great deal of investigative power. For example, as decided in *United States v. Calandra*, a grand jury "may compel the production of evidence or the testimony of witnesses as it considers appropriate, and its operation generally is unrestrained

---

[34]See, e.g., *Gollaher* v. *United States*, 419 F.2d 520 (9th Cir. 1969).
[35]*In re Groban's Petition*, 352 U.S. 330 (1957) and *United States* v. *Mandujano*, 425 U.S. 564 (1976).
[36]See, e.g., *Kirby* v. *Illinois*, 406 U.S. 682 (1972).

by the technical procedural and evidentiary rules governing the conduct of criminal trials."[37] In this vein, a grand jury can subpoena witnesses and evidence. However, it can also extend grants of immunity to certain individuals in exchange for their testimony, and it can find people in contempt for failing to cooperate with an investigation.

Subpoenas

subpoena *ad testificandum* A subpoena that compels a witness to appear before the grand jury.

subpoena *duces tecum* A subpoena that compels the production of tangible evidence (e.g., a suspected murder weapon).

Two types of subpoenas are available to grand juries: (1) a **subpoena *ad testificandum*** and (2) a **subpoena *duces tecum***. The former compels a witness to appear before the grand jury, and the latter compels the production of tangible evidence (e.g., a suspected murder weapon). The power of the grand jury to utilize both of these mechanisms is virtually unrestricted; however, there have been a few constitutional objections to their use.

First, some have argued that a subpoena to appear before the grand jury amounts to a seizure within the meaning of the Fourth Amendment. The Supreme Court acknowledged in *United States* v. *Dioniso* that being forced to appear before a grand jury may be inconvenient but not in comparison to the "historically grounded obligation of every person to appear and give his evidence before the grand jury."[38] Furthermore, Fourth Amendment restrictions on the grand jury's subpoena power "would assuredly impede its investigation and frustrate the public's interest in the fair and expeditious administration of the laws."[39]

As for tangible evidence, the Supreme Court has likewise held that a subpoena *duces tecum* does not amount to a Fourth Amendment seizure. However, according to the Court,[40] such a subpoena must comport with the Fourth Amendment's particularity requirement. In *United States* v. *Gurule*, the Tenth Circuit announced a three-prong test for ensuring that a grand jury subpoena satisfies the Fourth Amendment's reasonableness requirement: "(1) [T]he subpoena may command only the production of things relevant to the investigation being pursued; (2) specification of things to be produced must be made with reasonable particularity; and (3) production of records covering only a reasonable period of time may be required."[41]

It has already been noted that grand jury witnesses enjoy the Fifth Amendment privilege, but could being forced to appear before a grand jury itself be incriminating? Not surprisingly, people have objected to grand jury subpoenas for this reason. Few, if any, have succeeded, however. Why? Someone who is appearing before a grand jury does not know in advance what questions will be asked and, as such, cannot assert the Fifth Amendment privilege prior to his or her appearance.

Grants of Immunity

Even though witnesses appearing before the grand jury enjoy the Fifth Amendment privilege against self-incrimination, the grand jury can get around this. In particular,

---

[37] *United States* v. *Calandra*, 414 U.S. 338 (1974), p. 343.
[38] *United States* v. *Dioniso*, 410 U.S. 1 (1973), pp. 9–10.
[39] Ibid., p. 17.
[40] *Hale* v. *Henkel*, 201 U.S. 43 (1906).
[41] *United States* v. *Gurule*, 437 F.2d 239 (10th Cir. 1970), p. 241.

the grand jury can extend *grants of immunity* to witnesses in exchange for their testimony. A grant of transactional immunity prohibits future prosecution on the acts for which the witness testifies. In contrast, so-called use and derivative use immunity only bars the use of the witness's testimony against him or her in the future. If evidence is obtained after the fact, independent of the witness's testimony before the grand jury, then he or she can be charged.[42]

Findings of Contempt

contempt power The grand jury's authority to hold people in contempt of court for failing to appear before it. Civil and criminal sanctions can be imposed.

When someone is subpoenaed to appear before the grand jury but does not show up, the jury's contempt power can be utilized. That is, the grand jury can impose civil and criminal sanctions on the individual. For example, an individual who refuses to appear before the grand jury can be jailed until which point he or she agrees to appear. Note that the grand jury's contempt power is limited to compelling the presence of the witness, not his or her testimony. The witness who *does* appear can still invoke the Fifth Amendment privilege and not make a statement.

Challenging a Grand Jury Indictment

Restrictions on prosecutors' charging decisions were discussed earlier in this chapter. Restrictions are also placed on grand jury indictments. That is, it is possible to challenge a grand jury indictment on constitutional and similar grounds, including (1) lack of evidence, (2) misconduct by the prosecutor as the adviser of the grand jury, (3) unfair selection of grand jury members, and (4) use of different evidence at trial from that presented to the grand jury. When any of these circumstances exists, a grand jury indictment will be *quashed* or declared invalid.

There is considerable variation among the states as to what amount of evidence is necessary to secure a valid indictment. Some states hold to the probable cause standard. Others state that the grand jury can only issue an indictment when all the evidence before it would, if unexplained, warrant a conviction at trial. In Utah, an indictment can only be issued on clear and convincing evidence that a crime was committed and that the person charged committed it. In either case, a grand jury indictment can be quashed if the evidence relied on to obtain the indictment is insufficient. Also, if the evidence used to obtain an indictment is obtained in an unconstitutional fashion, the indictment can be quashed by essentially invoking the exclusionary rule.

Flagrant prosecutorial misconduct can also lead to an indictment being quashed. If, for instance, the prosecutor fails to supply the grand jury with exculpatory evidence, a subsequent indictment *may* be quashed but only if such misconduct violates existing law. There is, surprisingly, very little existing case law in this area. Indeed, the Supreme Court held in *United States* v. *Williams*[43] that federal courts cannot easily dismiss an indictment because of prosecutorial misconduct. "Because the grand jury is an institution separate from the courts, over whose functioning the courts do not preside, we think it clear that, as a general matter at least, no such 'supervisory' judicial authority exists."[44]

---

[42]*Kastigar* v. *United States*, 406 U.S. 441 (1972).
[43]*United States* v. *Williams*, 504 U.S. 36 (1992).
[44]Ibid., p. 47.

While the courts have been hesitant to quash indictments based on insufficient evidence and prosecutorial misconduct, discrimination in the selection of grand jury members is taken very seriously. As indicated earlier in this chapter, the composition of the grand jury must comply with the due process and equal protection requirements. When it does not, subsequent indictments can be quashed. The Court noted in *United States* v. *Mechanik* that "racial discrimination in the selection of grand jurors is so pernicious and other remedies so impractical, that the remedy of automatic reversal [may be] necessary as a prophylactic means of deterring grand jury discrimination in the future."[45]

variance When the prosecutor presents evidence at trial that departs significantly from that relied on by the grand jury for the purpose of issuing an indictment.

Finally, if the prosecutor presents evidence at trial that departs significantly from that relied on by the grand jury for the purpose of issuing an indictment, sanctions will be imposed. If this **variance** between the trial evidence and the grand jury evidence is minimal, the indictment will probably not be quashed. Interpreted differently, if the evidence presented by the prosecutor to secure an indictment is "in no way essential to the offense on which the jury convicted," the indictment will probably not be quashed.[46]

YOUR DECISION

1. Assume that the grand jury is investigating a major case of corporate fraud. Assume further that the grand jury issues a subpoena *duces tecum*, calling for "all understandings, contracts or correspondence between the Fabulous Widgets Company and all of its business partners, as well as all reports made and accounts rendered by such companies from the date of the organization of the Fabulous Widgets Company, as well as all letters received by that company since its organization from all of its business partners." Can this subpoena be considered sufficiently particular?

2. A grand jury returned an indictment against two women, charging them both with conspiracy to commit murder. Typically, a criminal *conspiracy* exists when two or more persons agree to commit a crime and then commit some sort of overt act in furtherance of that agreement. The grand jury was presented with a recorded telephone call between the two women, in which they agreed to murder their husbands. The grand jury was *not* presented with evidence that the women bought handguns for themselves. That evidence was introduced by the prosecutor at trial, however. The women were convicted and are now appealing their convictions, claiming that there was a variance between their indictment and the prosecutor's case. Will they succeed?

Summary

- Grand juries are closely related to prosecutors in terms of their charging decisions. Frequently, the grand jury serves as a means of formalizing the prosecutor's decision to charge.

- A grand jury is useful when the case in question is of great public and/or political significance, when its extensive investigative powers are helpful, when time is of the essence, and when one or more witnesses are hesitant to speak in open court, preferring the secrecy that surrounds grand jury proceedings.

---

[45]*United States* v. *Mechanik*, 475 U.S. 66 (1986), p. 70.
[46]See *United States* v. *Miller*, 471 U.S. 130 (1985).

- The size of a grand jury varies, depending on location. Typically, the smaller the grand jury, the higher the voting requirement. Grand jury selection pools must be representative in terms of race and gender.

- Grand jury proceedings are typically held in secret. Reasons for this secrecy include: (1) to prevent the escape of possible indictees, (2) to ensure freedom to the grand jury in its deliberations, (3) to prevent tampering with the witnesses who may testify, (4) to encourage persons who have information with respect to the commission of crimes to come forward, and (5) to protect the innocence of those who are ultimately exonerated by grand jury investigations.

- In general, an individual who is the target of a grand jury investigation does not have the right (1) to appear in front of the grand jury, (2) to have the assistance of counsel during the grand jury's investigation, (3) to be told he or she is the target of the investigation, or (4) to be reminded that he or she has the right to remain silent.

- Grand juries possess extensive investigative powers. They can issue subpoenas *ad testificandum*, which require witnesses to appear and testify, and subpoenas *duces tecum*, which compel the production of evidence.

- As part of their investigative powers, grand juries can also grant immunity and hold people in contempt.

- Just as there are constraints on prosecutors' charging decisions, there are restrictions on grand juries' indictment decisions; however, a grand jury indictment is rarely quashed.

- Only when there is evidence of serious prosecutorial tampering, discrimination in the composition of the grand jury pool, or variance between the evidence presented during the grand jury investigation and that presented at trial will a grand jury indictment possibly be quashed.

MODULE 14.3 · PLEA BARGAINING

Learning Objectives

- **Define plea bargaining.**
- **Outline the history of plea bargaining.**
- **Summarize the arguments for and against plea bargaining.**
- **Explain the plea bargaining process.**
- **Summarize the effects of plea bargaining on the court, the prosecutor, the defendant, and the victim.**

CORE CONCEPTS

Obtaining a guilty plea as the result of plea bargaining is the most common method of securing a conviction. The overwhelming majority—90%, by some estimates—of criminal convictions in the United States result from guilty pleas, rather than trials.

Moreover, these pleas usually derive from some bargaining between the defense attorney and the prosecutor. Both parties stand to gain something from a guilty plea: The prosecutor obtains a conviction, and the defense attorney usually succeeds in getting lenient treatment for his or her client.

Plea bargaining is essential to the administration of justice. If every defendant demanded his or her right to a jury trial and succeeded in such a demand, the criminal justice system would literally collapse. In this vein, arguments against plea bargaining are really like thought exercises; nothing can be done to eliminate plea bargaining because there are just too many criminals and not enough prosecutors, courts, and prisons.

At the same time, though, critics' views should not be dismissed. Consistent with what Americans are all taught, many people believe that judges and juries should determine guilt and that prosecutors and defense attorneys should only play a secondary role in this process. Plea bargaining essentially permits attorneys to decide the outcome of a case without ever going to trial. And it is well known that when two defendants face the same charge, the one who plea bargains invariably receives a lesser sentence than the one who does not.

Defining Plea Bargaining

plea bargaining The defendant's agreement to plead guilty to a criminal charge in exchange for reduced charge (charge bargaining) or sentence (sentence bargaining). Other concessions and inducements are possible.

There is no agreed-upon definition of **plea bargaining**, so the following subsections consider two definitions. The first is a specific definition found in *Black's Law Dictionary*, and the second is a more general definition.

A Specific Definition

Black's Law Dictionary provides a specific definition of *plea bargaining*. Namely, it is "the process whereby the accused and the prosecutor in a criminal case work out

The vast majority of criminal cases are settled by plea bargaining between the prosecution and defense.

Alexander Raths/Shutterstock

a mutually satisfactory disposition of the case subject to court approval. It usually involves the defendant's pleading guilty to a lesser offense or to only some of the counts of a multicount indictment in return for a lighter sentence than the possible sentence for the graver charge."[47]

It is useful to distinguish between charge bargaining and sentence bargaining. *Charge bargaining* refers to the prosecutor's ability to negotiate with the defendant in terms of the charges that could be filed. *Sentence bargaining*, by contrast, is when the defendant agrees to plead guilty in exchange for a less serious sentence. Charge bargaining is largely carried out between the prosecution and the defense. Sentence bargaining requires getting the judge involved because he or she usually hands down the sentence. In fact, there is even such a thing as *count bargaining*, in which the defense negotiates to have the defendant charged with fewer counts of a certain offense.

Black's definition first states that a plea bargain results in "a mutually satisfactory disposition." It is true, as will be noted later, that a plea bargain must be intelligent and voluntary, but it is not always satisfactory to both parties. For example, the prosecutor may simply be *forced* to present a favorable offer to the defendant because of procedural errors that would make it difficult to prove the state's case. Or the prosecutor may present the defendant with equally unfavorable choices. As one researcher observed, "[T]he right to reject the proposed plea bargain is largely chimerical. Fear of heavier sentence after trial and deference to advice of defense counsel might lead defendants to accept virtually all plea agreements."[48]

Black's definition of plea bargaining also states that each bargain must be "subject to court approval." While this is usually true, the plea bargaining process is mostly carried on between the defense and the prosecution with little judicial oversight. For example, prosecutors can do a great deal to drop or alter charges against an individual prior to bringing any subsequent agreement to the attention of the trial judge.

Finally, the foregoing definition of plea bargaining states that it "usually involves the defendant's pleading guilty to a lesser offense . . . in return for a lighter sentence." While this statement is true, it also obscures the reality that many concessions (i.e., besides a lighter sentence) can be offered to the defendant in exchange for a guilty plea. For example, sentence-bargaining concessions may include, but are not limited to, (1) the judge agreeing to impose certain probation conditions; (2) the prosecutor recommending a certain sentence to the judge; (3) the prosecutor agreeing not to invoke certain sentencing provisions, say, for multiple offenders; and (4) an agreement that the defendant will serve his or her sentence in a certain institution.[49]

A General Definition

In light of some of the shortcomings of the *Black's Law Dictionary* definition of plea bargaining, at least one authority has offered a more general definition: *Plea bargaining* is "the defendant's agreement to plead guilty to a criminal charge with the

---

[47]*Black's Law Dictionary*, 6th ed. (1990), p. 1152.

[48]Anonymous Author, "Plea Bargaining and the Transformation of the Criminal Process," *Harvard Law Review*, Vol. 90 (1977), pp. 564–595, 579.

[49]See, for example, H. S. Miller, W. F. McDonald, and J. A. Cramer, *Plea Bargaining in the United States* (Ann Arbor, MI: Inter University Consortium for Political and Social Research, 1978), p. 17.

reasonable expectation of receiving some consideration from the state."[50] This definition is far more inclusive in that it recognizes that several varieties of bargaining can actually take place. Several of these are considered throughout the remainder of this chapter.[51]

Arguments for and against Plea Bargaining

Historical accounts show that in the early days of English criminal justice, a jury would hear 12–20 felony cases in a single day.[52] Trials played out in a similar fashion in U.S. courts during the 1800s. Indeed, many early trials in the United States were carried out without lawyers for the defendant and even, in some cases, for the government.[53] As the U.S. legal system began to mature and lawyers became regular participants, trials slowed down and guilty plea rates increased out of necessity. According to one source, "[P]lea bargaining should be viewed as a natural outgrowth of a progressively adversarial criminal justice system."[54]

Despite its apparent necessity, plea bargaining was criticized extensively by early commentators. Some called it an "incompetent, inefficient, and lazy method of administering justice."[55] Others suggested that plea bargaining was just a means of avoiding trials for individuals charged with committing criminal acts. But as time went on, people came to realize the benefits of plea bargaining. Supportive arguments include the following:

- Plea bargaining is widely accepted because, despite certain drawbacks (discussed later), it benefits all members of the courtroom work group: the judge, the prosecutor, and the defense attorney (not to mention the defendant). Thus, the arguments in support of plea bargaining are really arguments concerning the *benefits* of reaching plea agreements. Each of these arguments needs to be viewed in context, however. In some situations, such as highly celebrated cases, the costs of plea bargaining may outweigh the benefits.

- Plea bargaining benefits the prosecutor because it provides him or her with a greater ability to dispose of a busy case load. District attorneys are often faced with limited resources and, as such, cannot prosecute every case that comes before them. Specifically, a district attorney may opt to pursue charges on cases that have a highly public element and/or are likely to result in guilty convictions. Cases that do not look promising may be prime candidates for plea bargaining. And according to one observer, plea bargaining may be favored by the prosecution simply because it allows the courtroom work group to further its

---

[50]Ibid., pp. 1–2.

[51]Much of the discussion that follows is based on D. D. Guidorizzi, "Should We Really 'Ban' Plea Bargaining? The Core Concerns of Plea Bargaining Critics," *Emory Law Journal,* Vol. 47 (1998), pp. 753–783.

[52]J. H. Langbein, "The Criminal Trial before Lawyers," *University of Chicago Law Review,* Vol. 45 (1978), pp. 263–316, p. 277.

[53]L. M. Friedman, *Crime and Punishment in American History* (New York: Basic Books, 1993), p. 235.

[54]Guidorizzi, "Should We Really 'Ban' Plea Bargaining? The Core Concerns of Plea Bargaining Critics," pp. 753, 760.

[55]A. W. Alschuler, "Plea Bargaining and Its History," *Law and Society Review,* Vol. 13 (1979), pp. 211–245, 211 (quoting the Chicago Tribune, April 27, 1928, p. 1).

"mutual interest in avoiding conflict, reducing uncertainty, and maintaining group cohesion."[56]

- Defense attorneys also benefit from plea bargaining. Public defenders, who are the most common type of counsel in criminal trials, face resource constraints similar to those of prosecutors. Thus, plea bargaining benefits public defenders by allowing quick disposition of cases. It also allows them to focus on cases that they perceive as being worthy of trial. Bargaining also benefits privately retained counsel because it speeds up the process, which translates into "more money for less work." This is not to suggest, however, that this is the prime motivation of defense attorneys. Many zealously guard the interests of their clients.

- Plea bargaining benefits the defendant perhaps more than the prosecutor or the defense attorney. The obvious reason for this is that the defendant generally receives a lesser sentence (or charge, which also affects the ultimate punishment) as a result of plea bargaining. On another level, as will be discussed later, the defendant loses his or her chance at an acquittal and, sometimes, important rights, including the right to a trial by jury. But the Supreme Court has said that these costs may be outweighed by the benefits of "avoiding the anxieties and uncertainties of trial."[57]

- The court also benefits from plea bargaining. The prompt disposition of cases saves judicial resources, as researching a plea bargain takes less time than holding a full-blown trial. In fact, to the chagrin of many, the victims of crime may even benefit from plea bargaining. A quickly reached plea bargain may give the victim the satisfaction of having the case closed sooner rather than later. Moreover, the victim may also not want to testify or risk the possibility that the prosecution will not succeed in obtaining a conviction.[58] Figure 14.4 summarizes the arguments for and against plea bargaining.

Apart from the obvious concern with the prosecutor and defense attorney effectively deciding a defendant's guilt, there are other problems posed by plea bargaining:

- In an effort to secure a conviction, the prosecutor will start with the most serious charge and work down. That is, the prosecutor may *overcharge* as a first step in the bargaining process. This negotiation process is much like that of buying a used car at a dealership, in which the dealer usually starts with a ridiculously high price but is willing to negotiate. In the end, however, few buyers end up purchasing a car for its fair market value. The concern with plea bargaining, then, is that the defendant will be encouraged to plead guilty to an offense that is more serious than that for which he or she would be convicted at trial.

- Plea bargaining may contribute to *inefficiency*. As one researcher observed, "[D]efense attorneys commonly devise strategies whose only utility lies in the threat they pose to the court's and prosecutor's time."[59]

---

[56]R. A. Weninger, "The Abolition of Plea Bargaining: A Case Study of El Paso County, Texas," *UCLA Law Review*, Vol. 35 (1987), pp. 265–313, 267, n. 5.
[57]*Blackledge* v. *Allison*, 431 U.S. 63 (1977), p. 71
[58]C. E. Demarest, "Plea Bargaining Can Often Protect the Victim," *New York Times*, April 15, 1994, p. A30.
[59]A. W. Alschuler, "The Prosecutor's Role in Plea Bargaining," *University of Chicago Law Review*, Vol. 36 (1968), pp. 50–112, 54.

Arguments for	Arguments Against
Contributes to cohesion in the courtroom work group	Behooves the prosecutor to choose the most serious charge from which to begin bargaining
Helps the prosecutor dispose of a busy case load	Contributes to inefficiency
Helps the public defender dispose of a busy case load	Wastes time; most defendants plead guilty anyway
Benefits the defendant by providing a reduction in charges and/or a favorable sentencing recommendation	Undermines the integrity of the justice system
Saves on judicial resources by avoiding the costs of going to trial	Decides the defendant's guilt without having a trial
May give the victim the satisfaction of having a prompt resolution of the case	Allows the criminal to get away with his or her crime
May benefit the victim who does not wish to testify at trial	An innocent individual may be coerced to plead guilty (i.e., legal versus factual guilt)

Figure 14.4

Arguments for and against Plea Bargaining

- Critics further contend that not only is plea bargaining inefficient, but it also wastes time. They claim that plea bargaining is not necessary to obtain guilty pleas and that most defendants plead guilty anyway, if they think it is highly likely that going to trial will result in a verdict of guilty.[60]

- Plea bargaining may undermine the integrity of the criminal justice system. Throughout this book, discussion has examined the complex rules of criminal procedure set forth by the U.S. Constitution and interpreted by the Supreme Court. Critics of plea bargaining claim that the practice circumvents these "rigorous standards of due process and proof imposed during trials."[61]

- Another reason that plea bargaining may undermine the criminal process is that it effectively decides the defendant's guilt without having a trial, an exhaustive investigation, or the presentation of evidence and witness testimony. As mentioned earlier in this section, the defendant's guilt is effectively decided by the prosecutor. One critic has argued that plea bargaining decisions result from improper considerations:

  > One mark of a just legal system is that it minimizes the effect of tactical choices upon the outcome of its processes. In criminal cases, the extent of an offender's punishment ought to turn primarily upon what he did and, perhaps, upon his personal characteristics rather than upon a postcrime, postarrest decision to exercise or not to exercise some procedural option.[62]

---

[60]P. Arenella, "Rethinking the Functions of Criminal Procedure: The Warren and Burger Courts' Competing Ideologies," *Georgetown Law Journal,* Vol. 72 (1983), pp. 185–248, 216–19.

[61]A. P. Worden, "Policymaking by Prosecutors: The Uses of Discretion in Regulating Plea Bargaining," *Judicature* Vol. 73 (1990), pp. 335–340, 336.

[62]A. W. Alschuler, "The Changing Plea Bargaining Debate," *California Law Review,* Vol. 69 (1981), pp. 652–730, 652.

- Plea bargaining may also allow criminals to get away with their crimes—or at least to receive lenient sentences. Furthermore, critics claim that providing reduced sentences may reduce the deterrent effect of harsh punishment. In both cases, plea bargaining may give the impression that defendants can negotiate their way out of being adequately punished for their crimes.

- Innocent individuals may be coerced to plead guilty. In such a situation, a plea bargain amounts to an admission of legal guilt, when, in fact, the defendant may not be factually guilty. An example of the pressure on innocent defendants to plead guilty is found in *North Carolina v. Alford*.[63] In that case, the defendant, facing the death penalty if he was convicted, pleaded guilty to the crime, but did not admit to all elements of it. His plea (and other similar pleas) was promptly dubbed the *Alford* Plea. Certain jurisdictions permit *Alford* pleas (also called "best-interests pleas"). A defendant who makes an *Alford* plea does not allocute, which means he or she does not—and indeed is not required—to explain the details of the offense for the judge.

> *Alford* Plea Also called a "best interests" plea, a defendant who makes an *Alford* plea does not allocute, which means he or she does not—and indeed is not required to—explain the details of the offense to the judge.

The Supreme Court's View on Plea Bargaining

Notwithstanding the competing views on plea bargaining, the Supreme Court has essentially laid the debate to rest by upholding the validity of the practice. In *Brady v. United States*, for example, the Court stated, "Of course, that the prevalence of guilty pleas is explainable does not necessarily validate those pleas or the system which produces them. But we cannot hold that it is unconstitutional for the State to extend a benefit to a defendant who in turn extends a substantial benefit to the State."[64] Next, in the case of *Santobello v. New York*, the Court offered the following argument in support of plea bargaining: "The disposition of criminal charges by agreement between the prosecutor and the accused, sometimes loosely called 'plea bargaining,' is an essential component of the administration of justice. Properly administered, it is to be encouraged."[65]

How, then, is plea bargaining to be properly administered? The following sections seek to answer this question. First, the plea bargaining process is described, and then the effects of plea bargaining, the rules concerning plea bargaining, and situations in which guilty pleas can be challenged are all discussed. The reader will develop an understanding of the complex practice of plea bargaining as it has been interpreted through the courts—most notably, the U.S. Supreme Court.

The Plea Bargaining Process

The prosecutor can make many different offers in order to secure a guilty plea. The most straightforward and common method is to reduce the charge or charges against the defendant. Other alternatives include dismissing other pending charges and promising to recommend a particular sentence.

---

[63]*North Carolina v. Alford*, 400 U.S. 25 (1970).
[64]*Brady v. United States*, 397 U.S. 742 (1970), pp. 752–753.
[65]*Santobello v. New York*, 404 U.S. 257 (1971), p. 260.

Assuming that what is offered by the prosecution is acceptable to the defendant, then he or she can make one of two pleas: a simple plea of guilty or a plea of *nolo contendere*. The former is akin to saying "I am guilty," and the latter is akin to saying "I do not contest this." Both pleas are effectively the same. The only difference is that the *nolo* plea cannot be used as an admission of guilt in a subsequent civil case.

Constitutional Rights during Plea Bargaining

Plea bargaining is a method of circumventing criminal trial, so not surprisingly, the rights available to the defendant during bargaining are not the same as those available at trial. There are, however, important rights that the defendant still enjoys during the plea bargaining process, including the rights to effective assistance of counsel and to be informed of exculpatory evidence. The defendant does not have the right to be present at important stages of the bargaining process, however.

The Sixth Amendment right to counsel applies during plea bargaining because charges have already been filed before bargaining commences. According to the Supreme Court in *Kirby* v. *Illinois*, the right to counsel attaches when, after charges have been filed, the "defendant finds himself faced with the prosecutorial forces of organized society, and immersed in the intricacies of substantive and procedural criminal law."[66] This means that the prosecutor cannot bargain directly with the defendant unless counsel has been waived.

The Sixth Amendment also requires that defense counsel be effective during the plea-negotiation process. This means that the defense attorney must, at a minimum, investigate the case so as to make an informed decision with regard to what sentences and charges are offered by the prosecution. To be effective, counsel must also ensure that his or her client understands the consequences of the plea bargaining process. This is not to suggest that the defendant can easily succeed in claiming ineffective assistance of counsel during negotiation, however. According to the Court in *Hill* v. *Lockhart*, the defendant must show "a reasonable probability that, but for counsel's errors, he would not have pleaded guilty and would have insisted on going to trial."[67]

The Supreme Court recently decided two more cases along these lines, reinforcing how important it is for the defendant to have effective assistance of counsel during the plea bargaining phase. The cases were *Lafler* v. *Cooper* and *Missouri* v. *Frye*.[68] In *Lafler*, the defendant rejected the prosecution's plea offer because his attorney told him—incorrectly—that the prosecutor could not prove intent to murder because the victim was shot below the waste. He was found guilty on all counts and sentenced to a minimum of 185 to 360 months in prison. Had he accepted the plea, he would have been out in 51-85 months. The accompanying Court Decision box discusses the *Lafler* case in more detail.

---

[66] *Kirby* v. *Illinois*, 406 U.S. 682 (1972), p. 689.
[67] *Hill* v. *Lockhart*, 474 U.S. 52 (1985), p. 58.
[68] *Lafler* v. *Cooper*, No. 10-209 (2012); *Missouri* v. *Frye*, No. 10-444 (2012).

COURT DECISION

The Logic behind the Right to Counsel in Plea Bargaining

Lafler v. *Cooper*

132 S.Ct. 1376 (2012)

Decision: The Supreme Court held that "if a plea bargain has been offered, a defendant has the right to effective assistance of counsel in considering whether to accept it. If that right is denied, prejudice can be shown if loss of the plea opportunity led to a trial resulting in a conviction on more serious charges or the imposition of a more serious sentence."

Reason: Where counsel's ineffective advice led to an offer's rejection, and where the prejudice alleged is having to stand trial, a defendant must show that but for the ineffective advice, there is a reasonable probability that the plea offer would have been presented to the court, that the court would have accepted its terms, and that the conviction or sentence, or both, under the offer's terms would have been less severe than under the actual judgment and sentence imposed.

a. Because the parties agree that counsel's performance was deficient, the only question is how to apply *Strickland*'s prejudice test where ineffective assistance results in a rejection of the plea offer and the defendant is convicted at the ensuing trial . . .

b. In that context, the *Strickland* prejudice test requires a defendant to show a reasonable possibility that the outcome of the plea process would have been different with competent advice. The Sixth Circuit and other federal appellate courts have agreed with the *Strickland* prejudice test for rejected pleas adopted here by this Court. Petitioner and the Solicitor General propose a narrow view—that *Strickland* prejudice cannot arise from plea bargaining if the defendant is later convicted at a fair trial—but their reasoning is un-persuasive. First, they claim that the Sixth Amendment's sole purpose is to protect the right to a fair trial, but the Amendment actually requires effective assistance at critical stages of a criminal proceeding, including pretrial stages. This is consistent with the right to effective assistance on appeal . . . This Court has not followed a rigid rule that an otherwise fair trial remedies errors not occurring at trial, but has instead inquired whether the trial cured the particular error at issue . . . Second, this Court has previously rejected petitioner's argument that *Lockhart* v. *Fretwell* . . . modified *Strickland* and does so again here. *Fretwell* and *Nix* v. *Whiteside* . . . demonstrate that "it would be unjust to characterize the likelihood of a different outcome as legitimate 'prejudice,'" . . ., where defendants would receive a windfall as a result of the application of an incorrect legal principle or a defense strategy outside the law. Here, however, respondent seeks relief from counsel's failure to meet a valid legal standard. Third, petitioner seeks to preserve the conviction by arguing that the Sixth Amendment's purpose is to ensure a conviction's reliability, but this argument fails to comprehend the full scope of the Sixth Amendment and is refuted by precedent. Here, the question is the fairness or reliability not of the trial but of the processes that preceded it, which caused

(continued)

**COURT
DECISION**
(continued)

respondent to lose benefits he would have received but for counsel's ineffective assistance. Furthermore, a reliable trial may not foreclose relief when counsel has failed to assert rights that may have altered the outcome . . . Petitioner's position that a fair trial wipes clean ineffective assistance during plea bargaining also ignores the reality that criminal justice today is for the most part a system of pleas, not a system of trials . . .

Where a defendant shows ineffective assistance has caused the rejection of a plea leading to a more severe sentence at trial, the remedy must 'neutralize the taint' of a constitutional violation . . ., but must not grant a windfall to the defendant or needlessly squander the resources the State properly invested in the criminal prosecution. . . . . If the sole advantage is that the defendant would have received a lesser sentence under the plea, the court should have an evidentiary hearing to determine whether the defendant would have accepted the plea. If so, the court may exercise discretion in determining whether the defendant should receive the term offered in the plea, the sentence received at trial, or something in between. However, resentencing based on the conviction at trial may not suffice, *e.g.,* where the offered guilty plea was for less serious counts than the ones for which a defendant was convicted after trial, or where a mandatory sentence confines a judge's sentencing discretion. In these circumstances, the proper remedy may be to require the prosecution to reoffer the plea. The judge can then exercise discretion in deciding whether to vacate the conviction from trial and accept the plea, or leave the conviction undisturbed. In either situation, a court must weigh various factors. Here, it suffices to give two relevant considerations. First, a court may take account of a defendant's earlier expressed willingness, or unwillingness, to accept responsibility for his or her actions. Second, it is not necessary here to decide as a constitutional rule that a judge is required to disregard any information concerning the crime discovered after the plea offer was made. Petitioner argues that implementing a remedy will open the floodgates to litigation by defendants seeking to unsettle their convictions, but in the 30 years that courts have recognized such claims, there has been no indication that the system is overwhelmed or that defendants are receiving windfalls as a result of strategically timed *Strickland* claims. In addition, the prosecution and trial courts may adopt measures to help ensure against meritless claims.

Next, the defendant enjoys the right to be informed of exculpatory evidence in possession of the prosecution. That is, if the prosecutor has evidence that casts doubt on the accused's guilt, he or she must inform the defense of that evidence. For evidence to be considered *exculpatory*, it must have a reasonable probability of affecting the outcome of the case. Evidence that is inconsequential to the question of guilt, which is clearly rare, need not be provided to the defense.[69]

Finally, as will be considered in an upcoming chapter, the defendant enjoys the right to be present at his or her own trial. However, this right does not apply in the

---

[69]*United States v. Bagley,* 473 U.S. 667 (1985).

context of plea bargaining. That is to say, no court has required that a criminal defendant be provided a constitutional right to be present during plea bargaining. This could change, but for now, all that is required is that the defense effectively communicates to his or her client the nature of the sentence or charges offered by the prosecution.

Recently, in *United States* v. *Ruiz*,[70] the Supreme Court decided that the defendant *does not* have the right to impeachment information relating to informants and other witnesses nor does he or she have the right to information supporting any affirmative defense that he or she might raise if the case went to trial. Thus, there are limitations to the defendant's rights during the plea bargaining process.

Acceptable Inducements by the Prosecution

prosecutorial inducements Offers made by the prosecution to the defendant.

The Constitution places few restrictions on offers the prosecution may make during the bargaining process, which are known as prosecutorial inducements. Since *Brady* v. *United States* was the first Supreme Court case to condone plea bargaining, it is a fitting point of departure before considering the offers prosecutors can make. The defendant in *Brady* was charged with kidnapping under a statute that permitted (1) a jury to recommend the death penalty if it saw fit *or* (2) a judge to sentence the defendant to life in prison, if guilt was determined via a bench trial. The defendant opted for a jury trial but then changed his plea to guilty and was sentenced to 30 years. He then argued that the statute effectively compelled him to plead guilty because of fear of the death penalty. The Supreme Court rejected this claim.

The reasoning the Court offered for its decision is somewhat complicated but important. Justice White emphasized that the statute in *Brady caused* the guilty plea but did not *coerce* it. He then emphasized that coercion is possible only when physical force or mental pressure is applied. This means that if "Brady was so gripped by fear of the death penalty or hope of leniency that he did not or could not, with the help of counsel, rationally weigh the advantages of going to trial against the advantages of pleading guilty,"[71] then his argument would have succeeded. However, Justice White found that the statute at most *influenced* Brady and that the coercion argument was exaggerated. In further support of his opinion, Justice White quoted an appellate court decision dealing with plea bargaining, *Shelton* v. *United States*:

> [A] plea of guilty entered by one fully aware of the direct consequences, including the actual value of any commitments made to him by the court, prosecutor, or his own counsel, must stand unless induced by threats (or promises to discontinue improper harassment), misrepresentation (including unfulfilled or unfulfillable promises), or perhaps by promises that are by their nature improper as having no proper relationship to the prosecutor's business (e.g., bribes).[72]

In short, a guilty plea resulting from an inducement from the prosecution, like a confession obtained in a police interrogation room, should not be involuntary. A guilty plea will be considered involuntary when it results from prosecutorial coercion

---

[70]*United States* v. *Ruiz*, 536 U.S. 622 (2002).
[71]*Brady* v. *United States*, 397 U.S. 742 (1970), p. 750.
[72]*Shelton* v. *United States*, 246 F.2d 571 (5th Cir. 1957), p. 572.

(e.g., physical force or strong psychological pressuring). If, by contrast, the prosecutor causes a guilty plea simply because the accused thinks that pleading as such is his or her best way of avoiding a long prison term, then the defendant cannot succeed by claiming such a plea is involuntary.

What, then, offers/inducements can the prosecution properly make? *Brady* answered this question only insofar as the Court held that the prosecutor cannot coerce a guilty plea. In *Bordenkircher v. Hayes*,[73] the Court attempted to offer a clearer answer. In that case, the defendant was indicted by a grand jury for forging a check for $88.30. The range of punishment was two to ten years in prison. The prosecutor offered to recommend a five-year sentence but threatened to seek an indictment under a habitual criminal statute if the defendant did not accept the offer. Since the defendant had two prior felony convictions, a conviction under the habitual criminal statute could have resulted in life in prison.

Somewhat controversially, in a 5–4 decision, the Supreme Court upheld the defendant's conviction under the habitual criminal statute on the theory that it resulted from a choice among known alternatives. Basically, the Court said that the defendant had the choice to accept five years in prison and neglected to take the opportunity. The defendant argued that his second conviction was vindictive, but the Court countered by stating that "the imposition of these difficult choices [is] an inevitable—'and permissible'—attribute of any legitimate system which tolerates and encourages the negotiation of pleas."[74]

Reduced to its most fundamental elements, the Court's opinion in *Bordenkircher* thus implies that the prosecution has great latitude in terms of being able to persuade the defendant to accept a plea, as long as the higher charges are authorized by law and are openly presented to the defense. This suggests, as well, that the prosecution may offer a charge or sentencing concession in exchange for the defendant agreeing not to appeal or claim that some constitutional right has been violated. The Court stated further:

> There is no doubt that the breadth of discretion that our country's legal system vests in prosecuting attorneys carries with it the potential for both individual and institutional abuse. And broad though that discretion may be, there are undoubtedly constitutional limits upon its exercise. We hold only that the course of conduct engaged in by the prosecutor in this case, which no more than openly presented the defendant with the unpleasant alternatives of forgoing trial or facing charges on which he was plainly subject to prosecution, did not violate the Due Process Clause of the Fourteenth Amendment.[75]

In a related case, *United States v. Goodwin*,[76] the Court reached a similar decision. The defendant was indicted on additional charges after plea negotiations broke down. The Court held that the prosecutor could file additional charges if an initial expectation that the defendant would plead guilty to a lesser charge proved unfounded. The Court refused to accept the defendant's argument that this prosecution was vindictive and, once again, gave broad authority to prosecutors in the plea bargaining process.

---

[73]*Bordenkircher v. Hayes*, 434 U.S. 357 (1978).
[74]Ibid., p. 364.
[75]Ibid., p. 365.
[76]*United States v. Goodwin*, 457 U.S. 368 (1982).

Nonetheless, certain prosecutorial inducements are *not* permissible. For example, the Supreme Court has stated that "a prosecutor's offer during plea bargaining of adverse or lenient treatment for some person *other* than the accused . . . might pose a greater danger of inducing a false guilty plea by skewing the assessment of the risks a defendant must consider."[77] Also, if the prosecutor flagrantly deceives the accused or fabricates evidence and/or starts rumors concerning the accused's level of involvement in the offense, a resulting guilty plea will be deemed unconstitutional.

Questionable Inducements

ad hoc **plea bargaining**
A term used to describe some of the strange concessions that defendants agree to make as part of prosecutors' decisions to secure guilty pleas.

Law Professor Joseph Colquitt has used the term *ad hoc* **plea bargaining** to refer to some of the strange concessions that defendants agree to make as part of prosecutors' decisions to secure guilty pleas. He states:

> Ad hoc bargains exist in at least five forms: (1) [T]he court may impose an extraordinary condition of probation following a guilty plea, (2) the defendant may offer or be required to perform some act as a quid pro quo for a dismissal or more lenient sentence, (3) the court may impose an unauthorized form of punishment as a substitute for a statutorily established method of punishment, (4) the State may offer some unauthorized benefit in return for a plea of guilty, or (5) the defendant may be permitted to plead guilty to an unauthorized offense, such as a "hypothetical" or nonexistent charge, a nonapplicable lesser-included offense, or a nonrelated charge.[78]

Colquitt also states that ad hoc plea bargaining "may involve neither a plea nor a sentence. For example, if a defendant charged with public intoxication seeks to avoid a statutorily mandated minimum sentence of 10 days in the county jail, the prosecutor might agree to dismiss the charges if the defendant agrees to make a monetary contribution to a local driver's education program."[79]

Judges can even get involved in ad hoc plea bargaining. Colquitt points to one shocking example of this method of bargaining run amok. The case, *Ryan* v. *Comm'n on Judicial Performance,*[80] involved a woman who was required to participate in a drug treatment program as a result of several narcotics convictions. The probation officer asked to have the woman removed from the program because she supposedly failed to follow program guidelines. At a hearing to decide on the matter, the woman, "who was wearing a low-cut sweater, bent over several times to remove documents from her purse. Thereafter the judge dismissed all criminal charges against her. When his clerk asked why the charges had been dropped, [the judge] replied, 'she showed me her boobs'."[81] The judge was subsequently removed from the bench. Some less extreme examples of ad hoc plea concessions, as well as some relevant cases, are described in Figure 14.5.

Statutory and Judicial Inducements

So far, the discussion has considered only what the prosecution can and cannot do as far as inducing the defendant to plead guilty. There have also been some interesting

---

[77]*Bordenkircher* v. *Hayes*, 434 U.S. 357 (1978) p. 365, n. 8.
[78]J. A. Colquitt, "Ad Hoc Plea Bargaining," *Tulane Law Review,* Vol. 75 (2001), pp. 695–776, 695.
[79]Ibid., p. 711.
[80]*Ryan* v. *Comm'n on Judicial Performance*, 754 P.2d 724 (Cal. 1988).
[81]Ibid., p. 734.

- Charitable contributions in lieu of fines or jail terms: *State v. Stellato* (523 A.2d 1345 [Conn. App.Ct.1987]); *Ratliff v. State* (596 N.E.2d 241 [Ind. Ct. App. 1992])
- Relinquished property ownership: *United States v. Thao Dinh Lee* (173 F.3d 1258 [10th Cir. 1999])
- Agreement to surrender a professional license or not work in a particular profession: *United States v. Hoffer* (129 F.3d 1196 [11th Cir. 1997])
- Voluntary agreement to undergo sterilization: *State v. Pasicznyk* (1997 WL 79501 [Wash. Ct. App. Feb. 25, 1997])
- Voluntary agreement to undergo surgical castration: *ACLU v. State* (5 S.W.2d 418 [Ark. 1999])
- Agreement to enter the army on a four-year enlistment: *State v. Hamrick* (595 N. W.2d 492 [Iowa 1999])
- Agreement not to appeal: *People v. Collier* (641 N.Y.S.2d 181 [App. Div. 1996])
- Shaming punishments, such as bumper stickers for convicted DUI offenders: *Ballenger v. State* (436 S.E.2d 793 [Ga. Ct. App. 1993])
- Agreement to seal the records of a case: *State v. Campbell* (21 Media L. Rep. 1895 [Wash. Super. Ct. 1993])
- Ordering offenders to surrender profits, such as from books written about their crimes: *Rolling v. State ex rel. Butterworth* (741 So. 2d 627 [Fla. Dist. Ct. App. 1999])
- Banishment to another location: *State v. Culp* (226 S.E.2d 841 [N.C. Ct. App. 1976]); *Phillips v. State* (512 S.E.2d 32 [Ga. Ct. App. 1999])
- Pleading guilty to nonexistent crimes (i.e., crimes that are not prohibited by law): *Bassin v. Isreal* (335 N.E.2d 53 [III. App. Ct. 1975])

Figure 14.5

Examples of *Ad Hoc* Plea Bargaining Concessions

Source: Adapted from J. A. Colquitt, "Ad Hoc Plea Bargaining," *Tulane Law Review* 75 (2001): 69. See Colquitt's article for a *thorough* discussion of various, sometimes stranger concessions made as a result of *ad hoc* plea bargaining (i.e., note 26).

statutory inducements
Statutes that offer incentives for pleading guilty.

judicial inducements
When a judge offers something to the defendant in exchange for a guilty plea. Most judicial inducements are prohibited.

cases dealing with statutory and judicial inducements. **Statutory inducements** refer to laws that provide lenient sentences in exchange for guilty pleas. **Judicial inducements** include actions by judges that influence the bargaining process.

With regard to statutory inducements, an illustrative case is *Corbitt* v. *New Jersey*.[82] In that case, the defendant was convicted of first-degree murder and sentenced to life in prison, as required by the state statute with which he was charged. However, the statute provided that if he decided to plead guilty to the crime, he could be sentenced either to life imprisonment or to a term of 30 years. The defendant claimed that the statute violated due process, but the Supreme Court upheld it in the spirit of consistency. That is, the Court stated that it could not permit prosecutorial bargaining as in *Bordenkircher* "and yet hold that the legislature may not openly provide for the possibility of leniency in return for a plea."[83] Furthermore, the Court stated:

> It cannot be said that defendants found guilty by a jury are "penalized" for exercising the right to a jury trial any more than defendants who plead guilty are penalized because they give up the chance of acquittal at trial. In each instance, the defendant faces a multitude of possible outcomes and freely makes his choice. Equal protection does not free those who made a bad assessment of risks or a bad choice from the consequences of their decision.[84]

---

[82]*Corbitt* v. *New Jersey*, 439 U.S. 212 (1978).
[83]Ibid., p. 221.
[84]Ibid., p. 226.

The Court also noted, though, that plea bargaining should be an *executive*, as opposed to *legislative*, function. That is, legislatures should not be permitted to decide "that the penalty for every criminal offense to which a defendant pleads guilty is to be one-half the penalty to be imposed upon a defendant convicted of the same offense after a not guilty plea."[85]

Traditionally, plea bargaining results from the prosecution and the defense reaching an agreement; the judge is usually not part of the negotiation process. Today, however, certain jurisdictions permit a degree of judicial involvement in the plea bargaining process. For example, the American Bar Association standards regarding guilty pleas permit judicial participation when it is requested but only for the purpose of clarifying acceptable charges and sentences. The judge cannot at any point, "either directly or indirectly, [communicate] to the defendant or defense counsel that a plea agreement should be accepted or that a guilty plea should be entered."[86]

In order to summarize the plea bargaining process, Figure 14.6 presents relevant portions of Rule 11 of the *Federal Rules of Criminal Procedure*. The procedures outlined are those by which the federal courts must abide.

Effects of Plea Bargaining

A plea bargain ultimately affects four separate parties: (1) the court, (2) the prosecutor, (3) the defendant (the latter, most often through the defense attorney), and (4) the victim. How plea bargaining affects these individual parties is discussed in the subsections that follow.

Effects on the Court

The court is not directly bound by a plea agreement. In deciding whether to accept the bargain, the court weighs the sometimes competing interests of the agreement and the public interest. Thus, if accepting a plea agreement poses a significant risk to the public—say, because a dangerous criminal will be spared prison and placed on probation (an unlikely event)—then the court has the discretion to deny it.

An illustrative case is *United States* v. *Bean*.[87] The facts were as follow: Bean was charged on October 22, 1976, with theft of property (i.e., a car) and with burglary of a habitation, in violation of state law. At the initial arraignment, Bean pleaded not guilty to both counts. On November 30, another arraignment was held on Bean's request. At this time, the court was informed that a plea bargain had been reached between the government prosecutor and Bean and his counsel. Bean would plead guilty to the theft count and cooperate with the prosecutor in investigating others involved in the burglary. In return, the prosecutor would move for a dismissal of the burglary charge. Judge Spears rejected the plea because the offense of entering a home at night where people were sleeping was a much more serious offense than

---

[85]Ibid., p. 227.
[86]American Bar Association, Standard 14-3.3[d], from *Standards for Criminal Justice*, 2nd ed., supp., vol. 3 (Washington, DC: American Bar Association, 1986).
[87]*United States* v. *Bean*, 564 F.2d 700 (5th Cir. 1977).

(a) **Entering a Plea.**

(1) *In General.*

A defendant may plead not guilty, guilty, or (with the court's consent) nolo contendere.

(2) *Conditional Plea.*

With the consent of the court and the government, a defendant may enter a conditional plea of guilty or nolo contendere, reserving in writing the right to have an appellate court review an adverse determination of a specified pretrial motion. A defendant who prevails on appeal may then withdraw the plea.

(3) *Nolo Contendere Plea.*

Before accepting a plea of nolo contendere, the court must consider the parties' views and the public interest in the effective administration of justice.

(4) *Failure to Enter a Plea.*

If a defendant refuses to enter a plea or if a defendant organization fails to appear, the court must enter a plea of not guilty.

(b) **Considering and Accepting a Guilty or Nolo Contendere Plea.**

(1) *Advising and Questioning the Defendant.*

Before the court accepts a plea of guilty or nolo contendere, the defendant may be placed under oath, and the court must address the defendant personally in open court. During this address, the court must inform the defendant of, and determine that the defendant understands, the following:

(A) the government's right, in a prosecution for perjury or false statement, to use against the defendant any statement that the defendant gives under oath;

(B) the right to plead not guilty, or having already so pleaded, to persist in that plea;

(C) the right to a jury trial;

(D) the right to be represented by counsel – and if necessary have the court appoint counsel – at trial and at every other stage of the proceeding;

(E) the right at trial to confront and cross-examine adverse witnesses, to be protected from compelled self-incrimination, to testify and present evidence, and to compel the attendance of witnesses;

(F) the defendant's waiver of these trial rights if the court accepts a plea of guilty or nolo contendere;

(G) the nature of each charge to which the defendant is pleading;

(H) any maximum possible penalty, including imprisonment, fine, and term of supervised release;

(I) any mandatory minimum penalty;

(J) any applicable forfeiture;

(K) the court's authority to order restitution;

(L) the court's obligation to impose a special assessment;

(M) in determining a sentence, the court's obligation to apply and calculate the applicable sentencing-guideline range and to consider that range, possible departures under the Sentencing Guidelines, and other sentencing factors under 18 U.S.C. §3553(a); and

(N) the terms of any plea-agreement provision waiving the right to appeal or to collaterally attack the sentence.

(2) *Ensuring That a Plea Is Voluntary.*

Before accepting a plea of guilty or nolo contendere, the court must address the defendant personally in open court and determine that the plea is voluntary and did not result from force, threats, or promises (other than promises in a plea agreement).

(3) *Determining the Factual Basis for a Plea.*

Before entering judgment on a guilty plea, the court must determine that there is a factual basis for the plea.

Figure 14.6

Elements of a Valid Guilty Plea under the Federal Rules of Evidence

Source: Federal Rules of Criminal Procedure, Rule 11.

the theft of an automobile. The Fifth Circuit Court of Appeals upheld Judge Spears's decision, stating:

> Without deciding what unusual circumstances may result in the refusal of a plea bargain being an abuse of discretion, we find that Judge Spears' action in this case was well within the scope of his discretion. A decision that a plea bargain will result in the defendant's receiving too light a sentence under the circumstances of the case is a sound reason for a judge's refusing to accept the agreement. . . . In this case, Judge Spears was faced with a man who was charged with burglarizing at night a home on Fort Sam Houston in Texas, while Lieutenant Colonel Robert W. Oppenlander, his wife, two daughters and one son were asleep inside. In addition, the presentence report indicated that Bean had previously been committed to four years in the Texas Department of Corrections for state charges of burglary and theft of a business at nighttime. Bean had also served twenty days for unlawfully carrying a weapon in San Antonio. Given this information Judge Spears was reluctant to accept a plea bargain that would allow Bean to plead guilty to only the theft of an automobile.[88]

Effects on the Prosecutor

The consequences of plea bargaining are of far greater magnitude for the prosecutor than for the court. Assuming the court accepts a plea bargain, whether it is a charge or sentence reduction, then the prosecutor must fulfill his or her part of the agreement. Note, however, that the prosecutor is not strictly obligated to fulfill his or her promises early in the plea bargaining process. More specifically, the prosecutor is not bound by the plea bargain prior to the point at which it is accepted by the court.

The prosecutor has a considerable amount of latitude with regard to fulfilling a plea bargain before it is accepted by the court. This should not be particularly surprising because before the court accepts (or rejects) the bargain, it is not formalized. When the court accepts the bargain, it becomes formalized, at which point the prosecutor must fulfill his or her promises.

A case dealing with the extent to which a prosecutor must uphold his or her end of the bargain prior to the point at which the court accepts it is *Mabry* v. *Johnson*.[89] In that case, the defense attorney called the prosecutor to accept a plea offer, but the prosecutor told him that the offer was a mistake and withdrew it. The prosecutor then offered a harsher offer in its place, one that would have resulted in a longer prison term. The Supreme Court upheld this practice, arguing that the plea agreement was reached with full awareness on the part of the defendant and "was thus in no sense the product of governmental deception; it rested on no 'unfulfilled promise' and fully satisfied the test for voluntariness and intelligence."[90] In an analogous decision, *Puckett* v. *United States*,[91] the prosecution agreed to a plea agreement, but then reneged when it became clear the defendant had aided a fellow inmate in another crime while awaiting sentencing. The Supreme Court sided with the prosecution.

In general, the prosecution is bound to its plea bargaining promises after the court accepts the bargain. An illustrative case is *Santobello* v. *New York*.[92] In that case, the

---

[88]Ibid., p. 704.
[89]*Mabry* v. *Johnson*, 467 U.S. 504 (1984).
[90]Ibid., p. 510.
[91]*Puckett* v. *United States*, No. 07-9712 (2009).
[92]*Santobello* v. *New York*, 404 U.S. 257 (1971).

defendant was indicted for two felonies. He first entered a plea of not guilty on each count. After subsequent negotiations, however, the prosecutor agreed to allow the defendant to plead guilty to a lesser offense. The defendant then withdrew his pleas of not guilty and agreed to plead guilty to the lesser offense. The court accepted the plea. At sentencing, however, a new prosecutor, who was unaware of what had transpired earlier, requested the maximum sentence. The defense objected on the grounds that the previous prosecutor promised not to make any particular sentencing recommendation. The judge then stated that he was not influenced by the second prosecutor's sentencing recommendation and imposed the maximum sentence.

In response to this turn of events, the Supreme Court declared that the sentence should be declared unconstitutional as a matter of due process. The Court stated that "when a plea rests in any significant degree on a promise or agreement of the prosecutor, so that it can be said to be part of the inducement or consideration, such promise must be fulfilled."[93]

Unfortunately, though, the Court was not altogether clear in terms of what remedy is preferable when the prosecutor breaches his or her agreement. In *Santobello*, the Court voided the defendant's conviction, but the Justices seemed mixed on the appropriate remedy for future cases. Some agreed that if the prosecution breaches its promise after the court has accepted the bargain, then it must be forced to uphold the bargain or the defendant should be able to withdraw the guilty plea. Others felt that the trial court should decide what remedy is necessary. The issue remains unresolved.

Some years after *Santobello*, in the case of *United States* v. *Benchimol*,[94] the Supreme Court seemed to change its opinion with regard to a prosecutor's breach of a plea agreement after the court has accepted it. In *Benchimol*, the prosecutor agreed to recommend a sentence of probation with restitution, but the presentence report mentioned nothing of the agreement. The defense attorney pointed out the error, and the prosecution agreed that an agreement had been reached. Even so, the court sentenced the defendant to six years. The defendant then sought to have his sentence vacated, and the court of appeals agreed. However, the Supreme Court reversed, holding that unless the prosecution supports a recommendation "enthusiastically" or sets forth its reasons for a lenient recommendation, the court is under no obligation to honor the agreement. According to the Supreme Court:

> It may well be that the Government in a particular case might commit itself to "enthusiastically" make a particular recommendation to the court, and it may be that the Government in a particular case might agree to explain to the court the reasons for the Government's making a particular recommendation. But respondent does not contend, nor did the Court of Appeals find, that the Government had in fact undertaken to do either of these things here. The Court of Appeals simply held that as a matter of law such an undertaking was to be implied from the Government's agreement to recommend a particular sentence. But our view of Rule 11(e) [of the *Federal Rules of Evidence*, which sets forth procedures for plea bargaining] is that it speaks in terms of what the parties in fact agree to, and does not suggest that such implied-in-law terms as were read into this agreement by the Court of Appeals have any place under the Rule.[95]

---

[93]Ibid., p. 262.
[94]*United States* v. *Benchimol*, 471 U.S. 453 (1985).
[95]Ibid., p. 455.

Effects on the Defendant

The defendant who accepts an offer to plead guilty often faces consequences besides a reduced sentence or charge. Important rights are often waived, such as the right to appeal, the right to a jury trial, and privilege against self-incrimination. Also, if the defendant supplies inaccurate information during the course of plea negotiations, he or she may not benefit from lenient treatment. Furthermore, in exchange for pleading guilty, the prosecution may require that the defendant testifies against a codefendant.

A significant Supreme Court case dealing with the latter consequence—that is, possible testimony against a codefendant—is *Ricketts* v. *Adamson*.[96] In that case, the defendant testified against both of his codefendants in exchange for a reduction in the charge he was facing. He was then sentenced on the reduced charge. After that, the codefendants' convictions were overturned on appeal. The prosecution then retried the codefendants, but the original defendant refused to testify at the second trial, claiming that his duty had been fulfilled. The prosecution then filed on information charging him with first-degree murder. The Supreme Court did not bar the first-degree murder prosecution because the original agreement contained a clause to the effect that the agreement would be void if the defendant refused to testify against his codefendants. Justice Brennan did acknowledge, however, that the defendant could have construed the plea agreement only to require his testimony at the first trial. The Court noted that the proper procedure, if such a situation would arise in the future, would be to submit a disagreement over the plea to the court that accepted the plea. That way, the expense of a further trial and appeals could be avoided.

At the other extreme, the defendant can sometimes *preserve* certain rights following a plea agreement. These types of arrangements are known as *conditional guilty pleas*. For example, New York law provides that an order denying a motion to suppress evidence alleged to have been obtained as a result of unlawful search-and-seizure "may be reviewed on appeal from a judgment of conviction notwithstanding the fact that such judgment of conviction is predicated upon a plea of guilty."[97] These types of agreements are rare, however. In *Tollett* v. *Henderson*, the Supreme Court stated that "[w]hen a criminal defendant has solemnly admitted in open court that he is in fact guilty of the offense with which he is charged, he may not thereafter raise independent claims relating to the deprivation of constitutional rights that occurred prior to the entry of the guilty plea."[98]

Effects on the Victim

While plea bargaining mainly occurs between the prosecution and defense, it is important not to leave out the victim. Victims are affected by plea bargaining in at least two respects. First, a plea agreement may give the victim a measure of closure relatively quick. On the other hand, a plea agreement may be viewed by the victim as lenient. That is, he or she may feel the offender was not adequately "punished" for

---

[96]*Ricketts* v. *Adamson*, 483 U.S. 1 (1987).
[97]N.Y. Crim. Proc. Law §§ 710.20 (1), 710.70 (2).
[98]*Tollett* v. *Henderson*, 411 U.S. 258 (1973), p. 267.

the offense in question. To address this problem, several states have laws that require victim involvement or input during the bargaining process.[99]

<table>
<tr><td>

YOUR DECISION

</td><td>

1. Assume that a prosecutor and a defendant are negotiating a plea agreement. In the negotiation, the prosecutor lies to the defendant, saying, "We have a videotape recording of you engaged in the crime. If you do not plead guilty, this evidence will be used against you at trial. No jury in its right mind would acquit you based on the recording. However, if you plead guilty to petty larceny, then you will be out of jail in no time flat." The defendant pleads guilty but later appeals his conviction, claiming that his plea was the result of prosecutorial deception. What should the court decide?

2. Judge Dubois has before her the prosecutor, defense attorney, and defendant in one of the cases slated to be heard in her court. The defense attorney and prosecutor tell the judge that they have reached a plea agreement and that Charles Down, the defendant, has agreed to plead guilty to manslaughter instead of first-degree murder. Judge Dubois then questions Down to ensure that the plea is voluntary, intelligent, and based in fact. During the questioning, Down begins to express reservations about the plea agreement and says, "On second thought, I don't want to plead guilty." Judge Dubois then looks at Down and says, "You should really plead guilty, because from the looks of things, you're going to get the chair if you don't." Down agrees to plead guilty but later appeals, arguing that his plea was not voluntary. How should the court rule?

</td></tr>
</table>

Summary

- Plea bargaining occurs when the prosecution offers some concession to the defendant in exchange for a guilty plea.

- Two common forms of plea bargaining can be discerned. The first, charge bargaining, occurs when the prosecutor offers to charge the accused with a less serious offense in exchange for a guilty plea. The second, sentence bargaining, occurs when the prosecutor promises the defendant a favorable sentencing recommendation.

- Plea bargaining is how most cases in the U.S. criminal justice system are disposed of. By some estimates, 90% of all criminal cases are plea bargained.

- Supporters of the practice claim that bargaining is necessary to ensure the orderly and prompt flow of criminal cases. Critics claim, among other things, that defendants are forced to give up important constitutional rights as a result of the plea bargaining process.

---

[99]U.S. Department of Justice, *Victim Input into Plea Agreements* (Washington, DC: U.S. Department of Justice, 2002). https://www.ncjrs.gov/ovc_archives/bulletins/legalseries/bulletin7/welcome.html (accessed March 26, 2012).

- Despite the Supreme Court's support for plea bargaining, it still requires that certain procedures be followed. First, the defendant must be represented by counsel and that counsel must be effective. Second, the defendant has the right to be informed by the prosecution of exculpatory evidence in the state's possession. Third, the prosecution can offer a wide range of inducements to the defense in order to secure a guilty plea, but those inducements cannot be coercive in nature. Fourth, there is some question about the propriety of so-called ad hoc plea bargaining: the practice of offering inducements to the defendant other than charge reductions and sentencing recommendations. Finally, statutory and judicial inducements for the defendant to plead guilty should be kept to a minimum.

- Plea bargaining affects four parties: (1) the court, (2) the prosecutor, (3) the defendant (most often through the defense attorney), and (4) the victim. It affects the court only insofar as the court has to decide whether to accept the plea. The prosecutor is affected by plea bargaining only after the agreement has been accepted by the court. The defendant often gives up certain rights by pleading guilty but can preserve certain rights pursuant to conditional plea agreement statutes. Victims get closure but may also be put off by agreements that are perceived as "soft."

MODULE 14.4 — GUILTY PLEAS

Learning Objectives

- **Outline the elements of a valid guilty plea.**
- **Explain the process for contesting a guilty plea.**

CORE CONCEPTS

Plea bargaining is not the only way to arrive at a guilty plea. Many defendants plead guilty to the charges against them even when no bargaining takes place. The bulk of this chapter focuses on plea bargaining; however, the section "Elements of a Valid Guilty Plea" is especially important for both types of guilty pleas: those that follow bargaining and those that do not. A sample of the plea form that is submitted to the court is presented in Figure 14.7.

Elements of a Valid Guilty Plea

Assuming the prosecutor offers an acceptable inducement to the defendant and assuming the defendant agrees to plead guilty in exchange for leniency, the judge still must determine that the defendant understands the plea. This is in addition to the need to determine that the plea conforms to statutory and other requirements, as discussed earlier. In *Boykin* v. *Alabama*, the Supreme Court held that it would be

PLEA FORM

CAUSE NUMBER:

STATE OF TEXAS   §   **IN THE MUNICIPAL COURT**
VS.   §   **CITY OF** _____
_____   §   _____ **COUNTY, TEXAS**

PLEA OF NOLO CONTENDERE

I, the undersigned, do hereby enter my appearance on the complaint of the offense, to wit: _____
_____
charged in Municipal Court Cause Number _____. I have been informed of my right to a jury trial and that my signature on this plea of *nolo contendere* (meaning "no contest") will have the same force and effect as a plea of guilty on the judgment of the Court. I do hereby plead *nolo contendere* to said offense as charged, waive my right to a jury trial or hearing by the Court, and agree to pay the fine and costs the judge assesses. I understand that my plea may result in a conviction appearing on either a criminal record or a driver's license record.

_____   _____
Date   Defendant's Signature

                                                     _____
                                                     Address

PLEA OF GUILTY

I, the undersigned, do hereby enter my appearance on the complaint of the offense, to wit: _____
_____
charged in Municipal Court Cause Number. I have been informed of my right to a jury trial and that my signature to this plea of guilty will have the same force and effect as a judgment of the Court. I do hereby plead guilty to the offense as charged, waive my right to a jury trial or hearing by the Court, and agree to pay the fine and costs the judge assesses. I understand that my plea may result in a conviction appearing on either a criminal record or a driver's license record.

_____   _____
Date   Defendant's Signature

                                                       _____
                                                     Address

PLEA OF NOT GUILTY

I, the undersigned, do hereby enter my appearance on the complaint of the offense, to wit: _____
_____
charged in Municipal Court Cause Number _____. I plead not guilty.

Initial One:

_____   I want a jury trial.
_____   I waive my right to a jury trial and request a trial before the Court.

_____   _____
Date   Defendant's Signature

                                                       _____
                                                     Address

Figure 14.7
Sample Plea Form

unconstitutional "for the trial judge to accept [a] guilty plea without an affirmative showing that it is intelligent and voluntary."[100] In order to determine that the plea is voluntary, the judge usually questions the defendant. As the Court noted in *McCarthy* v. *United States*:

> By personally interrogating the defendant, not only will the judge be better able to ascertain the plea's voluntariness, but he also will develop a more complete record to support his determination in a subsequent post-conviction attack. . . . Both of these goals are undermined in proportion to the degree the district court judge resorts to "assumptions" not based upon recorded responses to his inquiries.[101]

For a guilty plea to be valid, it must conform to three requirements: (1) It must be intelligent; (2) it must be voluntary, not coerced; and (3) it must be based in fact. That is, if the defendant pleads guilty to a crime he or she did not commit, then technically, the plea will be invalid. The following subsections consider the case law regarding these three important requirements.

Intelligence

In general, for a plea to be *intelligent* (i.e., understood), it must conform to specific requirements. The defendant must understand (1) the nature of the charge or charges of which he or she is accused, (2) the possible sentence or sentences associated with the charges, and (3) the rights he or she may waive if a guilty plea is entered. A person whose mental capacity is called into question may be declared incompetent at a pretrial hearing and treated in order to restore his or her competency. (The issue of competency is discussed further in the next chapter.)

In *Henderson* v. *Morgan*,[102] the defendant was charged with first-degree murder. However, he pleaded guilty to second-degree murder following an offer by the prosecution. Several years later, he sought to have his conviction voided on the grounds that at the time he entered his plea, he did not understand that one of the elements of second-degree murder was intent to cause death. The Supreme Court held that "since respondent did not receive adequate notice of the offense to which he pleaded guilty, his plea was involuntary and the judgment of conviction was entered without due process of law."[103] The element of intent in second-degree murder (i.e., the *mens rea*) was viewed as critical, which meant it should have been explained to the defendant.

It is not clear based on *Henderson* whether the *judge* must explain the elements of the offense to the defendant or whether this is the job of *counsel*. The Court intimated that if defense counsel explains the offense to the accused, then little else is needed: "[I]t may be appropriate to presume that in most cases defense counsel routinely explain the nature of the offense in sufficient detail to give the accused notice of what he is being asked to admit."[104] Nevertheless, the judge should at least inquire as to whether the defendant understands the charge.

---

[100]*Boykin* v. *Alabama*, 395 U.S. 238 (1969), p. 242.
[101]*McCarthy* v. *United States*, 394 U.S. 459 (1969), p. 468.
[102]*Henderson* v. *Morgan*, 426 U.S. 637 (1976).
[103]Ibid., p. 647.
[104]Ibid.

There are virtually no Supreme Court cases dealing with the defendant's understanding of the possible sentences that could result from a plea bargain. However, the *Federal Rules of Criminal Procedure* require that the defendant understand the consequences of the plea. This includes an understanding of the minimum and maximum sentences as well as applicable sentencing guidelines that the judge might be required to abide by.

Whether other consequences attendant to plea bargaining and sentencing have to be explained depends on the situation. On the one hand, at least one lower court has held that the defendant does not need to be informed of the loss of the right to vote.[105] On the other hand, failure to tell the defendant that deportation is a possible consequence of a guilty plea may result in a decision that such a plea is invalid.[106]

The rights *waived* as a result of plea bargaining are different than the rights *denied* as a result of plea bargaining. For example, loss of the right to vote is not a loss due to voluntary waiver; it is a consequence tied to being convicted (even if by guilty plea) of a serious crime. The rights *waived* are those the defendant would otherwise be granted by the Constitution but are essentially given up in exchange for lenient treatment.

The constitutional rights typically waived through plea bargaining are the right to trial by jury, the privilege against self-incrimination, and the right to confront adverse witnesses. By pleading guilty, the defendant forgoes having a trial, which is when these rights are frequently applicable. The privilege against self-incrimination, however, still applies outside the trial context, such as in pretrial custodial interrogations. Regardless, the defendant must be clearly informed of the constitutional rights that are waived as a result of plea bargaining. According to the Supreme Court in *Boykin* v. *Alabama*, there can be no presumption of "a waiver of these three important federal rights from a silent record."[107]

Voluntariness

In addition to the requirement that a plea be understood, it also must be voluntary. Even though a plea may be understood, it may have resulted from coercion, threats, physical abuse, or the like. Thus, the *Federal Rules of Criminal Procedure* require that a plea be "voluntary and not the result of force or threats or of promises (other than promises in the agreement)."[108]

Factual Basis

For a plea bargain to be valid, the plea must result from conduct that has a basis in fact. In other words, a defendant cannot (i.e., according to the courts anyway) plead guilty to a crime he or she did not commit. This means that the court should inquire about the crime in question by, perhaps, having the accused describe the conduct

---

[105]See, e.g., *People* v. *Thomas*, 41 Ill.2d 122 (1968).
[106]See, e.g., *Padilla* v. *Kentucky*, No. 08-651 (2010).
[107]*Boykin* v. *Alabama*, 395 U.S. 238 (1969), p. 243.
[108]*Federal Rules of Criminal Procedure*, Rule 11.

giving rise to his or her guilty plea. This does not always occur, but according to the Supreme Court in *McCarthy* v. *United States*:

> Requiring this examination of the relation between the law and the acts the defendant admits having committed is designed to protect a defendant who is in the position of pleading voluntarily with an understanding of the nature of the charge but without realizing that his conduct does not actually fall within the charge.[109]

Importantly, the Court in *McCarthy* did not state that a factual basis for the plea bargain is a *constitutional* requirement, only that there should be one.

The Court elaborated on this matter in a similar case, in which the defendant pleaded guilty but insisted on his innocence. The Court stated that "an express admission of guilt . . . is not a constitutional requisite to the imposition of a prison sentence even if he is unwilling or unable to admit his participation in the acts constituting the crime."[110] The Court upheld the man's plea but also pointed out the following:

> Because of the importance of protecting the innocent and of insuring that guilty pleas are a product of free and intelligent choice, various state and federal court decisions properly caution that pleas coupled with claims of innocence should not be accepted unless there is a factual basis for the plea . . . and until the judge taking the plea has inquired into and sought to resolve the conflict between the waiver of trial and the claim of innocence.[111]

Thus, while there appears to be no constitutional basis for requiring that a guilty plea be tied to specific criminal acts, the courts—including the Supreme Court—prefer to avoid guilty pleas accepted from otherwise innocent defendants. Unfortunately, it would be purely conjecture to estimate how many innocent criminal defendants plead guilty in order to "play the odds" and avoid potentially lengthy prison terms.

Contesting a Guilty Plea

The defendant may wish to contest the guilty plea he or she enters for several reasons, including the following: (1) If the plea was the product of coercion by the prosecution; (2) if the prosecution has failed to fulfill its end of the bargain; and (3) if other problems emerge, such as unconstitutional conduct on the part of law enforcement officials. A defendant who challenges his or her guilty plea does so in several ways, which include withdrawal of the plea and appeal.[112] Each mechanism is considered in a following subsection.

Withdrawing a Guilty Plea

Anytime the court refuses to accept a plea agreement reached by the prosecution and the defense, the defendant can usually withdraw the plea. Similarly, if the defendant

---

[109]*McCarthy* v. *United States*, 394 U.S. 459 (1969), p. 467.
[110]*North Carolina* v. *Alford*, 400 U.S. 25 (1970).
[111]Ibid., p. 38, n. 10.
[112]*Habeas corpus* review is also possible. This is discussed further in Chapter 15.

pleads guilty even when there has been no plea bargaining, he or she can seek to withdraw his or her plea. However, if the prosecution disagrees with the court's decision to refuse the plea, then the defendant might *not* be able to withdraw his or her plea.

Once a plea has been accepted by the court, then it can only be withdrawn in limited circumstances. The *Federal Rules of Criminal Procedure* provide that a plea can be withdrawn prior to sentencing if the defendant shows a "fair and just" reason for overturning the plea.[113] Fair and just reasons are the same as those mentioned at the outset of this section: involuntary pleas, prosecutorial breaches, and lack of evidence or similar deficiency. Once a sentence has been entered, however, the only methods to challenge a plea are to appeal and, to a lesser extent, to have a *habeas corpus* review (see Chapter 15). Also, many jurisdictions place a time limit on plea withdrawals; usually, withdrawal is not permitted once a sentence has been imposed.

Readers may recall the case of former Idaho Senator Larry Craig, who in 2007 was arrested in the Minneapolis-St. Paul International Airport on suspicion of lewd conduct in a public restroom. Craig quickly pleaded guilty to criminal charges but later attempted to withdraw his guilty plea, claiming that it was not knowing and intelligent. A judge denied his motion. Craig served out his term as senator and did not run for re-election.

Appealing a Guilty Plea

If the defendant moves to withdraw his or her plea and is denied this request, then an appeal is appropriate. However, if the withdrawal period has passed, then the only other method of appealing a guilty plea is through *direct* appeal. This creates something of a difficult situation for the defense. Since an appeal is mostly considered based on the trial court record, then the defendant has limited resources with which to prepare an argument. Namely, there is no transcript of a trial because by entering a guilty plea, the defendant elected to forgo trial. Thus, the only record left may be that from the arraignment or a similar pretrial proceeding. In sum, it is *very difficult* to succeed with a direct appeal of a guilty plea.

Fortunately, some states and the federal government permit appeals based on specific pretrial motions, such as a motion to exclude evidence on constitutional grounds. This is the case in New York and in other jurisdictions that maintain conditional plea mechanisms, as mentioned earlier. These issues aside, there are few Supreme Court precedents addressing appeals of guilty pleas. In *McCarthy* v. *United States*, the Supreme Court held that the trial court's failure to abide by proper arraignment procedure required reversal of a guilty plea on appeal. This is because the arraignment procedure—especially when there is no trial—"is designed to assist the district judge in making the constitutionally required determination that a defendant's guilty plea is truly voluntary."[114]

Note that the decision to appeal a court's denial of a motion to withdraw a guilty plea is not necessarily the same as an appeal of one's conviction. The former may go to the voluntariness of the plea. The latter may concern some other procedural matter, such as an improper search or seizure, and may be appealable,

---

[113]*Federal Rules of Criminal Procedure*, Rule 11.
[114]*McCarthy* v. *United States*, 394 U.S. 459 (1969), p. 465.

provided the defendant has not waived his or her right to appeal as a result of plea bargaining.

Finally, note that *plea bargaining* and *pleading guilty* are not the same. Plea bargaining often results in a guilty plea, but a defendant does not have to engage in bargaining to plead guilty. Regardless of how the guilty plea is arrived at, the defendant can still seek to withdraw the plea. By contrast, a guilty plea that is entered *without* plea bargaining is more appealable than one reached as a result of bargaining. In the latter instance, the accused often gives up important rights, such as the right to appeal.

YOUR DECISION

1. Bill Dover, a federal prisoner, filed a *habeas corpus* petition (i.e., a method of challenging his confinement; see Chapter 15), claiming that his guilty plea was not knowing and intelligent because of ineffective assistance of counsel. Specifically, Dover claimed that his attorney mistakenly advised him that if he pleaded guilty, he would become eligible for parole after serving one-third of his prison sentence. In actuality, because Dover was a second-time offender, he was required under the state law to serve one-half of his sentence before being eligible for parole. In other words, Dover claimed that he was not advised of the actual sentence that would result from his plea bargaining. Should he succeed with his petition?

2. Caroline Wynn pleaded guilty to federal drug charges and was sentenced to 247 months in prison by the U.S. District Court. At sentencing, the court neglected to inform Wynn of her right to appeal her sentence. Several months later, while Wynn was in prison, she filed a *habeas corpus* petition, alleging that the district court's failure to advise her of her right to appeal her sentence violated the express terms of Rule 32(a)(2) of the *Federal Rules of Criminal Procedure*, which provides that "[t]here shall be no duty on the court to advise the defendant of any right of appeal after sentence is imposed following a plea of guilty or *nolo contendere*, except that the court shall advise the defendant of any right to appeal the sentence." Wynn knew of her right to appeal at the time of sentencing but did not file an appeal. Now, she seeks postconviction relief. How should the court decide?

Summary

- Not just any plea agreement suffices. All plea agreements must be valid; that is, they must be knowing and intelligent, voluntary, and based in fact.
- A knowing and intelligent waiver is one in which the defendant understands the charge, the possible sentences, and the rights waived as a result of bargaining.
- A voluntary plea is one that is not coerced by the state.
- A plea agreement should be based in fact—that is, premised on conduct that actually took place. In other words, the defendant should not plead guilty to a crime he or she did not commit, although this clearly happens from time to time.
- The defendant can seek to withdraw his or her guilty plea. Doing so is fairly difficult once the court has accepted the plea. The defendant must show, for example,

that the plea was involuntary to have it withdrawn after the court accepts it. Next, if the defendant is denied a request to withdraw his or her guilty plea, he or she can appeal that decision.

- A guilty plea can sometimes be appealed, but this is increasingly rare because the defendant often agrees to waive his or her right to appeal as a result of plea bargaining.

Chapter Review

THE PROSECUTOR

Learning Objectives

- Understand the considerations going into the prosecutor's charging decision.
- Summarize restrictions that apply to the prosecutor's charging decision.
- Explain the concept of joinder and the reasons for it.

Review Questions

1. What is the role of the prosecutor?
2. What are some reasons for nonprosecution? What can be done to challenge a prosecutor's decision not to pursue charges?
3. What types of restrictions exist on the ability of the prosecutor to bring charges? Cite relevant cases.
4. What is joinder? Explain the differences between joinder of charges and joinder of defendants.

Key Terms

prosecutorial discretion
selective prosecution
pretextual prosecution

vindictive prosecution
joinder
severance

THE GRAND JURY

Learning Objectives

- Summarize the rules surrounding grand jury composition.
- Explain why secrecy in grand jury proceedings is important.
- Summarize the rights of grand jury witnesses and the targets of grand jury investigations.
- Describe the investigative powers of the grand jury.
- Explain the rules for challenging a grand jury indictment.

Review Questions

1. Explain some significant Supreme Court decisions with regard to the secrecy of grand jury proceedings.
2. Explain the rights of witnesses testifying before grand juries.
3. Distinguish among three types of investigative powers that grand juries possess.
4. Can a grand jury indictment be challenged? If so, how? If not, why not?

Key Terms

grand jury
true bill
subpoena *ad testificandum*

subpoena *duces tecum*
contempt power
variance

MODULE 14.3   **PLEA BARGAINING**

Learning Objectives

- Define plea bargaining.
- Outline the history of plea bargaining.
- Summarize the arguments for and against plea bargaining.
- Explain the plea bargaining process.
- Summarize the effects of plea bargaining on the court, the prosecutor, the defendant, and the victim.

Review Questions

1. What is plea bargaining? Can a defendant plead guilty without plea bargaining?
2. What are the reasons for the popularity of plea bargaining?
3. Summarize the arguments against plea bargaining.
4. What has been done in response to criticisms of plea bargaining?
5. Summarize the arguments in support of plea bargaining.
6. Explain the accused's constitutional rights during plea bargaining.
7. Explain how judges and statutes can induce guilty pleas.
8. Summarize the effects of plea bargaining on the court.
9. In what ways does plea bargaining affect the defendant?

Key Terms

plea bargaining

Alford Plea

prosecutorial enducements

ad hoc plea bargaining

statutory inducements

judicial inducements

MODULE 14.4   **GUILTY PLEAS**

Learning Objectives

- Outline the elements of a valid guilty plea.
- Explain the process for contesting a guilty plea.

Review Questions

1. Explain the elements of a valid guilty plea.
2. How can a plea of guilty be contested, if at all?

Chapter Synthesis Questions

1. Do prosecutors enjoy too much power or not enough? Explain your answer.
2. Grand juries do not investigate all types of crimes. Should they? Why or why not?
3. Compare and contrast the role of the grand jury with that of the traditional trial (petit) jury.
4. React to this statement: Plea bargaining is a necessary evil.
5. Should a defendant be allowed to contest a guilty plea? Why or why not?

15

TRIAL AND BEYOND

MODULE **15.4** APPEALS AND *HABEAS CORPUS*
Learning Objectives
- Summarize the types and effects of appeals.
- Explain the appellate process.
- Outline the *habeas corpus* process.

MODULE

15.1

RIGHTS TO SPEEDY AND PUBLIC TRIAL, IMPARTIAL JUDGE, AND TRIAL BY JURY

Learning Objectives
- **Explain the right to a speedy trial.**
- **Summarize the right to a public trial.**
- **Summarize the right to an impartial judge.**
- **Explain when the Sixth Amendment right to a jury trial applies.**

CORE CONCEPTS

Assuming a defendant does not plea bargain (or either plead guilty or nolo contendere), a trial will probably result. Thus, it is important to focus on constitutional rights during the trial stage. The four rights considered in this module are (1) the right to a speedy trial, (2) the right to a public trial, (3) the right to an impartial judge, and (4) the right to an impartial jury. Additional rights afforded to the defendant at trial are covered in module 15.2.

Right to a Speedy Trial

speedy trial A trial that meets with the Sixth Amendment's requirement for a speedy trial. A trial is no longer "speedy" when there is intentional delay that is prejudicial to the defendant's case.

The Sixth Amendment provides, in part, that "In all criminal prosecutions, the accused shall enjoy the right to a **speedy trial**." The federal "Speedy Trial Act"[1] plus statutes in every state also set forth a right to speedy trial. Unfortunately, though, it is not abundantly clear what the term *speedy* means. A number of court decisions have grappled with this issue over the years.

Somewhat surprisingly, it was not until 1966 that the Supreme Court addressed the Sixth Amendment's speedy trial provision. In *United States* v. *Ewell*, the Court identified three advantages associated with having a speedy trial:

1. It prevents excessive incarceration.

---

[1]18 U.S.C. Sections 3161–3174.

2. It minimizes anxiety experienced by the accused as a result of a publicized accusation.

3. It prevents damage to the defendant's case resulting from too much delay.[2]

Not only does the defense benefit from a speedy trial, but the government and even society at large benefit. Why? First, having a speedy trial provides the opportunity for a guilty verdict to be secured quickly (assuming, of course, that the defendant is guilty). Also, having a speedy trial minimizes the opportunity for an individual out on bail to commit additional crimes while awaiting trial. However, if the accused is kept in detention prior to trial, too much delay can take a financial toll on the government.

For the reasons just set forth, having a speedy trial can prove advantageous. However, this can be a double-edged sword. Having a speedy trial may promote efficiency, but too much efficiency may damage the defense's case. That is, if the defense is not given adequate time to prepare, then an erroneous guilty verdict could result. In *Ewell*, the Court stated that "[t]he essential ingredient is orderly expedition and not mere speed."[3]

When the Right to a Speedy Trial Applies

In *United States* v. *Marion*,[4] the defendants sought to dismiss the indictment against them by arguing that the government had known of their identities for three years prior to the indictment. More specifically, they argued that their Sixth Amendment's right to a speedy trial had been violated because the government was aware of them prior to their indictment and had delayed in initiating formal criminal proceedings. Their argument failed, however; and the Court held that the Sixth Amendment's guarantee to a speedy trial attaches only *after* the person (or persons) has been accused of a crime. The Court further stated that being accused of a crime did not necessarily mean that formal charges had to be filed. Namely, "[T]he actual restraints imposed by arrest and holding to answer on a criminal charge"[5] can be sufficient to amount to an accusation. This has since come to be known as the **accusation rule**.

accusation rule The requirement that a person must first be accused (i.e., charged) for the Sixth Amendment's speedy trial provision to apply.

What if a person is charged, has the charges against him or her dropped, and is then charged again at some point in the future? In *United States* v. *MacDonald*,[6] the Court held that the right to a speedy trial does not apply until the second set of charges is filed. In *MacDonald*, there were four years of delay between the dismissal of charges against the accused and a re-indictment on the same charges. According to the Court, "Following dismissal of charges, any restraint on liberty, disruption of employment, strain on financial resources, and exposure to public obloquy, stress, and anxiety is no greater than it is upon anyone openly subject to a criminal investigation."[7] The Court also observed that MacDonald had been "free to go about his affairs, to practice his profession, and to continue his life"[8] in the period between the two sets of charges, so the right to a speedy trial did not apply until the second set of charges was filed.

---

[2]*United States* v. *Ewell*, 383 U.S. 116 (1966).
[3]Ibid., p. 120.
[4]*United States* v. *Marion*, 404 U.S. 307 (1971).
[5]Ibid., pp. 327–8.
[6]*United States* v. *MacDonald*, 456 U.S. 1 (1982).
[7]Ibid., p. 9.
[8]Ibid., p. 10.

An interesting twist on *MacDonald* was presented in *United States* v. *Loud Hawk*.[9] In *Loud Hawk*, charges against the accused were dismissed but the prosecution appealed the dismissal. This action distinguished *Loud Hawk* from *MacDonald* because it suggested that the prosecution was not done accusing Loud Hawk. Even so, the Court still held that the defendant's right to a speedy trial was not implicated because he was granted unconditional release while the prosecution continued to mount its case. Thus, if an individual is accused but then released to go about his or her business *with no charges pending*, any attempt to claim a violation of the Sixth Amendment's speedy trial provision could prove difficult. However, if a person is released *while* charges are pending, a speedy trial argument could be successfully raised.

When the Right Is Violated

In general, the right to a speedy trial applies when a person has been accused and when too much time has elapsed between the criminal act and the point at which charges are filed. An important question has not yet been answered: Assuming the right to a speedy trial applies, when is the right violated?

The Supreme Court sought to answer this question in *Barker* v. *Wingo*.[10] In that case, the defendant did not assert his Sixth Amendment right until after the prosecution had sought 16 continuances, which lasted over five years. The Supreme Court announced a four-element test to assist in determining when the right to a speedy trial is violated: "(1) Length of delay; (2) the reason for the delay; (3) the defendant's assertion of his right; and (4) prejudice to the defendant."[11] According to the Court, none of these four criteria is, by itself, determinative. Instead, the courts must balance one against the others in deciding whether a Sixth Amendment violation has taken place. For example, if the delay is lengthy, but due to the defendant and not some other consideration, it is doubtful a court would hold that the right to a speedy trial was violated.

Right to a Public Trial

public trial A trial that is open to the public and/or complies with the Sixth Amendment's public trial provision. Courts can sometimes limit public access and the proceedings will still be considered public.

The text of the Sixth Amendment also guarantees the right to a "public trial." In *In re Oliver*, the Supreme Court stated, "The knowledge that every criminal trial is subject to contemporaneous review in the forum of public opinion is an effective restraint on possible abuse of power. . . . Without publicity, all other checks are insufficient; in comparison of publicity, all other checks are of small account."[12] Furthermore, "the presence of interested spectators may keep [the defendant's] triers keenly alive to a sense of their responsibility and to the importance of their functions."[13] This is what is meant by a **public trial**: It is one that is open to the public.

---

[9]*United States* v. *Loud Hawk*, 474 U.S. 302 (1986).
[10]*Barker* v. *Wingo*, 407 U.S. 514 (1972).
[11]Ibid., p. 530.
[12]*In re Oliver*, 333 U.S. 257 (1948), p. 271.
[13]Ibid., n. 25.

Oliver dealt expressly with criminal trials, but the Supreme Court has held that openness also applies to other hearings. For example, suppression hearings should be open to the public,[14] as should *voir dire*.[15] By extension, most other hearings—with the exception of grand jury proceedings, which are traditionally carried out in secret—should be considered public, as well.

Closing Trials to the Public

Most trials are open to the public, but not all of them are. Indeed, the defendant, whose interest is frequently served by openness, may want the trial closed to the public. This could be in an effort to minimize negative publicity, especially when the trial is for a heinous crime.

Sheppard v. *Maxwell*[16] illustrates the occasional conflict that can arise with the negative effects of trial publicity. In that case, the courtroom was packed with members of the public and media for all nine weeks of the trial. This made it difficult for people to hear one another. The press also handled and took pictures of evidentiary exhibits. The Supreme Court reversed the defendant's conviction, citing the "carnival atmosphere" of the trial in its decision.[17]

The government can also seek to close a trial to the public. In *Waller* v. *Georgia*,[18] the Supreme Court created a test for determining when the government will succeed in closing a trial to the public. The government must show (1) that there is an overriding interest, such as protection of certain witnesses; (2) that the closure is no broader than absolutely necessary; and (3) that reasonable alternatives have been considered.

Right to an Impartial Judge

impartial judge A judge who is capable of basing his or her decisions on the law and who has no conflict of interest or pecuniary stake in the outcome of the case. There is no constitutional right to an impartial judge. This right is a Supreme Court creation.

It is important to note that the Sixth Amendment speaks of juries, not of judges. But the Supreme Court has held that the due process clause of the Fourteenth Amendment guarantees a criminal defendant the right to trial by an impartial judge. This right applies in two situations:

1. A bench trial (also discussed in Chapter 1), in which the judge decides the defendant's fate instead of a jury

2. A jury trial, in which the judge acts solely as a trier of law (i.e., makes legal decisions, not factual ones)

The discussion begins with the right to an impartial judge and then moves into the more complicated issue of the right to trial by an impartial jury.

---

[14] *Waller* v. *Georgia*, 467 U.S. 39 (1984).
[15] *Presley* v. *Georgia*, No. 09-5270 (2010).
[16] *Sheppard* v. *Maxwell*, 384 U.S. 333 (1966).
[17] While the defense in *Sheppard* did not directly seek closure of the trial, it did make requests for a continuance, a change of venue, and a mistrial.
[18] *Waller* v. *Georgia*, 467 U.S. 39 (1984).

Though it is not constitutionally guaranteed, the accused enjoys the right to an impartial judge.

The Supreme Court first decided on the matter of an impartial judge in *Tumey* v. *Ohio*.[19] In that case, the judge of a municipal court was also the city mayor. In addition, he received the fines and fees that he levied against those convicted in his courtroom. The Supreme Court concluded that due process is violated when the judge "has a direct, personal, substantial pecuniary interest in reaching a conclusion against him in his case."[20]

Another impartial judge case was *Ward* v. *Monroeville*,[21] in which the fees/fines collected by the judge did not go to the mayor/judge but instead to the town's budget. The amount of money collected was apparently substantial. The Court concluded, again, that due process was violated, this time stating that "the mayor's executive responsibilities for village finances may make him partisan to maintain the high level of contribution from the mayor's court."[22] Contrast this decision with that of *Dugan* v. *Ohio*.[23] There, the Supreme Court held that due process was *not* violated because the mayor/judge was one of several members of a city commission and, as such, did not have substantial control over the city's funding sources.

Methods of Removing a Judge Who Is not Impartial

In most jurisdictions, either the defense or the prosecution can seek to have a judge removed *for cause*. That is, the individual seeking the judge's removal will argue that the judge is biased for or against a particular party to the case. Strangely, though, the only person who can remove such a judge is usually the judge himself or herself.

The second method of removing a biased judge is fairly rare. Some jurisdictions allow either party to a case to *peremptorily* remove a judge. This is akin to the jury selection process, which will be covered at length later in this chapter. Basically, the judge can be removed without any reason whatsoever. The number of peremptory removals, if permitted, is very small—usually one per case. If one judge has been removed, then the parties can only seek to remove the second judge with cause.

In most situations, the judge does not need to be removed at the request of another party. Responsible judges remove themselves when conflicts of interest exist. Indeed, most judicial codes of ethics require that a judge *recuse* (i.e., disqualify) himself or herself if, among other things, he or she has a personal bias or prejudice concerning a party, personal knowledge of disputed evidentiary facts concerning the proceeding, or some conflict of interest in the case

[19] *Tumey* v. *Ohio*, 273 U.S. 510 (1927).
[20] Ibid., p. 523.
[21] *Ward* v. *Monroeville*, 409 U.S. 57 (1972).
[22] Ibid., p. 59.
[23] *Dugan* v. *Ohio*, 277 U.S. 61 (1928).

Right to Trial by Jury

impartial jury A jury that is capable of making a decision based solely on the facts of the case.

As noted in the previous section, it is fairly easy to determine when a judge is impartial. After all, a judge is one person. Deciding on what constitutes an impartial jury is far more difficult and complex.

The right to a jury trial has always been recognized in the federal courts, but this right was not extended to the states until 1968 in the case of *Duncan* v. *Louisiana*.[24] The Court noted in that case that the right to a jury trial is "an inestimable safeguard against the corrupt or overzealous prosecutor and against the compliant, biased, or eccentric judge."[25] The right to a jury trial has therefore been incorporated, but subsequent decisions have restricted this right. The following subsections describe how.

Limitations on the Right

noncriminal proceeding rule The rule that limits juries to criminal trials.

First, the Sixth Amendment only applies to criminal proceedings; it does not provide a constitutional right to a jury trial in noncriminal proceedings. More specifically, there is no right to a jury trial in noncriminal proceedings that are nevertheless part of the "criminal" process (civil trials are of course by jury on a number of occasions and governed by the Seventh Amendment in federal cases). This has come to be known as the noncriminal proceeding rule. This rule stems from the Sixth Amendment, which states in part: "In all *criminal prosecutions*, the accused shall enjoy the right to a . . . trial, by an impartial jury" (emphasis added). Juvenile delinquency proceedings are not considered "criminal" in the Sixth Amendment sense.[26]

The right to a jury trial does not even apply to every criminal proceeding. The Supreme Court has also carved out a *petty crime exception* to the Sixth Amendment right to a jury trial. In *Duncan*, mentioned above, the Court expressly forbade jury trials for petty offenses, and in *Baldwin* v. *New York*, the Court announced its reasoning for this. It argued that the "disadvantages, onerous though they may be," of denying a jury trial for a petty crime are "outweighed by the benefits that result from speedy and inexpensive nonjury adjudication."[27]

What exactly is a *petty crime*? Unfortunately, there are no easy answers to this question, either. *Duncan* failed to define a *petty* offense, but in *Baldwin*, the Court concluded that any crime that can bring punishment of more than six months is no longer a petty one. This has come to be known as the six-month imprisonment rule; thus, defendants do not enjoy a right to jury trial when the punishment they face is less than six months in jail or prison.

six-month imprisonment rule The rule that limits jury trials to cases where more than six-months' incarceration in jail or prison is possible.

Jury Size and Voting Requirements

Many juries consist of 12 members, but the Supreme Court has stated that this is not a requirement. In *Williams* v. *Florida*, the Court stated that the 12-member jury was

---

[24] *Duncan* v. *Louisiana*, 391 U.S. 145 (1968).
[25] Ibid., p. 156.
[26] *McKeiver* v. *Pennsylvania*, 403 U.S. 528 (1971).
[27] *Baldwin* v. *New York*, 399 U.S. 66 (1970), p. 73.

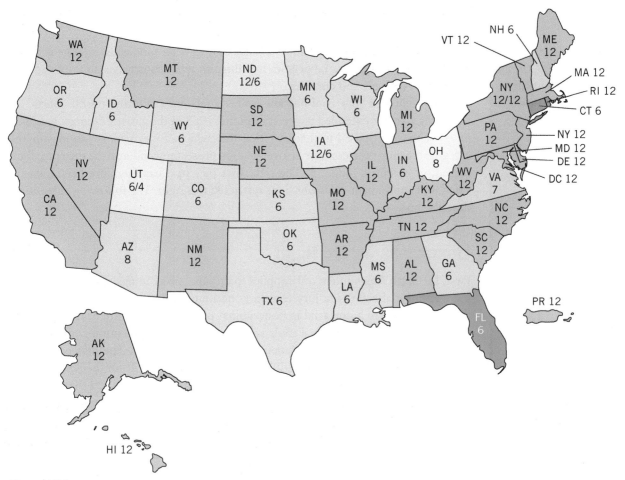

Figure 15.1

Jury Sizes by State for Misdemeaner Cases in Courts of General Jurisdiction

Source: D. B. Rottman and S. M. Strickland, *State Court Organization, 2004* (Washington, DC: Bureau of Justice Statistics, 2006).

a "historical accident" and "unnecessary to effect the purposes of the jury system."[28] The Court noted that a six-member jury would even provide "a fair possibility for obtaining a representative cross-section of the community, . . . [a]s long as arbitrary exclusions of a particular class from the jury rolls are forbidden."[29]

However, in *Ballew* v. *Georgia,* the Court concluded that a five-member jury was unconstitutional and found it unlikely that such a small group could engage "in meaningful deliberation, . . . remember all the facts and arguments, and truly represent the common sense of the entire community."[30] Thus, the appropriate size for a jury is anywhere between 6 and 12 members.

Jury size differs by state. See Figure 15.1 for a map of jury sizes by state, specifically for misdemeanor cases in courts of general jurisdiction (i.e., those with jurisdiction to try several types of cases, including more serious criminal cases). There is

---

[28]In *Williams* v. *Florida,* 399 U.S. 78 (1970), p. 102.

[29]Ibid.

[30]*Ballew* v. *Georgia,* 435 U.S. 223 (1978), p. 241.

more variability in misdemeanor jury sizes than felony, which is why the former is mapped (the vast majority of states require 12-member juries in felony cases).

As for voting requirements, a unanimous decision is not always required. In two companion cases, *Johnson* v. *Louisiana* and *Apodaca* v. *Oregon*,[31] the Court upheld a Louisiana statute that permitted 9 to 3 jury verdicts as well as an Oregon statute permitting 10–2 decisions. According to the Court:

> In our view, disagreement of three jurors does not alone establish reasonable doubt, particularly when such a heavy majority of the jury, after having considered the dissenters' views, remained convinced of guilt. . . . That want of jury unanimity is not to be equated with the existence of reasonable doubt emerges even more clearly from the fact that when a jury in a federal court, which operates under the unanimity rule and is instructed to acquit a defendant if it has a reasonable doubt, . . . cannot agree unanimously upon a verdict, the defendant is not acquitted, but is merely given a new trial.[32]

In short, guilt can be determined by less than an unanimous jury in certain jurisdictions. This is somewhat controversial, however, because according to the dissent in *Johnson* and *Apodaca*, permitting a less than unanimous decision diminishes reliability. Namely, jurors may not debate as fully as they may if a unanimous decision is required; that is, people may succumb to group pressure. See Figure 15.2 for a list of jury voting requirements by state, again for courts of general jurisdiction.

The *Voir Dire* Process

voir dire The process of selecting jurors for service. *Voir dire* proceeds through three stages: questioning by the judge, challenges for cause, and peremptory challenges.

jury panel The jury panel is the list of individuals drawn from the jury list. The jury panel consists of those individuals subpoenaed for jury service.

Voir dire is the process of selecting a jury from a **jury panel**. The jury panel is the list of individuals drawn from the jury list. The composition of the jury list varies from place to place. The norm for a jury list is a list of licensed drivers. The jury panel consists of those individuals subpoenaed for jury service.

It is important to understand that once *voir dire* commences, the concern is *not* to ensure that the jury represents a fair cross-section of the community. Instead, *voir dire* is concerned with the selection of jury members who can be *impartial*, as the Sixth Amendment requires. The term *voir dire* means "to see what is said." Thus, at this stage, the judge, prosecutor, and defense have an opportunity to review potential jurors for evidence of bias.

Voir dire can be simple or complicated. In some jurisdictions, the judge decides who will serve on the jury. The prosecution and defense merely suggest questions to the judge in these jurisdictions. Doing so speeds up the process and also helps ensure that jurors do not develop preconceived ideas about the case in question.

Usually, however, it is the attorneys who do the questioning. This process can take anything from a few hours to a few weeks. *Voir dire* during high-profile celebrity cases or in cases of particularly heinous crimes that are broadcast all over the national media can take several weeks. *Voir dire* can also take time because nothing precludes the attorneys from investigating jurors' backgrounds, interviewing their acquaintances, and even hiring social scientists who are experts in anticipating prospective jurors' probable decisions.

---

[31]*Johnson* v. *Louisiana*, 406 U.S. 356 (1972); *Apodaca* v. *Oregon*, 406 U.S. 404 (1972).
[32]*Johnson* v. *Louisiana*, p. 363.

State	Trial Type		
	Felony	*Misdemeanor*	*Civil*
Alabama	U	U	U
Alaska	U	U	5/6
Arizona	U	U	3/4
Arkansas	U	U	3/4
California	U	U	3/4
Colorado	U	U	U
Connecticut	U	U	U
Delaware	U	U	U
Florida	U	U	U
Georgia	U	U	U
Hawaii	U	U	5/6
Idaho	U	U	3/4
Illinois	U	U	U
Indiana	U	U	U
Iowa	U	U	7/8 or U
Kansas	U	U	5/6 or U
Kentucky	U	U	3/4
Louisiana	10/12*	U	5/6
Maine	U	U	3/4
Maryland	U	U	U
Massachusetts	U	U	5/6
Michigan	U	U	5/6
Minnesota	U	U	5/6 or U
Mississippi	U	U	3/4
Missouri	U	U	3/4
Montana	U	U	2/3
Nebraska	U	U	5/6 or U
Nevada	U	U	3/4
New Hampshire	U	U	U
New Jersey	U	U	5/6
New Mexico	U	U	5/6
New York	U	U	5/6
North Carolina	U	U	U
North Dakota	U	U	U
Ohio	U	U	3/4
Oklahoma	U	U	U
Oregon	5/6**	5/6	3/4
Pennsylvania	U	U	5/6
Rhode Island	U	U	U
South Carolina	U	U	U
South Dakota	U	U	5/6
Tennessee	U	U	U
Texas	U	U	5/6
Utah	U	U	3/4 or majority
Vermont	U	U	U
Virginia	U	U	U
Washington	U	U	5/6

(continued)

Figure 15.2

Jury Voting Requirements by State for Courts of General Jurisdiction
Source: D. B. Rottman and S. M. Strickland, *State Court Organization, 2004* (Washington, DC: Bureau of Justice Statistics, 2006).

West Virginia	U	U	U
Wisconsin	U	U	5/6
Wyoming	U	U	U

Key: U = Unanimous; *5/6* = 5 out of 6 jurors must agree (3/4. 7/8, etc., interpreted similarly)

*Some sentences

**Not capital cases.

Note: There are exceptions to these size requirements in each state. Also, where two voting requirements are listed, the voting requirement differs depending on the crime or the nature of the case.

Figure 15.2

(continued)

Voir dire usually begins with the judge asking questions—for instance, dealing with potential jurors' familiarity with the case, attitudes toward one or the other party to the case, demographic information, and so on. In high-profile cases, prospective jurors are often asked to complete a questionnaire intended to divulge information that might lead to their disqualification or excusal. This is often done to guide the attorneys in their *voir dire* questioning. The Supreme Court has upheld this type of questioning, noting that it is perfectly acceptable for the judge to question jurors about their knowledge and opinions concerning the case.[33]

The prosecution and defense are given unlimited opportunities to make challenges for cause. Convincing reasons can be found for the exclusion of potential jurors, some of which even have statutory origins. For example, if a member of the jury panel is related to the defendant, a challenge for cause will almost certainly succeed. Also, if the potential juror served on a past jury in a case dealing with a similar crime, a challenge for cause will probably succeed. If a potential juror stands to benefit financially from the outcome of the case, he or she will probably be excused based on a challenge for cause.

Peremptory challenges, by contrast, call for removal of potential jurors *without* any type of argument. Think of a peremptory challenge as a fallback measure. If, say, the defense fails with a challenge for cause to exclude a potential juror who it believes will be biased against the defendant, a peremptory challenge can be used. In fact, a peremptory challenge can be used to exclude a potential juror for nearly any reason. As the Supreme Court stated in *Swain* v. *Alabama*, the peremptory challenge "is often exercised upon the 'sudden impressions and unaccountable prejudices we are apt to conceive upon the bare looks and gestures of another,' upon a juror's 'habits and associations,' or upon the felling that the 'bare questioning [of a juror's] indifference may sometimes provoke a resentment'."[34] Peremptory challenges are numbered. How many are available depends on the state and the type of offense (see Figure 15.3).

It is generally unacceptable for the prosecution (and the defense) to exclude a potential juror based on race or ethnicity. In *Batson* v. *Kentucky*,[35] the Court decided that prosecutors can be called on to explain their use of peremptory challenges to exclude minorities. If the defense raises a *Batson* challenge, then the prosecutor will be

---

[33]*Mu'Min* v. *Virginia*, 500 U.S. 415 (1991).
[34]*Swain* v. *Alabama*, 380 U.S. 202 (1965), pp. 242–243.
[35]*Batson* v. *Kentucky*, 476 U.S. 79 (1986).

State	Number of peremptory challenges					
	Criminal					
	Capital		Felony		Misdemeanor	
	State	Defense	State	Defense	State	Defense
Alabama	12	12	6	6	3	3
Alaska	N/A	N/A	10	10	3	3
Arizona	10	10	6	6	6	6
Arkansas	10	12	6	8	3	3
California	20	20	20/10	20/10	10/6	10/6
Colorado	10	10	5	5	3	3
Connecticut	25	25	15/6	15/6	3	3
Delaware	12	20	6	6	6	6
District of Columbia	N/A	N/A	10	10	3	3
Florida	10	10	10/6	10/6	3	3
Georgia	10	20	6	12	2	4
Hawaii	N/A	N/A	12/3	12/3	3	3
Idaho	10	10	10/6	10/6	4	4
Illinois	14	14	7	7	5	5
Indiana	20	20	10	10	5	5
Iowa	N/A	N/A	10/6	10/6	4	4
Kansas	12	12	12/8/6	12/8/6	3	3
Kentucky	8	8	8	8	3	3
Louisiana	12	12	12/6	12/6	6	6
Maine	N/A	N/A	10/8	10/8	4	4
Maryland	10	20	5	10	4	4
Massachusetts	N/A	N/A	12/4	12/4	4	4
Michigan	N/A	N/A	12/5	12/5	5	5
Minnesota	N/A	N/A	9/3	15/5	3	5
Mississippi	12	12	6	6	6	6
Missouri	9	9	6	6	2	2
Montana	8	8	6/3	6/3	6/3	6/3
Nebraska	12	12	6	6	3	3
Nevada	8	8	4	4	4	4
New Hampshire	10	20	15/3	15/3	3	3
New Jersey	N/A	N/A	12	20	10	10
New Mexico	N/A	N/A	3	5	3	5
New York	N/A	N/A	20/15	20/15/10	10	10
North Carolina	14	14	6	6	6	6
North Dakota	N/A	N/A	6/4	6/4	6/4	6/4
Ohio	6	6	4	4	3	3
Oklahoma	9	9	5	5	3	3
Oregon	12	12	6	6	6/3	6/3
Pennsylvania	20	20	7	7	5	5
Puerto Rico	N/A	N/A	10/5	10/5	5	5
Rhode Island	N/A	N/A	6	6	3	3
South Carolina	5	10	5	10	5	5
South Dakota	20	20	20/10	20/10	3	3

Figure 15.3

Voir Dire Processes by State for Courts of General Jurisdiction *Source:* D. B. Rottman and S. M. Strickland, *State Court Organization, 2004* (Washington, DC: Bureau of Justice Statistics, 2006).

Tennessee	15	15	8	8	3	3
Texas	15	15	10	10	5	5
Utah	10	10	4	4	3	3
Vermont	N/A	N/A	6	6	6	6
Virginia	4	4	4	4	3	3
Washington	12	12	6	6	3	3
West Virginia	N/A	N/A	2	6	4	4
Wisconsin	N/A	N/A	6/4	6/4	4	4
Wyoming	12	12	8	8	4	4

Note: The following states/territories do not have a death penalty statute or have abolished the death penalty: Alaska, District of Columbia, Hawaii, Iowa, Maine, Massachusetts, Michigan, Minnesota, New Jersey, New Mexico, New York, North Dakota, Puerto Rico, Rhode Island, Vermont, West Virginia and Wisconsin.

Figure 15.3
(continued)

required to provide some other reason for excluding jurors other than race or ethnicity. However, this explanation does not need to be as convincing as one that would accompany a challenge for cause. It simply needs to be what the Court calls *race neutral.*

YOUR DECISION

1. Charles Pitt escaped from jail while awaiting his trial on narcotics offenses. He was apprehended by the police nine months later. He was then tried, convicted, and sentenced to prison for ten years. He has appealed his conviction, claiming that his Sixth Amendment right to a speedy trial was denied because of the nine-month delay. How should the appellate court rule?

2. Assume that during *voir dire*, the following exchange takes place between a defense attorney and a potential juror:

    DEFENSE ATTORNEY: Do you have any reservations against the death penalty?

    POTENTIAL JUROR: No, of course not. I firmly support capital punishment. I think we should execute all criminals.

    DEFENSE ATTORNEY: Do you think you can set aside your personal convictions for the purposes of this trial and make an objective decision based on the evidence?

    POTENTIAL JUROR: I suppose so. I think I could probably keep an open mind.

    Now, assume that the defense attorney seeks to exercise one of her challenges for cause and asks the judge to exclude this juror. The judge denies the request. Assuming that the remaining jurors are not as opinionated, do you think the resulting jury will conform to the Sixth Amendment requirements discussed thus far?

Summary

- The Sixth Amendment guarantees the right to a speedy trial.
- The right to a speedy trial applies once a person has been accused of a crime. If the defendant is charged, let go, and then charged again, the right does not apply until the second set of charges has been filed.

- Four criteria are used to determine when the right to a speedy trial has been *violated*: (1) too much delay between accusation and trial, (2) intentional delay, (3) whether the defendant asserts the right to a speedy trial, and (4) whether the delay is prejudicial. No criterion by itself is necessarily enough for the right to be violated, however.

- Criminal defendants enjoy the right to a public trial.

- The government may seek closure of a trial to the public, but to do so, it must show (1) that there is an overriding interest, such as the protection of certain witnesses; (2) that the closure is no broader than absolutely necessary; and (3) that reasonable alternatives were considered.

- The accused may seek closure of a trial, but only if an open proceeding will compromise the ability of the jury to make a fair decision.

- A judge cannot be considered impartial if he or she has a pecuniary interest in the outcome of a case.

- Usually, judges will remove themselves if they deem themselves less than impartial, but some jurisdictions permit the peremptory removal of judges. This allows counsel to remove one judge and request a second one.

- The defendant enjoys the right to trial by an impartial jury. However, the Supreme Court has held that this right applies only to criminal proceedings in which the possible punishment exceeds six months' detention.

- Jury size and voting requirements vary by jurisdiction, but as a general rule, the smaller the jury, the more unanimous the required verdict.

- Those selected for jury service are part of a jury panel. From the jury panel, some people are selected and required to go to a courtroom, where *voir dire* commences. *Voir dire* begins with the judge asking questions, some of which he or she is required to ask. Next, the attorneys on both sides will exercise their peremptory challenges and challenges for cause. The former are almost unrestricted but limited in number. The latter must be argued before the judge and are not limited in number.

MODULE

15.2 RIGHTS TO COUNSEL, CONFRONTATION, AND COMPULSORY PROCESS

Learning Objectives

- **Summarize the right to counsel.**
- **Explain the meaning of effective assistance of counsel.**
- **Explain the right to confrontation.**
- **Explain the right to compulsory process.**

CORE CONCEPTS Defendants enjoy additional rights at trial, including the rights to counsel, confrontation, and compulsory process. These are introduced throughout the remainder of this module. Still other rights at trial apply, such as double-jeopardy protection and the right to assert an entrapment defense, but we introduced these earlier on in the text, in the criminal law section. This module is concerned solely with the right to counsel, the right to confrontation, and the right to compulsory process, each of which can be rather tedious and complicated.

The Right to Counsel

The Sixth Amendment to the U.S. Constitution provides "in all criminal prosecutions, the accused shall enjoy the right . . . to have the Assistance of Counsel for his defense." The constitutional right of an indigent defendant to be represented by counsel was first announced in *Powell* v. *Alabama*.[36] In that case, the Supreme Court reversed the convictions of several indigent defendants who were not adequately represented by counsel at trial. Significantly, though, the Court based its decision on the Fifth Amendment's due process clause, not the Sixth Amendment:

> The right to be heard would be, in many cases, of little avail if it did not comprehend the right to be heard by counsel. Even the intelligent and educated layman has small and sometimes no skill in the science of law. If charged with crimes, he is incapable, generally, of determining for himself whether the indictment is good or bad. He is unfamiliar with the rules of evidence. Left without aid of counsel he may be put on trial without a proper charge, and convicted upon incompetent evidence, or evidence irrelevant to the issue or otherwise inadmissible. He lacks both the skill and knowledge adequately to prepare his defense, even though he may have a perfect one. He requires the guiding hand of counsel at every step in the proceedings against him. Without it, though he be not guilty, he faces the danger of conviction because he does not know how to establish his innocence.[37]

However, the right to counsel announced in *Powell* was not without limitations. It applied only to "capital case[s], where the defendant is unable to employ counsel, and is incapable adequately of making his own defense because of ignorance, feeble-mindedness, illiteracy, or the like."[38]

The Contemporary Sixth Amendment Approach

In *Johnson* v. *Zerbst*, the Court recognized the Sixth Amendment right to counsel in all federal prosecutions, stating that the Sixth Amendment "embodies a realistic recognition of the obvious truth that the average defendant does not have the professional legal skill to protect himself."[39]

But the Sixth Amendment's right to counsel was still not automatically extended to the states. In *Johnson*, the Court refused to apply its decision to the states, and this holding was reaffirmed a few years later in the case of *Betts* v. *Brady*, a case in which the Court held that "[t]he Due Process Clause of the Fourteenth Amendment does not incorporate, as such, the specific guarantees found in the Sixth Amendment."[40]

---

[36]*Powell* v. *Alabama* (287 U.S. 45 [1932])
[37]Ibid., pp. 68–69.
[38]Ibid., p. 71.
[39]*Johnson* v. *Zerbst*, 304 U.S. 458 (1938), pp. 462–463.
[40]*Betts* v. *Brady*, 316 U.S. 455 (1942), pp. 461–462.

It would not be until the 1963 decision in *Gideon* v. *Wainwright* that the Sixth Amendment right to counsel became incorporated. In that case, the Court recognized that "lawyers in criminal courts are necessities, not luxuries."[41] The reasoning behind *Gideon* is explored in the accompanying Court Decision box.

COURT DECISION

The Logic behind the Right to Counsel

Gideon v. *Wainwright*
372 U.S. 335 (1963)

Decision: The Supreme Court decided that "the right of an indigent defendant in a criminal trial to have the assistance of counsel is a fundamental right essential to a fair trial, and petitioner's trial and conviction without the assistance of counsel violated the Fourteenth Amendment."

Reason: The Sixth Amendment provides, "In all criminal prosecutions, the accused shall enjoy the right ... to have the Assistance of Counsel for his defence [sic]" We have construed this to mean that, in federal courts, counsel must be provided for defendants unable to employ counsel unless the right is competently and intelligently waived ...

... the Court concluded [in *Betts* v. *Brady*] that "appointment of counsel is not a fundamental right, essential to a fair trial. ..." ... the *Betts* Court refused to accept the contention that the Sixth Amendment's guarantee of counsel for indigent federal defendants was extended to or, in the words of that Court, "made obligatory upon, the States by the Fourteenth Amendment." Plainly, had the Court concluded that appointment of counsel for an indigent criminal defendant was "a fundamental right, essential to a fair trial," it would have held that the Fourteenth Amendment requires appointment of counsel in a state court, just as the Sixth Amendment requires in a federal court.

We think the Court in *Betts* had ample precedent for acknowledging that those guarantees of the Bill of Rights which are fundamental safeguards of liberty immune from federal abridgment are equally protected against state invasion by the Due Process Clause of the Fourteenth Amendment. This same principle was recognized, explained, and applied in *Powell v. Alabama* ..., a case upholding the right of counsel, where the Court held that ... the Fourteenth Amendment "embraced" those "'fundamental principles of liberty and justice which lie at the base of all our civil and political institutions,'" even though they had been "specifically dealt with in another part of the federal Constitution ..."

We accept *Betts* v. *Brady's* assumption, based as it was on our prior cases, that a provision of the Bill of Rights which is "fundamental and essential to a fair trial" is made obligatory upon the States by the Fourteenth Amendment. We think the Court in *Betts* was wrong, however, in concluding that the Sixth Amendment's guarantee of counsel is not one of these fundamental rights. Ten years before *Betts* v. *Brady*,

(continued)

---

[41]*Gideon v. Wainwright*, 372 U.S. 335 (1963), p. 344.

this Court, after full consideration of all the historical data examined in *Betts,* had unequivocally declared that "the right to the aid of counsel is of this fundamental character . . ." While the Court, at the close of its *Powell* opinion, did, by its language, as this Court frequently does, limit its holding to the particular facts and circumstances of that case, its conclusions about the fundamental nature of the right to counsel are unmistakable . . .

. . . reason and reflection, require us to recognize that, in our adversary system of criminal justice, any person haled into court, who is too poor to hire a lawyer, cannot be assured a fair trial unless counsel is provided for him. This seems to us to be an obvious truth. Governments, both state and federal, quite properly spend vast sums of money to establish machinery to try defendants accused of crime. Lawyers to prosecute are everywhere deemed essential to protect the public's interest in an orderly society. Similarly, there are few defendants charged with crime, few indeed, who fail to hire the best lawyers they can get to prepare and present their defenses. That government hires lawyers to prosecute and defendants who have the money hire lawyers to defend are the strongest indications of the widespread belief that lawyers in criminal courts are necessities, not luxuries. The right of one charged with crime to counsel may not be deemed fundamental and essential to fair trials in some countries, but it is in ours. From the very beginning, our state and national constitutions and laws have laid great emphasis on procedural and substantive safeguards designed to assure fair trials before impartial tribunals in which every defendant stands equal before the law. This noble ideal cannot be realized if the poor man charged with crime has to face his accusers without a lawyer to assist him. A defendant's need for a lawyer is nowhere better stated than in the moving words of Mr. Justice Sutherland in *Powell* v. *Alabama:*

> The right to be heard would be, in many cases, of little avail if it did not comprehend the right to be heard by counsel. Even the intelligent and educated layman has small and sometimes no skill in the science of law. If charged with crime, he is incapable, generally, of determining for himself whether the indictment is good or bad. He is unfamiliar with the rules of evidence. Left without the aid of counsel, he may be put on trial without a proper charge, and convicted upon incompetent evidence, or evidence irrelevant to the issue or otherwise inadmissible. He lacks both the skill and knowledge adequately to prepare his defense, even though he have a perfect one. He requires the guiding hand of counsel at every step in the proceedings against him. Without it, though he be not guilty, he faces the danger of conviction because he does not know how to establish his innocence.

Gideon dealt with a felony, which led the Supreme Court to conclude that the Sixth Amendment right to counsel applies only in felony proceedings. However, in *Argersinger* v. *Hamlin,* the Court held that the right to counsel also applies in misdemeanor cases. According to the Court, "The requirement of counsel may well be necessary for a fair trial even in petty-offense prosecution. We are by no means convinced that legal and constitutional questions involved in a case that actually leads to imprisonment even for a brief period are any less complex than when a person can be sent off for six months or more."[42]

This decision was then clarified in *Scott* v. *Illinois*,[43] in which the Court held that the right to counsel does not apply where loss of liberty is merely a *possibility*. In short, when there is no possibility of confinement, the Sixth Amendment right to counsel does not apply. A twist on the *Scott* decision was recently handed down in *Alabama* v. *Shelton*, in which the Court held that "[a] suspended sentence that may 'end up in the actual deprivation of a person's liberty' may not be imposed unless the defendant was accorded 'the guiding hand of counsel' in the prosecution for the crime charged."[44] *Shelton* differed from *Scott* because Shelton was placed on probation; Scott was not.

Waiver of the Right to Counsel

Although the Sixth Amendment provides for the right to counsel, accused individuals sometimes prefer to represent themselves. Indeed, according to the Supreme Court, criminal defendants have a constitutional right to represent themselves at trial.[45] This is known as a *pro se defense*. In reaching this decision, the Court noted that the Sixth Amendment only guarantees the *assistance* of counsel, not necessarily *representation* by counsel:

pro se defense When a defendant waives his or her Sixth Amendment right to counsel and defends himself or herself.

> The language and spirit of the Sixth Amendment contemplate that counsel, like the other defense tools guaranteed by the Amendment, shall be an aid to a willing defendant—not an organ of State interposed between an unwilling defendant and his right to defend himself personally. . . . An unwanted counsel "represents" the defendant only through a tenuous and unacceptable legal fiction. Unless the accused has acquiesced in such representation, the defense presented is not the defense guaranteed him by the Constitution, for in a very real sense, it is not his defense.[46]

The Court has also stated that the framers viewed the "inestimable worth of free choice" as more important than the right to counsel. Also, "[t]o force a lawyer on a defendant can only lead [the defendant] to believe that the law contrives against him."[47]

The Supreme Court has held that waiver of the right to counsel is one that the defendant takes, potentially, at his or her own peril. In *Iowa* v. *Tovar*,[48] the Court decided that a trial court was not required to warn the accused that waiving the right to counsel at a plea hearing involves two risks: (1) the possibility that valid defenses will be overlooked and (2) the accused will be deprived of advice as to whether a guilty plea is warranted.

Not every defendant who wishes to proceed without counsel is allowed to do so, however. In *Johnson* v. *Zerbst*,[49] the Supreme Court stated that a defendant may

---

[42] *Argersinger v. Hamlin*, 407 U.S. 25 (1972), p. 33.
[43] *Scott v. Illinois*, 440 U.S. 367 (1979).
[44] *Alabama v. Shelton*, 535 U.S. 654 (2002), p. 654.
[45] *Faretta v. California*, 422 U.S. 806 (1975).
[46] Ibid., pp. 820–821.
[47] Ibid., p. 834.
[48] *Iowa v. Tovar*, 541 U.S. 77 (2004).
[49] *Johnson v. Zerbst*, 304 U.S. 458 (1938).

only waive counsel if the waiver is "competent and intelligent." According to the Court in *Carnley* v. *Cochran*, "the record must show, or there must be an allegation and evidence must show, that an accused was offered counsel but intelligently and understandingly rejected the offer. Anything less is not a waiver."[50] The Court elaborated further in *Von Moltke* v. *Gillies*:

> To be valid such waiver must be made with an apprehension of the nature of the charges, the statutory offenses included within them, the range of allowable punishments thereunder, possible defenses to the charges and circumstances in mitigation thereof, and all other facts essential to a broad understanding of the whole matter. A judge can make certain that an accused's professed waiver of counsel is understandingly and wisely made only from a penetrating and comprehensive examination of all the circumstances.[51]

What constitutes a knowing and intelligent waiver is not always clear. However, in *Massey* v. *Moore*, the Court offered clarification by stating that "[o]ne might not be insane in the sense of being incapable of standing trial and yet lack the capacity to stand trial without benefit of counsel."[52] In *Godinez* v. *Moran*,[53] a case decided some years later, the Court held that a person who is competent to stand trial is also competent to waive counsel at trial as a result of pleading guilty. But in *Indiana* v. *Edwards*, the Court held that competency to stand trial was not the same as competency to represent oneself at trial, meaning the court can appoint counsel if it feels the defendant is not mentally competent to represent himself or herself at trial.[54]

In certain circumstances, while permitting waiver of counsel, the court can also require that *standby counsel* be available to the defendant—that is, an attorney who is standing by in order to assist the accused, if necessary. This was the decision reached in *McKaskle* v. *Wiggins*, in which the Court held that a judge can appoint standby counsel "to relieve the judge of the need to explain and enforce basic rules of courtroom protocol or to assist the defendant in overcoming routine obstacles that stand in the way of the defendant's achievement of his own clearly indicated goals."[55] When waiver of counsel is knowing and intelligent, a judge's decision to appoint standby counsel will not be unconstitutional as long as (1) the defendant retains control over the case and (2) the jury understands that the defendant represents himself or herself.

Effective Assistance of Counsel

effective assistance of counsel The requirement that a defense attorney must effectively represent his or her client.

If the Sixth Amendment's right to counsel provision was extended to indigent defendants with a blind eye, then some defendants would be convicted and others acquitted because of varying levels of competence among attorneys. All attorneys are not the same. Some, while authorized to practice law, prove to be totally ineffective in their duties. As such, the courts have grappled with what constitutes effective assistance of counsel.

---

[50]*Carnley* v. *Cochran*, 369 U.S. 506 (1962), p. 516.
[51]*Von Moltke* v. *Gillies*, 332 U.S. 708 (1948), p. 724.
[52]*Massey* v. *Moore*, 348 U.S. 105 (1954), p. 108.
[53]*Godinez* v. *Moran*, 509 U.S. 389 (1993).
[54]*Indiana v. Edwards*, 554 U.S. 164 (2008).
[55]*McKaskle* v. *Wiggins*, 465 U.S. 168 (1984), p. 184.

So, what constitutes effective assistance of counsel? The lower courts are somewhat divided in terms of how to answer this question, so it is necessary to focus on the Supreme Court's standard for deciding whether defense counsel's assistance is or is not effective. In the first key case addressing this question, *McMann* v. *Richardson*, the Court held that counsel is effective when his or her legal advice is "within the range of competence demanded of attorneys in criminal cases."[56] This is something of a vague standard, so the Court created a new test in *Strickland* v. *Washington*.[57] In that case, the Court held that a two-prong test must be applied in order to determine whether counsel is ineffective:

> First, the defendant must show that counsel's performance was deficient. This requires showing that counsel made errors so serious that counsel was not functioning as the "counsel" guaranteed the defendant by the Sixth Amendment. Second, the defendant must show that the deficient performance prejudiced the defense. This requires showing that counsel's errors were so serious as to deprive the defendant of a fair trial, a trial whose result is unreliable.[58]

The two prongs announced in this case are now known as the *performance* prong and the *prejudice* prong. With regard to the former, "The proper measure of attorney performance remains simply reasonableness under prevailing professional norms."[59] Defense counsel's performance will be considered adequate if he or she avoids conflicts of interest, serves as an advocate for the defendant's case, and brings to bear "such skill and knowledge as will render the trial a reliable adversarial testing process."[60] And with regard to the prejudice prong, the defendant must prove that "there is a reasonable probability that, but for counsel's unprofessional errors, the result of the proceeding would have been different."[61] In other words, the burden falls on the defendant to show that the outcome of the case hinged on the ineffective assistance provided by his or her defense attorney. If defense counsel acted ineffectively but such actions did not influence the outcome of the case, then a *Strickland* claim cannot succeed.

The Right to Confrontation

confrontation The defendant's Sixth Amendment right to be present at his or her trial, hear live testimony of adverse witnesses, and challenge such witnesses' statements in open court.

The Sixth Amendment also provides criminal defendants with the right to be "confronted with the witnesses against him." This right to confront one's accuser is manifested in three ways. The first method of confrontation is to allow the defendant to appear at his or her own trial. In fact, in *Illinois* v. *Allen*, the Supreme Court expressly stated that "[o]ne of the most basic of rights guaranteed by the Confrontation Clause is the accused's right to be present in the courtroom at every state of his trial."[62] The other two methods of confrontation extended to the defendant are to require the live

---

[56]*McMann* v. *Richardson*, 397 U.S. 759 (1970), p. 771.
[57]*Strickland* v. *Washington*, 466 U.S. 668 (1984).
[58]Ibid., p. 687.
[59]Ibid., p. 688.
[60]Ibid., p. 688.
[61]Ibid., p. 694.
[62]*Illinois* v. *Allen*, 397 U.S. 337 (1970), p. 338.

testimony of witnesses before the defendant and to permit him or her to challenge witnesses' statements in open court. Each of these methods of confrontation is considered in a following section.

The Defendant's Right to Be Present

The Supreme Court's opinion in *Illinois* v. *Allen* seems eminently sensible. Certainly, the defendant would be seriously hampered in his or her ability to confront adverse witnesses if he or she was not allowed to attend the trial. But allowing the defendant to be physically present in the courtroom may not be enough to satisfy the Sixth Amendment's confrontation clause. In particular, if the accused is not competent and is unable to understand what is taking place so as to be able to challenge the opposition, the Sixth Amendment may be violated. Given this, some Supreme Court cases have dealt with physical confrontation, and some have dealt with defendants' mental competence as it pertains to confrontation.

physical presence One of two confrontation requirements. In order to be "present at his/her trial," the defendant must be physically present (as opposed, for example, to appearing via closed-circuit television).

Physical Presence. Even though the Supreme Court's opinion in *Illinois* v. *Allen* suggests that the accused enjoys an unqualified right to **physical presence**, nothing could be further from the truth. In the cases decided after *Allen*, the Court placed significant restrictions on when the defendant is permitted to be physically present. By way of preview, the Court's decisions have indicated that the accused can only be present during critical proceedings. Also, the defendant's physical presence can be voluntarily waived or forfeited by failing to appear or by acting improperly.

First, even though *Allen* spoke of the right to be present "at every stage of [the] trial," the Court changed course in *United States* v. *Gagnon* and *Kentucky* v. *Stincer*.[63] In the former case, the defendant was denied physical presence at a meeting between a judge and juror, while in the latter, the defendant was not allowed to attend a pre-trial determination of a child witness's competence. The Court sanctioned the trial courts' actions in both cases. Generally, however, whether the defendant can be denied the right to be physically present at certain supposedly noncritical stages of the trial process depends on the nature of the communication in question and the hearing at issue.

Second, the defendant may not be physically present through waiver. That is, the defendant can waive his or her Sixth Amendment right to confrontation. Only the defendant can make this determination. In *Taylor* v. *Illinois*,[64] the Court held that the defense attorney cannot waive the defendant's right to be physically present without his or her consent. The defendant can waive his or her right to be present through an express request[65] or by implying waiver. As an example of an implied waiver, in *Taylor* v. *United States*, the Court decided that the defendant's refusal to return to the courtroom after a lunch recess, even though it was not an intentional waiver, could have amounted to a violation of his Sixth Amendment right:

> It is wholly incredible to suggest that [Taylor, the defendant,] . . . entertained any doubts about his right to be present at every stage of the trial. It seems equally

---

[63] *United States* v. *Gagnon*, 470 U.S. 522 (1985); *Kentucky* v. *Stincer*, 479 U.S. 1028 (1987).
[64] *Taylor* v. *Illinois*, 484 U.S. 400 (1988).
[65] *Diaz* v. *United States*, 223 U.S. 442 (1912).

incredible to us, as it did to the Court of appeals, "that a defendant who flees from a courtroom in the midst of a trial—where judge, jury, witnesses and lawyers are present and ready to continue—would not know that as a consequence the trial could continue in his absence."[66]

Finally, the defendant may not be permitted to be physically present at his or her own trial for reasons related to conduct. In *Illinois* v. *Allen*, for instance, the defendant was removed from his trial following repeated warnings by the judge to cease his disruptive behavior. The Supreme Court sanctioned the trial court judge's decision, holding that the right to be physically present can be waived if, after several warnings, the defendant acts "in a manner so disorderly, disruptive, and disrespectful of the court that his trial cannot be carried on with him in the courtroom."[67] The Court also noted, however, that the defendant can reappear in the courtroom when he is "willing to conduct himself consistently with the decorum and respect inherent in the concept of courts and judicial proceedings."[68]

Mental Competence. The Supreme Court has also held that the defendant must demonstrate **mental competence**. In other words, the conviction of an incompetent person is unconstitutional.[69] Specifically, due process—and by implication, the right to confrontation—is violated when the defendant cannot understand what is happening to him or her in a criminal trial.

mental competence One of two confrontation requirements. In order to be "present at his/her trial," the defendant must be not only physically present but also mentally competent. A defendant who is not mentally competent cannot adequately confront adverse witnesses.

The question of whether a defendant is mentally competent to stand trial was answered by a test announced by the Supreme Court in *Dusky* v. *United States*.[70] The test assesses whether the defendant "has sufficient present ability to consult with his lawyer with a reasonable degree of rational understanding—and whether he has a rational as well as factual understanding of the proceedings against him."[71] The burden of proving *incompetence* falls on the defendant.[72]

It is important to understand that this test for competency is different from the insanity defense discussed earlier in this text. *Competency to stand trial*—the type of competency considered here—deals with the defendant's ability to understand what is happening at trial (as well as at pretrial hearings, etc.). The *insanity defense* deals with the defendant's competence at the time he or she committed the crime. The competency to stand trial issue is narrowly concerned with the defendant's ability to understand what is happening and communicate with counsel.

The defendant's competency is usually considered in a separate pretrial hearing. This was the rule announced in *Pate* v. *Robinson*,[73] a case dealing with an Illinois trial judge's decision not to hold a hearing on the question of the defendant's mental condition, even though he had a long history of mental problems. The Supreme Court held that a hearing was necessary, noting that "[the Illinois court's] reasoning offers no justification for ignoring the uncontradicted

---

[66]*Taylor v. United States*, 414 U.S. 17 (1973), p. 20.
[67]*Illinois v. Allen*, 397 U.S. 337 (1970]), p. 343.
[68]Ibid.
[69]*Pate v. Robinson*, 383 U.S. 375 (1966).
[70]*Dusky v. United States*, 362 U.S. 402 (1960).
[71]Ibid., p. 402.
[72]*Medina v. California*, 505 U.S. 437 (1992).
[73]*Pate v. Robinson*, 383 U.S. 375 (1966).

testimony of Robinson's [the defendant's] history of pronounced irrational behavior. While Robinson's demeanor at trial might be relevant to the ultimate decision as to his [present] sanity, it cannot be relied upon to dispense with a hearing on that very issue."[74]

What happens to the defendant if he or she is declared incompetent to stand trial? Usually, the defendant will be hospitalized until his or her competency is restored, if it ever is. However, in *Jackson v. Indiana*,[75] the Supreme Court held that there are constitutional limitations on how long a defendant can be hospitalized for the purpose of restoring competency. That case dealt with a 27-year-old deaf-mute individual with the mental level of a preschooler, who was being hospitalized until the staff determined him sane. The Court concluded that it was likely the defendant's condition would *never* improve. Thus, the Court said:

> We hold . . . that a person charged by a State with a criminal offense who is committed [to an institution] solely on account of his incapacity to proceed to trial cannot be held more than the reasonable period of time necessary to determine whether there is a substantial probability that he will attain that capacity in the foreseeable future. If it is determined that this is not the case, then the State must either institute the customary civil commitment proceeding that would be required to commit indefinitely any other citizen, or release the defendant.[76]

Drawbacks of Being Present. Guaranteeing the defendant the right to be present at trial could be prejudicial—that is, it could be harmful. First, if the defendant is present but refuses to take the stand and testify (exercising a right guaranteed by the Fifth Amendment), the jury may conclude that he or she has something to hide. The Supreme Court has been so concerned with this possibility that it has prohibited the prosecution from calling attention to the defendant's refusal to testify[77] and even required judges to advise jury members that no adverse inferences can be drawn from a defendant's refusal to testify.[78]

The defendant's presence may also be prejudicial because by virtue of being in the courtroom, the defendant may remind jurors about the crime. It is often thought, in fact, that a defendant who is dressed in prison attire is not viewed the same, in the eyes of a jury, as someone dressed in a suit. An illustrative case concerning this matter is *Estelle v. Williams*, in which the Supreme Court held that a state may not compel the defendant to wear jail attire in the courtroom.[79] It concluded that a "constant reminder of the accused's condition implicit in such distinctive, identifiable attire may affect a juror's judgment."[80] This decision was extended to the sentencing phase in *Deck v. Missouri*,[81] where the Court held that defendants cannot be forced to wear leg irons during their capital sentencing hearings.

---

[74]Ibid., p. 385.
[75]*Jackson v. Indiana*, 406 U.S. 715 (1972).
[76]Ibid., p. 738.
[77]*Griffin v. California*, 380 U.S. 609 (1965).
[78]*Carter v. Kentucky*, 450 U.S. 288 (1981).
[79]*Estelle v. Williams*, 425 U.S. 501 (1976).
[80]Ibid., p. 504.
[81]*Deck v. Missouri*, 544 U.S. 622 (2005).

The Defendant's Right to Live Testimony

live testimony The confrontation requirement that adverse witnesses provide live testimony.

As mentioned earlier, the Sixth Amendment's mention of confrontation includes, according to the Supreme Court, the defendant's right to live testimony. That is, he or she enjoys the right to have witnesses physically appear in the courtroom to give their testimony. Even so, this right may be qualified for certain reasons. In fact, over 100 years ago, the Supreme Court stated in *Mattox* v. *United States* that the defendant's right to live testimony is "subject to exceptions, recognized long before the adoption of the Constitution."[82] The Court stated further:

> Such exceptions were obviously intended to be respected. A technical adherence to the letter of a constitutional provision may occasionally be carried farther than is necessary to the just protection of the accused, and farther than the safety of the public will warrant. For instance, there could be nothing more directly contrary to the letter of the provision in question than the admission of dying declarations. They are rarely made in the presence of the accused; they are made without any opportunity for examination or cross-examination; nor is the witness brought face to face with the jury; yet from time immemorial they have been treated as competent testimony, and no one would have the hardihood at this day to question their admissibility. They are admitted not in conformity with any general rule regarding the admission of testimony, but as an exception to such rules, simply from the necessities of the case, and to prevent a manifest failure of justice.[83]

The Supreme Court has considered several situations in which witness testimony can be admitted at trial without the physical appearance of the witness. First, if the witness, also known as the *declarant*, is unavailable because he or she is dead (as described in the previous paragraph), then an exception to the defendant's right to live testimony will be made. Similar exceptions are made when a witness is unavailable for other reasons, such as being in the hospital. Also, a witness may not be required to give live testimony if his or her statements fall under one of the established hearsay exceptions, permitting introduction of those statements by a third party. Each of these exceptions to the defendant's right to live testimony is considered in a following subsections.

Deceased Witnesses. In *Mattox*, already mentioned, the Supreme Court upheld the admissibility of a witness's past testimony from the defendant's first trial in the defendant's second trial because the witness died between the two trials. According to the Court, "To say that a criminal, after having once been convicted by the testimony of a certain witness, should go scot free simply because death has closed the mouth of that witness, would be carrying his constitutional protection to an unwarrantable extent."[84] The Court also stated, in relevant part:

> The primary object of the [confrontation clause of the Sixth Amendment] was to prevent depositions or ex parte affidavits, such as were sometimes admitted in civil cases, being used against the prisoner in lieu of a personal examination and cross-examination of the witness in which the accused has an opportunity, not only of

---

[82]*Mattox* v. *United States*, 156 U.S. 237 (1895), p. 243.
[83]Ibid., p. 243–244.
[84]Ibid., p. 243.

testing the recollection and sifting the conscience of the witness, but of compelling him to stand and face the jury in order that they may look at him, and judge by his demeanor upon the stand and the manner in which he gives his testimony whether he is worthy of belief.[85]

unavailable witness For purposes of confrontation, an unavailable witness is one who permanently moves to another country, cannot be located after a careful search by the prosecution, or suffers from a lapse in memory.

Unavailable Witnesses. The Supreme Court has held that an **unavailable witness**, for purposes of the confrontation clause, is one who permanently moves to another country,[86] cannot be located after a careful search by the prosecution,[87] or suffers from a lapse in memory.[88] In *Motes* v. *United States*, the Court stated that it would violate the Sixth Amendment "to permit the deposition or statement of an absent witness . . . to be read at the final trial when it does not appear that the witness was absent by the suggestion, connivance, or procurement of the accused, but does appear that this absence was due to the negligence of the prosecution."[89] In other words, if the prosecution fails to conduct a careful search for a certain witness and then claims that the witness is unavailable, then the defendant's right to live testimony will be violated.

In another case, *Barber* v. *Page*,[90] the Court considered whether statements by a witness who was not physically present at a preliminary hearing conformed to constitutional requirements, even though the witness was later found to be available and could have given testimony at the hearing. The Court stated that "a witness is not 'unavailable' for purposes of the exception to the confrontation requirement unless the prosecutorial authorities have made a good-faith effort to obtain his presence at trial."[91]

The state of Washington recognized a privilege that barred one spouse from testifying against the other without the other's consent. As a result, a wife did not testify in court at her husband's domestic violence trial. Instead, a tape-recorded statement to the effect that she was stabbed by her husband was admitted in court. In *Crawford* v. *Washington*,[92] the Supreme Court declared that the victim could not be considered unavailable. Consequently, it held that the accused's Sixth Amendment right to confrontation was violated. Some have argued that this case dealt a blow to the prosecution of domestic violence cases because it requires that victims must testify in person. In an analogous decision, the Supreme Court held that a state forensic analyst's laboratory report was testimonial and, as such, that the defendant should have been permitted to question its preparer during trial.[93]

Contrast *Crawford* v. *Washington* with the Court's more recent decision in *Davis* v. *Washington*.[94] In that case, a recorded 911 call from a victim was introduced into evidence. Davis challenged the introduction of the recorded call, arguing that not being able to confront the caller violated his Sixth Amendment right

---

[85]Ibid., p. 259.
[86]*Mancusi* v. *Stubbs*, 408 U.S. 204 (1972).
[87]E.g., *Ohio* v. *Roberts*, 448 U.S. 56 (1980).
[88]E.g., *California* v. *Green*, 399 U.S. 149 (1970).
[89]*Motes* v. *United States*, 178 U.S. 458 (1900), p. 474.
[90]*Barber* v. *Page*, 390 U.S. 719 (1968).
[91]Ibid., pp. 724–725.
[92]*Crawford* v. *Washington*, 541 U.S. 36 (2004).
[93]*Melendez-Diaz* v. *Massachusetts*, No. 07-591 (2009).
[94]*Davis* v. *Washington*, 547 U.S. 813 (2006)

to confrontation. The Supreme Court disagreed with his argument, holding that the confrontation clause does not apply to such statements. It went on to explain that ". . . statements are nontestimonial when made in the course of police interrogation under circumstances objectively indicating that the primary purpose of interrogation is to enable police assistance to meet an ongoing emergency."[95] In other words, the Court held that 911 calls are not considered the same as testimonial statements.

Nor are inquiries of wounded victims considered testimonial if the intent is to assist police with locating a perpetrator. In *Michigan* v. *Bryant*,[96] a shooting victim informed police that Bryant shot him. The victim died shortly thereafter, but the statement was introduced at trial (through the testimony of the officer who heard it) and used to establish his guilt. The Court observed that the victim's statements were "not testimonial . . . because they had a 'primary purpose . . . to enable police assistance to meet an ongoing emergency'."

Statements under Hearsay Exceptions. The death or unavailability of a witness is considered an exception to the defendant's right to live testimony. In either situation, the witness's statements are introduced by a third party. This is known as hearsay. Hearsay, as we defined it back in Chapter 5, is an out-of-court statement asserted for the truth of the matter. It is often introduced by someone who *hears* and then *says* (hence, the term *hearsay*) what the declarant said.

Hearsay is generally not admissible in a criminal trial. It is regarded skeptically because if the declarant is not available to be confronted and questioned by the defense, then there is no opportunity to question the truthfulness of his or her statements. The possibility also exists that the person communicating the declarant's statements may have misunderstood his or her intentions or forgotten exactly what he or she said.

hearsay exceptions
Exceptions to the rule that hearsay is not permissible in a criminal trial. Examples include excited utterances and present sense impressions.

Even so, there are several **hearsay exceptions**, which permit out-of-court statements made by declarants to be admitted at trial for the truth of the matter. On the surface, these exceptions seem to violate the defendant's right to live testimony. But the Supreme Court nevertheless permits hearsay in limited circumstances where the reliability of the statement is less in doubt. For example, the victim of a violent crime might yell or scream immediately after the crime. Due to the nature of this excited utterance, the declarant would not have time to think of a complicated lie or story. Thus, the statement is considered truthful and admitted as an exception to the hearsay rule. The reader is encouraged to consult an evidence textbook for a full review of specific exceptions to the hearsay rule. The following cases consider only two such exceptions.

One pertinent case is *White* v. *Illinois*,[97] which dealt with the admissibility of out-of-court statements made by a four-year-old girl. The prosecution argued that the statements should be admissible because of the "excited utterance" and "seeking medical treatment" exceptions to the hearsay rule. The former admits statements made in the "heat of the moment," while the latter admits statements made while an

---

[95]Ibid., p. 822.
[96]*Michigan* v. *Bryant*, No. 09-150 (2011).
[97]*White* v. *Illinois*, 502 U.S. 346 (1992).

individual is seeking medical treatment from a doctor. The Court held that the confrontation clause was not violated in this instance:

> A statement that has been offered in a moment of excitement—without the opportunity to reflect on the consequences of one's exclamation—may justifiably carry more weight with a trier of fact than a similar statement made in the course of procuring medical services, where the declarant knows that a false statement may cause misdiagnosis or mistreatment, carries special guarantees of credibility that a trier of fact may not think replicated by courtroom testimony.[98]

In another case, *United States* v. *Inadi*,[99] the Court decided on the admissibility of out-of-court statements from a coconspirator. The Court admitted the statements, claiming that they "derive much of their value from the fact that they are made in a context very different from trial, and therefore are usually irreplaceable as substantive evidence."[100] Stated differently, the Court thought that the out-of-court statements made by one co-conspirator to another should be admitted at trial because it would be difficult to replicate the conversation in a courtroom. As indicated in Figure 15.4, numerous other hearsay exceptions exist, as well. Indeed, even if a relevant exception does not exist, a court may still admit the hearsay, but such details are beyond the scope of this text.

The Defendant's Right to Challenge Witness Testimony

Part of the defendant's right to confrontation is the ability to challenge witnesses in the courtroom. This ability is manifested when each witness physically appears in court before the defendant. This type of confrontation permits questioning by the defense and is intended to submit the witness's account to relevant scrutiny. Also, the Court has held that the defendant can be limited in terms of the nature of the confrontation, which is usually accomplished through questioning—specifically, **cross-examination**. The rules of evidence dictate the limitations of cross-examination. Not all types of questions can be asked.

cross-examination
In-court questioning of a sworn witness by the opposing side's attorney.

Face-to-Face Contact. In *Coy* v. *Iowa*,[101] the Supreme Court considered the constitutionality of a state law that permitted the placement of a large opaque screen between the defendant and two young girls who testified that he had sexually assaulted them. The Court declared that the statute was unconstitutional because "the Confrontation Clause guarantees the defendant a face-to-face meeting with witnesses appearing before the trier of fact."[102]

Contrast *Coy* with *Maryland* v. *Craig*.[103] In *Craig*, the Court considered whether a statute permitting a witness's testimony via closed-circuit television was constitutional. The statute provided for such a procedure in cases in which the judge determined that face-to-face testimony would "result in the child suffering serious emotional distress

---

[98]Ibid., p. 356.
[99]*United States* v. *Inadi*, 475 U.S. 387 (1986).
[100]Ibid., p. 406.
[101]*Coy* v. *Iowa*, 487 U.S. 1012 (1988).
[102]Ibid., p. 1016.
[103]*Maryland* v. *Craig*, 497 U.S. 836 (1990).

Present sense impression. A statement describing or explaining an event or condition made while the declarant was perceiving the event or condition, or immediately thereafter.

Excited utterance. A statement relating to a startling event or condition made while the declarant was under the stress of excitement caused by the event or condition.

Then existing mental, emotional, or physical condition. A statement of the declarant's then existing state of mind, emotion, sensation, or physical condition (such as intent, plan, motive, design, mental feeling, pain, and bodily health), but not including a statement of memory or belief to prove the fact remembered or believed unless it relates to the execution, revocation, identification, or terms of declarant's will.

Statements for purposes of medical diagnosis or treatment. Statements made for purposes of medical diagnosis or treatment and describing medical history, or past or present symptoms, pain, or sensations, or the inception or general character of the cause or external source thereof insofar as reasonably pertinent to diagnosis or treatment.

Recorded recollection. A memorandum or record concerning a matter about which a witness once had knowledge but now has insufficient recollection to enable the witness to testify fully and accurately, shown to have been made or adopted by the witness when the matter was fresh in the witness' memory and to reflect that knowledge correctly. If admitted, the memorandum or record may be read into evidence but may not itself be received as an exhibit unless offered by an adverse party.

Records of regularly conducted activity. A memorandum, report, record, or data compilation, in any form, of acts, events, conditions, opinions, or diagnoses, made at or near the time by, or from information transmitted by, a person with knowledge, if kept in the course of a regularly conducted business activity, and if it was the regular practice of that business activity to make the memorandum, report, record or data compilation, all as shown by the testimony of the custodian or other qualified witness, or by certification that complies with Rule 902(11), Rule 902(12), or a statute permitting certification, unless the source of information or the method or circumstances of preparation indicate lack of trustworthiness. The term "business" as used in this paragraph includes business, institution, association, profession, occupation, and calling of every kind, whether or not conducted for profit.

Public records and reports. Records, reports, statements, or data compilations, in any form, of public offices or agencies, setting forth (A) the activities of the office or agency, or (B) matters observed pursuant to duty imposed by law as to which matters there was a duty to report, excluding, however, in criminal cases matters observed by police officers and other law enforcement personnel, or (C) in civil actions and proceedings and against the Government in criminal cases, factual findings resulting from an investigation made pursuant to authority granted by law, unless the sources of information or other circumstances indicate lack of trustworthiness.

Records of vital statistics. Records or data compilations, in any form, of births, fetal deaths, deaths, or marriages, if the report thereof was made to a public office pursuant to requirements of law.

Former testimony. Testimony given as a witness at another hearing of the same or a different proceeding, or in a deposition taken in compliance with law in the course of the same or another proceeding, if the party against whom the testimony is now offered, or, in a civil action or proceeding, a predecessor in interest, had an opportunity and similar motive to develop the testimony by direct, cross, or redirect examination.

Statement under belief of impending death. In a prosecution for homicide or in a civil action or proceeding, a statement made by a declarant while believing that the declarant's

Figure 15.4

Common Hearsay Exceptions

Source: Federal Rules of Evidence, Rules 803 and 804.

(continued)

death was imminent, concerning the cause or circumstances of what the declarant believed to be impending death.

Statement against interest. A statement which was at the time of its making so far contrary to the declarant's pecuniary or proprietary interest, or so far tended to subject the declarant to civil or criminal liability, or to render invalid a claim by the declarant against another, that a reasonable person in the declarant's position would not have made the statement unless believing it to be true. A statement tending to expose the declarant to criminal liability and offered to exculpate the accused is not admissible unless corroborating circumstances clearly indicate the trustworthiness of the statement.

Statement of personal or family history. (A) A statement concerning the declarant's own birth, adoption, marriage, divorce, legitimacy, relationship by blood, adoption, or marriage, ancestry, or other similar fact of personal or family history, even though declarant had no means of acquiring personal knowledge of the matter stated; or (B) a statement concerning the foregoing matters, and death also, of another person, if the declarant was related to the other by blood, adoption, or marriage or was so intimately associated with the other's family as to be likely to have accurate information concerning the matter declared.

Figure 15.4
(*continued*)

such that the child cannot reasonably communicate."[104] The Court upheld the statute, claiming that it did not violate the confrontation clause. It stated that a central concern of the confrontation clause "is to ensure the reliability of the evidence against a criminal defendant by subjecting it to rigorous testing in the context of an adversary proceeding before the trier of fact."[105] Furthermore, it held that the statute in question did "not impinge upon the truth-seeking or symbolic purposes of the Confrontation Clause."[106]

The Right to Compulsory Process

compulsory process
The Sixth Amendment requirement that criminal defendants enjoy the right to compel the production of witnesses and evidence. This is often accomplished via subpoena.

The compulsory process clause of the Sixth Amendment provides that the defendant can "compel" the participation of witnesses or the production of documents and other objects that are helpful to his or her defense. The right to compulsory process was incorporated to the states in *Washington v. Texas*, in which the Supreme Court stated that compulsory process protects "[t]he right to offer the testimony of witnesses, and to compel their attendance."[107] Furthermore, the Court stated:

We hold that the petitioner in this case was denied his right to have compulsory process for obtaining witnesses in his favor because the State arbitrarily denied him the right to put on the stand a witness who was physically and mentally capable of testifying to events that he had personally observed, and whose testimony would have been relevant and material to the defense. The Framers of the Constitution did not intend to commit the futile act of giving to a defendant the right to secure the attendance of witnesses whose testimony he had no right to use. The judgment of conviction must be reversed.[108]

---

[104]Ibid., p. 836.
[105]Ibid., p. 845.
[106]Ibid., p. 852.
[107]*Washington v. Texas*, 388 U.S. 14 (1967), p. 19.
[108]Ibid., p. 23.

Several state and federal statutes govern compulsory process, as do the *Federal Rules of Criminal Procedure*. Statutes and formal rules aside, at least two Supreme Court cases have considered aspects of the defendant's right to compulsory process. In particular, questions as to constitutional rights violations have been posed in instances in which the defense has been denied the right to subpoena a witness.

For example, in *Roviaro v. United States*,[109] the prosecution refused to provide the defense with the identity of a police informant. The Court recognized that the government had a significant interest in concealing the identity of the informant, mainly to further its efforts in combating the trafficking of illicit drugs. But the Court also found that the defendant's right to confrontation was denied by the prosecution's refusal to release the witness's identity. The informant was the only witness to the drug transaction for which the defendant was charged, so the defense clearly would have had a difficult time mounting an effective case without this witness.

Next, in *United States v. Valenzuela-Bernal*,[110] the defendant was charged with transporting illegal narcotics. He was arrested along with three other individuals who were unlawfully in the United States. Immigration officials concluded that two of the three aliens were not needed for the prosecution, so it deported them. The defendant then argued that his right to compulsory process was violated by the deportation. Surprisingly, the Court held that the government's interest in deporting illegal aliens and minimizing overcrowding in detention facilities outweighed the defendant's interest in mounting an effective defense. The Court concluded that the defendant did not offer a valid reason why the two deported witnesses were necessary for his defense.

The Right to Present Evidence

The Sixth Amendment's compulsory process clause appears only to grant the defendant the right to subpoena and question witnesses. However, in *Washington v. Texas*, the Supreme Court modified the definition of compulsory process to include the right of the *defense* to present evidence. The Court stated that compulsory process also guarantees "the right to present the defendant's version of the facts as well as the prosecution's to the jury so that it may decide where the truth lies."[111] Given this interpretation, the Court has more than once considered the constitutionality of restrictions placed on the defense's ability to present its case.

Decisions in Favor of the Defense. For example, in *Washington*, the Court decided on the constitutionality of a statute that prevented accomplices from testifying for each other. The statute was enacted out of fear that accomplices would give false testimony in order to benefit one another. The Court struck down the statute, stating that the defendant must be allowed to present the testimony of any witness who is capable of testifying.

---

[109]*Roviaro v. United States*, 353 U.S. 53 (1957).
[110]*United States v. Valenzuela-Bernal*, 458 U.S. 858 (1982).
[111]*Washington v. Texas*, 388 U.S. 14 (1967), p. 19.

In another case, *Chambers v. Mississippi*,[112] the Court overturned the conviction of a defendant who was not allowed to put three witnesses on the stand. The defendant, Chambers, had attempted to prove that another person, MacDonald, committed the murder for which he was charged. The three people Chambers wanted to put on the stand were those to whom MacDonald had allegedly confessed. The Court felt the witnesses' testimony should have been admissible, even though it would have been considered hearsay, because MacDonald "spontaneously" confessed to each person, making it likely that these individuals' testimony would be truthful and accurate. The Court felt that "the exclusion of this critical evidence, coupled with the State's refusal to permit Chambers to cross-examine MacDonald, denied him a trial in accord with traditional and fundamental standards of due process."[113]

In *Crane v. Kentucky*,[114] another related case, the defendant sought to present evidence that his confession was unreliable because it had been obtained when he was young and uneducated and had been interrogated at great length. The trial court excluded this evidence and the defendant was convicted. The Supreme Court reversed that decision, however, declaring that a state may not exclude "competent, reliable evidence bearing on the credibility of a confession when such evidence is central to the defendant's claim of innocence" because "[w]hether rooted directly in the Due Process Clause . . . or in the Compulsory Process or Confrontation Clause . . . the Constitution guarantees criminal defendants a 'meaningful opportunity' to present a complete defense."[115]

Decisions against the Defense. On a few occasions, the Court *has* sanctioned exclusion of certain defense evidence. For example, in *United States* v. *Scheffer*,[116] the Court upheld a trial court's decision to exclude polygraph evidence presented by the defense. The Court stated, "There is simply no consensus that polygraph evidence is reliable. To this day, the scientific community remains extremely polarized about the reliability of polygraph evidence."[117] Thus, the defense's ability to present its case can be restricted if the evidence it seeks to present cannot be considered reliable.[118]

Another important example of Court-sanctioned restrictions on the ability of the defense to present a case is *Michigan* v. *Lucas*.[119] In that case, the Court held that the defendant can be prevented from presenting evidence because of his or her attorney's misconduct. In this case, the trial judge in the defendant's rape trial excluded evidence about the victim's sexual history because the defendant failed to give notice of this to the prosecution within ten days of the trial, in violation of discovery rules. A similar decision was reached in *Taylor* v. *Illinois*, in which the Court sanctioned a lower court's decision to deny a defense witness's testimony because of providing short notice to the prosecution, again in violation of discovery rules.

---

[112]*Chambers v. Mississippi*, 410 U.S. 284 (1973).
[113]Ibid., p. 302.
[114]*Crane v. Kentucky*, 476 U.S. 683 (1986).
[115]Ibid., p. 690.
[116]*United States v. Scheffer*, 523 U.S. 303 (1998).
[117]Ibid., p. 309.
[118]See also *United States v. Salerno*, 505 U.S. 317 (1992).
[119]*Michigan v. Lucas*, 500 U.S. 145 (1991).

YOUR DECISION

1. Adam Fish was a soldier in the U.S. Army and stationed in Arizona. He was arrested and charged with the sale of marijuana, in violation of state law. Prior to his trial on this charge, Fish was discharged from the army and voluntarily left Arizona for New York. When the trial date was set, Fish's court-appointed attorney requested that he return to Arizona. However, because Fish lacked the funds necessary to travel from New York to Arizona, he did not appear in Arizona on the date set for trial. The trial proceeded without Fish's presence, and the jury returned a guilty verdict. After the verdict was rendered, Fish obtained the necessary travel funds and returned to Arizona in time for his sentencing. He was sentenced to not less than five or more than five-and-one-half years in prison. He is now appealing his conviction, claiming that his Sixth Amendment right to confrontation was violated. What should the court decide?

2. In the space of six months, the prosecution sent five subpoenas to a person it wished to testify at four separate trials. All five subpoenas were sent to the witness's residence, but the witness never appeared at trial. Can the witness be considered unavailable for confrontation purposes?

Summary

- Criminal defendants enjoy the Sixth Amendment right to counsel once adversarial criminal proceedings have commenced; this usually means once charges have been filed. Otherwise, when there is no possibility of confinement, the right to counsel does not apply.

- Like many constitutional rights, the right to counsel can be waived, but the court can appoint standby counsel in certain circumstances.

- The Supreme Court has interpreted the right to counsel to mean the right to effective counsel. Counsel is ineffective when specific errors are made that are prejudicial to the defendant's case.

- The right to confrontation refers to the ability of the defendant to face his or her accusers. This right is manifested in three ways: (1) by permitting the defendant to be present at trial, (2) by requiring live testimony, and (3) by allowing the defendant to challenge the government's witnesses through cross-examination.

- The defendant enjoys the right not only to be physically present but also to be mentally competent. Deciding competence hinges on whether the defendant is able to consult with his or her lawyer with a reasonable degree of understanding.

- Physical presence can be damaging to the defense, however, in cases in which the defendant does not testify or his or her being in court reminds jurors of the crime.

- The defendant's right to live testimony requires that witnesses appear in person. Recordings and the like are generally not permissible, but there are exceptions: (1) if the witness is unavailable because he or she is dead; (2) if the witness is unavailable for other reasons, such as by being hospitalized or confined to an institution; and (3) if the statement made by a witness who will not provide live testimony falls under one of the established hearsay exceptions, permitting introduction of those statements by a third party.

- The defendant's third guarantee for confrontation concerns the right to challenge witness testimony. The defendant can challenge witness testimony by engaging in cross-examination and recross-examination. Both forms of examination follow prosecutorial questioning and are intended to cast doubt on the witness's testimony.

- Compulsory process is another right enjoyed by a criminal defendant in the United States. It means that the defendant is legally entitled to compel the production of witnesses. This can be accomplished via a subpoena, if the witness will not voluntarily come forward.

- Compulsory process also extends to the production of physical evidence. However, there are restrictions that stem from the rules of evidence.

MODULE

15.3   SENTENCING

rehabilitation A goal of sentencing that consists of a planned intervention intended to change behavior (e.g., drug treatment); the process of restoring a witness's credibility.

CORE CONCEPTS

retribution A goal of sentencing that is concerned with punishing offenders based on the severity of their crimes (i.e., offenders "get what they deserve").

Incapacitation A goal of sentencing that is concerned with removing criminals from society, usually through incarceration.

Learning Objectives

- **Describe various sentencing goals.**
- **Distinguish between various types of sentences.**
- **Explain how the appropriate sentence is determined.**
- **Summarize constitutional rights enjoyed during sentencing.**

Once a person has been convicted at trial, he or she must be sentenced. Sentencing occurs at a separate, posttrial hearing but rarely for misdemeanor convictions. Individuals charged with misdemeanors are often tried and sentenced in the same hearing. When sentencing is carried out in a separate hearing, however, it is usually preceded by the judge requesting a *presentence report*. This report provides the judge with information concerning the defendant's pretrial record, financial characteristics, family status, employment status, and other factors that can be relevant in deciding on the appropriate sentence. The time needed to complete this report is the main reason for the time lapse between trial and sentencing. The report is intended to assist the judge in reaching his or her decision and is usually completed by a probation officer retained by the court.

Several sentencing options are available to the judge. The judge may impose a sentence and then suspend it, pending good behavior on the part of the defendant. The judge may also require the defendant to pay a fine or, in more extreme cases, to serve a term in prison. Probation or another method of supervised release is a possibility, as well. In any case, the type of sentence can hinge on the judge's own goal of sentencing—that is, his or her view as to the most important purpose of sentencing. The following section considers leading goals of criminal sentencing.

Four broad goals of sentencing can be identified: (1) rehabilitation, or reformation; (2) retribution; (3) incapacitation; and (4) deterrence, either general

deterrence A goal of sentencing that is concerned with punishing offenders such that they and others will be discouraged from committing crime.

specific deterrence When a sentenced offender is discouraged from committing additional crimes due to his or her sentence.

general deterrence When others besides the sentenced offender are discouraged from committing additional crimes due to sentencing practices.

indeterminate sentencing A sentencing strategy that gives the judge the authority to set the sentence.

determinate sentencing A sentencing strategy that permits the judge to set the sentence, and the sentence cannot later be altered by a parole board.

mandatory sentencing A sentencing strategy that takes discretion away from judges. The law, not the judge, sets the sentence.

sentencing guidelines State and federal rules used to set sentences based on offense severity and the offender's prior record. Sentencing guidelines achieve a balance between determinate and indeterminate sentencing.

or specific. Rehabilitation is a goal of sentencing that consists of a planned intervention intended to change behavior. Some people feel that a prison sentence can encourage offenders to see the "errors of their ways" and thus be rehabilitated. Rehabilitation is also used to refer to interventions such as drug treatment. Retribution is a goal of sentencing that is concerned with punishing offenders based on the severity of their crimes (offenders are supposed to "get what they deserve"). Incapacitation is concerned with removing criminals from the society, usually through incarceration. Specific deterrence refers to what it takes to discourage the offender from committing additional crimes. General deterrence refers to what it takes to discourage all would-be offenders from committing crimes.

Types of Prison Sentences

At least four types of sentences can be identified, some of which are closely related to one another.

Indeterminate sentencing gives the judge the authority to set the sentence. This form of sentencing empowers the judge to set the maximum sentence—that is, up to what the legislature will allow—or the minimum sentence for the offender to serve in prison. Under this system, a parole board usually ends up deciding the actual amount of time the offender will spend in prison.

With determinate sentencing, the judge is permitted to hand down a fixed sentence that cannot later be altered by a parole board. Determinate sentencing has the effect of treating all offenders similarly. It also has the effect of ensuring that criminals will be incarcerated for longer periods of time than may be permissible under indeterminate sentencing.

Mandatory sentencing is a form of determinate sentencing but differs insofar as it takes discretion away from the judge. "Three strikes" laws require mandatory sentencing. For example, under California's "three strikes" law, if a person who has two "strikeable" felonies on his or her record commits a third felony of any type, he or she will go to prison for life. The Supreme Court has decided that such laws do not constitute cruel and unusual punishment.[120]

Sentencing guidelines can be used to determine the appropriate sentence. They constitute the middle ground between indeterminate and determinate methods of sentencing. As such, they serve to reduce disparities in sentencing by recommending a certain term of imprisonment for a certain type of offender. Sentencing guidelines can be voluntary or involuntary, depending on state or federal law. Sentencing guidelines that must be followed exactly are known as *presumptive guidelines*.

The U.S. Sentencing Commission was created in 1984 to deal with sentencing problems in the federal courts. It put together a *sentencing grid* that federal judges use to determine appropriate sentences (see Figure 15.5). Both criminal history (i.e., horizontal axis) and offense level (i.e., vertical axis) are taken into account, such that a judge can set the appropriate sentence in months.

---

[120]*Lockyer* v. *Andrade*, 538 U.S. 63 (2003); *Ewing* v. *Andrade*, 538 U.S. 11 (2003).

SENTENCE TABLE (in months of imprisonment)
Criminal History Category (Criminal History Points)

Offense Level	I (0 or 1)	II (2 or 3)	III (4, 5, 6)	IV (7, 8, 9)	V (10, 11, 12)	VI (13 or more)
1	0–6	0–6	0–6	0–6	0–6	0–6
2	0–6	0–6	0–6	0–6	0–6	1–7
3	0–6	0–6	0–6	0–6	2–8	3–9
4	0–6	0–6	0–6	2–8	4–10	6–12
5	0–6	0–6	1–7	4–10	6–12	9–15
6	0–6	1–7	2–8	6–12	9–15	12–18
7	0–6	2–8	4–10	8–14	12–18	15–21
8	0–6	4–10	6–12	10–16	15–21	18–24
9	4–10	6–12	8–14	12–18	18–24	21–27
10	6–12	8–14	10–16	15–21	21–27	24–30
11	8–14	10–16	12–18	18–24	24–30	27–33
12	10–16	12–18	15–21	21–27	27–33	30–37
13	12–18	15–21	18–24	24–30	30–37	33–41
14	15–21	18–24	21–27	27–33	33–41	37–46
15	18–24	21–27	24–30	30–37	37–46	41–51
16	21–27	24–30	27–33	33–41	41–51	46–57
17	24–30	27–33	30–37	37–46	46–57	51–63
18	27–33	30–37	33–41	41–51	51–63	57–71
19	30–37	33–41	37–46	46–57	57–71	63–78
20	33–41	37–46	41–51	51–63	63–78	70–87
21	37–46	41–51	46–57	57–71	70–87	77–96
22	41–51	46–57	51–63	63–78	77–96	84–105
23	46–57	51–63	57–71	70–87	84–105	92–115
24	51–63	57–71	63–78	77–96	92–115	100–125
25	57–71	63–78	70–87	84–105	100–125	110–137
26	63–78	70–87	78–97	92–115	110–137	120–150
27	70–87	78–97	87–108	100–125	120–150	130–162
28	78–97	87–108	97–121	110–137	130–162	140–175
29	87–108	97–121	108–135	121–151	140–175	151–188
30	97–121	108–135	121–151	135–168	151–188	168–210
31	108–135	121–151	135–168	151–188	168–210	188–235
32	121–151	135–168	151–188	168–210	188–235	210–262
33	135–168	151–188	168–210	188–235	210–262	235–293
34	151–188	168–210	188–235	210–262	235–293	262–327
35	168–210	188–235	210–262	235–293	262–327	292–365
36	188–235	210–262	235–293	262–327	292–365	324–405
37	210–262	235–293	262–327	292–365	324–405	360–life
38	235–293	262–327	292–365	324–405	360–life	360–life
39	262–327	292–365	324–405	360–life	360–life	360–life
40	292–365	324–405	360–life	360–life	360–life	360–life
41	324–405	360–life	360–life	360–life	360–life	360–life
42	360–life	360–life	360–life	360–life	360–life	360–life
43	life	life	life	life	life	life

Zones (left margin): Zone A (levels 1–8 region), Zone B (level 9–10 region), Zone C (levels 11–12 region), Zone D (levels 13–43).

Figure 15.5

Federal Sentencing Guidelines

Source: U.S. Sentencing Commission, *Guidelines Manual* (Washington, DC: U.S. Sentencing Commission, 2010), p. 401. Available online: http://www.ussc.gov/Guidelines/2010_guidelines/Manual_PDF/Chapter_5.pdf (accessed January 4, 2013).

Determining the Appropriate Sentence

Determining the appropriate sentence almost always involves considering both the seriousness of the offense and the offender's prior record. Other factors that are considered include the defendant's possible threat to the community and his or her degree of remorse for committing the crime. Even age, family ties, employment status, and other demographic factors can come into play. Moreover, the defendant who pleads guilty may receive a different sentence than the defendant who is found guilty in a trial. A guilty plea suggests that the defendant is willing to admit what he or she did and, as such, should be treated more leniently.

Sentencing can also be determined by the number of separate crimes growing out of a single criminal act. If, for instance, a defendant is convicted of killing another person with a handgun, he or she may be sentenced for the killing as well as for unlawful possession of a handgun, if the law permits the latter. In such a situation, the judge may sentence the defendant to consecutive or concurrent sentences. With a concurrent sentence, the defendant serves time for both crimes at once. Consecutive sentences, by contrast, are served separately, one after another. In the murder example, the defendant would serve time in prison for the killing, and then when that term was completed, he or she would begin serving the sentence for possession.

Indeed, sentencing can be influenced by the defendant's degree of cooperation with the police. In *Roberts* v. *United States*,[121] the Court held that the sentencing judge was permitted to consider the defendant's refusal to cooperate with the police in investigating his crime. Still other factors, such as the offender's mental status, can be considered. In fact, it has been held that a mentally ill individual can be held in custody, such as in a mental institution, for a longer term than a traditional prison sentence for the crime charged.[122] This often happens following an insanity plea.

Most jurisdictions have what is known as the "going rate" for a criminal offense.[123] Usually, this is an unwritten, informal agreement between members of a courtroom work group (i.e., a judge, defense attorney, and prosecutor) as to what sentence a typical case merits. Usually, if the seriousness of the offense and the offender's background characteristics are known, one can predict with a fair degree of accuracy what sentence will be imposed.

A judge's sentencing decisions can also be influenced by *victim impact statements*. For example, Proposition 8, adopted by California voters in 1982, provides that "the victim of any crime, or the next kin of the victim, . . . has the right to attend all sentencing proceedings . . . [and] to reasonably express his or her views concerning the crime, the person responsible, and the need for restitution."[124] The Supreme Court has decided that testimony in the form of a victim impact statement is admissible.[125] The judge is then required to take the victim's or next of kin's statement into account when deciding on a sentence for the offender.

Death Penalty Sentencing.   The most serious punishment that can be imposed is *capital punishment*, or the death penalty. Prior to the 1970s, several executions were carried out each year. However, in 1972, the Supreme Court decided the landmark case *Furman* v. *Georgia*.[126] In that case, the Court held that the death penalty

concurrent sentence A prison sentence for two or more criminal acts that is served simultaneously.

consecutive sentence A prison sentence for two or more criminal acts that is served back-to-back.

---

[121]*Roberts* v. *United States*, 445 U.S. 552 (1980).
[122]See, e.g., *Jones* v. *United States*, 103 S.Ct. 3043 (1983).
[123]S. Walker, *Sense and Nonsense about Crime and Drugs*, 5th ed. (Belmont, CA: Wadsworth, 2001), p. 41.
[124]California Penal Code, Section 1191.1 (1996).
[125]*Payne* v. *Tennessee*, 501 U.S. 808 (1991).
[126]*Furman* v. *Georgia*, 408 U.S. 238 (1972).

was carried out in the United States in a way that amounted to cruel and unusual punishment, in violation of the Eighth Amendment. Then, in 1976, the Court reinstated the death penalty in *Gregg* v. *Georgia,*[127] holding that death is an acceptable sentence, provided the sentencing process is reasonable. See the accompanying Court Decision box for more on the Supreme Court's reasoning in *Gregg.*

COURT DECISION

The Logic behind the Death Penalty

Gregg v. *Georgia*
428 U.S. 153 (1976)

Decision: According to the Supreme Court, "the punishment of death for the crime of murder does not, under all circumstances, violate the Eighth and Fourteenth Amendments."

Reason: ". . . the concerns expressed in *Furman* that the penalty of death not be imposed in an arbitrary or capricious manner can be met by a carefully drafted statute that ensures that the sentencing authority is given adequate information and guidance. As a general proposition, these concerns are best met by a system that provides for a bifurcated proceeding at which the sentencing authority is apprised of the information relevant to the imposition of sentence and provided with standards to guide its use of the information . . . In the wake of *Furman,* Georgia amended its capital punishment statute, but chose not to narrow the scope of its murder provisions . . . Georgia did act, however, to narrow the class of murderers subject to capital punishment by specifying 10 statutory aggravating circumstances, one of which must be found by the jury to exist beyond a reasonable doubt before a death sentence can ever be imposed. In addition, the jury is authorized to consider any other appropriate aggravating or mitigating circumstances . . . The jury is not required to find any mitigating circumstance in order to make a recommendation of mercy that is binding on the trial court . . ., but it must find a statutory aggravating circumstance before recommending a sentence of death.

These procedures require the jury to consider the circumstances of the crime and the criminal before it recommends sentence. No longer can a Georgia jury do as *Furman's* jury did: reach a finding of the defendant's guilt and then, without guidance or direction, decide whether he should live or die. Instead, the jury's attention is directed to the specific circumstances of the crime: was it committed in the course of another capital felony? Was it committed for money? Was it committed upon a peace officer or judicial officer? Was it committed in a particularly heinous way, or in a manner that endangered the lives of many persons? In addition, the jury's attention is focused on the characteristics of the person who committed the crime: does he have a record of prior convictions for capital offenses? Are there any special facts about this defendant that mitigate against imposing capital punishment (*e.g.,* his youth, the extent of his cooperation with the police, his emotional state at the time of the crime). As a result,

(continued)

---

[127]*Gregg* v. *Georgia*, 428 U.S. 153 (1976).

while some jury discretion still exists, 'the discretion to be exercised is controlled by clear and objective standards so as to produce nondiscriminatory application' . . .

As an important additional safeguard against arbitrariness and caprice, the Georgia statutory scheme provides for automatic appeal of all death sentences to the State's Supreme Court. That court is required by statute to review each sentence of death and determine whether it was imposed under the influence of passion or prejudice, whether the evidence supports the jury's finding of a statutory aggravating circumstance, and whether the sentence is disproportionate compared to those sentences imposed in similar cases. . . .

In short, Georgia's new sentencing procedures require, as a prerequisite to the imposition of the death penalty, specific jury findings as to the circumstances of the crime or the character of the defendant. Moreover, to guard further against a situation comparable to that presented in *Furman,* the Supreme Court of Georgia compares each death sentence with the sentences imposed on similarly situated defendants to ensure that the sentence of death in a particular case is not disproportionate. On their face, these procedures seem to satisfy the concerns of *Furman.*

bifurcated trial Holding two separate proceedings in the death penalty context, one for determining guilt and another for determining the appropriate sentence (e.g., death or life in prison).

Determining whether death should be imposed is now frequently in the hands of a jury. Most state statutes call for, in essence, two trials. In legal parlance, this is called a **bifurcated trial**. In the first trial, the defendant's guilt or lack of involvement in the crime is determined. This is the traditional trial. Then, the jury sits for what is basically another trial to determine whether a death sentence should be handed down. The importance of such a procedure is that it allows a jury of the defendant's peers, not just a judge, to determine whether capital punishment is appropriate. Furthermore, the jury must take into account aggravating and mitigating circumstances. As decided in *Roberts v. Louisiana,*[128] failure to do so is unconstitutional. Importantly, though, if aggravating or mitigating circumstances presented to the jury are later found invalid, the Eighth Amendment will not necessarily be violated if a death sentence is imposed.[129]

In *Stebbing v. Maryland,* Justice Marshall described one state's approach to death penalty sentencing that relies on a jury's decision:

> Like most death penalty statutes, the Maryland statute begins by requiring the sentencing authority—either a judge or a jury—first to consider whether the prosecutor has proved, beyond a reasonable doubt, the existence of any of 10 statutory aggravating circumstances. . . . If the sentence does not find at least one aggravating factor, the sentence must be life imprisonment. . . . If the sentence finds that one or more aggravating factors exist, it then must determine whether the defendant has proven, by a preponderance of the evidence, that any of eight statutory mitigating factors exist. . . . If no mitigating factors are found, the sentence must impose death. If, instead, the sentence has found at least one mitigating factor, it must determine, by a preponder-

---

[128]*Roberts v. Louisiana,* 428 U.S. 325 (1977).
[129]*Brown v. Sanders,* 546 U.S. 212 (2006).

ance of the evidence, whether the proven mitigating factors outweigh the aggravating circumstances. If they do, the sentence must impose a life sentence. If the mitigating factors do not outweigh aggravating factors, the jury must impose a death sentence.[130]

Whereas a jury must take aggravating and mitigating factors into consideration when determining whether a death sentence is appropriate, it is not appropriate for a judge to do so. Such was the decision in *Ring* v. *Arizona*.[131] There, the Supreme Court held that allowing a sentencing judge, without a jury, to find aggravating circumstances necessary for imposition of the death penalty violated the Sixth Amendment's jury trial provision (incidentally, judges in some states can ignore jurors' sentencing recommendations in capital cases).

The death penalty is most commonly handed down for first-degree, premeditated murder. But whether death is the appropriate sentence for less serious offenses has raised some questions. The Supreme Court has answered these questions to some extent. For example, in *Coker* v. *Georgia*,[132] the Court held that a sentence of death for the crime of rape against an adult woman was grossly disproportionate and in violation of the Eighth and Fourteenth Amendments to the U.S. Constitution.

Other Important Sentencing Decisions. Several other recent decisions have sought to clarify the circumstances in which death and/or other types of sentences can be imposed. A handful of the cases and their holdings are as follows:

- *Woodson* **v.** *North Carolina*.[133] Decided on the same day as *Gregg*, the Court held that mandatory death penalty laws—that is, those that do not take aggravating and mitigating circumstances into account—are unconstitutional.
- *Ford v. Wainwright*.[134] The execution of someone who is insane violates the Eighth Amendment.
- *Harmelin v. Michigan*.[135] A life sentence without the possibility of parole for a first-time, nonviolent drug offender does not constitute cruel and unusual punishment.
- *Kansas* **v.** *Hendricks*.[136] Civil commitment was upheld for convicted child molesters who have served their sentences under the state's Sexually Violent Predators Act.
- *Apprendi* **v.** *New Jersey*.[137] Any fact, other than prior conviction, that increases the penalty for a crime beyond that allowed by statute must be submitted to a jury and proven beyond a reasonable doubt.
- *Atkins* **v.** *Virginia*.[138] The execution of a mentally retarded person violates the Eighth Amendment.

---

[130]*Stebbing* v. *Maryland*, 469 U.S. 900 (1984), p. 902.
[131]*Ring* v. *Arizona*, 122 S.Ct. 2428 (2002).
[132]*Coker* v. *Georgia*, 433 U.S. 584 (1977).
[133]*Woodson* v. *North Carolina*, 428 U.S. 280 (1976).
[134]*Ford* v. *Wainwright*, 477 U.S. 399 (1986).
[135]*Harmelin* v. *Michigan*, 501 U.S. 957 (1991).
[136]*Kansas* v. *Hendricks*, 521 U.S. 346 (1997).
[137]*Apprendi* v. *New Jersey*, 530 U.S. 466 (2000).
[138]*Atkins* v. *Virginia*, 536 U.S. 304 (2002).

- *Kansas* v. *Crane*.[139] Concerning the civil commitment of sexual offenders under Kansas's Sexually Violent Predators Act, such offenders cannot be civilly committed without having proof that they have serious difficulty in controlling their behavior.

- *Roper* v. *Simmons*.[140] The execution of offenders who committed their capital crime under the age of 18 violates the Eighth Amendment.

- *Deck* v. *Missouri*.[141] The constitution forbids the use of visible shackles during a capital trial's penalty phase.

- *United States* v. *Booker*.[142] Federal sentencing guidelines are advisory, not mandatory.

- *Carey* v. *Musladin*.[143] It was not unfairly prejudicial for trial spectators to wear buttons depicting the murder victim.

- *Rita* v. *United States*.[144] Sentences that fall within the federal sentencing guidelines are presumptively reasonable.

- *Cunningham* v. *California*.[145] State determinate sentencing laws violate the Sixth Amendment right to jury trial when they permit judges to impose enhanced sentences based on facts not found by a jury or admitted to by the defendant.

- *Kimbrough* v. *United States*.[146] The federal cocaine sentencing guidelines, like other federal sentencing guidelines, are advisory.

- *Baze* v. *Rees*.[147] A three-drug lethal-injection protocol does not violate the Eighth Amendment's prohibition of cruel and unusual punishment.

- *Graham* v. *Florida*.[148] Juvenile offenders cannot be sentenced to life in prison for non-homicide offenses.

- *United States* v. *Comstock*.[149] It is constitutionally permissible for the federal government to use civil commitment to keep a sexually dangerous federal prisoners confined beyond the date of scheduled release.

- *Miller* v. *Alabama*.[150] Life in prison without the possibility of parole for juvenile homicide offenders violates the Eighth Amendment.

Constitutional Rights during Sentencing

A convicted criminal enjoys several important constitutional rights during the sentencing process. First, the double-jeopardy provision of the Fifth Amendment, as discussed in Chapter 2, applies. Furthermore, the defendant is entitled to a reasonable

---

[139]*Kansas v. Crane*, 534 U.S. 407 (2002).
[140]*Roper v. Simmons*, 543 U.S. 551 (2005).
[141]*Deck v. Missouri*, 544 U.S. 622 (2005).
[142]*United States v. Booker*, 543 U.S. 220 (2005).
[143]*Carey v. Musladin*, 549 U.S. 70 (2006).
[144]*Rita v. United States*, 551 U.S 338 (2007).
[145]*Cunningham v. California*, 549 U.S. 270 (2007).
[146]*Kimbrough v. United States*, 552 U.S. 85 (2007).
[147]*Baze v. Rees*, 553 U.S. 35 (2008).
[148]*Graham v. Florida*, No. 08-7412 (2010).
[149]*United States v. Comstock*, No. 08-1224 (2010).
[150]*Miller v. Alabama*, No. 10-9646 (2012).

According to the Supreme Court, capital punishment is not considered cruel and unusual.

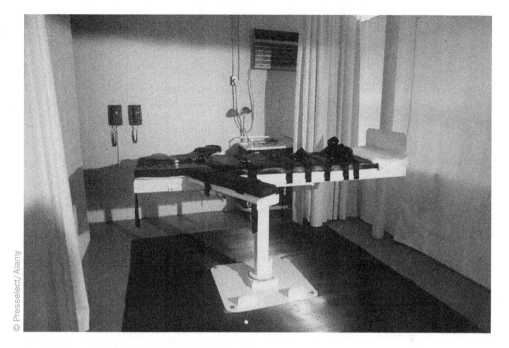

© Presselect/Alamy

punishment for his or her crime. Punishment that violates the Eighth Amendment, that is cruel and unusual, is unconstitutional. In other words, the punishment should reflect the seriousness of the crime. For example, in *Solem v. Helm*, the Court held that a life sentence for the defendant's seventh nonviolent offense was unconstitutional. The Court prohibited the sentence, stating that the defendant "received the penultimate sentence for relatively minor criminal conduct."[151]

The defendant also has the right to participate in the sentencing process. With the possible exception of misdemeanor sentencing, which may take place out of the presence of the defendant, the defendant has the right to be present during sentencing. Also, the defendant should be advised of his or her right to appeal. The defendant also has the right to have counsel present at the sentencing hearing to argue on his or her behalf. The Sixth Amendment right to counsel operates essentially the same way at sentencing as it does at trial.

The defendant also has the right to ask the sentencing judge to ignore past convictions that were obtained in violation of the right to counsel. For example, in *United States v. Tucker*,[152] the Supreme Court invalidated an individual's 25-year sentence because the sentencing judge arrived at the sentence by considering the defendant's past convictions, for which he was not afforded counsel. The Court stated:

> The government is . . . on solid ground in asserting that a sentence imposed by a federal district judge, if within statutory limits, is generally not subject to review. . . . But these general propositions do not decide the case before us. For we deal here not with a sentence imposed in the informed discretion of a trial judge, but with a sentence founded at least in part upon misinformation of constitutional magnitude. As

---

[151]*Solem v. Helm*, 463 U.S. 277 (1983), p. 305.
[152]*United States v. Tucker*, 404 U.S. 443 (1972).

in *Townsend* v. *Burke*, 334 U.S. 736 (1690), "this prisoner was sentenced on the basis of assumptions concerning his criminal record which were materially untrue." The record in the present case makes evident that the sentencing judge gave specific consideration to the respondent's previous convictions before imposing sentence upon him. Yet it is now clear that two of those convictions were wholly unconstitutional under *Gideon* v. *Wainwright*, 372 U.S. 335 (1963).[153]

In summary, a defendant enjoys at least three important constitutional rights during the sentencing process: (1) the right not to be put twice in jeopardy, (2) the right to a sentence that conforms with the Eighth Amendment's proscription against cruel and unusual punishment, and (3) the right to counsel at sentencing-related hearings, regardless of his or her ability to afford representation.

YOUR DECISION

1. Assume that a state law gives the trial judge authority to sentence to death a defendant convicted of a capital crime but also requires the judge to consider the jury's recommendation as to whether the death penalty should be imposed. Assume further that a man has been sentenced to death by the judge in his trial, even though the jury that convicted him recommended life in prison. The man appeals, claiming that the statute is unconstitutional because it does not specify the weight the judge must give to the jury's sentencing recommendation and thus permits the arbitrary imposition of the death penalty. He further claims that the judge should be forced to give "great weight" to the jury's recommendation. How should the appellate court rule?

2. Bill Smith committed and was convicted of two violent felonies in California. Once released, he promptly committed another felony, but it was not a violent felony. Instead, he stole merchandise from a big box store that made his actions constitute grand theft. The trial court convicts him and sentences him to life in prison under California's punitive three-strikes law, which it is permitted to do. Is Smith's punishment cruel and unusual? Why or why not?

Summary

- A sentence can range from a modest fine or supervised probation to life in prison or even death.

- Sentencing in the United States is carried out with one or more of four sentencing objectives in mind: deterrence, incapacitation, retribution, and rehabilitation. If a judge favors rehabilitation, he or she will probably be inclined to hand down a sentence of probation rather than imprisonment. Many judges and criminal justice commentators also believe rehabilitation is possible in a traditional prison environment. The aim of deterrence is to discourage others from committing crime by punishing the offender harshly. Finally, incapacitation and retribution simply remove the offender from the society and give him or her what is deserved.

---

[153]Ibid., p. 446.

- While a judge's goal or objective of punishment may guide his or her sentencing practices, other factors are considered, as well. Some of these factors include, but are not limited to, the crime in question, the defendant's prior record, his or her ties to the community and family, the defendant's employment history, whether he or she was convicted for many different crimes as opposed to one specific crime, the degree of the defendant's cooperation with authorities during the investigative stage, the defendant's mental status, his or her feelings of remorse, if any, and several other pertinent factors.

- Death penalty sentencing must be carried out with special care. The preferred method is to have a jury, not a judge, decide whether death is appropriate and to take into account aggravating and mitigating circumstances.[154]

- The death penalty is unconstitutional for young offenders but *is* sometimes appropriate for offenses other than first-degree murder. The Supreme Court has also handed down other important restrictions concerning death penalty sentencing.

- Excessive punishments can violate the Eighth Amendment's cruel and unusual punishment clause.

MODULE

15.4   APPEALS AND *HABEAS CORPUS*

Learning Objectives
- **Summarize the types and effects of appeals.**
- **Explain the appellate process.**
- **Outline the *habeas corpus* process.**

CORE CONCEPTS

The criminal process does not end with sentencing, at least with some offenders. Those who feel a mistake was made or a horrible injustice was done may elect to appeal their convictions. And in the event an appeal fails, the possibility exists for another challenge to the sentence, namely *habeas corpus*. This module is thus concerned with the rules surrounding appeals and *habeas corpus*.

appeal The practice of asking an appellate court to examine a lower court's decision in order to determine whether the proper procedure was followed or the correct law was applied.

Appeals

An **appeal** occurs when an appellate court, such as one of the federal courts of appeal, examines a lower court's decision in order to determine whether the proper procedure was followed or the correct law was applied. In other words, when a defendant appeals, he or she is claiming that the court made an error. Thus, the

---

[154]See *Ring v. Arizona*, 536 U.S. 584 (2002).

appeal guarantees that a defendant who is found guilty can challenge his or her conviction. Furthermore, the appeal guarantees that another judge or panel of judges, disconnected from the initial trial, will make the relevant decision.

Although appealing convictions is an important part of the criminal process, the Supreme Court has never held that doing so is constitutionally permissible. That is, nowhere does the U.S. Constitution specify that a certain number of appeals will be granted to each convicted criminal. In *McKane* v. *Durston*, the Supreme Court stated, "A review by an appellate court of the final judgment in a criminal case, however grave the offense of which the accused is convicted, was not at common law, and is not now, a necessary element of due process of law."[155]

Most appeals are posttrial in nature and filed by the defense, which is why this topic is being discussed at the end of this book. However, in some situations, the defense appeals a court's decision, such as on a motion to suppress evidence, during the trial. And in some instances, the prosecution can even file an appeal.

Types and Effects of Appeals

Despite the Supreme Court's view that appealing one's conviction is not constitutionally guaranteed, every state and the federal government has rules providing a certain number of appeals to a convicted criminal. At both the state and federal levels, a convicted criminal is usually granted at least one **direct appeal** (also known as an appeal of right).

direct appeal An appeal that is authorized by law.

An appeal of right, or a direct appeal, is automatically granted to the defendant by law. That is, an appeal of right *must* be heard by an appellate court. It is not up to the appellate court to decide whether to hear such an appeal. By contrast, the appellate court can decide, at its own discretion, whether to hear a **discretionary appeal**. Also, appeals of right are limited, but discretionary appeals can be filed several times, provided they are not redundant.

discretionary appeal An appeal that will be heard only if the reviewing court agrees to do so.

When a defendant appeals a decision, there are a number of possible consequences. In the typical appeal, the defendant seeks to correct a decision by the lower court that he or she perceives to be in error. In such an instance, the appellate court will either affirm or reverse the lower court's decision. It may also remand (i.e., send back) the case for further proceedings, consistent with its opinion.

trial *de novo* A type of appeal in which with appellate court holds a new trial as if the prior trial never occurred.

Another consequence of an appeal can be a **trial *de novo***. When the defendant appeals for a trial *de novo*, he or she is essentially requesting a new, independent trial at the appellate level. Trials *de novo* are rare. Furthermore, they are usually limited to appeals of decisions arising from misdemeanor courts of limited jurisdiction. Rarely, if ever, will a convicted felon succeed in obtaining a trial *de novo* in an appellate court. The primary reason for this is that an appellate court interprets the *law*, not the *facts*. It is the job of the trial court to determine guilt based on the facts.

Whether the defendant seeks a new trial or simply a review of the trial court's decision on some matter, he or she will not necessarily go free if a decision is returned in his or her favor. If, for example, the appellate court considers a lower court's decision not to exclude evidence and decides that the lower court's decision should be

---

[155] *McKane* v. *Durston*, 153 U.S. 684 (1894), p. 687.

reversed, this means the evidence should have been excluded, not that the defendant should be acquitted. For example, in the famous *Miranda* case,[156] the Supreme Court did not free Ernesto Miranda. Instead, it remanded his case for a new trial. He was subsequently found guilty and sentenced to more than 20 years in prison. It is, therefore, important when reading cases to understand precisely what the reviewing court is deciding. Rarely does an appellate court decide guilt; its job is to interpret the law and review the conduct of the trial court.

What happens to convicted defendants while they are appealing? In almost all cases, they serve out the conditions of their sentences. Assume, for example, that a defendant appeals his guilty conviction on the grounds that he was denied counsel at trial. Assume further that the defendant's appeal has merit. If he was sentenced to prison following trial, he will remain there until the appeal is heard, if it ever is. However, for a select few convicts, the judge will issue a *stay*, which means the convicted individual will not serve time before the appeal is heard. This is a rare situation and usually involves an individual who poses a low flight risk. The fact that most convicted criminals are considered flight risks further explains why stays of imprisonment are rarely granted.

Constitutional Rights during the Appellate Process

Even though the Supreme Court has held that appealing one's conviction is not constitutionally required, it has held, on a number of occasions, that when an appeal is permissible, the government must follow certain procedures. Specifically, the government must ensure that the defendant has (1) access to trial transcripts, (2) the right to counsel, and (3) the right to be free from government retaliation for a successful appeal. Before these procedural issues can be considered, though, the defendant must file *notice of an appeal*. An example of such a notice, from the U.S. District Court for the Southern District of California, is presented in Figure 15.6.

Ensuring That the Defendant Has Access to Trial Transcripts. In *Griffin* v. *Illinois*,[157] the Supreme Court considered whether an Illinois appellate procedure that required the defendant to produce transcripts of the trial—even if he or she could not afford to do so—violated the Constitution. The Court struck down the procedure, claiming that the government cannot impose a restriction on the right to appeal "in a way that discriminates against some convicted defendants on account of their poverty."[158] In a related case, *Entsminger* v. *Iowa*,[159] decided some time later, the Court invalidated a state procedure that allowed defense counsel, rather than an indigent defendant, to decide whether an appeal could continue with an incomplete trial transcript. An actual trial transcript order form is presented in Figure 15.7.

Ensuring the Defendant's Right to Counsel during Appeals. As has been discussed at some length in this text, criminal defendants enjoy the Sixth

---

[156]*Miranda* v. *Arizona*, 384 U.S. 436 (1966).
[157]*Griffin* v. *Illinois*, 351 U.S. 12 (1956).
[158]Ibid., p. 18.
[159]*Entsminger* v. *Iowa*, 386 U.S. 748 (1967).

Clear Form

NAME AND ADDRESS OF ATTORNEY

PHONE:

UNITED STATES DISTRICT COURT
SOUTHERN DISTRICT OF CALIFORNIA

TRIAL JUDGE   COURT REPORTER

)
)
)   CIVIL NO.
)
(Appellant/Appellee) Plaintiff   )
)
vs   )
)
)   NOTICE OF APPEAL (Civil)
)
)
_____)

(Appellant/Appellee) Defendant

    Notice if hereby given that

    Plaintiff   Defendant above named, hereby appeals to the United States

Court of Appeals for the: (check appropriate box)

    Ninth Circuit   Federal Circuit

from the: (check appropriate box)

    Final Judgment   Order (describe)

entered in this proceeding on the _____ day of   .20
Transcripts required   Yes   No.
Date civil complaint filed:

Date: _____

                                    Signature

Figure 15.6

Example of a Notice
of Appeal
Source: U.S. District Court,
Southern District of California.
Available online: http://www.
ca2.uscourts.gov/clerk/forms_
and_instructions/pdf/Form%20
A%20revised%203-11.pdf
(accessed December 27,
2012).

Amendment right to counsel under a number of circumstances. However, the Sixth
Amendment expressly states that this right only applies in *criminal prosecutions.*
Even so, the Supreme Court has required that counsel be provided to indigent defendants *on appeal* as a matter of either equal protection or due process. Interestingly,
though, the Court has also said that there is no right to self-representation at the
appellate stage.[160]

_____

[160]See *Martinez v. Court of Appeal,* 528 U.S. 152 (2000).

TRANSCRIPT ORDER FORM

PART I - To be completed by appellant within ten days of filing the notice of appeal

Short Title: _____   District: _____

District Court Number: _____   Circuit Court Number: _____

Name of Attorney: _____

Name of Law Firm: _____

Address of Firm: _____

Telephone of Firm: _____   Attorneys for: _____

Name of Court Reporter: _____   Telephone of Reporter: _____

PART II - COMPLETE SECTION A OR SECTION B

SECTION A - I HAVE NOT ORDERED A TRANSCRIPT BECAUSE

[ ] A transcript is not necessary for this appeal, or

[ ] The necessary transcript is already on file in District Court

[ ] The necessary transcript was ordered previously in appeal

number _____

SECTION B - I HEREBY ORDER THE FOLLOWING TRANSCRIPT:

(Specify the date and proceeding in the space below)

Voir dire: _____;   Opening Statements _____;

Trial proceedings: _____;   Instruction Cnf: _____;

Jury Instructions: _____;   Closing Arguments: _____;

Post Trial Motions: _____;   Other Proceedings: _____,

(Attach additional pages if necessary)

[ ] Appellant will pay the cost of the transcript.

My signature on this form is my agreement to pay for the transcript ordered on this form.

[ ] This case is proceeding under the Criminal Justice Act.

NOTE: Leave to proceed *in forma pauperis* does not entitle appellant to a free transcript. An order of the district court allowing payment for the transcript at government expense must be obtained. See 28 U.S.C. §753(f).

CERTIFICATE OF COMPLIANCE

I certify that I have read the instructions on the reverse of this form and that copies of this transcript order form have been served on the court reporter (if transcript ordered), the Clerk of U.S. District Court, all counsel of record or pro se parties, and the Clerk of the U.S. Court of Appeals for the Tenth Circuit. I further certify that satisfactory arrangements for payment for any transcript ordered have been made with the court reporter(s).

Signature of Attorney/Pro Se: _____   Date: _____

PART III - TO BE COMPLETED BY THE COURT REPORTER

Upon completion, please file one copy with the Clerk of the U.S. Court of Appeals and one copy with the Clerk of the U.S. District Court.

Date arrangements for payment completed: _____

Estimated completion date: _____

Estimated number of pages: _____

I certify that I have read the instructions on the reverse side and that adequate arrangements for payment have been made.

Signature of Court Reporter: _____   Date: _____

A-S Transcript Order Form 497

Figure 15.7

Example of a Trial Transcript Order Form

Source: U.S. District Court, District of Wyoming. Available online: http://www.wyd.uscourts.gov/pdfforms/tranord.pdf (accessed December 27, 2012).

The first case discussing the right to counsel during the appellate stage was *Douglas* v. *California*.[161] In it, the Court concluded that the government must provide an indigent defendant with counsel to assist in his or her appeals of right. The Court stated that "where the merits of the *one and only* appeal an indigent has as of right are decided without benefit of counsel . . . an unconstitutional line has been drawn between rich and poor."[162] The Court has also held that the Constitution requires counsel—particularly, effective counsel—for a nonindigent defendant in his or her appeals of right.[163]

Both *Douglas* and *Evitts* dealt with the right to counsel in appeals of right. By contrast, the Supreme Court has held that counsel is not constitutionally guaranteed in *discretionary appeals*. Specifically, in *Ross* v. *Moffitt*, the Court held:

> A defendant in respondent's circumstances is not denied meaningful access to the State Supreme Court simply because the State does not appoint counsel to aid him in seeking review in that court, since at that stage, under North Carolina's multitiered appellate system, he will have, at the very least, a transcript or other record of the trial proceedings, a brief in the Court of Appeals setting forth his claims of error, and frequently an opinion by that court disposing of his case, materials which, when supplemented by any *pro se* submission that might be made, would provide the Supreme Court with an adequate basis for its decision to grant or deny review under its standards of whether the case has "significant public interest," involves "legal principles of major significance," or likely conflicts with a previous Supreme Court decision.[164]

Timing of Defense Appeals

The defense can file an appeal at one of two stages: (1) prior to the reading of the verdict—that is, prior to adjudication; or (2) following adjudication. The typical appeal is filed after adjudication, but there can be reasons to file an appeal prior to adjudication, as well. Both types of appeals are considered in the sections that follow. However, the bulk of the discussion will focus on appeals prior to adjudication because the Supreme Court has imposed far more restrictions on these.

interlocutory appeal An appeal filed prior to adjudication.

final judgment rule The requirement that interlocutory appeals dealing with questions of the defendant's guilt (rather than questions of a constitutional nature) cannot be heard until after final adjudication.

Appeals Prior to Adjudication.

An appeal filed prior to adjudication is known as an **interlocutory appeal**. This type of appeal is governed by a complex and confusing body of case law. In simple terms, though, an interlocutory appeal will only succeed if it is important and unrelated to the cause of action. That is, it must deal with a critical constitutional question and have nothing to do with determining the defendant's guilt. Otherwise, the defendant will face what is known as the **final judgment rule**, which generally limits appeals until the court hands down its final judgment as to the defendant's guilt.

Cohen v. *Beneficial Industrial Loan Corp.* is perhaps the first noteworthy case in which the Supreme Court upheld certain interlocutory appeals: namely, "a small

---

[161]*Douglas* v. *California*, 372 U.S. 353 (1963).
[162]Ibid., p. 357.
[163]See *Evitts* v. *Lucey*, 469 U.S. 387 (1985).
[164]*Ross* v. *Moffitt*, 417 U.S. 600 (1974), pp. 614–615.

class [of preadjudication decisions] which finally determine claims of right separable from, and collateral to, rights asserted in the action, too important to be denied review and too independent of the cause itself to required that appellate consideration be deferred until the whole case is adjudicated."[165] This quote does not lend itself to easy interpretation, unfortunately. But clarification can be provided by considering some examples of cases in which the Court applied its ruling in *Cohen*. The following two cases illustrate *successful* appeals prior to adjudication, while the subsequent cases focus on *unsuccessful* appeals.

In *Stack* v. *Boyle*,[166] the Court held that the defendant could appeal a judge's decision rejecting his argument that bail was excessive, in apparent violation of the Eighth Amendment. The Court believed that the trial judge's decision on this matter was more or less independent of deciding the defendant's guilt. It also felt that delaying appeal until after adjudication would make it pointless; a bail determination after a guilty verdict would have virtually no bearing on anything.

In another case, *Abney* v. *United States*,[167] the Court held that a defendant could appeal a preadjudication order denying dismissal of his indictment on double-jeopardy grounds. The reason for this decision should be fairly obvious: If the protection against double jeopardy is to have any meaning, then a defendant who claims double jeopardy must be able to appeal before the second conviction is handed down. Otherwise, the appellate court would have to consider whether a defendant's Fifth Amendment protection was denied in *hindsight*, which is not a preferable approach.

An example of a preadjudication appeal that did *not* succeed can be found in *Carroll* v. *United States*.[168] There, the Court held that a defendant cannot appeal a decision on a preadjudication search-and-seizure motion until after final adjudication has taken place. In other words, the Court felt that an appeal of a decision addressing evidence critical to the defendant's case is not sufficiently independent of the trial.

In another case, *DiBella* v. *United States*,[169] the Court held that a judge's preadjudication decision not to suppress evidence following the defendant's assertion that his Fourth Amendment rights were violated was not appealable until after trial. The Court felt that "appellate intervention makes for truncated presentation of the issue of admissibility, because the legality of the search too often cannot truly be determined until the evidence at the trial has brought all circumstances to light."[170]

Why does all this matter? Uninformed readers of Supreme Court cases often wonder why some cases are appealed after final adjudication and others before. Understanding the restrictions imposed by the Supreme Court on preadjudication appeals is important because it helps readers trace the progress of particular cases. But because preadjudication appeals can impose serious delays, they are usually the exception, rather than the rule.

Despite the obvious time- and resource-saving benefits of restricting preadjudication appeals, requiring that most appeals be filed after trial can have serious consequences for defendants. Many defendants who are found guilty on serious charges

---

[165] *Cohen* v. *Beneficial Industrial Loan Corp.*, 337 U.S. 541 (1949), p. 546.
[166] *Stack* v. *Boyle*, 342 U.S. 1 (1951).
[167] *Abney* v. *United States*, 431 U.S. 651 (1977).
[168] *Carroll* v. *United States*, 354 U.S. 394 (1957).
[169] *DiBella* v. *United States*, 369 U.S. 121 (1962).
[170] Ibid., p. 129.

go to prison and are forced to pursue their appeals from there. Given that most appeals—especially those that raise constitutional questions and ultimately reach the Supreme Court—take several years, people who are wrongfully convicted can languish in prison. This is one of the weaknesses of the U.S. system of justice.

Appeals after Adjudication. Appeals filed after adjudication are subject to few restrictions. Indeed, there appear to be few Supreme Court cases addressing postadjudication appeals. Nonetheless, it is important to understand that postadjudication appeals are almost limitless in terms of their possible substance. Anything from the trial (i.e., as recorded in the transcripts) that the defense perceives to be in error can be appealed.

The constitutional rights violations that most commonly serve as the basis for an appeal (or appeals) involve convictions obtained by any of these means:

* A plea of guilty that was unlawfully induced or not made voluntarily with understanding of the nature of the charge and the consequences of the plea
* The use of a coerced confession
* The use of evidence gained pursuant to an unconstitutional search or seizure
* The use of evidence obtained pursuant to an unlawful arrest
* A violation of the privilege against self-incrimination
* The unconstitutional failure of the prosecution to disclose to the defendant evidence favorable to him or her
* A violation of the Fifth Amendment's double-jeopardy clause
* Action of a grand jury or petit jury that was unconstitutionally selected and impaneled
* The denial of effective assistance of counsel
* Denial of the rights to a speedy trial and appeal

Habeas Corpus

habeas corpus A means of challenging the constitutionality of one's confinement, best viewed as an alternative to appealing. *Habeas corpus* is a constitutional right (Article I, Section 9, Clause 2).

The most common method of challenging one's conviction is to appeal. However, filing an appeal or several appeals is not the only avenue of redress for a person who is wrongfully convicted. Another avenue is by means of a *habeas corpus* petition filed with the federal courts. This is known as a *collateral attack* and is a constitutional right.[171]

Habeas corpus (Latin for "you have the body") plays out as follows: First, the accused individual petitions one of the federal district courts and asks the court to issue a *writ of habeas corpus*, which literally means "you have the body." Portions of an actual petition for *habeas corpus* form are reprinted in Figure 15.8. Then, if the court decides to issue the writ, the petitioner is brought before the court so that the constitutionality of his or her confinement can be reviewed.

---

[171]U.S. Constitution, Article I, Section 9, Clause 2.

PETITION UNDER 28 U.S.C § 2254 FOR WRIT OF
HABEAS CORPUS BY A PERSON IN STATE CUSTODY

United States District Court	District:	
Name (under which you were convicted):		Docket or Case No.:
Place of Confinement:		Prisoner No.:
Petitioner (include the name under which you were convicted)	Respondent (authorized person having custody of petitioner) v.	
The Attorney General of the State of		

PETITION

1. (a) Name and location of court that entered the judgment of conviction you are challenging:
   (b) Criminal docket or case number (if you know):
2. (a) Date of the judgment of conviction (if you know):
   (b) Date of sentencing:
3. Length of sentence:
4. In this case, were you convicted on more than one count or of more than one crime?   ❑ Yes   ❑ No
5. Identify all crimes of which you were convicted and sentenced in this case:
6. (a) What was your plea? (Check one)
      ❑ (1) Not guilty ❑ (3) Nolo contendere (no contest)
      ❑ (2) Guilty   ❑ (4) Insanity plea
   (b) If you entered a guilty plea to one count or charge and a not guilty plea to another count or charge, what did you plead guilty to and what did you plead not guilty to?
   (c) If you went to trial, what kind of trial did you have? (Check one)
      ❑ Jury   ❑ Judge only
7. Did you testify at a pretrial hearing, trial, or a post-trial hearing?
      ❑ Yes   ❑ No
8. Did you appeal from the judgment of conviction?
      ❑ Yes   ❑ No
9. If you did appeal, answer the following:
   (a) Name of court:
   (b) Docket or case number (if you know):
   (c) Result:
   (d) Date of result (if you know):
   (e) Citation to the case (if you know):
   (f) Grounds raised:
   (g) Did you seek further review by a higher state court?   ❑ Yes   ❑ No
    If yes, answer the following:
    (1) Name of court:
    (2) Docket or case number (if you know):
    (3) Result:
    (4) Date of result (if you know):
    (5) Citation to the case (if you know):
    (6) Grounds raised:

(continued)

Figure 15.8

Example of a Petition for a Writ of *Habeas Corpus* Form

Source: Administrative Office of the U.S. Courts. Available online: http://www.uscourts.gov/forms/ao241.pdf (accessed December 27, 2012).

   (h) Did you file a petition for certiorari in the United States Supreme Court?   ❏ Yes   ❏ No

      If yes, answer the following:

      (1) Docket or case number (if you know):

      (2) Result:

      (3) Date of result (it you know):

      (4) Citation to the case (if you know):

10. Other than the direct appeals listed above, have you previously filed any other petitions, applications, or motions concerning this judgment of conviction in any state court?   ❏ Yes   ❏ No

11. If your answer to Question 10 was "Yes," give the following information:

   (a) **(1)** Name of court:

      (2) Docket or case number (if you know):

      (3) Date of filing (if you know):

      (4) Nature of the proceeding:

      (5) Grounds raised:

      (6) Did you receive a hearing where evidence was given on your petition, application, or motion?

         ❏ Yes   ❏ No

      (7) Result:

      (8) Date of result (if you know):

   (b) If you filed any second petition, application, or motion, give the same information:

      (1) Name of court

      (2) Docket or case number (if you know):

      (3) Date of filing (if you know):

      (4) Nature of the proceeding:

      (5) Grounds raised:

      (6) Did you receive a hearing where evidence was given on your petition, application, or motion?

         ❏ Yes   ❏ No

      (7) Result:

      (8) Date of result (if you know):

   (c) If you filed any third petition, application, or motion, give the same information:

      (1) Name of court:

      (2) Docket or case number (if you know):

      (3) Date of filing (if you know):

      (4) Nature of the proceeding:

      (5) Grounds raised:

      (6) Did you receive a hearing where evidence was given on your petition, application, or motion?

         ❏ Yes   ❏ No

      (7) Result:

      (8) Date of result (if you know):

   (d) Did you appeal to the highest state court having jurisdiction over the action taken on your petition, application, or motion?

      (1) First petition: ❏ Yes   ❏ No

      (2) Second petition: ❏ Yes   ❏ No

      (3) Third petition: ❏ Yes   ❏ No

   (e) If you did not appeal to the highest state court having jurisdiction, explain why you did not:

12. For this petition, state every ground on which you claim that you are being held in violation of the Constitution, laws, or treaties of the United States. Attach additional pages if you have more than four grounds. State the facts supporting each ground.

CAUTION: To proceed in the federal court, you must ordinarily first exhaust (use up) your available state-court remedies on each ground on which you request action by the federal court. Also, if you fail to set forth all the grounds in this petition, you may be barred from presenting additional grounds at a later date.

Figure 15.8
(continued)

Given that the Supreme Court hears a limited number of cases each term, it is unlikely that it will issue a writ. This leaves the defendant with the option of petitioning the federal district court. Also, it is important to remember that a *habeas corpus* petition must be limited to a constitutional claim. Finally, it is totally within the discretion of the court that is petitioned to decide whether the writ will be issued. The Constitution provides that the "privilege of the Writ of *Habeas Corpus* shall not be suspended," but this has been interpreted to mean that a defendant can *submit habeas petitions*, not that the defendant will necessarily get his or her day in court.

On several occasions, the Supreme Court has emphasized the importance of the writ. For example, in *Sanders* v. *United States*, the Court emphasized that "[c]onventional notions of finality of litigation have no place where life or liberty is at stake and infringement of constitutional rights is alleged."[172] Similarly, in *Kaufman* v. *United States*, the Court held that the writ is necessary to provide "adequate protection of constitutional rights."[173]

However, more recently, the Court has intimated that a *habeas corpus* review should be qualified. In particular, it has held that writs should not be liberally issued for claims arising from state courts. As the Court stated in *Stone* v. *Powell*, "Despite differences in institutional environment and the unsympathetic attitude to federal constitutional claims of some state judges in years past, we are unwilling to assume that there now exists a general lack of appropriate sensitivity to constitutional rights in the trial and appellate courts of the several States."[174]

These conflicting perspectives have influenced a number of important Supreme Court cases addressing the constitutional right to *habeas corpus*. Recently, the Court has placed limitations on the scope of the writ. Also, the Antiterrorism and Effective Death Penalty Act of 1996 has had important effects on *habeas corpus*. The following sections focus on some of these restrictions and modifications.

Restrictions on the Right to *Habeas Corpus*

The Supreme Court has restricted the right to *habeas corpus* in a number of ways. First, it has limited the types of claims that can succeed. In particular, the petition must raise a federal constitutional question. This ruling was applied in *Herrera* v. *Collins*,[175] in which the petitioner claimed that his death sentence should be vacated because new evidence pointed to his innocence. The Court held that the claim could not be heard on *habeas* review because it did not raise a constitutional question. The Court explained that "[i]n light of the historical availability of new trials . . . and the contemporary practice in the States, we cannot say that Texas' refusal to entertain petitioner's newly discovered evidence eight years after his convictions transgresses a principle of fundamental fairness."[176]

Second, the Court has held that *habeas* review may not be granted if the petitioner fails to submit a claim within the time frame specified by state law.[177] Third,

---

[172]*Sanders* v. *United States*, 373 U.S. 1 (1963), p. 8.
[173]*Kaufman* v. *United States*, 394 U.S. 217 (1969), p. 226.
[174]*Stone* v. *Powell*, 428 U.S. 465 (1976), p. 494, n. 35.
[175]*Herrera* v. *Collins*, 506 U.S. 390 (1993).
[176]Ibid., p. 411.
[177]See, e.g., *Kuhlmann* v. *Wilson*, 477 U.S. 436 (1986).

it is generally necessary for a convicted individual to exhaust all state remedies before a federal *habeas* review will be granted.[178] Finally, restrictions have been imposed in situations in which a prisoner filed multiple *habeas* petitions.[179]

The Right to Counsel in the *Habeas Corpus* Context

The Supreme Court has guaranteed the right to counsel in direct appeals of right, but not in discretionary appeals. Since *habeas corpus* is purely discretionary, the Supreme Court has held that no right to counsel exists, unless, of course, the prisoner can afford representation.[180] The Court has held, however, that federal prisoners have a "constitutional right of access to the courts."[181]

The Supreme Court has also held that a state cannot prohibit prisoners from helping each other prepare and submit *habeas corpus* petitions.[182] Moreover, the Court has held that an indigent *habeas corpus* petitioner is entitled to a free transcript of his or her trial to assist in preparing the appropriate paperwork.[183]

YOUR DECISION

1. Judge Lawson has before him two convicted criminals who are giving notice of their intent to appeal their convictions for robbery. The two are indigent and thus pursuing their appeals without the assistance of counsel. They request access to the trial transcripts, but Judge Lawson rules against them, claiming that because, in his view, their appeals are frivolous, it would be a waste of taxpayer funds to supply them with the trial transcripts. Is this action constitutional?

2. Ling Yu was convicted of first-degree murder and sentenced to death. The evidence against her consisted of the body of the victim, the murder weapon, and testimony from several witnesses that Yu spoke openly about wanting to kill the victim. Three years after her conviction, while she was awaiting execution on death row, new evidence was discovered, suggesting that Yu may not have committed the murder. The new evidence came in the form of a witness who was prepared to testify that Yu was with her in a different city on the night of the murder. Assume that Yu exhausts all state-level appellate mechanisms, to no avail, and decides to petition a federal district court for a writ of *habeas corpus*. Will her petition be heard?

Summary

- Once a sentence has been handed down, the convicted person can appeal.
- An appeal can also be sought prior to sentencing. This type of appeal is known as an interlocutory appeal.

---

[178]See, e.g., *Ex parte Hawk*, 321 U.S. 114 (1944).
[179]See, e.g., *Magwood v. Patterson*, No. 09-158 (2010).
[180]See, e.g., *Ross v. Moffitt*, 417 U.S. 600 (1974).
[181]*Bounds v. Smith*, 430 U.S. 817 (1977).
[182]*Johnson v. Avery*, 393 U.S. 483 (1969).
[183]*Griffin v. Illinois*, 351 U.S. 12 (1956).

- Most jurisdictions favor appeals after final adjudication, but sometimes it is necessary to appeal prior to conviction.

- Typically, the defendant is granted one appeal of right. Subsequent appeals are called discretionary appeals. They are discretionary because the appellate court decides if it wants to hear the appeal.

- An appeal rarely results in the defendant going free. What happens, in most cases, is one of two things: (1) The appellate court agrees with the trial court, in which case it affirms the lower court's decision; or (2) the appellate court reverses the trial court's decision. A reversal typically results in a new trial for the defendant, or a remand.

- The appellate process must be carried out such that the defendant's constitutional rights are respected. According to the Supreme Court, this means that the defendant (1) must have access to the trial transcripts; (2) must have access to counsel for appeals of right, though not necessarily for discretionary appeals; and (3) must not be retaliated against for exercising his or her right to appeal.

- *Habeas corpus* is another method challenging one's conviction. It is also known as a collateral attack. The Supreme Court has restricted the right to *habeas* review in a number of ways. First, it has limited the types of claims that can succeed. Second, the Court has held that a *habeas corpus* review may not be granted if the petitioner fails to submit a claim within the time frame specified by state law. Third, it is generally necessary for a convicted individual to exhaust all state remedies before a federal *habeas* review will be granted. Finally, restrictions have been imposed in situations in which prisoners have filed multiple *habeas* petitions.

- The Supreme Court has held that prisoners are not strictly entitled to counsel to assist in preparing their *habeas* petitions. They do, however, have constitutional access to the courts. In other words, the right to counsel is virtually nonexistent in the *habeas corpus* process, exists somewhat more so in the appellate process (i.e., mainly for direct appeals), and exists completely at trial.

Chapter Review

RIGHTS TO SPEEDY AND PUBLIC TRIAL, IMPARTIAL JUDGE, AND TRIAL BY JURY

Learning Objectives

- Explain the right to a speedy trial.
- Summarize the right to a public trial.
- Summarize the right to an impartial judge.
- Explain when the Sixth Amendment right to a jury trial applies.

Review Questions

1. Explain when the right to a speedy trial applies.
2. What criteria are used to determine when the right to a speedy trial has been violated?
3. Explain the term *public trial.*
4. When may the right to a public trial not apply?
5. Under what circumstances could a judge be considered *not* impartial (i.e., biased)? Cite relevant cases.
6. What methods are available for removing a judge who cannot be considered impartial?
7. When does the right to a jury trial apply?
8. Explain the jury size and voting requirements in your state.
9. Summarize the *voir dire* process.

Key Terms

speedy trial
accusation rule
public trial
impartial judge
impartial jury

noncriminal proceeding rule
six-month imprisonment rule
voir dire
jury panel

RIGHTS TO COUNSEL, CONFRONTATION, AND COMPULSORY PROCESS

Learning Objectives

- Summarize the right to counsel.
- Explain the meaning of effective assistance of counsel.
- Explain the right to confrontation.
- Explain the right to compulsory process.

Review Questions

1. When does the right to counsel apply?

2. Can the Sixth Amendment right to counsel be waived? If so, what are the requirements?

3. Explain the meaning of effective assistance of counsel.

4. In what three ways is the defendant's right to confrontation manifested?

5. Explain both elements of the defendant's right to be present. Cite pertinent cases.

6. How might the defendant's right to be present do more harm than good?

7. Explain the exceptions to the defendant's right to live testimony.

8. Explain the order and scope of questions in a criminal trial.

9. Explain both elements of the right to compulsory process.

Key Terms

pro se defense
effective assistance of counsel
confrontation
physical presence
mental competence

live testimony
unavailable witness
hearsay exceptions
cross-examination
compulsory process

MODULE **15.3**   SENTENCING

Learning Objectives

- Describe various sentencing goals.
- Distinguish between various types of sentences.
- Explain how the appropriate sentence is determined.
- Summarize constitutional rights enjoyed during sentencing.

Review Questions

1. Explain the goals of sentencing.

2. Identify several criteria used in determining the appropriate sentence.

3. What constitutional rights exist during sentencing?

Key Terms

rehabilitation
retribution
incapacitation
deterrence
specific deterrence
general deterrence
indeterminate sentencing

determinate sentencing
mandatory sentencing
sentencing guidelines
concurrent sentence
consecutive sentences
bifurcated trial

MODULE **15.4**   **APPEALS AND *HABEAS CORPUS***

Learning Objectives

- Summarize the types and effects of appeals.
- Explain the appellate process.
- Outline the habeas corpus process.

Review Questions

1. What guidelines has the Supreme Court imposed on the appellate process?
2. Summarize the relevant rules governing an appeal before and after adjudication.
3. What is *habeas corpus*? From where does this right stem?
4. Summarize four restrictions on *habeas corpus* petitions.

Key Terms

appeal	interlocutory appeal
direct appeal	final judgment rule
discretionary appeal	*habeas corpus*
trial *de novo*	

Chapter Synthesis Questions

1. Which trial right is most important and why?
2. What is the proper goal of sentencing and why?
3. Do convicted criminals get too many appeals? Why or why not? What about in death penalty cases?

A CONSTITUTION OF THE UNITED STATES AND AMENDMENTS

We the people of the United States

We the People of the United States, in Order to form a more perfect Union, establish Justice, insure domestic Tranquility, provide for the common defence, promote the general Welfare, and secure the Blessings of Liberty to ourselves and our Posterity, do ordain and establish this Constitution for the United States of America.

Article I.

Section. 1.

All legislative Powers herein granted shall be vested in a Congress of the United States, which shall consist of a Senate and House of Representatives.

Section. 2.

The House of Representatives shall be composed of Members chosen every second Year by the People of the several States, and the Electors in each State shall have the Qualifications requisite for Electors of the most numerous Branch of the State Legislature.

No Person shall be a Representative who shall not have attained to the Age of twenty five Years, and been seven Years a Citizen of the United States, and who shall not, when elected, be an Inhabitant of that State in which he shall be chosen.

[Representatives and direct Taxes shall be apportioned among the several States which may be included within this Union, according to their respective Numbers, which shall be determined by adding to the whole Number of free Persons, including those bound to Service for a Term of Years, and excluding Indians not taxed, three fifths of all other Persons.]* The actual Enumeration shall be made within three Years after the first Meeting of the Congress of the United States, and within every subsequent Term of ten Years, in such Manner as they shall by Law direct. The Number of Representatives shall not exceed one for every thirty Thousand, but each State shall have at Least one Representative; and until such enumeration shall be made, the State of New Hampshire shall be entitled to chuse three, Massachusetts eight, Rhode-Island and Providence Plantations one, Connecticut five, New-York six, New Jersey four, Pennsylvania eight, Delaware one, Maryland six, Virginia ten, North Carolina five, South Carolina five, and Georgia three.

When vacancies happen in the Representation from any State, the Executive Authority thereof shall issue Writs of Election to fill such Vacancies.

The House of Representatives shall chuse their Speaker and other Officers; and shall have the sole Power of Impeachment.

Section. 3.

The Senate of the United States shall be composed of two Senators from each State, [chosen by the Legislature thereof,]* for six Years; and each Senator shall have one Vote.

Immediately after they shall be assembled in Consequence of the first Election, they shall be divided as equally as may be into three Classes. The Seats of the Senators of the first Class shall be vacated at the Expiration of the second Year, of the second Class at the Expiration of the fourth Year, and of the third Class at the Expiration of the sixth Year, so that one third may be chosen every second Year; [and if Vacancies happen by Resignation, or otherwise, during the Recess of the Legislature of any State, the Executive thereof may make temporary Appointments until the next Meeting of the Legislature, which shall then fill such Vacancies.]*

No Person shall be a Senator who shall not have attained to the Age of thirty Years, and been nine Years a Citizen of the United States, and who shall not, when elected, be an Inhabitant of that State for which he shall be chosen.

The Vice President of the United States shall be President of the Senate, but shall have no Vote, unless they be equally divided.

The Senate shall chuse their other Officers, and also a President pro tempore, in the Absence of the Vice President, or when he shall exercise the Office of President of the United States.

The Senate shall have the sole Power to try all Impeachments. When sitting for that Purpose, they shall be on Oath or Affirmation. When the President of the United States is tried, the Chief Justice shall preside: And no Person shall be convicted without the Concurrence of two thirds of the Members present.

Judgment in Cases of Impeachment shall not extend further than to removal from Office, and disqualification to hold and enjoy any Office of honor, Trust or Profit under the United States: but the Party convicted shall nevertheless be liable and subject to Indictment, Trial, Judgment and Punishment, according to Law.

Section. 4.

The Times, Places and Manner of holding Elections for Senators and Representatives, shall be prescribed in each State by the Legislature thereof; but the Congress may at any time by Law make or alter such Regulations, except as to the Places of chusing Senators.

The Congress shall assemble at least once in every Year, and such Meeting shall be [on the first Monday in December,]* unless they shall by Law appoint a different Day.

Section. 5.

Each House shall be the Judge of the Elections, Returns and Qualifications of its own Members, and a Majority of each shall constitute a Quorum to do Business; but a smaller Number may adjourn from day to day, and may be authorized to compel the Attendance of absent Members, in such Manner, and under such Penalties as each House may provide.

Each House may determine the Rules of its Proceedings, punish its Members for disorderly Behaviour, and, with the Concurrence of two thirds, expel a Member.

Each House shall keep a Journal of its Proceedings, and from time to time publish the same, excepting such Parts as may in their Judgment require Secrecy; and the Yeas and Nays of the Members of either House on any question shall, at the Desire of one fifth of those Present, be entered on the Journal.

Neither House, during the Session of Congress, shall, without the Consent of the other, adjourn for more than three days, nor to any other Place than that in which the two Houses shall be sitting.

Section. 6.

The Senators and Representatives shall receive a Compensation for their Services, to be ascertained by Law, and paid out of the Treasury of the United States. They shall in all Cases, except Treason, Felony and Breach of the Peace, be privileged from Arrest during their Attendance at the Session of their respective Houses, and in going to and returning from the same; and for any Speech or Debate in either House, they shall not be questioned in any other Place.

No Senator or Representative shall, during the Time for which he was elected, be appointed to any civil Office under the Authority of the United States, which shall have been created, or the Emoluments whereof shall have been encreased during such time; and no Person holding any Office under the United States, shall be a Member of either House during his Continuance in Office.

Section. 7.

All Bills for raising Revenue shall originate in the House of Representatives; but the Senate may propose or concur with Amendments as on other Bills.

Every Bill which shall have passed the House of Representatives and the Senate, shall, before it become a Law, be presented to the President of the United States; If he approve he shall sign it, but if not he shall return it, with his Objections to that House in which it shall have originated, who shall enter the Objections at large on their Journal, and proceed to reconsider it. If after such Reconsideration two thirds of that House shall agree to pass the Bill, it shall be sent, together with the Objections, to the other House, by which it shall likewise be reconsidered, and if approved by two thirds of that House, it shall become a Law. But in all such Cases the Votes of both Houses shall be determined by Yeas and Nays, and the Names of the Persons voting for and against the Bill shall be entered on the Journal of each House respectively, If any Bill shall not be returned by the President within ten Days (Sundays excepted) after it shall have been presented to him, the Same shall be a Law, in like Manner as if he had signed it, unless the Congress by their Adjournment prevent its Return, in which Case it shall not be a Law.

Every Order, Resolution, or Vote to which the Concurrence of the Senate and House of Representatives may be necessary (except on a question of Adjournment) shall be presented to the President of the United States; and before the Same shall take Effect, shall be approved by him, or being disapproved by him, shall be repassed by two thirds of the Senate and House of Representatives, according to the Rules and Limitations prescribed in the Case of a Bill.

Section. 8.

The Congress shall have Power To lay and collect Taxes, Duties, Imposts and Excises, to pay the Debts and provide for the common Defence and general Welfare of the United States; but all Duties, Imposts and Excises shall be uniform throughout the United States;

To borrow Money on the credit of the United States;

To regulate Commerce with foreign Nations, and among the several States, and with the Indian Tribes;

To establish an uniform Rule of Naturalization, and uniform Laws on the subject of Bankruptcies throughout the United States;

To coin Money, regulate the Value thereof, and of foreign Coin, and fix the Standard of Weights and Measures;

To provide for the Punishment of counterfeiting the Securities and current Coin of the United States;

To establish Post Offices and post Roads; To promote the Progress of Science and useful Arts, by securing for limited Times to Authors and Inventors the exclusive Right to their respective Writings and Discoveries;

To constitute Tribunals inferior to the supreme Court;

To define and punish Piracies and Felonies committed on the high Seas, and Offenses against the Law of Nations;

To declare War, grant Letters of Marque and Reprisal, and make Rules concerning Captures on Land and Water;

To raise and support Armies, but no Appropriation of Money to that Use shall be for a longer Term than two Years;

To provide and maintain a Navy;

To make Rules for the Government and Regulation of the land and naval Forces;

To provide for calling forth the Militia to execute the Laws of the Union, suppress Insurrections and repel Invasions;

To provide for organizing, arming, and disciplining, the Militia, and for governing such Part of them as may be employed in the Service of the United States, reserving to the States respectively, the Appointment of the Officers, and the Authority of training the Militia according to the discipline prescribed by Congress;

To exercise exclusive Legislation in all Cases whatsoever, over such District (not exceeding ten Miles square) as may, by Cession of particular States, and the Acceptance of Congress, become the Seat of the Government of the United States, and to exercise like Authority over all Places purchased by the Consent of the Legislature of the State in which the Same shall be, for the Erection of Forts, Magazines, Arsenals, dock-Yards and other needful Buildings; -And

To make all Laws which shall be necessary and proper for carrying into Execution the foregoing Powers, and all other Powers vested by this Constitution in the Government of the United States, or in any Department or Officer thereof.

Section. 9.

The Migration or Importation of such Persons as any of the States now existing shall think proper to admit, shall not be prohibited by the Congress prior to the Year one thousand eight hundred and eight, but a Tax or duty may be imposed on such Importation, not exceeding ten dollars for each Person.

The Privilege of the Writ of Habeas Corpus shall not be suspended, unless when in Cases of Rebellion or Invasion the public Safety may require it.

No Bill of Attainder or ex post facto Law shall be passed.

[No Capitation, or other direct, Tax shall be laid, unless in Proportion to the Census or Enumeration herein before directed to be taken.]*

No Tax or Duty shall be laid on Articles exported from any State.

No Preference shall be given by any Regulation of Commerce or Revenue to the Ports of one State over those of another: nor shall Vessels bound to, or from, one State, be obliged to enter, clear, or pay Duties in another.

No Money shall be drawn from the Treasury, but in Consequence of Appropriations made by Law; and a regular Statement and Account of the Receipts and Expenditures of all public Money shall be published from time to time.

No Title of Nobility shall be granted by the United States: And no Person holding any Office of Profit or Trust under them, shall, without the Consent of the Congress, accept of any present, Emolument, Office, or Title, of any kind whatever, from any King, Prince, or foreign State.

Section. 10.

No State shall enter into any Treaty, Alliance, or Confederation; grant Letters of Marque and Reprisal; coin Money; emit Bills of Credit; make any Thing but gold and silver Coin a Tender in Payment of Debts; pass any Bill of Attainder, ex post facto Law, or Law impairing the Obligation of Contracts, or grant any Title of Nobility.

No State shall, without the Consent of the Congress, lay any Imposts or Duties on Imports or Exports, except what may be absolutely necessary for executing it's inspection Laws: and the net Produce of all Duties and Imposts, laid by any State on Imports or Exports, shall be for the Use of the Treasury of the United States; and all such Laws shall be subject to the Revision and Controul of the Congress.

No State shall, without the Consent of Congress, lay any Duty of Tonnage, keep Troops, or Ships of War in time of Peace, enter into any Agreement or Compact with another State, or with a foreign Power, or engage in War, unless actually invaded, or in such imminent Danger as will not admit of delay.

Article II.

Section. 1.

The executive Power shall be vested in a President of the United States of America. He shall hold his Office during the Term of four Years, and, together with the Vice President, chosen for the same Term, be elected, as follows:

Each State shall appoint, in such Manner as the Legislature thereof may direct, a Number of Electors, equal to the whole Number of Senators and Representatives to which the State may be entitled in the Congress: but no Senator or Representative, or Person holding an Office of Trust or Profit under the United States, shall be appointed an Elector.

[The Electors shall meet in their respective States, and vote by Ballot for two Persons, of whom one at least shall not be an Inhabitant of the same State with themselves. And they shall make a List of all the Persons voted for, and of the Number of Votes for each; which List they shall sign and certify, and transmit sealed to the Seat of the Government of the United States, directed to the President of the Senate. The President of the Senate shall, in the Presence of the Senate and House of Representatives, open all the Certificates, and the Votes shall then be counted. The Person having the greatest Number of Votes shall be the President, if such Number be a Majority of the whole Number of Electors appointed; and if there be more than one who have such Majority, and have an equal Number of Votes, then the House of Representatives shall immediately chuse by Ballot one of them for President; and if no Person have a Majority, then from the five highest on the List the said House shall in like Manner chuse the President. But in chusing the President, the Votes shall be taken by States, the Representation from each State having one Vote; A quorum for this Purpose shall consist of a Member or Members from two thirds of the States, and a Majority of all the States shall be necessary to a Choice. In every Case, after the Choice of the President, the Person having the greatest Number of Votes of the Electors shall be the Vice President. But if there should remain two or more who have equal Votes, the Senate shall chuse from them by Ballot the Vice President.]*

The Congress may determine the Time of chusing the Electors, and the Day on which they shall give their Votes; which Day shall be the same throughout the United States.

No Person except a natural born Citizen, or a Citizen of the United States, at the time of the Adoption of this Constitution, shall be eligible to the Office of President; neither shall any person be eligible to that Office who shall not have attained to the Age of thirty five Years, and been fourteen Years a Resident within the United States.

[In Case of the Removal of the President from Office, or of his Death, Resignation, or Inability to discharge the Powers and Duties of the said Office, the Same shall devolve on the Vice President, and the Congress may by Law provide for the Case of Removal, Death, Resignation or Inability, both of the President and Vice President, declaring what Officer shall then act as President, and such

Officer shall act accordingly, until the Disability be removed, or a President shall be elected.]*

The President shall, at stated Times, receive for his Services, a Compensation, which shall neither be increased nor diminished during the Period for which he shall have been elected, and he shall not receive within that Period any other Emolument from the United States, or any of them.

Before he enter on the Execution of his Office, he shall take the following Oath or Affirmation:- "I do solemnly swear (or affirm) that I will faithfully execute the Office of President of the United States, and will to the best of my Ability, preserve, protect and defend the Constitution of the United States."

Section. 2.

The President shall be Commander in Chief of the Army and Navy of the United States, and of the Militia of the several States, when called into the actual Service of the United States; he may require the Opinion, in writing, of the principal Officer in each of the executive Departments, upon any Subject relating to the Duties of their respective Offices, and he shall have Power to grant Reprieves and Pardons for Offenses against the United States, except in Cases of Impeachment.

He shall have Power, by and with the Advice and Consent of the Senate, to make Treaties, provided two thirds of the Senators present concur; and he shall nominate, and by and with the Advice and Consent of the Senate, shall appoint Ambassadors, other public Ministers and Consuls, Judges of the supreme Court, and all other Officers of the United States, whose Appointments are not herein otherwise provided for, and which shall be established by Law: but the Congress may by Law vest the Appointment of such inferior Officers, as they think proper, in the President alone, in the Courts of Law, or in the Heads of Departments.

The President shall have Power to fill up all Vacancies that may happen during the Recess of the Senate, by granting Commissions which shall expire at the End of their next Session.

Section. 3.

He shall from time to time give to the Congress Information of the State of the Union, and recommend to their Consideration such Measures as he shall judge necessary and expedient; he may, on extraordinary Occasions, convene both Houses, or either of them, and in Case of Disagreement between them, with Respect to the Time of Adjournment, he may adjourn them to such Time as he shall think proper; he shall receive Ambassadors and other public Ministers; he shall take Care that the Laws be faithfully executed, and shall Commission all the Officers of the United States.

Section. 4.

The President, Vice President and all civil Officers of the United States, shall be removed from Office on Impeachment for, and Conviction of, Treason, Bribery, or other high Crimes and Misdemeanors.

Article III.

Section. 1.

The judicial Power of the United States, shall be vested in one supreme Court, and in such inferior Courts as the Congress may from time to time ordain and establish. The Judges, both of the supreme and inferior Courts, shall hold their Offices during good Behaviour, and shall at stated Times, receive for their Services, a Compensation, which shall not be diminished during their Continuance in Office.

Section. 2.

The judicial Power shall extend to all Cases, in Law and Equity, arising under this Constitution, the Laws of the United States, and Treaties made, or which shall be made, under their Authority; - to all Cases affecting Ambassadors, other public Ministers and Consuls; - to all Cases of admiralty and maritime Jurisdiction; - to Controversies to which the United States shall be a Party; - to Controversies between two or more States; - [between a State and Citizens of another State;-]* between Citizens of different States, - between Citizens of the same State claiming Lands under Grants of different States, [and between a State, or the Citizens thereof;- and foreign States, Citizens or Subjects.]*

   In all Cases affecting Ambassadors, other public Ministers and Consuls, and those in which a State shall be Party, the supreme Court shall have original Jurisdiction. In all the other Cases before mentioned, the supreme Court shall have appellate Jurisdiction, both as to Law and Fact, with such Exceptions, and under such Regulations as the Congress shall make.

   The Trial of all Crimes, except in Cases of Impeachment; shall be by Jury; and such Trial shall be held in the State where the said Crimes shall have been committed; but when not committed within any State, the Trial shall be at such Place or Places as the Congress may by Law have directed.

Section. 3.

Treason against the United States, shall consist only in levying War against them, or in adhering to their Enemies, giving them Aid and Comfort. No Person shall be convicted of Treason unless on the Testimony of two Witnesses to the same overt Act, or on Confession in open Court.

   The Congress shall have Power to declare the Punishment of Treason, but no Attainder of Treason shall work Corruption of Blood, or Forfeiture except during the Life of the Person attainted.

Article IV.

Section. 1.

Full Faith and Credit shall be given in each State to the public Acts, Records, and judicial Proceedings of every other State. And the Congress may by general Laws prescribe the Manner in which such Acts, Records and Proceedings shall be proved, and the Effect thereof.

Section. 2.

The Citizens of each State shall be entitled to all Privileges and Immunities of Citizens in the several States. A Person charged in any State with Treason, Felony, or other Crime, who shall flee from Justice, and be found in another State, shall on Demand of the executive Authority of the State from which he fled, be delivered up, to be removed to the State having Jurisdiction of the Crime.

[No Person held to Service or Labour in one State, under the Laws thereof, escaping into another, shall, in Consequence of any Law or Regulation therein, be discharged from such Service or Labour, but shall be delivered up on Claim of the Party to whom such Service or Labour may be due.]*

Section. 3.

New States may be admitted by the Congress into this Union; but no new State shall be formed or erected within the Jurisdiction of any other State; nor any State be formed by the Junction of two or more States, or Parts of States, without the Consent of the Legislatures of the States concerned as well as of the Congress.

The Congress shall have Power to dispose of and make all needful Rules and Regulations respecting the Territory or other Property belonging to the United States; and nothing in this Constitution shall be so construed as to Prejudice any Claims of the United States, or of any particular State.

Section. 4.

The United States shall guarantee to every State in this Union a Republican Form of Government, and shall protect each of them against Invasion; and on Application of the Legislature, or of the Executive (when the Legislature cannot be convened) against domestic Violence.

Article V.

The Congress, whenever two thirds of both Houses shall deem it necessary, shall propose Amendments to this Constitution, or, on the Application of the Legislatures of two thirds of the several States, shall call a Convention for proposing Amendments, which in either Case, shall be valid to all Intents and Purposes, as Part of this Constitution, when ratified by the Legislatures of three-fourths of the several States, or by Conventions in three fourths thereof, as the one or the other Mode of Ratification may be proposed by the Congress; Provided that no Amendment which may be made prior to the Year One thousand eight hundred and eight shall in any Manner affect the first and fourth Clauses in the Ninth Section of the first Article; and that no State, without its Consent, shall be deprived of its equal Suffrage in the Senate.

Article VI.

All Debts contracted and Engagements entered into, before the Adoption of this Constitution, shall be as valid against the United States under this Constitution, as under the Confederation.

This Constitution, and the Laws of the United States which shall be made in Pursuance thereof; and all Treaties made, or which shall be made, under the Authority of the United States, shall be the supreme Law of the Land; and the Judges in every State shall be bound thereby, any Thing in the Constitution or Laws of any State to the Contrary notwithstanding.

The Senators and Representatives before mentioned, and the Members of the several State Legislatures, and all executive and judicial Officers, both of the United States and of the several States, shall be bound by Oath or Affirmation, to support this Constitution; but no religious Test shall ever be required as a Qualification to any Office or public Trust under the United States.

Article VII.

The Ratification of the Conventions of nine States, shall be sufficient for the Establishment of this Constitution between the States so ratifying the Same.

Done in Convention by the Unanimous Consent of the States present the Seventeenth Day of September in the Year of our Lord one thousand seven hundred and Eighty seven and of the Independence of the United States of America the Twelfth In Witness whereof We have hereunto subscribed our Names,

Go. Washington–Presidt:
and deputy from Virginia

New Hampshire

John Langdon
Nicholas Gilman

Massachusetts

Nathaniel Gorham
Rufus King

Connecticut

Wm. Saml. Johnson
Roger Sherman

New York

Alexander Hamilton

New Jersey

Wil: Livingston

David Brearley

Wm. Paterson

Jona: Dayton

Pennsylvania

B Franklin

Thomas Mifflin

Robt Morris

Geo. Clymer

Thos. FitzSimons

Jared Ingersoll

James Wilson

Gouv Morris

Delaware

Geo: Read

Gunning Bedford jun

John Dickinson

Richard Bassett

Jaco: Broom

Maryland

James McHenry

Dan of St. Thos. Jenifer

Danl Carroll

Virginia

John Blair-

James Madison Jr.

North Carolina

Wm. Blount

Richd. Dobbs Spaight

Hu Williamson

South Carolina

J. Rutledge

Charles Cotesworth Pinckney

Charles Pinckney

Pierce Butler

Georgia

William Few

Abr Baldwin

Attest William Jackson Secretary

In Convention Monday
September 17th, 1787.
Present
The States of
New Hampshire, Massachusetts, Connecticut, Mr. Hamilton from New York, New Jersey, Pennsylvania, Delaware, Maryland, Virginia, North Carolina, South Carolina and Georgia.

Resolved,
That the preceeding Constitution be laid before the United States in Congress assembled, and that it is the Opinion of this Convention, that it should afterwards be submitted to a Convention of Delegates, chosen in each State by the People thereof, under the Recommendation of its Legislature, for their Assent and Ratification; and that each Convention assenting to, and ratifying the Same, should give Notice thereof to the United States in Congress assembled. Resolved, That it is the Opinion of this Convention, that as soon as the Conventions of nine States shall have ratified this Constitution, the United States in Congress assembled should fix a Day on which Electors should be appointed by the States which shall have ratified the same, and a Day on which the Electors should assemble to vote for the President, and the Time and Place for commencing Proceedings under this Constitution.

That after such Publication the Electors should be appointed, and the Senators and Representatives elected: That the Electors should meet on the Day fixed for the Election of the President, and should transmit their Votes certified, signed, sealed and directed, as the Constitution requires, to the Secretary of the United States in Congress assembled, that the Senators and Representatives should convene at the Time and Place assigned; that the Senators should appoint a President of the Senate, for the sole Purpose of receiving, opening and counting the Votes for President; and, that after he shall be chosen, the Congress, together with the President, should, without Delay, proceed to execute this Constitution.

By the unanimous Order of the Convention
Go. Washington-Presidt:
W. JACKSON Secretary.

The Amendments to the Constitution of the United States as Ratified by the States

Preamble to the Bill of Rights

Congress of the United States begun and held at the City of New-York, on Wednesday the fourth of March, one thousand seven hundred and eighty nine

THE Conventions of a number of the States, having at the time of their adopting the Constitution, expressed a desire, in order to prevent misconstruction or abuse of its powers, that further declaratory and restrictive clauses should be added: And as extending the ground of public confidence in the Government, will best ensure the beneficent ends of its institution.

RESOLVED by the Senate and House of Representatives of the United States of America, in Congress assembled, two thirds of both Houses concurring, that the following Articles be proposed to the Legislatures of the several States, as amendments to the Constitution of the United States, all, or any of which Articles, when ratified by three fourths of the said Legislatures, to be valid to all intents and purposes, as part of the said Constitution; viz.

ARTICLES in addition to, and Amendment of the Constitution of the United States of America, proposed by Congress, and ratified by the Legislatures of the several States, pursuant to the fifth Article of the original Constitution.

(Note: The first 10 amendments to the Constitution were ratified December 15, 1791, and form what is known as the "Bill of Rights.")

Amendment I.

Congress shall make no law respecting an establishment of religion, or prohibiting the free exercise thereof; or abridging the freedom of speech, or of the press, or the right of the people peaceably to assemble, and to petition the Government for a redress of grievances.

Amendment II.

A well regulated Militia, being necessary to the security of a free State, the right of the people to keep and bear Arms, shall not be infringed.

Amendment III.

No Soldier shall, in time of peace be quartered in any house, without the consent of the Owner, nor in time of war, but in a manner to be prescribed by law.

*Language in brackets has been changed by amendment.

Amendment IV.

The right of the people to be secure in their persons, houses, papers, and effects, against unreasonable searches and seizures, shall not be violated, and no Warrants shall issue, but upon probable cause, supported by Oath or affirmation, and particularly describing the place to be searched, and the persons or things to be seized.

Amendment V.

No person shall be held to answer for a capital, or otherwise infamous crime, unless on a presentment or indictment of a Grand Jury, except in cases arising in the land or naval forces, or in the Militia, when in actual service in time of War or public danger; nor shall any person be subject for the same offence to be twice put in jeopardy of life or limb; nor shall be compelled in any criminal case to be a witness against himself, nor be deprived of life, liberty, or property, without due process of law; nor shall private property be taken for public use, without just compensation.

Amendment VI.

In all criminal prosecutions, the accused shall enjoy the right to a speedy and public trial, by an impartial jury of the State and district wherein the crime shall have been committed, which district shall have been previously ascertained by law, and to be informed of the nature and cause of the accusation; to be confronted with the witnesses against him; to have compulsory process for obtaining witnesses in his favor, and to have the Assistance of Counsel for his defence.

Amendment VII.

In suits at common law, where the value in controversy shall exceed twenty dollars, the right of trial by jury shall be preserved, and no fact tried by a jury shall be otherwise reexamined in any Court of the United States, than according to the rules of the common law.

Amendment VIII.

Excessive bail shall not be required, nor excessive fines imposed, nor cruel and unusual punishments inflicted.

Amendment IX.

The enumeration in the Constitution, of certain rights, shall not be construed to deny or disparage others retained by the people.

Amendment X.

The powers not delegated to the United States by the Constitution, nor prohibited by it to the States, are reserved to the States respectively, or to the people.

Amendments 11-27

Amendment XI.

Passed by Congress March 4, 1794. Ratified February 7, 1795.

Note: A portion of Article III, Section 2 of the Constitution was modified by the 11th Amendment.)

The Judicial power of the United States shall not be construed to extend to any suit in law or equity, commenced or prosecuted against one of the United States by Citizens of another State, or by Citizens or Subjects of any Foreign State.

Amendment XII.

Passed by Congress December 9, 1803. Ratified June 15, 1804.

(Note: A portion of Article II, Section 1 of the Constitution was changed by the 12th Amendment.)

The Electors shall meet in their respective states, and vote by ballot for President and Vice-President, one of whom, at least, shall not be an inhabitant of the same state with themselves; they shall name in their ballots the person voted for as President, and in distinct ballots the person voted for as Vice-President, and they shall make distinct lists of all persons voted for as President, and of all persons voted for as Vice-President, and of the number of votes for each, which lists they shall sign and certify, and transmit sealed to the seat of the government of the United States, directed to the President of the Senate;-the President of the Senate shall, in the presence of the Senate and House of Representatives, open all the certificates and the votes shall then be counted;-The person having the greatest number of votes for President, shall be the President, if such number be a majority of the whole number of Electors appointed; and if no person have such majority, then from the persons having the highest numbers not exceeding three on the list of those voted for as President, the House of Representatives shall choose immediately, by ballot, the President. But in choosing the President, the votes shall be taken by states, the representation from each state having one vote; a quorum for this purpose shall consist of a member or members from two-thirds of the states, and a majority of all the states shall be necessary to a choice. [And if the House of Representatives shall not choose a President whenever the right of choice shall devolve upon them, before the fourth day of March next following, then the Vice-President shall act as President, as in case of the death or other constitutional disability of the President.-]* The person having the greatest number of votes as Vice-President, shall be the Vice-President, if such number be a majority of the whole number of Electors appointed, and if no person have a majority, then from the two highest numbers on the list, the Senate shall choose the Vice-President; a quorum for the purpose shall consist of two-thirds of the whole number of Senators, and a majority of the whole number shall be necessary to a choice. But no person constitutionally ineligible to the office of President shall be eligible to that of Vice-President of the United States.

Amendment XIII.

Passed by Congress January 31, 1865. Ratified December 6, 1865.

(Note: A portion of Article IV, Section 2 of the Constitution was changed by the 13th Amendment.)

Section 1.

Neither slavery nor involuntary servitude, except as a punishment for crime whereof the party shall have been duly convicted, shall exist within the United States, or any place subject to their jurisdiction.

Section 2.

Congress shall have power to enforce this article by appropriate legislation.

Amendment XIV.

Passed by Congress June 13, 1866. Ratified July 9, 1868.

(Note: Article I, Section 2 of the Constitution was modified by Section 2 of the 14th Amendment.)

Section 1.

All persons born or naturalized in the United States and subject to the jurisdiction thereof, are citizens of the United States and of the State wherein they reside. No State shall make or enforce any law which shall abridge the privileges or immunities of citizens of the United States; nor shall any State deprive any person of life, liberty, or property, without due process of law; nor deny to any person within its jurisdiction the equal protection of the laws.

Section 2.

Representatives shall be apportioned among the several States according to their respective numbers, counting the whole number of persons in each State, excluding Indians not taxed. But when the right to vote at any election for the choice of electors for President and Vice President of the United States, Representatives in Congress, the Executive and Judicial officers of a State, or the members of the Legislature thereof, is denied to any of the male inhabitants of such State, [being twenty-one

*Superseded by Section 3 of the 20th Amendment.

years of age,]* and citizens of the United States, or in any way abridged, except for participation in rebellion, or other crime, the basis of representation therein shall be reduced in the proportion which the number of such male citizens shall bear to the whole number of male citizens twenty-one years of age in such State.

Section 3.

No person shall be a Senator or Representative in Congress, or elector of President and Vice President, or hold any office, civil or military, under the United States, or under any State, who, having previously taken an oath, as a member of Congress, or as an officer of the United States, or as a member of any State legislature, or as an executive or judicial officer of any State, to support the Constitution of the United States, shall have engaged in insurrection or rebellion against the same, or given aid or comfort to the enemies thereof. But Congress may by a vote of two-thirds of each House, remove such disability.

Section 4.

The validity of the public debt of the United States, authorized by law, including debts incurred for payment of pensions and bounties for services in suppressing insurrection or rebellion, shall not be questioned. But neither the United States nor any State shall assume or pay any debt or obligation incurred in aid of insurrection or rebellion against the United States, or any claim for the loss or emancipation of any slave; but all such debts, obligations and claims shall be held illegal and void.

Section 5.

The Congress shall have the power to enforce, by appropriate legislation, the provisions of this article.

Amendment XV.

Passed by Congress February 26, 1869. Ratified February 3, 1870.

Section 1.

The right of citizens of the United States to vote shall not be denied or abridged by the United States or by any State on account of race, color, or previous condition of servitude.

Section 2.

The Congress shall have the power to enforce this article by appropriate legislation.

*Changed by Section 1 of the 26th Amendment.

Amendment XVI.

Passed by Congress July 2, 1909. Ratified February 3, 1913.

(Note: Article I, Section 9 of the Constitution was modified by the 16th Amendment.)

The Congress shall have power to lay and collect taxes on incomes, from whatever source derived, without apportionment among the several States, and without regard to any census or enumeration.

Amendment XVII.

Passed by Congress May 13, 1912. Ratified April 8, 1913.

(Note: Article I, Section 3 of the Constitution was modified by the 17th Amendment.)

The Senate of the United States shall be composed of two Senators from each State, elected by the people thereof, for six years; and each Senator shall have one vote. The electors in each State shall have the qualifications requisite for electors of the most numerous branch of the State legislatures.

When vacancies happen in the representation of any State in the Senate, the executive authority of such State shall issue writs of election to fill such vacancies: Provided, That the legislature of any State may empower the executive thereof to make temporary appointments until the people fill the vacancies by election as the legislature may direct.

This amendment shall not be so construed as to affect the election or term of any Senator chosen before it becomes valid as part of the Constitution.

Amendment XVIII.

Passed by Congress December 18, 1917. Ratified January 16, 1919. Repealed by the 21st Amendment, December 5, 1933.

Section 1.

After one year from the ratification of this article the manufacture, sale, or transportation of intoxicating liquors within, the importation thereof into, or the exportation thereof from the United States and all territory subject to the jurisdiction thereof for beverage purposes is hereby prohibited.

Section 2.

The Congress and the several States shall have concurrent power to enforce this article by appropriate legislation.

Section 3.

This article shall be inoperative unless it shall have been ratified as an amendment to the Constitution by the legislatures of the several States, as provided in the

Constitution, within seven years from the date of the submission hereof to the States by the Congress.

Amendment XIX.

Passed by Congress June 4, 1919. Ratified August 18, 1920.

The right of citizens of the United States to vote shall not be denied or abridged by the United States or by any State on account of sex.

Congress shall have power to enforce this article by appropriate legislation.

Amendment XX.

Passed by Congress March 2, 1932. Ratified January 23, 1933.

(Note: Article I, Section 4 of the Constitution was modified by Section 2 of this Amendment. In addition, a portion of the 12th Amendment was superseded by Section 3.)

Section 1.

The terms of the President and the Vice President shall end at noon on the 20th day of January, and the terms of Senators and Representatives at noon on the 3d day of January, of the years in which such terms would have ended if this article had not been ratified; and the terms of their successors shall then begin.

Section 2.

The Congress shall assemble at least once in every year, and such meeting shall begin at noon on the 3d day of January, unless they shall by law appoint a different day.

Section 3.

If, at the time fixed for the beginning of the term of the President, the President elect shall have died, the Vice President elect shall become President. If a President shall not have been chosen before the time fixed for the beginning of his term, or if the President elect shall have failed to qualify, then the Vice President elect shall act as President until a President shall have qualified; and the Congress may by law provide for the case wherein neither a President elect nor a Vice President shall have qualified, declaring who shall then act as President, or the manner in which one who is to act shall be selected, and such person shall act accordingly until a President or Vice President shall have qualified.

Section 4.

The Congress may by law provide for the case of the death of any of the persons from whom the House of Representatives may choose a President whenever the right of choice shall have devolved upon them, and for the case of the death of any of the persons from whom the Senate may choose a Vice President whenever the right of choice shall have devolved upon them.

Section 5.

Sections 1 and 2 shall take effect on the 15th day of October following the ratification of this article.

Section 6.

This article shall be inoperative unless it shall have been ratified as an amendment to the Constitution by the legislatures of three-fourths of the several States within seven years from the date of its submission.

Amendment XXI.

Passed by Congress February 20, 1933. Ratified December 5, 1933.

Section 1.

The eighteenth article of amendment to the Constitution of the United States is hereby repealed.

Section 2.

The transportation or importation into any State, Territory, or possession of the United States for delivery or use therein of intoxicating liquors, in violation of the laws thereof, is hereby prohibited.

Section 3.

This article shall be inoperative unless it shall have been ratified as an amendment to the Constitution by conventions in the several States, as provided in the Constitution, within seven years from the date of the submission hereof to the States by the Congress.

Amendment XXII.

Passed by Congress March 21, 1947. Ratified February 27, 1951.

Section 1.

No person shall be elected to the office of the President more than twice, and no person who has held the office of President, or acted as President, for more than two years of a term to which some other person was elected President shall be elected to the office of President more than once. But this Article shall not apply to any person holding the office of President when this Article was proposed by Congress, and shall not prevent any person who may be holding the office of President, or acting as President, during the term within which this Article becomes operative from holding the office of President or acting as President during the remainder of such term.

Section 2.

This article shall be inoperative unless it shall have been ratified as an amendment to the Constitution by the legislatures of three-fourths of the several States within seven years from the date of its submission to the States by the Congress.

Amendment XXIII.

Passed by Congress June 16, 1960. Ratified March 29, 1961.

Section 1.

The District constituting the seat of Government of the United States shall appoint in such manner as Congress may direct:

A number of electors of President and Vice President equal to the whole number of Senators and Representatives in Congress to which the District would be entitled if it were a State, but in no event more than the least populous State; they shall be in addition to those appointed by the States, but they shall be considered, for the purposes of the election of President and Vice President, to be electors appointed by a State; and they shall meet in the District and perform such duties as provided by the twelfth article of amendment.

Section 2.

The Congress shall have power to enforce this article by appropriate legislation.

Amendment XXIV.

Passed by Congress August 27, 1962. Ratified January 23, 1964.

Section 1.

The right of citizens of the United States to vote in any primary or other election for President or Vice President, for electors for President or Vice President, or for Senator or Representative in Congress, shall not be denied or abridged by the United States or any State by reason of failure to pay poll tax or other tax.

Section 2.

The Congress shall have power to enforce this article by appropriate legislation.

Amendment XXV.

Passed by Congress July 6, 1965. Ratified February 10, 1967.

(Note: Article II, Section 1 of the Constitution was modified by the 25th Amendment.)

Section 1.

In case of the removal of the President from office or of his death or resignation, the Vice President shall become President.

Section 2.

Whenever there is a vacancy in the office of the Vice President, the President shall nominate a Vice President who shall take office upon confirmation by a majority vote of both Houses of Congress.

Section 3.

Whenever the President transmits to the President pro tempore of the Senate and the Speaker of the House of Representatives his written declaration that he is unable to discharge the powers and duties of his office, and until he transmits to them a written declaration to the contrary, such powers and duties shall be discharged by the Vice President as Acting President.

Section 4.

Whenever the Vice President and a majority of either the principal officers of the executive departments or of such other body as Congress may by law provide, transmit to the President pro tempore of the Senate and the Speaker of the House of Representatives their written declaration that the President is unable to discharge the powers and duties of his office, the Vice President shall immediately assume the powers and duties of the office as Acting President.

Thereafter, when the President transmits to the President pro tempore of the Senate and the Speaker of the House of Representatives his written declaration that no inability exists, he shall resume the powers and duties of his office unless the Vice President and a majority of either the principal officers of the executive department or of such other body as Congress may by law provide, transmit within four days to the President pro tempore of the Senate and the Speaker of the House of Representatives their written declaration that the President is unable to discharge the powers and duties of his office. Thereupon Congress shall decide the issue, assembling within forty-eight hours for that purpose if not in session. If the Congress, within twenty-one days after receipt of the latter written declaration, or, if Congress is not in session, within twenty-one days after Congress is required to assemble, determines by two-thirds vote of both Houses that the President is unable to discharge the powers and duties of his office, the Vice President shall continue to discharge the same as Acting President; otherwise, the President shall resume the powers and duties of his office.

Amendment XXVI.

Passed by Congress March 23, 1971. Ratified July 1, 1971.

(Note: Amendment 14, Section 2 of the Constitution was modified by Section 1 of the 26th Amendment.)

Section 1.

The right of citizens of the United States, who are eighteen years of age or older, to vote shall not be denied or abridged by the United States or by any State on account of age.

Section 2.

The Congress shall have power to enforce this article by appropriate legislation.

Amendment XXVII.

Originally proposed Sept. 25, 1789. Ratified May 7, 1992.

No law, varying the compensation for the services of the Senators and Representatives, shall take effect, until an election of representatives shall have intervened.

The Court Decision boxes throughout the book are edited versions of actual court cases decided by judges and justices across the country. We have edited their words into a simplified format that is easy to read and understand. "Briefing" a case is a method of reading, analyzing, and summarizing the key elements of these court cases. This is a short guide explaining how the process of briefing a case works. Please also refer to Chapter 1 for an explanation of the parts of a court opinion. We will use the following case as an example. A discussion of how to brief it and a sample brief follows the case.

People v. *Toler*
185 N.E. 2d 874 (Ill. 1962)

Supreme Court of Illinois

Prior History: Defendant (Toler) appealed the decision of the Criminal Court of Cook County (Illinois) convicting him of the unlawful sale of narcotic drugs and sentencing him to prison.

Disposition: Judgment affirmed.

Counsel: Julius Lucius Echeles, of Chicago, for the defendant.

William G. Clark, Attorney General, of Springfield, and Daniel P. Ward, State's Attorney, of Chicago (Fred G. Leach and E. Michael O'Brien, Assistant Attorneys General, and John T. Gallagher and Dean H. Bilton, Assistant State's Attorneys, of counsel,) for the state.

Judges: Mr. Justice Daily delivered the opinion of the court. Mr. Justice Schaefer, dissenting. Mr. Justice Klingbiel concurs in this dissent.

Opinion By: Daily

Defendant, Willie Toler, was indicted in the criminal court of Cook County on charges of having unlawfully sold narcotic drugs to Richard Tracy on June 8 and 11, 1959. Tracy, a Chicago police officer, had been introduced to defendant by Edward Unsell, a former fellow employee of defendant at a water-pumping station, and who was then working as a special employee of the State's Attorney's office. Defendant pleaded not guilty and waived a jury trial, but was subsequently found guilty after a bench trial and sentenced to the penitentiary for a term of not less than ten nor more than twelve years. Upon this writ of error the single contention made is that, under the evidence, defendant should have been discharged because he was entrapped into committing the crimes.

Past decisions of this court establish that entrapment constitutes a valid defense if officers of the law inspire, incite, persuade or lure a defendant to commit a crime which he otherwise had no intention of perpetrating…At the same time, however, it is equally well settled that officers may afford opportunities or facilities for the commission of crime, or may use artifice to catch those engaged in criminal ventures, and that the defense of entrapment is not available to one who has the intent and design to commit a criminal offense, and who does commit the essential acts constituting it, merely because an officer, for the purpose of securing evidence, affords such person the opportunity to commit the criminal act, or purposely aids and encourages him in its perpetration…

The testimony of the defendant paints a picture of an innocent man who, after being approached by Unsell some twenty times in an effort to get narcotics, finally succumbed to an appeal to his sympathy by Tracy. The latter told him that he worked for a dentist who had a son who was a narcotics addict, that he wanted some "good stuff," that he might need as much as three or four thousand dollars worth and that he wanted a sample. Defendant stated that he purchased narcotics, without profit to himself, to aid a narcotics addict who was sick… The proof introduced by the People reflects two sales of narcotics by defendant when the funds were shown to be available, and an intent and willingness on the part of the defendant to commit the crime, shown by his ready complaisance and quick access to substantial quantities of illegal narcotics. We are of the opinion that the officer and special employee did no more than afford defendant the opportunity to commit a criminal act of his own design, and that their actions did not constitute entrapment… The record also shows a circumstance hardly compatible with naivete and innocence, an elaborate system of delivery devised by defendant whereby the narcotics were never actually seen in his possession.

The judgment of the criminal court of Cook County is affirmed.

Dissent By: Schaefer

The evidence on the issue of entrapment in this case is not conflicting, and I think that it establishes that the defendant was entrapped. The police officer, Richard Tracy, testified as follows concerning the meeting at which Unsell introduced him to the defendant:

> "A. During the course of the conversation I told Mr. Toler I was working for a dentist and this dentist had a son that was a narcotic addict and because of the new prescription law it was impossible for this dentist to obtain narcotics legally for his son and the son was in need of narcotics, and we were looking for some good stuff, some good heroin, if we could get it off the street at least this occasion because he was in pretty bad shape; we didn't think he would live very long.

> Q.   Indicate how much you wanted?

> A.   I told—we talked about getting a very large amount, possibly three or $ 4000 worth of narcotics, and at that time I indicated to Toler I would like to buy a sample for approximately $ 100, and I asked him how much stuff he could get me for $ 100."

The defendant testified that he and Unsell were close friends, and that Unsell had approached him many times, telling him that he wanted narcotics for a friend who was sick and had only a year to live.

On cross-examination, the informer, Unsell, who was called as a rebuttal witness, testified as follows:

"Q. Isn't it a fact you told the defendant, Willie Toler here, you had a customer who needed some narcotics badly because he was ill and had about a year to live?

A. Not customer, No.

Q. Did you tell him anyone?

A. Yes.

Q. Whom?"

At this point the prosecution objected on the ground that the cross-examination was going beyond the scope of the direct, and the court sustained the objection saying "This is a rebuttal witness."

There is no showing in the record that apart from the two occasions involved in this case the defendant had ever had any transactions with narcotics or that he had any criminal record whatsoever. Under these circumstances I am of the opinion that the defense of entrapment was established and that the judgment should be reversed.

Mr. Justice Klingbiel concurs in this dissent.

While it is important to be able to read and understand a full court case, it is also important for you to be able to brief a case. A case brief is a short (usually one page or less) summary of the key components of a case. It is written in response to a few questions, such as:

1. What is the procedural history?
2. What are the facts?
3. What is the central issue at hand in the case?
4. What is the holding, decision, or disposition?
5. What is the reasoning the court offered in its opinion?
6. What is the essence of the dissent, if there is one?

Answers to these questions are invaluable, as they help you gain a complete grasp of a case. It is not enough to simply know what happened and what was decided. Case briefs help you identify the core issue at hand in each case. It is sometimes easy to lose sight of that issue, as cases can be long-winded, written in complex legalese, and presuppose that the reader already knows why the case is important. At the core of every case, though, is one or a few key issues. Case briefs also help you understand, in a "short and sweet" fashion, *why* the decision reached? Opinions tend to lay out the court's reasoning over several pages. A brief encourages you to "cut to the chase" and identify, in a sentence or two, what the court was thinking. The same holds for the dissent.

Appearing below is a brief of the *People* v. *Toler* case introduced above. Note that it is short. It is worth noting, too, that *People* v. *Toler* is itself a short case. The opinion and dissent are roughly two pages long. Other cases are much longer, making case briefing a challenge.

People v. *Toler*,
185 N.E.2d 874 (Ill. 1962).

Procedural History: This case is on appeal from the Criminal Court, Cook County to the Supreme Court of Illinois. The defendant was found guilty at the trial court.

Facts: Defendant Toler sold narcotics to an undercover police office, Richard Tracy. Toler had been introduced to the police officer by Edward Unsell, a friend of Toler and a special employee of the State's Attorney's office.

Issue: Was the defendant entrapped by Tracy and Unsell?

Holding: Conviction affirmed. Entrapment does not exist when a mere "opportunity to commit a criminal act of his own design" is presented to the defendant.

Reasoning: The court found an "intent and willingness" on the part of Toler to commit the crime when funds were shown to be available. In addition, the court stated that Toler's elaborate system of delivery indicated he was not simply a naïve and innocent victim.

Dissent: Justice Schaefer felt the defense of entrapment had been sufficiently established by the defendant. No evidence of Toler's propensity for criminal acts was presented. In addition, Toler was led to believe the drugs were for an ill patient with little time to live.

CASE INDEX

SUBJECT INDEX